Jim Flint
The Boy From Peoria

By Tracy Baim and Owen Keehnen

Edited by William B. Kelley and Jorjet Harper

Design by Kirk Williamson

Prairie Avenue Productions
Chicago, 2011

Cover photos of Jim Flint courtesy of Jim Flint

Cover illustration and book design by Kirk Williamson
Edited by William B. Kelley and Jorjet Harper

Images and photos used in this book provided courtesy of the following:
Jim Flint
Hal Baim for Windy City Times
Tracy Baim for GayLife, Windy City Times and Outlines
Louis Boroff
Mike Carter
Mike Denny
Maya Douglas
Kat Fitzgerald, www.mysticimagesphotography.com
Jennifer Girard Photography
John Hill
Lisa Howe-Ebright
Spike King
Marie J. Kuda
Jim Marks
Harley McMillen
MJ Murphy
Chuck Renslow
Christopher Reynolds
Tio's Photography
Jack Sitar
Mark Ward
Kirk Williamson for Nightspots and Windy City Times
Israel Wright
Other photographers from The Chicago Gay Crusader, Gay Chicago, GayLife,
Windy City Times, Outlines and Nightlines publications
All other photos courtesy of Jim Flint unless otherwise credited

First Edition, December 2011

Prairie Avenue Productions
1900 South Prairie Avenue
Chicago, Illinois, USA 60616-1321
editor@windycitymediagroup.com

Black-and-white and color editions available
Available in print and e-book form

ISBN-13: 9781466398405

ISBN-10: 146639840X

Dedications

Tracy Baim:
For Jean, and all those who persevere

Owen Keehnen:
For Carl, and for those who laid the foundation and those who continue to build

About the Authors

Tracy Baim is publisher and executive editor at Windy City Media Group, which produces Windy City Times, Nightspots, and other gay media in Chicago. She co-founded Windy City Times in 1985 and Outlines newspaper in 1987. She has won numerous gay community and journalism honors, including the Community Media Workshop's Studs Terkel Award in 2005. She started in Chicago gay journalism in 1984 at GayLife newspaper, one month after graduating with a news-editorial degree from Drake University.

Baim is the co-author of Leatherman: The Legend of Chuck Renslow. She is co-author and editor of Out and Proud in Chicago: An Overview of the City's Gay Community, the first comprehensive book on Chicago's gay history. And she is author of Where the World Meets, a book about Gay Games VII in Chicago. Her first novel is The Half Life of Sgt. Jen Hunter, about lesbians in the military prior to Don't Ask, Don't Tell. She also has an essay in the book Media Queered (Peter Lang, 2007).

Baim was executive producer of the lesbian feature film Hannah Free, starring Sharon Gless (Ripe Fruit Films, 2008). She was inducted into the Chicago Gay and Lesbian Hall of Fame in 1994 and was named a Crain's Chicago Business 40 Under 40 leader in 1995.

She lives with her partner, Jean Albright, in Chicago.

Inducted into the Chicago Gay and Lesbian Hall of Fame in 2011, writer and historian **Owen Keehnen's** fiction, essays, erotica, reviews and interviews have appeared in hundreds of magazines, newspapers and anthologies worldwide. With Tracy Baim, he was a co-author of Leatherman: The Legend of Chuck Renslow.

His gay novel The Sand Bar was released in 2012 by Lethe Press. He is the author of We're Here, We're Queer, a collection of more than 100 interviews with LGBTQ writers and activists who helped shape contemporary gay culture and the modern gay movement. Keehnen is the author of the horror novel Doorway Unto Darkness and the humorous gay novel I May Not Be Much but I'm All I Think About, available at e-gaymag.com.

In addition, he co-edited Nothing Personal: Chronicles of Chicago's LGBTQ Community 1977–1997 and contributed 10 essays to the groundbreaking, richly illustrated book of LGBTQ history Out and Proud in Chicago. He is also the author of the Starz series, a set of four books of interviews with the men of the XXX film industry.

Keehnen was on the founding committee of The Legacy Project and currently serves as board secretary for that LGBT history-education-arts program focused on pride, acceptance and bringing recognition to the courageous lives and contributions of international LGBTQ historical figures.

He lives in Chicago with his patient partner, Carl Blando, and their spoiled dogs, Flannery and Fitzgerald.

Table of Contents

Acknowledgments

We are very happy to once again profile a Chicago gay icon, Jim Flint. We completed this book right after our biography of Chuck Renslow, and there was a lot of overlap in the news and interview subjects between these two Chicago legends.

To finish this book in a short time frame, we called on more than 150 people to speak their own stories about Flint, the Baton, Redoubt, Annex 2 and 3, 3160, the Continental System, and other related Flint businesses and projects. We are very grateful for the time that people took to get back with us quickly and to share their memories of Flint and his impact in Chicago, nationally, and even internationally.

We also thank the Baton family and the Continental family, including Tim Gideon, Ginger Grant, Scott Palmer and Dan Neniskis. They shared stories and photos for use in this book.

Others who helped as research and photographic sources included Scott Burgh, Chuck Renslow, Marie J. Kuda, Harley McMillen, Lori Cannon, Alexandra Billings, Ann Perkins, Chris Badowski, Phil Hannema, Carrie Fairfield, Honey West, Mark Ward, Becky Menzie and Cheri Coons. For our research, we also used materials from Jack Rinella, the Leather Archives & Museum, Sukie de la Croix, The Chicago Gay Crusader, GayLife newspaper, Windy City Times and Outlines.

Jim Flint: The Boy From Peoria also would not have been possible without the full cooperation of its subject, Jim Flint, who turned 70 as we started the research and interviews that would be used in these pages. We told Jim that the book had to have it all, the good and the bad, so that we could provide a full and complete document of his life. He rarely complained, and fully supported our work.

Finally, we want to thank our amazing editors, William B. Kelley and Jorjet Harper, and our talented designer, Kirk Williamson, for their tireless efforts.

We are both very committed to continuing to uncover lost LGBT history in Chicago. Please join us on this stop in our journey, a look behind the lavender curtain and into the many-faceted life of Jim Flint, a true gay pioneer.

— Tracy Baim and Owen Keehnen

As I reflect back on the book's contents, I think of the many people who helped pave the way for me. I think of Dick Decker, my real friend, and the nights in Peoria when we would stop at Hunter's for the hot dogs, then ride around and kill time before going to Caterpillar. After that, it was off to the Navy and the base in Norfolk, Virginia. Then, following a brief stay, I was shipped to Pearl Harbor, where Brandy, Hanalei, Dina Jacobs and so many others made lasting friendships for me.

During my travels with softball and Continental, I met so many people who have left a lasting impression on my life. All the guys at Fritz in Boston, Billy Svetz, Steve Giuliano, Joe McGowen, Gary Staples, Freddie, Frank Snyder aka Butterfly always made it a great trip. There are also Jim O'Connor and Larry Hite, who opened up their homes in Provincetown and Naples. New York is where I met the late Chuck Dima as well as Bobby and Richie Diaz, Lady Catiria, Jose Disla, and Jeanette Valentino. Philadelphia was a blast with Tommy Garbino, Scottie, Vinnie Young, Bobby, Ralph and, of course, Bill Wood. In Pittsburgh, it was my lovely friend Nancy Pribich. San Antonio brought me Raphael Velasco, Stevie, The

Ambassador—Kourtney Devereux, Tandi and Erica Andrews. Houston was Errol Summons, Vince Sanchez, David Sandling, Ken Bailey and so many others.

In Dallas, Warren Williamson and John Keys. Ohio brought me my good friend Skip Mackall, who has helped change my life for the last 20 years, Denis Sabol and David Hudspeth. Dan Fraser and Cindy Barbalock from Orlando, as well as Danny, Leann, EJ, Kris Reynolds and Rachel. In Miami and Fort Lauderdale there were Alyson Thomas, Erika Norell, Don, Samantha, Electra, Zulema Romero, Derbis, Lola and, of course, the Elysian Guest House, where so many meetings have been held. Thank you, Corrie Boyd, Will at Tropics, Jim at Sidelines, and Tito at Boardwalk.

Tennessee was Wayne Chandler, Robbie Pedersen and Walter Patton. Atlanta was Tony Desario. In Norfolk, Virginia, I met Fred Asbell and Xavier Davis as well as Brandi Mizrahi. St. Louis was where I met Howard Meyer (I couldn't have done it without you) and Joe, who has always kept me on my toes. There were Tumara Mahorning, also from St. Louis, and Jodie Santana from Carbondale. In Indianapolis, there was Shawn and from Phoenix there was Brent Skoglund.

My life would not be the same without Eric and Keith from the Stonewall in Huntington and Atmosphere in Charleston, West Virginia. Go! Marshall, the thundering herd! Also from there were the very special Coty Lipscomb, Chris and Shelly, Olivia and Priscilla.

Two people who mean so much to me are Bob Waters and Ken Byrski from Detroit. They have been two of my dear friends for more than 40 years. Their friendship has always been there and never wavered.

Now to Chicago: There are so many people who have touched my life and made this city the best in the world! From my employees, to my companions and partners, Scott Palmer and Dan Neniskis. Then there is the greatest friend anyone could ever have—Ginger (Harry) Grant has been there for me always, even though we might disagree at times. There are Tim Gideon, Billy, Josh, my friends at Naha, Hanna and Paulo at the Coq d'Or in the Drake Hotel. Frank Zimmerman, a friend I have always needed. My political friends. My friends Bo and Eric, the kitty cats, Debbie and Kim, Ada and Trina. Antonio King; the Fraser family, Joe, Jackie and Nancy, and all their families and children; J.T. McWilliams; Sara Davis; Debbie; and, of course, John Twomey. There is Rick Welch, who has always been there, never wavering, even when we had differences. Brian (Dancer) Reams has always been there with good advice and friendship. All the sports associations that kept me busy in the early years. I owe so much to them.

I also want to thank Chicagoans Terrence Smith and of course Chuck Renslow.

And last but not least, I can't forget Lorenzo, Nick and Pat, and Tony at the Blues Club for their friendship.

— Jim Flint

Introduction

"Will it play in Peoria?" This common saying has been around in some variation for more than a century, with its roots possibly in the writings of (the apparently gay) Horatio Alger Jr. and certainly later in vaudeville and even politics. Based on its location and demographics, this quintessential Midwestern city in Central Illinois has been a launching pad for everything from theater and film, to products for the home, to presidential candidates.

Jim Flint was born in Mason City, Illinois, in 1941 and moved to Peoria as a toddler. Horatio Alger's stories of hard work leading to success are echoed in the life of young Jimmy, who was a product of both the good and the bad that the city had to offer. During his childhood, Peoria was well-known for its red-light district of brothels and other illegal activities. Flint leapt into this stream of humanity with eyes wide open, ready at age 8 to "shine shoes" for older men. He has no regrets about his childhood; instead, he boasts about how he took control of his own destiny, and never looked back.

Emboldened by his youthful money-making adventures, Flint became a paper boy and a carhop at Steak 'n Shake as well. The textbook entrepreneur joined the Navy at 17 and was a self-educated man of the world by his early 20s. He moved to Chicago in the early 1960s. After a few years of working for others and becoming one of the most popular bartenders in town—which included getting arrested numerous times in raids on the bars where he worked—Flint decided to start his own business. In 1969, the same year that the Stonewall riots in New York heralded the start of the modern gay-rights movement, Flint opened Smitty's Show Lounge, which in the months to come became the Baton Show Lounge.

The Baton was followed by the Redoubt, Annex 2, Annex 3, and 3160, among others. From its humble beginnings the Baton has become a world-renowned venue for the finest in the art of female impersonation. Flint has taken something that was often seen as a freak show and helped transform it into a profession worthy of respect both from the audience and from the performers. Famous figures in sports, politics and entertainment have attended performances, and many of them rush to the dressing room to be photographed with the cast. After 42 years, that stage—which began as a piece of plywood on top of 16 beer cases—has become an institution.

Flint was not content with just the world of impersonation. In 1976 he opened the Redoubt, a popular hardcore leather-uniform-and-western bar that endured four location changes and lasted well into the 1990s. Flint also opened the Annex 2, a dance-and-party bar where internationally acclaimed disc jockey Frankie Knuckles got his start. Flint followed this with Annex 3, a sports and (briefly) piano bar, and 3160, which is currently celebrated as a leading Chicago venue for cabaret entertainment. These diverse businesses, catering to seemingly separate populations within the LGBTQA (lesbian, gay, bisexual, transgender, questioning and allied) community, are more indicative of Flint's sense of unity. What on the surface seems very different, Flint sees as all manifestations of the larger LGBTQA community or, to use one of Flint's favorite words, family. We are one, despite our drag, which may be a gown, a harness or a softball uniform.

The personality it takes to navigate the myriad land mines placed by Chicago politicians, police, city inspectors and the Mafia also can create enemies even among people within your own community. Flint has a take-no-prisoners approach to running his businesses and the organizations he has headed. He admits to being strong-willed and big-tempered, but the vast majority of his close friends, customers, colleagues and players on his teams have remained dedicated and loyal friends across many decades. There is a charm about Flint that can usually smooth over the rough edges, especially for those willing to forgive any immediate arguments and flares of his temper.

Earlier this year, we published Leatherman: The Legend of Chuck Renslow, a book about a similar Chicago gay icon. In many ways, Flint and Renslow are polar opposites, while at the same time being two sides of one coin. Renslow, 12 years older than Flint, was also a role model for the younger gay man.

Both of them were boldly out gay business owners and activists at a time when many were closeted or used fake names. They were gay men who owned gay bars when most were either owned by the Mafia or by straights. They founded, ran or supported dozens of early gay movement organizations. Both of them created "chosen" families that became integrated with their families of origin, including their mothers. In fact, both Flint and Renslow became "fathers" to these new models of what a family can be. And both of them were very involved in politics—paying their dues literally and figuratively. Renslow ran to become a delegate for Edward Kennedy in the 1980 presidential race, and a few years later Flint ran for the Cook County Board, getting the most votes of any openly gay candidate in the city up to that time.

Flint also was a key early supporter and leader of gay sports in Chicago and nationally, helping put Chicago on the U.S. map for gay sports such as softball and basketball. The gay sports world has grown enormously over the years in Chicago, in no small part due to Flint's efforts. But his drive to win had a price, and Chicago's sports community was divided for many years between Flint's organization and a competing group.

Overall, Flint is something of an enigma to those not familiar with him. In his early years he was often dressed as "Felicia," a matronly Midwestern gal with an eye for the hot men.

His peak years of community involvement were from the late 1970s to the late 1980s. Since then he has focused primarily on his businesses and contests. In 1981, Flint began the Miss Continental pageant system, which has since spawned Miss Continental Plus, Mr. Continental and Miss Continental Elite. The Continental system has become a major part of his life.

At 70 years old, he is still intimately involved in all aspects of his businesses and groups. He travels extensively, visits regularly with dozens of friends, and maintains, to put it mildly, a complicated home life.

We learned a lot of interesting facts not just about Flint in working on this book, but also about the parallel growth of Chicago's lesbian, gay, bisexual and transgender community. In many ways, the transgender community and individual transgender people have moved beyond what the Baton has to offer. Flint is part of the reason transgender issues are more prominent today, thanks to his Baton performers and their appearances on talk shows during the 1970s and 1980s, including Phil Donahue's and Oprah Winfrey's. As his friend and attorney Ralla Klepak said, "He turned drag into dignity, into an art form for those not always headed for stardom."

We were also impressed with just how many people and organizations were positively influenced by the work of Flint. This included groups he founded and led, but also included groups he allowed to use his bar as a de facto community center for meetings, plays or benefit productions.

This former baton twirler from Peoria is an ultimate juggler, happiest when all his "batons" are flying through the air—preferably on fire, with Flint on roller skates for an added level of risk as well as showmanship.

It is our hope that this book provides insight into both Flint himself, an important part of Chicago's gay community history, and the role his bars, teams and contests played in highlighting Chicago's contributions to the national gay community.

—Tracy Baim and Owen Keehnen

1

Growing Up in Peoria, Entering the Navy

James William Flint was born at home on July 27, 1941, the fourth child of 24-year-old Pearl Marie Thomas Flint and 31-year-old Vern Flint, in Mason City, Illinois. Mason City is a small town in Central Illinois, halfway between Springfield and Peoria, and is home to the Cougars sports teams. The couple had been married on August 20, 1934.

In his later years, there has been scattered speculation that Flint claimed to be younger than his real age. The truth is, Flint had inadvertently lied for years about his age, but only by one day. "When I went into the Navy I had to get a copy of my birth certificate," Flint laughed. "And that was when I found out that July 27 was my birthday. My mother had always told me it was the 28th! So I'd been saying I was a day younger all along."

Though the Flint and Thomas family roots in Mason City can be traced back to before the turn of the 20th century, the economic situation of the early 1940s prompted the young couple and their small children to move to a relatively bigger city where there were more opportunities and more jobs.

The family moved 40 miles north to Peoria when Jim was about 2. His mother found work at Pabst Brewing Co. in Peoria Heights and his father, a mechanic, was soon employed at a Hudson car dealership.

"Everything I know about the Hudson cars was from when I was in fifth grade and my dad was supposed to wait for my mother to come home for her birthday," Flint said. "He got a little drunk on wine instead, so my mother took a coal poker and broke out every window on the car. She's where I get my temper from."

It was a big family: There were 13 children. Jim was the fourth, and all the children following him were hospital-born. His oldest sister is Darlene and then there were Florence (whom they called Sis), Robert, Jim and Dale (who died at about 7 months from pneumonia), followed by Serena, Doris, Merle, Dorothy, John, Everett and Ronnie.

Jim, Doris and Dorothy (who is mostly known as Skip) all agree that the family was a little dysfunctional. Their mother earned most of the money. Their father, as good as he was, was an alcoholic. He'd get drunk on muscatel. He was never an abusive father and he was always in a jovial mood.

"Mom was the disciplinarian. Dad would say, 'When Mom gets home you're going to get it,' and she spanked us. Sometimes she spanked us until she cried," said Jim's younger sister Doris.

"My mother was the breadwinner, and my dad sort of watched us," Jim recalled. "None of us can ever remember my dad putting a hand on us or hitting us or any of that. They were good for lecturing you or sitting you in a corner or putting soap in your mouth when you cussed. When I was 7, I got caught smoking a cigarette, and they made me smoke a foot-long cigar at the table. I've never smoked a cigarette since."

"My father gave me the nickname Skip because I used to skip a lot," Dorothy said. "My father had a glass eye, and Sundays, after services at the South Side Mission, he used to put his chair outside and sit. He sometimes would read the Bible, and he had a Howdy Doody puppet he would entertain us with. Then he'd tell us he could do magic and take his glass eye out. So I used to get real nervous when he did that—I used to skip all over the block, so they called me Skip."

Jim's grandmother was Assembly of God, Pentecostal. "That wasn't for me," Jim said. "My mom and dad were more Methodist, but mostly they just always tried to teach us the right thing."

"South Side Mission was where we went to Sunday school," said Dorothy, "but they also offered a lot of things for the community to do in the way of kid camps and activities."

They were also the ones who provided Thanksgiving and Christmas dinner for the Flint family. "I remember us as having to go to church every Sunday at the South Side Mission in Peoria. Dad's other rule was that you could not come downstairs in the morning until you were fully dressed," said Dorothy.

In due time, Pearl found a better job opportunity at the 286-room Hotel Père Marquette, a 14-story property built in 1926. Doris Flint explained, "She was a short-order cook there. She went to work at 3 or 4 in the afternoon and then worked until 1 in the morning and then would walk home. She always told us to never take a cab unless you have the money to tip, so she walked. Mom's big rules were that we had a curfew and that we always had to go to school."

"She pretty much worked nights," Dorothy said. "When we came home from school for lunch, she would oftentimes cut and curl our hair. Mom was always a stickler for going to school. She said she worked hard to support us, so the best thing we could do was go to school and get an education. We were very poor, and to make ends meet, my mother also sold Guardian Service—which were sort of pots and pans—and worked on commission, and you'd have parties to sell it, similar to Tupperware parties that came years later."

Before the family moved into public housing, they lived in a house at 191 Hickory Street. "We were there a short time and then moved to 423 Oak Street," Jim said. "That's where I went to Douglas Grade School with Richard Pryor for third, fourth and fifth grades. It was a strange area because right across from our house was the red-light district." Richard Pryor's grandmother and aunt ran a brothel. Later on in life, when he used to have fits of depression, he would come and stay at the brothels there," Flint said of Pryor. "It was home to him."

"I remember when we were living in that house, my mother would send me to the bakery because you could get day-olds at half price," Jim said. "To get there I had to walk through that alley, and all the red lights were on, and I never knew what all those red lights meant until later on in life.

"One time at Christmastime my mother put a red wreath on the door. I was outdoors playing and this gentleman came over and asked me, 'Who's in this house?' And I said, 'Just my two sisters.' Then the guy went up on the porch and started banging on the door, and my sister said, 'Who is it?' The man said, 'I just talked to your brother and he said there are two of you girls.'

"She screamed he'd better get off the porch or she'd cut his heart out. She told my other sister to call the police, but we didn't have a phone so she ran for help. When my mother came home, the police were there and everything. We never had a red wreath after that."

The Peoria Journal Star reported in March 2006 that "prostitution has long been associated with Peoria. From the heady days of the 1930s and 1940s, when GIs would come to Peoria looking for fun, to decades later when residents and police largely ignored those on the 'merry-go-round' [an area of South Peoria where men wanting sex for cash would drive in circles seeking prostitutes], sex was always for sale. … Things began to change in the early 1950s, when a federal report chronicled 132 brothels in and around 'Aiken Alley' in what is now Southtown." Old Aiken Alley and Prairie Street were known for prostitution from the 1920s to the 1970s. Gangsters and bootleggers hid their merchandise in Prairie Street brothels. Tunnels connected buildings through basements and cellars.

Being Different

Jim was always different from other boys. More than anything, he didn't engage in games with the other children. He wanted to be with the adults. As a child, there was only the slightest inkling of the "Felicia" to come: "The only time I had dressed up was when my mother and everyone had gone to school or work and I would pull the bedsheets off the bed and act like it was a gown."

By the time Jim was in sixth grade, the family moved to public housing at the Harrison Homes on the far South Side of Peoria. According to the Peoria Housing Authority, the Harrison Homes were built in 1942 to provide housing for Peoria's working families. The Harrison Homes currently have 158 apartments on 31 acres of land.

"They were actually nice, and they had some strict rules," recalled Doris. "You could not have excessive trash, and your yard area had to be clean and orderly. No garbage outside the cans, that sort of thing. There were a lot of kids around and we were always outside if we could be."

Dorothy explained: "If your screen or window was broken, you had to repair it right away or they would repair it and charge you for it. Your yard couldn't have any litter in it, and they had a curfew. You couldn't be out after certain hours. They were very strict and people actually went around and checked."

"Trewyn Park was nearby, and there was a sand pit there, and we all used to hang out there. We used to love to jump in the sand pit and roll down it," laughed Doris. "We also used to go to the Illinois River. My brother Merle and I would jump the train that went over the Illinois River, and then the big thrill was to jump off the train into the river and then swim back home. Merle was very daring. It took me a while to get up my courage, but I finally did it."

Jim saw another advantage to the relocation. "The great thing about moving there was, I got the chance to have a paper route and started peddling the Peoria Journal [which was to become the Peoria Journal Star in the mid-1950s] at age 8," Jim said.

"I had about 330 papers I delivered every morning. I kept that route for four to five years, and that was about the only time I recall my mother ever hitting me. One morning it was cold and snowy and I was whining to have my sister get up and help me come and peddle papers, and she wouldn't do it. We made such a racket my mother started hitting me with a belt, but I couldn't feel anything since I had my coat on and everything."

This is also when Jim started learning about sex—at age 8. "I was a shoeshine as well," he recalled. "On weekend mornings at 8 or 9, I'd go up and down Adams Street in Peoria. They [the adult men Jim met] rarely made me shine shoes. I just carried the box. But they gave me money for other things. I'd go out doing that until 9 at night.

"I always made my own money. It started when some guy offered me money. I enjoyed it and that was that. No one was ever arrested. At that age there were so many perverts who wanted to touch you or grab you or play with you. I was sexually assaulted in ways that I just never realized at the time.

"I was very advanced for my age. There was also a guy I had a huge crush on when I was 9 or so. Then there was my Sunday school teacher, who I loved to watch play basketball. Every week I would go and watch the South Side Mission basketball team. Of course then I also got to hand out the towels in the shower room."

This eventually led to Flint's return to his old neighborhood near Aiken Alley. "I worked in a brothel there for several months when I was 13. There were 16 or 17 girls in the house and then me. A lot of the professors would come over from Normal [where Illinois State University is located] or from Bradley University [in Peoria]. They'd come in and play around with you for a while. They would rub me down with alcohol to be sure I was clean. I did that after I had the paper route and before I started working at Steak 'n Shake [a chain that was founded in 1934 in Normal, Illinois].

"I knew how hard my mother worked and I wanted to help out," Jim said. "I remember I went over to see my mother, and my last brother, Ronnie, was being born. I went in and asked the other cook where my mother was. He said, 'Your mother went to the hospital.' I asked, 'What's the matter?' He said, 'I think she's going to have a baby.' She left work, went to the hospital, and four hours later had the baby. Two days later she was back at work with the baby [Ronnie], which she put in a dishpan and kept right there in the hotel kitchen. She had all of us and she had a responsibility to provide for us."

At one time, a woman, Gracie Snyder, lived with the family. "Gracie used to work with my mother [at the Père Marquette] and they caught her drinking and fired her," Dorothy said. "My mother used to feel sorry for a lot of people, so Gracie came to live with us, and she was always drunk, and we used to have to hide her so my mother wouldn't see her. Because otherwise my mom would have never let her take care of us.

"In the back of the house we had a stoop where she used to sit, and people would stare. It was later I found out they were looking because she wasn't wearing underwear. I always thought it was on account of her being drunk. She was a nice lady, but we were the ones who took care of her."

Doris added, "Mom let her stay with us. We used to tell people she was our nanny. We used to play awful pranks on her. When she used to get drunk, sometimes she'd pass out, and then we'd take her and put her in other people's cars."

In this large household, Doris and Dorothy were the cleaners. Dorothy recalled, "I was immaculate, and my older brother Merle used to call me crazy because I was always washing and waxing the floors."

"I remember we moved when I was in eighth grade, because everyone else was going to Manual High School and I had to go to Central," Doris said. "So I told them all that if I had to go there, I was going to drop out. Well, Jim said, 'No, you're not. I'll fix it, I will get you in Manual.' Well, he didn't, but he went out and bought me all these beautiful clothes so it wouldn't be so hard going to a new school.

"Jim was always doing stuff for us. That continued for years. In fact, when I got married, Jim picked out my wedding gown with me, paid for it, and walked me down the aisle."

Do Fries Come With That Shake?

Flint's most auspicious foray into the working world began when he was in junior high. It was then that he donned his white pants, white shirt, bow tie and paper corner hat to begin working as a carhop. "At about 14, I lied about my age and started working at Steak 'n Shake. It was hard work but it was fun. We only got paid a dollar a night. At that time Steak 'n Shake was all carhops," he said.

Steak 'n Shake is known for premium burgers and milkshakes. "The word 'steak' stood for STEAKBURGER. The term 'shake' stood for hand-dipped MILK SHAKES," the company states on its website. The site explains that founder Gus Belt was "determined to serve his customers the finest burgers and shakes in the business. To prove his point that his burgers were exceptionally prime, he would wheel in a barrel of steaks (including round, sirloin and T-bones) and grind the meat into burgers right in front of the guests." This gave rise to the chain's popular slogan, "In Sight It Must Be Right."

By the time Flint joined the corporation, there were several of the popular fast-food chain's outlets in Peoria. "The first one I worked at was on North Adams, and they closed that, and then I worked the one on South Adams," Flint said. "They would hire 15 of us, and whoever was best-dressed and with the nicest-polished shoes would be the ones who got to work. It was always a race to see who was going to come in first, second and third, and I always got one of those top three positions.

"If you didn't really want to work that night, someone would always want your shift. The other option was to go peel potatoes all night. I did that once and that was enough for me. It was a good place to work. I used to go home with $35 or $40 a night and all but a dollar of it from tips, and that was in the 1950s. That was big money back then. I always would give my mother extra money, too, so she could help the rest of the kids.

"Sometimes when they were short of help at the original Steak 'n Shake in Normal, they'd drive one or two of us over there and we'd work the night. Then I started training carhops in new places like Indianapolis. The best rules for being a good carhop are 'be nice' and 'be fast.' At that time, the service at Steak 'n Shakes was three to five minutes, but it's not like that anymore.

"I remember one night when the curb manager was out talking to customers in a car, and of course I ran out to take the order, and the guys in the car said, 'We'll take a chocolate shake and a blow job.' I almost died. These were two of the H____ brothers, who were known around town as picking on the gays, kind of teen thugs. When the one brother said that, I said, 'Sir, I can get you your chocolate shake, but we don't serve the other,' and ran away.

"I remember going over and counting all my tickets and just being so upset because I thought I was going to get fired, especially with the curb manager right there. But he walked around and he said, 'You handled that very nicely.'

"Everybody sort of wondered about me and who I was, because we had these two lesbians in town—Jean, and I cannot recall her lover's name. She owned [a hotel] where my dad sometimes worked, the bank building and three or four other businesses. She always drove a brand-new Eldorado Cadillac convertible, and they would only let me wait on them. She'd be in her man suit with her tie, and her girlfriend was always dressed just right, and everybody was always saying, 'Why does she just let you wait on her?' I never knew what to say, so I just said, 'I don't know, I guess I just give good service.'"

'We Are the Peoria Girls ...'

Flint recalled another important event from that era. "One night, I was about 13, and it was a Monday," he said. "I was walking down Main Street, and this carload of five kids came by and were yelling 'sissy' and 'fag.' I didn't know what it all meant but I was still petrified. Monday night was the night everyone was downtown shopping. I thought someone was going to see me and hear all this stuff being yelled at me.

"The guys calling to me said to come on and get in the car. I did. I thought for sure I was going to get beaten up, but it was better than just standing there and thinking about people from school seeing all this going on and recognizing me.

"Turned out it was a carload of gay guys doing the yelling. That was the night I really found out there were others like me. Bob Burton, Dick Woosley, Harold, Eddie Billingsley. After that night, life was so much easier. That's when I got to meet all the gay kids in Peoria.

"Before we had any place to go, the gays would all meet on the courthouse stairs. There was an all-night place called Thompson's Restaurant across the street, so we'd go over and get coffee or meet a date or whatever, and then we'd go across the street. The more femmes of us would do a kick line on the courthouse stairs and sing, 'We are the Peoria Girls, we wear our hair in curls, and when we walk down Main, we drive all the men insane ... .' It was a riot.

"The gay kids sort of raised me in Peoria, and it was also around that time that this Spanish gay kid in Peoria called me Felicia for the first time. He kept calling me that, and I said, 'Why are you calling me that all the time?' and he said, 'That means happiness.' Of course I liked that." (Felicia is derived from the Latin word "felix," which means "happy.")

One of Flint's friends from that era, Dick Decker, recalled that time in Peoria. "Oh, yes, that courthouse square was a very cruisy area," Decker said. "There was a cement coping wall that was about 2½ feet high that ran around the courthouse square. Guys used to sit there and the cars would go around the square and slow down. It was dangerous, but it was very popular."

Flint continued: "It was also back when I was 14 that I met Nick and Donna. Donna worked with my mother at the Père Marquette, but she and her husband also owned a bar on Main Street called the Quench Room [631 West Main Street], and so I asked Nick if he would mind the gay kids coming in there, and he said, 'No, you're all welcome here.'

"I remember I always had to go in the back door because my uncle worked at the gas station across the street. So, little by little, the gays took over the Quench Room and turned it into a gay bar. It was every Friday and Saturday, and boy, it was just wonderful."

"It was a wild place," recalled Decker. "I started going there when I was in my late teens, and that was where I met all my dear friends. It was a piano bar and I remember we would all stand around the piano and sing.

"There was also the Merrimac Lounge. It was a husband and wife [the Peppers] that ran it. I'm not sure why they let us in. Maybe they just thought we would spend a lot of money there, and we did. All the stools were covered in zebra skin. It was a narrow bar that ran the full length of the bar, front door to back. There were booths on the side. Everything was zebra print. I remember at Halloween they would have a costume contest and we'd all come in drag.

"In high school nobody teased Jim, even though he was the majorette. He led the band, and no one could twirl like he could. He was always so effervescent and so fun that every time you hung around with him, you knew you were going to have a good time.

"He was never teased as far as I can recall. He was just himself. I was teased in high school, and I was closeted! I would get things, like in my yearbook it would say, 'To My Favorite Gal,' and then 'Gal' would be crossed off and they'd write 'Pal.' I always knew Jim would be successful. He always had that air about him like nothing was going to stop him."

Flint said he did pirouettes in the high-school hallway, "just over-the-top gay things and no one ever teased me. I was always popular with the popular girls, and so the boys knew I'd never put in a good word for them if they teased me."

Eventually they built a new Steak 'n Shake next to the Quench Room, and Flint became the curb manager there. "It was all very convenient," he said. "The gang would come by sometimes when I was working and run across the parking lot in their high heels and all that nonsense. By then people were starting to understand that I was gay."

According to the article "Gay in Central Illinois" on the BoiMagazine.com website, the Quench Room on Main Street was an "ominous tavern just blocks from Bradley University [and] was the longest lived gay bar in Peoria's history, up until the late 1990s [before] changing over to a straight bar."

Flint said the other bars they frequented were the African-American bars Harold's Club and the Blue Shadow. Harold's was on Washington Street, and the Blue Shadow was on Hamilton Boulevard. "Somehow they understood our cause," Flint said.

Harold's Club has also achieved fame for other reasons. According to his Yahoo! Movies biography, high school dropout and teen father Richard Pryor began his career as a nightclub comedian at Harold's Club, which was reportedly owned by the most powerful black man in town. Harold's was also known for live jazz.

Flint's fascination with drag entertainers may have started with John Casey, who came to Peoria to perform at the strip joints. "He was a queen, and nobody ever knew he was a queen, and he would start hanging around with us guys. I was so fascinated," Flint said. "I can't think of his stripper name. When he would dress up and I would see him heading down the street to work, I would always think, 'Oh, my God, that's a man.' I couldn't believe such a beautiful woman was a man."

Mom, I've Got Something to Tell You

Flint eventually decided that he needed to come out to Pearl, his mom, or rather the decision was made for him.

"Right after my 14th birthday I had to go home and tell my mother I was gay," he said. "At that time, my mother was the head cook at the Père Marquette Hotel. I got caught coming out of the hotel about 4:30 in the morning. Of course the house detective recognized me and said, 'Don't one of your family members work here?' I said, 'Yes, sir, my mother. This was a friend of my family I was visiting.'

"I didn't sleep all night, but I waited until my mother got up. She had worked the night before until about 1, so it was about 11 when she got up. I said, 'Mother, I have to talk to you,' and we went out on the porch. She said, 'What's the matter?' I said, 'Well, I got to tell you something.'

"We went on for about a half-hour before I could tell her, and I finally said, 'Mom, I don't know if I'm normal or what, but I don't like women. I like men, and last night I went to a hotel with a gentleman and I got caught coming out of there by the house detective. I told him it was a friend of our family, and he wanted to know if you knew I was there, and I said yes. I just wanted to let you know I am different.'

"She said she didn't know that's what it was, but she knew I was different because I never wanted to play with toys or kids, I always wanted to be with the adults. She said she didn't understand it, but not to tell my father. So then I thought, Well, if I am going to do anything, it's time that I get out on my own, because I couldn't keep it a secret after that.

"So, when I was 15, I moved out of the home and got a one-room in a rooming house up by Methodist Hospital. And then when I was 16, I got a job there as an orderly."

Drum Major: Flint's Sporting Life Begins

With school colors of orange and black, the Manual High School Rams were huge in the sports arena. When Jim Flint attended the school, it was on Lincoln Avenue in Peoria and was a Central Illinois football powerhouse, undefeated in 1958 as well as 1959 and in his post-Manual years of 1960 and 1962. Coach Ken Hinricks is in the Illinois High School Football Coaches Hall of Fame. Basketball titles for the school came in the 1990s. Notable Manual Rams alumni include former NBA players Frank Williams, Al Smith and Howard Nathan, former basketball player and coach Sergio McClain, and American Sportscasters Association Hall of Fame announcer Jack Brickhouse.

Flint was a drum major at Trewyn Middle School and then at Manual High School. "For the band, I wore the black pants (which always upset me because the girls had the shorts) and then an orange vest and the big hat," Flint said. "I had some fringe. I remember walking down Main Street in all the parades and hearing 'Oh, Mommy, look, there's a boy doing that.'

"The first time I came to Chicago was with the band. I was probably 15 or so at the time. We performed at Soldier Field, and when I did, I thought, If I ever get out of Peoria I am moving to Chicago. I snuck out of our hotel when we were there and went to the Lincoln Baths [a notorious gay bathhouse at 1812 North Clark Street]. It was dirty and filthy, raunchy but full of beautiful people. I got back to the hotel before anybody knew I'd been gone all night. Although I was way underage, they didn't care, that guy [at Lincoln Baths] didn't check anybody. As long as you had the money. It was illegal anyway. That was before they had the big raid [by the police]. I also went to Bughouse Square. I'd heard about the Lawson YMCA, but I didn't go there."

Flint was in the Manual class of 1959, and though not exactly out, Flint wasn't closeted, either. "Everyone thought I was different —not bad, just different," he said. "In my junior year, I was a drum major in the band and got elected again to the student council. After the election, the principal called me into his office and said, 'You have to start setting an example, because you're on the student council, so your clothes have to be this way, and you need to behave this way.' I said, 'You know, my clothes may never be new or never be designer, but they'll be clean, and as to how I act, I am myself.' They elected me and he didn't like it, and I remember I cried all the way home. Two weeks later I quit school and finished up my GED in the Navy."

Though Flint would eventually move on, Steak 'n Shake would remain a big part of his life and work ethic. As of 2011, he still fills out Steak 'n Shake comment cards.

"I most certainly do," he said. "One time we were in Michigan City and we went to the bathroom, and the toilet was blocked, and there was a sign that said, 'Toilet blocked, use the sink.' I went out and asked for a comment card and said, 'I want one because what you have in there is unacceptable.' Sure enough, I sent the card in and called Indianapolis, and they told me they would send me complimentary coupons. I said, 'I don't need coupons—this was my job and how I learned, and I still care about the company.'"

Flint related several instances of sending both good and bad comment cards about regional locations of the business. "That was my first real job, and they taught me how to work, and I still take pride in it. I have a Steak 'n Shake T-shirt and I wear it with pride," he said.

In the Navy

Flint's father had warned him about the military draft. He told his sons it would be better to enlist in the Navy than be drafted into the Army, so Jim followed the advice. His enlistment was covered in the Peoria Journal, in an article headlined "2 Boys Go Navy, 1 Takes Air Force." It noted that "James W. Flint, 17, of 2826 W. Grinnell St ... will be discharged the day before his 21st birthday" because he was signing up under the "minority enlistment" program.

"Two weeks after I turned 17, I joined the Navy," Flint said. "I came up to Camp Porter in the Great Lakes Naval Training Center. Camp Porter was the new barracks at Great Lakes. I was lucky because I was made the company clerk, so boot camp was very easy for me. I was doing all the clerk duties so I didn't have to do all the heavy lifting and calisthenics.

"I also noticed the more I was there, the more I looked at guys. We had a great group of guys we went through boot camp with. I was so honored to be in the Navy. When I got my first leave, my mother came up with my sister Darlene and we came into the city. They were both so proud of me.

"When I got out after nine weeks of boot camp, I went home for five days before I went off to my first assignment. I got on a Capital Airlines plane to Little Creek, Virginia—it was really Norfolk, but the amphibious base is in Little Creek.

"I will never forget. It was my first time up in an airplane. I was in full uniform and the plane started to land at Washington National as a stopover, and all of a sudden we were flying over the river and I thought we were going to land in it. In full uniform I let out a scream. Everyone turned and looked, and I was so embarrassed, what with being in uniform and all. But I was scared. I thought we were going to go down and crash right in that river.

"When we got there, they started assigning us to different places. I got the Operations Division. I lucked out again. It was all down on the waterfront and we had our own barracks, and there were only 37 guys in the division, and only 18 of us stayed in the barracks all night.

"Every time a ship would come into port, we would perform the services and have to go out and be sure they had the right flags up, and the harbor pilot went aboard and made sure they went through all the right procedures to get into port. It was kind of interesting to know all the LSTs [Landing Ships, Tank] and all the LSDs [Landing Ships, Dock] and all the amphibious warfare things.

"I was there about four months when the third-class yeoman left and they couldn't get another yeoman in to take his job. He was the head yeoman in the division, so the captain said, 'I'm going to make you in charge.' Then I had to run the whole office. I had to do all the assignments, say who was doing inspections, anything that was wrong. I had to send the letters or go on board and make sure they did certain things. It was a lot of work, and finally they sent two seaman apprentices in to help me.

"It was a good division. I got to meet the harbor pilots. They were all chief petty officers and they were all good to me. We just stayed away from the base, but we had to go onto the base to eat. After I burned out three clutches on the car, the captain wouldn't let me drive anymore, so he'd always make someone drive me.

"When we were there, I got to know everybody. It was soon apparent that there were so many gays on the base that at one time I thought that being gay was the first qualification for being in the Navy. So we'd all meet at lunch—the guys from the captain's office or the CO's or the disbursing clerk.

"We'd all start walking in, and the Marines would go and open the door and say, 'Here come the girls.' Then we'd walk right ahead because we all had early chow passes. So we could go to the head of the line. None of us hid it. We were just ourselves and nobody bothered us or anything. I think the ones who really hid it were the ones who had the problems. It was such a great life I never wanted to leave there."

Flint went to the Continental gay bar right after he got to Norfolk. "As soon as I got there, I had to meet gay people," he said. "It was right in town on Boush Street. The Continental was such a great bar. It was booths around the sides and a long narrow circular bar in the middle. To the side was a piano where they could have a singer. It was dark and nice, and up front they had a little grill with the best hamburgers in the world. You could eat there, play there, and get lucky there.

"The Thomas Nelson Hotel was right across the street, and right behind it was the Navy YMCA. And if you couldn't make it there, you would run across the street to the hotel, because the downstairs washroom was always busy with people looking. Around the corner was the Peppermint Lounge, and we used to go over there, too.

"At 11:30 or 11:45 the shore patrol would make the final go-through, and the bars all closed at 12, so you made your final play right then. Then we would always have parties out at Ocean View or Virginia Beach or somebody's house.

"If you left there with somebody, you always had to be careful because the vice always watched you out front. There was a cop there named Robinette and he loved to catch gay guys. Especially two gay guys in a hotel room together. He'd break the door down and everything. It sort of makes you wonder about him."

Losing Dad

Flint's schedule changed and he started getting off duty at 2 p.m. each day. He thought about planning for the future, and that plan included saving money. But first he started as a volunteer at DePaul Hospital in Norfolk, in the emergency room. One Saturday afternoon, the mother superior took Flint in the private elevator up to where the chapel was for the nuns.

"She took me in there and told me my dad was dying and that she didn't know if I would be able to get back in time to be with him or not," Flint said. "They took me in and prayed for me. Then I went back to the base and they sent me right away to Peoria.

"First off, though, I was on Capital Airlines again, so I had to stop in Washington, and because the plane was overloaded, they didn't know if they would get me out, with the delays and everything. In one of the restaurants, I was talking to a United pilot and telling him my story, and he said, 'Come with me,' and he got me right on and flew me home. I got there about an hour after my dad had passed away.

"My dad was an alcoholic, a good man but an alcoholic. He [also] went into a TB [tuberculosis sanitarium] center for about five years in Chicago. And when he got out, my mother said it's either her and the kids or him and the liquor.

"He chose her and the kids and didn't drink anymore and was having such a great life. Everything was going well. It was like he had really turned his life around. Then my dad was helping do something and fell off a chair and got a blood clot—it went to his brain and it killed him."

Dorothy recalled: "I remember when Jim came home when my dad died, and I had never seen a dead body, and Jim said, 'You have got to go up and see your dad.' I was scared to death. He knew that, for me, I had to see Dad dead in order to let go and go through grieving. It was then that Jim really became the dad in the family."

Jim explained, "I told my mother I would help her as much as I could, so I went back and got a job at Norfolk General Hospital in the psychiatric department because a friend of mine, a guy we always used to call Salome, worked there."

Dorothy added: "Financially Jim helped out a lot. He was sending us money, and we moved from the projects into this big house with maybe five bedrooms. It was great because for the first time I didn't have to share my bedroom with my two brothers and sister. It was just my sister and I sharing a room.

"We got a phone but we weren't allowed to use the phone until we did our homework unless it was an emergency, so we didn't use the phone. We finally had a TV, but we couldn't watch it because our homework had to be done first. I thought, Oh, this is a great house and we have all these things, but we can't use any of them."

Shocking Treatment

In the aftermath of his father's death, Flint returned to Norfolk and his work in the Navy and at the hospital. "The hospital work was such a trip," he said. "I thought some of the patients' families were more in need of the psychiatric help than the patients were. When I started there, a lot of the Navy wives would try and kill themselves just to get their husbands home from duty in the Navy. They would put them through the electric shock treatments, which I thought was just the most horrible thing in the world, but I would have to hold them down. Then there was insulin therapy."

According to Wikipedia, insulin shock or insulin coma therapy was a form of psychiatric treatment in which patients (usually diagnosed as schizophrenic) were repeatedly injected with large doses of insulin to produce daily comas over several weeks. Seizures sometimes occurred before or during the coma. Each coma would last for up to an hour and be terminated by intravenous glucose.

Patients undergoing this treatment required continuous supervision, since there was a danger of hypoglycemic aftershock. Typically, insulin injections were administered six days a week for about two months. Insulin coma therapy and electro and cardiazol/metrazol were collectively known as the shock therapies.

"Once in a while there were gay patients," Flint said, "but whenever anyone was in psychiatric need they would send them there—but mostly the military hospital didn't handle that. If there were [gays], there was nothing we could do to help them." Flint could not personally put himself forward to patients as a gay man in order to mitigate their situation.

Flint said the work was terrifying. "I thought, My God, I'm lucky my mother understood me, that I was different, but for people who grow up like that, it was awful," he recalled in WTTW's 2008 film Out & Proud in Chicago. "And to sit there and watch the shock treatment and have to participate in some of that was even more … .

"There were patients that were gay and they were there because their parents put them there thinking there was a cure for this, and some went through extensive shock and insulin therapy … . You're there for nursing care and to help them and watch that they don't hurt themselves, because at the time they were just walking around like a zombie after these treatments. But you certainly couldn't come out and say, you know, 'I'm gay' or that sort of thing. You'd be out of there fast … ."

Mental health professionals as well as the general public considered homosexuality to be a mental illness at the time. It was listed by the American Psychiatric Association in its Diagnostic and Statistical Manual of Mental Disorders (the DSM) until 1974.

Sometimes there were other barbaric or absurd methods to "treat" gays and lesbians. One doctor who practiced during this period said he could treat lesbians by teaching them how to apply cosmetics, giving them a styled haircut and hiring a fashion consultant. Other times, the measures were more drastic. In 1955 in Sioux City, Iowa, 29 men suspected of homosexuality were committed to mental asylums as a preventive measure authorized by the state.

Flint said his hospital unit had 36 to 42 patients each night. "You met some of the nicest people there, and some of the strangest," he said. "I remember we had this one guy who was in traction, and [Flint's colleague] Salome and I would always play around with people. Salome looked at the traction and leaned close and said, 'Look, Jim, if you look you can see the ships coming in.' So I jumped up and looked and said, 'Oh, my gosh, you can see three of them.' So this family all jumped up and looked at the traction like they could actually see ships, too. I looked at Salome and said, 'Do we have the right person in the bed?'

"Another time we were back in seclusion, where they put the patients who got violent. They would put them in padded cells so they didn't hurt themselves. I was putting this harness on a woman to calm her down and she kicked me right in the gut. It kept hurting so bad I went down to the emergency room, and they said, 'Oh, young man, that's not from the kick. Your appendix has ruptured.' So they rushed me to Portsmouth Naval Hospital [in Portsmouth, Virginia] and they operated on me within an hour. The doctor said to me if it would have been a couple more hours I may not have made it.

"The worst thing about being in a naval hospital is, after you are well, they keep you because they always need help around the hospital. So they were keeping me and keeping me and keeping me before I could be sent back to duty. So I called the captain and said, 'Sir, they won't let me out of here.' He said, 'I'll make a call,' and I got out. That night I got out and went to the Continental bar.

"When I walked in, the owners, Jack and Manny, got up on the microphone and said, 'Guys, look, Flossie is back.' Everybody turned around and looked, and there were five guys from my division. I about fainted. So there was nothing to do then, so I just started talking and carrying on, and little did I know I would end up going out with every one of those five guys."

Flint's exploits with Navy men were well known to his sisters.

"As a kid, I remember two holidays," Dorothy said. "I always thought it was Halloween because after Jim joined the military and he would come home, he always brought a bunch of guys. Then later he'd come in and they would be all these women with big hair. I always asked my mom, 'Why are these people dressed like this? Where are they going?' She would always say to me, 'Oh, it's Halloween. There's a Halloween party that they're going to.' So I always thought he came home for Halloween, and then for Christmas because we always saw him for Christmas."

In the Navy Again: Going to Hawaii

After serving in the Navy, Flint was released in the early 1960s. He moved in with his sister Darlene and her husband, Andy, in St. Louis and started working for Steak 'n Shake as a manager on Riverview Boulevard. After a while, he started to miss the military. "I liked the gay bars in St. Louis but it wasn't doing anything for me," Flint said. "I felt like I was just sort of floating. Then I was going by the post office one day and saw 'RE-ENLIST RE-ENLIST' in the windows. So I did.

"When I re-enlisted, they sent me to Honolulu, to Pearl Harbor in Hawaii. I was there about 18 months. It was fabulous. The gay kids were great. We used to hang out at this bar called Le Coq d'Or. One room was all knotty pine and games and a pool table, and the other room was a long piano bar. Then they had red booths all around it, and each booth had a telephone so you could call the other booths. The real hot spot, though, was The Glade nightclub on Hotel Street [152 North Hotel Street]."

According to the website thegladeproject.com, for a documentary of the period: "The performances of the glamorous female impersonators at The Glade nightclub on Hotel Street in Old Chinatown were a must-see for tourists, military personnel from around the world and local families. The main attraction was a beautiful Mahu known as Prince Hanalei—fire dancer extraordinaire ... . Straight and gays alike mixed on Hotel Street to enjoy some of the most beautiful Mahus (Asian and Pacific Islanders of the Pacific Rim). For the performers at The Glade, great pride was taken in the crafting of elaborate gowns and wardrobe adorned by Asian/Pacific Islander men .... .

"Just as Hawai'i began its new status as the 50th State [August 1959] there came along a strong Americanization/westernization influence. Modernization brought with it a shift in attitude towards the Asian/Pacific Islanders and the cultural identity of Mahus. By default, ai'kane (same-sex lovers) in general also began to be treated differently. These groups, who once enjoyed a large amount of acceptance, now suffered discrimination, stigmatization and violence. The Hawai'i State Legislature passed a law in the early 60s, on police recommendation after a series of articles in the local Honolulu Advertiser newspaper, that declared that Mahus could be arrested for 'dressing to deceive'. A white card labeled with the words 'I am a boy' or 'I am a male' had to be pinned on the chest of each Mahu ... . Over time, higher levels of violence toward Mahus and ai'kane increased to a critical mass ... ."

In 2011, former Baton Show Lounge performer Dina Jacobs explained her experience in Hawaii during this period. "The first time I did drag was Valentine's Day 1964," she said. "One of my friends lived in the projects and told my cousin and I we couldn't come to the party unless we came in drag, so having balls the size of coconuts, we did.

"My cousin came as the bride, and I came as the mother of the bride. My cousin (Shawn Luis) is also an entertainer who worked at the Baton for a while. Four of us cousins all do drag, but Shawn and I are the only entertainers.

"We grew up in Hawaii among all women, my mother and aunts. We always thought we were one of them. They treated me soft, and so I had the compassionate side of being a woman and the biological side of being a man. Drag was second nature to me. "When I was a junior in high school, Jack Cione, who had a club in Waikiki called The Clouds, was having auditions for a drag talent show, and I ended up being the emcee. Eventually I went to The Glade, which was a huge show bar with a three-piece combo ... there was no pantomime, no lip-syncing—it was all done live.

"Because of prejudices against the queens, we couldn't have real jobs, and so, many of us became prostitutes. The government started to see it as a real problem, so they had this law where if you were a male drag prostitute you had to wear a sign around your neck that said 'I am a boy.' They thought they could humiliate us into not being in drag anymore, but it didn't work. People were regularly beaten by the police, as though they could beat it out of us. The vice squad was doing that nightly, and if they caught you out at night alone—watch out."

Baton Show Lounge emcee Ginger Grant added: "A problem with the 'I am a boy' thing was, it was during the Vietnam War. They were all hooking on the street, and ships would be in, and the boys were all prettier than the real girls, and then surprise, surprise. When they'd be out hooking, the queens would wear their hair down in the front to cover the 'I am a boy' badge, and then they'd shout 'maka'i' [police] when someone saw a cop, and they'd flip their hair back so the badge was visible, then the police would go by, and then they would bring their long hair around to cover the badge again.

"There was an area called Hotel Street. On one side was the females, and the queens were on the other. Nobody crossed. One time this car was going around calling the queens mahus and my friend said, 'Ginger, get inside.' I said, 'What do you mean?' and she just repeated, 'Get inside.' This was a dark back street and there were probably 50 queens there, and suddenly they were all gone.

"That car came around the block a second time, and from the dark of this alley came garbage cans and bricks and everything else, and those queens smashed that car and the guys in it. Don't fuck with the mahus.

"At the same time, if the police caught the mahu without their badge visible, they would take them down to River Street; sometimes the water would be up and sometimes not, but the police would pick them up and throw them over that wall into the water whether the water was low or high."

Flint remembered his own time going to The Glade drag shows. "I met all the kids and queens there," he said. "It was the first time I ever really saw good drag. There was a high stage in the back and lots of terrific entertainers. Brandy Lee was probably the first one I ever saw sing live, and could she handle an audience. It was such a trip going downtown to Hotel Street from the base, because it was all dirt roads. Then down on Hotel Street, this block was all gay kids and queens, and then on that side was all hookers.

"A lot of the entertainers I had for the Baton who were from Hawaii were the contacts I met from when I was over there. The entertainers were so great. There was The Glade, and the Rains up the street, and then of course in Waikiki we had Hula's and a bar right underneath it called the Hideout. .... Then when I got out of the Navy, I kept going back there every year. I always thought I was going to make my life there."

From Pleasure Island to Treasure Island

Flint's naval career came to an abrupt end.

"I was at a big gay party," Flint said. "Somebody must have wanted us out of the Navy, because they made a call and turned us all in. They gave Naval Intelligence every one of our names. There were, I think, 37 of us."

One by one they were called in and sent to Naval Air Station Treasure Island, an artificial island in San Francisco Bay where the military had facilities.

"They were either going to break us or let us out," Flint said. "We stayed in the brig at Treasure Island for six weeks. Everyone was asking me if I was going to stay in the Navy or leave, and finally I decided not to fight it. Sitting there looking at San Francisco every night, I wanted to go and be a part of that.

"This was stupid. I was being punished for being myself. I was doing a good job and this is what I got. I wanted to be gay, so after a while I said I was going, and they gave me a general discharge under the gay issue."

Flint stayed in San Francisco for two short weeks. The boy from Peoria felt too removed from his Midwestern roots. "I missed Chicago," he said. "I lived with twins there [San Francisco], Ross and Randy Miller. They were two of the wildest guys I ever met. I got a small job at a sandwich shop but soon realized I couldn't do it. It wasn't me. I didn't have friends there, not like I had back in Illinois."

Homesick, Flint returned to Illinois and lived with his Aunt Dorothy (his mother's sister) and her husband, Walter, in Waukegan, Illinois, north of Chicago. They were like another set of parents to him.

More Hospital Work

Flint quickly found employment at St. Therese Hospital, 2615 Washington Street in Waukegan. St. Therese was built in 1929 by the Missionary Sisters Servants of the Holy Spirit, also called the Holy Spirit Missionary Sisters. Beginning in the 1950s, it became a safety-net hospital for the poor. (In 1985 the name was changed to St. Therese Medical Center, and it is now Vista Medical Center.)

"My favorite was Sister Kateria," Flint said. "She was someone I absolutely fell in love with. She was the head nun on our ward.

"Once she was demonstrating to the student nurses how to use the defibrillator paddles. She had me lie down to demonstrate and thought the thing was off. It wasn't. When she touched me with the paddles I bounced up at the jolt, and ever since I've said that's where I got my extra spark of life.

"She and I were there in intensive care along with Fannie, the nursing assistant. We had so much fun, but we were hard-working. We were always so busy from tracheotomies to craniotomies to heart-attack patients. Eventually I moved into the hospital [after living with his aunt and uncle]. I worked as a technician and scrubbed in for some of the emergency surgeries, especially on Saturdays.

"I really became involved with spirituality there as well. The more I got into the Catholic faith, the more I thought I would like to be a nursing brother in a mission and go into one of the seminaries. I was always interested in Catholicism and helping others and just the whole ceremony of the Catholic Mass. I wanted to be a part of that.

"The feelings grew stronger in Waukegan, but I thought about something like that even working in the hospital in Norfolk. It was always something I thought about doing when I got out of the Navy. In Waukegan I started going to Mass a lot.

"I still hadn't been baptized in the Catholic religion and still wanted to do it and then eventually become a brother. That never happened. There were other things in store for me. It was thrilling to help patients and see them get better, but you also got to see a lot of death. I was with Nat King Cole's father the night that he died there in 1965."

(Nat's father, the Reverend Edward James Coles, died February 1, 1965, and Nat died just two weeks later, on February 15. One of Nat's adopted children, the actor Nat Kelly Cole, born in 1959, died in 1995 of AIDS complications.)

"Another night there was a big car wreck," Flint said. "The misery became too overwhelming, especially with living there as well. I wanted to have a little fun, so I came to Chicago for a weekend. I experienced the nightlife and fell in love. I knew I couldn't do it at the hospital any longer."

Jim (right) with his dad and brother Bob.

Jim Flint's parents, Pearl Marie (Thomas) Flint and Vern Flint.

Jim's dad, mom and sister Florence.

Jim and his siblings and a cousin, from left: Florence, Jim, Bob, Darlene, and cousin Junior.

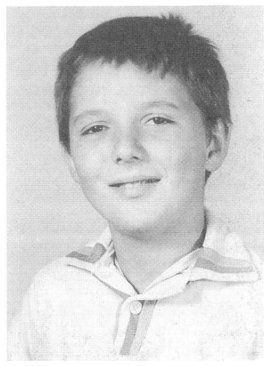

Jim Flint: The boy from Peoria.

UNITED STATES OF AMERICA
OFFICE OF PRICE ADMINISTRATION

771 022 CN

WAR RATION BOOK No. 3 *Void if altered*

NOT
VALID
WITHOUT
STAMP

Identification of person to whom issued: PRINT IN FULL

James W. Flint

(First name)   (Middle name)   (Last name)

Street number or rural route *131 HICKORY ST*

City or post office *PEORIA*   State *ILLINOIS*

AGE	SEX	WEIGHT	HEIGHT	OCCUPATION
2	MALE	30 Lbs.	3 Ft. In.	

SIGNATURE *JAMES WILLIAM FLINT*

(Person to whom book is issued. If such person is unable to sign because of age or incapacity, another may sign in his behalf.)

WARNING
This book is the property of the United States Government. It is unlawful to sell it to any other person, or to use it or permit anyone else to use it, except to obtain rationed goods in accordance with regulations of the Office of Price Administration. Any person who finds a lost War Ration Book must return it to the War Price and Rationing Board which issued it. Persons who violate rationing regulations are subject to $10,000 fine or imprisonment, or both.

OPA Form No. R-130

LOCAL BOARD ACTION

Issued by _____

(Local board number)   (Date)

Street address _____

City _____ State _____

_____

(Signature of issuing officer)

Flint's war ration book from his childhood years: at age 2, when he weighed 30 pounds.

Flint's mom, left, with his Aunt Dorothy and Uncle Wally.

Jim at the Steak 'n Shake on Main Street in Peoria around 1958-59, with his friend Nellie.

2 Boys Go Navy, 1 Takes Air Force

Two 17-year-old Peoria youths Wednesday enlisted in the Navy and a 19-year-old youth joined the Air Force. All were sent to Chicago for final processing.

Signed to minority enlistments in the Navy were James W. Flint, 17, of 2826 W. Grinnel St., and Jerry L. Ramos, 17, of 1410 Livingston St. Each will be discharged the day before his 21st birthday. Raymond P. McMillan Jr., 19, of 2624 N. Springdale Ave., enlisted in the Air Force for four years and will be enrolled in an electronics school.

Above: Flint, 17, enlisted in the Navy in 1959. This unmarked clipping is believed to be from the Peoria Journal newspaper.

Right: Flint's appointment as a recruit petty officer at U.S. Naval Training Center Great Lakes.

In the Navy: Flint is pictured, second row from bottom, second from left, in this U.S. Naval Training Center 1959 photo.

Flint (right) and two Navy friends.

Flint's honorable
discharge from the Navy,
November 16, 1960.

Counterclockwise from top right:
Jim's sister Florence and her daughter Billie in the 1960s.

Jim with his grandma Edna Thomas (left) and mother, Pearl, in front of the Candlelight Dinner Playhouse, 5501 South Archer Avenue in Chicago, which was featuring The Unsinkable Molly Brown.

Jim's sister Margaret in the 1970s.

Jim's mother, Pearl (left), with her siblings Martha, Willard and Dorothy, plus Jim's sister Doris (2nd from right), in 1973.

Flint and his siblings gathered with their mother for this photo from 1985. Back row, from left: John, Dorothy, Doris, Merle, Serena, Jim, Bob. Front: Ronald, Pearl, Margaret and Darlene.

Jim's mom Pearl with her siblings, 1985: Dorothy, Willard, Floyd, Pearl and Martha (front). In 2011, Willard is the last remaining sibling.

Jim and his siblings in 2001. Back row: Darlene, Serena, Dorothy, Doris, John and Jim. Front: Florence, Margaret and Ronald.

2

Annex, Chesterfield, Sam's and Other Clubs

Jim Flint worked at numerous gay clubs in Chicago before opening his first bar in 1969. The Chesterfield, at 2831 North Clark Street near Diversey Parkway, was one of those clubs. It was a Mob-owned club that featured female-impersonator shows by the time Flint worked there.

Jim Henritze, a manager at The Chesterfield, moved to Chicago from Florida in 1962 for work. "It was impossible to find work there because of the Cuban Missile Crisis," he said. "I worked here at a restaurant on Lawrence for about eight months and used to come to The Chesterfield.

"I was friendly there with a woman named Opal Carlson, who was 36 inches tall and who used to be a dice girl at the Century [gay bar] across the street. Dice girls were outlawed just before that—basically no money was involved, you'd [roll the dice] for free drinks. Anyway, when that ended, the Syndicate took care of her and moved her across the street to The Chesterfield, where she worked as sort of a hostess, just sitting at the door greeting people.

"She got me a job there tending bar. When owner Nick Dallesandro had a gallbladder infection, his wife came to me and asked me to run the place for him until he got better. I hired my lover at the time, Ray Bell, as a bartender, as well as a daytime bartender, Barney Branson.

"During that time, a bunch of us went down to the Nite Life to see Gail Sherman, and we thought about bringing a drag show to The Chesterfield, but figured it would never happen. Nick thought it was a good idea, so he went to the police commander down at Town Hall, and suddenly we could do it. I hired three entertainers—Jackie Lynn, Mitzi Monet and Criss Cross. I couldn't hire four, but I told Roby Landers that once Nick let me, that she could come on as well."

Henritze said there were a front and a back bar, and by the back bar there was a raised stage for an organist. "So we adapted and rebuilt that stage to be against the back wall, and then eventually the bar was opened up into a sort of V shape with the stage at the back," Henritze said. "We had a great sound system and curtains that opened and closed electronically, and we put in lights and were all set to go on Saturday night.

"Well, that Thursday, Roby Landers opened her show at the My-O-My down on Clark and Wrightwood. That was a struggling straight bar that put on a drag show to drum up business. Their stage was basically wood on a bunch of orange crates. It was a Syndicate place, too, and not associated with the My-O-My down in New Orleans. The My-O-My here was only open a few months.

"Once she got a chance, Roby came to The Chesterfield because what we had was so much nicer. Well, she took over the show. She and I clashed. She was the boss of the stage show but I was the manager of the bar. She announced that while she was onstage no drinks would be served. Well, we clashed right there. I said, 'You're here for the show, but the bar isn't here for you.' I went to Nick. He backed me up, since he didn't want to lose the money. Roby clashed with Criss Cross as well. That's eventually why she [Criss] left.

"At The Chesterfield we had a 4 [a.m.] license and did three shows at 10, 12 and 2. The show was about an hour. The show at The Chesterfield evolved, and eventually there was Roby Landers, Vicki Marlane, Jackie Lynn, Mitzi Monet, Lee Lorraine and Tillie.

"Jackie Knight would do guest spots. She came from a place farther north on Sheridan at Wilson called the Chit Chat, which was a lesbian bar but that had shows there. Nite Life could get away with it [drag shows] because it was a tourist place. There was also the Front Page downtown, and they had some drag shows on the q.t. They were always getting raided.

"At the time, a Greek woman owned the building The Chesterfield was in. We were paying $175 in rent, but if we bought the building the mortgage was $250. I told Nick he was nuts not to do it. So he did and it ended up in a couple months a building up the street came up for sale, and that was where the Annex was, so he bought that as well. The Annex was nicer. It was much newer. Nick never trusted us, so he brought in his two nephews to run the places. I left in 1965."

Another star of the era, who wished to remain anonymous, elaborated on the shows at The Chesterfield as well as around town. "I remember Jim [Flint] from The Chesterfield," the performer said. "I did comedy and lip-synced to Shirley Bassey, Judy Garland and Judy Canova. I worked as a nurse during the day, and then periodically I'd do some of the shows at night. I worked The Chesterfield sometimes, sometimes the Mob-owned Talk of the Town, and My-O-My farther down on Clark.

"At The Chesterfield, I remember working with Criss Cross (who I never got along with), and Tillie the Dirty Old Lady, who would do Sophie Tucker. Vicki Marlane would strip as well as lip-sync, at least strip down to what was allowed, which was G-string and pasties. Mitzi Monet was another stripper/lip-sync act who was very good, but we didn't get along, either. There was Jackie Lynn, Lee Lorraine. Lee Lorraine was a comedienne and was known as the French Pussycat.

"I met Roby Landers when she did a bit at Shoreline 7, and that was when she got me hired at My-O-My. It would have much more elaborate numbers. The place was not all that beautiful but it had a stage that was an elevated sort of half circle, and if you had five or six of us onstage it was a little crowded. Despite that, we did production numbers.

"Roby would do things from South Pacific. Roby actually left My-O-My when she got hired at The Chesterfield. Bee Lo Beau was at My-O-My, too, Ray Bourbon, Skip Arnold, TC Jones. Mickey Sellis was the male lead, and I remember he and Vicki Marlane did a wonderful version of 'Slaughter on Tenth Avenue.' Sometimes they would even do plays on Sundays as a sort of matinee.

"I did a lip-sync there to 'Limehouse Blues' that was very popular. There was usually a production, and then in between were duets and trios, and it ran about an hour to an hour and a half, and in between there would be duets and numbers—'Sisters' from White Christmas was popular, and Judy at Carnegie Hall. I remember a big production we did to 'Hava Nagila.'"

Flint Moves In

When Flint worked in the Chicago suburbs, he made the trek down to visit Chicago gay bars. One day he walked into The Chesterfield. Looking across the bar, he saw this gorgeous

Italian kid, and that was when thoughts of being a missionary started to really fade.

"I fell in love," Flint said. "I was talking to this kid, and he told me they were opening this bar just up the street called the Annex [2865 North Clark Street] and they were looking for bartenders. I asked if the boss was there now. So I walked up there and talked to him.

"I told him I had experience and named some places. It wasn't true. I had experience, but not on that side of the bar. He asked how long it would be before I could get there and be ready for work. I said I could be there in a week. So I gave my notice at St. Therese's [Hospital]."

In early 1965, Flint moved to Chicago and got a place at a rooming house across from Illinois Masonic Hospital, which is near Wellington Avenue and Halsted Street. He had enough money to rent the room for a week.

Flint thought as a security measure he'd better get a second job, so he began working as an operating-room tech at Illinois Masonic. "At that point I was still going to be a nurse and wanted to keep that field open. It just never worked out. I went to night school at Northwestern and took some classes but then I said, This is too much, I can't do it."

When he later started working at the Annex, Flint knew how to operate a bottle opener and could figure out a rum and Coke or a gin and tonic, but that was about the extent of his bartending skills. In WTTW's 2008 film Out & Proud in Chicago, Flint confessed: "Somebody came in and asked me for a screwdriver, so I went into the toolbox and gave him a screwdriver. And the owner came flying back there—actually it was the manager, the owner's nephew Skip—and said, 'I thought you said you knew how to tend bar.' I thought I was going to be fired on the spot, but I talked my way out of that, and so they kept me."

Keeping Flint despite his inexperience proved a wise business move. Nick Dallesandro, who owned both the Annex and The Chesterfield, soon discovered Flint's ability to draw and, more importantly, keep a clientele. "Eventually I worked at both," Flint explained. "They were in the same block. I did all the pre-work at the Annex to get it all ready, and then I would go down to The Chesterfield and open it up and then go back to the Annex."

Not only was Flint a reliable worker, he also had some very smart ideas about increasing business. "I started opening Mondays from 7 p.m. to 4 a.m. There was nobody there, and so I would get one or two people and then three or four people. So then I started ordering pizzas at around 11. The next thing I knew, I had 25 or 30 people every Monday. And we all had a good time, and then around 1:30 a chef named Jim from a place on Sedgwick started bringing ribs when he got off work. It started turning into a real party.

"The Annex was a small, narrow bar—straight back, and there was a stage at the back," said Flint. "Annex and Chesterfield were both 4 o'clock bars and both featured a similar design, except The Chesterfield was longer and bigger. The Chesterfield was also a narrow bar in the shape of a V, with the bar branching out as it went back to the free-standing stage behind the bar.

"The bars had windows in the front, but no other signs. I know the Annex had just 'the Annex' outside, nothing more, nothing but the name. They didn't want to draw attention. The less people knew, the better. The people who needed to know could find it. The same with the Century across the street. Neither one had a back door, so patrons came in off the street."

"The gays were finding it by word of mouth in the community. That's how you usually found a place. I know in some cities, like Milwaukee, all the bars had blue lights. They wouldn't have any windows," Flint told WTTW.

The entertainment at the Annex was the John Conrad Trio and the drag comic Skip Arnold. Bradley Osborn's 2006 essay "Skip Arnold Takes Final Bow" (see queermusicheritage.us) describes the pioneering drag comic Ralph "Skip" Arnold as a true legend. The Navy veteran and Kansas City native performed in Chicago at venues such as The Chesterfield, The Trip and the Alameda as well as at clubs in San Francisco, Toronto, Fort Lauderdale, Pittsburgh (as Magnolia Calhoun) and elsewhere.

In the essay, Osborn captures a classic Arnold warm-up joke: "Two men were conversing in a bar and one of the men began making fun of the other's suit. The man in the suit said, 'It's not my fault. I sent my wife to Cox's department store to buy a seersucker suit and instead she went to Sears and asked for a cocksucker.'" Another bit involved Arnold's accompanist, who would play "Fairy Tales Can Come True" beneath a portion of his monologue while Arnold would recite homosexual versions of classic children's stories.

As evidence of this performer's talent, a two-sided 45-rpm single of Skip Arnold material exists. The disc was actually recorded live at the Annex. Side A is 6 minutes, 5 seconds long and is "Welcome to Fairieland" by Skip Arnold, alias Mother Goose. Side B is a 6-minute routine called "Snow White vs. The Watch Queen." This rare recording is on Fairieland Records, a production of DAARKO Productions Inc.

"Skip could drink a whole bottle of Rock and Rye in one night," Flint said. "He was 6 feet 5 and not pretty, but very humorous and talented. I idolized him. He was wonderful. He would perform in drag and it was all gay humor. I think he moved back to Kansas City after Chicago."

"Skip Arnold was a sort of Carol Channing and Don Rickles all rolled into one," said Jim Henritze. "I'd seen him in Kansas City at the Jewel Box. Also at the Annex was the John Conrad Trio—a three-piece band with bass, piano, and drums. John played the piano."

"John was probably the best pianist I had ever heard," said Flint. "It was music six nights a week with the John Conrad Trio. They backed Skip Arnold all the time, and so when he'd take a break, they'd take over."

Though Arnold was a drag performer, down the street at The Chesterfield was the bona fide drag show. The Annex had a drag show, "but not drag patrons," Flint said. "There were not as many drag patrons in those days. A lot of people were afraid to go out on the street.

"Roby Landers was in The Chesterfield revue, Jackie Knight (who was beautiful) and Jackie Lynn … to tell you the truth, Jackie Lynn was so filthy, they used to get her down in the dressing room and somebody had to cut off her underwear, it was so bad."

Also on the lip-syncing bill were Terri Page, Vicki Marlane, Criss Cross and Mitzi Monet. "Libby Reynolds was also there, and Libby was the one who was in the big Confidential magazine exposé with Raymond Burr," Flint added. "Criss and Mitzi were there before Roby, and they went off to the Blue Dahlia [at 5640 West North Avenue]. Roby was the lead, she did a lot of comedy. You didn't tangle with her. Roby did all the sewing for the show.

"We all lived upstairs. That's where I moved after the rooming house. There were five apartments up there. Roby, Jackie Knight, Terri, Libby and myself all had separate apartments there. It wasn't all over The Chesterfield; a Chinese restaurant was on the bottom floor of the space beside The Chesterfield, and some of the apartments were over that. Nick Dallesandro owned not only The Chesterfield but the building as well. We all both rented from him and worked for him."

Tillie the Dirty Old Lady was another featured performer at The Chesterfield during this time. In an article on the ChicagoPride.com site from December 23, 2005, "Tillie, the DOB From Chicago Passes Away," Jason P. Freeman managed to capture a bit of a late Chicago legend after knowing the performer in her older years: "'The dirty old bitch from Chicago,' he said while pulling out handfuls of costume jewelry from a Ziploc bag. Once all his gaudy rings were in place on his fingers, he then produced a fiber-optic coaster that flashed different colors when you set a glass on it. … He removed the blue straw from the drink I had just given him and replaced it with a plastic penis. 'Do you like my dick?' he asked.

"As I moved in closer to examine these favors, which he had with him every time he came in, his scent assaulted my nostrils. Sweet and pungent in powder, the assailing aroma extended around him in a fifty-foot radius, he was wearing perfume. That was the last time I ever referred to him as 'him.'

"Then she ordered another drink. … In between sips she'd share stories of her 1950s female-impersonator fame to anyone who would listen. And she had pictures to show off too. I think the bar she performed at was called Chesterfield's … . Ms. Foozie once flailed out her fingers and wrists, bedazzled with bogus [baubles], and offered up, 'Tillie, any one you want.' The old lady had no shame. She took the biggest ring on Foozie's finger and dumped it in her Ziploc bag … ."

The renowned female impersonator and performer David de Alba, who used the early Chicago stage name of Heri Del Valle, was also a star of the era. "My first performance was at The Chesterfield Club in Chicago, one of the nicest bars I have ever performed in," he told GayBay.net. "Being new, I was allowed to perform every Sunday on their Talent Night. Roby Landers, the emcee/performer, was very good at his craft, however, he never liked me. … In those days, everybody pantomimed to recordings. The exception was acts like Skip Arnold, who worked live as an emcee for drag shows. I did not like to pantomime, so I sang over Judy Garland recordings. It sounded like a duet … ."

Felicia Is Born

They had "turnabouts" about once every six months at The Chesterfield. Turnabouts were a special treat where the bartenders did drag and the drag performers tended bar. They became very popular, and they were also the origin of "Felicia."

"I had never done drag before, except for dancing around in the sheets as a kid," Flint explained. "I called myself Felicia and I twirled the baton, so my first drag outfit was actually a majorette uniform. So that turnabout at The Chesterfield was my gay-bar debut as a baton twirler and my gay-bar drag debut. Later on, I had my first gown at a turnabout at The Chesterfield as well, a big gown with big hair. I thought I was so pretty.

"Once I was doing a guest spot at the turnabout at The Chesterfield, and it wasn't Felicia's debut but maybe the turnabout after it. I wanted to make it special, so I was going to twirl flaming batons. I was getting ready to go on, and I'd just put the alcohol in the ends of the baton, and Roxanne picked up the baton, and when she did, the alcohol went all down the middle and so when they lit it the whole damn thing caught on fire. The curtains started on fire and I was beating it out with my hands, and finally we got it out.

"So after all this, Roby asked me if I was ready to go on. I said I couldn't, my hands hurt. She said, 'The show has to go on,' so I went out and started twirling. My hands were so badly burned they blistered. I couldn't work for a while. I couldn't even tend bar. I thought I was going to get fired, but Nick Dallesandro gave me the time off until my hands healed."

"Oh, yes, I remember that. It wasn't just the curtains but the ceiling decorations that started to burn, too. It spread from the center outward," said patron and photographer A.J. Epstein.

The Chesterfield and the Annex were both managed by Nick's nephews. Skip Dallesandro ran the Annex, and Bobby Dallesandro ran The Chesterfield. It was widely suspected at the time they were on the fringe of the Mafia, but nothing was certain. "I know one time they said the payments weren't in, and they [the Outfit boys] came behind the [Chesterfield] bar at 2:30 in the morning and cleaned all of our registers out and left us a dime, a nickel and a quarter in each register to work with," Flint said.

Jim Henritze added, "The Mob controlled what brands of liquor we would carry. Basically you could own a bar, but there was a collection of unsavory characters who had control over certain areas, and that group who came on were your partners. They knew the right people and you had to work with them to survive."

"Every once in a while at The Chesterfield around 3 a.m., we'd get a call to open the back door," said Flint. "It would be the booze we were using for the next week. Three Feathers, Corby's De Luxe, Crown Velvet and Falstaff beer. VO and CC, all those call brands would be the same liquor. We would just pour their liquors into the bottles we had. It was all the same. Whoever was pushing it, that's what we served.

"That's how the Mob operated. John Gattuso's brother Andy was Falstaff. We didn't have just that—those were the liquors we had to carry. In addition, we did Bud and Miller's, but Falstaff was the one they told us we had to serve, and that's what we served. The jukebox was something else that was always Mafia, supposedly."

Henritze added, "I remember two weeks after I started at The Chesterfield, this black Cadillac pulled up and Benny Allegretti got out with four bodyguards and walked in and took Nick to the back office. After a couple minutes they came out and cleared all the money out of the two front registers and the two back registers and then went back out to the car and pulled away. Nick was like that, though. He always kept putting off his payments. He'd always say, 'I'll get to it,' so that caused some problems."

"I always found out—whether they were Mob or not—if you were honest, they trusted you," Flint said. "Evidently Nick trusted me, because every night I would have to do all the cash registers—count them out, and then I would have to put tape this way and then that way and sign my name on it. If they trusted you, you could do anything."

One Monday night, Flint was tending bar at the Annex, and about 17 motorcyclists pulled up. "It was these leather guys, and I got a ball bat and put it right there beside me," Flint said. "I don't know what I would have done with it. It [the cyclists coming in] turned out to be one of the best things that ever happened. It helped bring a lot of new guys to the Annex. They started coming up to visit me on Monday nights.

"I remember the first time I went to the Gold Coast, though. The doorman took one look at me and said, 'Honey, that's right—just go walk around in a circle and go right back out.' I wasn't the sort of patron they had in mind. Next time I went back, they were a little nicer."

Flint brought bartender Sam Olin to The Chesterfield. He'd met Olin at the Gold Coast. Ray Bell was also a bartender at The Chesterfield. Bartenders at the Annex included Ronnie and Big John. Ronnie went with female impersonator Libby Reynolds, and John went with female impersonator Tara Montez.

Community activist William B. Kelley recalled Dwight Menard, an Annex bartender. "He was very nice and smart, and if I recall he was a music student," Kelley said. Menard was a church organist and in the Allegro Handbell Choir. He figured as a bartender in an appellate case in which the Annex successfully contested a license revocation, known as Easy Life Club v. License Appeal Commission, 310 N.E.2d 705 (Ill. App. 1974).

"I recall it as being a very popular bar, and sometimes on the weekend you were barely able to get through. I also remember Dallesandro sitting at the door checking IDs," Kelley said. He remembered The Chesterfield less clearly: "It was popular as well. I didn't go there more than once. I remember the stage in the back, and I believe I even saw Felicia perform there. I remember how the stage was fancily draped with curtains."

New Friends

Soon Flint got to know leatherman and entrepreneur Chuck Renslow, who owned the Gold Coast leather bar, and his crowd. And on July 26, 1965, Sam Olin bought Flint his first tattoo for a birthday present. The ink was done by a tattoo legend who was Renslow's then-lover, the late Cliff Raven (Ingram), at the Cliff Raven Tattoo Studio on Belmont Avenue.

"Cliff did all my tattoos," Flint said. "I have two spiders, one on each pectoral muscle. Being out of the Navy, one of the spiders was port and one was starboard. I have a lion on my left bicep because I am a Leo, and my Cubs tattoo on my lower right leg."

After moving out from above The Chesterfield, Flint moved in with Dick Decker, a friend from Peoria. "I moved up to the city and we moved in together on a place on Surf," Decker said. "It was only for a few months. I never saw him. He worked all the time. Jim was always working, always on the go."

"Dick Decker was from Peoria and a year behind me in high school," Flint said. "His sister was in my class and she always joked that I was the one who turned him gay. After a few months, Dick moved in with a guy named Mike Montgomery, and after a bit he went back to Peoria.

"I moved to 2828 North Pine Grove and roomed with the wildest guy in Chicago. His name was Jerry Condon and he was a florist working for himself—Jerry Condon's Flowers. One time Jerry said, 'Let's have the leather boys over for breakfast.' So at 5 a.m. they all came on their bikes with all the racket and such. Two days later, the landlord talked to Jerry and said, 'Your lease is coming up very soon—I think it's time for you to look for someplace else to go.' Then I moved into a studio on the 400 block of St. James Place in Lincoln Park. I lived there alone for a while."

At The Chesterfield, Flint also worked with a guy who was destined to be a workmate and employee for years to come, Richard "Richie" Saunders.

Flint explained: "I took Richie Saunders with me everywhere I went. Richie used to be a model in Hollywood. During the war. And when Joan Crawford couldn't get anyone to clean her house, Richie would get together a bunch of the gay kids to go over and clean her house for parties and things and serve drinks. Then, when he left there, he came here and started working at the Lake Shore Club and the Nite Life and eventually The Chesterfield. That's where I first met him.

"One night the door opened, and in comes this person wrapped all around and around in a scarf with a big hat. I will never forget the first time I worked with him. He said, 'This is your area, and across this line is my area—and by the way, sweetie, I think you should go to the bathroom and take off some of that makeup.' When he said that to me, I thought, Who the hell is this? That was Richie."

"Richie hated the straights," Flint said. "So, women would come in with the straights, and Richie would stick out his tongue at them or he'd get them in an argument and I'd have to jump over the bar and calm things down. Richie would say anything to anyone. It's a wonder I didn't get plastered a few times jumping in to break up things he'd start. If he didn't like you, Richie would take a booger out of his nose and wipe it on your glass."

The Raids

The downside of tending bar in the 1960s was the odds of being in a raid.

"My first experience going to jail was at the Annex in 1965," Flint said. "This girl came in and she was wearing a lot of makeup. I said, 'I can't serve you,' and Skip [Dallesandro] said, 'You've got to serve her,' and insisted. The minute I did, the arresting officer, Gene Benjamin, and his partner came out, and I went to Town Hall [the police station at 3600 North Halsted Street] and was put in a tank with 18 other guys.

"I was scared to death. I was wearing a pair of high men's shoes with open heels at the time. They told me, 'We'll have you out in a few minutes, Felicia,' that's what Skip said. 'We'll come and get you.'

"I was the only one arrested. I was scared out of my mind. I sort of suspected he knew she was underage, and that I'd get arrested. I felt like I was bait for the cops, to give them somebody to arrest so they could make their quota. They let me out that night about three or four hours later."

Jim Henritze remembered when the beat cop would come around for his money. "Nick would hide in the back room and say, 'Tell him I'm not here.' In those days there was a drop right at Town Hall," Henritze said. "One time they came in after Nick didn't pay and busted me for serving a minor. These two kids came in and I was just starting my shift, and not two minutes later two cops came in and walked right to them and asked for ID.

"Well, when they hauled me off to Town Hall, the affidavit they wanted me to sign was already filled out along with this story of how they came in with fake IDs and I took them, and one of them grabbed the IDs when he saw the cops and ran in the back and flushed them down the toilet. None of that happened. In other words, the bust was all planned and written out ahead of time. So Nick came into Town Hall, paid the cops what he owed, and the case was dismissed. It didn't even come to trial. That's how corrupt it all was back then."

"I'd heard that they raid the bars from time to time," Flint said. "Every time there was a raid, they put your name in the paper and all the patrons' names in the paper. The Tribune was the big one for that. Most of the stories about careers being ruined were after the Lincoln Baths raid [see Chapter 3]. Careers were ruined, teachers lost jobs, a couple people committed suicide. That happened when I was here. When the Louie Gage's Fun Lounge raid occurred, I was still in Peoria. Some people changed careers and became clerks at Marshall Field's, things like that.

"People would always tell me that if you smoke, always have a pack of cigarettes and

$25 on you. I never smoked but I always had $25 on me. Usually, when you were busted, you went over on Maxwell Street [police station] first and then to 11th and State [police headquarters], but sometimes because of being on Clark Street you went to Town Hall."

The longtime bar employee and writer Richard Cooke also remembers the raids. "I worked the coat check at the Annex and also across the street at Ruthie's," Cooke said. "That's where I met Eddie Dugan, when he was bartending at Ruthie's. It was really good money working coat check in those days, so I did it all through school. I'd work one night Annex and then Ruthie's, back and forth. I was working coat check before I even turned 21.

"When you got raided, the cops came in, the music went off, the overhead lights went on, everyone lined up against the wall, and the cops went down the line picking out who they were going to take or who they didn't like the look of. I remember when I was at Ruthie's, and every bar at that time had to have a window on the front so the police could look in— well, at Ruthie's that window was near the coat check, and part of my duty was to look out for the squad cars. When I saw one pull up, I nodded to Ruthie in the back, and he would send the bouncer out with an envelope. They were all on the take back then."

Flint recalled the second raid he was in, while working at The Chesterfield. "The plainclothes policeman came in and bought two or three people a drink," Flint said. "I served them all a drink and went to the Hollywood Restaurant, and when I got back I could not figure out what was going on. The next thing I know, someone is yanking my collar and the cop says, 'This is him, he's the one who was serving the drink.'

"At that time, another thing they always used to arrest you for was, they'd buy somebody a drink, and the minute you'd serve it the vice cop would arrest you for solicitation of prostitution and [being the] keeper of a disorderly house. They never hit the straight bars with that, only the gay bars.

"I guess that night when it started, the cop came behind the bar, and Sam Olin said, 'You'd better not be back here, the owner isn't going to like this,' and he said, 'Well, the owner isn't going to like this, either,' and pulled out his badge and said, 'This is a raid.' They told us we were all going to jail and made us line up against one wall.

"Poor Roby [Landers] had just come down from upstairs in a pair of red pajamas to get a pack of cigarettes out of the machine, and the cop said, 'Get her, she was here last time as the emcee of the show.' They took Tillie and all the girls in drag. There was something like 28 of us.

"When we got to 11th and State we were photographed and processed. The thing that was funny was, every time they took one of the girls out of the tank, we'd all start singing their theme song. When I went in, they started singing 'These Boots Are Made For Walkin'.' The cops started yelling, 'Shut them fags up, it's 4 in the morning.' The patrons who were not in drag were arrested that night as inmates of a disorderly house."

"The raids in those days were terrible," added Chuck Renslow. "They always used to say, when you go in a gay bar, stand by the door so you get a seat in the paddy wagon."

Flint said he would go to court and everybody else would be found not guilty. "However, they wouldn't find me not guilty. They kept filing it and reinstating it. I think they [the Dallesandros] were trying to say that I was really soliciting for prostitution. They were using me, trying to bargain me through the court system as a way to find me guilty so I'd be gone. Then they could say, 'Hey, the bartender who was a bad element is gone, we didn't know what was going on.' In that way they could reopen.

"They were trying to use me as the scapegoat to get the bar license back after the raids. That's the way it worked. You could go to court and be found not guilty, but when you went before the liquor commission you would be found guilty and you had to close. When all that was going on is when I hired attorney Ralla Klepak." (See Chapter 3.)

In the 2008 WTTW film, Flint said about local attorneys: "Renee Hanover, Ralla Klepak, and Pearl Hart were all great." Speaking of Klepak, Flint explained: "She was there any time of day you called her. She could come and be with you and was just so reassuring. 'Oh, don't worry.' You were terrified and didn't know what was going to happen. In those days it might mean your name was going to come out in the paper, people worried about losing jobs.

"Renee was just like Ralla. She'd sit down and she'd just say, 'Don't worry about it, I'm going to take over, just calm down.' Because of them, things went much more smoothly."

The Media Underground

The Mattachine Midwest Newsletter of the 1960s was an important communication tool for the growing Chicago gay movement. But unlike later gay newspapers and magazines, the newsletter had difficulty even being carried at gay bars, unless there was someone sympathetic working there. Gay bars like the Annex and The Chesterfield were straight-owned or Mob-controlled, and they didn't care about gay rights.

In an interview with gay historian Jack Rinella, activist Ira Jones explained: "[The bars] were in business simply to make money. They had absolutely no interest in the gay lifestyle or the gay community, or gay rights for individuals in the community. They could only comprehend making money off of gays, and exploiting them, ripping them off. They had no more interest than the man in the moon in gays at all.

"The only way that it [the newsletter] came in was if somebody worked at the bar … . But that influence could creep in, and the newsletter could be kept under the bar, I well remember, at the Annex, and Chesterfield's, and places like that in the early '60s. The bartenders would keep the newsletter under the bar, and the customers would come and say, 'Has the Mattachine newsletter arrived yet?' And he would say yes, and he would slip him one."

The Hub of Activity

At the time The Chesterfield and the Annex operated, the area around the intersection of Clark Street and Diversey Parkway was quite a hub of activity. There was the ever-popular Ruthie's at 2835 North Clark, and then 2850 North Clark, and finally 3231 North Clark. Shari's was on the northeast corner of Clark and Surf streets.

"Ruthie's, like Shari's, was a circular storefront bar on the east side of Clark down near Diversey," said frequent patron Richard Johnson. "Since it was a round bar, we mostly kept moving around and around. One exception, though, was we used to sometimes cram in on the north side of the back of the bar and have a big gropefest, but pretending we were all just standing there. It was a jukebox bar. I think it was even five plays for 25 cents. These were the beginning years of my gay life, having come out in Omaha, Nebraska, in 1966 when I was in college."

Gary Chichester recalled in a 2010 Gay Chicago column, "Gary Chichester: A Remarkable

Life," by Sukie de la Croix, that the first gay bar he could get into while underage was a place on Clark Street called the Orange Cockatoo. That was back in the late 1960s when Clark and Diversey was the gay hub and the hustlers worked Diversey Parkway and Pine Grove Avenue. Chichester explained: "Before you go in the bars, you did street cruising. And there was a coffee shop down there called the Hollywood, which underage kids would hang out in. It was an opportunity to meet and mingle."

After The Chesterfield closed, the area continued to flourish, perhaps reaching its peak in the 1970s. New gay bars quickly arose around Clark and Diversey: Ruthie's; Shari's; Bughaus Saloon (2570 North Clark Street), which was later Take One; Big Red's (642 West Diversey Parkway); Cheeks (2730 North Clark—go-go boys every night!); Dickie's (674 West Diversey), which later became Piggen's Pub. Meanwhile, El Dorado ("The Latin Touch"), Company, and later Harlequins were all consecutive bars at 2683 North Halsted Street. There was the strangely named Le Trolls (2838 North Broadway) as well as the Grapevine (2548 North Clark) and K's on Klark (2568 North Clark), which later became Molly's Follies, a juice bar.

There was a piano bar, the Virgo Out (formerly the Checkmate), at 2546 North Clark. At the time, the Checkmate was one of the few gay-owned bars.

Another bar that opened in the area was the Knight Out (2936 North Clark), which was billed as Chicago's friendliest with the slogan, "Drinkin', Rappin', and Other Carryin' On," and "what's not to love with those summer of 1975 drink specials Wine Coolers .50 and Malt Liquor .30!" In the front part of the Knight Out, a small gay bookstore, the Stonewall Memorial Bookshop, operated for several years, before the later free-standing bookstores opened that catered to gay and lesbian literary tastes. (Gay activist Gene Janowski had opened the Stonewall shop in the mid-1970s, later turning it over to Knight Out owner Harold Meyer, who changed the name to the Source.)

There was also the Snake Pit (2628 North Halsted), billed in ads as "Chicago's answer to The Stork Club," which also begat the first punk dance bar. (See Chapter 13.)

Dave Riley captured his experience of the area in a 1996 interview with Jack Rinella. "Century had a piano bar. So did Chesterfield, at the time," he said. "I made a phony ID, used a Xerox machine and plastic. I think every kid did it back then with the selective service [draft] card. It worked. ... Century, Chesterfield, Annex, and then right where the parking garage is, that building ... was the Orange Cockatoo. It was somebody's side door or something. ... People used to joke, 'At the Orange Cockatoo, any cock will do.'"

Longtime gay columnist Jon-Henri Damski tried to evoke the spirit (though perhaps not quite accurately) of the nearby Lincoln Park a bit more in remarks quoted in a 1997 piece by Neal Pollack for the Chicago Reader. "Twenty years ago, this is where the park began," Damski said. "We started here. Men would be out all along the wall. All the way up from Clark and Diversey. We're talking about hundreds. You could always sleep in the park because 20 years ago, as soon as it was night, this was all gay territory, right down to the rocks, down to the harbor there. In the '70s you were home free for miles along the lake. Foster to Oak Street Beach. We just controlled this whole space. The Alexander Hamilton statue, in those days, guys went up there and cruised at night. It was a meeting hall. You didn't have the fag-bashers. They didn't come until '82, in the Reagan years, when people would start to beat you up for being in the park. But then people didn't know about us. This place was ours at night."

Marge Summit recalled the area. "I would go to the Volleyball, which was a women's bar up north [on the west side of the 2100 block of North Clark Street]," she said. "I remember going up to The Chesterfield with the girls, which is what I called my guy friends at the time. I call myself a gay woman and not a lesbian, and believe me, there is a difference.

"Anyway, there was Don (Donna May), Joey (Sophie), Michael (Maria) and Frank (Francis). The doorman looked at me and said, 'You can't get in without a skirt,' because if they got busted it would be because of me cross-dressing in pants. When the doorman said that, I turned and said, 'See, Donna May, I said you should've worn a skirt.'

"I also would go to a lesbian bar called Midget Inn out on Kedzie and Montrose. The first floor was a regular small bar, and in the center was a stairway, and then you went up these stairs in the back and it was a place for gay women. It was pretty cool. We had our own jukebox and bar up there. The only thing was, when they raided it, you had to kick out the screens and jump out the second-floor windows and run. Mostly, in those days, though, we would hang out at each other's apartments, which was a lot easier.

"Sometimes we'd go to Calumet City, which was pretty much Perversion City with all the gay bars on State Line (Mr. B's, the Bank Vault, the Music Box, the Pour House, Our Place) and all the hookers on State Street. In the Indiana papers at the time, there would be stuff saying, 'Be careful when you go on State Line Road because the faggots are jumping out of the trees to get you.' That was the way of thinking back then. It was just ridiculous."

Sam's Wants You!

After it was clear to him that his ongoing legal battles regarding his arrests at the Annex and The Chesterfield were a setup, Flint bade the Dallesandros adieu and went to work for Sam's at 1205 North Clark Street. That bar had been out to recruit the popular bartender from the Annex and The Chesterfield even before the raids.

"I couldn't figure out why they wanted me to come work there, because Sam's was probably the most popular gay bar in town at the time and had all these beautiful bartenders," Flint said. "I was just this chubby kid. The three owners were Wally Fleischmann, Jerry Fleischmann and their brother-in-law, Al Waldman. They didn't trust anybody at that time, so they always had somebody behind each register watching everything you did.

"Sam's was old and it looked dirty, but it wasn't. Every week we had a new toilet because somebody either stopped it up or broke it somehow. It was a rectangular island bar that looked like it could fall apart at any time.

"There was not much room around the perimeter of the bar, and when all the 2 o'clock bars closed, it got very tight in there because Sam's had a 4 o'clock license. Believe me, we had to get the traffic going one way or you weren't going to get around. You could get two or three hundred people in there—squeezed around. It could take a half-hour to get from one end of the bar to the other. They didn't care about things like occupancy [limits] in those days."

Jim Henritze added: "Sam's was painted black on the outside, with windows. There were beer cases all around and a rectangular bar in the middle. There was paneling on the walls that went up about 7 feet, but the ceiling was high."

"Sizewise, Sam's was about the same as the Annex and The Chesterfield," Flint said. "There was a jukebox in the back by the two bathrooms, which were by a back door off the alley. Most of the closet cases [closeted gay men] came in the back door. The bathrooms had

Ladies and Men on them, but since we didn't really allow women they were both unisex.

"That was the only thing I never liked about it, was the only women who could ever come in the bar were straight women that one of the owners knew or were talking to. Sam's would not let lesbians in the bar. It was an unspoken rule. The clientele was mostly white, but never excluded blacks. The jukebox featured Diana Ross and The Supremes, Frank Sinatra— 'That's Life,' 'Fly Me to the Moon,' 'Ain't No Mountain High Enough.' In the front were two little round windows that were too high to see through."

"I remember Sam's most because it was a great bar to go to pick up guys and to get picked up," said satisfied Sam's customer Jerry Leppek. "You could stand there and see two lines of people—those across sitting at the bar, and the line of people behind them standing against the wall, and then everyone moving in a circle between those two rows.

"You saw a lot of people from a lot of different angles by just staying in one spot. One of the first times I was there, this beautiful hunk of a man came up to me and said, 'You want to go fuck?' and I said yes, and on the way out he asked a few more people, and the evening was memorable because it was my first orgy."

"It was always very popular. I was down in Hyde Park at the time so I didn't get there as often," recalled Bill Kelley. "It was right by the subway at Clark and Division, which wasn't yet known as the Red Line. It was called the North-South Line and went from Howard to 63rd. There was a rear entrance so people could come in without being seen.

"It was busy every night of the week but it was very seedy, undecorated and never looked like anything special. I recall it as having a tin ceiling. There were a lot of drunks that hung out there as well. I remember the Fleischmanns, who were considered part of the Mafia by most people. They were sort of loud and brash, nice but frank, sort of 'what you see is what you get.'"

In a 1995 interview with Jack Rinella, attorney Ralla Klepak explained: "Sam's was owned by the Fleischmann brothers ... . One day one of the Fleischmann brothers came to me and said, 'We'd like you to represent us, and we'd like to put you on retainer.' I said, 'No, thank you.' They said, 'You know, name your price, you want $1,000 a month, just to be on call in case we call you?' And I said, 'No, thanks.'

"When they asked why, I said, 'Because word has it that you're a Syndicate bar, and I don't represent the Syndicate—I represent the patrons.' He said, 'Sure we can't change your mind?' I said, 'That's right, I don't want anything from you, and you can't have anything from me.'"

Jim Henritze added: "They also owned a bathhouse out on Western called Man's World [4740 North Western Avenue]. Wally was handsome as hell, and when my partner Kenny used to go down to Sam's, Kenny had a pink Cadillac convertible and Wally would always tell him he was too drunk to drive, and then Wally would take his car keys and go drive around chasing skirts.

"They were good owners, though. When they got the 30-day suspension in 1968, they paid all the employees for the time and they got vacations. They did a lot of things that were unheard of at the time. They were fair, but you'd better not steal. They could be very rough."

"Later on, Wally told me that I was probably the only bartender they ever trusted. After a while they moved me to the front station. You only got the front station if you were the top ringer [sold the most drinks]," said Flint. "I didn't understand it because I was nellie and effeminate and played with everybody's ears, and the other three or four guys were all so beautiful. I guess they were too busy always trying to get laid.

"It was long hours, nights from 7 to 4 and on Saturday from 7 to 5. You never stopped, because those times beer was 55 cents and a mixed drink was 75 cents, and on a good weekend on Friday and Saturday we would go through close to 400 cases of beer. You didn't slow down. Like the bars before, I was making good money for the time—$150 to $170 a night."

Flint said he recommended most of the men who came to work there. Bartenders were Lundy Fisher, Al Hamill, Carl Forrester, Sam Olin, Philip DeCamp, Stan Walker, Bill, Mike Dudek and Richie Saunders.

"Lundy Fisher was the day bartender at Sam's," Flint said. "He knew how to manage a bar. He had a huge following—bartenders had followings in those days. He told me not to put my tips in my tip jar so they [the Fleischmanns] could see what I made. I said, 'Lundy, I don't care if they see what I make, they can watch me. I am doing it for my customers, and if they don't like it they can talk to the customers.' If I remember right, Lundy retired when Sam's closed."

"I remember Lundy Fisher and that foghorn voice of his," said Jim Henritze. "After I got out of the bar business, I was the juice man. Lundy called me Jimmy Juice because that was my job. I sold the juice to bars."

Flint recalled several of his fellow bartenders in greater detail. "Carl Forrester was gorgeous. He came from Waukegan," Flint said. "One year for Halloween we dressed up as Pierrot and Pierrette. We painted our bodies blue, and he had the tights on, and I had the tutu. We spent all day doing that damn costume. We went to the State Fair together. Carl and I and a bunch of us just piled into one car, and when we got there and opened the door we all just sort of fell out. We had a lot of fun together. That whole gang at Sam's was like family.

"Philip DeCamp. We used to call him Bucky Beaver because his teeth used to stick out in front. Beautiful man. Mike Dudek was gorgeous as well and he ended up in Palm Springs. I practically stalked Al Hamill. He was a whore, though. He had a different one every night, and if he could have two or three a day, he did. He lived in what is now the Tokyo Hotel. His pants and shirt were always pressed. He'd always walk through that door perfect.

"Sam Olin was probably my best friend at the time. I remember one time I went to Philadelphia with him to see his family, and they didn't know he was gay, so I spent the whole day in the hotel waiting for him. I just wanted to be around him. He was so quiet but there was just something about him that people loved. We were never lovers, but I sure wanted to be.

"Richie [Saunders] worked one end of the bar and I worked the other, and he never liked to open a bottle and he never liked to make change. So, one day he went on his break, and we left a nickel, a dime and a quarter and took all the bottles out and left just a little bit in each bottle.

"People would order things and say, 'I ordered a screwdriver and this tastes like gin.' He'd say, 'No, it was vodka.' Well, there was no vodka there; he was just pouring whatever he had in there. When people would give him money, he'd tell them to get change because he didn't feel like bending down to get more. When somebody would complain about a spill, he'd throw a rag at them and say, 'You spilled it, you wipe it up.'"

Stan Walker recalled Saunders: "Oh, God, Richie. I remember one time Richie was downtown at one of the big theaters for a matinee—which meant he was fooling around sucking guys off in the bathroom. He would bring a shopping bag so he could stand in the shopping bag in the stall and bend over and blow the guy, so when cops or ushers checked under the partition they'd only see one set of feet. Anyway, he left his dentures on the back of the toilet, and I guess he had to go down there and pick up his teeth in the lost-and-found box at the theater.

"Things like that happened to Richie all the time. He was a trip. He was the sloppiest bartender I have ever seen. Never wiped down his bar, never cleaned up spilled drinks, nothing. He was fun, though, a great storyteller."

"I trained Stan Walker as a bartender during the big snow of 1967," said Flint. "That winter was a trip because Sam's was the only bar people could get to because of the subway. So the owners were out buying beer every day. We must have served 100 different kinds of beer. Since no delivery trucks could get through, it was whatever they could bring in, that was what we served. I never worked so hard in my life. I could make it in to work because by that time I was living at the Tuscany Hotel at 1244 North Dearborn, which really wasn't a hotel; it was apartments. I lived there when I worked at Sam's."

"I moved to Chicago with a pair of jeans, a white T-shirt and a sweater and not much cash," laughed Walker. "I went into Sam's and met a bartender named Philip DeCamp. We dated for a while, but it didn't work out, so then he tried to get me banned. He went on so much about it, they eventually let him go. By then I was working as a busboy at the Water Tower Inn until I became a waiter there.

"During that blizzard [of 1967] they were running out of everything. It was horrible. I stopped in Sam's, and Jim told me they were looking for a bartender. I said I had no experience, but Jim and Wally and Al could tell I was good with people.

"It was pretty simple—shot, beer and mixes. It was mobbed all the time. It was long and narrow. The walls were grooved, simulated wood paneling, and the rest of the interior was so basic. I have no idea why it was so popular.

"Inside there was the bar and then a row of people on the stools and then another row behind them leaning against the wall, with only room for one row of people to move between, and that always had to move clockwise, or you were going to have problems. It was always so loud. I became an expert at reading lips there.

"Since the day I started, Jim called me Twiggy. I think it was because Twiggy was starting to be popular, and the name just stuck. Anyway, this guy came in one night and asked me out, and Jim said he didn't trust him. So he told this guy he was going to go on the first date with the two of us and that the guy needed to come to my apartment at such and such a time and bring Champagne, that he would be there to supervise. And this guy agreed to it! It just amazed me. Jim had a way of just making most every situation memorable.

"We were always being watched there, not just by guys cruising us. I mean the owners. There were stacks of beer cases in the front and in the back, and that's where Wally and Al would sit, one at the front door and one at the back door. They'd check IDs but mostly they were watching us at the cash registers. Watching all the time.

"I lived at the Tuscany Hotel, too. I didn't know Jimmy lived there when I moved in. Jackie Day, who was a Sam's regular, told me about the place. It was kind of an old and funky place but it was affordable and was mostly young people and so convenient, right near Clark and Division."

Flint explained the situation at the Tuscany Hotel. "You paid rent either by the week or month. It was very much a community," he said. "We hung out and went out for breakfast.

"I remember this one guy who used to come into Sam's. He'd been after me for six or seven weeks. He'd wait for me every night after work, but I was scared of him so I'd never go with him. He was beautiful and persistent, so one night I took him back home to the Tuscany Hotel, and that was the first night I realized there were those Outfit guys who liked gay guys. He started undressing and the first thing he did was take off his gun. I had no idea. I thought I was going to get killed."

Flint spoke a bit about the clientele as well. "Sam's was a bar that had everything. An old man could find a hustler, and everything in between," he said. "It was always crowded.

"It went in shifts. You had a group that came in at 7 in the morning and stay until noon, then you had the noon people who would stay until 4 or 5. Then there were the after-work people that would come in, and they'd stay until 8 or 9. Then you would notice the ones that went home after work and came out at 9 or 10 and stay until about 1. Then you would have the ones who would be home all day and then come out from 1 to 4. It ran in shifts like that."

Well-Known Customers

Dan Dailey, a 6-foot-3 Hollywood movie legend, star of such films as It's Always Fair Weather and There's No Business Like Show Business as well as the TV series The Governor & J.J., used to come into Sam's. "He was a pain in the ass, he only wanted a certain kind of gin, and of course we didn't serve that kind of gin," Flint said. "They would let his girlfriend in when he showed up. It wasn't really his girlfriend. She would find tricks for him to go home with and be with him after he got in drag. Dan Dailey was a cross-dresser."

"Shecky Greene used to come into Sam's," said Bill Kelley, a claim verified by Flint. Chicago comic Greene is best-known for his long and varied career as a stand-up comic and for frequent guest-starring work on TV.

"The clientele at Sam's ranged from the richest to the poorest people," said Flint. "We had a guy named Jim Manley who owned the Surrey Bar off of Michigan. Wealthy, wealthy man. He helped start the Gold Coast Art Fair years ago [in 1957]. It didn't make much difference how wealthy he was when it came to tipping. He came in every night, and you knew you were going to get a quarter from him every time."

Flint said mass murderer Richard Speck, who broke into the townhouse that doubled as a dormitory at 2319 East 100th Street and tortured, raped and murdered eight student nurses in a July 1966 spree, was another Sam's customer. Flint claimed he came into Sam's the night before his rampage. "He was here, all right. He used to hustle in there. He was a male hustler. I'd seen him in Sam's maybe two or three times," Flint said.

(According to Wikipedia, Speck spent only a few days in Chicago. This was enough time for him to have gone to Sam's.)

Hugh O'Brian, best-known for his starring role on the ABC-TV series The Life and Legend of Wyatt Earp, came into Sam's one night, Flint recalled. "He was straight, but he came in one time when he was doing Cactus Flower in town, because Louis, his assistant, brought him to visit," Flint said. "One night after that, we all got together and went to see him in the show."

Future Bistro bar owner and Chicago legend Eddie Dugan was a very popular bartender at Ruthie's, which in one location had been the Orange Cockatoo. Dugan also tended bar at the Inner Circle (at its Armitage Avenue location prior to its 1842 North Wells Street and then 233 East Erie Street locations), where portions of the Warren Beatty movie Mickey One were filmed in the mid-1960s.

"When Eddie was at Inner Circle, we decided we were going to do this campy campaign like we were running for something." Flint said. "One night he would have a big campaign to come see him bartend at the Inner Circle, and then I would do one to come and see me bartend at Sam's. I'd try and get people to vote for me, and he would try to get people to vote for him.

"He was a giant of a person. It was hard not to love Eddie. He made everybody he talked to feel like a million dollars. The fake campaign was fun and it brought business to the two bars, and it also gave even more of a sense of community to it all."

More Sam's Memories

Flint smiled when he recalled his years working at Sam's.

"I loved Sam's," he said. "It was never a job—it was a game and I was onstage, and certain songs would come on and I had a bunch of hats above the bar, and I'd grab one. I'd do songs like 'I'd Rather Be Blue' or 'That's Life' and make up my own gay words to it. It was a good way to make money and make people laugh. I was the show."

However, Flint's stint at Sam's was not a continuous run. "I actually got mad at Al [Fleischmann] one time when he wouldn't give us a pay raise, so I went to work for Chuck Renslow at the Gold Coast for about three weeks. I probably would've stayed at the Gold Coast, I liked Chuck Renslow better than I liked [Gold Coast part-owner] Herbie Schmidt—but there were other factors. Wally Fleischmann was a straight man, and I was very much in love with him.

"After I left Sam's, every day he came up the street to the Gold Coast and asked me to come back. To get away from him, I went out to the 21 Club [a gay bar and restaurant at 3042 West Irving Park Road]. There was a little gay area out there. It was out near the lesbian bar Lost and Found [3058 West Irving Park Road] and the Blue Pub [3059 West Irving Park Road]. They were all in that block.

"I was probably only there a couple weeks. Then he followed me out there, so I finally gave in and came back to Sam's. He could see how I felt and knew I was good for business. He definitely played himself to get me back."

Flint recalled being arrested three times while working at Sam's. "All three arrests, somebody would come in and I'd serve them a drink," Flint said. "It's so funny. All of my arrests have since been expunged, but almost every arrest record I have is identical to the one before. Literally, you could have photocopied it and changed the date and that was about it, like I was signing copies.

"I remember one time in a Sam's raid they took 87 of us. The funny thing was, if they didn't arrest you at Sam's, they'd do a raid up north later on in the night. They knew, when people heard about Sam's, they would run north because that's where they'd go to drink, and that's how news traveled. What happened a lot was, then people would get arrested up there instead."

Stan Walker recalled one night during the 1968 Democratic National Convention. "That was probably the most memorable night I had working at Sam's," Walker said. "The troops were in town in full gear—in the Jeeps with bayonets and guns, going through the intersection of Clark and Division.

"One night there was a cop car parked out in front of Sam's because they had tear-gassed some people who were demonstrating earlier. So when they threw tear gas to break up the mob and protesters, the tear gas got sucked in the exhaust fan of the bar, and everyone came pouring out of the bar and into the line of fire of these protesters, who were throwing a Molotov cocktail at the cop car as well as other things. Then the protesters ran back in the bar and out the back. That was probably the craziest night there."

According to Flint and other bar owners, bars were also closed down during at least part of the Democratic National Convention on the orders of Mayor Richard J. Daley.

First Love

Flint's first serious lover relationship was with Warren Williamson. "He came in Sam's every night," Flint said. "He was this butch, butch guy who would be standing there. I thought, Why is he interested in me?

"He kept asking me to go out. At Sam's, it was funny: If you just wanted a regular night off, you couldn't get it off, but if you said to Wally, Al or Jerry, 'I'm so horny tonight I gotta get laid,' then they'd let you off. They understood that more than anything."

Williamson explained how he came to Chicago. "I moved to Chicago from New York City, where I'd been for about four years. I was relocated," he said. "I was working for Standard Oil as a corporate travel manager. In fact, they were building the Standard Oil Building when I moved here in January 1968 [the building, now called the Aon Center, was completed in 1973].

"I found a place, a one-bedroom for $100 a month with everything included, at 1100 North LaSalle, which was about a block away from the Gold Coast when it was on the 1100 block of North Clark, and about two blocks from Sam's. I still remember the Etienne murals in that second location of the Gold Coast when they moved up the block. [Etienne was one of the names used by artist Dom Orejudos, who was Chuck Renslow's lover.]

"I remember when I went to Sam's, I liked Jimmy right away. He was just so nice, so helpful, and he bought me a beer. I was new in town. I wasn't looking for a relationship, but there it was. We used to like to go to a 24-hour Chinese restaurant, the Little Rock Garden, just north of Sam's on Clark, but I still had to get up early because of work."

After they began to date, Flint moved out of the Tuscany Hotel, and they moved in together at 1100 North LaSalle Street, Apartment 102.

"Well, he never technically moved in," said Williamson, "but he stayed over a lot. He bought us a couple of jade rings, and we were very together for almost all of 1968. "There are so many memories. I remember Jimmy taking me to the St. Patrick's Day Parade, which I thought was a big deal in New York, but Chicago's was huge. I remember as a joke I gave him a big orange T-shirt to wear for the day, and he wore it because I gave it to him, which was sweet. I remember thinking how funny it was to see him in orange in the midst of all that green.

"When I was at 1100 North LaSalle, they still had one of those old-fashioned switchboards downstairs where you plug in calls to the different rooms. An ex-nun ran it, and when I was living there, I would have guys down every weekend from the Great Lakes Naval [base], since that was during the Vietnam War. Anyway, one time I was going by and this ex-nun switchboard operator said to me, 'Mr. Williamson, I think you must be about the third-most-popular USO in the city.'" (USO stands for the United Service Organizations, a private group that provides support to U.S. military members.)

The MLK Riots

During the riots that followed the April 1968 assassination of Dr. Martin Luther King Jr., Flint remembered they had to lie on the floor of the apartment because of the Molotov cocktails (bombs) and all of the violence. "You could reach out our window and touch the guardsmen," Flint said of the nearby activities.

"I remember it was a Friday, and we had some people coming over that night," Williamson said. "I was on the first floor, a corner apartment right there on Maple and LaSalle, and about one block or so behind the building was Cabrini-Green [public housing projects], which was insane during those riots.

"That day I was working at 500 North Michigan, and we went on the roof of the building at sunset, and I remember looking out at the city and thinking it looked like Nero's Rome with all the fires. Standard Oil received some bomb threats, so they let us off early.

"That night we still had our party. Why, I don't know. There were National Guardsmen in the streets. People were shot. The A&P grocery store across the street was burned to the ground. We had curtains and shades on the window but we didn't dare stand up, so we were there with our guests playing board games on the floor.

"The next day I went down to Ace Hardware and got some horseshoe nails and wire and started nailing the wire to the windows. I wasn't going to have Molotov cocktails coming through the window. The building manager started yelling that I couldn't do that, and I just said sue me."

"They still have the wire over the windows on that building," said Flint. "I think of that night many times when I pass it."

Different Paths

Flint smiled when he recalled his time with Williamson. "I'm not a great cook but I started trying to make something when he came home from work," Flint said. "I wanted to do everything to please. When he'd get up at 7:30 or 8 to go to work, I'd always get up and try to lay out his clothes because this guy was so great.

"We had been going out for a little bit over a year, year and a half. A friend of mine got us tickets to see Phyllis Diller at the Empire Room at the Palmer House. We had a few drinks and I said, 'Let's stop in at the Croydon Circle.' So we stopped in for a few more. We ended up at the bar and Warren said, 'I think it's time to go home.' I said, 'Warren, why don't you go home? I feel like staying out tonight, I work six nights a week.' He didn't see it that way.

"We finally went home and we were laying in bed talking, and I said, 'You know, Warren, the difference is that you met me as a bartender and you wanted me at that time, but I don't think you really want a bartender. You want somebody 9-to-5 or maybe not as flamboyant as I am.' I went on and on.

"We laid there for an hour, an hour and a half, two hours and finally I just got up. He asked, 'What are you doing?' I answered that I was leaving. He said, 'What do you mean you're leaving?' I said, 'I am going to leave, I'll be back tomorrow when you are at work to pick up my clothes. Everything else is yours,' and I walked out."

Williamson said Flint had "gypsy feet." "He tended to stray a lot," he said. "Not that he didn't want to be in a relationship, I think he did. But everything was just so free-wheeling at the time. Everything was constantly available and especially for him, since he was so popular at Sam's. It was funny—I came into this not wanting to be in a relationship, and he came in wanting to be in one, and things turned out different for both of us.

"It wasn't him deciding to move on. I could see things weren't going to change. He couldn't be faithful. He had people all around him all the time, and I got tired of it. Who could blame him? That was a magic decade after Stonewall [the Stonewall gay uprising in New York was in June 1969] and before AIDS—everything was so wide open and he was in the middle of it all."

"A year later I knew I'd made a mistake," a tearful Flint acknowledged, "but you can't go back, and of course he had met a guy named Bob, who was in Second City Motorcycle Club, which was one of the leather clubs. I was the president of the Chicago Knight Motorcycle Club."

Williamson and his partner, Bob, the person he dated after Flint, have been together 41 years as of 2011.

Flint described his recent reconnection with Williamson. "When I talked to him about being interviewed for this book, he asked me if I still had our scrapbook," Flint said. "I told him I never could have gotten rid of our scrapbook. It had things from our first night at dinner at The Trip and then we went home. Our first night doing Japanese and our first night doing this and that. Pictures. I said, 'Yeah, I still got it.'" Flint teared up again. "When I called him the other night it was reliving all that and it made me realize I should have never left him. And it was all because of me being stupid.

"He's a Gemini and he was born the same day as my mother. I am a Leo. Typical Leo. I love the nightlife, I'm strong and abrupt. I like to make decisions, although every once in a while I like to have a guy who can make a decision for me, who can pick the wine off the wine list. When I called, he said he was just thinking about me. I asked if he had a nice birthday and he said he was thinking of Pearl, my mother."

"Boy, I loved her," Williamson said of Pearl Flint. "She was just a Southern Illinois country girl, and I knew her favorite beer and would always have it ready when she came into the Baton after being out all afternoon. She was very laid-back and accepting. Nothing bothered her. Her motto was pretty much 'live and let live.' She was easy to be around, and the great thing about Pearl was, you always felt that she liked you. I think they were most alike in that Jim always took care of his people, like Pearl was the breadwinner and raising all those kids. Same thing. He always had a soft spot for folks."

Clark and Division

The area around the intersection of Clark and Division streets on Chicago's Near North Side was big for gay nightlife in the late 1960s. There were Sam's, Still of the Night, Shoreline 7, Jamie's, the Gold Coast and the Hollywood Bowl, the business that moved into the Gold Coast's original space after the Gold Coast moved up the street to 1110 North Clark. Eateries included the Hasty Tasty restaurant, BG's at the other corner, and the ever-popular Feast on a Bun. Additional places of interest in the area were Club 69 (69 West Division Street), Club 169 (169 West Division) and Scarlet Ribbons (a "private club" at 169 West Division), Figaro's Lounge at 7 East Oak Street, and Gus's Pub at Rush Street and Bellevue Place.

A man using the name "Bob" recalled a neighborhood mainstay, the Shoreline 7, in

Sukie de la Croix's August 13, 2003, "Chicago Whispers" column in Windy City Times. "The Shoreline 7 at 7 West Division was rumored to be owned by Al Capone's brother Ralph, but was actually owned by Ralph Marco," Bob said. "The bar was really called the Shoreline, but on the matchbooks it said Shoreline, then underneath 7, then West Division, so everyone called it the Shoreline 7."

Warren Williamson said the Still of the Night bar was raided a lot, "so the talk was to go into the bar, get your beer, and then go stand by the phone booth inside. Then if there was a raid, you could run inside the phone booth and technically you would be on Bell Telephone property and not in a gay bar. You could always say you stepped inside to make a phone call and not get busted. People could be pretty ingenious when it came to avoiding the raids."

"Still of the Night was one of the only bars that ever got closed because of discrimination against non-homosexuals," Flint said. "The owner used to stand at the door and say, 'Are you a homosexual?' If you said yes, he'd let you in.

"One night the cops came to the door and he asked, 'Are you homosexual?' The cops flashed their badges and busted them. Ernie and Dutch were bartenders there. It was a wild place. [One] night someone cracked and threw two bottles of poppers into the air conditioning system. That was the sort of thing that happened at Still of the Night."

"That corner [of Clark and Division streets] was so raunchy," laughed Flint. "Ding Hoe was on the corner, and next door to Sam's was the Little Rock Garden, which was another Chinese restaurant. For the bartenders, it was great because when Sam's was packed, and we couldn't get in the john, we'd run next door and they'd let us use their bathroom."

Jerry Pagorek recalled the action in the Clark and Division neighborhood. "I'd just gotten out of high school, and what I remember more than the bars was the area," he said. "Everyone ran around and worked the street. Sam's was right there on Division, and that was always packed. Jamie's was on Clark just south of Division, and the Gold Coast was right there. The Mark Twain Hotel saw a lot of action.

"There was a small counter restaurant right next to Jamie's called Feast on a Bun, and we used to go there and do drugs in back by the cooler. The drag queens did their makeup back there. I remember two in particular that hung around there were Alphonsa, a big, thin African-American drag queen, and her plush sidekick Sheba, who always had her hair in a French twist. They were ringleaders. Everyone hung out on the streets around there and would carry on when the city tour buses would come by.

"Sometimes we'd go out to Lou Gage's [Louie's Fun Lounge, run by Louis Gauger] on Mannheim Road. We hung out in Bughouse Square a lot, too. That was wild with the hustlers and the cruising. There was even a guy there who sold liquor out of the trunk of his big black Lincoln, so you didn't even need to be old enough to go to the bars."

Bill Kelley also shared memories of this part of town. "Oh, it was unforgettable," he said. "There was Sam's on the northeast corner. The Ding Hoe restaurant was on the southeast corner on Division, and it was either right next door to or part of the Mark Twain Hotel, which was a place for trysts. The Syndicate drag bar Talk of the Town was right there. There was also the all-night sandwich place Feast on a Bun, which was a big hangout for street cruisers, transvestites and hustlers. Jamie's was right there as well.

"There was the Shoreline 7. There was the old-style Chicago diner Ricketts Restaurant as well, on Clark at Oak, and that was open late, and although it wasn't gay it had a big gay clientele because of the late hours and location. One block south of Ricketts was Bughouse Square, where there were so many hustlers and lots of cruising, so gay men could go there and pick someone up whether they wanted paid sex or free sex. There was also another all-night coffee shop at Dearborn and Division.

"With all these elements converging, there was also a police presence in the area, and there would be periodic sweeps."

Jerry Leppek said the area was even referred to, with a warning, during a "marital relations" discussion at Notre Dame, where he was attending school. The married couple leading the talk said, "Always be sure to make up at night and never go to bed angry, or your husband might end up at Clark and Division in Chicago." So, of course, Leppek said he immediately thought, I have got to go there, "and I moved to Chicago and that's right where I went. It was the center of everything when I first came to Chicago. You walked up out of the subway and you were there.

"I was moving here with my boyfriend at the time, named Ron. He came ahead, and when I got here, all the stuff was gone from the apartment and nothing had been paid with the money I gave him. He'd gone through my things and taken what he wanted and disappeared. I was left high and dry. Well, I found some friends who helped me out, and they decided that to cheer me up they were going to take me out, so we all went to the Shoreline 7. I went and got drinks and beers for everyone and when I turned around, there was Ron, who immediately said, 'I didn't take anything, it must have been the landlord,' which told me right away that he'd taken it.

"Well, I slammed the drinks down, and he ran and locked himself in the women's bathroom. That's when I met Jim Flint, who was also at the bar that night. He stepped right into it. Jim somehow managed to calm me down and got us more drinks and had someone sneak Ron out. His doing that prevented me from getting in a lot of trouble, because who knows what I would've done. I was that mad."

"I remember when Sam's lost their license," said Stan Walker. "That made no sense, since I had seen a white envelope pass hands, so I know the police were getting paid, but supposedly someone didn't get their envelope. Actually, I think the police just needed some good press, and a raid on a gay bar was always good.

"Someone came in, supposedly asked to buy someone a drink, and it was a charge of solicitation. The patrons were let go one by one, once they gave the cops their name, but they were still waiting outside to see what was going to happen.

"They had all the bartenders line up, as well as Al and Wally. Then they ushered us all in the paddy wagon one by one. As we went in, I remember each of us turned and did a bow, and the crowd applauded. They brought us to the station, and I remember Wally and Al were in a separate cell, and we could hear them yelling, 'Oh, he's gonna fuck me in the ass,' and all this crazy stuff.

"I remember the cops actually being pretty good-natured at the station. They served us bologna sandwiches on white bread and coffee. They even brought us some porn for some reason, porn magazines, which was sort of surprising. It was all dismissed but, as a result of that, the bar lost their license and was closed for a year and a day." This would have been a decision by the city's liquor commissioner.

Chicago, the One and Only

After the closing of Sam's, Flint went to California with several guys, including fellow bartender Sam Olin. But once again the boy from Peoria missed the Midwest. After a few weeks Flint returned and, soon after, found work at the Drake Hotel as a waiter at the Club International.

"We both worked there," said Walker. "It was supposedly a nice members club, but the setup was insane. It was on the second floor, but the kitchen was in the basement, and the connecting passages were either a very slow elevator or a spiral staircase built for one. So we were carrying these huge trays with covered dishes up and down this winding staircase. There was also a kitchen off the dining room, but that only had salads and ice cream. Everything else went to the basement kitchen. Hot fudge sundae—ice cream in the adjoining kitchen, hot fudge downstairs in the basement. As I said, the setup was insane."

"It was an all-private club, and the waiters had been there forever," laughed Flint. "I went there to get hired and lied my way through it. Then when he hired me, I admitted to the headwaiter that I didn't know French service with the gloves and everything but said I could learn it. He said, 'You're being honest with me, so I'm going to give you a try.'

"I told him I had a buddy who needed a job who was also a good waiter, and that was Stan. A lot of the waiters were very jealous of us. We'd serve very fast and worked well as a team. We moved up to the No. 2 team. We'd always slip the chef a little tip and a bartender a tip so we'd get our food and drinks faster. Stan would get hungry and say, 'Go down there and see if you can get us something to eat. Those Greek chefs, they love you.' So I would go down and get us prime rib or something. They would give us anything.

"One night when Ann Landers was in there with her husband and we were waiting on them, she was up and over talking to these people, and she came back to the table and called me over, and I said, 'Yes, Miss Landers.' She said, 'My food is a little cold.' I said, 'Yes, ma'am, I'm sure it is. If you would have sat down when I served it, I'm sure it would have been warm.' When I said that, the captain came flying out of the back. I thought he was going to fire me, but he said, 'You do not speak to guests like that.' I said, 'Very good, but I just did.'"

The Normandy Inn

When the Fleischmanns discovered they were going to lose the Sam's location because of the late-1960s Sandburg Village development, they bought an old restaurant a bit farther south and decided to open a bar at 744 North Rush Street.

"Even though Sam's was demolished to make way for Sandburg Village, that lot stayed vacant for years before anything was built there," Bill Kelley said.

When the waiter-duo of Jim Flint and Stan Walker left Club International, the two parted ways. "I went to work downtown at a commodities clearing house, H.S. Kipnis, and worked at night tending bar at King's Ransom [20 East Chicago Avenue] before moving out to San Francisco," Walker said. "I've managed bars there—the Pendulum; the Lion Pub; Toad Hall, the first bar in the Castro before everything took off in 1971–72; the Trocadero Transfer; the Woods Resort in the Russian River area; and the Stud. I guess Sam's was the one that started it all."

Flint moved on to the Normandy Inn. "After a bit, the Fleischmanns opened a bar at Chicago and Rush called the Normandy Inn, and I went there," Flint said. "When I came in, I told them they had the bar all in wrong. I told them to tear it down and redo it, since they had the drink stations on the wrong side. The way they had it you couldn't watch the door." They redid the bar following the star bartender's advice.

"Something I liked about tending bar there was, I was always the setup man. They let me open the bar, order the booze that wasn't picked by the Mob, and let me hire or recommend most of the bartenders.

"The place was enormous. There was a coat check in the front. It was carpeted, with a long bar and a stage on the side where they eventually had dancing. They also had two or three pool tables and a bowling machine. There was also a jukebox and then booths all around."

The Normandy "was very popular," Bill Kelley said. "I remember it as being much plusher and nicer than Sam's. I seem to recall some carpet and upholstered chairs, flocked [textured] wallpaper. It was probably twice as big as Sam's."

The Twirling Tradition

"The Normandy was when I started twirling the baton all the time," laughed Flint. "They'd play a song, and I would go up and down the bar and collect seventy or eighty dollars every time. I made big money. A big night at the Normandy was five or six hundred dollars, and that was in the late 1960s.

"It was like at Sam's. I felt like a star. If you rang the highest key, you had the front section, that's the way it worked. At Sam's I'd have big hats I'd put on and lay across the beer cooler and perform, and at the Normandy I had the baton. Being behind the bar was my stage."

"These Boots Were Made for Walkin'" was one of Felicia's first songs. However, the most popular Felicia song at the time was "Abergavenny," which was on the jukebox at the Normandy.

"I used to twirl my baton and go up and down the bar when that played, collecting tips," Flint said. "One night we had this new bartender and Sam told him, 'When Jim starts, get out of the way.' So I threw it up and did a flip and the thing came down and hit the poor kid right in the head. I was throwing my baton there, too, I wasn't just rolling it over my knuckles.

"Whenever anybody wanted me to twirl, they would go play that damn song. I twirled to that for years." ("Abergavenny" is an upbeat song with a marching tempo. Named for a town in Wales, the word means "mouth of the River Gavenny," and the song was a 1968 European hit for British singer Marty Wilde. It found some success in the U.S., landing in the Top 50 in August 1969.)

Chicago activist Joe Loundy was interviewed about the Normandy by Jack Rinella in 1995. "It was huge, and jammed with people," Loundy said. "I remember it made such an impression because I had never seen so many people together all at once, and they were obviously having a great time. I felt like I was Dorothy, just in from Kansas. I had never seen anything like that.

"They had the jukebox, and at one point they put on this type of marching music, and the bartender grabbed a baton, and marched up and down behind the bar twirling the baton, and it was only years later that I pieced it together. That was Jim Flint, and that's why Jim Flint's bar was called the Baton, because early on, Jim Flint did this thing, twirling the baton when they played the march music."

Flint said the best thing about working for Sam's and the Normandy was that you got to know every bar owner on Rush Street and you could go into any of the clubs. "They all knew me because I worked for the Fleischmanns," Flint said. "I also liked that it was on Chicago and Rush so I could go shopping every day before work. It was a big place and I saw everybody. I liked that part of it. I could socialize, be the center of attention, and make money, lots of money.

"Despite the shopping, I was still saving my money, but if you were working six or seven nights a week, you didn't have that much time to go out and spend it. There were some Sundays where I would wake up and I would still be serving drinks in my sleep. Almost every night after work, we used to go to the Little Corporal on Wacker and Wabash and sit in those big red booths. We'd never leave there until 5 or 6 in the morning."

Kitty Sheon

Though it was right in the thick of gay doings with the Lawson YMCA a few blocks away, the Normandy got a lot of the more closeted guys from Kitty Sheon's, 745 North Rush Street, across from the Normandy. The advertisements at the time declared "Kitty Sheon—The Name Says It All."

"Kitty Sheon's had a dress code and you had to have a suit and tie to get in," Flint said. "If you looked at Kitty herself, she looked like Mayor Daley in drag. Her husband was a captain in the police force. I don't think she ever got raided.

"The biggest scare Kitty ever had was when they were playing The Leather Boys [a 1964 British film featuring a gay motorcyclist] at a theater on Chicago Avenue. We all decided to go—all the bartenders of Gold Coast, Jamie's and Sam's. We had our leather jackets on and were ready to see the movie and decided to stop in at Kitty Sheon's to see [bartenders] Eddy Jacobs and Tommy.

"When we walked up, Pat, the black lady who worked the door, didn't know what to say. She let us in. Otherwise Tommy and Eddy would've never gotten served anywhere else [at any other gay bar] in town if they hadn't [let us in]."

On the website for his film Quearborn & Perversion, a 2008 documentary on the early history of lesbian and gay life in Chicago, Ron Pajak wrote: "Kitty was the proprietress who ran a tight ship—no touching allowed. Despite the fact that her bar served as a haven for gay men, she would patrol the bar for any 'shenanigans,' an innocent hand on another man's arm, for example. Once spied, she would march up to the perpetrators, grab one man's wrist, remove the hand from the arm and place it gently back on the bar in front of him."

In a June 25, 1992, Jon-Henri Damski column in Windy City Times, the Chicago journalist talked with bartender Sophie about the bar. "In those days, Kitty Sheon's … was the premier gay men's bar in town. Where gentlemen met gentlemen after work, a jacket and tie required.

"Some of the old-time restrictions, which didn't allow men to hold hands, kiss, or dance together, were still in play. As Sophie remembers, 'Your seat at your bar stool was yours alone. If you tried to change seats, or move around, they would ask you to leave. There was no overt cruising. You never gave your real name, your real phone number. And above all, you never told anyone where you worked in the daytime.'"

Let's Dance

"Toward the end of working at the Normandy, I asked the owners for a raise because we were still only making $55 a week but working 60 hours," said Flint. "I thought we deserved at least $80. Wally wanted to give it to me, but the other two didn't. "I decided to start looking. I contacted a couple people and we got the Baton started [in 1969]. The Fleischmanns found out about it, and saw that as a conflict of interest, and I had to quit. I was actually still working at the Normandy when I started it.

"I remember Wally's wife telling him not to let me leave and saying that if I left, the bar was going to close. He told me that and said, 'My wife wants you to stay,' but I said, 'It's too late, Wally. I have to go.'"

Not long after Flint left the Normandy, there was picketing outside the popular gay nightspot—not because of his departure, but for the right to dance. The protest resulted in the Normandy Inn becoming the first bar where same-sex dancing was allowed in Chicago.

As stated in The Electronic Encyclopedia of Chicago by the Chicago Historical Society: "Following the June 1969 Stonewall riots in New York City, a more militant gay liberation organization formed at the University of Chicago. This group sponsored a citywide dance at the Coliseum Annex in 1970, the first public lesbian and gay dance (aside from the annual Halloween drag balls) held in Chicago. Shortly thereafter, the university group merged with the newly founded Chicago Gay Liberation (CGL) and led a successful picketing campaign to force the Normandy on Rush Street to become the first gay bar in Chicago to obtain a dance license and to permit same-sex dancing."

Noted gay historian John D'Emilio elaborated on this topic in an essay in the 2008 book Out and Proud in Chicago: An Overview of the City's Gay Community and also on the website Outhistory.org. Referring to the April 18, 1970, showdown at the Coliseum Annex, he wrote on the website: "Chicago Gay Liberation ... rented the Coliseum, a structure near 16th and Wabash that, in bygone days, had hosted professional hockey and basketball games, roller derby, and major political conventions. It was a huge space! And, most importantly, it was public space in every sense of the word. This was pushing the boundaries and taking a big risk.

"Folks were scared. Might the police invade the place? Was there the danger of a 'giant bust'? Renee Hanover, the lawyer for the gay groups, pressed hard on the police to make sure nothing would happen. The police did show up and patrol the area on April 18th, but there were no arrests and no interference.

"The dancing crowds didn't quite fill the place, but 2,000 people came, making this perhaps the biggest openly acknowledged queer gathering in Chicago history. 'The dance floor was filled with laughing faces,' reported Mattachine Midwest's newsletter. Its writer waxed eloquent about the dance. It 'introduced freedom as the remedy that will end the closet as a way of life. The faggots came out for their public, the band was great, the vibes were beautiful. … The revolution has just begun, and the dances are part of it.'

"One thing leads to another, as my mother often warned me. In this case, the heady pleasures of a few dances led straight to the door of a popular local bar. The weekend after the Coliseum dance, gay and lesbian liberationists showed up with picket signs outside the Normandy Inn, near Chicago and Rush Streets. The flyers they distributed listed their demands: 'Gay people can dance both fast and slow ... no arbitrary dress regulations ... no discrimination against women.'

"The Seed, a local alternative radical newspaper, reported that the Normandy was 'nearly empty' that weekend, as protesters kept patrons away and 'convinced the owners they would have to take the wishes of Gay people seriously.' The owners caved in, and other bars quickly responded as well. For queer Chicagoans, dancing had come to stay."

Bill Kelley explained the picketing as a sort of jujitsu move. "The picketing was against the bar to allow same-sex dancing, but the bar couldn't do that because of the police," Kelley said. "So what was actually happening was, the picketing was putting pressure on the bar to get a new dispensation from the police. We couldn't do that, but they could. They had a good relationship with the police. The picket also worked because people would not cross a picket line to go into a gay bar for fear of drawing unwanted attention. So people weren't necessarily not crossing the picket line out of sympathy, but out of fear of exposure."

In a 1996 interview with Jack Rinella, local bar legend Chuck Rodocker recalled: "I picketed. I think they did it two or three nights, and I was there for one night. I think it was the second night or something. It was a party. You know, that's where the action is. I mean, you're talking no more than maybe a half dozen businesses. Like I say, there was the King's Ransom, Normandy, for drags there was the Blue Dahlia way out on North Avenue. And then there was the Alameda. So we were probably drinking up at the Alameda [5210 North Sheridan Road] and said, 'Oh, there's a party down at the Normandy. Let's go.' So that's probably what happened ... . I don't think I carried a sign. I'm trying to think actually what the signs would have said, too, and I can't recall that, either. But I do remember it being a fun event. Yeah, I don't think anybody was real mad."

"I remember after those protests we were allowed to dance," said patron Richard Johnson. "I specifically remember dancing there to 'Band of Gold' by Freda Payne. That was the first place we actually could dance in Chicago in a gay bar without being arrested. Prior to that, if you were dancing in a bar, the manager would come over and either make you stop or ask you to leave. In fact, a group of us used to drive to a roadside bar up in Kenosha called Lydia's just so we could dance. It also helped that near the Normandy was a drugstore on Rush and Chicago where we got the real original Snap Crackle Pop poppers so that we could dance and carry on all night!"

Flint in Acapulco, 1966.

Flint as Felicia at a "turnabout" at Chesterfield bar, circa 1965. Lower two photos are with Richie Saunders.

Flint as Felicia, 1960s.

Flint does leather, late 1960s.

Flint as Felicia, 1960s.

Flint as Felicia, white gloves and all.

This page: Flint as Felicia, 1960s.

Flint at Chesterfield bar, 1965.

Popular Sam's bartender Stan Walker also worked with Flint at Club International.

Warren Williamson, Flint's first serious boyfriend, and Flint, 1968.

3

Police and the Law

In the 1960s and 1970s, gay bars experienced pressure from all sides: the police, building and fire inspectors, and the Mafia. Bar raids were a common occurrence, and to stay in business, payoffs were the norm.

Corruption among the police and in other city departments was virulent and pernicious. Some of those hired to serve and protect were simply serving themselves, causing a breach of trust that even caught the attention of the Richard Nixon White House. Some forms of corruption will probably never go away completely, but without such a high level of exploitation, by the mid-1980s most gay and lesbian bars in Chicago were able to survive and thrive.

In a 2008 interview for WTTW, the Public Broadcasting Service affiliate in Chicago, Flint told filmmakers Alexandra Silets and Dan Andries that in the early 1970s, the payoff rate was about $1,800 per month to police and $1,800 to the Mafia. "How that shifted from person to person, I don't know, but that's what I know that I handed them in two envelopes," Flint said. "I had to do that before I even had to pay my rent. Because I couldn't afford an apartment, I had to live in the basement here [the Baton]. Those were hard years back then.

"I remember the owner [of a previous bar Flint worked for] giving an envelope to the police. That was in 1968. I remember this distinctly because five days later the sergeant came in and said, 'I'm sorry, you have to close,' and he said, 'What do you mean, I have to close? I just took care of you.' 'The word downtown is that all gay bars are closed during the Democratic convention. Either you close or we make sure you close.' Because somebody had the fear that the gays would team up with the hippies and Yippies, so we ended up closing." Not all gay bars were closed during the convention, but both Flint and Chuck Renslow recalled that some of them were closed.

In this chapter we look more closely at the police and legal issues Flint faced throughout his business career. Elsewhere in this book we address the Mafia-related profiteering. Many of the specific arrests Flint experienced are documented in the chapters on his various bars.

When Flint started going to gay bars in Chicago in the mid-1960s, he was well aware of the high-profile police raids that swept up many of his peers.

One of the most notorious was in 1964 on Louie's Fun Lounge (commonly known as Louie Gage's), at 2340 North Mannheim Road in Leyden Township. There were 109 people, including six women, arrested in the raid, conducted by officers under Cook County Sheriff Richard B. Ogilvie. The Chicago Tribune on April 24, 1964, printed the names and occupations of those arrested. Louis Gauger, the bar's owner, was among those arrested. The Tribune reported April 28 that Gauger was an "avowed friend of Tony Accardo, crime syndicate figure."

The Tribune did a story April 27 specifically about the teachers and school officials who were arrested, "Boards to Get Vice Raid Data on 8 Teachers," and it again listed their names and where they taught. The next day the Tribune reported that at least two of them had quit.

The Tribune's account read in part: "Lt. James Donnelly said that many of the men carried powder puffs and lipsticks, and that some wore wigs. The lounge has catered to sex deviates from all over the nation, Donnelly added, and has been raided many times in the last 15 years by police of the state's attorney's office and the sheriff's department."

This was a final straw for some gays, and Mattachine Midwest, an independent organization that borrowed from the name of the once-national gay Mattachine Society, was formed out of the anger generated by this raid and other police harassment.

That same year, the Lincoln Baths, 1812 North Clark Street, were raided. One of the raids was documented in the June 14, 1964, issue of the Chicago Tribune in an article titled "33 Men Seized Thru Vice Raid on Bathhouse." Two years later, on March 6, 1966, the Tribune reported that another 32 men were arrested there. The 1964 article listed the professions of those arrested, but only one name. The 1966 article listed all the men's names and their ages, addresses and occupations. The article said an undercover detective witnessed lewd acts being performed in the steam room. It also said the business was controlled by members of the crime syndicate.

Here are excerpts from the 1964 raid article: "Thirty-three men, including a County physician, two teachers, and two attorneys, were arrested early yesterday in a vice raid on the Lincoln Baths ... . [A detective] saw four men performing indecent acts in a steam room. [Lieutenant Thomas] Kernan said the bathhouse has been a national meeting place for perverts. ... He said files of the bathhouse confiscated in the raid listed various meeting places for perverts throughout the United States."

Sergeant James Reilley of the Police Department's prostitution unit was in charge of the 1966 raid, and he said the patrons of the bathhouse were "required to show identification and to sign a register," the Tribune reported. The police also said the bathhouse was controlled by the Mafia, including Michael "The Fireplug" Glitta and Lawrence "The Hood" Buonaguidi.

Some men arrested in these raids lost their jobs or their families, or both. And some were said to have committed suicide.

Mattachine Midwest Responds

The Mattachine Midwest Newsletter provided some of the only fair coverage of the bar raids of the 1960s. It reported that Central Vice police raided the Annex and Sam's on August 20, 1968. Flint is not sure of all the exact dates of his arrests, but he was arrested while working at both the Annex and Sam's in the 1960s. Note that the August 20 raids were eight days before the Democratic National Convention in Chicago—very likely these raids were a show of force to intimidate some of the city's gay bars into closing during the convention that year.

The September 1968 issue of the Mattachine Midwest Newsletter had a cover article, "Cops Ride Again," that read in part:

"During the week preceding the Democratic convention, police activities in the homosexual community resulted in the sending of a letter from Mattachine Midwest to Police Superintendent [James] Conlisk, followed by two press releases. ...

"After interviewing victims and eyewitnesses, we felt that a protest had to be made.

Victims were selected at random on a 'you, you and you' basis. One cop actually groped a customer in one bar. ...

"The following week, the whole world saw the hatred and violence of which Chicago's police are capable [at the convention]. Whether one's sympathies are with the demonstrators or not, the police tactics during the week of the convention, and especially on August 28 and 29, belong in a history of Nazi Germany. ...

"To our surprise, many of the gay community were present in Lincoln and Grant parks, collecting signatures on our petitions and observing police and demonstrators. They confirm that the police action was entirely out of line with any 'provocation' (which in most instances amounted to name-calling in reply to police name-calling). ...

"Our September 19 membership meeting [at The Trip] is to be a semi-public hearing on the homosexual community and the police situation, and other problems. ... "

In the same month as the Democratic National Convention, Chicago hosted the annual meeting of the North American Conference of Homophile Organizations, which helped to bring national gay activists into the city for the convention as well. Those in town for the NACHO conference included Dr. Franklin Kameny. (He died October 11, 2011, at age 86, as this book was being prepared for publication.)

An ad in September's Mattachine Midwest Newsletter warned readers about the police: "Remember, your local police are armed and extremely dangerous," and it was signed "A Concerned Citizen, and Taxpayer." It was aimed at local residents because it was published after the Democratic convention.

The newsletter also ran a news release about the raids and the "harassment and arrest of 17 patrons and employees of two bars catering to homosexuals. The arrests, which occurred on Tuesday, August 20, were marked by increased plainclothes and uniformed police surveillance and the intimidation of other homosexual bars.

"At one bar, a bartender was arrested on a charge of solicitation for prostitution after he replied indifferently to a question whether a certain patron 'could be trusted.' Three bar patrons were arrested on charges of public indecency. Police demanded identification of all customers regardless of age. Reliable witnesses report that one plainclothesman was himself guilty of public indecency [at Sam's] and was rebuked for it prior to the arrests.

"At the other bar, ten patrons picked at random and three employees were arrested on 'public indecency' and related charges. As an apparent attempt at justification, one policeman allegedly told an arrestee that he was part of a minority group and should expect to be treated like it.

"Homosexual bars have been subject to similar harassment for several years, despite the fact that in Chicago (and elsewhere in Illinois) homosexual acts between consenting adults in private are not illegal. The latest wave of police harassment comes on the heels of the fourth annual North American Conference of Homophile Organizations, held here in August, which resolved to work vigorously to change such police practices."

An open letter to Superintendent Conlisk was also included in the newsletter, signed by Mattachine Midwest President Jim Bradford, Vice President William B. Kelley, Secretary Jerome Carter and Treasurer Paul Baker.

The letter read in part:

"We are writing to protest vehemently the current wave of police harassment of homosexual bars and their patrons, and to demand that you call a halt to it. ... [We] are tired of receiving 'special' treatment as a minority group in Chicago. ... Unfounded arrests, trumped-up charges, entrapment and constant surveillance of homosexuals and their social institutions must stop."

That same newsletter issue also provided a three-page guide on the rights of citizens if arrested, and suggestions on what to do if arrested.

Mattachine Midwest kept up the attempted pressure on police for several more years, until more organizations and individuals took up the cause.

Nixon's Justice

President Richard Nixon was not a fan of Chicago Major Richard J. Daley, and not just because they were in opposite political parties. Nixon blamed Daley for his loss to John F. Kennedy in the 1960 presidential race.

Nixon had a way to pay Daley back. He used his Justice Department to go after corrupt members of the Chicago Police Department.

The December 31, 1972, issue of the Chicago Sun-Times reported on the crackdown: "Chief of Traffic Clarence E. Braasch and 23 other policemen were named Saturday in the most inclusive indictment ever returned against personnel of the Chicago Police Department. A special federal grand jury accused the 24 of conspiring to extort monthly cash payoffs from 53 Near North Side taverns, nightclubs and restaurants. The total take was said to be several hundred thousand dollars."

Four additional officers were charged as co-conspirators. Braasch and 13 others also faced perjury charges. There were also four unindicted co-conspirators, bringing the total implicated to 32. Those four unindicted co-conspirators reportedly testified against their colleagues.

All the accused police officers worked under Braasch at the 18th District ("East Chicago Avenue") police station, 113 West Chicago Avenue, from 1966 to 1970. Almost everyone who worked in Braasch's vice detail was involved. (Another police station farther west on Chicago Avenue was known as the West Chicago Avenue station.)

This was the police district that included many of the era's top gay bars, including the drag bar that Jim Flint had opened by that time, the Baton Show Lounge.

The Sun-Times printed a list of the businesses named by the special federal grand jury as victims of the alleged police shakedown. The list included these gay bars:

>Aggie's Gold Coast Lounge, 501 North Clark Street (owned by Chuck Renslow)
>Baton Show Lounge, 430 North Clark Street
>Bentley's, 640 North State Street
>G.C.'s (also known as Gerry's Club and Gold Coast), 2265 N. Lincoln Avenue
>>(also co-owned by Chuck Renslow at a different time)
>Haig, 800 North Dearborn Street
>Ifs, Ands or Burt's, 5 West Superior Street
>Inner Circle, 1842-44 North Wells Street
>King's Ransom, 20 East Chicago Avenue
>New Jamie's, 1110 North Clark Street
>Nite Life, 955 North State Street

Normandy, 744 North Rush Street
Togetherness, 61 West Hubbard Street

Some of these bars, including New Jamie's, were owned by the Mafia and were paying off the police for protection from raids. Some were gay-owned and paying off both the police and Mafia for protection as part of a "street tax" common on the Near North Side. Several of the bars had folded by the time of the trial.

The Chicago Gay Crusader, in its September 1973 edition, noted that "several of the Chicago Avenue vice officers have been the subjects of repeated complaints over the years to Chicago gay groups by victims of alleged prostitution and public-indecency frame-ups."

Among the 53 businesses were also an "elite" list of allegedly Mafia-owned bars, what Braasch called the "Big 10," which were reportedly to be protected along with gambling interests in exchange for the money, according to the September 12, 1973, issue of the Chicago Tribune.

The Justice Department's Strike Force on Organized Crime was headed by Sheldon Davidson. The U.S. attorney on the case was James R. Thompson, future governor of Illinois, with Assistant U.S. Attorney Dan K. Webb—who was the U.S. attorney 10 years later when charges were brought against alleged Mafia members accused of shaking down gay bars.

Some gay bar owners did testify in the Nixon-era Chicago Police case, but Chuck Renslow and Flint did not cooperate, though they were brought in by authorities.

"I went before the grand jury [on March 13, 1973], and they asked me if I was paying off," Renslow said. "I said yes. They said, 'To who?' I said, 'I don't know.' They gave me a list of pictures; I knew them right away, but I didn't identify any." The judge asked Renslow why he wouldn't cooperate, and he said he was worried about implicating himself because bribes were illegal.

Renslow's own FBI file notes that he admitted that payoffs were made to police in the 18th and 20th districts, but that he "will not furnish any information about the police because he fears the police and did not want to become a target of their rage."

Flint said he was locked up for about 18 hours in an effort to force him to testify, but his lawyers helped him avoid it.

"I said, 'Judge, I can't testify because I don't know these policemen as Jim Flint—I run a bar for female impersonators and I live as a woman [Felicia],'" Flint said. "At about that time [the judge] started banging his gavel and calling for a recess, so we went to his office in the back and he said, 'What's this all about, young man?' and I said, 'Sir, I live as a woman, I cut my hair out of respect for your courtroom.' … He said, 'We don't need your testimony.'"

Flint said that excuse would not have been enough in itself to stop him from testifying, but somehow it did get under the judge's skin and Flint was excused. Webb, the assistant U.S. attorney, "just looked at me like he could have killed me," Flint said.

Flint said he knew of the police payoffs even before he opened his own bar. When he worked at other gay bars in the 1960s, he saw the police send representatives to collect the money.

"There was a bagman in the area that would come to all the bars and would take it," Flint said. As soon as he opened the Baton (and later the Redoubt), the payoffs started, to both police and Mafia.

After the Braasch arrests, Flint said the police payoffs did mostly stop.

The federal government also tried to get well-known lawyer Ralla Klepak to testify against police. Klepak helped LGBT clients, including Flint. Two of the primary vice squad officers who were up on charges phoned her and tried to entrap her, she said, and when she recognized that she was talking to the two vice squad officers who were the known bagmen for the 18th District, she said she told them to stop calling her and playing games. The next week, she was visited by the feds and asked to turn over her files on the Baton, Renslow and others, but she refused, saying they were clients' files and confidential.

Klepak was then subpoenaed before the federal grand jury, and she told the jurors and prosecutor that she had nothing to say. She asked why the bars were raided if they were paying off the police, and she said that she would be called by a bar owner only when the bar was raided.

Klepak was then summoned before U.S. District Judge James B. Parsons and granted immunity, but when she told a friend who was a judge that she had been granted immunity and still had nothing to say, that judge told her, "You need a lawyer or they will destroy you." Over Klepak's protestations that she did not need a lawyer to tell the grand jury she had no personal knowledge of any payoffs, reluctantly Klepak accepted the offers of friends and attorneys R. Eugene Pincham and Lawrence E. Morrissey to represent her.

Klepak said she was called before the grand jury eight times. "They threatened me; they told me they would indict me for income tax evasion and perjury if I did not say what they wanted me to say," she remembered. "I was told if I didn't lie they would indict me.

"During the last time I was called to the grand jury and continued to answer that I had no personal knowledge about the allegations as to bar payoffs, I finally said, 'Wait, there is something I have to say: I am tired of being threatened that if I do not lie I will be indicted for perjury, amongst other things.' They quickly got me out of there so fast!

"Some of the biggest and brightest lawyers were representing others in that case, and they called me and said my testimony would help their own cases, showing how the feds were pressuring people. They never did touch me, but after that occurred, I stopped practicing criminal law in the federal court and started to switch away from criminal court and transitioned to other areas. Since that experience, I have no respect for the feds because of how they handled that case—and I used to think that the feds were the 'good guys.'"

In an apparent revenge move against gay bars, even against those whose owners did not testify, city authorities tried to revoke their licenses because of the alleged bribery. The Chicago Gay Crusader reported in October 1973 that U.S. Attorney Thompson and Cook County State's Attorney Bernard Carey defended the bars, "saying that the immunity given operators in exchange for their testimony prevented such revocation action," and the city backed down.

But Mayor Richard J. Daley did not help matters any when he tried to blame the public for the corruption. In a September 5, 1973, news conference, Daley said he was not defending corruption, but that it is a "two-way street. Some people have to be corrupt in order to corrupt the policemen," as reported in the September 6 Chicago Tribune.

Braasch and 18 of the former vice squad members were found guilty of conspiracy to commit extortion. Braasch and 10 others also were found guilty of perjury. The sentence for Braasch was six years in prison. Others were given sentences of anywhere from 18 months to four years. Four officers were acquitted.

In parallel to the Braasch trial, 13 other former vice policemen and their ex-commander from the 15th District in the Austin area were also indicted on similar charges, this time involving 30 bars. One gay bar, the Blue Dahlia, 5640 West North Avenue, was named as having paid $300 monthly from 1966 to 1970, according to the September 1973 issue of The Chicago Gay Crusader.

In 1975, the U.S. attorney's office and the FBI were continuing their probes of police corruption. A March 13, 1975, Chicago Tribune headline said it all: "2 Policemen Are Subpenaed in Extortion of Gay Bars." This time the corruption allegations involved the 14th (Shakespeare), 23rd (Town Hall) and 20th (Foster Avenue) districts on the city's North Side.

In 1986, two former Cook County sheriff's officers were sentenced to 15 years in prison each, according to a Sun-Times report on July 19 of that year. The U.S. district judge who sentenced them, James F. Holderman, had been a prosecutor on the Braasch trial. He said at the trial that he had hoped his earlier work would help deter future wrongdoing, but he said clearly it did not. Ten years later, in 1996, seven 15th (Austin) District police officers were charged in a new series of corruption scandals.

What a Drag

The October 1973 issue of The Chicago Gay Crusader covered multiple stories related to gays and the law: the Braasch police corruption trial, the city gay-rights bill hearing, and a judge's overturning of the city's anti-drag law.

Flint had to make an end run around that law when he opened the Baton in 1969, and more than three decades later his bar almost got shut down as part of the city's attempt to crack down on strip clubs. (See more details later in this chapter.)

On September 20, 1973, Cook County Circuit Judge Jack I. Sperling, who was a former Chicago alderman, ruled against the Chicago ordinance banning cross-dressing, as in men wearing "women's" clothing and vice versa. The judge sat in the North Youth Court, and he ruled that the ban violated the U.S. constitutional right to equal protection, among other rights.

Ominously, the Gay Crusader report noted that "unless the judge's ruling is appealed by the city and then upheld by a higher court, it has no binding effect upon any other judges and may or may not be followed by them in any other transvestite case."

Later, Cook County Circuit Judge David Shields, sitting in Jury Court, decided to ignore Sperling's ruling, and in August 1974 he declared that the cross-dressing ban was constitutional. The Chicago Tribune reported August 8 on his ruling that "the ban is within the police powers of a community provided by the federal and state constitutions because it affects only public conduct." The Northwestern University Legal Assistance Center had argued that it was impossible to define what is men's or women's clothing, but Shields said the law is about "the intent to conceal his or her sex," not about fashion.

Other cross-dressing cases were also pending during that time period, according to the Gay Crusader's August 1974 report on the Shields ruling.

The 1973 case before Sperling had been argued by lesbian attorney Renee Hanover, who represented four young Mexican-American cross-dressers (who went by the names Melinda, Mona, Tanya and Tammie), all aged between 17 and 20, who were arrested after complaining to police about harassment against them at El Jalisciense, a bar in the Pilsen neighborhood at 2200 West 21st Place, on August 21, 1973. They were charged with violating Section 192-8 of the Chicago Municipal Code, which barred someone from wearing clothing of the opposite sex "with the intent to conceal his or her sex." The "conceal" phrase had been added to the law in 1943. The possible fine was from $20 to $500.

The original 1973 ruling had led to a proposal to repeal the law in the City Council. But even though there was not clarity on the law, it was rarely enforced and was eventually repealed on January 11, 1978, when the Chicago City Council removed the cross-dressing language from the Municipal Code. According to the change, the following language was removed from the code, which dealt mainly with the public appearance of a person: "or is in a dress not belonging to his or her sex, with intent to conceal his or her sex, or in an indecent or lewd dress, or who shall make any indecent exposure of his or her person." The remaining law was mainly about describing what body parts could not be exposed in public (such as genitals, pubic hair, buttocks, female breasts, etc.).

The change had been recommended by the City Council Committee on Police, Fire, Personnel, Schools and Municipal Institutions, chaired by Alderman Ed Burke. The proposed ordinance had been signed by Mayor Michael Bilandic on October 26, 1977, and the rewriting was done to "bring it in compliance with recent decisions of the United States Supreme Court," according to the City Council Journal, January 17, 1978. After it passed out of committee 10–1, it then passed the City Council 36–5. (Of those voting against, three were aldermen who in later years backed the city's gay-rights ordinance: Burt Natarus, Martin Oberman and Dick Simpson. This may have been because the overall ordinance, of which the language deletion was one feature, was still a moralistic effort.)

Just as with the end of the unofficial but police-pressured ban on same-sex dancing that decade, it became easier for most LGBTs to navigate on the edges, even if they were still targeted for police harassment, anti-gay violence, and loss of work and family. There was at least some legal hope, even if there was still a long way to go.

For Flint, the cross-dressing ban did not hurt his business, as his performers were safely "entertainers" who did cross-dressing as an art form. But in the bar's first few years, once the performers were offstage, and especially when they were outside the bar, they were at risk for arrest.

"In those days there were all kinds of rules for female impersonator shows," said attorney Klepak. "In Florida, maybe you could wear some men's clothes and a woman's blouse. But during intermission you had to change into male clothes. All kinds of rules, like you couldn't dress in clothes perceived to be from the opposite sex. All these stupid rules cops could arrest you for."

The March 23, 1979, issue of GayLife carried a letter written by lesbian activist Christine Riddiough (today a resident of Washington, D.C., where she continues her activism) protesting police harassment of that kind: "A few weeks ago in a vice-squad raid aimed primarily at female prostitutes, two female impersonators from the Baton were arrested. This kind of action by the police should make all of us outraged both at the kind of tactics the police use, and about the targets of this kind of repression.

"This police action raises other complex issues for the women's and gay movements and brings up questions that have been a source of tension for some years now. What should be our attitude toward female impersonators, drag queens, the more 'outrageous' parts of the gay community? What role should they play within the movement?

"Quentin Crisp's autobiography, The Naked Civil Servant, illustrates this further. Because they are so visible, they have often drawn the scorn and abuse of homophobes. They have also been used by the media to portray the gay community as a whole—for example, pictures of gay/lesbian pride parades have often featured drag queens."

Riddiough noted that within the gay and lesbian community, there is often bias against female impersonators, including antagonism by women who feel drag queens can be sexist. She said even if there is sexism, that alone "shouldn't mean a complete rejection of drag queens. Doing that is too similar to the homophobia of the non-gay society. ... Tede [Mathews] in [the documentary] 'Word Is Out' says it best, 'We're all born naked so anything we wear after that is drag.' ... We've still got some consciousness raising to do within the community—if we expect the police and the rest of the straight world to accept us, we've got to be more accepting and unified ourselves."

Despite the Chicago law, however, Flint's more-than-16 arrests in bar raids were never about drag. They were usually for being a "keeper of a disorderly house," serving liquor to an undercover "underage" plant from police, or similar charges.

Flint explained his first arrest in the 1960s, for serving someone underage. Flint was only in his 20s then, and he told WTTW he remembered getting his hands cuffed: "I was petrified. And when they threw me in that drunk cell with about 18 other people, it was even more petrifying. And of course I had a drag name, Felicia ... . Thank God, that time I only had to stay in there for four hours."

Later arrests were even more terrifying, as most of them were part of larger raids on bars, with multiple people arrested. During one raid on dozens of people at the Chesterfield, the police had about 10 paddy wagons ready for the patrons they were arresting.

From all his arrests, Flint said he remembers the horrible bologna sandwiches served to arrestees and the normal routine, which was to let the prisoners out at noon, from police headquarters at 1121 South State Street. He told WTTW he remembers the prisoners screaming and carrying on, "especially the drags, because everyone [workers downtown] was out on their lunch hour and your makeup would be cracking, so they all wanted to embarrass you. That was really the only time they'd let you out was 12 o'clock. So you usually got in there around 2 or 3 in the morning and you'd spend a nice little time there on that hard bench."

Though mostly minor, those charges did put Flint at risk as he tried to move from being a bartender to being a bar owner. In order for Flint to open a bar, he needed to make sure his record was clean.

Moving On Up

Four attorneys represented many of the LGBT persons arrested in various bar raids and entrapment cases during the 1960s and 1970s: Pearl Hart, Paul R. Goldman, Ralla Klepak and Renee Hanover. Ed Mogul also provided invaluable advice, but more behind the scenes.

After one of his 1960s arrests at a gay bar, where he had been hired only recently to tend bar, Flint called Klepak for help.

"I get a call one day, and Jim comes in to see me. I didn't know him from Adam," Klepak said. "Before then, I would never represent these cases because they [the bars] had their own lawyers, lawyers who worked for the Syndicate."

Klepak said that, of the attorneys who did help gays, Goldman was known "for never trying a case. He would compromise, he would settle, he would have his clients plead guilty or cut deals. I was stubborn. If my client did not do anything wrong, I would not compromise. I would ask for a jury if I had to, and people knew this." Goldman died in 1986, one month before his 80th birthday. While he was practicing, he financially sponsored ONE of Chicago, the local chapter of ONE Inc., and furnished meeting space for it in his office and elsewhere.

There was a branch courtroom upstairs above the 18th District police station. "Every summer it was so crowded, with 40 or 50 people a day," Klepak said. "They were arrested for all kinds of things, including in gay bar raids, public sex, masturbating in public, exposing themselves, being at the baths, etc. Most of the gay bar raids were in that district, but some were in outlying districts, like Lost & Found was. So, in the summer, court was crowded, in a large auditorium.

"There was a concerted effort to arrest gays and cross-dressers, to categorize sex criminals and homosexuals. This harassment was supported by Mayor [Richard J.] Daley and the archdiocese, because they saw these places as a plague, an abomination. It was almost unheard of for a gay person to own their own gay bar or restaurant [in the 1960s].

"Into this era enters Jim Flint. Jim was from a small town, he had been in the Navy ... he was the sweetest guy, a typical small-town guy. I had been representing these drug dealers, all kinds of people, and in walks Jim Flint. I had a lot of patrons [of gay bars] hire me, but Jim was the first employee of a bar to hire me. He explained that the bar had been raided and he was in Criminal Court. This had been going on for months and case after case was being dismissed, except for Jim's; he was last. They were all represented by a lawyer for the bar's owner.

"As a bartender, Jim was charged with being the keeper of a disorderly house. The case was before Judge William Sylvester White, a black man, in Criminal Court. Judge White was a dignified man, a smart and good judge. But Jim sees all the others getting not-guilty verdicts, 40 or so of them, but not him. I told Jim he was going to be scapegoated, that he was going to be the one conviction, and as the last hired he was the disposable one to convict."

Klepak agreed to represent Flint to fight to make sure such a criminal conviction would not taint the rest of his life. She did a brave thing, telling the judge there was an image of the court being corrupt, so she wanted a new judge. She said she pressured to have a pretrial conference with the state's attorney, and Judge White refused. Then she pressured and had a meeting with the judge explaining that the court would be viewed as tainted because the lawyers said there had been a deal made.

Flint's case was tried before a different judge, and Klepak got it dismissed. She still believes that, had the case gone before the original judge, Flint would have been the sacrificial lamb.

"I felt there really had been a deal, so I did what was best for my client," she said. "Jim and I were both scared. The win was an emotional catharsis for both of us. I thought what they were doing to him was terrible. When I met him, I knew this would affect the rest of his life.

"As the years go by, Jimmy always remembers and says, 'She saved me.' Who knows what would have happened to him? Look at all the good things he has done. He never took anything from anybody; he can still say that. He earned his success and gave dignity to people."

Later, Klepak helped Flint expunge his arrest records.

Fighting for the Right to Stay Open

Klepak also tried an important case in the late 1960s against The Trip bar, 27 East Ohio Street, and her work helped make it easier for bars to survive while they fought in the courts. Prior to this case, a Chicago bar that had its license revoked after a raid was required to close during its appeal of the revocation, because the police would seize the bar's liquor license off the wall.

"You couldn't open until you were found not guilty, and after criminal court you had to go before the liquor commission," Klepak said. "They could still rule against you even if you won in criminal court.

"That happened with The Trip. Two guys [Dean Kolberg and Ralf Johnston] opened The Trip. It was a really classy place; it was like a house, with multiple stories. There was a piano, a pool table, dancing, games, next to where Pizzeria Uno was. It was mainly straight [at first], but on Sundays it was for private parties, mainly so guys could dance together. If you had a [membership] card, you could get in."

The Trip was rented by the cast of the hit stage show Man of La Mancha for a cast party. This was likely the November 1967 production at the McVickers Theatre, starring Keith Andes.

"There was dancing, etc.," Klepak said. "A vice squad cop somehow got in and raided it. The whole cast was arrested except the lead. [The owners] called me. They were charged with being the keepers of a disorderly house because boys were dancing with boys and touching each other." William B. Kelley, who worked for Klepak at the time, remembers hearing that the vice officers were able to enter after one of them stopped a would-be patron on the sidewalk, somehow obtained his Trip membership card, and used it to gain admittance.

Klepak was familiar with Greek restaurants. Sometimes they were called "bouzouki" joints, from the Greek musical instrument of that name. The male waiters would line-dance to the music. Klepak asked two musicians and some waiters to come to court and do their thing, to show that it's the same thing, men dancing, and therefore the arrests violated the U.S. Constitution's guarantee of equal protection.

"I said, 'This is what my clients were doing, in the same district as Greek Town, and yet my clients were arrested, and there were no arrests in Greek Town,'" Klepak said. "The case was thrown out. The judge asked me for a favor, to have the lead actor sing 'Impossible Dream.' The actor was there and did sing it, and the judge cried."

The next step for The Trip was to go before the Chicago Local Liquor Commissioner. The whole process was drawn out. "The commission said The Trip was still a disorderly house, because they were not Greeks, they were fucking homosexuals," Klepak recalled. "It may have been private, they said, but if a cop got in, the public could have gotten in."

Klepak appealed and, after she decided to claim this was a constitutional issue, the Illinois Supreme Court allowed her to skip the Appellate Court and go right to the Supreme Court.

"I had remembered in law school they said a license was a 'privilege,' that you can't demand it," Klepak said. "But once you have a license, it is a property right. And you can't take someone's property away without due process. So by viewing it as a property right, you can't take it off the wall of a bar until they are convicted. Up until then, they could just close you down by taking the license."

Technically, as explained in a 1969 opinion written by the highly regarded Justice Walter V. Schaefer, the Supreme Court based its decision on the unconstitutionality of the

Legislature's practice of differentiating among cities as to whether a liquor licensee could continue doing business until its administrative appeal of a license revocation was decided. Before the Supreme Court decision, a Chicago licensee had to stay closed, but a licensee in other Illinois cities could stay open during its administrative appeal.

The court also held that Chicago's License Appeal Commission had waited too long to uphold The Trip's license revocation and therefore had lost jurisdiction to do so. The case is known as Johnkol Inc. v. License Appeal Commission, 247 N.E.2d 901 (Ill. 1969).

Even though The Trip won this precedent-setting case, it had taken a long time and a huge amount of money—for rent (on the closed bar) and for lawyer fees. The owners owed Klepak $100,000—some of that because she had hired famed lawyer Elmer Gertz and Wayne Giampietro of his office to be co-counsels, based on Gertz's Supreme Court experience.

"I always wanted to own my own bar, so I said, 'Consider me your partner until you pay off your bill,'" Klepak said. She helped Kolberg and Johnston through some renovations and upgrades, to make The Trip more popular and successful, and they were eventually able to pay off their debt to her.

Klepak got a taste for the bar business, so she was instrumental in opening up an elegant club, Togetherness, for all genders and races, at 61 West Hubbard Street. Flint was also associated with Togetherness prior to opening his own bar, the Baton.

Marching Against Harassment

Even after the police-payoff trial, there continued to be police and city harassment of gay bars under Mayor Richard J. Daley and Mayor Michael Bilandic, who took over after Daley died in 1976.

However, Flint said he experienced no arrests or incidents at his Redoubt leather bar. "We could have gotten busted," he said. "We had a sex room downstairs, but the cops just didn't bother us. There were payoffs available. We opened around 1976."

During Bilandic's election effort, when he was facing off against newcomer Jane Byrne, Flint's Baton Show Lounge was raided. This was considered a common thing during election season, as politicians tried to show they were for law and order and cleaning up the "deviates."

In early February, Flint and one of his performers were arrested, and after the arrest Flint flew to Hawaii for a break from the stress of the arrest. The New Flight was raided the same night, and the Chatterbox was next. These incidents were reported in Ira Jones' "Ira's Eye on Chicago" column in the GayLife edition of February 16, 1979.

"Is there any coincidence that gay bars are always raided approximately 30 days before every election in Chicago?" questioned GayLife Publisher Grant Ford in the same edition.

The arrests received TV and print news coverage, and Howard Goodman, owner of the New Flight, hosted a meeting at My Brother's Place, a gay restaurant at 111 West Hubbard Street. Other gay business owners and media attended, and as a result, the Gay and Lesbian Coalition of Metropolitan Chicago appointed an ad hoc committee to investigate the incidents.

This group seems to have been dormant for several months until more raids happened.

Raids that occurred between May 12 and 20 were covered by Stephen Kulieke for GayLife's May 25, 1979, edition: "Carol's Speakeasy at 1335 N. Wells was the site of the most serious police action when eleven men were arrested for disorderly conduct" in the early morning hours of May 19. At around 1:15 a.m., the police entered the bar to check for underage drinkers. But then the doors were locked and patrons were told they could leave shortly. Soon, the floodlights were switched on and the estimated 550 people were told, "It would be to your advantage to leave."

Once outside, patrons shouted against the harassment and soon the police began the arrests. Kulieke also said that photographer Dave Veltkamp was attacked when he tried to take photos of the situation. Veltkamp was handcuffed, struck in the stomach with a nightstick, and his film was confiscated, Kulieke said. The photographer was bleeding from a head injury, but he was not treated immediately. He later was in the intensive care unit at Henrotin Hospital for two days. There were other injuries and arrests as well.

Carol's Manager Richard "Mother Carol" Farnham had been arrested on May 12 for keeping a disorderly house. On May 19, the New Flight, 420 North Clark Street, was raided and two bartenders were arrested. GayLife reported that other bars had also said they were visited by police, including Dugan's Bistro, 420 North Dearborn Street, and the Ranch, 112–14 West Hubbard Street. The article said there were also unconfirmed reports of police visits to several other bars, including Flint's Baton Show Lounge.

The match had struck kindling. Within a week, plans were taking shape for a march against police harassment.

The timing was also politically important, since the raids had taken place just one month after Jane Byrne took office April 16, 1979, as the city's first female mayor. Many gays had backed Byrne's election as a change from business as usual, and they were upset that these crackdowns now came in the early weeks of the new administration. A March 2, 1979, GayLife report on Byrne's election win was titled "Gays cheer news of Byrne upset," and it said Byrne "sought for and received considerable support from Chicago's active gay community."

On May 19, a few hours after the Carol's raid, about 75 people gathered at the Belmont Avenue and Broadway office of Dignity, Chicago's gay Catholic group, to plan a response to the raids. They called for a May 21 communitywide meeting. According to GayLife, Flint said at that meeting that this "is the first time I've seen so many bar owners and media representatives together in one room. We've had our difficulties in the past but today I'm proud of us."

At that May 21 meeting at Second Unitarian Church, 656 West Barry Avenue, hosted by the citywide Gay and Lesbian Coalition, a group of about 350 people voted overwhelmingly to stage a march Tuesday, June 5, against the police harassment. An ad hoc committee was formed, "Gays and Lesbians for Action," to organize the protest. Jim Flint and Doris Shane, a supervisor at a health-care facility, were selected to co-chair the group. More than 100 volunteers met at the Baton on May 24, and Flint and Shane held a news conference May 25 at the Executive House hotel, 71 East Wacker Drive.

Bar employee Delilah Kenney of the Baton, who co-chaired the Gay and Lesbian Coalition of Metropolitan Chicago with David Boyer of Carol's Speakeasy, said the May 21 meeting boasted more unity than she had ever seen in the gay community, according to GayLife. "People know we are out there, but not really how numerous we are," said Flint. "The march also is to educate, to focus on our rights."

GayLife Publisher Grant Ford reported at the May 21 meeting that he had contacted Mayor Byrne's office and was told Byrne would not tolerate police harassment, and that she would launch an investigation about the recent raids. Attorney Renee Hanover told the audience she had met with Cook County Board President George Dunne, who told her he was "very concerned" about the harassment, according to a May 25 article by George Buse in GayLife.

The June 1, 1979, issue of GayLife reported on plans for the nonviolent march: "In response to Mayor Jane Byrne's now famous campaign slogan 'One Chicago,' the planners chose 'One Chicago for Gays and Lesbians Also' as the motto for the march. Earlier last week leaders attended the Chicago Police Board meeting to raise some probing questions about recent police bar raids, and alleged use of excessive force, entrapment and selective arrests in dealing with gay businesses and their patrons."

The Police Board meeting took place May 22, and John Donovan from Mayor Byrne's office also attended. GayLife reported May 25 that the meeting "was in great contrast to the stormy meeting held May 16 between 18th District Commander Joseph McCarthy and Joe Murray of the 13th District Gay Caucus." Those two were also at the May 22 meeting.

Chief of Patrol Earl Johnson said he will "discipline all officers who harassed, whether physically or verbally," patrons at the bars. James Casey of the Office of Professional Standards said he would investigate cases of alleged police abuse. Gay attorney Larry Rolla suggested that the police have sensitivity training on gay issues, and Donovan pledged the mayor's support for such a program (which did in fact happen).

Acting Police Superintendent Dan Nolan, at the police meeting, said that citizens should report any police abuse to the Office of Professional Standards.

Gays and Lesbians for Action asked businesses to give $50 for the upcoming march and also asked them to close between 6 and 9:30 that evening. Logistics committee leaders were Tony Lewis, Sean Reynolds and Dennis Murphy. Jim Bussen and Sherry Carpenter chaired publicity, and Woody Lorenz, Felix Morales and Chris Riddiough headed the media committee.

The June 5 march began at Bughouse Square (formally known as Washington Square Park), on the corner of Walton and Clark streets, at 6 p.m., and marchers headed south on Clark to the Daley Center Plaza for a rally. GayLife's June 8 edition estimated there were 2,000 participants, including 44th Ward Alderman Bruce Young, who used the opportunity to state his support of a city gay-rights bill.

Before the march, representatives from Gays and Lesbians for Action also had an extended discussion with Mayor Byrne on a wide range of grievances. Co-chair Doris Shane said Byrne "was concerned enough to call us in before the march. She assured us she was asking for investigations of the harassment charges and allowed real openness to gay problems."

Marchers wore green, regarded as the color of nonviolence, and some 150 monitors helped keep the peace. Chicago police also provided heavy protection, according to GayLife, with many officers on foot for the march. There were also police on horses.

"Singing gay lyrics to familiar tunes and chanting slogans as they marched, gays and lesbians presented exuberant and energetic faces to onlookers, some of whom joined in the high spirited proceedings," GayLife reported. "Taking charge at the plaza rally, Flint introduced the speakers, which included Alderman Young and [43rd Ward] Alderman Martin Oberman.

"Singer Ginni Clemmens led the ralliers in singing the civil-rights favorites of other days: 'We Shall Not Be Moved' and 'We Shall Overcome.' In the singing of the latter, the crowd joined raised hands in a very moving moment. A sad note of the rally was a memorial singing of the song 'G-A-Y,' written by Chicago gay community performer Diana 'Straight-as-an-Arrow,' who passed away on June 5.

"Among the speakers was Chuck Renslow, gay businessman, who said, 'We have but one enemy and that's ignorance and stupidity. We are here to overcome both. A great American [President Franklin Delano Roosevelt] once said, 'All we have to fear is fear itself.' [Years] ago we would have been afraid to come here. Now we aren't afraid. Leaders in the straight community are listening to us here.'"

The Tribune's report of the protest was brief, and on Page 5 of the June 6 edition: "A group of homosexuals marched Tuesday from Washington Square on the Near North Side to the Daley Center Plaza in the Loop to protest police raids on bars and businesses patronized by gays. … The demonstration was to protest at least 12 recent raids on gay owned and patronized taverns and other businesses in the New Town area, said Gays and Lesbians for Action co-chairmen James Flint and Doris Shane."

The Tribune estimated there were 1,500 people, "mostly men in their 20s and 30s," gathered for the event.

Flint, who praised the police support of the event at the time, said that years later he found out there were hundreds or possibly even thousands of other police nearby, on Wells Street, ready to come squash the march if protesters got out of hand.

Another interesting facet of the timing of these raids and protests is that this was also the same period of time that the FBI was using gay bar owners as undercover allies in its effort to catch Mafia shakedown perpetrators. Flint was among those who was forced to testify against the Mob in the 1983 trial about events of 1978–79, but Flint was not paying off at the time. Meanwhile, during the late-1970s FBI investigation, his bar was also being raided by the police.

More Harassment

While Jane Byrne's administration dramatically reduced the number of raids on gay bars, there were still some incidents that outraged the community.

During a raid on a predominantly African-American gay bar, the Rialto Tap, 14 West Van Buren Street, on December 28, 1979, a hundred men were arrested on various charges of prostitution. In a January 4, 1980, GayLife cover story, Stephen Kulieke reported that Byrne responded "with strong words of criticism which received extensive coverage on local TV and radio and in the daily papers."

Byrne said the police energies would be more wisely spent on "true crime." Kulieke also reported a police source as saying Byrne had sent a memo on the topic to the police and that there would be upcoming meetings between the police and the gay community.

Chuck Renslow's Gold Coast bar was raided once during Mayor Harold Washington's tenure as mayor. It was claimed that the warrant was sought after an anonymous tip telling police that sex was taking place in the bar. In the September 28, 1983, raid at the bar, at 501 North Clark Street, seven customers were charged with public indecency, and a bartender was charged with keeping a disorderly house.

Officials in other city departments also conducted harassment, and sometimes expected payoffs.

The December 3, 1978, issue of Gay Chicago reported on the indictment of 29 city Buildings Department inspectors. Other Chicago media also covered the indictments, which alleged that inspectors demanded bribes from bar owners. The Chicago Sun-Times and the Better Government Association had cooperation from bar owners in the sting operation that led to the indictments. Several gay bar owners were among those who cooperated, and the FBI later said that at least 100 other city inspectors could be implicated in the crackdown.

In the 1983 Mafia trial, a former city employee confirmed corruption in the Buildings and Fire departments under Mayors Richard J. Daley and Michael Bilandic.

The corruption did not end there, as headlines in subsequent years would indicate: "Extortion Routine for City Inspectors, Trials Have Shown" (Tribune, July 2, 1979); "19 Charged in City Inspector Payoffs" (Sun-Times, August 6, 1986); "City Inspectors Plead Guilty in Payoffs" (Sun-Times, September 16, 1986); and "Fire Inspector Guilty of Extortion" (Tribune, June 10, 1987). And, of course, several Chicago aldermen have been taken down in corruption trials, even the popular pro-gay Alderman Clifford P. Kelley.

Flint experienced some inspector issues, but because he had some political connections, including a sister who worked for the city, he was less affected than others.

"I think the fireman I was having problems with was just a guy that was homophobic," Flint said of one incident related to an alleged fire code violation. "He would just hit me for simple stuff. I went to the station nearby and got a commander. He asked for a 2-by-4, pounded in some nails, went and got the guy and said, 'What's wrong with that?' That finished that.

"With the city Building Department, it was simple things. I felt for a while I was being harassed because of being gay, but not because of payoffs. But there was a guy who worked there at the Building Department—he and his wife liked the show [at the Baton], so he sort of looked after me."

Legal Issues

As a man with multiple businesses, and involvement in a wide range of organizations, Flint knew and relied on a number of lawyers who were sympathetic to gay causes. Ed Mogul, a behind-the-scenes attorney for many gay individuals, businesses and nonprofit groups (including Gay Horizons and Howard Brown Memorial Clinic), also helped Flint around issues that members of Flint's family faced in Illinois and Indiana.

"He was very concerned about their welfare," Mogul said. "He was like an uncle to them all, with any problems they had. Jim struck me as a small-town boy who made it in the sophisticated big city, but was always careful to take care of the folks back home. He was very generous with his hospitality for them, and his concern and support for them. Not just his immediate family, but his extended family."

Mogul said that Flint "more than anybody took care of the transsexuals that most of the rest of the gay community were indifferent or hostile to." Mogul added that his own transsexual clients were among the most harassed people he dealt with.

"These kids were hated by their families," Mogul said, "and they had only each other to turn to. They made their living by selling themselves on the street. And they were stupefying themselves with glue-sniffing. This was the early 1970s. I was interested in helping those young trans and others who had been rejected by everybody, and who had no one to turn to. They had fallen prey to some of the worst elements of the vice squad."

Flint was also a leader in a 1985 battle with the city about a new nickel-a-drink tax on bars. The tax had been imposed in December 1984 as part of numerous revenue recommendations by Mayor Harold Washington's administration.

Gay bars seemed to lead the opposition against the "pour" tax, a $10 million city tax on liquor by the drink. Bar owners said the tax would be a bookkeeping nightmare as well as unfair if liquor stores were not also taxed.

Flint organized bar owners into a new group to fight the tax, and the first meeting was held at the Baton on January 26, with more than 50 restaurant and bar owners attending. A larger meeting was held March 4 at the Park West music venue, 322 West Armitage Avenue. Flint had gathered support from more than 300 bar owners, gay and straight.

Flint also organized a meeting with Ira J. Edelson, a senior fiscal policy adviser for the city, and sent an open letter to Edelson that was printed in GayLife on February 14. Flint, signing his name as the organizing chairperson of the new Tavern Owners Association, asked for a review of the overall licensing structure in the city, to make it fairer to all businesses.

Touché bar owner Chuck Rodocker said that, while the tax was not a gay or straight issue, gays would be more affected "because our bars are social centers."

The tax was repealed quickly in April 1985 after strong opposition.

Flint also used his clout to fight for bars outside the city limits. In 1985, Bubbles Bistro, which opened that January, was facing harassment from suburban Niles officials. Malcolm Silverman, the owner of the bar, filed suit in U.S. District Court in October 1985 against the village of Niles. Flint wrote a guest view in the November 14 issue of GayLife:

"What happens in the village of Niles is important to every gay man and woman in Chicago and it is especially important to all owners of gay establishments in Cook County. We 'city people' tend to ignore what's happening in the suburbs as not being relevant to us, but what is happening to the owner of Bubbles Bistro and his customers is relevant to all of us.

"According to what I understand, the Village President, Nicholas Blase, is using every means available to him to see that there is no gay bar in his town, as if the town personally belonged to him. The police department of Niles is using its manpower and resources to harass the owner and his customers.

"The latest incident this weekend involved a jurisdictional question of who can tell the President of Niles what he can or cannot do. A court appeal allowed the bar to remain open but the police would not allow anyone to enter the bar without threat of arrest. Niles has been referred to as the 'All American Village' for its ability to assimilate a variety of ethnic minorities; and yet who do we find leading the city, but a highly prejudiced man whose own background should make him keenly aware of the dangers of discrimination against any group of people.

"The Bubbles incident owes a debt to our own history when the owners of The Trip, a gay bar, fought all the way to the [Illinois] Supreme Court for the right to remain open on a licensing appeal issue. Yet Village President Nicholas Blase has his own interpretation of the Supreme Court ruling—let them remain open, but surround the place with cops so that none can get in.

"All the bar owners in Cook County need to take notice of these new tactics by governmental officials. In addition, our community needs to take an aggressive stance that we will not allow this type of discrimination to occur against us; and to let these officials know that we will march on the city hall to express these concerns, and that we will financially contribute to a defense fund to fight their actions. What happens in Niles affects all of us, for any discrimination against one is discrimination against all."

Bubbles closed in Febuary 1986.

A New Kind of Drag Ban

Flint faced another legal fight in 2006 when the Chicago City Council was revamping the 1957 zoning code, but left the archaic adult-entertainment definition intact. The ordinance became a focal point in the fight by the city to limit certain proposed strip clubs, and the Baton almost became an unintentional casualty.

The wording of the new zoning ordinance—Section 17-17-0104-A(4) of the Municipal Code of Chicago—originally said that an "adult entertainment cabaret is a public or private establishment which (i) features topless dancers, strippers, (ii) male or female impersonators; (iii) not infrequently features entertainers who display 'specified anatomical areas,' or (iv) features entertainers who by reason of their appearance or conduct perform in a manner which is designed primarily to appeal to the prurient interest of the patron or entertainers who engage in, or engage in explicit stimulation of, 'specified sexual activities.'"

Such businesses needed a "special use permit" if they operated in a business or commercial district, and they could not be located within 1,000 feet of schools, churches, parks or residential areas. Alderman Tom Tunney of the 44th Ward told the Chicago Sun-Times on April 1, 2006, that this covered "95 percent of the land in Chicago," making it almost impossible to exist. This would have forced the Baton to move, possibly outside the city.

Flint and his political allies acted to amend the law. Tunney sponsored the change, which was supported by 46th Ward Alderman Helen Shiller and 42nd Ward Alderman Burton L. Natarus. The Baton is located in the 42nd Ward.

On December 13, 2006, the City Council eliminated the words "male or female impersonators" from that law. The motion to amend the law passed 39–1 (Alderman James Balcer voted no, other aldermen did not vote).

"I partnered up with other aldermen, and did what was necessary to get it done," said Shiller. "I know that on different issues that impacted gays or African-Americans, I always made a point of sticking my nose into it, for the best outcome."

Natarus said the fight for the Baton to stay in business on Clark Street was just part of his job. "The Baton is considered just nice, pleasant, enjoyable entertainment," the now-former alderman said. "Jim has an outstanding legacy, and the Baton is wonderful entertainment. I've been there, I think it's a wonderful place."

Why did Flint put up with all the police, city and Mafia harassment? He said Chuck Renslow, who was a mentor, helped create new paths for gays to own their own businesses.

Flint told WTTW in 2008 that he may have started a gay bar a bit too early for the times, but he "never gave up because a lot of people can't do what I'm doing and a lot of people can't fight for themselves because of jobs, family or whatever. The thing about me is that I've been an open book since I was about 13 years old, so there wasn't much more they could tell about me. [The] nice thing about it, on the other hand, was now everybody in town knows you. … It has its advantages. But that's why I never gave up. I just never was a quitter."

Flint also realized one way to confront the harassment, or to avoid it altogether, was to increase his involvement in politics. So, he ran for office, which he believed helped protect him from the same level of harassment he had previously survived.

2 More Teachers in Raid Quit; Others Off Duty

Three Chicago area school teachers had resigned and two others and two school officials were off duty yesterday as the result of a vice raid early Saturday on the Fun lounge, 2340 N. Mannheim rd., Leyden township.

They were among eight school teachers and officials seized in the raid, in which 103 men and six women were arrested by sheriff's police under Richard Cain, chief investigator for Sheriff Richard B. Ogilvie.

Won't Renew License

Meanwhile A. L. Hornick, administrative assistant to Seymour Simon, county board president and liquor control commissioner for unincorporated areas, announced that Simon would not renew the liquor license for the tavern, which will expire at midnight Thursday.

It was announced that Norman Gee, 25, of 38 Washington st., Oak Park, has resigned as a 5th grade teacher in Longfellow Elementary school, Oak Park.

It was disclosed that Roger Born, 26, of 195 Harvey st., Wood Dale, quit his position as a teacher in Parkside school, Roselle.

Another of those arrested, Norris Angel, 24, of 2025 Pine av., Des Plaines, had resigned Saturday night as a teacher in Lincoln Junior High school, Park Ridge, altho he denied any wrong doing.

Board to Meet

Clair G. Grindstaff, 33, of 1637 Chicago av., Evanston, personnel director for elementary school district 39 in Wilmette, was reported "off duty" pending a meeting with the school board last night. It was reported he will be given an indefinite leave of absence.

John Kutcosky, 31, of 45 Forest av., Riverside, was granted a temporary leave pending investigation by the school board for Riverside-Brookfield High school, where he has been teaching.

Charles Rolinski, 35, of Lake Zurich, teacher in Palatine Junior High school, was suspended pending investigation by the school board and his court hearing.

It was announced that Herbert P. Jensen, 56, of 225 E. 1st st., Elmhurst, was being relieved of his duties as principal

of Jackson Junior High school, Villa Park, pending investigation of his arrest in the raid.

Melvin Anglin, 30, of Algonquin, teacher in Dundee Community High school, Dundee, another of those arrested, continued teaching. School officials said they were convinced he would be acquitted, and that he claimed all he knew was that he was going to a night club.

Will Appear May 15

The 109 persons arrested are to appear in West District court in Oak Park May 15, most of them on disorderly conduct charges. The proprietor, Louis Gauger, 53, avowed friend of Tony Accardo, crime syndicate figure, will face several charges.

Col. John Bucher, police director of personnel, said he was investigating the arrest in the Fun lounge of one of his clerks, Michael Gavigan, 26, of 8432 Throop st. Forest preserve district officials said they were investigating the arrest there of a painter employed by the district, Robert Zahnen, 41, of 5712 N. Moody av.

The Chicago board of election commissioners said George A. Kapellas, 24, of 7700 Cornell av., would be dismissed as a Democratic election judge in the 20th precinct of the 8th ward as a result of his arrest.

April 28, 1964, Chicago Tribune coverage of the raid on Louie's Fun Lounge. Many gays, including some teachers, lost their jobs as a result of this and other 1960s-era raids.

32 Seized in Raid on North Side Bath

Thirty-two men were arrested early yesterday in a raid on a north side bath house which police said is controled by vice overlords of the crime syndicate.

Sgt. James Reilley of the police prostitution unit led eight detectives in the raid on the Lincoln Baths, 1812 N. Clark st., after an undercover detective entered the basement establishment and said he witnessed lewd acts being performed in the steam room.

Two Are Cited by Cops

Reilley said Michael [The Fireplug] Glitta, near north side vice boss, and Lawrence [The Hood] Buonaguidi, a near north side gambler and strip show operator, are among gang figures who control the bath house.

Lincoln Baths does about $1,000 worth of business a week, Reilley said, and attendants get large tips from patrons to encourage anonymity. Some patrons have been subjected to blackmail, he said.

In a similar raid on Lincoln Baths on June 13, 1964, 33 men were arrested, some of whom also were caught in yesterday's raid, Reilley said.

Keeper Is Seized

Of those arrested yesterday, six were charged with public indecency, lewd acts, and being inmates of a disorderly house.

Fred Braxton, 51, of 8925 Harper av., was charged as a keeper of a disorderly house. The others were charged with being inmates.

Reilley said the patrons were required to show identification and to sign a register.

Those arrested and the names and addresses they gave were:

Jerome Champagne, 39, of 222 E. Delaware pl., a dentist; William Cohen, 38, of 1443 Astor st., department manager of a chain store; Byron Cook, 44 of 1211 Mohawk dr., Elgin, social worker; David Driscoll, 27, of 2422 Church st., Evanston, an accountant; David Dunn, 28, of 1414 E. 59th st., a student at the University of Chicago; Edward Filemann, 45, of 3120 N. Kedzie av., an accountant; and Daniel Graat, 28, of 2400 Roosevelt rd., Broadview, a production planner.

Sherwin Goldman, 34, of 200 Ridge av., Evanston, a salesman; Holmes Hardin, 31, a teacher from Maryland; Robert Hembree, 41, of 2109 Farragut av., a field representative for an auto manufacturing company; Thomas Jagielski, 28, of West Allis, Wis., a student; Dennis LeBouton, 29, of 500 Fullerton pkwy., a buyer; Jay Merrill, 55, of 1510 N. Harlem av., River Forest, office manager of an auto agency.

Danny Miller, 25, of De Kalb, Ill., an instructor at Northern Illinois university at De Kalb; James O'Neil, 25, of 1216 Marengo av., Forest Park, a student at De Kalb.

Harold Helln, 59, of Hobart, Ind., a bartender; Kenneth Gray, 39, of 1140 N. La Salle st., a display man for a department store; Hugo Ly, 28, of 441 Barry av., a printer; Eric Koernke, 50, of Jackson Mich., a florist; Robert Williams, 34, of 106 W. Oak st., a sculptor; Joao Penna, 25, an airline reservations clerk.

Kenneth Neville, 25, of 530 Diversey av., an employe in the credit department of an oil company; Eugene Conley, 45, of 4211 N. Leavitt st., a truck driver; Melvin Davis, 42, of 666 N. Clark st., a hotel desk clerk.

William Miller, 48, of Mundelein, an electronics inspector; Roland Munroe, 35, of 1244 N. Dearborn st., a factory worker; Robert Keith, 25, of 5757 Sheridan rd., an office worker; Arthur Alexander, 49, of 7423 Ridge av.; Samuel Reynolds, 29, of 1032 N. Dearborn st., an advertising salesman; Thomas Freeman, 45, of 3222 Berteau av.; and Thomas Connell, 49, of 4527 N. Malden av., an elevator operator.

All will appear March 14 in Central District court.

March 6, 1966, Chicago Tribune article about a raid on Lincoln Baths. Flint knew about these raids as he began his own work in Chicago's gay business world.

Menu for The Trip, a bar and restaurant that was raided by the police in the 1960s.

The 1973 Chicago Police corruption trial made big headlines, including this coverage in the Chicago Sun-Times.
Courtesy of M. Kuda Archives

Chief of traffic indicted with 23 other policemen

By Art Petacque
and Hugh Hough

Chief of Traffic Clarence E. Braasch and 23 other policemen were named Saturday in the most inclusive indictment ever returned against personnel of the Chicago Police Department.

A special federal grand jury accused the 24 of conspiring to extort monthly cash payoffs from 53 Near North Side taverns, nightclubs and restaurants. The total take was said to be several hundred thousand dollars.

In addition, Braasch and 13 others were charged with perjury.

Later Saturday, Police Supt. James B. Conlisk Jr. ordered the suspension of Braasch and all of the other newly indicted policemen who had not been suspended previously. He said the suspensions are effective New Year's Day.

The suppressed indictment, returned Friday and announced Saturday by U.S. Atty. James R. Thompson, named four additional Chicago policemen as unindicted co-conspirators, bringing to 28 the number implicated in the alleged shakedown.

All named with Braasch, including the unindicted co-conspirators, formerly served under him as vice investigators when he commanded the East Chicago Avenue Police District, now called the 18th Police District, from 1966 to 1970.

The 23 persons indicted with Braasch are: Sergeants Edward J. Barry, Carl Flagg, John M. Geraghty, Howard L. Pierson, Joseph A. Schillinger and Thomas D. West, and Patrolmen Daniel H. Armstrong, Thomas D. Battistini, Natale R. Cale, John Catalano, William F. Demke Jr., Martin D. Eshoo, Edward F. Finn, Philip R. Grana, Thomas M. Lazar, Edward McGee, Lowell E. Napier, Emmanuel P. Russell, Harry R. Salvesen, Steve L. Seno, William D. Swallow, Costenz Troche and Mike Zakoian.

One of those indicted, Napier, resigned from the force during the investigation.

Those named in the perjury count with

CAPT. CLARENCE E. BRAASCH

Braasch are Geraghty, Armstrong, Demke, Eshoo, Flagg, Grana, Lazar, Pierson, Russell, Schillinger, Swallow, Troche and West.

Those named as unindicted co-conspirators are Lt. Robert Fisher, currently head of the Area 2 stolen-auto unit and formerly a vice co-ordinator under Braasch; Sgt. John Cello Jr., and Investigators Salvatore Mascotino and Edward Rifkin, who worked on the vice squad under Braasch.

The 23 men indicted with Braasch and the four unindicted co-conspirators constituted virtually the entire vice detail under Braasch during his tenure as East Chicago district commander.

The indictment set no dollar figure on the extent of the alleged extortion racket. But The Sun-Times learned independently that Federal Bureau of Investigation agents found the payoffs totaled about $300,000 in the 1966-1970 period.

And Thompson confirmed at a Federal Building press conference that the alleged

Turn to Page 10

From 1966 to 1970
Name shakedown victims

Following is the list of establishments named Saturday by a special federal grand jury as being victims of the alleged police shakedown racket from 1966 to 1970. Some of the places are now out of business.

Aggies Gold Coast Lounge, 901 N. Clark. Alfie's, 900 N. Rush.

Barnaby's, 7 W. Tooker Pl. Baron Lounge, 629 N. Clark. Baton Lounge, 430 N. Clark. Bentivy's, 640 N. State. Bowery, 1504 N. Wells. Buddy's Fun House, 1117 N. Dearborn. Bunny Inn, 1148 N. Clark. Burke's, 105 W. Division. B-29, 715 N. Clark.

Cabaret, 930 N. Rush. Cousins, 166 E. Superior. Croydon Circle Lounge, 616 N. Rush.

East Inn, 206 E. Superior. Erin Club, 701 N. Clark.

Filling Station, 12 W. Maple.

Gap, 2 W. Division. Gin Mill, (also known as Jay's), 1021 N. Rush. G. C.'s (also known as Gerry's Club and Gold Coast), 2265 N. Lincoln.

Haig, 800 N. Dearborn. Hennessy's, 12 W. Elm. Hungry I, 1333 N. Wells.

If Ands or Buts, 5 W. Superior. Imprint, 235 E. Ontario. Inner Circle, 1842-1844 N. Wells.

Irish Mike's, 644 N. State.

King's Ransom, 20 E. Chicago.

Liberty Inn, 661 N. Clark.

Midas Touch, 1520 N. Wells. Mother's, 26 W. Division. Mr. Jones, 53 E. Chicago. My Place, 11 E. Delaware.

New Janie's, 1110 N. Clark. New Twist Lounge, 612 N. Clark. Normandy, 744 N. Rush.

Orange Tree, 1166 N. State. Oxford Pub, 2261½-2263 N. Lincoln.

Pokey, 833 N. Clark.

Queens Paradise, 620 N. Clark.

Rush Over, 900 N. Rush. Rush Up, 907 N. Rush.

Sammy's 1205, 1205 N. Clark. She-Nannigan's, 16 W. Division. Spartan Room, 1117 N. Dearborn. Spirit of 76, 26 W. Division. Store, 1036-1036 N. State. Stork Lounge, 59 E. Walton.

Togetherness, 61 W. Hubbard. Tony's Cellar, 909 N. Rush. Twist Lounge, 637 N. Clark. Upstairs Queen, 19 E. Chestnut.

Wagon Wheel (also known as The Hayride), 1901 N. Clark.

The September 1973 edition of The Chicago Gay Crusader also covered the police corruption trial.

Chapter 192 of Municipal Code Amended Concerning Public Morals.

The Committee on Police, Fire, Personnel, Schools and Municipal Institutions submitted the following report:

CHICAGO, January 11, 1978.

To the President and Members of the City Council:

Your Committee on Police, Fire, Personnel, Schools and Municipal Institutions, to which was referred (October 26, 1977) an Ordinance signed by Mayor Michael A. Bilandic amending Chapter 192, Section 192-8 of the Municipal Code of Chicago by rewriting it in order to bring it in compliance with recent decisions of the United States Supreme Court, begs leave to recommend that your Honorable Body *Pass* the said proposed Ordinance, *as amended* by your Committee, which is transmitted herewith.

This recommendation was concurred in by 10 members of the Committee, with 1 dissenting vote.

Respectfully submitted,
(Signed)   EDWARD M. BURKE,
Chairman.

On motion of Alderman Burke the proposed ordinance *as amended* transmitted with the foregoing committee report was *Passed*, by yeas and nays as follows:

Yeas—Aldermen Roti, Kenner, Sawyer, Wilinski, Humes, Adduci, Vrdolyak, Huels, Kwak, Madrzyk, Burke, Barden, Shannon, Kellam, Joyce, Stewart, Lipinski, Rhodes, M a r z u l l o, Z y d l o, Ray, Washington, Cross, Hagopian, Keane, Gabinski, Mell, Frost, Laskowski, Aiello, Casey, Gutstein, Pucinski, Schulter, Saperstein, Stone—36.

Nays—Aldermen Barnett, Lathrop, Natarus, Oberman, Simpson—5.

Alderman Madrzyk moved to *Reconsider* the foregoing vote. The motion was *Lost*.

The following is said ordinance as passed:

Be It Ordained by the City Council of the City of Chicago:

SECTION 1. The Municipal Code of the City of Chicago, Chapter 192, Section 192-8 is hereby amended by deleting the language in brackets below and adding the language in Italics as follows:

192-8. Any person who shall appear, [in a public place in a state of nudity], *bathe, sunbathe, walk or be in any public park, playground, beach or the waters adjacent thereto, or any school facility and the area adjacent thereto, or any municipal building and the areas adjacent thereto, or any public way within the City of Chicago in such a manner that the genitals, vulva, pubic, pubic hair, buttocks, perineum, anus, anal region, or pubic hair region of any person, or any portion of the breast at or below the upper edge of the areola thereof of any female person, is exposed to public view or is not covered by an opaque covering,* [or is in a dress not belonging to his or her sex, with intent to conceal his or her sex, or in an indecent or lewd dress, or who shall make any indecent exposure of his or her person] shall be fined not less than twenty dollars nor more than two hundred dollars for each offense.

SECTION 2. This ordinance shall be in full force and effect from and after its passage.

_____

The Chicago cross-dressing law was not changed officially until 1978, though an earlier court decision did rule against the law.

Jim "Felicia" Flint and Chuck Renslow judge a costume contest in Milwaukee, late 1970s. Both Flint and Renslow were called to testify in the police corruption trial.

The May 1979 police raid on Carol's Speakeasy sparked community outrage.

GayLife News/Editorial
236-7575
GayLife Advertising/Classifieds
236-0889

GayLife

40¢

Friday, May 25, 1979   The Midwest Gay Newsleader   Volume 4 / Number 49

Mob storms SF city hall

By George S. Buse

Dan White, fifth from left, accompanied to jail by police

Police hit Carol's, other bars

By Stephen Kulieke

Inside GayLife

Police enter Carol's Speakeasy

GayLife News/Editorial
236-7575
GayLife Advertising/Classifieds
236-0889

Friday, June 1, 1979

The Midwest Gay Newsleader

Volume 4 / Number 50

COMPLIMENTARY 40¢

GayLife covered the before-and-after of the June 1979 march, co-chaired by Flint, to protest police harassment of gay bars.

June 5 march plans take shape

Co-chairs of the Coalition flank co-chairs of Gays and Lesbians for Action at Friday, May 25 press conference at the Executive Hostel. Left to right: David Boyer, Doris Shane, Jim Flint, Dennis Murphy.

What's going on here

Hubbard Street Dance Company rehearses their high-energy show

Read about two sizzling Chicago dance troupes on page 15

Polish Princess hits the road

Detroit and Toronto roll out the royal red carpet

Turn to the Midwest section page 7

Inside GayLife

Dennis Murphy (right center, rear) leads a logistics session to plan for the June 5 march.

March monitor training dates

GayLife

Friday, June 8, 1979

The Midwest Gay Newsleader

Volume 4 / Number 51

COMPLIMENTARY 40¢

'We are gay, we are proud'

Chicago's gay people protest police harrassment, lack of action on gay rights

by George S. Buse

Marchers proceed down Clark Street 2000 strong

Free concert planned in Lincoln Park

Jim Butson leads crowd in cheers at Daley Center

"One Chicago for Gays and Lesbians Also" was the banner in front of the June 1979 protest march. Photo courtesy of the Chicago History Museum.

Jim Flint leads the 1979 march against police harassment.

4

The Mafia World

Jim Flint's ability to navigate the Chicago business world of the 1960s through the 1980s made him a true survivor. Not everyone made it out with business—or life—intact.

The Mafia, also known as the Mob, the Syndicate or the Outfit, controlled most bars in Chicago during that era, and before. This underworld is documented in many books, including interviews with gay businessman Chuck Renslow in the 2011 book, Leatherman: The Legend of Chuck Renslow. Flint did not escape harassment from city licensing authorities, police and the Outfit, but he figured out how to be a survivor.

Flint was in the FBI's cross hairs at least twice. The first time was in the early 1970s when police corruption trials were taking place, because he had been paying "protection" money to the police on the city's Near North Side. He did not testify, even though he was paying off. Next, in 1984, Flint was forced to testify in a trial of accused Mafia men, but because he said he did not pay them off (during the years under investigation) he testified but said nothing incriminating.

Flint has often discussed those scary days, but his memory is that he did not even testify in the case against the Mob, that he gave just a few short answers and was let off to watch the Cubs in yet another failed season. But Flint did testify, along with other prominent Chicagoans including GayLife Publisher Grant Ford, bar owner Steve Rempas, Woody Lorenz, Ira Jones, and attorney Renee Hanover (some testified for just the grand jury, some in just the trial itself).

Another person who testified was Robert Hugel, owner of the Glory Hole gay bar. He was reportedly in the U.S. marshal's witness protection program, and he has not been seen in Chicago since the trial. In 2011, the U.S. Marshals Service would not confirm what happened to Hugel.

(Stories about the Mafia connection to gay bars are also included in Chapter 2.)

Mother Carol

One person who could not testify was the Carol's Speakeasy bar manager, Richard Carrol Farnham, known as "Mother Carol," who died September 30, 1979, at age 37, soon after he stopped wearing a wire for the FBI for the activity alleged in the Mafia trial. Few at the time even knew Farnham was under investigation (the trial was not held until four years later), and everyone believed he had died just as a result of a wild and unhealthful lifestyle. The cause of death was cirrhosis of the liver.

In a Chicago Reader story of January 11, 1980, on Farnham's death, writer Grant Pick detailed the high cost of Farnham's lifestyle: "In March 1978, Carol checked into Augustana Hospital for liver ailments stemming from his drinking. Farnham's doctor told it to him straight: if you stop drinking now, you've got seven years left to live; if you don't, you have two years. Carol's answer was to host a booze party in his private room, amid the banks of flowers his friends had sent." (The Farnham piece is also included in Pick's collection of interviews, The People Are the News [Northwestern University Press, 2009].)

Farnham continued his heavy partying. Did he wear a wire in 1978–79 for the FBI because he knew he was dying? Did he increase his consumption of drugs and alcohol because he was scared for his life in more ways than one? Did he try to help the FBI as a way to help other gay bars, even though it would probably be from the grave?

GayLife nightlife columnist Ron Helizon (who later owned his own bar, and who died in 2011) wrote about Farnham's death in his October 5, 1979, column. "We all have memories of this burly Irish guy who seemed to celebrate St. Patty's day every day. Carol did it his way through all his ups and downs, and when things were not going well he was always able to come up with a bigger and better idea," Helizon wrote.

In that same edition of GayLife, George Buse wrote that Carol's Speakeasy was the bar that Mother Carol "raised from obscurity to one of the gayest show places in town." Farnham was raised in Aurora, Illinois, and left the mainstream world around 1970 to be part of the show business world in Chicago's bars. His first time in drag was for the closing night of Ruthie's bar, when the club lost its lease. His second time in drag was for Jim "Felicia" Flint's Halloween ball in the early 1970s. Friend Jim Sykes told Buse that on one Halloween night Farnham and Flint showed up in the same outfit, but in different colors.

In 1972, Farnham took over Lee Stanley's straight bar at 2519 North Halsted Street and called it the Coming Out Pub; it eventually was known as Carol's Pub. This is where he became Mother Carol. In October 1976 the bar moved and became Carol's in Exile at 3510 North Broadway, but that lasted just a few months. On October 13, 1978, Fred Kramer opened Carol's Speakeasy at 1355 North Wells Street, and for nearly a decade it was among the top gay bars in the city. Farnham was the bar's manager until his death in 1979.

The bar's success attracted anyone looking for a handout: city inspectors, police and the Mafia. But it was the police raids that received the most attention while Farnham was alive. Despite the payoffs, Carol's was raided, in part because the neighborhood was gentrifying and wanted the gays out. In May 1979, during the year in which Farnham died, Carol's experienced a high-profile police raid. While other bars also suffered raids, the raid on Carol's particularly enraged the gay community and sparked Jim Flint and others to organize a 2,000-person march June 5, 1979, down Clark Street from Bughouse Square to the Daley Center Plaza. (This event is detailed in Chapter 3.)

Farnham's Mass was celebrated at Our Lady of Good Counsel Church in Aurora. His mother, Lillian Windisch, and sister, Pat Barnes (the Reader said her last name was Barkes, but the ad said Barnes), took out a full-page ad in the October 5, 1979, issue of GayLife thanking the community for their "great concern and prayers during his illness and death. We feel he loved you all very much and would want you to remember him as he was—a thoughtful and loving person."

Just weeks before he died, Farnham was wearing a wire for the FBI, taping the "protection" money requests from several alleged mobsters. Flint was among those who thought the death of Mother Carol was suspicious, but because he died so long before the trial, and just a month after his last FBI recording, no one at the time knew to connect his death to the investigation. But Farnham was "one of the wildest people I knew," Flint said, so Farnham's death certainly could have been unrelated to the investigation.

When the payoff trial was finally held, four years later, the defense tried to have Farnham's testimony thrown out because he was dead and could not be cross-examined, but his recordings were allowed into evidence.

History of Mob Involvement

It was well-known in Chicago's gay community that the Mafia owned or controlled most gay bars. Even into the 1980s, there were straight men taking the money at the doors of numerous gay and lesbian clubs, and the vendors used by the bars were often owned by the Syndicate (for towels, the jukebox, alcohol, etc.).

The Chicago Tribune's crime reporter Bob Wiedrich wrote on September 30, 1973, that "in a certain North Side police district, crime syndicate operators of a network of homosexual bars have been cavorting with vice detectives and some of their bosses for almost a decade." In his October 4 column that year, "Cops, Pols, Mob in Gay-Bar Payoffs," Wiedrich went after the "unholy alliance" among police, politicians and the Mob. The column details extortion, blackmail and skimming of cash.

Wiedrich also wrote: "[I]n a network of 20 nightclubs and bars catering to the specialized recreational needs of homosexuals, the mutually avaricious interests of these groups are interwoven in a tragic tapestry of corruption. In short, thieving lawmen and politicos have joined forces with crime syndicate gangsters to prey on some of society's most vulnerable members—the gay people."

A 1973 issue of the Mattachine Midwest Newsletter, published by one of the city's first gay-rights groups, reported on the story, noting that "Wiedrich's column was generally non-judgmental about gays although the tone was a bit patronizing. He made no mention of gay bars not owned by the mob … ."

The Indictment

On December 7, 1983, indictments were announced in Chicago's U.S. District Court in the case of the United States of America vs. Joseph DiVarco, 72, also known as "Caesar"; Joseph Arnold, 66; Frank DeMonte, 55, also known as "Babe"; Peter Dounias, 62, also known as Pete Dumos; and John Matassa, 32.

The indictments came from a joint investigation by the FBI and the U.S. Justice Department's Organized Crime Strike Force.

Chicago Tribune writer Rudolph Unger reported December 9, 1983, that Arnold had allegedly succeeded DiVarco as "overseer of the Rush Street nightclub district. While Rush Street was mainly a strip of heterosexual clubs, the area also includes a number of gay bars on or around Clark Street on the Near North Side."

The mainstream and gay media reported on the indictments and the ongoing trial. For this book, we also looked at the testimony in the trial, obtained from documents held in the National Archives and Records Administration's Chicago regional archives. Some of the proceedings included undercover testimony from former mobster Ken Eto, who turned informant after he was the victim of a "botched assassination attempt in February," the Tribune reported.

The men who were accused of shooting Eto were later found murdered. One was Johnny Gattuso, a Cook County sheriff's deputy who also was among gay bar owner Chuck Renslow's contacts in the Mob. The other was Jasper Campise.

The five indicted men were accused of demanding protection money from four gay bars, two of them owned by Jim Flint. Flint's bars were the Baton at 436 North Clark Street and the Redoubt at 65 West Illinois Street. The other bars were Richard Farnham's Carol's Speakeasy, 1355 North Wells Street, and Robert Hugel's Glory Hole Tavernia, 1343 North Wells Street. The payoffs tracked by the FBI happened between December 1978 and August 1979. Farnham died in September 1979. Flint said the New Flight bar, at 420 North Clark Street, was also under FBI investigation for these payoffs.

The U.S. attorney charged that Dounias received $300 from Hugel, and Arnold got $5,200 from Farnham. Dounias also allegedly asked Flint for "safety money" at the rate of $500 a month.

Both DiVarco and Arnold had ties to the trial 10 years earlier that took down dozens of Chicago police officers, including Capt. Clarence Braasch of the 18th ("East Chicago Avenue") Police District. Braasch and his team were convicted of extorting money from businesses, including some owned by the Syndicate. In a September 12, 1973, Chicago Tribune report on the Braasch trials, a witness said DiVarco and Arnold owned a shirt store called Shirts Illustrated that was among those paying off the police.

The tangled web thus included gay bars and other businesses paying off both the police and the Mafia, and then the Mafia also paying off the police.

Bars that operated prior to the 1980s were mostly either Mafia-owned or required to pay off the Mafia and police to stay in business. Art Johnston and his partner, José "Pepe" Peña, said they were not very aware of this when they opened Sidetrack in 1982, and they, like many bar owners, benefited from the battles fought by Flint and Renslow, among others, against the payoff system. Johnston met Peña when Peña was tending bar at Shari's, 2901 North Clark Street, in 1973, and they believed that the club was owned by the "Outfit," but the reality of that fact still was not clear to the couple.

"We were really not very aware of the historic need for gay bars to be connected to somebody important," Johnston said. "We were just naïve. In some ways we were fortunate that we opened [Sidetrack] at the right time when that dynamic was no longer in play. We had very few examples come into our lives." Johnston did remember one difficult time: They experienced veiled threats when they tried to change their vending machine provider.

The police also tried to harass Sidetrack out of existence. "They said, 'If you're the fag owner of this fucking fag bar we're going to close you down, we've got enough fags over here,'" Johnston recalled. This was Halsted Street circa 1982 and 1983.

In the book Leatherman, Renslow readily admits paying off the police and Mafia: "That was the reality of having a bar in Chicago at that time. I got lucky. I had some protection early on. In all fairness, they didn't want to own you—they just wanted a little bit, they just wanted their cut. It was maybe a couple hundred a month. Like clockwork on the first of the month or whatever, two bagmen in silk suits would come around asking for money. Then there were other things, like we had to use the Outfit's jukebox company."

Many 1970s bars were paying off the Mob, and the Club Baths chain, which had an operation in Chicago at 609 North LaSalle Street, was also reportedly paying off the Mob.

Even Flint admits now that in the past he had paid protection money to people he believed to be from the Mafia. But he said that during the period the FBI was investigating (1978–79), he had refused to pay off, even at risk to his own life. Flint's trial testimony articulates this in great detail. The prosecution tried to get Flint to admit that these were illegal payoff attempts and that he felt threatened, even though he did not pay. The defense said the fact that Flint was not hurt was evidence that there was no real threat: Flint didn't pay, and Flint wasn't hurt.

Flint said he was visited by people he believed were Mafia members who told him not to testify and that he should tell other bar owners the same thing. Hugel had since sold the Glory Hole; he went into witness protection, and did testify at the trial.

Defense attorneys said there were no "implied threats" with the payoffs, and the money was voluntarily given by the bar owners to help the bars fight crime and police harassment in the neighborhood.

Flint Provides a Statement

Flint gave a statement to Peter Dounias' attorney Adam Bourgeois Sr. in an attempt to avoid testifying in the pending case. The statement was made and signed on December 13, 1983, just after the indictments, but months before the actual trial, which started in September 1984.

What follows is what Flint swore to on December 13, 1983, as owner of the Redoubt and Baton bars:

"In 1978 or 1979, I was approached at the front door of the Baton, a nightclub which I own. I have owned it since 1971. My clientele is very mixed. It was in the summer '78 or '79. Two men talked to me at the door and said something about safety money. The total conversation took about five minutes. I got real nervous. I didn't want to talk. It was around 7:00 or 7:30 at night. It had to be around the time we opened and we opened at 8:00.

"The men were big. It would be very hard for me to pick out these men.

"About 2 or 3 months later, the FBI sent two agents to see me. They said that other bars were cooperating in giving evidence of shakedowns. I said there's nothing to cooperate for because I am not being shaken down. One of the agents asked if I could be shaken down and I said if they used force, anyone in his right mind could be shaken down.

"I told them that I had been approached. The agents asked me if the men said they were from the syndicate. I said no. Anyone could come along and say they were from the syndicate. They had about five or six photographs with them. I recognized one of the photographs and told the agents that it could have been one of the people.

"I was never asked to look at a line-up. My identification of the person in the photograph was not a positive one. If I were asked today to pick out the men who approached me in '78 or '79, I doubt if I could identify them.

"The second visit I had was about a month later. Only one of the men returned. I told him that the FBI had been around. It had to have been in the evening around the same time.

"The man asked me whether I had made up my mind about paying the money. I told him that I wasn't going to pay anyone off. He said he'd get back to me. I never heard from him again. He stayed only 3 or 4 minutes.

"The FBI came back many times. I told them about the second visit. They showed me the same photographs. I think I said it could be the same man. I'm not sure what I said.

"I could not truthfully say I could identify anyone.

"The FBI kept asking me about some Caesar guy. I told them I don't know him. I told them that I never heard the name before.

"The only one of the defendants I know is Joe Arnold and I only know him from television. I saw his photo on TV when he was shot. I don't know any of the other defendants.

"Both visits I had were very brief.

"The men were dressed in sports shirts and slacks. One had a hat. It was summer. At no time was I threatened by anyone.

"The month before I was visited I received a phone call. The caller said someone would be coming to see me. I asked what about and the person said you'll find out when the person comes. I did not recognize the voice of the caller.

"When the two people came neither said that they had been the caller.

"I could not recognize the voice of either of the two men as the voice of the caller.

"I don't think that I told the FBI that Pete had called me.

"Neither of the men said they were gay.

"The conversations were never more than 3 to 5 minutes.

"After reading this statement I will sign and date it."

Flint signed and dated the document December 13, 1983, in front of Bourgeois and at Bourgeois' law office in Suite 852 at 53 West Jackson Boulevard in Chicago.

The Trial

The judge for the 1984 extortion trial was Prentice H. Marshall. Though he was a Democrat, in 1973 President Richard Nixon, a Republican, nominated Marshall to the U.S. District Court for the Northern District of Illinois. He was one of Nixon's very few Democratic picks for judge.

A grand jury had been appointed in September 1981 by Judge Frank McGarr, but the indictment was not returned until December 7, 1983. The trial was slow to come. The defendants were out on bond from December 1983 until the trial date.

The defendants' attorneys tried to get the case dismissed because of the delay, in part because some witnesses had died and one was missing (Hugel, who was actually in witness protection). Farnham was not the only witness to die. Kenneth Cameron, owner of the Over 21 adult bookstore, at 1347 North Wells Street, died in a boating accident in California in 1983; he was a confidant of Farnham and Hugel. But the judge allowed the case to move forward, ruling it was within the statute-of-limitations period for the charges.

Douglas Roller and Mitchell Mars of the U.S. Department of Justice's Organized Crime Strike Force were the main prosecuting attorneys in the case. The U.S. attorney overseeing the prosecution was Dan K. Webb.

Much of the evidence in the case was based on audio- and videotapes of activity at the Odds and Ends, at 913 North Rush Street on Chicago's Near North Side. Defendants DiVarco and Arnold ran the store and met with their colleagues and alleged victims there. Other recordings were taken at Carton's restaurant, 900 North Rush Street.

U.S. Attorney Webb filed a motion before the trial, noting that the government intended to use "evidence of other crimes, wrongs, or acts" in its case. This included Arnold's alleged attempt to extort monthly "protection" money from a gay bar owner in June 1977; evidence that some of the defendants collected a "street tax" from Ken Eto; and evidence of Arnold's conversations in 1979 involving intimidation of a witness before a federal grand jury in Chicago.

Defendant Dounias' attorney, Bourgeois, said the trial was "more a case of distortion than extortion," according to the September 20, 1984, GayLife newspaper account of the trial. GayLife's Paul Cotton reported that Bourgeois said gays were "subject to terrorism both from law and outlaw." The attorney gave a brief history of gays, saying a barrage of police raids was causing "havoc" for gay businesses, including a gay bookstore Dounias himself owned on Ohio Street. Cotton reported that the attorney said the new visibility of gays made them "natural targets" for attacks by "fag bashers," hustlers and muggers.

Bourgeois said his client, Dounias, was able to rid his own area of these elements, so naturally he wanted to assist others. Bourgeois said that Richard Farnham of Carol's Speakeasy had been willing to pay "for someone to intercede for him ... for muscle … to keep these elements out of his bar."

DeMonte's lawyer, Patrick Tuite, said his client was also just helping fellow businessmen to keep "undesirables" out of the clubs.

The Glory Hole

But Robert Hugel, in his testimony, countered these assertions. He had not heard of "fag-bashing" and said he was not harassed by police.

Hugel was owner and operator of the Glory Hole during the time of the alleged shakedowns. He owned the gay bar from 1972 to 1979 at 1343 North Wells Street. Hugel testified that the liquor he served came from South Shore Liquors, Continental and "Judgendall" as it was listed in the transcripts. This was probably Judge & Dolph, a longtime liquor distributor in Chicago.

Hugel testified in court that one of his employees, disc jockey Hubert Belcher, gave him a note on November 22, 1978. The note had been dropped off, and it told Hugel to "get in touch with Johnny at Carton's Restaurant on Rush," about a mile from the Glory Hole. Hugel said, "I was quite upset." He said he went to Carol's bar to speak to Farnham about the note. He was getting increasingly nervous, so he contacted the FBI. He met with the officials November 27, 1978, gave them the note, and agreed to cooperate with the authorities.

The next day, on November 28, he went to Carton's to meet "Johnny," who was not there. On November 29, Hugel was at his bar, and Over 21 bookstore owner Ken Cameron came in. His store was two doors away from the Glory Hole. Hugel returned to Carton's on November 30, 1978, wearing a recording device and aware that there were FBI agents also in the restaurant.

His November 30 tape, recorded at Carton's, was played at the trial. Dounias said on the tape to Hugel: "Listen, you know we got an association here in the district, you understand? You're not a member of the association, you got to come in." Dounias asked for $400 a month, but after Hugel complained, Dounias came down to $300. Dounias received $200 in FBI cash through Hugel the next day and Hugel complained he did not have more.

Dounias said: "Listen, it's not that bad, 'cause the other guys are rougher than I am, you know what I mean, they're dirty mother-fuckers." Hugel said: "I'm scared. I am." Dounias replied: "You don't have to be scared. Nothing to be afraid of. You understand? All you have to do is, it'll pick up [business]. Don't worry about it, you hear? Give me the hundred, gotta have the hundred before the 10th, all right?"

Jurors heard the tapes of the conversations. Hugel said he had fears for himself and his business. For the $300 a month they asked for, Hugel said he expected "for them to leave me alone." He said he did not want to pay the money and he did not expect any services in exchange for the payment. He also said he did not have need of protection.

Mother Carol's Testimony

Richard Farnham may have died just after taping incriminating evidence against the defendants, but his participation was allowed by the judge, through statements he made and the evidence he collected on tape for the FBI.

The government's evidence included taped conversations and statements to the FBI including:

— Statements made by Farnham on November 22, 1978, to Hugel that Farnham, like Hugel, had been approached by two men who wanted $1,000 per month for protection.

— Statements made by Farnham on December 16 and 18, 1978, to special agents of the FBI detailing conversations Farnham had with defendants DeMonte, Dounias and Matassa concerning their demands for protection payments.

— Statements made by Farnham on July 10, 1979, to FBI agents that, after having met DeMonte and Matassa on that date, Matassa was the individual who had earlier contacted him about the Glory Hole tavern owner's ability to make monthly payments.

The prosecutors said Farnham's statements "will be extensively corroborated by independent evidence, including Hugel's testimony regarding defendant Dounias' shakedown efforts, recorded admissions made by defendants DeMonte, Arnold, and Matassa to Farnham during surveilled meetings" and other tape recordings.

The Farnham account of the harassment, taken down by FBI agents Roy Lane and Tommie Canady on December 16 and 18, 1978, reads as follows:

"Richard Farnham, also known as Carol, 3171 North Hudson, Chicago … provided the following information:

"Farnham advised that since October 13, 1978, he has been the manager of Carol's Speakeasy, 1355 North Wells, Chicago … . Carol's Speakeasy is a gay discotheque which serves liquor. Several suppliers of Carol's Speakeasy are Anhauser [Anheuser] Busch Inc., Miller High Life, Inc. and Pabst Brewery Inc.

"Farnham stated that in mid November, 1978, he received a telephone call at home from Frank DeMonte, also known as Babe, a long time acquaintance of Farnham's. Babe requested Farnham to meet with him later that day at Carton's restaurant, 900 North Rush Street, Chicago, Illinois.

"Farnham continued that later the same day he met Babe at Carton's Restaurant. Babe stated that he (Babe) was upset with Farnham because Farnham did not go to Babe to receive approval to operate Carol's Speakeasy. Babe explained that Carol's Speakeasy was in 'Ceasar's' district and that it was necessary for Farnham to do the right thing. Babe told Farnham that they wanted $1,000 per month from the Speakeasy for protection. When questioned about the payment, Babe told Farnham that it was protection money and that part of the protection would be to keep others from extorting the Speakeasy. Babe added that it was a good thing he (Babe) interceded on behalf of Farnham as 'they' wanted to take Farnham for a ride. Babe continued that they could be rough and that they would have busted up the Speakeasy. Babe wanted the payment by December 15, 1978 and told Farnham that he (Babe) could be reached through telephone number (312) 889-9430.

"Farnham further advised that when Babe told Farnham about 'Ceasar,' Babe stated that 'Ceasar' has his office in a sundry store across the street called Odds and Ends. Babe added that the store was just a front and that future payments made by Farnham could be made at the store or someone from the store would come to the restaurant to receive the payment. Farnham told Babe that they were coming on strong to which Babe replied that guys are now getting out of prison and are going to work again. Babe said they were also operating a betting parlor down the street.

"Farnham stated that a few days after the above meetings, he was visited at the Speakeasy by a Peter … and an unknown male who said they were friends of Babe's. Peter inquired about the owner of the tavern next door, The Glory Hole. Peter wanted to know about the owner and amount of business done by The Glory Hole. Peter added that the owner of The Glory Hole, Bob, had to do the right thing. Farnham described the unknown male as being short, stocky, white and approximately 55 to 60 years old.

"Farnham continued that a short time later, he was visited by another unknown male who again said he was a friend of Babe's. The unknown male questioned Farnham about Bob, the owner of The Glory Hole Tavern. The unknown male wanted to know how much Bob could afford to pay per month. The unknown male also asked about the owner of Alfie's, 900 North Rush Street, Chicago. Farnham described this unknown male as being a white Italian, short, stocky build and approximately 30 years old.

"Farnham advised that on December 14, 1978, he received a telephone call from Babe regarding the payoff. A meeting was scheduled for 2:00 PM on December 19, 1978 at Carton's Restaurant.

"Farnham added that he has had conversations with Bob, owner of The Glory Hole Tavern, regarding having to make protection payments.

"Farnham was then shown photographs of the following individuals: Frank DeMonte, also known as Babe; Ken Eto; James LaPietra; Joseph Arnold; Peter N. Dounias; Tommy Campione; Marshall Caifano; Joseph DiVarco; Vincent Solano; Andy Pasha; unknown white male.

"Farnham identified the photograph of Frank DeMonte as being Frank DeMonte, also known as Babe. He also identified the photograph of Peter N. Dounias as being the Peter who questioned him about the owner of The Glory Hole Tavern."

The government also alleged that on August 23, 1979, Farnham met with John Matassa at Carol's. Special Agent Tom Canady posed as Farnham's partner in the club. "Matassa came to collect money for DeMonte; Farnham told him he couldn't pay just then because business was poor," the prosecutors stated. "FBI surveillance shows that upon exiting Carol's, Matassa met with Pete Dounias. Farnham died of natural causes in September 1979."

Farnham's payments were listed as follows:

12/18/78: DeMonte/Arnold at Carton's, $600
12/22/78: Arnold, Odds & Ends, $400
02/15/79: Arnold, Odds & Ends, $700
03/21/79: Arnold, Odds & Ends, $700
04/12/79: Arnold, Odds & Ends, $700
05/17/79: Arnold, Odds & Ends, $700
07/10/79: DeMonte/Matassa, 4818 W. North Ave., $700
08/23/79: Matassa, Carol's, $0

Flint Testifies in Mob Trial

The court transcripts for the case show prosecuting attorney Douglas Roller questioning "James William Flint," owner of the Baton Show Lounge and Redoubt Lounge, as one of the government's witnesses. The Baton was incorporated as R & K Shack Inc. (which reflected the initials of Ross Downs and Ken Overly; Downs and Overly had started out their business where the Baton is now at 436 North Clark and they were the names on the Big Basket/ Shack license). Flint's first day of federal-court testimony was September 19, 1984, in the courthouse at 219 South Dearborn Street.

Flint said that in 1979 he used Continental, Romano and Capital liquor distributors.

Flint was asked about William Mann, a bartender at the Baton who, in late May 1979, said he had spoken with Flint about the men who were coming to ask for safety money. Flint said the men had spoken to Mann, with Flint 15 or 20 feet away. Flint said he believed one of the men was Peter, as in Peter Dounias, but Flint never said he was 100 percent sure of the identification of the men in the bar. According to the statement provided by Bourgeois, Flint had at one time identified a photo of Dounias as among the men, but he later said he was not sure.

After the May 1979 visit, Flint testified, he received a phone call from someone he had never heard before, the call coming from Carton's restaurant. The lawyers then asked Flint about his grand jury testimony of October 17, 1979. There followed some behind-the-scenes discussions between the judge and the prosecuting and defense attorneys about whether Flint's grand jury testimony would impeach his current testimony that he did not know the caller.

Flint had told the grand jury, "Back in 1971 I had my first encounter with Joe Arnold. That was when I was with another establishment, which nothing came of. … I got a call also from Joe at home. He said I would be contacted by the next person."

Defense attorneys said that even if Flint knew Arnold, that did not mean he could identify his voice on the phone. But Flint told the grand jury the caller, Arnold, had identified himself.

After the discussion ended, Flint was allowed back into the courtroom, but the jury remained outside. Attorney Roller then asked Flint if he was acquainted with Joseph Arnold.

Flint: I've heard the name, yes. That's what the caller said his name was when he called.

Roller: Are you acquainted with Joseph Arnold?

Flint: I am not fully acquainted with him but just from a telephone call.

Roller: Have you prior to 1979—had you ever met with him?

Flint: Years ago, I met him once.

Roller: So at the time of the telephone call in 1979, you were acquainted with Joseph Arnold?

Flint: Yes.

Roller: And the telephone call—did you place it or did you receive that telephone call?

Flint: I received a call.

Roller: Where were you when you received it?

Flint: At home.

Roller: Did the person calling you identify himself?

Flint: Yes.

Roller: How did he identify himself?

Flint: By his name.

Roller: And which was?

Flint: Joe Arnold.

Roller: And is that—did you understand the individual that identified as Joseph Arnold to be the same Joseph Arnold you were already acquainted with?

Flint: I don't know if I could truthfully say that because I didn't know his voice. I only met him once. That was about eight years before that.

Roller: Do you know any other Joseph Arnolds?

Flint: No, I don't.

Roller: You only know one Joseph Arnold?

Flint: Yes.

Roller: Exactly what did he say when he called?

Flint: He said that some gentleman would be coming in to see me.

Roller: In regards to identifying himself?

Flint: Oh, he said his name.

Roller: He just said this is Joe Arnold?

Flint: Yes.

Roller: What did he say to you at that time?

Flint: That some guys would be stopping by the club to see me.

Roller: After that telephone call, did anyone come to any of your establishments?

Flint: Yes.

Roller: Which one?

Flint: The Baton.

Roller: And approximately what time of day?

Flint: Around 7:30 in the evening.

Roller: How long after your telephone conversation with this individual who identified himself as Joe Arnold did this occurrence take place?

Flint: A few days.

Roller: How many individuals were there?

Flint: Three or four.

Roller: Had you seen any of these individuals that came on this occasion before?

Flint: I think—I assume they were the same guys as before.

Roller: Not assume. Did you recognize anyone who came the second time?

Flint: Yes, yes. They were the same people.

Roller: The same people as when?

Flint: That were there before.

Flint: That spoke to Mr. Mann?

Flint: Yes.

Roller: That you overheard?

Flint: Yes.

Roller: Did you have a conversation with one of those individuals?

Flint: Yes, I did.

Roller: And to the best of your recollection, what did you say to him and what did he say to you?

Flint: He asked me about safety money.

Roller: Did he say anything further to you about safety money?

Flint: No. Just that was I going to come up with it.

Roller: During the course of this conversation, was any money at all mentioned?

Flint: Money? Yes.

Roller: Amount of money?

Flint: $300 and $200.

Roller: What do you—$300—

Flint: For the Baton and 200 for the Redoubt.

Roller: What did you say to the individual?

Flint: That I wasn't going to get involved in that.

After more discussions about photos and process, Roller continued his questioning of Flint.

Roller: Now, Mr. Flint, during the year 1979, you were interviewed by special agents of the FBI, were you not?

Flint: I was.

Roller: And did that interview take place at approximately—during the same approximate time period as you have been testifying about?

Flint: Yes.

Roller: And did they show you certain photographs at that time?

Flint: I [can't] remember if they showed me the photographs there at the grand jury, but I was showed photographs right about that time.

Roller: Agents showed you photographs right about the time of this occurrence, did they not?

Defense attorney Bourgeois pointed out that the photos were in an envelope dated August 21, 1979, and Roller confirmed that this was the date Flint was shown them. Flint said he did recall agents showing him the photos.

Roller: And at that time, did you pick out a photograph and tell the FBI that that was the individual that had come to your bar?

Flint: I believe I did.

Roller: At this time, I'm going to show you several photographs. I would like for you to look at them one at a time, sir, and determine if you recognize the photograph that you pointed out to the FBI at the time that they talked to you in 1979. Do you understand?

Flint: Yes, I do.

Roller: I place them in front of you. Look at each one in order, place it face up to the side after you have looked at it. Have you looked at them, sir?

Flint: Yes.

Roller: Do you see the photograph that you pointed out to the FBI when they exhibited those photographs to you?

Flint: Yes, I think so.

Roller: Would you show it to me, please. You have handed me two, Mr. Flint. Which one?

Flint: I believe it was this one that I showed them.

Flint said the man in the photo was the one he saw speak to Mann at the Baton and the same one who returned after Flint was called at home by Joseph Arnold. Flint spoke to the man at his bar, and the man was accompanied by other men.

Roller: What did he say to you and what did you say to him, sir?

Flint: About safety money for the Baton and the Redoubt.

Roller: What did he say?

Flint: That I was—was going to pay it.

Roller: What did you say?

Flint: I said no, I was not going to pay it, I was not getting involved in that.

Roller: Were any amounts mentioned by either one of you, amounts of money during this conversation?

Flint: 300 and 200 [for the Baton and Redoubt, respectively].

Roller: … and what did these two amounts relate to? What were they? …

Flint: Safety money.

Roller: Did you say anything further to this individual on that day?

Flint: Yes, I said I wasn't going to get involved because the FBI was there, and I went through this before, and I was not going to do it again.

Roller: Did this individual respond in any fashion at that time?

Flint: I believe he said don't worry about it.

Roller: Thereafter did he and the people that came with him depart the Baton Show Lounge?

Flint: Yes.

Roller: Did there come a time when you saw this individual again, sir?

Flint: Yes.

Roller: Approximately how—where did you see this individual again?

Flint: At the Baton.

Roller: Now, did you know this individual by any first name?

Flint: He said Pete the one time.

Roller: All right. Did Pete come back to this—back to the Baton Show Lounge?

Flint: Yes.

Roller: When?

Flint: A month later or so.

Roller: A month after the meeting you just described?

Flint: A few weeks. I can't be sure.

Roller: Approximately?

Flint: Yes.

Roller: Did he come alone or was there anybody else with him?

Flint: Several people.

Roller: Did you have a conversation with him?

Flint: Yes.

Roller: Who was present?

Flint: I was.

Roller: Was anyone else present during this conversation with Pete?

Flint: No.

Roller: To the best of your recollection, what did he say to you and what did you say to him?

Flint: Was I going to come up with the money, and I said no. I said I was getting farther behind, and I said the FBI was here and I was not going to get involved. That's how it ended.

Roller: During the events you just described, that you have testified to so far today, what was your state of mind, sir?

Flint: Oh, I was probably shaken up.

Roller: Not probably. What was … your state of mind?

Flint: I was shaken up. … I was shaken up a little.

Roller: All right. When this Pete used the term safety money, what did you understand that to mean?

Flint: Probably nothing. Shakedown.

Roller: What was your understanding of the term you testified was used, that term being safety money. What was your understanding of that term? What was it?

Flint: A shakedown.

Roller: After the third occasion of this individual you identified as Pete came to the Baton Show Lounge, did he ever return?

Flint: No.

Roller: And you testified that … you paid him no money?

Flint: I paid no money to anybody.

Roller: Did you do anything between the second and third visits by Pete?

Flint: Did I do anything? I don't understand what you mean.

Roller: Did you do anything in regards to the demand for safety money?

Flint: Oh, yes, I laid some money aside.

Roller: What do you mean by laid money aside?

Flint: I took some money out of my personal account and put it in an envelope.

Roller: How much money did you do that with?

Flint: $500.

Roller: And when did you do that?

Flint: Oh, towards the first of August, middle of August, somewhere in that area.

Roller: When did you do it regards to the visits by Pete?

Flint: After the second visit.

Roller: So between the two visits?

Flint: Yes, sir.

Roller: And where was that money located at?

Flint: It was in my desk drawer.

Roller: At the Baton Show Lounge?

Flint: Yes.

Roller: So when … Pete came on the third occasion, you had the money there?

Flint: No, that was after the third. I had the money—he never came back after I put the money there.

The prosecution completed its questions, and then Arnold's attorney Herbert Barsy asked to question Flint about the phone call. Meanwhile, the judge was deciding whether to allow this testimony to be given before the jury. Roller said that FBI tape recordings show that Arnold admitted to calling Flint, in a conversation with DeMonte on May 29, 1979, in which Arnold told DeMonte: "He [Flint] was supposed to call me. He didn't call me. I called him the other night. What do you think I called him on the telephone. I called about 11:00 o'clock at home from the house." Roller said a further recording June 1 confirmed that Arnold did not just call Flint, but that he spoke to him.

Judge Marshall ultimately allowed the phone call to be admitted and asked Roller to question Flint about the caller in front of the jury. Many of the same questions were asked again of Flint, but this time with the jury hearing his answers.

Attorney Bourgeois then cross-examined Flint briefly. Bourgeois pointed out that Flint, during the questioning, originally pointed to two potential photographs to identify "Pete," so he asked Flint more about the description of the person who came to his bar. Roller continued his questions to Flint, and the testimony was pretty consistent with what Flint had said earlier without the jury in the room.

More Flint Testimony

Flint returned to the trial the next day, September 20, 1984.

Bourgeois asked Flint about the Baton and its clientele. Flint said it was mixed gay and straight, about 15 percent gay and 85 percent straight, while the Redoubt was a gay bar. Flint said that since the 1979 alleged shakedown, the Redoubt had moved to Halsted Street. The attorney asked how many gay bars there were in 1978 or 1979, and Flint estimated 45 or 50, plus gay and adult bookstores and other gay businesses.

Bourgeois asked, "Now, some of these establishments were having difficulty with the police, isn't that correct?"

Roller objected to this, so the judge asked Bourgeois to limit the question to Flint's own bars.

Bourgeois: Well, your own establishments, the Baton did have some difficulty with the police, isn't that correct?

Flint: Not in that year, no, sir.

Bourgeois: Not in 1979?

Flint: I don't believe so.

Bourgeois: Well, don't you recall that on March 2, 1979, the police came into your establishment?

Flint: I don't recall it.

Bourgeois: And don't you recall that there were some arrests on that occasion?

Flint: I know that we have had one or two, but I don't know what year it was.

Bourgeois: I see. Let me refresh your recollection. It occurred on March 2, 1979. Let me show you something here. I'm going to show you, Jimmy, what is your file from the city of Chicago, with reference to your license at the Baton … .

Flint: Okay, I remember it, I thought it was earlier, yes.

Bourgeois: But it was in '79.

Flint: Yes.

Bourgeois then asked Flint about the New Flight, a gay bar at 420 North Clark Street, a short distance from the Baton. The New Flight was owned by Howard Goodman, who died at age 51 on October 9, 1980, following a yearlong illness. This was after the FBI was looking into extortion, but four years before the trial. Goodman was a vocal critic of police harassment, according to his October 17, 1980, GayLife obituary. He had opened the bar more than three years earlier with his sister Harriet Freeman and brother Bob Goodman, who continued to operate the bar for several years after Howard died.

Bourgeois: And they [the New Flight] had some problems with the police also at about the same time, didn't they?

Flint: Many, yes.

Bourgeois: Yes. Now, you also had trouble with the Building Department and the Fire Department with respect to alleged violations in your establishment, did you not?

Flint: Yes.

Bourgeois: Now, when the police came into your establishment, isn't it a fact that in addition to the arrests, that they carded all the customers?

Flint: No, that's not true.

Bourgeois: They did not card the customer—

Flint: They didn't card the customers. They have, other places.

Bourgeois: I see. Is that a police tactic that you know of personally?

Flint: I've heard it happening in other places but it has never happened in my place per se.

Bourgeois: When you say other places, do you refer to gay places?

Flint: Yes.

Bourgeois: Now, do you recall in May of 1979, that a committee was formed by gay people to protest police harassment in gay bars?

Flint: Yes, I'm aware of that committee.

Bourgeois: And you were a member of that committee, were you not?

Flint: Chairperson, yes.

Bourgeois: You had a series of meetings, as a matter of fact, did you not?

Flint: We did.

Bourgeois: And at one point, you organized a march, didn't you?

Flint: Yes, I did.

Bourgeois: And you organized a march, and you had a hundred volunteers at the Baton one night who were going to supervise the march, is that right?

Flint: That's very true.

Bourgeois: And you also organized a committee that met with Mayor Byrne, isn't that right?

Flint: That's true.

Bourgeois: And Byrne heard the committee's story and agreed to do something about it, isn't that right?

Flint: That's true.

Bourgeois: And as a result, the harassment at the gay bars stopped or lessened, isn't that right?

Flint: That's true.

Bourgeois, who was known to have gay clients at his law firm, asked if Flint knew whether the police commander of the 18th District had been removed because of the activist efforts in which Flint participated, but Flint said he did not know if the transfer was because of the protests.

Bourgeois asked Flint if he had heard of the term "fag basher." Flint said he had not.

Bourgeois: Do you know of the problem of people who—men who pick on gays and who hang around gay establishments, and either rob or assault gays as they are leaving?

Flint: I've heard of that, yes.

Bourgeois: Yes. And, now, your business at the Baton was fairly successful at that time, was it not, in 1978 and '79?

Flint: That's true, yes.

Bourgeois: And it continues to be a successful place today, isn't that correct?
Flint: Yes.

Bourgeois asked his client, Peter Dounias, to stand up, and asked Flint about their meetings in 1979. Bourgeois admitted that Dounias was the one to visit Flint, and said his client told Flint, "The Flight has had some problems. As you know, they were going to close. We took care of it and they are not closing now." Flint said he was not sure if Dounias was the man who said that to him in 1979, but he did remember the New Flight conversation. Bourgeois showed Flint his grand jury testimony to refresh his memory of the incidents five years earlier.

Bourgeois also asked Flint about his appearance in an interview with John Drummond of WBBM-TV, the Channel 2 CBS local station in Chicago. Flint told Drummond that no one had ever threatened him, and he confirmed that in his testimony. He also said that since the original request for safety money, he had not experienced any threats at home or at his businesses.

Roller asked for a redirect-examination opportunity and then asked Flint about the committee he chaired, the 1979 march against police harassment and the subsequent meeting with Mayor Byrne, which all occurred prior to the safety-money requests. Roller said that therefore "you had no need on the behalf of—on behalf of other people to go to anyone else to seek help with that police problem, did you?" Flint said, "I don't believe so."

One taped reference to Flint paid Flint a compliment. When Arnold and DeMonte discussed Flint's not calling Arnold back, this exchange took place, as recorded by the FBI:

"And that Jimmy Flint …" Arnold said.

"Oh, he's got balls," said DeMonte.

"That motherfucker, he's got balls, that Jimmy Flint," Arnold added.

Other Testimony

Another witness in the trial was Steven Rempas, a Chicago dentist and co-owner of the Loading Zone, a gay bar at 46 East Oak Street. The FBI visited Rempas on May 29, 1979, and he agreed to cooperate in the investigation. Taped conversations between Joseph Arnold and Frank DeMonte on May 30, 1979, showed that Arnold had had a tip that the FBI had approached "three dentists who owned a gay bar."

Rempas allowed an FBI agent to pose as a business partner. Rempas testified that he told his business associate James Graves about this setup, and Graves told Joseph Arnold, his longtime associate. Arnold told DeMonte, in the May 30 meeting recorded by the FBI, that "we gotta stay away from" the Loading Zone altogether, for fear of FBI connections.

Former GayLife newspaper Publisher Grant Ford, who by 1984 was pastor of Holy Covenant Metropolitan Community Church in Hinsdale, Illinois, also testified at the trial. He said he had still been at GayLife when the alleged shakedowns occurred, and he testified to basic questions of what "gay" is, and that there were growing numbers of gay businesses in the late 1970s.

Ford was asked about Richard Farnham and the high-profile raid on Carol's Speakeasy in May 1979. Ford said he had met with Farnham several times that year, including a meeting at the office of GayLife, and also at the committee that formed in response to the police harassment. Ford said the committee was chaired by Jim Flint and Doris Shane.

Ford also testified that his reporter and photographer wrote about the raid at Carol's, and a story was published in GayLife. Ford said that after the story, he and others attended a meeting that also included representatives of the Police Department's Office of Professional Standards.

Bourgeois asked Ford about the meeting the committee held with Mayor Jane Byrne. "Our main concern [was] about police action that was taking place in a number of the bars, that had taken place shortly after her election. And we were frustrated about it, and asked if she could help us find some relief," Ford testified. "The general result of that conversation was that the harassment ceased."

Bourgeois also asked Ford about "fag bashing" and a group Ford co-founded called Volunteers for Human Rights, which operated from 1978 to early 1980. "One of our main projects was in response to personal violence against gay people. We worked with the Whistle Stop program," Ford said. "And we also organized patrols to watch for any incidents against gay people. These patrols worked mostly in the New Town area [the eastern Lakeview neighborhood], and we saw a considerable decrease in crimes of personal violence against gay people."

Ford and other witnesses were called to establish the tenor of the times for the gay community. The defense wanted to prove that their clients were merely providing a necessary defense against police, the allegedly corrupt city Buildings and Fire departments, and criminal elements. The defense said the money was given voluntarily, without threat of violence. The defense also argued that since Flint experienced no violence in the months after the safety-money requests, there was no real threat.

The prosecution tried to show that the accused were not helping anyone but themselves, taking their share of the gay pie. The prosecution also argued that the reason no violence happened was that the defendants were aware the FBI was snooping around the area.

A 'Fruit Parade'

The defense attorneys appeared at times very homophobic. In the October 4, 1984, issue of GayLife newspaper, reporter Paul Cotton said that "defense attorneys attacked—in both visible and vulgar style—the credibility of gay government witnesses, what one attorney called a 'fruit parade.'"

Dounias' attorney Adam Bourgeois and attorney Santo Volpe, who represented Matassa, mentioned homosexuality, but in different ways.

"How does anyone become a criminal because of what's on some fag's mind?" said Volpe, according to GayLife. "Some fruit who only in his own mind is afraid has become the subject of a federal case. A federal case should be a federal case, not a fruit parade."

Bourgeois had his own take on the gay angle: "People who are gay have had to live a lie, and living a lie is a life of fear. Bob Hugel had led a life of deception. The only fear he felt was stage fright." The attorney said Hugel wanted out of the bar business anyway and "took the FBI for a ride."

There were other interesting things reported in the trial, as noted in the government recordings.

— On May 30, 1979, Arnold referred to "fruits" in an apparent reference to the opening of a new club. Later, an unidentified male alluded to Carol, who, he tells Arnold, is "very,

very close" to the owner of another bar. He also told Arnold of another gay bar that almost closed because the doorman would not admit "straights." (That is believed to have been Still of the Night.)

— On May 31, 1979, an unidentified male cautioned against bothering gays because he felt they were dangerous. Arnold cited the shooting of Mayor George Moscone and Supervisor Harvey Milk in San Francisco. The killings, by Dan White, had occurred the previous year, on November 27, 1978. White was found guilty of involuntary manslaughter on May 21, 1979, 10 days before this recording, so it may be that Arnold was referring to the riots in San Francisco by persons outraged that White was acquitted of first-degree murder. Those events were called the "White Night Riots," in which 61 police officers and 100 rioters and gay residents were hospitalized.

— On June 1, 1979, Arnold told DiVarco that he spoke to Jim Flint, whom they referred to as "the Tat, the Baton" ["Tat" may have been short for Baton or tattler] and he said Flint invited him to join the gay pride parade later that month.

Harassment by officials of the city of Chicago was also mentioned in testimony by defense witness Frank Barnes, who was the city's chief Building Code enforcement officer during the time of the alleged payoffs in 1978 and 1979. GayLife reported September 27, 1984, that Barnes testified that "on orders from the Mayor's Office and the building commission under the [Mayor Richard J.] Daley and the [Mayor Michael] Bilandic administrations he led teams of nine to 10 building code inspectors, accompanied by uniformed police, into gay bars during early evening hours, writing tickets on the spot for any violations. He said 'quite a few' establishments were shut down through such tactics." (Daley died in 1976 and was succeeded by Bilandic, who served until Jane Byrne was elected on April 16, 1979.)

Barnes testified that one of the bars visited by his team was Carol's Speakeasy.

Closing Arguments and Verdict

An unexpected development came just before closing arguments in the nine-day trial. GayLife reported that "DiVarco walked out of the courtroom after his attorneys surprised prosecutors—just minutes before closing arguments were to begin—with city records showing that the gay bar Jamie's, 1108 N. Clark, which DiVarco allegedly had conspired to shake down in 1979, had been demolished in 1976." The plot thickened: In the tape recordings, Arnold and DiVarco were allegedly pressuring Jamie's owner John Gattuso for payments, but the purpose was unclear, and Gattuso was found murdered after the Eto assassination attempt in which he was implicated. (DiVarco, known as crime boss "Caesar," died of a heart attack in 1986 at age 74.)

Prosecutor Roller's closing arguments clarified the charges against the defendants. Arnold, DeMonte and Dounias were charged with a conspiracy, "agreeing to extort—not extorting, agreeing to," Roller said. Meanwhile, Dounias also was charged with attempting to extort, not extorting. And the defendants Arnold, DeMonte and Matassa were charged with attempting to extort in regard to the Farnham payments.

On September 27, 1984, the jury returned only one guilty verdict, against Dounias on Count 2, and the remaining three defendants—Arnold, DeMonte and Matassa—were found not guilty on all counts. The jury deliberated for just 10 hours in the case.

The judgment order in the court files says Dounias received a sentence of six years in prison and was found guilty because he "knowingly, willfully, and unlawfully attempted to obstruct, delay, and affect commerce, and the movement of articles in commerce, that is, alcoholic beverages, by extortion, did unlawfully attempt to obtain property, approximately $100.00 in United States currency, which was not due and owing the defendant. In violation of Title 18, United States Code, Section 1951."

Section 1951 of Title 18 of the U.S. Code—the Hobbs Act—reads in part: "Whoever in any way or degree obstructs, delays, or affects commerce or the movement of any article or commodity in commerce, by … extortion or attempts or conspires so to do, or commits or threatens physical violence to any person or property in furtherance of a plan or purpose to do anything in violation of this section shall … " be guilty of an offense against the United States.

Dounias had received $100 from Robert Hugel at Carton's on December 11, 1978. He received a six-year sentence for that $100 safety payment. The maximum penalty was 20 years and a $10,000 fine.

Arnold, DeMonte and Matassa were found not guilty of extorting some $5,200 from Richard Farnham, among other charges. Attorneys were apparently successful in convincing the jury that Farnham sounded relaxed and friendly in the taped conversations—that he was not being threatened.

Dounias was found not guilty of extorting from Flint, even though he was given six years for the Hugel charge.

Looking Back

Flint does believe there was a hit ordered on his life during the Mafia investigation. "A woman who worked at the Oak Tree restaurant told me they had talked about it," Flint said. "That's when I went and talked to Joe Arnold and said, 'I'm not paying off, why is there a problem?' He said, 'No, you're OK.' Later a big guy came to the bar, said he was Mafia, I don't know if he was. He said, 'Tell these bar owners they better be quiet or somebody's going to get hurt.' I talked to the other bar owners. That's the last I heard of him. That was before the trial."

Flint admits he had paid off police and Mafia in the past, but he says he did not during the time under investigation by the FBI in 1978 and 1979.

Flint says that while he was afraid of the Mafia and those who could have been from the Mafia, he was never asked by the FBI, nor did he ever consider, going into witness protection, as Robert Hugel had done. Flint says he was not paying off, so he didn't need witness protection. But his not seeking such protection may also have been because he had built up such a strong business reputation in Chicago, and because of the close-knit relationship he had with so many friends and family members. He would have lost all of that, had he gone into witness protection. Flint did the reverse—he kept a high profile, and one year after the Mafia trial he even decided to run for a seat on the Cook County Board. These days, he feels that his high profile has kept away people who previously would have tried to intimidate him.

Richard Farnham, "Mother Carol," died September 30, 1979. This is coverage from GayLife newspaper, October 5, 1979.

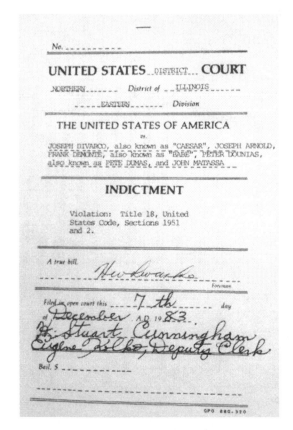

The December 7, 1983, indictment of five alleged mobsters by the FBI. Flint was forced to testify in the trial.

Robert Hugel, owner of the Glory Hole gay bar, went into federal witness protection and testified in the Mafia trial.

Flint's two-page statement prior to testifying in the Mafia trial. This statement was taken December 13, 1983, and Flint testified at length several months later.

Statement of James Flint given to Adam Bourgeois in the Office of Adam Bourgeois on December 13, 1983, at 2:00 P.M. at 53 W. Jackson Boulevard, Suite 852, Chicago, Illinois 60604

My date of birth is 7/27/41. My Social Security # [redacted] I own the Redoubt. 666-1969.

In 1978 or 1979, I was approached at the front door of the Baton, a nightclub which I own. I have owned it since 1971. My clientele is very mixed. It was in the summer of '78 or '79. Two men talked to me at the door and said some hing about safety money. The total conversation took about five minutes. I got real nervous. I didn't want to talk. It was around 7:00 or 7:30 at night. It had to be around the time we opened and we opened at 8:00.

The men were big. It would be very hard for me to pick out these men.

About 2 to 3 months later, the FBI sent two agents to see me. They said that other bars were cooperating in giving evidence of shakedowns. I said there's nothing to cooperate for because I am not being shaken down. One of the agents asked if I could be shaken down and I said if they used force, anyone in his right mind could be shaken down..

I told them that I had been approached. The agents asked me if the men said they were from the syndicate. I said no. Anyone could come along and say they were from the syndicate. They had about five or six photographs with them. I recognized one of the photographs and told the agents that it could have been one of the people.

I was never asked to look at a line-up. My identification of the person in the photograph was not a positive one. If I were asked today to pick out the men who approached me in '78 or '79, I doubt if I could identify them.

The second visit I had was about a month later. Only one of the men returned. I told him that the FBI had been around. It had to have been in the evening around the same time.

The man asked me whether I had made up my mind about paying the money. I told him that I wasn't going to pay anyone off. He said he'd get back to me. I never heard from him again. He stayed only 3 or 4 minutes.

-1-

The FBI came back many times. I told them about the second visit. They showed me the same photographs. I think I said it could be the same man. I'm not sure what I said.

I could not truthfully say I could identify anyone.

The FBI kept asking me about some Caesar guy. I told them I don't know him. I told them that I never heard the name before.

The only one of the defendants I know is Joe Arnold and I only know him from television. I saw his photo on TV when he was shot. I don't know any of the other defendants.

Both visits I had were very brief.

The men were dressed in sports shirts and slacks. One had a hat. It was summer. At no time was I threatened by anyone.

The month before I was visited I received a phone call. The caller said someone would be coming to see me. I asked what about and the person said you'll find out when the person comes. I did not recognize the voice of the caller.

When the two people came neither said that they had been the caller.

I could not recognize the voice of either of the two men as the voice of the caller.

I don't think that I told the FBI that Peter had called me.

Neither of the men said they were gay.

The conversations were never more than 3 to 5 minutes.

After reading this statement I will sign and date it.

Signature:

Dated: December 13, 1983

Reserve space below for notations by minute clerk

Jury returns verdict in open court. We, the Jury, find the defendant not guilty in counts 1 and 4. Guilty as charged in count 2. Court enters judgment on the verdict. Time for defendant to file post trial motions extended to October 18, 1984. Government to answer by October 29, 1984. Order cause referred to the probation department for a presentence investigation. Sentencing set for November 7, 1984 at 9:00 a.m. Same bond to stand.

The jury verdict in the Mafia case, from the National Archives files.

GayLife newspaper reported the verdict on October 4, 1984.

3 freed, 1 found guilty in gay bar shakedown

By William B. Crawford Jr.

THREE REPUTED crime syndicate figures were acquitted by a federal jury Thursday on charges that they shook down owners of taverns frequented by homosexuals. A fourth defendant, Peter Dounias, 62, was found guilty of attempted extortion.

A jury in the courtroom of U.S. District Judge Prentice H. Marshall acquitted Joseph Arnold, 72; John Matassa, 32; and Frank DeMonte, 55. The defendants had been charged with one count each of conspiracy and one count of attempted conspiracy.

The jury reached its verdict after 10 hours of deliberations over three days.

Marshall set sentencing of Dounias for Nov. 7. The maximum penalty for attempted extortion is 20 years and $10,000.

Douglas Roller, chief of the Chicago strike force on organized crime, and coprosecutor Mitchell Mars had contended in the weeklong trial that the four defendants, and a fifth man, Joseph DiVarco, 72, a convicted felon whose rackets domain includes the Rush Street nightclub district, shook down owners of four taverns that catered to homosexuals.

MARSHALL DISMISSED a single charge of conspiracy against DiVarco Monday. He threw out the government's case against DiVarco after defense attorneys produced records showing that a tavern from which DiVarco allegedly extorted payoffs in 1979 had been razed three years earlier.

The conviction of Dounias evidently stemmed from the testimony of Robert Hugel, former owner of the Glory Hole, 1343 N. Wells St., a bar once frequented by homosexuals. Hugel, who agreed to wear a tape recorder after he learned of the payoff scheme, testified that Dounias told Hugel that he would be required to pay $400 a month.

Hugel testified that he feared for his life after Dounias told him on Nov. 30, 1978, "We got an association here in the district, you understand? You're not a member of the association, you got to come in."

ADAM BOURGEOIS, Dounias' attorney, contended at the trial that the tavern owners were not extortion victims, but willingly made payoffs because they were being harassed by police and their customers were being assaulted by anti-gays who gathered near the bars at closing time.

But Roller and Mars contended that the defendants threatened to harm the bar owners and their business if payoffs were not made.

The Chicago Tribune's coverage on September 28, 1984.

5

Politics

The history of Chicago's Democratic Party is filled with division and rancor. Those problems reached a new low in the 1980s during the "Council Wars" that pitted independent Democratic Mayor Harold Washington against "Regular Democrats" (also known as the Democratic Machine) headed by Alderman Edward R. Vrdolyak.

Prior to the 1980s, the Regular Democrats pretty much controlled everything in Chicago. Richard J. Daley had served 21 years as mayor and ruled the city with an iron fist. He held total political sway over vast areas of the city, and that included anyone wanting to do business there.

Daley was first elected mayor in 1955, just prior to the radical 1960s and a growing gay movement in the Windy City. Chuck Renslow, who opened a photo studio in the 1950s, knew the lay of the land right away. He was asked for a "donation" to Daley's campaign in order to smooth the way to get his photo studio license. As he opened a gay bar and other businesses, it was just a part of the cost of doing business to pay off politicians, city inspectors, police and the Mafia.

Into this environment skated Jim Flint from Peoria, Illinois. When he began working at gay bars in the 1960s, he too saw the way things were done. He witnessed owners of the bars making payoffs, and once he opened his own bar, the Baton, in 1969, he simply went along to get along.

With the Regular Democrats in charge, and with a weak independent opposition, many gay leaders and business owners aligned themselves with the Regulars or with some moderate Republicans. (From 1870 to 1980, Illinois had state representative districts with three representatives and a cumulative-voting system to elect them. The cumulative-voting system facilitated minority-party inclusion, and thus a moderate Republican such as pro-gay state Representative Susan Catania was able to hold office in the otherwise predominantly Democratic city.) Some gays certainly tried to support independent Democratic forces, which were gaining in strength in the 1970s, but to own a business meant a whole other level of problems for those not part of the "Machine."

South Side Alderman Clifford P. Kelley, of the 20th Ward, was the first alderman to step up for gay rights, by being the first to sponsor a city gay-rights bill, in 1973. Kelley, who is African-American, was also a frequent guest at gay political events and benefits in the 1970s and 1980s, often at the invitation of Jim Flint or Chuck Renslow.

Meanwhile, Flint and Renslow both attended mainstream Democratic Party events, to make sure to be seen as leaders who could wrangle votes and money. And eventually, both men ran for office, making history as early pioneers of gay electoral politics.

First Steps

Flint remembers his father's teaching him the importance of voting. His father voted for Harry S. Truman over Thomas E. Dewey in the 1948 presidential election, and at first Dewey was considered such a shoo-in that it was reported in the Chicago Tribune that "Dewey Defeats Truman," in a now-famous erroneous headline. His father told little Jimmy that the incident showed how important every vote was.

"Let this be a lesson to you, always vote," his dad said to him. "From then on, I always was involved in politics. I got more involved in the Democratic Party when I moved to Chicago," Flint said.

One of Flint's earliest political activities in Chicago was volunteering in the areas where he lived, operated his businesses, or had political allies. This included activism in the 42nd, 44th and 46th wards.

A January 7, 1976, GayLife article by Les Trotter reported about one such Flint involvement, when his bar hosted a meeting of the 43rd Ward Gay Caucus. The article also noted that state Representative Susan Catania would be resubmitting a gay civil-rights bill to the Illinois General Assembly on January 14.

An important ally of gay rights during this time was the Alliance to End Repression. The Illinois Gay Rights Task Force (later called the Illinois Gay and Lesbian Task Force, or IGLTF) grew out of the Alliance's own gay-rights group, which had been formed by mostly non-gay Alliance members. Future gay leaders also had Alliance backgrounds, including John Chester, who would become a "godfather" to Flint. In his GayLife column, Trotter noted that Alliance member Betty Plank was "the perfect example of the type of deed that can be performed by our non-gay allies in the struggle not only to obtain our rights, but in those areas of discrimination that affect gays and non-gays alike."

IGLTF was a very political group. It rated candidates for election and lobbied for local and state gay-rights bills. In the March 1982 primary, for both Cook County and Illinois offices, the group rated the candidates on a range of gay issues. Of 450 candidates in the March 16 primary, 28 completed the IGLTF questionnaire, and 14 were ranked high on gay-rights issues.

In that same election, GayLife endorsed dozens of candidates, including some in the Republican primary. The newspaper endorsed both Adlai Stevenson III as a Democrat for governor and Republican James R. Thompson for the same race. It did the same in the lieutenant governor's race, with Grace Mary Stern the Democrat and Susan Catania the Republican. In other races, GayLife backed Harold Washington in the 1st Congressional District, both Democrat George Dunne and Republican Bernard Carey in the race for Cook County Board president, and mostly Democrats for state representative and senator.

Among state reps that year, 8th District candidate Jesse White received strong gay support.

John Chester remembers taking Flint to one of Flint's first mainstream Democratic fundraisers, a house party for then-state Senator Richard M. Daley's race to become the Cook County state's attorney in 1980. "This was at a large apartment down in Hyde Park, and there were lots of people," Chester said. "Jim and I were there. Jim wanted to know about where Daley stood in terms of the gay community. Daley was taking questions, and Jim stood in the front row of people. I was right behind him.

"I pushed him to ask Daley a question—I poked him two times. Then Jim asked him what would he do on gay issues. This was the first time, at a regular straight event, that he was asked this. Daley gave a very good answer, that gays and lesbians were part of the community; if they had concerns about how they were treated, he would be interested in working it out. Jim was so stunned that he did it and got a good answer—and the hostess came over and said, 'I'm glad you raised the question.'"

The late political activist and business owner Dewey Herrington, a leader in the Lakeview business community, was interviewed in 1995 by Jack Rinella about Chicago's gay community. Herrington, like many people active in the 1970s, said Jim Flint and Chuck Renslow were "really hard workers … I have a lot of respect for them."

Another of Flint's political activities was service as vice president of the 46th Ward Democratic organization, even though he did not actually live in the ward. He got the post because of all the help he did to elect Jerome Orbach as alderman.

Flint also remembers going with John Chester to hand out election fliers for state Representative Catania in the South Side's Robert Taylor Homes public housing project. He was a poll watcher for the first time in that 1970s race.

Flint gave time in the late 1970s to Regular Democrats, including Cook County Board President George Dunne and 1st Ward Alderman Fred Roti (who served in office 23 years until he was indicted in 1990 on racketeering and extortion charges). Flint said he was told that that was the only way to get someone hired by the city, and Flint wanted to help one of his sisters (Dorothy) get work. Once he volunteered, she got a job in the Chicago Department of Streets and Sanitation downtown.

Prairie State Democrats

In April 1982, political activists felt compelled to form their own organization, and by later that year they adopted the name Greater Chicago Gay and Lesbian Democratic Club. The group changed its name to the Prairie State Democratic Club a few years later.

Though there were some progressives involved in the group, and it eventually did endorse the openly gay Ron Sable for 44th Ward alderman and even Harold Washington in his mayoral re-election bid, the group was always tied more closely to the Regular Democrats.

Ultimately it folded around 1988 as more progressive voices took a dominant role in Chicago and the LGBT community. But for several years, the Prairie State club played an important role in showing the mainstream political community that the gay vote, and gay dollars, mattered.

For its launch event, the group kicked gay political activism up a big notch.

The Greater Chicago Gay and Lesbian Democratic Club hosted a free "Political Pride '82 Rally" on October 1, 1982, at the historic Bismarck Hotel, site of numerous large mainstream political events in the past. Between 600 and 800 people were at the event, and Jim Flint was the master of ceremonies.

The special guest speaker was the Reverend Troy Perry, founder of the Metropolitan Community Churches. The Windy City Jazz Band, the Windy City Gay Chorus and disco singer Angela Clemmons ("Give Me Just a Little More Time") performed.

"If everyone goes out of here with the enthusiasm I got, we'll have the strongest gay Democratic club in America," Flint said at the event.

Harley McMillen, who temporarily chaired the group and was also executive director of Howard Brown Memorial Clinic, was quoted in the October 7, 1982, issue of GayLife newspaper: "We made politicians decide whether to support us by appearing."

Flint read a letter from Mayor Jane Byrne at the start of the event: "Best wishes for a successful inaugural rally of the Greater Chicago Gay and Lesbian Democrats. It is heartening to see your fine organization become as involved as it has in Chicago's political concerns, and I hope you continue your fine work." Byrne had a previous commitment, but Chicago Consumer Services Commissioner Karen Petitte spoke for her at the event.

The most high-profile attendee was Alderman Ed Vrdolyak, president of the Cook County Democratic Party. (In 1987 he became a Republican, after he had recanted his earlier gay-rights support.)

"Fellow Democrats," Vrdolyak said at the start of his remarks, acknowledging the common ground between himself and the largely gay audience. He went on to praise the Cook County Dems for adopting a platform that included a sexual-orientation non-discrimination clause.

Alderman Cliff Kelley received a standing ovation for his sponsorship of the city gay-rights ordinance. State Senator Dawn Clark Netsch was also well received. Others attending included state Senator William Marovitz; state Representatives Daniel O'Brien, Woods Bowman, Ellis Levin and Jesse White; and Aldermen Ralph Axelrod and David Orr. Axelrod's electoral opponent, community activist Charlotte Newfeld, also attended the event.

City Treasurer Cecil Partee, committeeman of the 20th Ward, also spoke. "You have witnessed here tonight all the components of history, past, present, and future ... human rights, human rights, human rights," he told the crowd.

White said he was disappointed in the news that the Salvation Army was turning down Toys for Tots money raised by the gay Chicago Knight Motorcycle Club (of which Flint was leader; see Chapter 13). Almost 30 years later, White still remembers the disappointment he had in the homophobia the Salvation Army exhibited. At the time of the event, White was running against pro-gay Republican Elroy C. Sandquist Jr.

Alderman John Merlo, of the 44th Ward, received some boos when he took the stage, partly because he ran a campaign perceived as anti-gay. As a state legislator Merlo had not been a co-sponsor of the state's gay-rights bill, and during that time he also had not bothered to answer the candidates' questionnaire of the Illinois Gay Rights Task Force. Merlo had defeated gay candidate Michael Harrington for an aldermanic seat that had been held for 10 years by independent Democrats. Merlo won the 1981 special election for a two-year aldermanic term by a 4–1 margin (9,892 to 2,364) over Harrington. Merlo did not seek re-election in 1983, instead backing Bernie Hansen for the post. He said part of his reason was that he felt the ward was still independent in its politics, according to GayLife, December 16, 1982.

In December 1983, a year later, about 100 people attended the Gay Dems group's holiday party held at Flint's Redoubt bar. Several elected officials were there, including Senator Marovitz, Representatives Levin and White, Aldermen Bernard J. Hansen (who had replaced Merlo) and Jerome Orbach, as well as Merlo himself, who was still 44th Ward committeeman. Some candidates for office also attended the party.

Flint was an administrative assistant to state Representative Jesse White for nine years and has supported White in all his campaigns over the course of more than 30 years. One benefit Flint hosted was held March 7, 1978, for White's state representative campaign. On October 31, 1980, Flint, John Chester and William B. Kelley jointly paid for and signed an ad in GayLife for White in the 13th District race for state representative, along with Republican Elroy C. Sandquist Jr. and Democrat Daniel P. O'Brien (at that time, each district still had three representatives).

Jesse White is now Illinois secretary of state, and he still fondly remembers the support Jim Flint and Chuck Renslow gave to his early state representative campaigns in the 1970s. "Today I tell people, once you've been segregated, once you have experienced discrimination, you know how badly it makes you feel, you never want to do it to another human being. It is the ugliest card in the deck," said White, who is African-American. "When it comes to the gays, my attitude is the same. There is a big, wide, wonderful world and we should live with peace and harmony, no matter what."

When White was a state representative, he was one of only a handful of 1970s legislative supporters of gay rights. As secretary of state decades later, he helped lobby for the gay-rights bill, which finally was signed into law in 2005. "When I was a lawmaker it was not fashionable, not popular to support gay rights. We were castigated because we thought it was the right thing to do. ... I had experienced segregation and discrimination ... so it was easy for me to support [gay rights]."

Leadership

On December 7, 1982, the Greater Chicago Gay and Lesbian Democratic Club elected its first board members and officers: Chuck Renslow was president, Tom Stabnicki vice president, Angelo Galicia secretary and David Toland treasurer. Jim Flint was elected fundraising chair, Jerry Williams membership chair, Bill Essler public relations chair and Michael Harrington political action chair. Victor Jones, Harley McMillen and Richard Noland (a Gay Chicago columnist) were elected at-large members.

Renslow, publisher of GayLife newspaper starting in 1980, was quoted in a story about the elections, in the December 16, 1982, issue of GayLife: "This organization is extremely important to the present political climate. It's time to make change in the Democratic Party, and the way to make those changes is from within."

Stabnicki was president of the American Federation of State, County and Municipal Employees Union Local 2081, and coordinator of AFSCME's gay caucus, and he was a member of the gay branch of the Democratic Socialists of America.

The new group did have a range of Democratic opinions, but was mostly white and overwhelmingly male. The group even had an internal debate, in November 1982, about whether to be known as an "Independent" or "Regular" Democratic group. It agreed not to have either affiliation.

In May 1983, in a contested election, Chuck Renslow was given a second term as president, Stabnicki was elected vice president, Angelo Galicia secretary, Dave Toland treasurer, Michael Harrington political action committee chair and Jim Flint fundraising committee chair. Janis Malone was elected to head the membership committee, and Bob Dachis was elected to head publicity. More elections were delayed until the June 1 meeting, when Harley McMillen was elected to an at-large post. John Chester, president of the Organization to

Promote Equality Now (Chicago's first gay political action committee), was elected for the first time to the Gay Dems board, and Victor Jones was re-elected.

On May 3, 1984, the group held new elections. Renslow was elected to his third term as president, and Flint was elected vice president (a position he had temporarily filled when Stabnicki resigned). Jack Delaney was elected secretary, Jim Serritelli was elected political action committee chair (Harrington was switched to an at-large post), Dave Toland was elected treasurer, Wendell Roberson membership chair, Angelo Galicia fundraising committee chair, and Jerry Williams public relations chair. Melvin Simmons and Karen Boehning-Cimmarusti were elected to at-large posts.

The group at this point reported having 92 members, including the officers.

Flint used his annual July birthday event as a fundraiser for the Gay Dems that year, besides hosting other fundraising activities.

The June 9, 1983, issue of GayLife reported that the group also created two ad hoc committees: the Appointments Committee to work with the administration of Mayor Harold Washington (who was elected that year) to focus on gay and lesbian appointments to city positions, and the Racism and Sexism Committee.

Lesbian activist Sarah Craig was so concerned about the lack of women in gay groups that she wrote a letter to her "sisters" urging them to get involved. Craig herself participated in numerous groups, including the Gay Dems organization.

"Jim is a very passionate guy," Jerry Williams said of Flint's political activism, including his work with the Gay Dems group. "At that time, what turned into our gay leadership, there were only a few willing to stand and be out; Chuck Renslow, Jim Flint, Ira Jones and Michael Harrington were among the only few who were willing to do this. Jim and Chuck had lived through the dark period where the Mob controlled all the bars. I never experienced that. I was in one bar raid at [the] Hideway in Forest Park, years ago. It was kind of scary, though the names were not in the paper. But raids were rare by then, in the early 1980s." Williams said that many of his friends were still very closeted at that time and that they questioned why he was being so out and involved. They were worried about their careers. Meanwhile, Williams took a prominent staff role at Gay Chicago Magazine.

Why was Flint so out? "I think Jim was a visionary," Williams said. "It didn't matter, he was going to be who he was, regardless of how society looked at us. He was very proud."

The late Jim Serritelli was interviewed in 1995 by Jack Rinella about Chicago's gay political efforts. Serritelli, who had worked for Alderman Jerry Orbach, said he saw Flint and himself as "political conservatives, when it comes to economics, and social liberals. At least that's my opinion of Jim. He may have a different opinion of himself. But that's what I think of him. And it's just that we had a lot of the same agenda, how politics should be run. … I introduced him to my alderman, Jerry Orbach. And they hit it off. They hit it off very well. As a matter of fact, they hit it off so well, Jim sponsored some fundraising events for my alderman."

Endorsements

The 1983 city races were the first high-profile test of the Greater Chicago Gay and Lesbian Democratic Club. GayLife Publisher Renslow was also president of the Gay Dems, and the newspaper did run a lot of letters and guest views about endorsements that differed from the paper's endorsements and from the Gay Dems' endorsements.

Chicago used to have both a primary and a general election for city races. But that was changed a few years after Harold Washington turned the party upside down in 1983: He defeated incumbent Mayor Jane Byrne and State's Attorney Richard M. Daley in a three-way race. GayLife newspaper reported that all three candidates received some gay support.

Byrne did appear to be the gay favorite, in part because she attended the gay group's February 10 candidates forum and Washington did not.

"It was a historic moment when Jane M. Byrne stepped up to the podium at the Greater Chicago Gay and Lesbian Democratic Club's candidates forum," reported GayLife on February 17. The incumbent mayor thought it was important enough to attend a gay endorsement session—and history was being made. About 400 people attended the session, which was not all rosy for the mayor. Activists did challenge the progress of the gay agenda under Byrne.

Washington and Daley both sent representatives to the forum. Hyde Park community activist Al Raby was speaking for Washington, while state Senator Dawn Clark Netsch represented Daley. All three candidates also answered the group's lengthy questionnaire on gay and AIDS issues (AIDS started to affect the community in 1981), and GayLife printed those responses.

The Greater Chicago Gay and Lesbian Democrats endorsed Byrne in the primary, but the group's bylaws required it to back candidates on the Democratic ticket only, so that meant it could not support her when she decided to run a write-in candidacy after she lost to Washington in the primary. At the group's March 22 endorsement session for the general election, Washington received 51 of the 60 votes of those attending the meeting. Alderman Cliff Kelley spoke in favor of Washington at the event.

Some gay and lesbian activists placed an ad titled "Gays and Lesbians United for Washington" in the February 10, 1983, issue of GayLife. Those signing the ad were Chris Cothran, F. Jay Deacon, Martha Fourt, Barry Friedman, Hannah Frisch, Renee Hanover, Michael Harrington, Victor Jones, David Kline, Jim Lovette, Ron Sable, Tom Stabnicki, Paul Stensland and Elaine Wessel.

In that year's primary, GayLife endorsed Byrne, but then the paper backed Washington in the general election against Bernard Epton (despite Byrne's write-in effort).

In the primary, GayLife also backed Jerry Orbach over incumbent 46th Ward Alderman Ralph Axelrod and over independent Charlotte Newfeld. In the runoff between Orbach and Newfeld, GayLife Publisher Renslow personally endorsed Orbach, while reporter Karlis Streips had a column endorsing Newfeld. GayLife, as a newspaper, backed Orbach. Flint, like GayLife, was usually supporting the Regular Democrats, and did so in this race, too.

In the 44th Ward, GayLife backed Bernie Hansen, who won.

After the elections, the Greater Chicago Gay and Lesbian Democrats, the Illinois Gay and Lesbian Task Force and the Gay and Lesbian Branch of the Democratic Socialists of America sponsored a free rally for the community to celebrate activism. The event was May 18 at Paradise, the gay disco at 2848 North Broadway.

Within weeks of Washington's election victory, the City Council Wars began. The "Vrdolyak 29" aldermen (Chicago has 50 wards) made power grabs and opposed anything Washington tried to accomplish. The Greater Chicago Gay and Lesbian Democrats adopted a resolution in May calling for an end to the infighting, and GayLife, in an editorial, told the council to clean up its act.

In 1984, the Greater Chicago Gay and Lesbian Democratic Club made another round of endorsements, including Alan Cranston for U.S. president (over Walter Mondale, Gary Hart, Jesse Jackson and George McGovern), Philip Rock for U.S. senator (over Paul Simon), and Larry Bloom for Cook County state's attorney. Rock had the advantage that Jerry Williams, a Rock volunteer, was also a leader of the Gay Dems group. At that meeting the group also endorsed state Representative Jesse White for re-election, and Jim Flint represented White onstage.

Paul Simon won the primary over Rock, so most organized gays and lesbians backed him in that fall's successful general election. Among those listed on an endorsement ad for Simon in the November 1, 1984, issue of GayLife were Jim Flint, John Chester, Chris Cothran, Jack Delaney, Martha Fourt, Nancy Katz, Harley McMillen, Chuck Renslow, Ron Sable, Al Wardell, Elaine Wessel, Jerry Williams and dozens more. Simon was also backed by a wide range of progressive groups.

When Alderman Orbach ran for the 46th Ward committeeman's seat in 1984, he also received gay backing, and one large fundraiser held at the Park West included gays and straights together in historic ways. "Old-time politicians" and many other groups were represented there, reported columnist Ron Ehemann in GayLife on March 8. "But the real show—planned, booked, and emceed by the gay master of entertainment, Jim Flint—was the unexpected." Cabaret singer Nan Mason, comedian Pudgy and Baton star Chilli Pepper entertained the crowd. Despite any issues audience members might have had with gays, Chilli won over the crowd, Ehemann said: "By the end of Chilli's third number, the outstretched hands clutching dollar bills were connected to every group and ethnicity in attendance."

The special guest at the event was Cook County State's Attorney Richard M. Daley, who praised Orbach from the stage for his leadership role on gay rights. Ehemann said there was a "gasp" from parts of the room when Daley made the pro-gay comments.

Growing Pains

Renslow was an easy target for a new breed of activists pushing for passage of a long-stalled gay-rights ordinance in Chicago. By 1985, his ownership of GayLife, Man's Country bathhouse, the Gold Coast leather bar and other businesses, added together with his presidency of what was now known as the Prairie State Democratic Club, meant that some people felt he had too many conflicts of interest and too much power.

A front-page article by Tracy Baim in the March 7, 1985, issue of GayLife spoke to this conflict, in the pages of Renslow's own paper. In the next issue, Renslow had a front-cover response to the allegations, and he ran a letter that he sent to the Prairie State Democrats, announcing his resignation as board president. Jim Flint, as vice president, would take over as president.

The crux of the matter was that ACTION (A Committee To Impel Ordinances Now) was upset that the Prairie State Democrats group voted unanimously against working with ACTION because it disagreed with the new group's approach. At the March 4 ACTION meeting, attendees voiced their concern about Renslow's comments in the Reader newspaper saying gays should "take a back seat" and allow politicians to work quietly for the ordinance. Renslow was echoing the recommendations of the elected officials who spoke to ACTION in February. All four aldermen (Cliff Kelley, Martin Oberman, Bernie Hansen and Jerry Orbach) told ACTION that lobbying on the gay-rights ordinance should be "quiet."

ACTION members voted to produce their own newsletter in competition with GayLife and to start a letter-writing campaign against the paper.

Renslow defended himself in his open letter to the community. He said gay allies in the City Council counseled the community "not to visibly stir the waters and risk a backlash from the conservative right. These aldermen advised us to push quietly, behind the scenes," especially given the paralysis caused by Council Wars. Renslow also noted that the Prairie State vote had been unanimous and that his own personal views are not the same as those voted on by a membership group.

Renslow also made it clear he thought ACTION was being influenced in its direction by community activist Charlotte Newfeld, a straight woman who came close to defeating Orbach for the 46th Ward post.

In his letter to Prairie State, Renslow said: "I know I am leaving the club in the good hands of our Vice President, Jim Flint. Having worked closely with Jim … I have nothing but confidence in his dedication and energy."

By May, the Prairie State Democrats voted to join ACTION as a coalition member. Flint said at the time: "ACTION seems to be moving in the same directions as we are. There's [just] a difference in the leadership... ." GayLife reported May 23 that ACTION had also told Newfeld not to speak on its behalf, which likely influenced the Prairie State group's vote.

In May 1985, Flint was elected by the Prairie State group as its president, Jerry Williams as vice president, Donna Wood as secretary, Dave Toland as treasurer, Chuck Renslow as political action chair, Jimmy Smith as fundraising chair, Bob Bearden as public relations chair, and Jim Serritelli, Ben Allen and Ira Jones as at-large members.

A gay Republican group, CARGO (Chicago Area Republican Gay Organization), was also active by the mid-1980s.

Sidetrack bar co-owner Art Johnston was just getting involved in politics in the 1980s, after the Prairie State Democrats had formed. But he did attend one meeting, and his view was that it had a "top-down" structure, not a participatory democracy. He said he felt Flint echoed this style. He said he soon sought out different types of political groups and activism.

Electoral Politics

While Flint was president of the Prairie State Democratic Club, he also decided to take the plunge and run for office himself.

His choice was big and bold, just like a showgirl: a citywide race for one of 10 Chicago seats on the Cook County Board. The county had not yet been divided into County Board districts, but was divided only between Chicago and the rest of the county, which meant Flint had to campaign in all 50 Chicago wards to have a chance to win. But with so many running, any candidates who did not have the backing of Harold Washington or the Regular Democrats, led by Alderman Ed Vrdolyak and George Dunne, were at a disadvantage. Despite Flint's support of many Regular Democratic candidates in the past, he did not get Regular Democratic backing in the 1986 Democratic primary, and he also did not have the endorsement of Mayor Washington—though he came close.

Flint had been considering a run for office earlier. In a March 1985 interview with WMAQ-TV reporter Carol Marin, Flint casually mentioned he might run for 44th Ward alderman in 1987. The feature was about the Baton and included an interview with Flint in his dressing room.

Flint was among the first people who ran as openly gay candidates for office in Illinois, or anywhere in the country. In the 1970s, a few openly gay people had run in Chicago:

— Michael Bergeron ran to be an openly gay at-large delegate to the 1972 Democratic National Convention.

— In 1974, two radical gays tried to run for alderman, Don "Red Devil" Goldman in the 44th Ward and Nancy Davis in the 43rd Ward.

— Gary Nepon mounted a serious campaign for state representative in the North Side's 13th District in 1977.

— GayLife Publisher Grant Ford ran for 44th Ward alderman in 1979 (the campaign started in 1978).

— Michael Harrington ran for 44th Ward alderman in 1980.

— Chuck Renslow ran to become a Democratic National Convention delegate for Ted Kennedy's 1980 presidential run.

— Tim Drake, a Republican, ran to become a delegate for John B. Anderson's 1980 presidential race.

Of those who ran, only Drake was successful, and that was just as a delegate for someone who later became an independent candidate after falling behind in Republican primaries. Renslow had amassed an impressive list of supporters in his delegate bid, but he (and Kennedy) fell short; Jimmy Carter was renominated as his party's pick, and he lost to Ronald Reagan that fall. Gary Chichester and Delilah Kenney were Renslow's campaign managers, and Jim Flint and Alderman Cliff Kelley were listed among dozens of supporters in a March 3, 1980, GayLife advertisement.

In 1985, Flint decided to run to become a member of the Cook County Board of Commissioners.

Even though he received the most votes of any gay candidate up to that point in Chicago history, they were not enough for Flint to overcome the clout of candidates who were endorsed either by the Regular Democrats or by Mayor Washington's coalition. This was ironic and upsetting to Flint, since for a decade he had in fact been working to help elect Regular Democratic candidates, as well as some independents and moderate Republicans.

Flint filed more than 5,000 signatures in December 1985 to put his name on the March primary ballot. He made his initial campaign announcement during a fundraising event for the AIDS agency Chicago House. He was inspired to run after attending the National Association of Gay and Lesbian Democratic Clubs meeting in San Francisco in July 1984 and a later meeting of the executive committee in Fort Lauderdale, Florida.

At the first event, held right before the Democratic National Convention and attended by about 200 people from 46 gay and lesbian Democratic clubs, Flint was elected president of the Midwest Region for the group. At the second event, members discussed how to attract more gay and lesbian candidates for public and party office.

"We need to have gay people running for office in Chicago," Flint told GayLife.

Jim Serritelli, interviewed in 1995 by Jack Rinella, spoke about being with Flint and Renslow in San Francisco for the gay convention and the Democratic one. "Jim Flint and myself were on the [Democratic] convention floor," Serritelli said. "Through the generosity of [Cook County Treasurer] Ed Rosewell, he was able to get us passes to go on the convention floor. …

"It was really being proud to be a gay person, and just going over there at the Democratic National Convention. I mean, we were involved in all the committees, with the gay activists, and stuff through all over the United States. And they're trying to get their platform erected and stuff.

"But there's nothing like Chicago politics. It's like, they really don't know how to get things done. I'm probably talking out of turn, but it's like myself, Chuck, and Jim were all going to the backrooms, smoke-filled rooms, so to speak, we're trying to cut deals with people, 'Why don't we try and do this? Why don't we try and do this?' They're not used to that stuff. We got some of the stuff done, but, I mean, not the way we would have liked to. But it was really, really nice being at that convention."

This was a time of peak activism for Flint, and the cover of the December 5, 1985, issue of GayLife newspaper tells the story very well: There were four articles on the cover page, and Flint had a connection to all of them. His announcement for County Board was one; the main story was "Chicago comes out for Chicago House," an event Flint helped organize and emcee; U.S. Senator Paul Simon planned a meeting with gays—Flint, John Chester, Jack Delaney and others attended; and the final story was about the death of Andrea Nicole from cancer.

Nicole died in Honolulu on November 27. She was a regular cast member at Flint's Baton Show Lounge who had been Miss Gay Illinois in 1980 and Miss Gay Chicago in 1982. Flint had flown Nicole to Chicago a few weeks prior to her death so that she could be a judge for his annual Costumes on Review. At the Chicago House event, a collection was made in Nicole's memory for a fund at the agency; Flint gave $500 that evening for the cause.

Flint campaigned hard throughout all areas of the city. By this point he was very active with Operation PUSH, and he went to many campaign rallies at African-American churches on the South Side of the city. He also opened a campaign office at 814 North State Street on January 11, 1986, with an estimated 200 supporters. Among those at the kickoff were state Senators Dawn Clark Netsch and Bill Marovitz; state Representatives Ellis Levin and Woods Bowman; and Alderman Jerry Orbach. Gay Democratic and Republican activists also attended to show their support.

Flint's first campaign poster was "Gay Vote, Gay Clout, Register to Vote."

Though he was already president of Prairie State, Flint did of course also go for the group's endorsement—he and fellow County Board candidate Lilia Delgado received Prairie State's backing. Delgado was never "out" as a lesbian during that part of her career, but now that her children are grown, in 2011, she is out of the closet. Also endorsed by Prairie State in that race were Edward Mazur, Daniel O'Brien, Sid Ordower and Bobbie Steele.

There was obviously a controversy about Flint's receiving the endorsement from his own group, and some community members questioned the strength of the endorsement session since only about 25 members showed up to vote.

Prairie State also endorsed Cook County Treasurer Edward Rosewell, a somewhat closeted gay man who was supportive of gay rights, in his re-election bid. The group gave its support to several other candidates in state, county and local races as well.

Flint received other important endorsements from organizations and individuals. The then-powerful Independent Voters of Illinois–Independent Precinct Organization (IVI-IPO, also known as just IVI) backed his candidacy. Flint lobbied to get Mayor Washington's backing, but did not succeed. Delgado was among the 10 candidates Washington did endorse.

Flint said the IVI endorsement "is very important to me personally," according to the January 30, 1986, issue of GayLife, "because the IVI stands for the ideals that are at the center of this campaign—fair and open government and a voice for the previously disenfranchised."

The IVI endorsement wasn't easy, because Flint had ties to the Regular Democrats. He told the IVI group that he has "chosen in the past to approach my political work less in terms of the candidate's party affiliation and more in terms of the candidate's commitment to the people and issues I am concerned about—I consider myself to be an independent working within the Democratic Party."

GayLife noted: "He went on to describe his reasons for moving to a more independent stance in the wake of the Democratic National Committee meetings where minority caucuses were dissolved and an openly lesbian candidate from Chicago, Chris Riddiough, received no support from the Illinois delegation."

The most historic endorsement Flint received was from the Chicago Sun-Times newspaper—at a time when it was owned by Rupert Murdoch (his company purchased it in 1984). The paper said this in backing Flint on March 12: "James W. Flint, a Near North tavern-owner who has waged an aggressive, issues-oriented campaign keyed to plans for improved health care, better management of revenue, and weeding out bureaucratic layers obstructing county government."

The Sun-Times also ran a profile of Flint on February 24. The paper said some political observers consider Flint's run "as the first real test of whether an openly gay candidate can be elected." Political consultant Don Rose told the paper that previous gay losses could have been because campaigns were small and poorly funded, the opposite of Flint's effort. "Now, we'll see whether a well-financed but openly gay candidate can reach outside the gay community and find support," Rose said.

Flint's Baton Show Lounge was a favorite of Sun-Times gossip columnist Irv Kupcinet, so when he ran for office, he was mentioned as "an avowed homosexual running for Cook County Board" in the March 5 "Kup's Column." Just a mention in Kup's column was a big deal in those days.

One of Flint's campaign proposals was to avoid cuts at Cook County Hospital, which would negatively affect people with HIV/AIDS and others needing county care.

GayLife ran an editorial backing Flint in its January 30, 1986, edition—which turned out to be the paper's last issue, as it was unable to compete with the new paper in town, Windy City Times, founded in September 1985 by several former GayLife employees and writers, including Jeff McCourt (a freelancer who had been seeking to buy GayLife), Bob Bearden (sales manager), Drew Badanish (production manager) and Tracy Baim (managing editor). Flint did not get along with McCourt, and he later had issues with how McCourt covered his campaign for Cook County Board.

That January 30 issue of GayLife also carried a quarter-page ad by Citizens for Flint, with names of community members backing his race. Those listed (in the order on the ad) were IVI-IPO, Representative Woods Bowman, Representative Ellis Levin, Ron Ehemann, Larry Rolla, Victoria Cazel, Ralla Klepak, Steve Jones, Tom Stabnicki, Rose Pohl, Pearl Flint, Gary Chichester, Mary Ann Johnson, Harley McMillen, Ollie McLemore, Dorothy Ellis, Greg Moore, Linda Leslie, Dewey Herrington, Jon Weiss, Adrene "Big Red" Perom, Judy Walker, Irene Raczka, Bill Williams, David Taylor, Towanna, Dan DiLeo, Ira Jones, Chuck Renslow, JoAnn Di Cory, Janet Zimmerman, John Chester, Erin Criss, Bob Cohn, William B. Kelley, Gwen Angster, Judy Perovski, Marie J. Kuda, Robert Koral, Ralph P. Gernhardt, Barry Flynn, Joseph Loverix, Melvin Simmons, Gene Janowski, Jack Delaney, Coleman, Jenna McKeenan, Steve Wakefield, Mary B. Powers, Lennie Malina and Steven Feinstein.

The list was a cross-section of leaders and activists, Regular Democrats and independents, friends, family, employees and colleagues of Flint from organizations in which he was involved.

By March 13, Flint's campaign ads had more political support, and the ads also included a quote from Booster Newspapers reporter Greg Hinz: "If Jim Flint does well, it will signal the birth of political clout for the gay ghettos on the North Side. If he fares poorly, it's back into the closet." (This did not prove to be true, but no one had a crystal ball to know for sure.)

In addition to his IVI-IPO endorsement, Flint listed backing from Operation PUSH, NARAL (the National Abortion Rights Action League) of Illinois, Prairie State Democratic Club, Gay Chicago Magazine, the Asian Express, and the Philippine News. The politicians on his endorsement ad were state Senator Bill Marovitz, state Representatives Ellis Levin and Woods Bowman, and Aldermen Wallace Davis Jr., Ed Smith, Danny Davis, Bernie Hansen and Jerry Orbach. Aldermen Wallace Davis, Smith and Danny Davis all represented heavily African-American wards.

Representative Levin issued a statement supporting Flint, saying his "background and qualifications are among the most varied and solid I've ever examined. He knows how to get things done quickly and efficiently." The letter ran in GayLife on January 16, 1986.

Chicago's gay community has never been very easy to wrangle. While Flint managed to get support from across the city, his support was far from unanimous in the gay community. There were few high-profile leaders during that era, and Flint was an easy target for those who accused him of self-promotion and conflicts of interest. The letters section of Windy City Times had points and counterpoints from people who either supported Flint or were not impressed.

Windy City Times endorsed Flint in his race for County Board (along with Lilia Delgado, Bobbie Steele, Sid Ordower, John Fraire, Charles Bernardini and Republican Susan Catania). WCT also had an editorial about the Flint race March 13, 1986, trying to address the conflicting views. It was written by Tracy Baim, co-author of this book, and read in part:

"This week's letter titled 'Political Movements' makes an important point—we must unify in the face of outside pressures and internal differences. With the March 18 primary elections less than one week away, our gay and lesbian votes have the potential to influence several key races.

"In the most visible race for gays and lesbians, Jim Flint is running as an openly gay candidate for Cook County Board of Commissioners (Democrat from the city). While there are people in our community both strongly for and against Flint, we must unify. This is an election many local, county and state politicians will be looking at to see if the 'Gay Vote' really means something. We must show all onlookers that we have unity despite healthy disagreements. ...

"Many people outside our community would like to see Flint fail miserably, and to use that failure against us. Our votes, at least 10 percent of the population, do matter. Politicians viewing next Tuesday's election must clearly see our power. ...

"With the far-reaching impact of AIDS on gays and lesbians, each election brings an added importance. We are not merely voting for equal opportunities and non-discrimination. We are voting for our lives."

Jim Flint's Race

John Chester and Harley McMillen were co-chairs of Flint's election bid, and Jerry Williams was campaign manager. Erin Criss and Jan Berger also had leadership roles in the race, often accompanying Flint to the dozens of campaign stops a week.

Criss, who worked for local gay media, met Flint when she first moved to Chicago around 1980. He was among her clients when she sold ads for Gay Chicago and GayLife, and their friendship grew. She traveled with him to sports tournaments, hung out at his bars and then, like many of Flint's friends, joined the effort to get him elected. Criss said that she and Jerry Williams were the campaign's only paid staff.

"He was a gay man running countywide," Criss said. "People did not know what to make of Jim. He had a lot to say. No one expected him to be successful, but everyone was intrigued. We marched in the St. Patrick's Day Parade and gave out palm cards and fliers. I don't remember anything that was negative. I was surprised how well he did."

Jerry Williams first met Flint as a customer at the Baton. Williams had worked at Eddie Dugan's Bistro, which was near the Baton downtown. But he got to know Flint much better through the Greater Chicago Gay and Lesbian Democratic Club around 1982. First inspired by Jimmy Carter's 1976 race for president, Williams worked for state Senator Phil Rock in his various races, and he said he gravitated more to Regular Democratic officials in part because some of them (Jerry Orbach, Bernie Hansen and Ed Rosewell) had encouraged gays like him to organize.

"We knew we were not going to win the Cook County race," Williams said. "But we were trying to set the bar. We took the campaign seriously, we designed brochures, etc., that other candidates even copied."

Flint had a hard time getting a critical mass of gay support for a variety of reasons. First, people were afraid a loss would hurt the community, so they were angry he would run in such a difficult race. Second, Flint had alienated some in the community through his aggressive and competitive style. And third, there was still residual homophobia and transphobia in the gay community, and some people voiced concern about having a "drag queen" or owner of a female-impersonator bar in a high-profile political race. That sentiment was echoed even years later when people remembered Flint putting on his makeup for Carol Marin in that 1985 TV interview.

"Inside the gay community, I think Dan DiLeo and Ralph Paul [Gernhardt] at Gay Chicago took the campaign seriously, because they took Jim seriously, and Chuck Renslow was very supportive. I am sure he wished he could do more," Williams said. "But Jeff McCourt [then publisher of Windy City Times] basically told us, 'Oh, yeah, we'll cover the campaign, but on the entertainment page, because Jim's an entertainer.' But Jim said to me we're in this to win."

Flint agreed that it was hard to get widespread support among gays. "I have to tell you, this community, as much as I love our community, they are still very split and jealous of anyone that seems to do something different," Flint said. "A lot of them were not supportive. Mainly because I was a female impersonator at the Baton and they didn't want that image. ...

"A lot of lesbians supported me and Prairie State Dems supported me, and certain people in the bar world supported me. Some pockets of gays supported me. No one attacked me, they just didn't get involved. I don't think a lot of them voted at that time. I think we still have a problem with gays and lesbians not getting out to vote. I say, How are you going to sit and complain about anything? We have got to know our power!"

Sidetrack bar's Art Johnston said he did donate to Flint's campaign, as an important step for the community. However, he felt the campaign was more about mainstream good-government politics, not about the gay community.

But Johnston remembers some people who did not support Flint: "Most people were more self-conscious about images, with leather and female impersonators. But I am glad Jim did it. Nobody thought he had a prayer. But the things about his personality made him both a success and caused problems. Jim is willing to leap into things headfirst and alone, even though the chances of winning were next to none. He would say, 'I'm a showgirl, I've got to be onstage.' The campaign was another chance to be onstage. He took it all on and he did it. There is no question it helped raise the visibility of gay people in Chicago."

One Southwest Side campaign stop was promoted in an area newspaper with a sensational headline, something along the lines of "transsexual bar owner to speak." Williams said they were terrified to go, but nothing bad happened. At that event, Flint said those attending mainly asked questions about the Cubs and Sox rivalry, and his opinion on lights at Wrigley Field.

Williams remembers running into Mayor Washington frequently along the campaign trail (he was not up for re-election, but he was campaigning for his candidates). At one stop the last Sunday before the election, at Providence of God Church on the South Side, Washington asked Flint to come over to his car.

Williams said that Washington said, "My advisers were wrong, they said you wouldn't campaign anywhere on the South Side. I've seen you at every place I have been." After the race, Flint and Williams met with Washington in his City Hall office. He told Flint he was impressed with the campaign and would endorse him if he ran again. But Washington died the next year. "I believed Mayor Washington, and I think Jim would have been on the County Board had Harold lived," Williams said.

Kit Duffy, Mayor Washington's liaison to the gay community, said such a meeting among Flint, Williams and Washington was "very possible, and it's very possible he would have said he would back him the next time. I know Harold was pretty horrified I had endorsed Flint; he said, 'You want to explain yourself?' Harold was a doll in terms of letting me do what I wanted to do; after, he would ask for an explanation. In retrospect, I should have asked for his OK.

"I told him this is the guy who is really very much in the process of changing his whole concept on racial issues, and he would be an incredible service provider, have a service office like no other. I said, 'You want to continue with [John] Stroger running things, or you want someone to come in with roller skates twirling a flaming baton and really open it up, like a pile of dynamite, he would blow holes open in the process and silence of this board.' He probably would have endorsed Flint the next time."

Duffy said she thinks the campaign helped open Flint's eyes to the African-American community, especially once he went to Operation PUSH. Some white gays had stereotypes about blacks, especially in the Byrne-Washington battle for gay votes, Duffy said. There was a lot of racism in that campaign, and some gays played into that, though others simply believed in supporting Byrne as a pro-gay incumbent. But once Washington was elected, some gays formerly influenced by the campaign's racism came around, she said.

"One of the things Harold did, when they got to know him, he was real serious about the whole fairness issue, and people changed their minds about him and racial issues generally," Duffy said.

On March 10, 1986, Washington sent a letter addressed to the Flint campaign. It read:

"I wish to congratulate Jim Flint and his supporters on your campaign for Cook County Board. Your candidacy has reached thousands throughout the city and spoken to the issues which effect us all. Your candidacy has helped to wipe away old prejudices and to build new coalitions.

"The Flint candidacy has made a bold step toward leading lesbians and gay men onto the path of progressive, independent political action. I urge Jim Flint, his supporters, and the gay and lesbian community to continue your involvement in the political process. It is through this process that all minorities will achieve an open government which responds, with fairness, to everyone."

Flint said he had some of his biggest events and fundraisers in predominantly African-American wards. "A lot of the black ward committeemen couldn't understand how I got votes in their ward, because I was gay." Flint said. "The one thing I understood from that race—is, that's why I got all diverse [better understanding of racial diversity issues].

"I went to First Church of Love and Faith on 87th, Reverend Lucius Hall let all the candidates come in. I think that's the first time I left a church and felt God was in me. It was inspirational. I was always accepted at the churches. In the Spanish wards, too." Hall's previous affiliation had been with the Reverend Clarence Cobbs' long-running First Church of Deliverance. Cobbs' church was well-known as welcoming gay people, who composed a significant part of its congregation, and Cobbs, who was widely regarded as gay himself, was politically influential in City Hall.

Flint's run for office "opened a lot of eyes," Williams said. "It was becoming OK to be out and gay, other than on Pride Day. I think people saw it as a sign that we can do this. More people started to get involved in various levels of politics and organizations and I think it opened the door for [future successful campaigns by] Larry McKeon, Tom Chiola and Sebastian Patti, etc. It demonstrated you can be openly gay and totally involved at every level of the community.

"I don't necessarily think that a lot of these people would attribute that to Jim, but Jim definitely kicked the door down—on skates. Gary Nepon and others ran before, but I don't think they did the fundraising and footwork and actually organized and had materials as much as Jim did. We raised at least $100,000. We got more than 40,000 votes."

Williams said he admires Flint for just taking the leap on so many projects. "I know very few people like him," he said. "I don't have the cojones he has. I have always been in the background. He used to encourage me to run for something. I don't have that kind of fire in my belly. I'd hate to get beat.

"The night of the primary, I knew we weren't going to win, but it was still hard. We had a campaign party at the North End [a bar at 3733 North Halsted Street]. Jim went home to take a nap, I told him I'd meet him. I stayed at the campaign office until late; and he was livid with me, that I was not at the party. I walked into North End, and I almost burst into tears, there were a lot of people there. It was nice to see. Jim made a beeline at me, hugged me, and he was very appreciative of me during his remarks. He's a remarkable person. Everything he's done in his life."

Harley McMillen, as co-chair of Flint's race, has fond memories of their travels together. McMillen also worked as a bartender at Flint's Redoubt leather bar.

"At one time, I was working for Jim Flint and Chuck Renslow at the same time," McMillen said. "I think I was the only person in Chicago that had that kind of a reputation, since there was always an underlying tension between the two. I think Jim was never sure how much he could trust me since I was part of the 'Renslow Family'—although for me that never interfered with our friendship. I got along real well with his female impersonators and I was always a welcome guest backstage when I was director of the Howard Brown Memorial Clinic.

"Jim has had a real positive impact on the gay community as well as the politicians in Chicago—the old-time politicians. To go from a drag queen twirling a baton to where he is now, he has really been a successful story. I can only have good thoughts about him."

John Chester, Flint's other campaign co-chair, first met Flint when Chester was involved in Illinois Gay and Lesbian Task Force work in the 1970s. "My politics were independent liberal lakefront; where we found agreement was in the oppression that was coming to the gay and lesbian community," Chester said.

"There were certain Democratic principles—such as providing for people in need—that he and I agreed on. Jim's politics, personally, were probably more liberal; but if you wanted to own a bar in those days, or anything like that, you had to get involved in the [Democratic] Machine. There were no other choices."

Chester said that, while he did help Flint with the county campaign, Flint "was his own campaign manager; Jim is a strong-willed person." Chester said Flint was shy about doing general campaigning at public places such as train stops, but that he did go to churches and many other events. "He put time in on it, and I was able to work him through a stump speech—he was pretty good at delivering that," Chester said. "He was a little bit shy as a candidate; that might sound strange."

Chester said the campaign had a very positive political impact for the gay community. "He really presented very nicely," Chester added. "He spoke very well. The community talked a better game about involvement, before AIDS, than they almost always delivered. But Jim went out and did it."

Contrarian columnist Jon-Henri Damski, who was not a fan of Flint, wrote "A Post Mortem" about the race in the April 3, 1986, issue of Windy City Times. It read in part:

"[Flint's] 45,000 plus votes were 10 times more than any other openly gay candidate has ever received [in Chicago], but his 2,000 or so in wards like the 44th were about the same as novice Gary Nepon's totals eight years ago. But it is not realistic to compare a three-person race with bullet votes with a 30-person citywide race in a vote-for-10 situation. …

"Flint ran a credible, professionally staffed campaign. [But his] campaign never caught fire or came alive inside his core constituency of lesbians and gays. He railed and huffed and puffed at us, but only got a limp response from us. Flint is too [scarred] and battered from so many intramural wars inside our community: from the Knight club and Tavern Guild to softball and Gay Dems."

Flint's sometime attorney Ralla Klepak said she believes Flint was just "ahead of his time" in running for County Board.

Rainbow Coalition

Flint and Jerry Williams also went to meetings in heavily African-American areas of the city, including visits to Operation PUSH. "We would go to Operation PUSH, on the South Side, and [they] endorsed him for Cook County Board—we went to the founding convention for the Rainbow Coalition," Williams said.

In 1984, the Reverend Jesse Jackson took a public, pro-gay position at the Democratic National Convention, so the Prairie State Dems sent a letter of thanks to him in 1985. Eventually, out of that campaign, Jackson founded the Rainbow Coalition, to bring racial minorities, poor people, farmers, working moms, union members, gays and lesbians and others together. Flint and Williams attended the founding of that group in Washington, D.C. They were gay representatives.

"Unfortunately, our involvement with it crumbled because, for all of the talk of inclusion that they have, the only thing they wanted from us was Jim's money and my work," Jerry Williams told interviewer Jack Rinella in 1995. "We went to the national board meeting— Jim was on the original board of the Rainbow Coalition—and we went to their board meeting and were treated so rudely and actually held in an elevator as a security risk by some of Jackson's bodyguards, and I mean, we were on a first-name basis with Jesse Jackson.

"We were treated so rudely, and Reverend [Willie] Barrow was very, very shocked when she heard and saw what was happening to us, and Jim told her, you know, 'We don't accept treatment like this and you cannot call yourselves a Rainbow Coalition when you're excluding colors. If you wanted an all-black board you should have asked for an all-black board. If you didn't want gay inclusion you should have said you don't want gay inclusion. Because why are we working to be treated like this?' And [we] told her it was bullshit, and we walked out of the meeting."

Even though the Reverend Willie Barrow rescued them, Flint never forgave Jackson for the bad treatment—despite the fact that Jackson did not authorize it. "Jesse was leaving messages all over D.C. for him, and Jim didn't call him back," Williams said.

Lilia Delgado's Race

More than two decades after her near-miss to become elected as a Cook County commissioner, Delgado spoke openly for this book, to set the record straight about her campaign. At the time, she felt she had to be closeted because of her two daughters and an ex-husband. But unlike some closeted politicians who run to the right and act homophobic, Delgado ran a very pro-gay race. She received the backing of Mayor Washington and many major community leaders and groups. It was an open secret that Delgado was a lesbian, but the gay media respected her privacy because she was not hypocritical about the topic.

Delgado was a key player in the 1980s battles for cable and telecommunications rights in Chicago, and she was seen as a strong consumer advocate on those issues. As with Flint, the County Board race was both her first and last campaign for public office. She got a very bad taste of the nastiness and even risks of violence that faced anyone who did not play the political game.

"Harold Washington asked me to run," Delgado said. "He wanted to see what an independent Latina woman could do; I was the first to run countywide." The other Latina woman in the race, Irene Hernandez, tried to get Delgado kicked off the ballot, even though Delgado's father had helped raise money for her in previous campaigns. "I learned a lot in that campaign. Certainly a lot of political leaders are not what they appear to be."

Some independent Latino leaders did back Delgado, but she was quite disappointed in those who followed the Regular Democrats in lockstep.

Delgado said that Mayor Washington knew she was a lesbian, and he did not have an issue with it—though he was surprised, since he had his own stereotypes about what a lesbian was. But she felt she could not be out, because she had recently emerged from a difficult divorce and worried about her daughters Jessica, 5, and Liza, 10.

Her daughters are grown now and fully accepting of their mother. And now Delgado is a grandmother of three. "When Flint met the girls, he fell in love with little Liza. She loved the ballet and Shakespeare, so she met Flint and they clicked," Delgado said.

Flint remembered how Delgado always was nice to him and gave a hug during the campaign, and he thanked her at the time for that. Most of the opposition treated people in very unfriendly ways. Her daughters had a positive impression of Flint, and in later years Delgado would socialize with Flint—and her daughters both held their bachelorette parties at Flint's Baton Show Lounge.

Delgado said Flint raised a lot of money for a lot of politicians, and he felt that would be reciprocated—but it was not. "He was very disappointed," she said. "They would be rude and ignore him. But I never did that to anyone. Jim and I remained friends."

After Delgado lost, she was appointed by Washington as one of four members of the Chicago Cable Commission—she was the only non-attorney on the commission, and she fought hard to make sure that cable television franchise deals were the best for the citizens, including support for public-access channels. She also helped make sure that both women and minority requirements were included in the contracts. Delgado served eight years on the commission, under Washington, under Mayor Eugene Sawyer and briefly under Mayor Richard M. Daley.

The battle for cable rights in Chicago is a long and complicated one, and gays and lesbians were at the forefront of the activism that started during the Byrne administration and carried on for many years. For example, gays and lesbians were a key coalition partner in the Citizens' Cable Caucus of the early 1980s. Network Lambda was formed in 1981 to push for a gay-inclusive agenda for the pending wiring of the city for cable. What citizens wanted was to make sure minorities, women, and gays and lesbians were given opportunities to both receive and create their own original programming.

According to a GayLife editorial of October 20, 1981, the Illinois Gay and Lesbian Task Force and GayLife were also pushing for a ban on anti-gay job discrimination by cable companies; inclusion of gays and lesbians on city committees and boards that dealt with cable; and no official censorship of programs beyond existing censorship laws.

Several months later, on February 12, 1982, GayLife reported that a leading cable ordinance sponsor, Alderman Ed Vrdolyak, agreed to drop the controversial word "indecent" as a category of shows that could not air in the city. Activist William B. Kelley met with Vrdolyak to lobby for the change. Gays were worried the term was too vague and could be used against pro-gay shows.

Earlier, gay concerns about cable inclusiveness had found support in a group called the Citizens Committee on the Media, which along with the IGLTF had origins in the Alliance to End Repression. Active at the time in the IGLTF, Kelley became involved in the CCOM as an advocate for gay concerns and helped to lobby for a gay-inclusive cable enabling ordinance.

When the ordinance-prescribed Chicago Access Corporation was formed in 1983 to administer the city's newly authorized public-access cable channels, Mayor Jane Byrne named Kelley as one of its incorporators. He served as a CAC officer and board member until 1990 and received the group's Spirit of Access award in 1988. Delgado was also a CAC board member. The CAC's public-access system is now known as Chicago Access Network Television, or CAN TV.

The County Board Results

There were 30 people running for the 10 primary slots in the 1986 County Board race. No matter how hard Flint campaigned, he was hindered by a lack of Regular or independent Democratic organizational support. He received 46,128 votes, or 1.48 percent of the votes cast. While it was a low percentage, it was still the largest number of votes an openly gay candidate had ever received up to that point in the state's history, and no candidate among the many running received even as many as 10 percent of the votes.

Delgado placed 11th in the tight field, despite her backing from Washington. She had 122,794 votes, or 3.94 percent. Incumbent Board President George Dunne had the most votes, 270,744, or 8.68 percent of the votes.

In the general election, the Democrats all won: Dunne, Jerry "Iceman" Butler, John Stroger, Samuel Vaughn, Charles Bernardini, Bobbie Steele, Irene Hernandez, Frank Damato, Marco Domico and Rose-Marie Love. (Of those, Steele, Stroger, Vaughn, Butler, Bernardini and Dunne were backed by Mayor Washington in the primary. IVI backed Bernardini, Stroger, Ordower, Delgado, Flint and Steele in the primary.)

The 1986 Democratic primary for state offices saw the Democrats' divisions coming back to haunt them—this was the year that two slated party regulars were defeated in the primary by followers of anti-gay, right-wing Lyndon LaRouche Jr. In that upset, Mark Fairchild defeated George Sangmeister for lieutenant governor, and Janice Hart defeated Aurelia Pucinski for secretary of state. Neither of the LaRouchies won in the general election. In the wake of the primary-election debacle, independent voters blamed the Regular Democratic organization for selecting a slate of candidates based on loyalty versus qualifications or ability to win.

The party was in shambles for a long time. This was reflected by the mood at the May 1987 annual party dinner, which the Sun-Times described as more like a wake. The paper noted that party leader Ed Vrdolyak was not even paying attention during the speeches: "The dinner could have been a platform for a presidential prospect who has had little exposure in Illinois, Rep. Richard Gephardt of Missouri, but it went to naught. Few in the audience paid attention to Mr. Gephardt, following the lead of Mr. Vrdolyak, who held court in an aisle. He talked to gay activist Jim Flint during the congressman's speech."

Jerry Williams recalled that event. "Jim was introduced to Ed, as owner of the Baton, with gay sports teams, etc., and you could see Ed's eyes were wide open," Williams said. "Jim challenged him to have a gay softball team play the City Council. Jim was totally serious, and Ed says, 'I'll get back to you.' It never happened. I was standing next to Jim, this was the chairman of the Democratic Party. Flint went up to Jerry Orbach, and Orbach asked what he was talking to Ed about. Flint said he challenged him to a softball game. I thought Orbach was going to shit his pants," because of how bold this was for Flint to have suggested.

The Impact of Flint's Campaign

Flint's vote totals show that he did receive votes in all 50 Chicago wards. The impact of his race, given its coverage and support from mainstream media and groups, can't be overestimated, especially looking back at results historically.

What follows is the final Board of Election Commissioners report on votes for Flint by ward on March 18, 1986 (with the name of each ward's alderman who held office at the time of the vote):

Ward 1 (Fred Roti)	742
Ward 2 (Bobby Rush)	776
Ward 3 (Dorothy Tillman)	540
Ward 4 (Timothy Evans)	1,401
Ward 5 (Lawrence Bloom)	1,986
Ward 6 (Eugene Sawyer)	1,048
Ward 7 (William Beavers)	596
Ward 8 (Marian Humes)	1,036
Ward 9 (Perry Hutchinson)	845
Ward 10 (Ed Vrdolyak)	868
Ward 11 (Patrick Huels)	885
Ward 12 (Aloysius Majerczyk)	983
Ward 13 (John Madrzyk)	1,101
Ward 14 (Ed Burke)	763
Ward 15 (Frank Brady)	863
Ward 16 (Anna Langford)	617
Ward 17 (Allan Streeter)	935
Ward 18 (Robert Kellam)	1,436
Ward 19 (Michael Sheahan)	1,024

Ward 20 (Cliff Kelley)	588
Ward 21 (Niles Sherman)	1,094
Ward 22 (Frank Stemberk)	475
Ward 23 (William Krystyniak)	1,053
Ward 24 (William Henry)	653
Ward 25 (Vito Marzullo)	521
Ward 26 (Michael Nardulli)	654
Ward 27 (Wallace Davis)	669
Ward 28 (Ed Smith)	878
Ward 29 (Danny Davis)	944
Ward 30 (George Hagopian)	791
Ward 31 (Miguel Santiago)	518
Ward 32 (Terry Gabinski)	697
Ward 33 (Richard Mell)	726
Ward 34 (Wilson Frost)	859
Ward 35 (Joseph Kotlarz)	692
Ward 36 (William Banks)	862
Ward 37 (Frank Damato)	725
Ward 38 (Thomas Cullerton)	786
Ward 39 (Anthony Laurino)	710
Ward 40 (Patrick O'Connor)	622
Ward 41 (Roman Pucinski)	792
Ward 42 (Burton Natarus)	973
Ward 43 (Martin Oberman)	1,611
Ward 44 (Bernie Hansen)	2,211
Ward 45 (Gerald McLaughlin)	811
Ward 46 (Jerry Orbach)	1,424
Ward 47 (Eugene Schulter)	1,086
Ward 48 (Marion Volini)	1,095
Ward 49 (David Orr)	1,228
Ward 50 (Bernard Stone)	935

When taken individually, by ward, it's difficult to see how this race would have had an impact for gays, but Flint's vote turnout was impressive in a city where aldermanic races can be won by single or double digits. A margin of several hundred or a couple of thousand votes could influence an election, so some aldermen no doubt took note of the votes Flint had garnered across ethnic, racial and geographic boundaries.

Perhaps even more important about the timing of Flint's loss was that it came less than four months before a full vote on Chicago's gay-rights ordinance—a vote that failed, but that galvanized the Chicago gay community to come back even stronger, for Ron Sable's 44th Ward race, and for all of the allies on the City Council.

Mike McRaith, who knew Flint mostly through the Windy City Athletic Association men's basketball league, is also well aware of Flint's political background. McRaith was director of the Illinois Insurance Department for six years, and in 2011 he was appointed by President Barack Obama to be director of the Federal Insurance Office.

"I try to remind people, and I believe this very deeply, that people like Jim, who ran for office in the mid-1980s, just by running made significant progress in the world for our community," McRaith said. "I was in college through 1987, but I was aware, as a native of Evanston, Illinois, that an openly gay man was running for office in Cook County.

"At that time, someone like me, who was oblivious to my own sexuality—to have somebody openly gay putting himself into the public eye, as a candidate for office in our county, was groundbreaking. It moved our community forward, winning or losing. Having someone prominent, known in the city and the community, run was a milestone for us as a community. For me it's always important to remember all of those people who fought so hard."

Tom Chiola may be the person in the best position to estimate Flint's impact, since Chiola, in 1994, was the first openly gay man to win an elected office in Illinois. He won a Cook County Circuit Court subcircuit race along the lakefront in Chicago. "I see any pecking at the door to try to open it as being a net positive," Chiola said about Flint. "It got the issue of openly gay candidates out there."

In 1996, Sebastian Patti became the first openly gay candidate to win countywide, for a Circuit Court seat—10 years after Flint first tried to win a county race.

In 2006, exactly 20 years after Flint ran for office, Debra Shore became the first openly gay person to win a nonjudicial post countywide, by winning a seat on the board of the Metropolitan Water Reclamation District of Greater Chicago. She received 225,051 votes in the primary, and then more than 800,000 in the general election.

The 1987 Race: Sable and Washington

Less than one year after Flint lost, on February 24, 1987, the openly gay Dr. Ron Sable faced off against incumbent 44th Ward Alderman Bernie Hansen for a City Council seat and lost by 1,616 votes—Hansen won by 12,009 to 10,393, or 53.61 percent to 46.39 percent.

Sable's race was concentrated geographically but, like Flint, he did not have unanimous support from the gay community. In fact, there were bitter divides within the community over Hansen. Some considered him pro-gay, while others felt it was time for a seat at the table. In 1991, when Sable ran again against Hansen, he lost by a wider margin, 8,098 to 4,365 (64.98 percent to 35.02 percent), because Hansen had done even more to shore up his gay, and especially gay business-owner, support by then.

Sable was a key leader in the formation of a new group, the Lesbian and Gay Progressive Democratic Organization, which hoped to lead the city's gay community into a new era of progressive politics. While the group did not last long, it did spearhead an important campaign for Sable. And in October 1988, the group took out an ad in Outlines newspaper listing its choice for the Democratic presidential ticket (Michael Dukakis) and listing a range of pro-gay and gay Democratic leaders.

The Prairie State Democrats, headed by Flint, did in fact endorse Sable in the 1987 race, but it was not an easy vote. Flint personally supported Hansen because he felt Hansen had been a strong community ally. The previous year, Flint had wanted people to vote for him as the gay candidate, but in the Sable race, Flint found himself opposing the gay man running.

In its endorsement pamphlet, the Prairie State group ran photos for some candidates (Mayor Washington, Orbach in the 46th, Cliff Kelley in the 20th, and even political action chair Chuck Renslow), but not one of Sable. Its endorsement of him was also shorter in word count, seeming rather tepid compared to the straight men and women the group backed. It read: "Dr. Sable, a co-founder of the Sable/Sherer A.I.D.S. Clinic at Cook Conty [sic] Hosptial [sic] is making his first attempt for elective office. Dr. Sable, an openly gay candiate [sic], has been active in various community organizations and in the struggle for gay rights for many years. Dr. Sable has promised to bring honest and affective [sic] leadership to the 44th Ward." Meanwhile, the Orbach wording was very enthusiastic, starting with "Orbach has clearly served the Lesbian and Gay Community since he was elected Alderman in 1983." Kelley's wording said, "His record is solid."

The Prairie State pamphlet also had an address from Flint to the community. It read in part: "I am proud to present to the community the endorsements of the Prairie State Democratic Club. These endorsements demonstrate the truely [sic] independent and progressive nature of PSDC. As a group we have endorsed the re-election of Mayor Washington, as well as, endorseing [sic] aldermanic candidates from both sides of the splintered City Council. We have demonstrated, once again, that it is important for us as a community to reach beyond our own unique diversities to build and nurture coalitions with other communities while continuing our support of those who have supported us."

In that same election, Jane Byrne tried to unseat Harold Washington, but despite another bitter battle, she lost again. The Prairie State Democrats endorsed Washington this time around. This appears to be the last election in which Prairie State endorsed candidates.

Washington had done a lot to win over the gay vote in his second election, including the issuance of Gay Pride Day and Gay Pride Week proclamations starting in 1983, attending the 1984 post-Pride Parade rally in Lincoln Park, and pushing for the gay-rights ordinance. He also appointed the first liaison between the city and the gay community, Kit Duffy, and started a Committee on Gay and Lesbian Issues. In May 1985, Washington received a rousing reception when he attended the first annual Glynn Sudbery Awards, an event sponsored by the IVI-IPO's gay and lesbian caucus and named for the IVI-IPO's first gay chief executive, who died of AIDS in 1984.

Byrne, meanwhile, did not come out strongly against the Roman Catholic archdiocese when it lobbied against the gay bill in 1986, and this lost her some gay support. An August 7, 1986, Chicago Sun-Times article by Basil Talbott Jr. discussed the situation of Flint, Byrne and the gays:

"So far, attempts to organize politically around the issue of homosexual rights have failed in Chicago. Over the last decade, three declared gays have run for public office and flopped.

"James Flint ran the best of the three campaigns but still came out 26th in a field of 28 [really 30] candidates for Democratic nomination to the Cook County Board on March 18. The City Council voted down a gay rights ordinance 30–18 last week, prompting Flint to pledge to get even this fall and spring.

"Byrne has been the most visible candidate touched by Flint's backlash. She endorsed the proposal in office, but since has distanced herself from it. When Flint lobbied to call it up, she was noncommittal.

"'My position has not changed, but I was not for calling up the ordinance,' Byrne explained Monday in an interview. 'There was no consensus of religious groups. More input is needed. It was too soon to pass it because of disagreement with the cardinal.'

"Flint, an admirer of Byrne, hinted she could lose gay support: 'Some (gays) will still favor Jane Byrne because of what she has done in the past. Others will look at the new movement, and her silence on the ordinance.' Flint noted that Mayor Washington worked for the ordinance. ...

"Between Flint and Joseph Cardinal Bernardin, Byrne went with the cardinal. She also noted, 'There has been a backlash on AIDS through fear created by more headlines.'"

Byrne did ride in the Pride Parade after she was out of office, and many gays did vote for her in her 1987 comeback bid against Washington. In the heavily gay 44th Ward, for example, she easily defeated Washington, with 12,661 votes to his 9,155—though the ward's Regular Democratic alderman, Bernie Hansen, was among Washington's City Council opponents, the "Vrdolyak 29," and had his own influence in turning out votes.

Citywide, Washington defeated Byrne 53.5 percent to 46 percent. In the April 7 general election, Washington beat Illinois Solidarity Party candidate (and former Democratic Party leader) Ed Vrdolyak 53.8 percent to 42.8 percent (Republican Donald Haider received 4.3 percent). Some questioned whether Richard M. Daley was behind the last-minute withdrawal from the race by Daley ally Tom Hynes.

The Gay-Rights Ordinance

Coinciding with all of the other political activism and campaigning of the era, the Chicago gay and lesbian community was waging a fight to pass a comprehensive city gay-rights ordinance, later known popularly by its unofficial name, the Human Rights Ordinance.

In the 1970s, Chicago gays and lesbians were working to pass gay-rights protections at city and state levels. Some were also lobbying for federal protections, but the main focus was local.

Clifford P. Kelley, the African-American alderman of the South Side's 20th Ward, was perhaps the biggest ally of city gay-rights supporters in the 1970s, having sponsored the first city gay-rights bill in 1973. He connected the dots on discrimination and was inspired to get involved on gay rights after he heard presentations on the topic at a Young Democrats meeting and at a Democratic platform hearing. The presentations were organized by a small group called Illinois Gays for Legislative Action, led by Larry Gulian and William B. Kelley.

The October 1973 issue of the Mattachine Midwest Newsletter had an article about state and local gay-rights efforts. It started by noting that Illinois had been the first state to repeal its anti-sodomy law, and "Chicago has the opportunity to be one of the first major American cities to enact official legislation forbidding discrimination against homosexuals in employment, housing, public accommodation and dress." The article explained that this would involve a series of amendments to the city's Municipal Code.

Alderman Kelley introduced those amendments, and the co-sponsors at the time were Aldermen Eugene Sawyer (6th Ward), William Cousins (8th Ward), Robert Wilinski (7th Ward—he had won a special election in 1972 and was out by 1974), Anna Langford (16th), Jimmy Washington (28th), Seymour Simon (40th), Bill Singer (43rd), Marilou Hedlund (48th) and William Shannon (17th). Alderman Leon Despres (5th) oddly co-sponsored repeal of the cross-dressing law but not the other proposed amendments. Michael Bilandic (11th), a future mayor, did not sponsor the measures. Neither did 42nd Ward Alderman Burt Natarus, later a supporter of gay rights.

It would take another 15 years for the Human Rights Ordinance to pass, under former Alderman Sawyer, who had become mayor after Harold Washington died in office.

The Illinois Gay and Lesbian Task Force, Illinois Gays for Legislative Action, and the Gay and Lesbian Coalition of Metropolitan Chicago were among the early groups lobbying for gay rights in the city and the state. But a lot of the efforts were not structured; they were person-to-person, by business owners and activists. Jim Flint and Chuck Renslow, persons connected to so many groups and businesses, were two of those who pushed both independently and through groups to pass a gay-rights law in Chicago.

The efforts in that decade were mostly stymied because Mayor Richard J. Daley controlled the City Council, and his successor, Michael Bilandic, had little interest in changing the status quo. Mayor Jane Byrne, elected in 1979, did make some progress on gay rights, including city employment nondiscrimination and proclamations for gay pride. But the furthest the gay-rights ordinance went during her four years was getting reported favorably by the City Council's Human Relations Committee.

The lack of progress was in part because of the overall negative climate on gay rights, but also because the gay community was still in its activist youth.

By 1983, when Mayor Harold Washington was first elected, more aldermen were willing to take a public stand for gay rights. Most of them were from the independent side of the City Council, Washington's "21" versus Vrdolyak's "29" members. But a few of the 29 were from areas of the city with heavy gay populations, so they crossed lines on this one issue to be supportive of gay rights. These Regular Democrats included 44th Ward Alderman Bernie Hansen and 46th Ward Alderman Jerry Orbach. Independent and pro-Washington 43rd Ward Alderman Martin Oberman was also a strong ally.

In a June 23, 1983, feature on gay political groups, GayLife noted that IGLTF co-chairperson Al Wardell expected to work with the Greater Chicago Gay and Lesbian Democratic Club on city gay rights: "Wardell expects this to be complementary rather than a competitive effort, particularly because of the power struggle going on in the Chicago City Council. As an affiliate of the Regular Democratic Organization, the gay Democratic club should have entrée to the 'Vrdolyak 29' and their allies, Wardell thinks, while the Task Force will maintain the long and productive relationship it has had with such current Washington backers on the Council as aldermen David Orr and Clifford Kelley."

The backroom maneuvering for a gay bill heated up in 1984, and activists tried to force the bill once again out of the Human Relations Committee, where it had been stalled. Gay activist Jim Serritelli told interviewer Jack Rinella in 1995 that Aldermen Hansen and Orbach tried to get a vote in October of that year, but their intent was leaked by a newspaper reporter, which caused a backlash, pushing the vote back more than a year.

According to Serritelli, the reporter saw that gay activists Jim Flint, Chuck Renslow and Bill Kelley were at the City Council meeting to witness the ordinance being brought out of the committee. Serritelli said that once the story was printed about the committee move, the bill itself was dead in the water for the next council meeting, "because once it got out into the public, it just wouldn't come out [for a full council vote]. No one would vote for it."

This is a confusing account, however, because if a committee were going to report a bill favorably at a council meeting, the normal procedure would be to take a council vote on it at the same meeting—or if two aldermen moved to "defer and publish" it, a vote would be delayed until the next meeting. But in that case it would be the deferral motion itself, not the discovery of any activists' presence, that would give opponents time to organize and most likely would have alerted any reporter to the issue.

There had also been confusion because Alderman Cliff Kelley believed the ordinance was in the same status as in 1979, when it had been reported favorably by the City Council's Human Relations Committee. But 8th Ward Alderman Marian Humes had said she believed it was not still viable and had to pass through the committee again.

The effort to push for a gay-rights ordinance continued in 1985. Burned by the public backlash the previous autumn, aldermen lobbying for the bill told gay activists at a February 1985 meeting of the new umbrella group ACTION (A Committee To Impel Ordinances Now) to do "quiet" lobbying. But ACTION was a confrontational group impatient with old-style politics. The aldermen at that meeting were Cliff Kelley, Martin Oberman, Bernie Hansen, and Jerry Orbach, plus a representative from David Orr. These were representatives from both the Washington 21 coalition and Vrdoyak's 29, and they agreed on this quiet strategy.

"You need to quietly and effectively lobby the aldermen that are in the direction of the ordinance," Hansen said, according to a February 7, 1985, GayLife report on the meeting by Tracy Baim. Alderman Kelley said that drawing in the media and calling attention to the bill could bring out anti-gays, and that having it fail could be devastating. However, Oberman was a bit more optimistic, saying that even a failed vote could have a positive outcome: It could let the community know who its true allies were.

This split in tactics reflected a true split occurring on a larger scale in the Chicago gay community. The year 1985 was a pivotal year, as numerous AIDS groups formed and thousands of new "LGBT" activists took to the streets and the boardrooms—and to the City Council.

Flint and Renslow, allied with many of the Regular Democrats, took their cue from the Regulars. They wanted that behind-the-scenes approach to secure gay rights, and they had no reason to believe that strategy would not work. Given the destructive Council Wars that were raging, there was little hope for much of Washington's agenda to pass, so if aldermen from both sides of the aisle were saying to work quietly, that seemed like a solid strategy—for the time being.

By 1986, the community was losing its patience, and with AIDS claiming even more gay men, there was a strong eagerness to push the ordinance through to a vote—no matter what the outcome. It also helped that a court ruling had mandated redrawing some ward boundary lines and that in 1986 special elections, four Vrdolyak allies had gone down to defeat, tipping the City Council balance to an even 25–25—and Washington's could thus be the tie-breaking vote if enough of his forces supported the ordinance. Some former Vrdolyak allies also switched allegiances to Washington.

Jim Flint's County Board race had just ended earlier that year, and, according to Jerry Williams, when Flint and Williams met with Washington after the defeat, Flint said Washington was impressed with his 50-ward turnout and asked what he could do for the community. The duo didn't hesitate. They said, "Get the gay-rights bill passed."

"Harold said he didn't have the kind of support needed to pass it. I said, 'Bullshit, you got elected.' He looked at us like we were crazy," Williams said. "He said, 'All right, use your skills and lobby the aldermen and get a count, just you two do this [Flint and Williams], and then work through Kit Duffy [Washington's gay liaison] and let me know what's going on. Don't tell anyone, it has to be quiet.'" This was in May or June, and indeed a "quiet" effort to pass the bill was going on behind the scenes.

"Jim and I were at City Hall almost every day," Williams said. "We had a count of around 32 for us. Then it leaked that the vote was going to happen."

Despite some hope for the gay bill that year, once word was out about a vote, a big obstacle to the efforts emerged when Cardinal Joseph Bernardin, the Roman Catholic archbishop, inserted himself and the church into the ordinance debate.

"Up until June 25, lobbying for passage of the bill was done primarily behind closed doors," Windy City Times reported at the time. "Bar owner and former Cook County Board candidate Jim Flint joined with several other community members and Mayor's liaison Kit Duffy in working for aldermanic support.

"But June 25, when it appeared there could be enough votes [to pass that day], Ald. Cliff Kelley (20th), who introduced the legislation in 1973, failed to give enough advance warning about the vote to the other aldermen. After June 25, the bill was out in the open, and Mayor Harold Washington called for its passage during his speech at the 17th Annual Gay and Lesbian Pride Rally and to the local media. What followed was a strong anti-bill campaign by some religious leaders … ending with the diocesan statement July 8" in opposition to the gay-rights ordinance.

On July 9, 1986, hundreds of activists descended on City Hall for a proposed vote, only to find that Bernardin had given a letter to all 50 aldermen stating opposition to the bill as worded—it did not have an exemption for religious institutions. There were also hundreds of protesters outside City Hall who were opposed to the proposed law and calling for a quarantine of people with AIDS.

Flint asked Duffy for a place to make calls to the archdiocese, since he said he had "dirt" on some of the priests, so Duffy said she gave him a space to work near the mayor's office. "It is easily true that Flint and Williams were very involved for the first vote," Duffy said. "But Harold wanted to get away from this brokered system of votes, where you had to have a connection to City Hall to get things done—whether for an ordinance or to fix a pothole.

"We needed to broaden out who was working on gay rights, so we expanded the number of people involved, to include people like Jonathan Katz, Jon Simmons, etc." Katz was a University of Chicago gay activist, and Simmons was head of Joseph Holmes Dance Theatre. Simmons later worked as gay liaison for Mayor Eugene Sawyer and as director of the city's Advisory Council on Gay and Lesbian Issues under Mayor Richard M. Daley.

In covering the rancorous debate, the Chicago Tribune appeared to give credibility to rumors about Mayor Washington's own sexual orientation. Couching the wording carefully, the paper said July 10 that "the mayor's opponents have missed no opportunity to push a whispering, rumor campaign aimed more at Washington personally."

But in actual editorials, the Tribune went further in covering the rumors, saying it was its job to report rumors, even if not proved to be true. It also editorialized against the gay-rights bill, using convoluted logic that being gay was a "choice" and not an "accident of birth," apparently forgetting that religion is also a choice. In her July 17 Windy City Times editorial, Tracy Baim wrote: "We support Mayor Harold Washington on this issue—whether he is gay or not. The Tribune should be ashamed … ."

The cardinal's last-minute lobbying, despite being seen by some as a violation of church-state separation (though church officials said they viewed their goals as a matter of religious freedom), caused the bill to be delayed. Gay activists were upset, and Jim Flint was pictured in the Tribune pointing angrily at the aldermen for the delay.

Even though everyone knew a vote would go down to defeat, with Bernardin's letter influencing six or more of an original 27 expected gay-rights votes, most of the vocal gay community was unified in demanding a vote July 29. There was something the bulk of the community could finally come together around: a push to "know" who the true allies of gay rights were, so that they could work to defeat opponents in the 1987 City Council election.

"Every alderman has to come up for election," Flint told the Tribune. "We intend to make this an issue of support or nonsupport in 1987."

The July 17 Windy City Times reported on the City Council maneuvers, in an article by Tracy Baim and William Burks: "At the Council meeting, in an unprecedented aldermanic pow-wow with the gay and lesbian community, several elected officials met in a large group with rights supporters to discuss the bill changes and possible compromise amendments, hastily drawn to console the Archdiocese." A compromise was voted down, and a delay to July 29 was approved.

"We have an enemy now not only in some of these aldermen but I think the cardinal who came out so hard against us," Flint told the Tribune. "He has unified our community and our next move will be political." Flint's photo was also among those included with the Tribune's coverage, with a caption that read: "Ald. Clifford Kelley (20th), who voted for the ordinance, confers with gay activist James Flint (seated)."

As a result of the cardinal's letter, new strategies took shape.

The July 11 issue of the Tribune further elaborated on the pending City Council gay vote. Jerry Williams, Flint's campaign manager in the 1986 County Board race, was quoted as being in favor of a vote. "Even if it's going to be defeated, let's go ahead and see who goes for it. If it goes down, we can identify who is against us, then organize and go after them in the council."

In advance of the July 29 vote, Mayor Washington's gay liaison, Kit Duffy, scheduled meetings with various religious groups (Alderman Bernard Stone had been swayed against the gay bill by an Orthodox Jewish group), and Jim Bussen, national president of the gay Catholic group Dignity, joined other community activists including Bill Kelley and Larry Rolla in meeting with Bernardin and archdiocesan officials. The Reverend Michael Place, Bernardin's chief policy adviser, was among them.

Those activists were working on compromise wording, but many in the community opposed compromise language. Compromise was being sought on the extent to which churches and their affiliated institutions might be exempted from the wording of the ordinance—even though at least the churches themselves most likely would automatically be exempted under the Constitution with regard to their own religious employees. A similar legal controversy is still alive today nationwide—one example being 2011's dispute between Illinois officials and several Illinois dioceses' Catholic Charities organizations over their adoption and foster-care programs' compliance, as state contractors, with the state's ban on discriminating against civil-union couples. As it turned out, Bernardin ended the 1986 meeting after he and Bussen had a heated exchange; thus, there was no compromise with Bernardin, and he withheld support of the gay bill.

An open letter to the City Council, Washington and Bernardin was printed in the July 26 edition of Windy City Times, calling for no compromise unless any compromise language were judgment-neutral about sexual orientation. It was signed by about two dozen community activists including Chris Cothran, Marie Kuda, Achy Obejas, Armando Smith, Linda Bubon, Thomas Donelan, Florencia Carolina, Mary Mack, Nettie Sabin and Paul Stensland.

Some 150 people attended a community meeting held about two weeks before the planned vote, at Good Shepherd Parish Metropolitan Community Church, 615 West Wellington Avenue. Prearranged speakers included Kuda, Bussen, Al Wardell, Sarah Craig, Cothran, attorneys Vince Samar and Sabin, and Jim Flint. Dr. Ron Sable and attorney Renee Hanover also addressed the crowd.

Flint told the group he was upset there were not more businesspeople getting involved in the gay-rights push. He received loud applause for his proposal calling for gay- or lesbian-owned businesses to shut down for two hours during a planned candlelight vigil July 27 at the Daley Center, across from City Hall. "Tell them they take our money 365 days a year, and they can close for two hours for the rights of gay men and lesbians," Flint said.

Sidetrack co-owner Art Johnston, in one of his first political efforts, organized CTA (Chicago Transit Authority) buses to take people to the rally. Johnston opposed pushing businesses to close; instead, he asked them to sponsor the buses as a way to support the rally and get their customers downtown and back.

"I said, 'Guys, show me how getting the bars to close is going to get people there,'" Johnston said. "I said, 'It does not work that way. But it will piss off bar owners,' who to this point had been the funders of the movement.

"I suggested, 'Leave bars open, and let's get the bars to make a donation to get buses.' People would meet at the bars to get a bus, to bring them to Daley Plaza, and when the rally was over, the bus would take them back to the bars. The bar owners were happy." Seeing CTA buses surrounding the Daley Center Plaza was a nice symbolic sign for those attending the rally.

An estimated 2,000 to 3,000 people attended the July 27 rally, and some businesses did close for the event. The event was organized by Mary Mack, with sound assistance by Lee Newell and stage managing by Gary Chichester. Flint was emcee.

There were dozens of speakers, including Peter Kessler, past president of Congregation Or Chadash; Achy Obejas of the Mayor's Committee on Gay and Lesbian issues; Sister Donna Quinn, executive director of the National Coalition of American Nuns; Angela Van Patten, a board member of Legacy, a group serving older gay men and lesbians; Dr. Adrienne J. Smith of the American Psychological Association; Alderman Bernie Hansen; Art Johnston; Dr. Ron Sable; Chris Cothran; Marie J. Kuda; Rob Sherman, regional director of the American Atheists; Windy City Gay Chorus member Peter Daniels; Republican 1st Congressional District candidate Joe Faulkner; and Sister Deborah Barrett of Catholic Women for Reproductive Choice.

The Windy City Gay Chorus, Chicago Gay Men's Chorus and Artemis Singers sang. Lesbian singer Paula Walowitz performed her original song "We Are Not Alone" and led the crowd in Holly Near's "We Are a Gentle, Angry People" ("Singing for Our Lives"). Flint, Obejas, Jon Simmons, Cothran, Kit Duffy, Dewey Herrington and the Reverend Ninure Saunders joined together onstage with sign interpreter Diana Thorpe in singing "We Shall Overcome."

The gay-rights bill failed in 1986, as expected. Hundreds of activists lined up early July 29 for seats in the council chamber. The vote was 18 for, 30 against, with two aldermen absent (Ed Burke and Miguel Santiago). There was both anger and a commitment to press on, as people filed out of the chamber singing "We Shall Overcome."

Alderman Anna Langford was a crowd favorite when she declared she cast her vote for gay rights "proudly." As she left the chamber, she shouted at the anti-gay Reverend Hiram Crawford that he was a "sanctimonious bigot."

Those who backed the gay-rights bill were Aldermen Bobby Rush (2nd Ward), Dorothy Tillman (3rd), Tim Evans (4th), Larry Bloom (5th), Anna Langford (16th), Cliff Kelley (20th), Jesus Garcia (22nd), William Henry (24th), Luis Gutierrez (26th), Wallace Davis Jr. (27th), Danny Davis (29th), Percy Giles (37th), Burt Natarus (42nd), Martin Oberman (43rd), Bernie Hansen (44th), Jerry Orbach (46th), Marion K. Volini (48th), and David Orr (49th)

Those against were Fred B. Roti (1st Ward), Eugene Sawyer (6th), William Beavers (7th), Marian Humes (8th), Perry Hutchinson (9th), Ed Vrdolyak (10th), Patrick Huels (11th), Aloysius Majerczyk (12th), John S. Madrzyk (13th), Marlene Carter (15th), Allan Streeter (17th), Robert T. Kellam (18th), Michael Sheahan (19th), Niles Sherman (21st), William Krystyniak (23rd), Juan Soliz (25th), Ed Smith (28th), George Hagopian (30th), Terry Gabinski (32nd), Richard Mell (33rd), Wilson Frost (34th), Joseph Kotlarz (35th), William J.P. Banks (36th), Thomas Cullerton (38th), Anthony Laurino (39th), Patrick O'Connor (40th), Roman Pucinski (41st), Gerald McLaughlin (45th), Eugene Schulter (47th), and Bernard Stone (50th).

More than two decades later, Mell's daughter Deborah came out as a lesbian, and he even supported gay marriage and attended his daughter's wedding ceremony to her partner Christin Baker in Chicago in 2011. (The couple were legally wed in Iowa.)

Those absent were vacationing Aldermen Miguel Santiago (who was said to be avoiding the vote; he ran for mayor in 2011, losing to Rahm Emanuel) and Ed Burke, who was reported to have left the chamber for a court appearance.

The Final Push for Rights

After the gay-rights bill's 1986 defeat, Ron Sable's race for 44th Ward alderman received a boost in support, even though it was against Hansen, who voted for the bill. Some people blamed Hansen and 46th Ward Alderman Orbach for "weak" support in not convincing more of their allies to vote for the bill. Even former Mayor Byrne experienced collateral damage, as gays were angry she did not speak up against Bernardin and for the gay bill.

In the 47th Ward, Tracy Baim organized a gay group (47th for All) to pressure Alderman Schulter on his views, and other aldermen were also strongly urged to reconsider their votes during and after the 1987 aldermanic elections. Sable had lost, but not by many votes, so it showed that the gay community was nipping at the heels of power.

In the meantime, gays joined most of the city in mourning the death of Mayor Washington on November 25, 1987. His sudden death created a power vacuum, and a compromise candidate emerged in 6th Ward Alderman Eugene Sawyer. The Regular Democratic aldermen knew they could not pick one of their own to be mayor, so they selected a candidate they agreed would be easier to defeat in the 1989 special mayoral race. Alderman Tim Evans was viewed as too strong, so Sawyer was the consensus candidate.

Sawyer, who had voted against the gay bill as alderman, eventually proved to be a strong ally for the gay community, but he was not able to create a coalition as Washington had done, and Richard M. Daley won the mayoralty in 1989.

Meanwhile, gay rights had come to Chicago in 1988.

In the fall of 1988, another vote was taken on the newly minted "Human Rights Ordinance." This time, on September 14, the vote was 21–26, three more yeses than before. Aldermen Ed Burke, Dick Mell, and Patrick O'Connor had switched sides. But the longtime gay ally, Alderman Cliff Kelley, and Alderman Wallace Davis were caught in a federal prosecutorial sting in 1987 and they had now been forced out of office.

Kelley's 20th Ward replacement, Ernest Jones, did not vote for the gay bill, and neither did Davis' replacement, Sheneather Butler. But Ronald Robinson, who took Sawyer's seat once he was promoted to mayor, voted yes.

Helen Shiller, who defeated incumbent Jerry Orbach in the 46th Ward, also voted yes. Kathy Osterman, the new 48th Ward alderman, also voted yes, as did new 43rd Ward Alderman Edwin Eisendrath. Alderman Raymond Figueroa, who replaced Santiago in the 31st Ward, also voted for the ordinance. The new 8th Ward alderman, Keith Caldwell, continued the anti-gay pattern of Marian Humes (which she had established by then, even though she had been an original supporter of the bill in 1973).

Not voting this time were Victor Vrdolyak (Ed's brother, who had taken over the 10th Ward seat), William Henry and Lemuel Austin (who had replaced Wilson Frost). Henry had voted for the bill in 1986. William Shaw, the replacement for 9th Ward Alderman Hutchinson, who had voted no, was himself rabidly against the gay bill, holding a Bible above his head while he spoke against it.

There was a quick call for a new vote, and on October 15, 1988, Mayor Sawyer reintroduced a Human Rights Ordinance in the City Council.

Intense lobbying by a new wave of activists spearheaded the new efforts. Flint said he was lobbying behind the scenes with some of the Regular Democrats, but by this point there were many parallel efforts happening. The victory, coming after 15 years, happened on December 21 in a 28–17 vote that was met by loud cheers in the packed City Council chamber. The victory was the result of votes from all sides of the council.

Those voting yes were Bobby Rush (2nd Ward), Dorothy Tillman (3rd), Tim Evans (4th), Larry Bloom (5th), Ronald Robinson (6th), Keith Caldwell (8th), Patrick Huels (11th), Mark Fary (12th), Edward Burke (14th), Marlene Carter (15th), Anna Langford (16th), Jesus Garcia (22nd), William Henry (24th), Juan Soliz (25th), Luis Gutierrez (26th), Sheaneather Butler (27th), Danny Davis (29th), Ray Figueroa (31st), Percy Giles (37th), Patrick O'Connor (40th), Burt Natarus (42nd), Edwin Eisendrath (43rd), Bernie Hansen (44th), Helen Shiller (46th), Eugene Schulter (47th), Kathy Osterman (48th), David Orr (49th), and Bernard Stone (50th). Langford was so excited that Carter—who had called gays "sissies" before—had switched that she jumped up to hug her.

Those voting against were Fred Roti (1st Ward), William Beavers (7th), Robert Shaw (9th), Victor Vrdolyak (10th), John Madrzyk (13th), Allan Streeter (17th), Michael Sheahan (19th), Ernest Jones (20th), William Krystyniak (23rd), Ed Smith (28th), George Hagopian (30th), Lemuel Austin (34th), William Banks (36th), Thomas Cullerton (38th), Anthony Laurino (39th), Roman Pucinski (41st), and Patrick Levar (45th).

Joseph Kotlarz (35th) abstained, and Robert Kellam (18th), Jesse Evans (21st), Terry Gabinski (32nd) and Richard Mell (33rd) were absent. (Mell was in Hong Kong.)

The ordinance took effect February 17, 1989.

The successful vote came just two months before the February 28, 1989, special mayoral primary, so activists said this actually helped their efforts. The three major candidates for mayor—Sawyer, Daley and Tim Evans—were all asked to help lobby their allies on the City Council, and they did not disappoint. (A fourth major candidate, Alderman Larry Bloom, backed out late in the mayor's race.)

While Flint, Renslow and some others from the Prairie State Dems era of activism did continue their lobbying efforts, the main final sprint to the finish line was by the new group—Town Meeting—and its main ordinance liaisons Art Johnston, Rick Garcia, Laurie Dittman and Jon-Henri Damski, known as the "Gang of Four." Flint ally Jerry Williams had taken a job at Gay Chicago magazine, so he took a back seat to the new lobbyists, and Flint said he just quietly made calls to his allies on the City Council.

Town Meeting said Sawyer delivered the most conversions from no to yes votes. He was asked to lobby Carter, Henry, Austin, Butler, Caldwell and Beavers—only Beavers did not switch his vote. Evans was asked to convert Jesse Evans and Ed Smith, but neither was swayed. Daley was asked to pressure Huels, Fary and Kotlarz. Kotlarz abstained and Huels and Fary changed to yes. Daley claimed not to have lobbied, but Rick Garcia said he believes Daley's emissaries, Hansen and Osterman, worked on Daley's assigned targets.

In all, eight aldermen had switched their votes in just three months: Caldwell, Huels, Fary, Carter, Henry, Butler, Schulter and Stone. Unfortunately for Sawyer, he did not win re-election, despite his efforts to help the gay community.

The ordinance did have two slight changes to placate some wavering aldermen: A limited religious exemption was added, and a statement was added that said the ordinance does not advocate a particular "lifestyle or religious view." Ironically, some activists who participated in this strategy were among those who had denounced other activists' proposals for a religious exemption before the bill failed two years earlier.

In her January 1989 Outlines newspaper account of the final victory, Tracy Baim wrote that Town Meeting "was made up primarily of two groups: a core group of four activists who essentially 'quarterbacked' the Ordinance; a second, larger, flexible group of about 20 people who met on a regular basis to discuss strategy and the 'next step' to take."

The larger group included Carole Powell, Vince Samar, Vern Huls, Al Wardell, Sue Purrington, Alison Brill, Ron Sable, Peggy Baker, Chris Cothran, Larry Rolla and Donna Quinn—some of these were straight allies with political experience.

There was a large celebration the night of December 21 at the Ann Sather restaurant on Belmont Avenue.

Flint and Renslow, and their colleagues from Prairie State Dems, were not formally asked to be part of Town Meeting. No one was actually asked—the meetings were public and promoted through fliers and articles in gay media. Some of the leaders such as Flint likely expected at least some measure of respect that would have meant an invitation to be part of the new group. On the other hand, disdain or even antagonism toward earlier activists was not uncommon within Town Meeting.

But things moved fast and furiously between July 1986, when the bill lost, and the winter of 1988, when it won. During the same period, new AIDS activism and organizations were arising. Dozens of new groups, small and large, were springing up to meet the community's wide-ranging needs.

What is interesting to reflect on is that even those who said they were opposed to "closed-door meetings" and behind-the-scenes lobbying had to acknowledge, at some point, that they had to operate out of the public and media eye to get the bill passed. Looking back, Kit Duffy, Rick Garcia and Art Johnston all say there was some measure of secrecy needed—the same kind of secrecy that Flint and others used in order to protect their lobbying in prior years. The difference in 1988 was that there were just many more people, and more aggressive people, who had come forward to work on the bill, from a wider diversity of the LGB and T communities.

"It could be that the Gang of Four rejected the old guard entirely," Duffy said. "I would personally have had a more open process, but I also did not want to be 'this is how it should be.' You give people the tools and let them make the decisions. I would have made sure there were roles carved out for the Flints, Renslows, Ira Joneses, etc."

Rick Garcia had just moved to Chicago in 1986, so he did not really have either the baggage of past political work here, nor the knowledge of the big "players" in the community, though he had had contacts for several years with some Chicago political and religious activists while he was still living in St. Louis. He and Flint never got close, but Garcia said he does respect the work Flint did.

"In 1986, the tenor of the community and activism changed dramatically, politically," Garcia said. "There was not a split, just two very different paths. There wasn't necessarily a power struggle between independents and Regulars; it was just a change. His politics and mine are night and day, but what I admired about him was that here you had Regulars, and they did an excellent job in the way that politics was done in their day.

"One of the things I am very grateful for is people, those Regulars, who set a firm foundation for the Regulars to come and bring the ordinance over the finish line. They had developed relationships with a number of aldermen. Flint, as a businessman, was not shy or retiring, by any means, and really gave visibility to gays. It was not the way some of us liked to do politics, it is not the way some of us do it today. But at the time, it was pioneering."

Garcia remembers sitting in the balcony for that City Council vote in 1986, and within just a few months afterward the scene had changed: "I look back on this—here you have Jim and others who have given their body, blood and soul for the movement, and the next thing you know, where are they? Being new, maybe there was a desire on the part of some people to ice them out, but folks I worked with, we weren't very conscious about that."

Garcia also said Town Meeting discussions were often very heated and there was rarely unity among those involved. The lack of continuity in attendance from meeting to meeting meant that ultimately a few people had to take control, or nothing would get done, he said.

He also said there is "no question" that people like Flint and Renslow lobbied their connections at City Hall, each time the ordinance came up for a vote. Looking back from the perspective of 2011, Garcia said that victory in 1988 would not have happened without the foundation built by Flint, Renslow and others. "They set a very firm foundation. We were able to come in and finish," Garcia said.

The Gang of Four's Art Johnston also does not feel there was a conscious effort to shut anyone out of the ordinance battle. However, very few of the previous leaders of the effort to pass the bill were contacted to play a role in the new strategy.

"Kit Duffy and others reached out and brought in fresh faces," Johnston said. "Jim had been very successful, but when he is not running the show, you don't see him as part of a team or group. Chuck and Jim just let themselves not be a part of it. Maybe they would have expected an invite to a meeting as opposed to a group call. It's very possible they felt there was not sufficient respect, given their history."

Johnston said a lot of behind-the-scenes work did eventually have to happen—there were just too many activist cooks in the kitchen. "But the difference with these new leaders is, these people emerged and rose through the ranks, they didn't take charge because they owned a business. It was much less of a top-down thing," Johnston said.

A New Day

Flint has continued his political involvement since those heated 1980s. Richard M. Daley, once he became mayor, initially had a bumpy relationship with the gay community. He was planning to attend a 1989 meeting at the Ann Sather restaurant. Members of the community were upset with progress on gay issues and AIDS funding, and Daley knew he was walking into a hornet's nest. Flint said he was among about a dozen activists who met with Daley before the event.

"I told him, 'You're going to go and a lot of people are going to try and embarrass you, and when they do, the rest of the gay community is going to fall back in line with you.' That's exactly what happened," Flint said. In fact, the event was so charged that Daley walked out, but within a few years he was able to smooth over relations and during his time in office did much to advance gay rights in Chicago.

Flint was also a huge supporter of Carol Moseley Braun in most of her races, especially when she ran successfully for the U.S. Senate in 1992.

Flint took out personal ads for the aldermanic races in 2011, including ads for the openly gay James Cappleman in his race to fill the seat vacated by Alderman Helen Shiller in the 46th Ward.

Flint's relationship to the 46th Ward had already come a long way. He had been strongly against Helen Shiller when she ran against Flint's friend Jerry Orbach in the 1980s. But after a few years, Flint began to see Shiller as an ally. He's not sure exactly what caused that shift, but in part it was because Shiller started aligning herself with Mayor Daley on issues Flint cared about. She also helped Flint's Baton Show Lounge when a city ordinance threatened to hurt clubs with female impersonators. (See Chapter 3.) Flint even backed Shiller over Cappleman in Cappleman's first 46th Ward race, because Flint remained loyal to Shiller. But once Shiller retired, Flint felt free to endorse Cappleman.

He also strongly admires the city's first openly gay alderman, Tom Tunney in the 44th Ward—a post that Flint once briefly coveted in the 1980s. He said Tunney, who was appointed by Mayor Daley to fill the seat vacated by Bernie Hansen in 2002 and has been elected three times since, is a true example of an alderman who is about service, including sweeping the streets himself and pulling weeds when needed.

Flint received a letter from new Chicago Mayor Rahm Emanuel on the occasion of Flint's 70th birthday, July 27, 2011:

"I am delighted to offer my sincere best wishes to you on your 70th Birthday. This is a very special milestone of which you should be quite proud.

"During your lifetime, you have watched the world undergo enormous change and progress. Along the way, you have shared your knowledge, joy and wisdom with family, friends and neighbors.

"I am pleased to join your loved ones in wishing you an enjoyable birthday celebration. May you have many wonderful memories of this joyous day."

Looking back just 25 years, to a time when there were almost no openly gay or lesbian candidates, Flint is proud of how far the community has come, even if he didn't win his first and only race: "We now have two [openly gay] aldermen, three state reps and numerous judges—I tell everybody, I am always bragging about Chicago's gay and lesbian community now that we are finally getting through some of our pettiness and backing the candidates we have. Not many places have what we have, with so many elected officials and judges."

Coverage of the launch of the Greater Chicago Gay and Lesbian Democratic Club in the October 7, 1982, GayLife. The "Political Pride '82 Rally" was held October 1 at the Bismarck Hotel.

City Treasurer Cecil Partee, committeeman of the 20th Ward, spoke at the October 1, 1982, gay Democratic event
Courtesy of GayLife archives.

Gary Nepon ran unsuccessfully for state representative in 1977. He was one of the first openly gay candidates in Illinois.
Courtesy of GayLife archives.

The Reverend Troy Perry (left), founder of the Metropolitan Community Church movement, with Harley McMillen and Jim Flint onstage at the "Political Pride '82 Rally."

Thomas E. Corcoran
City Treasurer

PRAIRIE
STATE
DEMOCRATIC
CLUB
ENDORSEMENTS

1987

PRESIDENT'S ADDRESS
JIM FLINT

MAYOR WASHINGTON

Charles Renslow
Political Action Chair

Jerry Orbach
Alderman 46th Ward

Clifford Kelley
Alderman 20th Ward

Dr. Ron Sable
Alderman 44th Ward

Joseph C. Faulkner
Alderman 8th Ward

Bob Perkins
Alderman 43rd Ward

David Orr
Alderman 49th Ward

Robert Remer
Alderman 48th Ward

GLORIA CHEVERE
City Clerk

The gay Democratic group changed its name to Prairie State Democratic Club. Shown is a flier promoting its 1987 endorsements.

Jim Flint, Jim Serritelli and Chuck Renslow all attended the Democratic National Convention in San Francisco in 1984.

The Chicagoans posed for a photo with political activist and future San Francisco City Supervisor Harry Britt during the Democratic National Convention in 1984.

A gathering of Chicago political activists, early 1980s. Flint is at left, next to Steve Rosenberg. The woman is Kathy Byrne, daughter of Mayor Jane Byrne. Jerry Williams is center, followed by Jim Serritelli, Chuck Renslow and David Toland.
Photo courtesy of Chuck Renslow

Flint at a fundraiser for 46th Ward Alderman Jerry Orbach (right), mid-1980s.

Jim Flint with Mike Quigley in Quigley's unsuccessful bid to defeat Helen Shiller for 46th Ward alderman. Quigley later was elected a commissioner on the Cook County Board, and is now a U.S. congressman. From left: Steve Jones, Mark Siefker, Quigley, Flint, Doug (last name unknown) and Bill Bergfalk.
Photo by Spike King

Political activists dressing up for a cause: John Chester (left) and Jim Flint, 1980s.

From left: Alderman Ed Vrdolyak, Cook County State's Attorney Richard M. Daley and Mayor Harold Washington at a rally for the national and local Democratic Party ticket in 1984.
Photo courtesy of Chuck Renslow

Presidential candidate Walter Mondale at a Chicago rally for the national and local Democratic Party ticket in 1984.
Photo courtesy of Chuck Renslow.

Flint meets U.S. Senate candidate Paul Simon (left) in 1985.

Cook County Treasurer Edward J. Rosewell, who was closeted about his sexuality but supportive of gay rights.

The campaign launch event for Jim Flint's 1986 race for the Cook County Board. From left: John Chester, Dawn Clark Netsch and Flint.

Erin Criss at the Flint campaign launch.

Judge Michael Kelly with Flint at the campaign launch.

Jerry Williams (left) staffs the phones for the campaign kickoff.

CHICAGO'S **GayLife**

Volume 11, Issue 25   *"A DECADE OF TRADITION AND INTEGRITY"*   Thursday, December 19, 1985

CITY CONTRACT INCLUDES PROTECTION FOR GAYS

By Jennifer Kapuscik

The city has reached a tentative agreement with the American Federation of State, County, and Municipal Employees on a contract that contains clauses protecting gay men and lesbians from job discrimination, according to mayoral liaison Kit Duffy.

Duffy told GayLife that the tentative contract reached late last week would go further in protecting the rights of gay and lesbian workers than the mayor's executive order, banning discrimination on the basis of sexual orientation, because it includes specific provisions for enforcement. The contract reflects what has become traditional support by labor for gay rights in employment.

An executive order banning discrimination against gays in city employment was issued first during the Byrne administration. Duffy recalled that when she was first appointed by Mayor Harold Washington she was asked by the Illinois Gay and Lesbian Task Force to look into the status of the executive order. She discovered, upon asking, that most department heads, including the head of the personnel department, were not aware of the order.

In June of 1984, Mayor Washington reaffirmed the executive order protecting gays and lesbians in city employment. There have been no official complaints of discrimination against gays since the order first went into effect. Says Duffy, there is still a problem with harassment of gay employees, or those perceived to be gay, that should be addressed.

The Federation contract is expected to be ratified by the city council within the next few weeks. The non-discrimination clause is not expected to stall approval. The equal protection language in the new contract is not dissimilar to clauses in other city contracts.

The value of this particular protective contract, according to Duffy, is that it will apply to all clerical, semi-professional, and

See CONTRACT page 5

Gay Democrat files for County Board.

Prairie State Democratic Club president Jim Flint files petitions bearing over 5,000 signatures to assure his spot on the March primary ballot as a Democratic candidate for County commissioner. Flint is the first openly gay candidate to run for county office.   Photo by Erin Criss.

GayLife covered Flint's campaign filing in its December 19, 1985, edition.

JIM FLINT FOR COOK COUNTY BOARD PUNCH 147

Flint rides in the St. Patrick's Day Parade downtown, campaigning for office.

An advertisement in the January 30, 1986, GayLife newspaper (its last edition) for Flint's campaign.

One of the fliers for Flint's campaign.

An advertisement in the March 13, 1986, Windy City Times newspaper for Flint's campaign.

A campaign poster for Lilia Delgado, a lesbian who also ran for County Board that year (she was not out as a lesbian at the time).

Chuck Renslow had also run a campaign in 1980 to be a Democratic National Convention delegate for Senator Ted Kennedy, and Flint supported his business colleague.

The March 13, 1986, election edition of Windy City Times had the paper's endorsement of Flint (top) along with ads for Flint and Lilia Delgado.

The Independent Voters of Illinois–Independent Precinct Organization endorsement of Flint in his race for County Board.

Chicago Sun-Times

Rupert Murdoch, Chairman

Robert E. Page, President and Publisher

Frank Devine, Editor

Kenneth D. Towers, Managing Editor

R. K. Gaur, Editor of the Editorial Pages

10 for County Board

Chicago Democrats face a rare opportunity to advance good government in Tuesday's primary contests for city nominations to the Cook County Board. For the first time in decades, voters have a realistic chance of nominating 10 city-based commissioners of the Cook County Board, not all of whom were hand-picked choices of the party organization.

There are 30 candidates running at-large within the city for the 10 nominations, and the unprecedented fragmentation of party support gives rise to hopes that several independents (those not slated by the party) will be among the winners.

Our 10 choices include some supported by the party, some not; some endorsed by Mayor Washington, some not.

We drafted our recommendations with two questions uppermost: By virtue of their abilities and interest in county issues, are these the 10 most qualified of the 30 candidates? Do they represent a diversity of economic and social interests? We offer these choices confident that we were faithful to those criteria.

In the order their names will appear scattered on the ballot:

● **Jerry "Iceman" Butler**, legendary rhythm-and-blues singer, an entertainer at a stage in life where he wants to make a meaningful commitment to public service. He deserves that chance.

● **Charles Bernadini**, attorney and former elections fraud unit chief for the state's attorney, with a history in anti-machine politics that assures his ability to

act forthrightly and with independence.

● **George W. Dunne**, also seeking renomination as board president, who merits retention as arguably the county's most knowledgeable and experienced official.

● **John H. Stroger Jr.**, an attorney and veteran of 15 years on the board, who emerged as a strong voice on matters dealing with County Hospital.

● **Irene C. Hernandez**, a veteran of 12 years on the board, who helped guide renovation at Oak Forest Hospital.

● **Edward H. Mazur**, a City Colleges behavioral sciences professor whose academic background would invigorate an often stagnant board.

● **Daniel P. O'Brien**, a former legislator who became Dunne's primary antagonist on the board, who deserves retention because he is the only commissioner who comes close to balancing Dunne's political shrewdness and parliamentary guile.

● **Sidney L. "Sid" Ordower**, a former congressional aide and former leader in the Jewish Council on Urban Affairs, who would pursue creation of neighborhood health centers.

● **James W. Flint**, a Near North tavern owner who has waged an aggressive, issues-oriented campaign keyed to plans for improved health care, better management of revenue and weeding out bureaucratic layers obstructing county government.

● **Bobbie L. Steele**, an elementary school teacher who would fight for patronage reform, women's advancement and cutting fat from the sheriff's budget.

The Chicago Sun-Times endorsement of Flint's campaign.

```
     F I N A L   C U M U L A T I V E   R E P O R T
     3/24/86  21: 2:29
                    PRIMARY ELECTION
          CITY OF CHICAGO, COOK COUNTY ILLINOIS
               TUESDAY, MARCH 18, 1986
```

The final results for the 1986 race, with Flint finishing near the bottom.

COUNTY COMMISSIONERS -DEM-	COUNT	PERCENT
Jerry (Iceman) Butler	215292	6.90
Charles R. Bernardini	153272	4.91
Stephen T. Hynes	98506	3.16
Michael Patrick Hogan	95876	3.07
George W. Dunne	270744	8.68
Frank A. Damato	132098	4.24
John H. Stroger, Jr.	196824	6.31
Michael L. Nardulli	116850	3.75
Irene C. Hernandez	135026	4.33
Frank D. Stemberk	114750	3.68
Samuel G. Vaughan	161586	5.18
Marco Domico	129186	4.14
Rose-Marie Love	127975	4.10
Charles R. Bowen	51522	1.65
Edward H. Mazur	115117	3.69
Carmine Castrovillari	35479	1.14 -
Daniel P. O'Brien	86849	2.79
William J. Donohue	54288	1.74
Sidney L. (Sid) Ordower	109529	3.51
Mary Therese Dunne	79066	2.54 -
John Fraire	21341	.69 -
Joseph McAfee	46493	1.49
Robert J. Mercurio	29821	.96 -
Lilia T. Delgado	122794	3.94
CANDIDATE WITHDRAWN		
Gregory J. Wojkowski	59943	1.92
James W. Flint	46128	1.48
Ginger E. Andrews	41867	1.34 -
John T. McGuire	58117	1.86
Chester T. Stanislawski	68529	2.20
Bobbie L. Steele	143577	4.60

Windy City Times

Volume 1, Number 31   **Chicago's Gay and Lesbian Newsweekly**   May 1, 1986

Flint's vote tally cuts across ward lines

The final Chicago vote breakdown by ward for the March 18 primary shows openly gay Cook County Commissioner candidate Jim Flint, Democrat from the city, with support from each of the 50 wards. These votes numbered in the hundreds in wards headed by Ed Vrdolyak (10th) and Ed Burke (14th), and more than a thousand in the heavily-gay wards of Bernard Hansen (44th) and Jerome Orbach (46th).

Flint began his campaign for Cook County Commissioner late last year, holding fundraisers in the gay community and reaching out to people all over the city. With extensive campaigning and networking with other candidates, Flint received the support of several key organizations, in addition to the *Chicago Sun-Times.*

Flint campaigned as an openly gay candidate with an emphasis on issues important to small business owners as well as gays. He strongly emphasized the need for comprehensive AIDS funding and care, and lobbied for increased services at Cook County Hospital.

While he did not come close to being among the top 10 candidates to gain spots in the general election this fall, Flint did accumulate more than 40,000 votes from across the entire city. The following are the ward-by-ward breakdowns for Flint's race. Figures were provided last week by the City of Chicago; precinct breakdowns were not yet available. [The aldermen listed are those which held the office before the election.]

Ward 1 (Ald. Fred B. Roti)	742 votes
Ward 2 (Ald. Bobby L. Rush)	776
Ward 3 (Ald. Dorothy Tillman)	540
Ward 4 (Ald. Timothy C. Evans)	1,401
Ward 5 (Ald. Lawrence S. Bloom)	1,986
Ward 6 (Ald. Eugene Sawyer)	1,048
Ward 7 (Ald. William M. Beavers)	596
Ward 8 (Ald. Marian Humes)	1,036
Ward 9 (Ald. Perry Hutchinson)	845
Ward 10 (Ald. Edward R. Vrdolyak)	868
Ward 11 (Ald. Patrick Huels)	885
Ward 12 (Ald. Aloysius Majerczyk)	983
Ward 13 (Ald. John S. Madrzyk)	1,101
Ward 14 (Ald. Edward M. Burke)	763
Ward 15 (Ald. Frank J. Brady)	863
Ward 16 (Ald. Anna R. Langford)	617
Ward 17 (Ald. Allan Streeter)	935
Ward 18 (Ald. Robert T. Kellam)	1,436
Ward 19 (Ald. Michael Sheahan)	1,024
Ward 20 (Ald. Clifford P. Kelley)	588
Ward 21 (Ald. Niles Sherman)	1,094
Ward 22 (Ald. Frank D. Stemberk)	475
Ward 23 (Ald. Wm. F. Krystyniak)	1,053
Ward 24 (Ald. William C. Henry)	653
Ward 25 (Ald. Vito Marzullo)	521
Ward 26 (Ald. Michael Nardulli)	654
Ward 27 (Ald. Wallace Davis, Jr.)	669
Ward 28 (Ald. Ed H. Smith)	878
Ward 29 (Ald. Danny K. Davis)	944
Ward 30 (Ald. George J. Hagopian)	791
Ward 31 (Ald. Miguel A. Santiago)	518
Ward 32 (Ald. Terry M. Gabinski)	697
Ward 33 (Ald. Richard F. Mell)	726
Ward 34 (Ald. Wilson Frost)	859
Ward 35 (Ald. Joseph S. Kotlarz)	692
Ward 36 (Ald. William J.P. Banks)	862
Ward 37 (Ald. Frank A. Damato)	725
Ward 38 (Ald. Thomas Cullerton)	786
Ward 39 (Ald. Anthony C. Laurino)	710
Ward 40 (Ald. Patrick J. O'Connor)	622
Ward 41 (Ald. Roman Pucinski)	792
Ward 42 (Ald. Burton F. Natarus)	973
Ward 43 (Ald. Martin J. Oberman)	1,611
Ward 44 (Ald. Bernard J. Hansen)	2,211
Ward 45 (Ald. Gerald McLaughlin)	811
Ward 46 (Ald. Jerome M. Orbach)	1,424
Ward 47 (Ald. Eugene Schulter)	1,086
Ward 48 (Ald. Marion K. Volini)	1,095
Ward 49 (Ald. David D. Orr)	1,228
Ward 50 (Ald. Bernard L. Stone)	935

While Flint did not come close to winning, this chart, in Windy City Times of May 1, 1986, showed that he received votes from all 50 wards.

OFFICE OF THE MAYOR

CITY OF CHICAGO

HAROLD WASHINGTON
MAYOR

March 10, 1986

To the Flint Campaign:

    I wish to congratulate Jim Flint and his supporters on your campaign for Cook County Board. Your candidacy has reached thousands throughout the city and spoken to the issues which effect us all. Your candidacy has helped to wipe away old prejudices and to build new coalitions.

    The Flint candidacy has made a bold step toward leading lesbians and gay men onto the path of progressive, independent political action. I urge Jim Flint, his supporters, and the gay and lesbian community to continue your involvement in the political process. It is through this process that all minorities will achieve an open government which responds, with fairness, to everyone.

                 Sincerely,

                 Harold Washington
                 Mayor

Mayor Harold Washington did not back Flint in his race, but he did congratulate his campaign on a well-fought race.

Several thousand people attended a rally July 27, 1986, at the Daley Center to push for a vote on the city's gay-rights ordinance. From left: Sign language interpreter Diana Thorpe, Jon Simmons, Achy Obejas, Dewey Herrington, Kit Duffy, T. Chris Cothran, the Reverend Ninure Saunders and Jim Flint. The group is singing "We Shall Overcome." (Simmons, Herrington and Cothran have passed away.)
Photo by Tracy Baim.

28th Ward Alderman Ed Smith (left) held a forum on gay rights in his ward and invited, to his left, 44th Ward Alderman Bernie Hansen, Jim Flint and T. Chris Cothran to debate the issues.
Photo by Tracy Baim.

At a November 1988 City Council hearing on the gay-rights bill, from left: Laurie Dittman, Rick Garcia and Art Johnston. Behind them, to the right, is Kit Duffy.
Photo courtesy of Windy City Times archives.

16th Ward Alderman Anna Langford speaks up for the gay-rights ordinance, December 21, 1988, when it finally passed, 28–17. Seated at left is 48th Ward Alderman Kathy Osterman.
Photo by Mike Carter

Eugene Sawyer was mayor at the time the ordinance passed in 1988. He is pictured celebrating the passage with his gay liaison, Jon Simmons (left), Alderman Anna Langford and former Alderman Cliff Kelley (right), who had long championed the bill in the City Council.
Photo courtesy of Windy City Times archives

Mayor Eugene Sawyer campaigns in 1988 before the Lesbian and Gay Progressive Democratic Organization, a short-lived alternative to the Prairie State Democratic Club.

Jim Flint was in the first class of inductees into the Chicago Gay and Lesbian Hall of Fame, in 1991. He's pictured with Mayor Richard M. Daley.

14th Ward Alderman Edward Burke gives Flint a City Council certificate honoring his 60th birthday, in 2001 at the Park West.

Flint is pictured here with Mayor Richard M. Daley and other political activists and Hall of Fame inductees at the city's first Gay and Lesbian Hall of Fame ceremony, in 1991. From left: Carol A. Johnson, Ralph Paul Gernhardt (representing Gay Chicago Magazine, which was also inducted), Adrienne Smith, Jerry Williams (representing Gay Chicago), John Balester, William B. Kelley, Richard Turner, Ron Nunziato, Nancy Reiff, Dan Dever, Mayor Daley, Renee Hanover, Max Smith (back), Jon-Henri Damski, Chuck Renslow, Jim Flint, Marie J. Kuda and Art Gursch (representing Ortez Alderson, his lover who was inducted; Alderson had died in 1990 of AIDS complications).

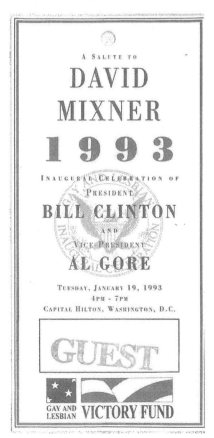

A SALUTE TO

DAVID MIXNER

1993

INAUGURAL CELEBRATION OF PRESIDENT

BILL CLINTON

AND

VICE-PRESIDENT

AL GORE

TUESDAY, JANUARY 19, 1993
4PM - 7PM
CAPITAL HILTON, WASHINGTON, D.C.

GUEST

GAY AND LESBIAN VICTORY FUND

Left: Flint attended Bill Clinton and Al Gore's 1993 inauguration events in Washington, D.C., including this special event hosted by the Gay and Lesbian Victory Fund and honoring gay activist David Mixner.

Below: Flint meets Vice President Al Gore, 1990s.

The Democratic National Convention was held in Chicago in 1996. There was a huge LGBT event at the Museum of Contemporary Art during the convention. Flint is pictured at the event, which featured special guest Tipper Gore.

Tipper Gore and Jim Flint at the gay event during the Democratic National Convention in Chicago, 1996.

Mayor Rahm Emanuel sent this letter to Flint honoring him on his 70th birthday, July 27, 2011.

OFFICE OF THE MAYOR
CITY OF CHICAGO

RAHM EMANUEL
MAYOR

July 27, 2011

Mr. James William Flint
432 North Clark Street
Suite 100
Chicago, Illinois 60654

Dear Mr. Flint:

I am delighted to offer my sincere best wishes to you on your 70th Birthday. This is a very special milestone of which you should be quite proud.

During your lifetime, you have watched the world undergo enormous change and progress. Along the way, you have shared your knowledge, joy and wisdom with family, friends and neighbors.

I am pleased to join your loved ones in wishing you an enjoyable birthday celebration. May you have many wonderful memories of this joyous day.

Sincerely,

Rahm Emanuel

Mayor

6

The Sporting Life

For a drag queen from Peoria, sports has played a surprisingly important role throughout Flint's life.

"I never played sports as a kid," Flint said. "That's why when I got involved it was a shock. Although I'm a devout Cubs fan, I watch football, and sports was always a part of my life, I was never a player." Like many young gay men, Flint stayed away from sports because he feared harassment and rejection, and because of the stereotype about gays. "Although I found out later there were a lot of gay players in the major leagues," he said.

While Flint was a drum major at Peoria Manual High School, his team won Illinois state titles. Alum Jack Brickhouse began his career by broadcasting games from that school. "We were very competitive," Flint said of his high school. "I was always like that. I wanted to be better, in anything. When you come from nothing, and you have 13 kids in your family, and are very poor, and you worry if you're going to get a toy for Christmas or whatever, you just want to be better, you want some of the things that other people had."

Ultimately, Flint overcame many stereotypes to be in the top tier of important sports figures in the LGBT community.

Flint's first connection to the burgeoning world of gay sports started in the 1970s when his various bars sponsored gay teams playing in straight leagues. This included women's and men's softball. The Lincoln Park Lagooners, the Chicago Softballers 16-inch league, and the Lesbian Community Center's softball and volleyball teams were among the first formal attempts to organize gays and lesbians into sporting and recreational activities.

As the Gay Athletic Association started to take shape in the late 1970s, Flint soon became a part of the group, sponsoring teams through his Baton, Annex and Redoubt bars. (GAA later became the Metropolitan Sports Association and is now the Chicago Metropolitan Sports Association, or CMSA.)

On Labor Day weekend in 1979, Flint drove to Milwaukee to see the third year of the North American Gay Alliance (they later added Amateur and Athletic to their name to become NAGAAA) Gay World Series. They played 12-inch softball at the event, not the traditional Chicago 16-inch style. Flint's competitive nature was engaged. He returned to Chicago interested in fielding a team to compete in the World Series.

But GAA was not ready to add 12-inch softball. Flint and an ally were allegedly forced off GAA's board, according to GAA records, although Flint said he was never actually on the board. Flint had already started a 12-inch team in the new Windy City Athletic Association. WCAA had been formed over the winter of 1979–80 by Gary Magida, Al Busker, Frank Bostic and Vince Butz. Bostic was the first commissioner of WCAA, and Flint was the second.

More than 30 years later, CMSA and WCAA (now known as the Athletic Alliance of

Chicago) are still competing on the area sports scene, even though the rivalries have lessened and CMSA is the dominant league. The new AAC has only a few sports, and no softball.

But in the 1980s and 1990s, those rivalries were intense and personal, and the competition threatened to tear apart Chicago's LGBT sports community. Once Flint left GAA, WCAA went full force toward the goal of national softball competition, first in the men's division and later in the women's.

By 1983, Chicago was even hosting the Gay Softball World Series, just four short years after Flint had watched the Los Angeles Rusty Nails team win that Milwaukee World Series match.

The love of sports has followed him from his youthful dedication to the Los Angeles Dodgers, because he likes a winner, even to his frustrated loyalty to the Chicago Cubs as a season ticket holder for many years. But he has also put his glove, ball and bat where the action is, leading a gay sports league in Chicago and following it through to the national stage.

GAA/MSA Begins

GAA/MSA preserved a historical summary of the league's early years. GAA was incorporated in Illinois on December 31, 1979. Its first 16-inch softball season was the summer of 1979, ending October 7 in its own local "World Series" championships, with the One Knighters defeating New Flight for the title. The founding GAA board members were Alex Bell, Dan DiLeo, Karen Dillion, Sam Molinaro, Gail Parzygnat, Angelo Rios, Joyce Rzeppa, Kerry Sabinske and Tyrone Sinclair. Molinaro was the president and Sinclair the treasurer. In April 1980, according to the summary, the board members were Bell, DiLeo, Jim Flint, Bill Maggio, Molinaro, Adrene "Big Red" Perom, A.J. Piraccini, Rios and Sinclair. Molinaro was once again president, with Rios vice president, Bell secretary, Piraccini treasurer and DiLeo was chairman of the board.

But by the summer of 1980, there was controversy. Flint tried to recruit new board members sympathetic to his goals of 12-inch softball in a 16-inch town, and also wanted to move games to downtown ball fields. As a result Flint and Tyrone Sinclair (who had been GAA softball commissioner in 1979) were out after losing a "vote of confidence," and Maggio resigned. The vote was actually held at the Baton Show Lounge, but Flint did not attend. Flint's membership was not revoked, but it is unlikely he renewed it after being voted off the board. The next month, the GAA board was listed as Bell, Arthur Johnston, Ed Lund, Molinaro, Perom, Piraccini, Rios, Eddie Shelton and Jody Upp.

"The MSA didn't want to do 12-inch softball," Flint said matter-of-factly. To play in national tournaments, which was Flint's goal, he wanted to have his teams in a 12-inch league.

WCAA Begins

In parallel with all of this, the Windy City Athletic Association actually was already formed, as reported in GayLife newspaper's issue of April 11, 1980. Though it started playing in 1980, the WCAA was not officially incorporated in Illinois until February 4, 1982. Its members were playing men's 12-inch softball at Margate Park (the part of Lincoln Park adjacent to Margate Terrace). Flint's Redoubt bar sponsored teams that summer in both GAA 16-inch and WCAA 12-inch softball, but he reportedly pulled his 16-inch team after the GAA board vote.

Flint said that several men asked him to get involved with WCAA in 1980. "I said I can get a team, so I did go out of my way to help them put the four teams together to do a league. After going to Milwaukee with them to see the quality of play, I liked it. Sam Molinaro wouldn't do 12-inch softball [in GAA]."

The May 16, 1980, issue of GayLife ran a letter signed by WCAA officers "Frank, Mike, and Vince" that announced WCAA's founding. Their full names were Frank Bostic, Mike Bradley and Vince Butz. The letter read in part:

"Men and women of the gay community:

"On May 6, 1980, the Windy City Athletic Association (WCAA) held its first general meeting at Carol's Speakeasy. … The purpose and intent of that meeting was to generate community interest and support for the league, and to kick-off the first softball season—not to conduct a political forum. [The letter mentions that some problems and issues were brought up, but not specifically what they were.]

"In the early Fall of 1979, shortly after Gay World Series III, and through the winter of 1979/1980, a group of people began formulating plans to organize a softball league in Chicago. This group felt that it was about time for Chicago to join the ranks of other cities and inaugurate organized competition for the gay community. The Chicago gay community is ready for organized sports—note the success of LPL, volleyball, Chicago Softballers (both organizations having entered teams in the WCAA), GAA softball, and various bowling leagues. These activities did not start big, but grew slowly over the seasons to their present degree of success and continue to expand. …

"The immediate goal of WCAA is its first successful season. It also hopes to achieve a long-range goal of national prominence for Chicago gay softball. … The home field of the WCAA is diamond no. 2, located in Lincoln Park, just north of Wilson and East of Lake Shore Drive. The WCAA will be playing on Sundays from May 18 through June and Saturdays during July and August. …" (While WCAA called this Margate Park, it was actually near Margate Park; Diamond 2 was on what is called Lawrence Field Athletic Area.)

GAA 16-inch softball had started just one year earlier and was played in Lincoln Park between Wellington and Oakdale avenues, near the Belmont Rocks. (It moved to Margate Park in 1983.) No Flint bars were listed as season sponsors in 1979, but in 1980 he had a Redoubt team in GAA. In 1981, no Flint teams were listed with GAA softball, but he again had a Redoubt team—in WCAA.

Also that summer, the Lincoln Park Lagooners hosted a national volleyball tournament, possibly the first national gay sports tournament Chicago has hosted.

WCAA was voted into NAGAAA in April 1980—which would have been the same month Flint joined GAA's board, according to GAA/MSA, and around the same time WCAA launched its 12-inch league. But Flint said he was not on GAA's board and he was also not a founder of WCAA—he came on board later and simply had teams in both GAA and WCAA that summer.

The first board of WCAA had the following officers: Commissioner Frank Bostic, Assistant Commissioner Mike Bradley, Secretary Keith March and Treasurer Vince Butz.

Bostic and Bradley attended NAGAAA meetings in April 1980 and submitted WCAA for membership. WCAA was approved 8–0 for entry, thus becoming the representative of NAGAAA's ninth member city. Flint was commissioner in 1982, with Garry Magida as commissioner in 1983 during the World Series.

The April 11, 1980, issue of GayLife confirms that WCAA did start its first 12-inch league that summer and that the league winner would compete in the Gay World Series that year. The article reports that after individuals attended the 1979 World Series, they returned to Chicago to discuss formation of a competitive 12-inch league, which resulted in the formation of WCAA after GAA declined to add 12-inch play.

The World Series

WCAA was off and running in the summer of 1980. Redoubt won the WCAA championship that August in a game against the Gold Coast Softballers, so Redoubt represented Chicago in the 1980 Gay World Series held in Los Angeles. The L.A. Griffs won that tourney, and Flint was enamored of the whole experience. He returned to Chicago and sponsored numerous WCAA softball teams over the years. In 1981, Dugan's Bistro, sponsored by Eddie Dugan's popular disco, represented WCAA in the World Series in Toronto. Dugan's team had defeated Flint's Redoubt team to win the tournament spot. As a consolation, Redoubt traveled to New York's Big Apple Invitational Tournament in September.

"The World Series had to be competitive. You could only have one team from each city," Flint said. "My first experience was in 1980 in L.A. To see more than 1,000 people cheering the last two teams was amazing, like the World Series of baseball."

Flint didn't just sponsor or coach teams; he also played. "I was forced into it," he said. "We were playing in a straight tournament, and our pitcher was having trouble with the wind, and I took over and pitched nine games that day. I got hooked. I mainly pitched in straight leagues and coached the bases in the gay leagues."

At NAGAAA's spring 1982 meeting in San Francisco, the team from host city New York decided that it was not ready to run the seventh annual World Series in 1983, and WCAA Commissioner Flint stepped up and said Chicago would be able and willing to host the event. Other WCAA reps at that April 1982 NAGAAA meeting were Assistant Commissioner Greg Cobra and Sergeant-at-Arms Joe Clarke.

Chicago was awarded the bid and hosted the 1983 Gay Softball World Series at the fields in Lincoln Park near North Avenue Beach. But Flint clashed with the host committee and did not fully participate in that series, though WCAA did. One of the WCAA teams was sponsored by Art Johnston's bar Sidetrack, which ended up winning the 1983 tournament, even though Johnston was active in the GAA group.

In its report on the series, GayLife's September 7, 1983, edition noted: "Clutch hitting, a tight defense, aggressive base running, and a super-positive attitude shaped the four-leaf clover the Chicago Sidetrack 12-inch softball team needed to outperform 15 other competitors in Gay World Series VII in Chicago." The Chicago team defeated Atlanta's Pharr Library Gators 6–4 in the finals.

Events during the week included parties at Touché, Sidetrack, Carol's Speakeasy and Paradise, plus meetings at the Best Western Lake Shore Drive Hotel and a closing banquet at the Bismarck Hotel.

"I did not even associate with that World Series," Flint said. "I helped get it and then, over some conflict with Garry Magida and Bob Strada, I said 'you guys go do it the way you want to' and then I backed off." Magida was WCAA assistant commissioner at the time, and he was tournament director for the World Series in Chicago.

WCAA and Commissioner Flint did host the NAGAAA meeting in Chicago on March 24–26, 1983, a few months prior to the tournament. Flint also used his annual birthday party on July 27, 1982, as a fundraiser for the Gay World Series. The birthday event was a progressive series of parties at Flint's bars: Annex 2, the Baton and the Redoubt.

Since its founding, NAGAAA had dealt with a conflict over rules covering gay vs. straight players. The group alternated between a 100 percent gay rule and an 80 percent gay and 20 percent straight rule (known as the 80/20 rule). Flint wanted no rules to apply, but at the very least wanted some compromise to allow heterosexuals to play, because many of his teams had been integrated over the years, having played in both gay and non-gay leagues and tournaments. The rule was so strict that even if your team was accepted under the 80/20 rule, the non-gays still could not play at the World Series. For the Chicago 1983 event, NAGAAA kept to the 100 percent gay rule, so a team that had straight players during the season would not qualify.

"I never believed in discrimination, so I was always on the other side of it," Flint said. "I thought, What better way of bringing straights to understand us than play with them, go to the bars and socialize [with] us? Phil Runions and his family, they raised more money than any gay person in the league. When it came to basketball, we couldn't have even started the league if I didn't get two of my straight friends to get two teams in the league with us."

Flint had some straight players on his softball teams and knew that those players would not be able to compete in the World Series. At one NAGAAA meeting the debate lasted more than five hours, with some teams threatening to pull out of the World Series if straights were allowed in.

"Almost every team I knew of had straights," Flint said about that era. "Even in later years some teams had eight or more." Sometimes they were the better players, but not always. "It was the opposite, in the 1970s, for women, where it was the gay women's teams that were the best and straights wanted to play on the better teams. One straight woman came to me after four years and wanted to play for my team, just to finally win."

Three decades later, there are still bitter feelings over the GAA-WCAA split. A few years after WCAA started its 12-inch league, GAA/MSA started a 12-inch division. This only heightened the competitiveness, which then infected the women's leagues when WCAA added a women's division and some MSA teams switched to WCAA.

"The bitterness came because we were a more competitive league," Flint said.

Flint was a representative to NAGAAA's national meetings for many years. The Chicago rivalries transferred to NAGAAA, and Johnston and Flint were often on opposite sides of arguments, including the time when MSA tried to get its men's and women's divisions into the Gay World Series. MSA had added men's 12-inch softball in 1986. Its women's 12-inch league had already begun by then. MSA men eventually won the right to play in NAGAAA, but it was hard-fought and controversial. When WCAA added a women's division, and MSA women were already in NAGAAA, there was a repeat battle, with MSA as the insiders trying to keep out the new women's league. Eventually, both the men's and women's divisions from GAA and WCAA were allowed into NAGAAA.

NAGAAA has changed in many ways since those early days. It added the women's division in 1985, and that division grew so large that in 2008 the open division (which is mostly men but does allow women players) and the women's division split off and now hold separate World Series in two different cities. In 1988, the men's/open division added a recreational title, and in 1992 it created A, B and C divisions. By 2002 there was even a D division.

Flint was against adding even the C division, saying that the World Series began to lose its unique claim to being the best of the best. "People move down to lower divisions just to win trophies. There are too many teams and divisions to enjoy the event," he said, adding that he sat out the tournament in 2011, when it was back in Chicago for the first time since 1983. Was it odd not to be involved? "Not at all," Flint said. "When I told Sam Coady and Suzi Arnold [two longtime WCAA athletes and leaders] I was leaving WCAA, around 2005, I had no regrets. If I didn't have Miss Continental [Flint's annual series of contests around the country; see Chapter 11] and my business, maybe it would be, but no, I don't miss it."

The rivalry between MSA and WCAA was strongest among the men and was mainly focused among some of the leadership of the leagues. There were rumors spread about Flint's stacking his teams with straight players, or bending the rules to allow late-season roster additions, having players flown in for games, and more. Flint said people just did not understand his competitive nature, and a lot of the rumors were not true. He said many gay teams had straight players, not just his, and that he followed the rules set by NAGAAA, even when gay players on his team were upset that their straight allies could not play.

"I hope it all keeps going," Flint said. "I learned more from the women than the men. The women had much more sportsmanship, played aboveboard. The women taught me a lot. The biggest disappointment was in separating the women's and men's World Series now. I lost my best friend in Boston when they were trying to vote women out. I said, 'No, we can't, we need to stay together.' They held it off but years later they did split it off, it got just too big."

Flint said Synergy, which first won the World Series women's title for MSA in 1989 in Atlanta and then switched to WCAA and won in 1990 in Pittsburgh, was "probably the greatest women's team around. They played for me for five years." Synergy attended multiple World Series, coming close even when it did not win. In 1987 it placed second in San Francisco's World Series. Player Susan Crawshaw remembered scoring the winning run on a close play at the plate in Pittsburgh and said, "Jim scooped me up in his arms, gave me a huge smooch, and carried me off the field. I bet he did that with a lot of the girls."

While Flint fought long and hard to keep MSA men out of NAGAAA's World Series, insisting on a one-league rule, he said it was because he feared it would hurt one of the leagues back home. But both MSA and WCAA retained strong men's softball leagues for years, until the 2000s when MSA's became the main gay softball league in town.

Points of View: Women's Sports Memories

Jan Berger is one of the key early leaders of sports in Chicago's LGBT communities through both GAA/MSA and WCAA.

"I met Jim on a softball field," Berger said, "although our relationship went far beyond that, politically, and other things developed as time went on. Jim's competitive, he likes to win."

Berger transferred from MSA to WCAA to start the women's softball division for Flint's league. "As softball started to become more competitive in Chicago, there was the split into two leagues, and Jim reached out to me to run the league he ran, to bring the team [Synergy] to WCAA," Berger said. So Berger left MSA, where she had been one of the founders of women's softball with Peg Grey, to be part of a league that was more competitive, especially in A-level women's softball (at the time, NAGAAA had just one division each for men and women, so it was competitive A-level ball).

An issue also arose regarding the size of the softball. With the earlier men's battle, it was 16 inches vs. 12 inches. Now the issue was that nationally the competitive women's teams were playing 11-inch softball, so Chicago was hurt by the fact that MSA at the time ·played just 12-inch. For this reason as well, Synergy left to be part of WCAA's new 11-inch women's division in 1990, and the team once again won the World Series title for Chicago.

There was a struggle to have the second league's women's teams recognized for NAGAAA competition. This hearkened back to the original battle over allowing the MSA men in for the World Series. Art Johnston and Peg Grey represented MSA, and Jim Flint and Jan Berger represented WCAA. "At times it was competitive and uncomfortable, and cyclical," Berger said. "Both [Flint and Johnston] were very professional, but there was a lot of frustration. There were hurt feelings. But I never think it got nasty personally; professionally it was nasty on both sides. But Jim is a politician and tends to be pretty pragmatic, as does Art."

After women started playing in NAGAAA, there was a battle to have only one league represented from Chicago, Berger said. "There were a lot of hurt feelings. Jim and I wanted two leagues for women repped. The reality was that Synergy was the most competitive team in Chicago and had the best chance of bringing the title to Chicago. Jim and I were well-known in NAGAAA, and we were running a national softball tourney in Chicago every Memorial Day. The politics helped to get the approval for two leagues."

In the wake of the struggle, NAGAAA agreed to have two women's reps, with Berger repping WCAA and Grey repping MSA.

"Over the years it became less contentious," Berger said. Many friends and even partners split between the leagues. "For the most part people remained friends. There was some contention for a while. A few years later the women's teams played each other, but because many of us were dating people from the other side, we got along, it was not political."

Berger said there were rumors about straight players on men's teams across the country, and it was always more of an issue for the men's teams. "It was an uncomfortable, contentious conversation," Berger said. "But some of the 'straight' men were bisexual, and some were doing everything with Jim anyway—people who were part of Jim's life every day. Whether they were bisexual was never clear. I spent a lot of time with these people. It was a jealousy issue from other teams, and it was at a time in our gay history that was unclear as to definitions of sexuality. Also, there were questions about 'do we integrate or do we segregate?'

"But we were by far not the only city that struggled with this. This was on the men's and women's sides. Synergy had a straight woman on the team, a sibling of a gay player. We had the same conversations about straight players, although it was less important with women."

Berger added that "Jim was not stacking the team. These were people who were very much in their social realm, they spent personal time with them. It was a matter of people saying they had good players. WCAA men had very good teams, so it was a mixture of jealousy. It was a time in our gay world history when we all came together, but even then, there were very few African-American players, locally or nationally."

Berger spent a lot of time at Flint's bars, in part because they sponsored the teams as well as fundraisers to send teams to the World Series. "I was very close to many of the performers. I spent an enormous amount of time there," she said. "For a number of years, Jim was one of my closest friends. I co-chaired some of the benefits—they got me onstage; what little I know about makeup today, I learned from them. I still go in there probably once a year and am welcomed by a number of the performers as their little sister. I learned that birdseed is a great substitute for breasts," for performers impersonating women.

Berger said Flint is a businessman, but still very generous, opening his businesses to benefit many causes, including WCAA and individual teams.

Berger also traveled with Flint to other cities, not just for gay sports but also to follow professional football teams. She has many good memories of those vacations, which included Disney World side trips, New Orleans, Tampa Bay, the Caribbean and other places. "One year we were carrying a microwave oven from city to city so Jim could stay on his diet," Berger recalls. "He would pick a day or two to go off diet, even though we carried that microwave all over the country."

Marcia Hill is one of Chicago's most important sports leaders. She has been part of MSA for most of its three decades, including some years as president of the group. She also played in the women's sports leagues. She saw Flint when she played in WCAA's women's basketball league, but never had much direct interaction with him. She did hear stories from Sam Molinaro, Art Johnston and other early GAA/MSA leaders.

Hill said that in 1983, the year WCAA hosted the Gay World Series, MSA started its first women's softball league. She recalled that MSA women were first allowed into NAGAAA for the World Series in 1985. Synergy won the World Series women's title in 1989 for MSA, she added, but then Flint, as sponsor, moved the team to WCAA, and it won the title for WCAA in 1990.

Hill said she remembers when WCAA tried to take over MSA's Park District fields by applying for the permits before MSA did, but the MSA people were able to stop the change. The fields MSA used by the late 1980s were actually the original fields WCAA had used. The competitiveness does still affect some of those who endured it, Hill said, noting that they still discuss it today with rancor.

Suzanne Arnold is a longtime athlete and an important early leader on the national lesbian sports scene, as a player in multiple sports including softball and basketball. She was also a leader in WCAA and the 2006 Gay Games in Chicago, and she first met Flint through NAGAAA in 1988. Arnold is also in the NAGAAA Hall of Fame as well as the Chicago Gay and Lesbian Hall of Fame.

"We called Jim 'lobby boy', because he was always lobbying behind the scenes, in the lobby of the NAGAAA hotel," Arnold said. "After I moved to Chicago in 1990, I started working with him in 1991 because he sponsored my softball team, the Baton Showgirls. Jim sponsored a ton of teams. Our team was very involved in fundraising, especially for the World Series. At one time he may have had six teams. He is very competitive. He favored his competitive teams, and we [as a recreational team] were OK with that."

Arnold helped run the WCAA softball league in 1992 and 1993. She worked closely with Flint on the board and said she had fun with the group. She was director of women's softball and basketball, and assistant commissioner of WCAA.

Arnold was in Milwaukee playing for a men's team when NAGAAA added the women's division, so she helped pave the way for women to play in the World Series. The first tournament with a women's division was in 1985 in Milwaukee, and the San Diego Spoilers won the first women's championship.

Arnold missed the most intense battle years between MSA and WCAA, but she did witness the NAGAAA battle over letting the WCAA women's division in. MSA argued against it, but WCAA was successful.

Arnold said the women's teams never had a big issue with straight players, although there was a rule of just two per team. She remembers Flint telling her he flew some players in from Detroit to play for his teams, and saying that the men's teams were more threatened than the women's teams by straight players. "Straight women were not threatening to us," Arnold said. "After the women voted to allow two straight players, I came down to the lobby in the Boston hotel, and I was verbally attacked by the open-division people [primarily men]. They attacked me for letting the women vote to allow two straight players." The men's division later changed to allow two straights as well.

Arnold said that WCAA "was one of Jim's loves. He reveled in it. He loves sports. Cubs, Bears, softball and baseball—kind of interesting that an old drag queen would love sports so much. He loved the league and making things happen. He ran it when I was there.

"We had one falling-out. Around 1993, we didn't have a women's team going to the World Series. He was livid. He wouldn't even talk to me for a long time. No one wanted to go. The Synergy team disbanded, the one competitive team wasn't going; a lot were retired, or split up, so no one wanted to go, take a week off work, spend the money. He didn't speak to me for a long time. That was part of his competitiveness. He kept saying he was going to give up softball, and he did, he totally did by the mid-2000s."

WCAA itself dropped its softball divisions in the mid-2000s and filed voluntary corporate dissolution papers on January 31, 2011. Some people associated with WCAA formed a new organization, incorporating as the Athletic Alliance of Chicago on November 26, 2010. The sports the alliance has in 2011 are beach volleyball, darts, floor hockey, volleyball and women's basketball.

"Like anything, there is some positive and negative to Jim's impact," Arnold said. "He helped NAGAAA grow." She pointed to Flint's concern that the World Series was just becoming another tournament, now that it has multiple divisions. "Jim brought some really good competitive teams and he elevated the level of playing. There was an A-division team that brought straight players, and people were sick of them; I am not sure Jim's guys ever even won [NAGAAA], but he brought competitive teams. That was important to people, that the level of play was higher. For the founders it was really important." (On the NAGAAA website, the list of men's teams that have won does not include any Baton, Annex or Redoubt winners, but Flint's teams did push up the level of play.)

"The other side of the argument is that NAGAAA is now all-inclusive and empowers people who are not as athletic," Arnold said. "But people like Jim and some of the founders, they need to be competitive. He made people think about things. He created issues by pushing the envelope. I agree with Jim that they should not have added the other lower divisions. It became so big and split the men and women, and it somewhat dilutes the effectiveness of local tournaments, because people can't afford to go to lower tournaments; and the tournaments raise money for the leagues."

Arnold said her favorite WCAA memories include the annual Follies shows at the Baton, which served as fundraisers for the league and for the teams going to the World Series. The dances were choreographed, and the Baton girls helped the lesbians with their makeup. "Jim is extremely generous. When he believes in something he really goes for it. He would even have seamstress people make costumes, to make it successful. He doesn't do anything halfway."

The nice thing about WCAA, Arnold said, was how well the men and women got along. They shared softball fields, socialized at the same sponsor bars, went to Follies shows together, and hung out together at the World Series. She said she misses that, because the LGBT community can often be so divided and cliquish.

Edith Nieves began her Chicago gay softball days in the MSA women's league in the early 1980s. She knew Flint as a sponsor of numerous women's softball and other sports teams. "When Jimmy decided to add women's softball at WCAA, I went with him," she said.

Nieves was a leader of the women's softball division for a few years and ran teams in WCAA. While with MSA, she rarely interacted with the men's teams, but she said that once she joined WCAA there was a lot more interaction between the genders, and she liked that camaraderie. This was true at the annual Follies benefits for WCAA teams, too.

"Jimmy had a real passion for the community," Nieves said. She also did not see his competitive nature as getting in the way of his support for the overall community. "There was a component that was about a need to win, but I never saw him treat teams differently, whether they won or lost."

Nieves said that opponents of some of the more winning teams would often complain about "ringers" or better players, but that came with the territory.

Flint's travel agency, River North Travel, was also an important support for the teams needing to travel to tournaments and the World Series.

Nieves pointed out that some people don't understand some of Flint's quirks, such as the fact that he never says goodbye when ending a phone conversation. "Jimmy always cracks me up; you have to know him so you are not offended. It's just the way he is. He's on the phone all day," Nieves said. "He really has a soft heart, but he does not always show it when you first meet him. He is very businesslike, but he has a great sense of humor. Jimmy's a great guy, but when it comes to all sorts of choices, he has made some good choices, some bad. But the majority of the time, Jimmy has made really good choices and has been fair for the community. But there are always two sides. Jimmy's not perfect, and he has some regrets, but he has done so much."

The relationship Nieves had with Flint was close enough that he is the godfather of her son Christopher, who turns 18 in 2012. "My son admires Jimmy," Nieves said. "And so do I."

Nancy Pribich is a leader in the Pittsburgh-area sports scene as part of the Steel City Softball League and her Pittsburgh Millhunks team. The Millhunks team never won a World Series, but it hosted the tournament. She began playing in the World Series in 1982—women can play on the "men's," otherwise known as "open," teams.

She said she enjoyed competing against Flint's teams over the years. "He is very, very, very competitive," Pribich said, laughing. "I think that when someone is very competitive, it leads into their personal life, and to his success in business."

Pribich and Flint clashed over games and rules, but she said that never got in the way of their three-decade-long friendship. They were especially at odds over the World Series and its evolving rules on including straight players. "I am adamantly against straight people playing in the Gay World Series," she said. "I have nothing at all against straight people playing with us in any other tournament; we have gay tourneys all over the U.S. all year long. But one time a year, gays should have the right to play against gays, against their own. There is nothing wrong with that.

"For every straight player you have, you have a gay person sitting on the bench again. Through most of our lives we sat on the bench; we should not have to in our own Gay World Series. Second, if you are truly straight, and truly supportive of the gay community, gay bars, functions, as a whole, then you would be more than glad to sit out for one day so gays can compete against gays. You can coach a base, keep score, root for your team, but see them compete."

Pribich said she was at "great odds with Jim on this. We fought about it all the time. But I admire that about him—he and I both liked each other, we could argue adamantly, I mean strongly on that issue and we are able to keep our 30-year friendship."

Pribich said there were rumors about many of the teams having straight players, and she thinks Flint probably did use some, but mainly because of his strong feelings about the rule. But she also said Flint's teams were never caught with any straight players, and other teams were, and that Flint was not one to break the rules. "I don't know one way or the other if he had straight players, but he was never caught, kicked off or fined," she said.

Pribich remembers the heated discussions when the NAGAAA meeting was held in Pittsburgh, at which it was debated whether MSA should join since WCAA already represented Chicago. "I'm not sure what I thought then—but I'm not sure that was the right way to go, simply because NAGAAA had territories given out to leagues. So if you let two leagues in, it is going against the rules and bylaws because then you have no need for territories."

One of the things Pribich does every year is produce the World Series Talent Show, a popular event that raises funds for an AIDS charity in the host city. She said Flint has always helped her create a great show.

Another strong memory she has of Flint is their shared love of gambling. At tournaments, when they needed a break, they would sometimes drive one or two hours just to get to a casino to gamble.

Raquel Rodriguez faxed her comments for this book. She said she had a difficult upbringing, coping with economic hardship, racial discrimination and other barriers. She found a home in softball and played for teams sponsored by the lesbian bar Augie/C.K.'s, 3726 North Broadway. That was in the 1970s, and raids on gay and lesbian bars were still happening, and some bars were still paying off police.

Rodriguez played several infielder positions in 16-inch softball. During that time, she met Jim Flint as well as his alter ego Felicia, while having drinks at the Baton. "I truly adored Felicia," Rodriguez said. "When I saw Felicia, I saw my mother." She said Flint taught her not to judge people by their genders, the color of their skins or their sexual orientations. Flint helped her to live a "self-taught" life, because as a man in drag, he showed her in living color the truth in "'I am who I am.' Knowing Jim Flint gave me the strength to be free. After all, he is my den mother, Felicia."

Sports Memories: The Men

The most visible men in Chicago's gay sports world of the 1980s were Jim Flint, Sam Molinaro and Art Johnston, co-owner of Sidetrack bar. There were certainly other prominent sports men and women, but Flint, Molinaro and Johnston were the most visible adversaries in the battle between WCAA and GAA/MSA. Molinaro preferred not to speak directly for this book, his feelings still strong about the GAA-WCAA battles. As two powerful bar owners, Flint and Johnston also sponsored multiple teams in multiple sports and leagues, not just softball, but also bowling, basketball, volleyball and more.

Sidetrack opened in 1982, a critical time in the Chicago community. Flint's bars had already been open for several years (the Baton opened in 1969), and Johnston was a relative newcomer to Chicago's scene. But the sports leagues were just starting to really take off, and the AIDS plague years were just beginning. The growth of the Chicago LGBT communities took several parallel paths in that decade (sports, politics, health activism, the arts, etc.), and Flint and Johnston always seemed to be on opposite sides of the tracks, whether it was sports, politics or activism. They did come together for some unifying demonstrations and protests, but for the most part they faced each other down in pitched battles.

"I knew Flint's name, and I knew very little about female impersonators," Johnston said, adding that he remembers Flint from Tavern Guild fundraisers and meetings that were held at the Baton. "Almost everything that happened for the benefit of the community happened out of the bars. People who worked in bars were the majority of people who were out of the closet," Johnston said.

Johnston, like Flint, attended the Gay World Series in Milwaukee in 1979, and this piqued his interest in sports. "I didn't know about gay sports stuff," he said. "I came home hoping to find a way to be involved. I read some pieces in Gay Chicago about GAA softball. I walked over to where they played; it was not even on regular fields, it was near the Belmont Rocks. I got interested. Then I was hired to work weekends at Carol's Speakeasy. I asked them about sponsoring a softball team. They used to have one but had nobody to run it. They said they would sponsor one if I could put one together. I quickly discovered that there was a titanic clash of wills between Jim Flint and a number of other folks trying to run the league. This was 1980.

"The guy who seemed to run everything was Sam Molinaro. Sam asked me to come to a meeting of the softball league at the Baton in 1980. I got there and discovered this meeting was an attempt by a number of people to change the officers on the board. That evening there was a vote of confidence and Jim Flint was voted off the board of GAA at his bar, the Baton. Jim had strong ideas about how he wanted things to go. Part of it is he wanted them all to move to Grant Park [downtown], and people didn't want to go there; it was too big and distant. Everyone in GAA played 16-inch—women played on mixed teams, there was no women's league yet. Jim was voted off GAA, and at that point Jim pulled his teams from the league."

Johnston said Flint was clearly interested in having his teams travel to tournaments, and in that case they had to be playing 12-inch ball, which GAA did not yet offer. Chicago was the founding home of 16-inch softball, so it took a lot of work to get the city behind 12-inch teams. It was a very different game, including the use of mitts and different rules, as well as going against the Chicago tradition of 16-inch.

WCAA hosted the 1983 Gay World Series in Chicago, though Johnston recalled that

Flint backed off from involvement after a disagreement with the leadership. Sidetrack had a team in WCAA, and it ended up in the World Series. It won the title, and the team started to travel to tournaments. It faced some boos from competitors who said Chicago had a bad reputation (supposedly for unsportsmanlike behavior, cheating and other problems) around the country.

Johnston was on the board of MSA when it later decided to add a 12-inch division. "We resisted a long time," Johnston said, but MSA eventually capitulated because of so many requests from players, including those disillusioned with WCAA, according to him. Once MSA joined NAGAAA, Johnston said, he had to enforce the strict no-straights rule NAGAAA had at the time, and he recalled that some of his players were upset with the situation and eventually gravitated back to WCAA.

Initially, MSA had said it would sanction 12-inch softball but not to compete at the World Series. But later its teams wanted that chance, so MSA had applied for standing with NAGAAA, to which WCAA already belonged. Flint and WCAA strongly resisted this, arguing that it would dilute both leagues. MSA's teams did want to play in other tournaments, but they often found the doors to registration closed by WCAA and Flint, Johnston said. Eventually, this meant that MSA had to go for NAGAAA qualification because it wanted to be in other tournaments that used NAGAAA status as a standard of entry.

Johnston was the MSA rep charged with convincing NAGAAA to allow a second Chicago men's league to join. "Judge Mike McHale insists I learned all my political skills from softball, in an effort to get enough cities to get us into NAGAAA," Johnston said. "It was a longtime battle. It took over a year or so." Johnston spoke to people around the country. He took Chicago columnist Jon-Henri Damski with him to the meeting to document the events, but they had a plane mixup at O'Hare International Airport and ended up being late for the cocktail party the night before the vote. Nevertheless, MSA avoided a tie, getting into NAGAAA on a 14–12 vote.

Johnston was also in the heat of the battles over straight vs. gay players. At the time, NAGAAA still had a "no straights" rule that was upsetting for some players. He pushed to have NAGAAA adopt the North American Gay Volleyball Alliance rule that allows for teammates to be questioned about a player's sexuality, but not direct questions to the player. This seemed to him a better solution, and that rule is still in place today (except now NAGAAA does allow two straight players per team).

The new rule was used in the controversial Seattle World Series that resulted in a lawsuit against NAGAAA by players who were disqualified. NAGAAA won the lawsuit in June 2011 when U.S. District Judge John Coughenour ruled in Seattle that the group could legally limit the number of non-gay players, basing his decision in part on the U.S. Supreme Court ruling allowing the Boy Scouts of America to exclude gays. So, ironically, an anti-gay victory was used to justify an anti-straight rule.

After the men's 12-inch teams were developed, women's 12-inch soon followed in MSA. It was not as hard to get the MSA women accepted in NAGAAA because NAGAAA already included an "open" or men's division. Later, when WCAA added women's softball, there was the familiar MSA-WCAA battle, but with the sides reversed: MSA trying to keep WCAA's women out of NAGAAA. But WCAA won that fight.

"I don't believe that the fights hurt softball. It probably helped, because we had 12-inch and 16-inch. There was enormous competition between Jim and Sam Molinaro and WCAA and GAA—to add teams, to add sports, to bring people in," Johnston said. "It resulted in

MSA's success—it is the largest amateur gay sports organization in the world. Some of that comes from that aggressive work that Sam did and from the competition of wanting to add a sport before WCAA did, to get a bar to sponsor a team in GAA, not WCAA.

"Some of it was not pleasant, and was not good sportsmanship, or good for the community. But that same competition didn't hurt with two strong gay choruses in Chicago [the Windy City Gay Chorus and the Chicago Gay Men's Chorus]."

Mike McHale started playing softball in the winter of 1989, at a time when MSA used to host a Winter Snowball softball tournament. He quickly became a leader in MSA, joining the board of directors and helping run men's softball. His leadership skills eventually also translated to his career, when he became one of a handful of openly gay judges in Illinois.

McHale attended NAGAAA meetings as MSA's rep after the controversial 1980s votes to allow both MSA and WCAA leagues into NAGAAA. But he was well aware of the rancor between the leagues. Most of what McHale knows is secondhand, gathered from those who lived through those difficult years, including rumors of fluid rules, umpires yanked from games, no locked rosters, and exceptional players—known as ringers—flown in for late-season matches. But he did experience the rift firsthand when WCAA sent a letter to MSA teams, to people's home addresses, on March 17, 1997. The letter was from Timothy Keeney, WCAA's director of men's softball. The letter was an attempt to encourage cross-league play in order to give top A- and B-division teams competitive play in town to better prepare for the World Series.

Based on similar arrangements in Washington, D.C., and Philadelphia, Keeney said the concept "calls for WCAA upper division teams to play MSA upper division teams. We truly believe that this could eliminate our current problems and are willing to workout [sic] the details of playing fields, umpires, scheduling, etc." The problem he referred to was that "the number of A and B division level softball players had dwindled nationwide and with our unique situation here in Chicago [meaning two leagues], our pool of upper division players is even more deluded [sic]."

McHale said MSA teams were upset with the proposal and refused the cross-division offer. At that point MSA was getting larger, and WCAA was suffering from dwindling numbers of top teams.

McHale also remembers a highly charged situation in the 1990s, when WCAA tried to get MSA's fields at Margate Park. While WCAA had been the first to use the Margate Park fields in the early 1980s, MSA had had the fields for years and knew how the system worked—the man who operated the field house would ask for a "contribution" to his daughter's dance troupe. Then a permit would be issued.

Somehow, that year WCAA had gotten to the field-house manager first and got the permits. McHale, who worked for the Cook County state's attorney, said he told the manager that some people might be interested in how he asked for a contribution before issuing permits. MSA got its permits back for the season. WCAA played at nearby Clarendon Park (bordering Lincoln Park, just west of Clarendon Avenue and just south of Wilson Avenue).

But McHale said he also understands that Flint was an early champion of gay rights in Chicago and that it probably "wasn't easy. He probably dealt with a lot of discrimination, keeping the Baton open. I respect that, and it's all a part of gay rights, moving people forward. I respect the man for sticking his neck out and being visible when it wasn't easy. I just wish his competitive sports needs had taken a different path. He was notorious. … But I'll admit,

I don't know Jim personally. I had to deal with some of the things in sports, I had to take refugees from WCAA. But I can respect him for standing up and supporting gay sports. I don't have anything against him personally."

Tom Chiola, who in 1994 became the state's first openly gay elected official when he won a judicial race in Chicago, participated in the gay sports leagues during the heated MSA-WCAA softball wars of the 1980s. He started his gay softball years with MSA's 16-inch league. He then played 12-inch for WCAA, but after concern about how competitive and serious team members were, he transferred to MSA's league, once it started 12-inch softball.

"What I remember all these years later is how highly competitive he was—Jim definitely wanted to win," Chiola said.

"WCAA seemed to be a stacked league," Chiola said. "Jim definitely found the best players, and there were always rumors about where he was getting his players. One guy I remember, the rumor was he was being flown in from Miami on weekends to play."

Chiola, who also joined the MSA board of directors, said he switched to MSA for two reasons. First, he wanted the more social aspects of softball, not the supercompetitive way WCAA was run. Second, that focus on winning often meant humiliation, as teams were often losing by the "slaughter" rule of a lopsided victory (if a team was far enough ahead at a certain point, the game would be stopped). "I just wanted to get out and have a fun day. I didn't mind winning—I liked winning, too," Chiola said. "But if we didn't win, it wasn't the be-all and end-all. We had an awful lot of fun in the 16-inch league because of the crazy rivalries between Sidetrack and Roscoe's, etc. But we always had fun. The 12-inch [WCAA] league did not have the same attitude and experience. People found their niche. So the highly competitive could go to WCAA, and win at any cost. The social ones could find MSA."

Bob Strada has known Jim Flint since about 1980. He played both for and against Flint's teams, and in some ways their relationship was strained by their own styles of play.

Strada managed Flint's Redoubt softball team, which went to the World Series in 1980 as the first Chicago team to play there. Strada came into the season too late to play for the team that year, but his partner did play for the Redoubt.

This was at a time when MSA still played only 16-inch, and WCAA played 12-inch, the standard for the World Series.

"I recall some debate about NAGAAA and MSA-WCAA," Strada said. WCAA, which was already in NAGAAA, "was trying to ask, why two associations in one city, separating talent and separating people? The thought process was, Jimmy was running the show of WCAA; as the money person and commissioner, he was Windy City. The other organization had been 16-inch, then had other sports, volleyball, bowling, but not 12-inch. And when they started 12-inch, they were not interested in the national scene of NAGAAA, they just wanted to have an in-city Sundays league, championship, etc. Eventually their players did want the national level and that caused the strife between MSA and WCAA on the national scene."

In 1983, with MSA still only offering 16-inch, Strada played for MSA's Art Johnston but on a Sidetrack team in WCAA. "Sidetrack had a team in WCAA under my managing, with Jack McGowan as a figurehead of managing," Strada said. "When I was managing Sidetrack in WCAA, the relationship was a little strained, as competitors on the field, but with civility. There were times, with Jimmy, throughout the 30-plus years I have known him, that you have your close periods, and then something might take place, nothing drastic enough to be enemies, but we're not as close."

Strada played for other Flint teams over the years. In fact, he said the board of MSA questioned him at length when he wanted to switch leagues, because its members assumed he was there to sabotage their league.

"Jimmy played an immense role in the sports scene," Strada said. "Art Johnston, Sam Molinaro and Jimmy were the three major people. If not for them in the early 1980s," sports would not have progressed as quickly as it did in Chicago's gay community.

Strada said that while Flint is a competitive person, he eventually cooled down about Strada's leaving WCAA. "It would be a competitive game when we played in a tourney outside of the city of Chicago. Emotions were high. We both wanted to beat each other. [But] when we did win the World Series in 1983 for Sidetrack, I recall Jim being in the stands in Lincoln Park, cheering for us. In 1990, when the MSA team was close to winning in Pittsburgh, he was there rooting for us," Strada said.

Sam Coady started his involvement with Chicago gay sports through the WCAA men's softball competitive team Christopher Street in 1987. He was quickly recruited by Flint to play on his Annex 3 Blues team for the 1988 WCAA season. Up until that year, the Bob Strada–managed Annex 3 Reds teams had always won in the league, but in 1988, Coady said, his Annex 3 Blues won and represented WCAA at the NAGAAA World Series in Dallas. The team finished fifth at the national tournament.

"My early memory of Jim with sports is that he was definitely a competitive person, so there were times people would say, 'He's going to fly in a ringer,'" Coady said, adding that while Flint sometimes did this for straight players, nine times out of 10 it was just to help a gay player who couldn't afford to travel for a tournament.

Coady knows that several teams had straight players, including some of Flint's, but he does not recall any of them playing for Flint's team at the World Series events. Coady played for Flint teams in both gay and straight leagues, so it was common for there to be crossover. "For me, it wasn't that big of a deal," Coady said. "The more competitive the gay players got, the less it was a big deal. One player does not make a difference."

Coady was a key part of WCAA's early men's basketball leagues, and he credits Flint with being an important organizer and sponsor at both the league's founding in 1988 and the annual tournament started soon after. That tournament, now called the Coady Classic, is still run under the auspices of the WCAA (under the group's new name AAC), while the men's league plays for CMSA.

Coady served on the WCAA board in the 1990s, including the period when Flint was commissioner. "Jim was always very supportive of two things. First, ensuring that there were always women's leagues alongside the men's leagues. We would travel to tourneys and the teams were very supportive of each other. The men's and women's divisions very much interacted. That happens much less so in CMSA. The other thing is, he did outreach to minority communities. He would be out putting out fliers in Latino or heavily African-American bars, looking for athletes. Very few other sports leaders did that type of outreach. He had a desire to have more minorities playing. He'd get to know South Side bar owners and get them to sponsor teams." Coady said Flint also encouraged the formation of teams in other cities as well, when he visited for Continental events or other tournaments.

Coady said that while Flint "definitely wanted his teams to win, he also usually sponsored recreational teams at the same time. He wanted his competitive teams to be very good and win, go all out, practice in winter, find facilities to practice in, going to more tourneys, shake the bushes to find players, etc. He was much more willing to be supportive to have that winning team than any other sponsor I know. He was a top-notch sponsor, regardless of the level of play."

Coady also has warm memories of the time when Flint managed the Annex 3 Blues team. Flint did not have a lot of base-managing experience, so he often gave conflicting directions to base runners. "One hand would be waving the player to go home, the other to stop," Coady said. "He was always colorful."

At times, Flint and Coady had disagreements, a "love/hate relationship," Coady said, but he always appreciated Flint as a sponsor. "He was very good at marshaling resources for gay and lesbian sports," Coady said. "His amount of passion and drive and pulling in these other sponsors to get teams and leagues going was pretty unmatched."

Coady also remembers attending many benefits Flint hosted for players who needed help with health expenses, including a player for his Synergy women's team.

Once, Coady said, he was with Flint at the Water Tower Place shopping mall, and Flint was wearing his full-length fur coat. An animal-rights protester confronted Flint, asking him if he knew how many animals had died to make that coat. Coady said Flint responded quickly, "Do you know how many men I had to sleep with to get this coat?" The woman was stunned speechless.

Several years ago, with CMSA's board numbers dwindling, Coady said he approached the group to join its board with the goal of perhaps merging CMSA and WCAA. Coady said he did this on his own, not necessarily with any support from Flint or WCAA. His efforts were rebuffed, however, when CMSA voted against his board membership.

Chicago athlete Mike McRaith started playing for MSA and WCAA in the early 1990s. He also was the Illinois Insurance Department's director for six years before taking an Obama administration post in 2011 as director of the Federal Insurance Office at the U.S. Treasury Department.

McRaith played tennis and football for MSA and basketball for WCAA.

"I heard about the divisions between the leagues in the political context, where some of the same people had different views about politics in the community, and different advocacy organizations or political action committees were set up by different individuals, trying to serve the same purpose," McRaith said. "But I did hear about the sports rivalry as well.

"As an outsider to the dispute, my view was always that we have common objectives and should not allow personal differences to interfere with those objectives. Working together, we're always going to be stronger than if we're separated."

McRaith graduated from law school in 1990 and soon heard about WCAA's basketball league. "As someone who had played basketball my entire life, and as someone who was learning how to be an adult but also a gay person, being able to combine basketball with this was a tremendous affirmation and tremendous opportunity, and I have appreciated it ever since," he said.

McRaith's initial interaction with Flint was only as a player, and Flint was the organizer of a team that usually had some of the best players. "I was in my rookie year and I remember feeling like that guy, Jim Flint, had really organized a good, talented team, and a tough-to-defeat team," McRaith said. "He soon 'recruited' a group of us for his top team, a group that remains very close today: Tony Miller, Sam Coady, myself and others. We were kind of the organized opposition, and every year we would try to field a team to defeat Jim's teams."

"The rivalry stayed on the court. I learned Jim was a very competitive guy when it came to sports. He did not like losing. We had trouble beating his teams, but we did beat them on occasion, and he was generally displeased with the outcome. But he was such a warm and engaging personality, that was sometimes prickly for sure, but always interesting, and once we left the gym and were hanging out someplace, he was always entertaining and fun to be with."

McRaith said the issue of straight players in the basketball leagues was never the big deal it was in softball. There were straight players then, and there still are today, in gay basketball. "We played with and welcomed straight players on every team, so that issue was never one that I felt or that, as far as I am aware, my teammates felt was determinate of a game or the league," McRaith said. "To this day, the league, basketball, has such a broad diversity in terms of ethnic, demographic, socioeconomic, it's really in some ways a melting pot. Basketball as a game draws such a diverse cross section of the city's population. People would bring their buddies from college, brothers, brothers-in-law, nephews, grandfathers and sons, etc., so that issue of gay and straight, as far as I am aware, was never determinative of the outcome of a game or league. It did not rise to the level as it did with softball leagues."

Greg Moore, like so many other gay men of the era, met Jim Flint through softball, around 1983. Moore played in WCAA, but not originally for one of Flint's teams. Soon he found himself playing for Flint, and he said Flint was a "terrific sponsor—he always made sure the teams were outfitted really well. We usually had two sets of uniforms. He bought us bat bags. A lot of the younger players couldn't afford that stuff on their own.

"He always traveled with the teams. Some of my best memories are going to tournaments all around the country: San Francisco, Kansas City, Norfolk, New York City, Boston, Atlanta several times, Minneapolis, Milwaukee, all over. A lot of my travel experience has been playing ball, because we were going with Jimmy's teams. It was a lot of work to get teams together to do that much traveling. He was always enthusiastic."

Moore, who now lives in Orlando, played in NAGAAA for Flint, and in 2011 he was still playing World Series softball when the annual event came to Chicago. He played WCAA softball from 1983 to 1991.

"We had some straight players that would go in tournaments, but they couldn't play in the World Series," recalled Moore. "But we pretty much embraced them; to us on the team, it was not an issue. I remember we were friends with these players, they were not ringers. Phil Runions, who is straight, was just [in 2009] inducted into the NAGAAA Hall of Fame, the first straight person inducted in. Phil would go to the World Series with us, even if he couldn't play and was ineligible. That says a lot right there. He was not in it to be a ringer.

"I still play in NAGAAA. I was a founding member of the Orlando softball league, and I've seen straight players and all they do is play ball. The team members barely know their names, they don't socialize or go to the bars; that's the true test right there."

Moore noted that "people always said Jim stacked his teams; I'm not sure how many of Jimmy's teams even won tournaments. The old Sidetrack won; but I am not sure his teams even were winning much. The MSA-WCAA battles could only happen in Chicago. It's just the way Chicago is, also because of the size of the city. You couldn't do that in Orlando. We don't have the players to support that kind of rivalry. I was never interested in that. I just wanted to play ball and have fun.

"I had as much fun off the field as on. Back then, we would go barhopping in our ball uniforms, and everyone flocked around the players. These days, these kids, they play ball, get [dressed] up before they go to the bars. In the old days we'd just go in uniform to the Annex or Redoubt, all sweated up in our uniforms, then go to Sidetrack, Bulldog Road, etc."

By the time Moore played in WCAA, Flint was winding down as a player and focused more on being a coach and sponsor. "As a coach, he had a great knowledge of the game, was very opinionated and passionate; he would not hesitate to mix it up with umpires," Moore said. "He has a competitive streak—it's just insatiable. He was extremely competitive, still is, very headstrong. He's an entertainer. He kind of brought the entertainment spotlight to how he did softball. He wanted to win, everybody does; he was as much about having fun as going out, doing stuff after the game. There was a social element to it. It was a lot more than just softball. But he would go toe-to-toe with you."

Moore said that sports was important in changing the image of gays in the eyes of the straight world, who only thought about sex and bathhouses when it came to gay men, especially when AIDS started. "But there was also another story to be told, and that was that we were just as good athletes as straight athletes," Moore said. "We could be just as competitive. This carried us through the 1980s. At tournaments and such in the 1980s, I didn't think we got the media coverage we deserved. There was a story to be told, it was not all about just sex in the gay community, there was so much more we did as a community.

"I'm in my mid-50s now, and I kind of preach this to the younger guys. They are amazed I am still playing and competing. I'm the second-oldest guy in the Orlando league. They ask, 'How come there are not more players your age playing?' I tell them, 'It's because they're dead, don't you get it?' Most of them didn't make it [because of AIDS]. A whole bunch of them didn't make it. Softball helped a lot, it stabilized me, it kept me focused. I developed lifelong friendships."

Moore, who has had a long career in the private security business, calls Flint a "trailblazer. He had the idea to do it. He's the one that opened the door for everybody else. You've got to have that spark, that idea, that vision. That's the real thing—he had the vision to see what this thing could be. Who would imagine this thing would have gotten this big? In the 1980s World Series, there were maybe 40 teams; now the men's alone is more than 170 teams.

"His legacy is, he gave—he had the vision, he envisioned where this thing could go. I am not sure he even knew how big it could become. There is gay bowling, tennis, kickball leagues, gay darts, etc. A lot of that is because they saw the success and fun and cohesiveness that gay softball brought. It was all because of people like Jimmy in the late 1970s who started all this stuff. You had to start somewhere."

Moore also related several stories about how Flint helped him mature as a young gay man. This story was echoed by other young players who saw Flint as a father figure, one who tried to develop them not just as softball players, but as gay men in the world. It was not about sex; it was about being men and broadening horizons.

"He nurtured me from a young man into my 30s," Moore said. "This was during those impressionable 20-year-old years. He'd pick me up and we'd get on a plane and fly to New York for the weekend, and go see Pudgy in New York City. We'd end up in Pudgy's room and partying and drinking, and fly back a couple days later.

"There was one time Jimmy and I were having dinner at the Pump Room at the Ambassador East Hotel, and we both wore our fur coats in there—back when you could wear a fur coat—and I told Jimmy I was going to Hawaii, that a guy was going to take me. He said, 'If you let that guy take you to Hawaii, then don't talk to me anymore.'

"I said, 'Start now,' and I slammed my napkin down, put on my fur, and Jimmy chased me. This was an exclusive place to eat; he chased me out. We had words. He called me all night long, said it was 'OK if you go.' Of course I went.

"I was known as his sidekick, but nothing was going on. I had a new Jeep. People thought Jimmy bought it for me. So maybe Jimmy was jealous, though I was never in a relationship with him. We were best friends.

"Danny [Flint's partner], he didn't want to do anything, I was always up to go. To the racetrack, or wherever. Danny was not going to go. Jimmy knew he could count on me to go. For weekends, there would be a gay political convention in L.A., he'd say 'let's go.' Jimmy could get me to run around anywhere."

Moore related a story about attending the Miss Universe pageant in St. Louis with Flint; Ray West, a male stripper; and three female impersonators, Roski Fernandez, Andrea Nicole and Cherine Alexander. They flew to St. Louis for the pageant. "The three of us were in tuxes, and the girls were all in Bob Mackie gowns. We flew in a helicopter around to see the sights. It was my first copter ride. We had a limo that took us everywhere. It pulled up in front with big searchlights. Roski Fernandez and two of the girls were foreign, so they looked like dignitaries; we played it up and went barhopping in St. Louis, it was crazy. We also used to go to St. Louis and go to Busch Stadium and watch the Cardinals play because Jimmy had friends there who had tickets."

"We went in with the girls and everyone would just turn and look at us because the queens were so beautiful, and dressed immaculately," said Moore.

Moore is still friends with Flint, and said "Flint had an amazing impact on me. The words I would use to describe Flint are 'trailblazer' and 'visionary' when it came to softball. He put his money where his mouth was. He wanted to see it done right. He didn't quibble about it. There were guys that would go on trips who did not have a pot to piss in, and Jimmy would buy them dinner. He had the same effect on hundreds of people."

Mike Meismer is from Metamora, Illinois—near Peoria, where Flint was raised— and it was softball that brought the two native sons together in Chicago. Meismer was 23 when he met Flint, around 1984, on the softball diamonds.

"He was a mentor, and I always looked up to him for guidance," Meismer said. "Then around 1985, Jim asked me to be on his bowling team with him and Danny and Jim's sister Flo and her husband, Fred. It was at Marigold Lanes. I pitched on his Annex Blues softball team. After two years or so, I formed my own team as captain; then I became assistant commissioner for WCAA in 1988–89. Jim was commissioner then. That was fun.

"I got to travel a lot with him for NAGAAA, playing in tournaments. We always had such a great time together. We were like a big family, the softball teams. There were not as many divisions of teams as there are now. Bob Strada had a team and we traveled in the same circles, like a big family unit. We did Thanksgivings and Christmases together. I played in NAGAAA in one of the World Series, for the Christopher Street team around 1988."

Meismer said he never quite understood the rift between MSA and WCAA: "It felt like it was between Art and Jim. They had different views about how things should be run. I never got into the politics part of it. I didn't understand it."

Flint's role in Chicago was as a "key figure for the national gay sports scene," Meismer said. "I got to go to NAGAAA meetings when I was assistant commissioner, and Jim was definitely a person that everybody listened to. Jim was an outspoken person people looked for. He always made his presence known."

Meismer is not as active in sports these days, but when he does watch games, he sees a difference in the social spirit. "There was more heart in it in the early days. After a game, the entire group, not just one team, but all the teams, would go to a host bar. We would all interact, it was on a much smaller scale. It was more about camaraderie, everybody getting together. You knew their names from other teams. It was like a professional league that no one else had," Meismer said.

As AIDS started its devastating path through the gay community, Meismer said everyone was learning how to be safe. But it was already too late for some gay men. "Jim was very upset about AIDS," Meismer said. "Jim lost some really good friends early on. He knew better than I did ... I could see he was really caring about it. I was so new to the scene, so I wasn't into the politics of it. I see today what a pioneer he was."

As for Flint's competitive nature, Meismer said "it didn't bother me to think they were stacking the team, when they went to the NAGAAA level, and people would question it, but I didn't like to get into it. Here we are all trying to be equal, but [we're] discriminating if someone is straight. Who wouldn't recruit a good ballplayer? They were recruiting good players. I think teams from other cities were doing the same thing. Phil Runions played, he was straight, but he was a teddy bear. He was one of the nicest guys I ever met, and a great player. I would have loved to play alongside him. I don't think people felt threatened or that he shouldn't be playing in the leagues. For me it wasn't an issue."

Meismer said he and Flint had a falling-out when Meismer took his team to MSA. It was at a time when WCAA was struggling to field four teams, which was the minimum requirement for a league to be represented at the World Series. "It really hurt Jim at the time," Meismer said. "Somehow Jim managed to pull two new teams together and they had four. In MSA, we didn't have as much fun. It was like leaving family. The following year, or maybe that year, I moved to Texas. ... I always had a friendship with Jim regardless. We still talked.

"When I moved back in the late 1990s from Dallas, I looked back and went, 'Wow, Jim has helped so many people.' Don't get me wrong, Jim likes to do things his way, and did things early on; who doesn't? But he helped move people and the gay lifestyle ahead. And personally he has helped people, he's employed how many people? People were sick in the hospital and Jim was there for them. He's done so much for so many people. He did it his way, but I don't know how anybody could do that today. It was such a burden to go through. He was such an integral part of everything. We take it for granted, but people like him are what really got us to where we are today, both on the political and sports scenes."

Joe Fraser and JT McWilliams are two other men who view Flint as a father figure. "They both think they're my kids. They call me every day of the week and go places with me all the time. They really think they are my kids," Flint said. "I met JT when he was a 17-year-old waiter at El Jardín on Clark and Buckingham. Then he played ball for me. El Jardín was a big part of my life then. It was the place I constantly hung out. ... We'd go there after ball practice."

"I met Jim in 1986 at El Jardín restaurant with my friend JT McWilliams," Joe Fraser said. "Back in those days I was very homophobic. I came from a Catholic high school and in those days I didn't know anyone who was gay. I didn't remember people being out in high school. You may have suspected that they were gay, but you didn't know. Jim opened the eyes of me and maybe 15 or 20 of my friends. Really, he has gone a long, long way in helping me to break down barriers and prejudices I had. I consider him part older brother, part father, and part good friend.

"Back in 1986, JT was supposed to go to Cubs spring training down in Arizona and for whatever reason he ended up not being able to go, so Jim said, 'I've got a spot available,' and so I said, 'I'll go.' The thought never occurred to me not to. And that day starting at the airport for the next few days all I did was laugh, laugh, laugh. We laughed our asses off for four solid days."

Fraser, McWilliams and Flint were also all softball players and met through 16-inch straight leagues. Fraser said that at one point around 1988, Flint challenged them to a 12-inch game, and Fraser's team was cocky, thinking it would be easy to just switch to another size of softball. They were crushed by Flint's team. Eventually the leagues got mixed in, and Fraser said it was a nice blend, with players from 16-inch and 12-inch together.

Fraser played for Flint's teams in both gay and straight leagues. But because he is straight, he could not travel to some of the gay tournaments. As a straight man in a gay league, Fraser made a lot of friends. Flint also sponsored straight softball teams at local parks. "As we merged together, it was a great thing. You take these guys, with these preconceived notions that gay players can't play, and they kicked our ass. It was an eye-opening experience for a lot of people. It was pretty cool to see the progression from straight vs. gay to mixed leagues and teams. It was a pretty good blend," Fraser said.

Fraser feels the gay/straight rule is reverse discrimination, "but I understand too that it's an opportunity if for gay players it is their only option to play ball, and straight players knock them out of a position," Fraser said. "But it was not a ringer issue, it was about friendships. Nobody was that good to be ringers, it's not like we had major-league players. They were just good, solid ballplayers who played all season long."

Fraser also played in Flint's basketball leagues.

Rick Welch is a Chicagoan who played for Flint's teams over the years, and also worked for him at 3160 bar and River North Travel.

"I was 17 when I met Jim, around 1963," Welch said. "I met him at Sam's bar in Chicago. He was bartending. Sometimes he would throw up the baton and people would buy him a Bacardí and Coke. One day he said to me, 'What can I get you?' They were cracking down on underage drinking, and he asked if I had an ID, and I said no. He said goodbye."

Welch moved to California in the 1970s, but met up again with Flint at a 1985 softball tournament in Milwaukee. Flint contacted him about putting together a team in Chicago. Welch moved back to Chicago and pitched for the Baton Blues. When Welch wanted his own team in 1989, Flint sponsored it, as the Annex Wrecks.

"Jim was a terrific sponsor," Welch said. "He always gave us two uniforms and paid the fees. The highlight was when my team beat his [other] team—it just about killed him. We wound up going to Philly and placed second in the early 1990s World Series, and he was very happy my team did well. Then I started umpiring in WCAA and was captain of my own team, and we'd go to all the softball meetings."

Welch said he has many funny and interesting stories from his travels with Flint, including cruising men and a driverless car moving off with Flint chasing. Flint would even stay in a hotel lobby if Welch had company back in their shared hotel room during out-of-town meetings and tournaments. "Only a true friend would do this for you," Welch said.

"Jim would do anything to promote softball," recalled Welch. "We'd go to bars to see if they would sponsor. He went to NAGAAA meetings twice a year religiously. He had a very big part in the growth of gay softball. [At NAGAAA], he spoke up, said what he thought, he put his 2 cents in. He was very outspoken, a few people were outspoken. He would lobby for votes, he went to every World Series for years. He became a NAGAAA Hall of Famer, not so much for his teams, but because of his participation, sponsorship and dedication to the gay community and softball."

Another NAGAAA Hall of Fame honoree is Bill Svetz, a Boston-based sponsor of the nationally known Fritz softball teams in that city. Svetz had many stories to share about Flint. Their teams competed against one another at tournaments, but their friendship survived the rivalry.

"Jim was a board member in NAGAAA, and he was very active and vocal," Svetz said. "He always expressed himself, and he was the same on the softball field. He was energetic; he was a player, and he used to coach, then he was a manager and sponsor. He was an extremely vital part of the organization. It was 23 teams, now it is more than 180 teams. Chicago was an early city in NAGAAA, and Jim was an important part of it. Jim used to entertain during tournaments, running on the stage, on roller skates—to see a man that size roller-skating was a sight to be seen."

Svetz said there has always been controversy at NAGAAA, some because of the gay/straight issue. "This created a lot of concern. Some cities had too many straights; the World Series was designed for the best gay athletes because of the stigma gay people have: of dancing, cooking, not being an athlete. We always said two straight players should be allowed, because we felt that people were part of the community, and you could have two straight players. Jim always felt it was OK to have more straight players because some had played in the gay leagues for years."

Svetz said that, as with any friend, he and Flint "sometimes have our differences, but in the long run we always come back together."

Mike Denny met Flint in the 1980s at a July 4 weekend softball tournament in Chicago hosted by WCAA. Denny was visiting from Atlanta and he saw "Felicia," Flint's alter ego, onstage that night at the Baton. "I couldn't believe it. He was on roller skates with a baton, and a fake penis, and he lifted his skirt," Denny said. "It was the start of a long friendship."

When Flint decided to open an Atlanta version of his Chicago leather bar Redoubt, he asked Denny if he would work there as a bartender, and Denny said yes. He also helped at the Baton Atlanta bar as well. Both bars eventually closed.

Denny's softball teams frequently played against Flint's teams at tournaments. "He is a great competitor, he was incredible," Denny said. "People look at him today, he has not changed much physically, and they say he does not look like a softball player. He was a pitcher and a tough competitor, and a pretty good athlete. He talked a lot. Chicago teams had a reputation: 'Hate those Chicago teams, they talk so much.'" Denny also played on teams sponsored by Flint's Atlanta bars.

Denny played in NAGAAA and said there were rumors in every league about straight players; Atlanta had the same problems as Chicago. "People have pros and cons whether they approve of straight players or not. His teams were no different," Denny said.

Asked about the role of sports for gay men in the 1980s, Denny said it was "the best thing. I am 50 now. I really miss that in my life. I wouldn't want to dedicate that time again; we also like baseball, the Cubs, Braves, and Jim said, 'What would we do without sports?' That's always stuck with me. For me personally, it wasn't your stereotypical gay thing people thought of. I ran into people from all walks of life that didn't get to experience it. Some of the best times of my life, trips, meeting Jim, would not have happened without sports, that camaraderie."

Denny told of one story with Flint when both men were sick, Denny from hepatitis B and Flint recovering from a heart attack. The two were driving from Atlanta to Savannah and ran out of gas 10 miles outside of their destination city. They had to walk a mile for gas, both not feeling well, but laughing at their run of bad luck.

John Keys met Flint back in 1994, at a softball tournament in Atlanta. Keys was living in Dallas at the time and then moved to Chicago in 1997. Keys played for Flint's competitive Chicago Blues team for about five years.

"Little did I know at the time that he would become such a wonderful friend, away from softball," Keys said. "He has been a personal mentor, a teacher of life lessons, and he holds a special place in my heart forever. He showed me business smarts, was politically aware, and most importantly he taught me about humanity and the importance of benevolence. He showed me through his own actions of generosity, he always donated his time and his money to the community. He's always taken a strong political stand and has been passionate in his beliefs. He's led by example."

Keys has many stories about traveling with Flint to tournaments around the country. "In Phoenix he insisted on staying at the casinos on the Indian reservation until the last possible second," Keys said. "When we sped to the airport to turn the car back in, there was a big, long line, so he went to the other side and ran over the spikes and popped the tires. But we didn't miss the flight."

Keys said Flint "exposed me to some of the finer things in life. I had an underprivileged background, and he exposed me to things I wouldn't have thought of. He helped mold me into the gentleman I have become. He has been such an influential person in my life and I will forever be grateful for the life lessons he taught me."

Bob Nicholson, as co-owner of the Chicago gay bar North End for 16 years, sponsored many sports teams and events. He also played 16-inch softball in GAA prior to opening his bar in 1983.

"I started attending the WCAA meetings, when teams were forming, to make sure they knew we were interested in sponsoring an A team in their league," Nicholson said. "I wasn't much into 12-inch softball, more with 16-inch. The following year, 1984, we had our first team. About that time I met Jim. The decision we made to put a team in WCAA was a good one, all around, and I met many fine people. For whatever reason that year, people came back to the bar after games. It seemed like joining that organization got the bar off to a real solid start. Three-fourths of the league came in there on Sunday afternoons. We were considered a sports bar, and we backed all kinds of sports."

Nicholson said he did not get involved in the GAA-WCAA split and that North End sponsored teams in both leagues. When MSA added 12-inch softball, Nicholson did play in that league because that was where he first played in 1979.

What impressed Nicholson about Flint was his national vision for sports. "I had never heard of the NAGAAA Gay World Series. Jim to me put the game more on a national perspective, not just Chicago or the Midwest," Nicholson said. "I think I played my first World Series in 1987. I started going to some of the tournaments. I never realized softball existed outside of our area—that gay people played. I give credit to Jim—both leagues really prospered, up until recently. I compare it to the Chicago White Sox and the Cubs. North End always had two teams; the players got along."

Nicholson turned to umpiring, once his playing days were ending. "I umpired some games at Clarendon Park for WCAA, I think the Thursday-night league. In 1999, when Jim had a tournament here called the Windy City Classic, he let me umpire, my first tournament. I credit him with giving me the confidence to keep doing that. To this day, I'm still doing it, in 2011, umpiring," Nicholson said, adding that he was an umpire at the 2011 Gay World Series in Chicago. "I credit Jim for my softball career and to a greater extent my umpire career." This is his 10th World Series as an umpire, and he played in 14 as a player.

What about Flint as a player? "He was a pitcher—a fine pitcher, and with a very competitive streak," Nicholson said. "All players at some point get competitive—get angry at times, you play to win. If there's a mistake, you let them know, whether an umpire or on your team. I go by the old adage, It's fun to play the game, but a lot more fun to win than lose."

Larry Scantland, a former Chicagoan who played in—and wrote newspaper articles about—the gay sports leagues in the 1980s, has good memories of the role Flint played in his life.

"Most people looked at Jim as this guy who was always mad about something," Scantland said. "Yes, he was competitive, but he was also one of the most sensitive men ever. He put his money, his businesses and his reputation on the line each season to make sure gay athletes got to play gay sports. He may not have been the most cordial or the most liked, but if you are able to look at the man and not the persona, then you see what a great man he was. He led by example. He played most of his sports and he did his best to make it as competitive as he could.

"He never liked to fail and I would say that even his harshest critic would be hard-pressed to not say they respected Jim for taking gay sports to a new era. When I really was down and out, I had Jim to turn to and he saved me. He gave me a life, and today I am stronger and more confident because of him. I just wish that all the people would see him with my eyes and see the champion he truly is."

Jim O'Connor is another good friend of Flint's from their gay softball days. O'Connor played for Fritz of Boston, but never at NAGAAA. Rather, he played against Flint's teams in other tournaments across North America.

"My impression of Jim is that he is very dedicated to sports," O'Connor said. "Sometimes it could get nasty, but Jim was always for the good of the whole thing. He always had competitive players and good teams."

O'Connor remembers not just the games, but the off-field good times with Flint. "Jim's one of the greatest guys," he said. "Look at all he has done over the years, especially with the Baton, and pageants all over the country. He's probably created more jobs and successes than anybody I know."

Straight vs. Gay

GayLife newspaper covered the debate over whether any straight players should be allowed in the NAGAAA World Series. In articles, columns and letters, people called attention to what they considered the hypocrisy of the gay leagues' discriminating against straights, while others said it made the leagues special and a safe place for gay men to compete.

On April 24, 1981, GayLife reported on NAGAAA's meeting in Toronto. At that meeting, NAGAAA added the third and fourth A's for "Amateur Athletic" and rejected a proposed change from the 100 percent gay rule back to the 80/20 rule. The Chicago delegation made a motion to rescind that 100 percent rule.

An anonymous man wrote to GayLife for its issue of August 27, 1982: "I am proud to be playing with a group of guys who happen to have two straights on the team. ... What is supposed to happen in participatory sports has happened to our team: we have grown to love and respect each other. ... Now as the season culminates, and it is very possible our team will move on to San Francisco [for the World Series], we gays must say to these people: 'Sorry, but you're not gay. You can't participate. Sure, you helped us get where we are, but you're not up to NAGAAA's norms.' What a travesty!"

GayLife columnist Ron Ehemann wrote about the NAGAAA rules twice in 1982, first on April 16 and then again on May 14. He wrote in part:

"Discrimination is wrong. It's a shame gay people don't believe it. ... In March, 11 members of the North American Gay Amateur Athletic Alliance (NAGAAA) met in San Francisco to lay policy for the upcoming season. As last year, they passed a rule that is blatantly discriminatory and therefore wrong.

"The 80/20 rule, which was formerly in effect, states that NAGAAA will not recognize a team unless at least 80% of its members are gay. To make matters worse, even if a team complies with these prejudicial requirements, none of the non-gay members may play in the league's World Series. Last year and again this year, an even worse 100% rule was adopted.

"I'm told that Chicago representatives proposed the elimination of that 100% rule during the meeting in San Francisco and favored at least a return of the 80/20 rule. Los Angeles and New York joined in the effort. But NAGAAA wouldn't do it."

In his second column, Ehemann interviewed Jack McGowan, the founder of the gay Community Softball League in San Francisco. McGowan had moved to Chicago and was an important part of early gay softball in the Windy City, too. He saw how some San Francisco teams initially bowed out of the World Series because of the rule, a rule he opposed. But he said the rule is important not because straight players are all better, but because there are more straight people overall, and therefore more good players.

McGowan told Ehemann that straights are attracted to gay leagues because of better fan participation, more money spent on the competition, bigger events, and better social parties. McGowan said the 80/20 rule does more to prevent gay rejection than it does to promote non-gay discrimination—and, he said, it's legal. Some courts had allowed for discriminatory rules in athletics for African-American, Japanese-American and Native American teams.

William B. Kelley, consulting editor for GayLife at the time, wrote an op-ed on the topic for the September 3, 1982, edition. He said it is the right of a private volunteer league to decide who can play: "Since statistically there are more non-gay than gay people alive, there are also more good non-gay players than gay ones, and a 'gay' team that was truly open to all players would inevitably be dominated by non-gay jocks. In real life, of course, this won't happen until homophobia is vanquished, but, to the extent that it does begin to happen, some gay players will be crowded out.

"Those same gay players, by and large, would not be accepted in their openness by most amateur or professional teams in the larger community. Therefore, they would be victimized by homophobia in the outside world and by muted group consciousness in their 'own' world."

Growing Pains

Flint was interviewed in the April 16, 1982, issue of GayLife. The article noted that Bob Strada was manager of the Annex 2 team and Greg Cora was manager of the Redoubt team, both in the WCAA softball league. WCAA also had two volleyball teams and eight bowling teams at that point. Flint also was sponsoring a women's softball team for the 13th year and a women's volleyball team for the eighth year, both in straight leagues.

On May 21, 1982, Flint, as commissioner of WCAA, wrote a sports column for GayLife about WCAA's third season of 12-inch softball starting at Margate Park. He reported on the scores of the games and how the teams performed. Teams were sponsored by the Redoubt, Touché, the Gold Coast, Annex 2, Paradise, and the Unicorn. Redoubt and Annex 2 were Flint's bars. That same issue had the scores for GAA 16-inch as well, with teams named Sidetrack, His 'n Hers, Dandy's, the Closet, BJ's, the Other Side, Bushmen, Touché, Big Red's, Baskets, New Flight, 905ers, and Piggen's.

Flint told GayLife that Chicago won the 1983 World Series bid by presenting a more realistic budget than other cities. Flint also explained that 100 percent of the players had to be gay, and the definition was "a predominant sexual interest in the same sex, including gay men and lesbians."

During the buildup to the 1983 Gay World Series in Chicago, GayLife reported on fundraising efforts alongside reports of Sidetrack's dominance in the WCAA league on its way to winning the league championship and a berth in the World Series, which the team also won. WCAA Gay World Series VII Chairman Arturo Agurto announced fundraisers for the series, including a benefit called The Wiz at Carol's Speakeasy on July 24, 1983, plus a variety show hosted by Cesar Vera at the Paradise bar.

That same summer, Chicago also hosted the North American Gay Volleyball Association's Midwest Regional Tournament on July 30–31 at Lane Technical High School. GAA was the host of the event.

Jack "Irene" McGowan, the founder of the gay Community Softball League in San Francisco, moved to Chicago and participated in sports leagues and sponsored teams for his Irene's Diamonds gay bar, but he also wrote about sports for Windy City Times. In his November 21, 1985, column, he used his space to attack WCAA's style vs. MSA. He opened his column with Charles Dickens' classic "It was the best of times, it was the worst of times," comparing the French Revolution period in Europe to the gay sports scene in Chicago in 1985.

He said MSA was older and therefore more structured and successful. At the time, MSA had 68 bowling teams, 12 basketball teams, distance running, 18 volleyball teams and 26 softball teams. It had about 1,000 athletes in all. He said MSA had a corporate structure and generally steered clear of infighting. He also had kind words for Sam Molinaro, who was in his ninth year as leader of MSA.

WCAA, McGowan said, was a "younger and more tumultuous organization" with six softball teams and 34 bowling teams. He claimed WCAA "seems more dedicated to the individual ambitions of its leaders than to the growth and good of its membership" of about 270. McGowan alleged illegal elections, resignations, physical threats, fake names, election boycotts, illegal members and more.

In the December 5, 1985, issue of Windy City Times, Joe DiMartino, WCAA commissioner, defended WCAA against McGowan's charges, which he said should have come with a disclaimer noting that McGowan had an obvious conflict of interest in writing the story to begin with.

"McGowan has been a member of the Windy City Athletic Association since its incorporation … and has supported the association until this past summer," DiMartino wrote. "During this past softball season Jack dropped out of WCAA due to several disagreements with and decisions made by the officers of the association. Further adding to Jack's displeasure with the WCAA was his ineligibility to vote in our recent election due to Jack not having submitted a membership application or payment of the fee for annual membership in the association.

"With these facts in mind, I find his article giving overwhelming praise to the Metropolitan Sports Association while characterizing WCAA as an organization 'dedicated to the individual ambitions of its leaders' as completely personal, biased, and unfair. Although WCAA is a younger organization and at times its members are a bit more volatile, any general statement depicting all present and past leaders of WCAA as only concerned with their own individual ambitions is an insult to all those who have served the association fairly and with integrity. …

"Some of Jack's allegations may very well be valid and some changes may indeed be necessary in WCAA, but the intent and use of these methods to discredit a particular organization is inexcusable and an affront to every member of WCAA, many of whom he has participated side by side with since 1982."

Flint himself did leave and return to WCAA a few times, including his 1985 return as commissioner of the league, with Donnie Welsh as assistant commissioner, John Lyrla as secretary, Rudy Johnson as treasurer and Phil Runions as sergeant-at-arms. This was in November 1985, when Flint was also gearing up for his race for the Cook County Board.

WCAA also participated in the first Gay Olympics games, founded in San Francisco by Dr. Tom Waddell. A court decision forced the organizing group to remove the word "Olympics" from the event's name, so the name was changed to Gay Games, but that didn't stop the first games from happening in San Francisco in 1982. The WCAA softball championships featured Flint's Annex 2 team defeating Chuck Renslow's Gold Coast team in a tight 6–5 game, which meant Annex 2 would be representing Chicago in the Gay Games men's softball division.

For that first Gay "Olympic" Games, WCAA's Jim Russell was Chicago chairman of the National Torch Run, the kickoff for the Gay Games. The run was from New York City to San Francisco, ending at the start of the games on August 29, 1982. GAA's Sam Molinaro and WCAA's Flint were also listed as contacts for Chicago runners in the April 23, 1982, issue of GayLife.

Because the Gay Games used the standards of NAGAAA for players, Flint was upset that two of his players (Dwayne Metzger and John Hale) were forced off the roster for the Gay Games. (Future Gay Games, including the 2006 event in Chicago, did not discriminate based on gender or sexual orientation.)

Mainstream Sports and the Chicago Cubs

Flint's love of the Chicago Cubs is what connects him with a wide range of gay and non-gay friends. One is Sara Davis, an 88-year-old, lifelong Cubs fan who met Flint in the late 1970s at a Cubs game at Wrigley Field.

"He took me to Puerto Rico, St. Louis, and also we met in San Diego," Davis said. "I am so happy he is in my life; not because of what he did, but because he is a genuine, great person for everybody else. He is a warm, caring gentleman."

"He used to go a lot on the road with me, to spring training" for the Cubs, Davis added. While Flint has lately not had as much faith in the Cubs, he and Davis still share their love of the team. And Davis has taken her neighbors at an independent living facility in Chicago's north suburbs on visits to Flint's Baton Show Lounge. "They loved it," she said.

"I am straight," Davis said. "But I have relatives I don't even tell I mix with gays, because they are such bigots; they think someone can change. Jim told me once, he was born with this, but he doesn't flaunt it. He said to me, 'Don't you think I would want to be married and have kids?' They [gays] take care of you—they are just nice, decent people. Everybody's got to do what they have to do. I don't hold anything against those people. I am so proud to know him and be a friend."

Davis treasures stories that include gambling in Colorado with Flint, going to Houston for games, spring training in Arizona, San Juan, and a notorious trip to San Diego for a Cubs series that could have led to a playoff berth. This was 1984, and the Cubs were eight outs away from winning against San Diego. First baseman Leon Durham allowed a hit to dribble through his legs, and the San Diego Padres won the game, and the series. The cursed Cubs were once again waiting for next year.

Davis said she and Flint were upset about the game, and upset with the hotel rooms, and when they returned after a night of baseball and drinking, Davis pressed the manager to see the better rooms, and made a big scene out of it. "I said, 'Sir, may I talk to you?" Davis said, as she pointed to a photo in the hotel brochure. "I said, 'Can you show me a room like that [the better one]?' I said, 'You have fraudulent ads.' I said a lot of shit, and we left there."

"Jim's just a great person, not because of the help he has given me," Davis said. "I wouldn't trade him for all the straight guys." Davis' husband died when their daughter was just 7, and she never remarried. She said her daughter likes Flint a lot and is very open-minded, which could be from Flint's influence on her.

Carol Hadden is another of Flint's long list of heterosexual women admirers and friends. She met him in 1984 on a plane to Pittsburgh, where they were both going to watch the Cubs potentially clinch an entry into the playoffs. "We were all excited about being where the Cubs would finally bring home an opportunity for us to go to the playoffs, which never happened," Hadden said.

"When you are sharing the same somewhat limited interests, you befriend people, and through that we became friendly. Jim would go to the Stadium Club at Wrigley—both he and I are season ticket holders of long standing—so we would enjoy each other's company at the ballpark, and then at that time I actually enjoyed going to his bar, the Baton, and I actually continued to support the Baton and his Miss Continental beauty pageant.

"In fact, on one occasion in the early days before he had more high-profile people, I was a judge for that pageant. Being a judge—I loved it. I loved the event. He put so much of himself into it, and all the competitors put so much of themselves into it, it was quite an occasion. It is very special, as is Jim. He's just a hardworking, wonderful person."

Hadden also mentioned that her daughter, who was in her teens when Hadden met Flint, was among those lucky few thousand who were able to legally wed in California before Proposition 8 was passed in 2008, and has been with her partner for 18 years. Hadden said she feels fortunate to know Flint, through sports, politics and his businesses.

Flint combined his sports loves one year when he got a Cubs tattoo during the Gay World Series in Los Angeles, while at Dodger Stadium. It was the last of the major-league parks he had not been to. "In 1988 I got the Cubs tattoo," said Flint. "My other tattoos were all done by Cliff Raven. That [Cubs tattoo] wasn't [done by] Cliff, but it was at his shop in Los Angeles [Tattoo Works/Cliff Raven Studios]. I was there because Dodger Stadium was the last stadium I hadn't been in and we were out there playing the Gay World Series and I thought, I am going to get a Cub tattoo to commemorate being at every park in baseball."

Baton performer Mimi Marks has often said that the true test for a transwoman in Chicago is Wrigley Field. "If you could walk through Wrigleyville during a Cubs game and not get 'spooked,' and not have anybody call you out, you were the 'girliest' girl, you made it. [The first time I did it] I called [a friend] and said, 'I am at a Cubs game on first base, 11th row. I made it. I'm a girl!'"

Marks also used to attend Bulls games frequently. "Dennis Rodman used to get her tickets," Flint said. "She would go with [well-known Baton performer] Cezanne a lot. One day Dennis gave two other ladies the tickets. So the ladies got to the door and said, 'Dennis Rodman has left tickets for us at the door.' The guy at the box office said, 'Oh, you're in the show with Mimi,' and those ladies said, 'What show?' and the ticket man said, 'Well, aren't you impersonators at the Baton?' Dennis told me those women were dumbfounded."

The Sports Legacy

Flint's sports life these days mainly revolves around the Cubs, Bears and other mainstream competitions. WCAA, under its new name, the Athletic Alliance of Chicago, has changed into a more social league, with no more softball. But Flint's impact on Chicago's sports scene is indelible, especially when it comes to teams that could compete on a national stage. Both WCAA and MSA grew to include many sports beyond softball, with national and international championships coming out of Chicago. That competitive spirit may have alienated some players, but it also helped attract others to the gay sports movement.

After those hard-fought 1980s, Chicago would never go back, and it continues to be a leader in the LGBT sports movement. The annual Coady Classic gay men's basketball tournament is the largest of its kind in the world, and grew out of WCAA. Some of WCAA's past sports leaders, including Sam Coady and Suzanne Arnold, helped run the Gay Games in Chicago in 2006.

And in 2011, nearly 30 years after the Gay World Series was first played in Chicago, with WCAA's Sidetrack team winning, the World Series returned to Chicago. Once again Sidetrack won, this time in the masters division, and this time as a representative of MSA.

Sidetrack owner Art Johnston appreciates the legacy Flint provided as a business owner. "I said then, and I say now, that I am proud to be a gay businessman in Chicago, in the activist tradition like Chuck Renslow and Jim Flint. I say it and I mean it. I have great admiration for what Jim has accomplished, keeping his business running as long as he has. I am proud to be in the same community as Jim. We are not chummy by any means. But I recognize and salute Jim doing stuff for a long time.

"History is made by people who show up, and he has been showing up, and more than showing up, for many years. We have a different style in many things. He is a feisty guy, who was not going to be held back, not even by something like the Mafia. I have enormous admiration for Jim. Even at the height of the feuds between us—anybody who was against Sidetrack, Jim would be on their side—if I had fallen ill, there would have been a troupe of female impersonators performing in a benefit."

Reminiscing about some of the high-profile leaders of that 1980s-era sports world, Flint said he was never that close to Molinaro. As for Peg Grey, who died in 2007, he said he always thought she didn't like him, but she invited him to a cancer benefit one year, and after that they got along. About Johnston, Flint said that while they were not close, they did work together on some projects, including one when the bars were trying to keep Coors products out because of the company's anti-gay legacy. But they've never had a conversation about the past, and it will probably stay that way.

Despite the enemies he made through sports, "to this day my greatest friends that I have in my life I met through athletics and sporting events," Flint said. "They are true friends. We were going out and going to tournaments. What we had was the bars. The black community was built around the churches; we were built around the bars. But the sporting events gave you a little more activity to participate in without going to a bar every night of the week. I think it was healthy and it was great for people.

"In the 1980s, when players started getting sick with AIDS, a lot of players were affected. It got to be when I would go to a tournament, I didn't want to ask where people were. I could go down a list and name them all. It affected leagues all over the country. Rusty Russell, he started Chicago's first candlelight march, as sick as he was. He would come to games, and he was an inspiration. You can't desert your friends."

Sports played a role in community building, "it moved us further towards acceptance," Flint said. "I had women's teams in gay leagues in the 1970s, at straight leagues in Lake Shore Park. Anybody who played would tell you there was no animosity, everybody partied with each other at gay or straight bars after the games." Flint said the only times there were issues were when gay guys would beat straight guys, and sometimes egos were bruised.

Flint played an important role in building the gay sports community, both in Chicago and nationally. Flint was the first Chicagoan voted into the NAGAAA Hall of Fame, in 2000. When he travels now, he never goes to a gay bar unless it sponsors sports teams or has a female impersonation show. "My greatest friends come from softball—my longtime friends," he said.

Flint sponsored sports teams in straight leagues, including some prior to the formal organization of a gay sports community. This is a Flint women's softball team, sponsored by the Baton, circa mid-1970s.

Flint wearing a jacket for his Redoubt softball team, Windy City Athletic Association (WCAA), early 1980s.

8   GayLife / Thursday, November 4, 1982

Flint reelected WCAA commissioner

Windy City Athletic Association Commissioner Jim Flint has been reelected to that position for the 1983 season.

In balloting on Oct. 19, the group also reelected two other incumbent officers—Pat Griffin as treasurer and Joe Clarke as Sergeant-at-Arms. Gary Magida won the office of assistant commissioner from a field of four candidates, and Rod Moore beat out another candidate for the position of secretary.

The WCAA has just entered its bowling season, with 14 separate teams competing in weekly play. Most of those teams, according to a group spokesman, represent area bars.

WCAA was founded in 1979 as a five-man group. It has since grown to incorporate dozens of participants and encompasses softball and bowling. The spokesman said volleyball and basketball are also being looked into. WCAA teams have participated in tournaments across the country, including the last three World Series of gay softball, held in Los Angeles in 1980, Toronto in 1981, and San Francisco in 1982.

Information about the organization can be obtained from P.O. Box 14142, Chicago 60614. WCAA membership costs $10 per year.

This November 4, 1982, GayLife newspaper clip shows Flint securing his second term as WCAA commissioner (he was the group's second commissioner).

Vince Butz, a founder of WCAA.

Flint with his winning Annex 2 WCAA softball team, early 1980s.

Above: Mike Denny (center, back row) with a mix of players from Chicago and out-of-town teams, at a 1980s softball tournament.
Photo courtesy of Mike Denny

Right: Mike Denny and Jim Flint.
Photo courtesy of Mike Denny.

Flint with his Annex 3 Blues team, 1987
Photo courtesy of Windy City Times/Outlines

Flint with Annex 3 Reds team, 1988.
Photo by Lisa Howe-Ebright

Flint with the Annex 3 Reds, late 1980s.

Flint with the Harold's Cougars basketball team, 1988, when it won first place in the WCAA league. Sam Coady is to Flint's left.
Photo by MJ Murphy

Flint with the Baton's Dina Jacobs, who was an excellent softball player, late 1980s.

This Gaylife December 5, 1985, clip shows the leaders of Chicago's gay sports community at the time.

Flint with WCAA men and women softball players, including Jan Berger (hand raised) and Edie Nieves (left) in the 1980s.
Photo courtesy of Windy City Times/Outlines

The Synergy softball team first played for the Metropolitan Sports Association, winning the Gay World Series title, then switched to WCAA and again won the title. This is a late-1980s photo.

Flint with the winning Synergy team, 1989, in San Francisco.
Photo by Jim Marks

The Redoubt volleyball team, 1980s.

Flint at a Cubs game at Wrigley Field.

Flint with his darts team, circa 1990.

Flint with his Irish team at the 1993 Southern Shootout tournament in Birmingham, Alabama.

Flint with the Annex 3 Blues, 1990s.

The Annex 3 Blues in the Cactus Cup V in Phoenix, Arizona, 1998.

Flint in Wrigley Field for the Closing Ceremony of Gay Games VII in Chicago, 2006. Behind him, from left, are Joey McDonald, José Peña and Art Johnston.

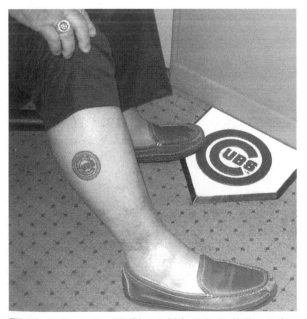

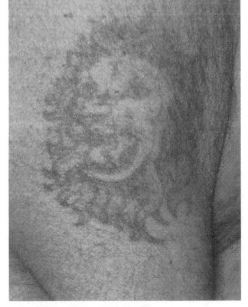

Flint's Cubs tattoo (left), and his tattoo (a lion, since Flint is a Leo) by Cliff Raven.

7

Baton: In the Beginning

In the late 1960s, most gay and lesbian bars in Chicago were owned either by non-gays or the Mafia—or both. Two of the very few bars of the era that were not in that category, according to Jim Flint, were the Checkmate, at 2546 North Clark Street, and Chuck Renslow's Gold Coast. In many ways, seeing that Renslow could make it as a gay bar owner gave Flint the nerve to try.

"Chuck really was a mentor. He made the paths for us," said Flint. "If it wasn't for him, gays owning their own bars might have taken a lot longer."

Flint's decision to open his own gay bar was gutsy, but perfectly in character. Ex-lover Warren Williamson recalled Flint as always being ambitious and having aspirations of that sort. "He was a workaholic," Williamson said. "When he was at Sam's [tending bar], I remember even then he was planning to open his own place somewhere down the line. And when Jim wanted something, there was no stopping him."

So Flint gathered together with Dwight Smith and Sam Olin to see about opening a place. Olin had lived in California since Sam's closed in 1968. (Olin was an employee and not the owner or namesake of Sam's.) Olin had opened a bar out there, but wanted to return. He told Flint to talk to Chuck Renslow and see what Renslow said.

"Dwight was a good customer. He was secure. Dwight had some money and so did Sam and I," said Flint. "Chuck came on, too. When it first opened, it was named Smitty's Show Lounge, after Dwight Smith, because he could get a liquor license and I couldn't at the time because of all my arrests."

So, with four owners, Smitty's Show Lounge opened in March 1969 at 430 North Clark Street, at the corner of Hubbard Street on Chicago's Near North Side. The group rented the space from Julius Friedman. "We didn't have a lease, everything was a handshake with him," Flint said. "My former bosses, the Fleischmanns, wanted to keep me working for them. I was a huge draw at the Normandy. There weren't many things I was good at, but I was good at tending bar. I knew how to keep my crowd and was probably one of the best bartenders in the city at that time. So they were after [Julius Friedman] to not let me rent this spot. Mr. Friedman said, 'No, everybody has to have a chance to make it, and if he can make it he should.'"

Attorney Ralla Klepak recalled: "Bea Holland used to work in a nightclub in Old San Juan that I represented, called Main Street, owned by two ladies from California, Kay and Marion. After her gig there, she returned to playing piano bars in Manhattan. When Smitty's opened, they wanted a sophisticated piano-bar player and I suggested Bea and called her in New York and offered her the intro for the job. Chuck Renslow hired her."

Flint also hired piano-playing vocalist Tony Zito, who was in the original Chicago production of Hair. His job at Smitty's was his first job after his military service in Vietnam.

The talent may have been good, but the Clark and Hubbard location wasn't exactly inviting. In those years the Baton was in a neighborhood that less than a decade before had been called the city's "worst half-mile."

"Those first years were rough," Flint said. "At the time, the River North area was a nameless and seedy area. We had SROs [single-room-occupancy residential hotels] and wino bars all over. People were afraid to come down here—seedy hotels, prostitution hotels, Indian bars, transient bars. Bars where the women would get up and strip for a bottle of wine. It wasn't a pleasant area to be in back in 1969. I remember two really nasty bars next to one another on Clark and Ontario—the Queen's Paradise and the Baron Lounge. They always talk about the Normandy, but at the Baron Lounge gay couples could dance together even before that, mainly because they didn't care what you did. There were sex acts going on under the booths, people passed out in chairs, there was everything there."

"Oh, yeah," explained Warren Williamson, "in that area you could look out at any time of day and see winos passing Thunderbird [cheap fortified wine] to each other."

"Well, nobody was coming down to Smitty's," Flint said. "Nobody knew who Smitty was, and Dwight wanted to sell out [his shares] and go to California. He was the first to drop out. That was early on, maybe a month or two into it. The name changed from Smitty's Show Lounge to the Baton Show Lounge once Smitty was out of the deal. Probably in April, or at least by summer of 1969, it became the Baton, and right around that time I started the show. I performed in the street, roller-skating back and forth across Clark with my baton to get people to notice. I'd have traffic backed up two blocks sometimes, but I had to let people know we were here, and it was cheap advertising.

"The fact of nobody coming down there was actually how the Baton show got started in the first place. We had to do something. I said, 'I am going to start a show.' So I got Lady Baronessa, Jodie Lee and Samantha George and put 16 beer cases down and a couple pieces of plywood on top of them. We got a spotlight and a curtain and we did a show."

First Class

Lady Baronessa was a Latina queen who went on to eventually become Miss Gay America in 1974. She passed away from AIDS complications in October 1992. Lady Baronessa's full "name" was The Lady Baroness María Andrea del Santiago. "We called her Barry," Flint said. "Everything about her was a baroness or a Spanish countess. Carlos was her real name."

"Lady Baronessa taught me how to really feel a song and lip-sync," said female impressionist Dina Jacobs. "She made you believe. After watching her, I began lip-syncing. I never thought of it as really an art before her. Lady Baronessa was so spot on—easily one of the best, if not the best, pantomime artist I'd ever seen. She was singing 'Top of the World' by The Carpenters and 'Eres Tú' in Spanish. She wasn't costumed like everyone else; she wore more regular clothes, but when she hit that stage she owned it. She just grabbed you. People would just throw money at her."

Samantha George was also in the first cast at the Baton. She was also known as Jimmy Humphries. "She was a young black kid and used to help make gowns for me as well," Flint said. "He's still around. He'd do Melba Moore." "Walk a Mile in My Shoes" was the big song Flint remembers George doing. Recorded by Elvis Presley and Billy Eckstine among others, the song was about racial intolerance.

Jodie Lee's persona was Liza. Flint recalled the night a 17-year-old Lorna Luft came into the Baton. "She didn't drink," Flint explained, "but she couldn't believe how much Jodie looked like her sister. She said it gave her chills."

Performer Sabrina Sabo recalled: "Jodie Lee was sort of heavily into drugs. There were times she'd do things that were crazy. Other times she'd do things like not show up, and that was something you never did at the Baton."

"One time we couldn't find her and she was discovered lying across her grandfather's grave out in the cemetery. And then they put her in Lakeshore Psychiatric Hospital," explained Flint. "We went to visit her and they wouldn't let her have visitors. Joanne [Baton waitress Joanne De Corey] had visited her earlier that afternoon, so I asked what the problem was. Apparently Jodie Lee had taken all the old women in there, teased their hair up, put makeup on them, and rolled them up and down the hallway telling them they were Miss America. That disturbed some of the families, so they wouldn't let Jodie have any visitors. Years later we heard she'd passed on."

Along with those three, Flint performed as Felicia. "I was a comedian, not very pretty, but more comic drag. Mostly I was emcee," Flint said. "The first Saturday night we did it, I was overwhelmed. It was our best night for business. We did it again the next Saturday and it went well again. Baronessa said we should do it on Fridays and Saturdays, and I gave in. When that went over, we eventually added Sundays. It kept on going and eventually got to five nights a week." (For more about the regular Baton cast members, see Chapter 8.)

In "A Slice of History: The Near North" from the February 22, 1980, GayLife newspaper, Roger "RJ" Chaffin described the drastic transformation that had occurred in the River North area. He wrote: "Having just left Normandy's, Jim Flint opened the doors to one of the most successful female impersonation clubs in the country. Jim (perhaps better known as Felicia) was also the first person in Chicago to put boys on stage for dancing and stripping. Go-go boys were a big attraction at the old Baton for several months."

One of the most popular go-go boys/strippers at the Baton at the time was Tony Lewis. He would later also become one of the most popular of the Baton's leading men, as well as a core member of Renslow's Family. (Chuck Renslow's family was a collection of lovers and friends who lived in communal style at different Chicago locations over the years. These included their six-flat building on Belmont Avenue near Clark Street, which was nicknamed the Black Castle, as well as the opulent Dewes Mansion on Wrightwood Avenue.) Other go-go boys in this chapter of the Baton history were Little Jimmy and Ricky Love.

Bartender Warren Williamson explained a bit about the bar demographics in those early days. "The mix of people was so strange," he said. "You had the drag thing going on and the lesbians, and then in the back you had a pool table, and that back area was more leather. This was when it was still on the corner [430 North Clark], and The Shack was where the Baton is now [436 North Clark]. That corner space was a mix of everything. Back there, playing pool, was where I met my lover of 41 years. He walked in and I was tending bar, and I saw him through the haze of smoke above the pool table and I knew he was the one."

When the Baton moved from the corner space to the new location a couple of doors up the street, it inherited the décor of what was formerly The Shack. The Shack had a Hawaiian motif with a thatched roof over the bar, which stood in the back corner of the room. Tables were made from long slabs of wood. It had been the R & K Shack (for Ross Downs and

Ken Overly). The switch occurred only months after the Baton had opened. Flint explained, "After we moved, we didn't change the bar much at all. It looked that way for a while."

Giving a little back story on the place, Renslow Family member David Cardwell said in a 1996 interview with Jack Rinella that he left Renslow's Sparrow's bar to work at The Shack "to try to save it because the business had gone down. It opened as The Shack, which didn't have a liquor license. It was a juice bar, and it was supposed to attract underage hustlers. It was a bust. It opened in the summer and only lasted a few months." The nonalcoholic Shack featured dancing, live music, a pool table, food and a coffeehouse atmosphere.

"We wanted to open up the Sugar Shack, and it was a teenage bar, but it didn't work," explained Renslow. "When you are just selling soft drinks, the markup is so low we just couldn't make enough to make the rent. It had sort of a surfer look because that was what was popular at the time, especially with the younger teens, who we wanted as a crowd."

Ross Downs and Ken Overly were the names on the Big Basket/Shack license. Renslow said that the duo tried to acquire ownership from him. Along with his adopted son Patrick Finnegan Renslow, Chuck Renslow met with the Downs-Overly lawyer and secretly recorded what he said were threats that were made against him, which allegedly included someone saying they "had more muscle behind them than Renslow did." Renslow then played the tape (which Renslow still claims to have in his safety deposit box) for Outfit man Johnny Gattuso, who got a "gentleman named Tiny" to beat up Overly and Downs right on Clark Street in front of The Shack while Gattuso stood on the sidewalk and smiled and waved the squad cars on.

R & K Shack Inc. is still the corporate name Flint uses today. However, following the failed attempt to gain ownership, Overly and Downs became very scarce. Flint said, "I don't know what ever happened to them," a statement echoed by Renslow. Soon after the 1970 incident, The Shack closed and the Baton moved to the 436 North Clark address.

Renslow added, "So we moved Smitty's Show Lounge, which had become the Baton, to that new location." The former location of the Baton became a leather-and-Levi's bar, the short-lived Ramrod, and everything settled down for a while—a very short while.

More funds were needed for various things, and Sam Olin didn't have or was unwilling to spend any more money, so he dropped out, the second of the four original partners to leave within only a few months after the Baton's opening. That left Renslow and Flint.

"When Felicia took over at the spot of the Baton," Renslow said, "I still owned [the license for] that spot but it was when Jim Thompson [the future Illinois governor] was a prosecutor, and he was out to get [Mayor Richard J.] Daley and was investigating everything—bars, payoffs and everything.

"I was scared because technically it was in another name, but I gave it to Felicia because I didn't want to get in trouble with the Gold Coast because of having a subterfuge license, meaning a license where I am the owner but it is in someone else's name. That's a subterfuge license. I had that going on already with the Gold Coast, and I really didn't want to stretch my luck by doing it with the Baton as well. Finally, with all the investigations going on, I just said to Jimmy, 'Here, you take it,' and I walked away from it." (President Richard Nixon appointed James R. Thompson as U.S. attorney for the Northern District of Illinois in the early 1970s. See more on this topic in Chapter 3.)

While all of this was happening in the early 1970s, the investigations by Thompson continued. As Flint explained, "He [Renslow] had his issues and I had my issues, and so he decided to focus on the Gold Coast and I got sole ownership of the Baton." Since the Baton was R & K Shack Inc., Flint became president of that corporation. By this time Flint had also had his previous arrest record expunged and could have the liquor license in his own name.

Growing the Baton

There was plenty of action behind the scenes, but the Baton's stage show was continuing to capture greater attention as well. "I owe a lot to Roby Landers," laughed Flint. Landers worked with Flint at The Chesterfield and opened the House of Landers right beside the el tracks at 936 West Diversey Parkway. "Every time the train would go by, Roby would say, 'There goes that bitch again on her roller skates.' People started getting curious and wondering what Roby was talking about, so that was good publicity. People started coming south to see what this Felicia and her gang were all about."

Despite the word of mouth, building a clientele was not easy. "Things were really tough for a while," said Warren Williamson. "With the payoffs and the cost of running the place and the staff, he [Flint] didn't always know if he was going to make payroll or not. But he always did. I'd see it be so low that he had me jump in a cab and go to the liquor store and get one bottle of bourbon and one bottle of gin, because that's all he'd have the money for, but he always made sure his people were taken care of."

Flint said that in the early 1970s, the crowd "was anyone and everyone. We stayed open until 4 and had pool tables, and when we didn't have shows, people could play pool. The music was good. We had a movie night. That was popular then. The Gold Coast and Carol's had one. It was like what karaoke is today. The bar still really wasn't profitable. I still lived in my room upstairs above the bathrooms, which was probably a 6-by-10 room. I showered in the basement because I couldn't afford to pay people, pay the rent and rent an apartment.

"I had three older guys who liked me very much. They were tricks who liked me in drag. They were supporting me and always giving me money. They always offered to help me if I got into trouble. That was my life for years. I've never been ashamed of anything I had to do to get by. Later I offered to pay them back, but they didn't want it back. I could never have made it in those early years without that.

"The Baton could also not have survived without the lesbian community. Like I said, it was so rough down here—but the lesbians weren't afraid. They saved the Baton."

Williamson agreed. "Lots of lesbians came to the Baton in those days—especially Sunday afternoons, that's all the place would be. It was nothing for me to be the only guy in there. I remember, too, the popular lesbian drink at the time was sloe screws," he said.

Flint said a lot of the women were from sports teams. "I knew a couple that played softball, and they said, 'Jim, would you be willing to sponsor us?' I said, 'Sure,' so I sponsored one team and eventually had a second team," he said. "For years we took first and second place. Because I supported them, they in turn supported me, and I was very thankful. Most gay women loved the performers, and the performers loved it. Jan Zimmerman, Kathy Kelly, Cheryl Landers, Angie—those were some of the softball ladies."

Crime and Punishment

Both the gay and mainstream media covered an October 23, 1973, shooting at the Baton. A woman shot the bartender and ran. Several lesbian patrons and patrolman Robert Murphy followed until they caught up with her on LaSalle Street, where she allegedly fired at the officer. He then shot and killed her.

"After one of the softball games, there was a murder. All the ladies were there," explained Flint. "We had a movie night and all the women were there. We heard gunshots. We came running out, and the bartender, John, got shot in the back. He was asking a woman to leave because she was being a nuisance, and she shot him. We called 911. Some of the women went after her and she ran into the doorway of 505 North LaSalle, and the cops came and surrounded it, and she opened fire on them, and so then they opened fire on her and she was killed. It was the anniversary of the night her husband broke up with her and told her he was gay. She had all these bullets in her pocket. She was going out to hurt somebody that night. Some of the women's softball team followed the woman until the cops got there."

Bartender John Staley was treated and released to recover from his wounds. He was actually off duty at the time he was shot, according to the November 1973 issue of The Chicago Gay Crusader. The woman, later identified as Joanne Popiwchak, 31, accused Staley of having cheated her earlier that day and then shot him. Popiwchak was said to be a legal secretary and divorced mother of two boys.

Flint told the media he did not recognize Popiwchak as a regular at the bar, and members of Chicago Lesbian Liberation also said they did not recognize her.

Ralla Klepak recalled the first time she really saw the aggressive masculine side of Felicia come out. "One day he was on the stage as Felicia, throwing his flaming baton while on roller skates. A guy heckled him, and Jim threw off his wig, jumped down and threw the guy out of the bar," Klepak said.

"That kid was throwing ashes all over the customers." Flint explained. "I jumped off the stage and threw off my wig and my roller skates and got him up to the door, and he swung at me and I hit him. My mistake was, I didn't call 911. If I'd have called 911 it would've been nothing, but he went out and said I brutally attacked him and I was operating with the Syndicate and all this stuff. So they hauled me in that night. When they got me in the paddy wagon, this big black guy we used to call Tits came into the paddy wagon with me. He wasn't arrested, he was there to support me. The cop said, 'What is this guy here for?' And Tits said, 'I'm just here to make sure you don't bother him because, if you do, every black guy on the West Side is going to be over here.'

"We got robbed a couple times," explained Flint. "One night Chilli Pepper came running back and said, 'We're getting robbed,' and I said, 'Oh, Chilli, you've got to be kidding.' She said, 'No, we're getting robbed.' She said China [Nguyen] was on the stage, and I looked out, and here's [waitress] Joanne De Corey stuffing all her money in her underpants. They tried to take tips, too.

"Then I came out, and all of a sudden the guy went to hit me with a gun. There were three of them and they had been sitting there all night, and this was like 1 or 2 in the morning. He told me to hit the floor, and I said, 'You've got to be crazy,' and I started running across the stage.

"All the girls had left the stage except for China, who was still back in the chorus singing 'Lullaby of Broadway.' Dina and Chilli had left, and China was singing the chorus all by herself. Every time we go to her house, we will start teasing her and start singing 'Lullaby of Broadway.'

"I ran upstairs to the dressing room and called the police, and they came and caught the guys. All they actually got was $25. In those days, every two or three hours I would clear out the cash register. When they told me to get on the floor, one of the reasons I ran was that I still had all that cash in my pocket. It was armed robbery. They got prosecuted."

Dina Jacobs recalled: "When it broke out and before we even knew the place was getting robbed, Chilli had left the stage, grabbed her coat and purse, and was out the back in the alley. I remember they were out onstage, and Jan Howard asked what was happening since she could never see, and Audrey Bryant looked up and said, 'We're getting robbed, bitch!'"

Another time, Flint spied a police lieutenant in the bar. "It was clear who he was," Flint said. "I said to all the girls, 'Do not, and I repeat do not, talk to that person.' So Dolinda [Ko'], a naïve little entertainer from Hawaii, was up there and talking to him. Andrea [Andrea Nicole, another entertainer] said, 'Jim, I think we're going to have a problem.' Evidently Dolinda gave him her phone number, and about 20 minutes later he came back with two uniformed police officers. I will say he was discreet. He arrested Ko' so quietly that no one even knew it, because at the front table was Joan Rivers and [closeted Chicago Tribune "Tower Ticker" gossip columnist] Aaron Gold. It was an arrest as a solicitation."

Flint added: "Aaron Gold used to always come in and ask Gay Chicago to keep his name out of print because he was getting too much heat from the paper." The irony of a gay gossip columnist asking not to be photographed or gossiped about did not go unnoticed.

(In 2000, when asked who Gold was, poet and lyricist Rod McKuen wrote on his official website: "The talented Aaron Gold wrote a very popular and much quoted daily newspaper column for the Chicago Tribune until his very untimely death from AIDS [in 1994]. More important to me, he was a good and generous friend. Aaron was a loving father and a great asset to Chicago where he spirited much charity work and boosterism for the city.")

There was another, much more unexpected and disturbing incident involving a Chicago police officer. "When we used to have the Traffic Division over here [54 West Hubbard Street] and my sister Skip was tending bar part-time in the daytime, this policeman liked her," Flint said. "One night he told her that she was going to go with him. She said, 'No, I'm not,' and he pulled a gun on her. As I was coming down the street in a cab with my mom and my younger sister, I looked and thought, 'Oh, my God, I wonder what's going on down there.' There were all these police cars, and when the police told me what was going on and asked me what I wanted to do, I said to get him out of here and never let him in here again, and it's over. And that was it."

Dorothy "Skip" Flint explained the story further. "They used to have a pool table over there, and the police used to come over on lunch and play," she said. "They would come in and play pool if they got off work, or if they had a court case and had to waste a few hours. If they were working, they'd have a pop or something, but if they were off duty they'd have a beer. I was friendly with everybody. I didn't notice the guy that much.

"Then one night we were going out to eat—my mom, Jim and myself. Jim didn't have anyone to work the door. I said I'd do it, since they were going out for Chinese food and I don't like it that much. So I was working the door, and the guy came in, and I said, 'What are you doing here, you usually come in during the day?' He said, 'I just stopped by and was hoping you could get off so we could go out.' I told him I couldn't go out, I was working. Then he came around like he wanted to tell me something, and he had a gun, and he put it to my side and said, 'No, you are going out with me.' I repeated that I had to work, and he said, 'No, you're going with me.'

"I thought he was just playing around, but then he called the bartender over and pulled the gun on him. He said, 'She's going with me or someone is going to get hurt.' I was more scared for him than for me. Luckily it was winter, so I said, 'Well, if I am going with you I need to go get my coat, so you wait here and I'll be right back.' I went to the office and dialed 911. By the time I came down, there were cops everywhere, and they'd already pulled him out."

Flint's beloved sister Dorothy came to Chicago by way of St. Louis. "I lived in New Mexico and was married with a kid, and then I got divorced," she said. "After I divorced, I had my son and lived with my mom in St. Louis. It wasn't until I got there that I found out I was pregnant. Jim was my brother, and after my father died he became like a father. After my divorce and I moved up here, he became my friend.

"Jim had a three-bedroom place by [University of Illinois] Circle Campus at 720 South Carpenter. It was Jim and my mother, myself and my two children [Earl and Michelle], and my younger brother Ronnie. I've worked for Jim on and off for years. I also worked for the city—that was my job for 12 or 13 hours a day. Then weekends I'd be at the Baton. I didn't start working for him as my main job until I retired. Right now I take reservations three days a week and answer phones, and then on Saturdays I help him seat people. I used to like tending bar during the day, but then Jim decided to only open at night and ended the day business."

"After the Baton had been open a while, [Mobster] Johnny Gattuso came to me and said he wanted the bar," explained Jim Flint. "I said, 'Johnny, I can't, my sister is in it with me.' She wasn't, but my sister Skip (Dorothy) worked at City Hall with Johnny's wife, Shirley. Skip used to sometimes say to me, 'You know that guy from Falstaff beer, John Gattuso, he stares at me every day that he comes to the office.' Years later, I finally told her what I'd said. She was not real happy with me. That could have been the trigger which kept the Mob from moving in on the Baton."

"Jim told me that—eventually," added his sister Dorothy. "I didn't know this until years later, after Johnny died. I worked for City Hall for Streets and Sanitation. Johnny knew everybody, and his ex-wife Shirley worked as my secretary, and he used to come in, and I knew of him but was never much involved. He had married her cousin, but Shirley had something like six kids with him, so they were still very close.

"He would come in and just stare at me. So after a few times, I said, 'Shirley, are you and your ex-husband having problems? Why is he here all the time? He is just sitting and staring at me.' It was making me uncomfortable. Finally I told her she had to tell him to stop coming in. It was only about two weeks later that he ended up dead. I didn't know Jim had said that [she was co-owner of his bar]. To me, it looked like he [Gattuso] was trying to get too much involved in things going on, and I was dealing with a lot of union issues at the time. I just didn't trust him. That's why I wanted him to stop coming in, but then Jim told me that about the Baton, and it made more sense."

(Johnny Gattuso was Mob-affiliated. According to a Chicago Tribune article on

December 3, 1989, by Ronald Koziol: "Jasper Caprise and John Gattuso, the two who botched the murder of mobster Ken Eto in 1983, paid for that mistake with their lives. Both were repeatedly stabbed to death, then stuffed in the trunk of a small car." Their bodies were found July 14, 1983. According to a June 6, 2006, piece in the Chicago Tribune by staff reporters Jeff Coen and Rudolph Bush as well as staff reporter Matt O'Connor, Eto, known as "Tokyo Joe," turned on the Mob after surviving the hit. Eto crawled into a pharmacy and called 911. Eto had been targeted after his conviction on gambling charges—the Mob feared he would testify against them. Eto was placed in the witness protection program, and died of natural causes in Atlanta in 2004.)

Special Guests

In "Felicia Does It 'My Way': Baton Boasts Best in Female Impersonation," by Fred Alexson in the April–May 1975 issue of The Chicago Gay Crusader, the bar and its performers were profiled.

"After 5½ years ... I decided to go on my own, and I have to thank Chuck Renslow because he helped me to get my own place, the first Baton on the corner of Clark and Hubbard. Chuck is responsible for many people making it on their own," Flint told the Crusader. "I'm indebted to Lady Baronessa, Peaches, Jodie Lee and Jan Howard because these four entertainers stuck by me and put up with me during a period in my life when I really didn't know what I was doing. I almost went bankrupt two or three times, but we kept trying, and now five years later we're still here."

Alexson's piece continued: "The current cast at the Baton is certainly the most star studded ever, presenting the Versatile Polynesian lovely Dina Jacobs (Miss Gay Chicago 1975); the Personality Plus of Miss Gay Illinois 1975, Peaches; the Blonde Goddess Bombshell Jan Howard; the Redheaded Vamp and Miss Gay Chicago 1974 Chilli Pepper; the Fiery Fire Goddess and Countess of Hong Kong China Nguyen; the Liza Minnelli look alike Jodie Lee; the Queen of Motown and Soft Soul, Leslie Rejeanné; and the Lady of Sophisticated Elegance, Audrey Brian [also spelled Bryant]. All these superlatives and a few more apply in each case, and while each of the entertainers is uniquely talented, all are distinctly original and appreciated for their differences by audiences who make them all stars."

The story also mentioned that in addition to the regular cast, in the previous few years the Baton had also been a venue for well-known entertainers and engaging special guest artists Michael Greer, Charles Pierce, Craig Russell, and Tiffany Jones.

The string of guest appearances at the Baton began with the legendary Charles Pierce (1926–1999) performing at a fundraiser for the groups ONE of Chicago and Mattachine Midwest in May 1973. (ONE of Chicago was the local chapter of the Los Angeles–headquartered ONE Inc., which was one of the earliest U.S. homophile organizations.) Pierce is best known for his dead-on and hilarious impersonations of such Hollywood legends as Bette Davis, Joan Crawford, Mae West, Katharine Hepburn, Jeanette MacDonald and many more. A Chicago Gay Crusader piece on the entertainer at the time of the benefit said (perhaps with more than a wink), "It's no wonder people like Rudolf Nureyev and John Gielgud run to see him." When Pierce came to town, he was also a popular draw at Man's Country, a men's bathhouse and entertainment complex owned by Chuck Renslow.

From July 3 to 15, 1973, Michael Greer gave 10 and 12 o'clock shows at the Baton.

Greer was another "gay/K-Y circuit" entertainer who also appeared in Chicago at Man's Country. According to his Internet Movie Database biography, Greer (1943–2002) was best-known for his work as Queenie, the prison drag queen in the stage and film versions of Fortune and Men's Eyes in 1967 and 1971, and he had also been featured in the 1969 film The Gay Deceivers, about two men avoiding Vietnam service by saying they are gay. One of his best-known personas was Mona the Mouth, in which he would dress up as Mona Lisa and hold a gilded picture frame in front of himself as he did his comedic monologue. This shtick eventually evolved to include another persona as Gainsborough's "Blue Boy."

Greer was followed at the Baton by the booking, on July 18, 1973, of Craig Russell (1948–1990). "He's Mae West, Peggy Lee, Barbra Streisand, Judy Garland, Carol Channing. He's the fabulous female impersonator Craig Russell," read The Chicago Gay Crusader advertisement. Variety praised him: "Russell leaves the more frenetic pace to Jim Bailey. With precision gestures and vocal inflection, Russell is as good if not better." Russell performed Wednesdays through Sundays for a few weeks with showtimes at 10 and 12:30.

According to Wikipedia, Russell was born in Toronto and became president of Mae West's fan club as a teen, and worked briefly in Los Angeles as her secretary. Returning to Toronto, he pursued his career as a stage performer. By 1971, he was a regular performer in Toronto gay clubs and had a burgeoning international following. His impersonations included Carol Channing, Peggy Lee, Judy Garland, Marlene Dietrich, Bette Midler, Tallulah Bankhead, Barbra Streisand, Shirley Bassey, Bette Davis and even notorious homophobe Anita Bryant. While performing, Russell always spoke and sang in the voices of the celebrities he was impersonating. In 1977, he starred in the film Outrageous!, which led to his winning the Best Actor Award at the Berlin International Film Festival. A decade later he starred in the sequel, Too Outrageous! Although he publicly identified as gay, Russell married his close friend Lori Jenkins in 1982. In 1990 he died of a stroke related to complications of AIDS.

"I found Craig Russell in Toronto and I brought him here [to the Baton] and asked him to come work for me," said Flint. "He came, and I got him on the Tom Snyder show, and that's when he really made it big. Then he got very heavy on coke and went on Channel 7 one time on the morning show, and they did an interview with him and he was so drunk. The producer of the show got fired, and he [Russell] got banned from the network. He went to West Germany to work for the rest of his life.

"The last time I saw him, they took him off the plane at O'Hare and he came here, and you would have thought he had mayonnaise in his hair, it was so filthy. Chilli took him in the back and combed it all down. He was out of control, sitting at the bar and throwing money everywhere. I called my friend who was a police officer in the district, and they took him over to the River North Best Western and checked him into a room and put his money in the safe. The next day he got up and got on an American flight, and that was the last I ever heard of him. What a great entertainer, though. Jim Bailey could do two or three imitations—this kid could do something like 30 voices. It's a shame.

"I got so mad. One time we were in Boston doing a show when the Baton was on tour, and Jim Bailey was being interviewed in the other room. I remember when he walked out, the station manager said, 'Do you want to meet the entertainers (meaning us)?' He said, 'I don't associate with them.' Like he was above it all. I said to him, 'You are very good, but Craig [Russell] is a lot better."

Tiffany Jones (Kenneth Whitehead) made special guest-star appearances at the Baton as well. "She was one of the most beautiful drag stars you've ever seen," Flint said. "The Texas Tornado, they called him. He did roller skates in a nun's habit, and he is also the only white person I know who could pull off doing Diana Ross, and then two minutes later he would come out as someone else entirely."

Jones hosted the show at the Copa in Houston and toured extensively, playing, among other places, the Club Baths, and was extremely popular in Provincetown. One of Jones' favorite lines was, "I see we have a number of straight people in the audience today. I love straight people; they're so obvious!"

In Body Positive and on the site thebody.com, Dennis Rhodes wrote of the late Jones: "For years, his signature closing was Charles Aznavour's lovely ballad, 'Tell Me If You Can, What Makes a Man a Man,' which defiantly confronts hostility and discrimination against gay people. Resplendent in drag, Tiffany would elegantly remove one thing at a time until he was in his bikini briefs. Then he would throw on a pair of old jeans, boots, and a cowboy hat, now the picture of masculinity, and crumple his wig in his hand while looking heavenward. That number elevated a cheap and funny drag show to something approaching art."

Jones was one of those to die in the early years of the AIDS epidemic.

"Pudgy was another one who appeared on a Baton stage a few times," Flint said. "I met her as a waitress at Toffenetti's [restaurant] next to the [Greyhound] bus station. We all just thought she was so funny and talented. We all worked to get behind her and get her popular. She played places like The Trip and some of Chuck's [Renslow] places, and I had her here."

The wisecracking waitress, whose real name was Beverly Wines, was compared by many to Totie Fields. She played lots of big clubs, where her insult brand of humor was extremely popular. She was working her regular gig as the comedy star of X-Burlesque, a show at the Flamingo Hotel in Las Vegas, when, at the end of the night, she went home, sat in her favorite chair and died of heart failure on Christmas Eve of 2008.

In addition to stars on the stage, there were plenty in the audience as well, as Flint recalled. "One time [singer/songwriter] Rod McKuen was in here, and he went up to my light man Billy Cooper and said, 'Stop flashing those lights, you're taking the beauty away from those girls.' Rod came in with Rock Hudson," Flint said. "The last time Rock was here, he'd gotten robbed by a hustler at the Ambassador East, and so they called me. Rock always liked those little blond hustlers from Texas, and so I had to go over there and get him out of there [the hotel] before the police came or anything. That was probably 1982 or '83. He was sort of secretive at the Baton, but, you know, even people who didn't know what gay was knew he was gay—especially in Hollywood. It was just one of those things."

Flint recalled many more celebrity sightings in town and at the Baton. "We'd hang out at Punchinello's ["Chicago's watering hole for Broadway buffs"] on Rush near Oak, or the Croydon Circle in the Croydon Hotel [at 616 North Rush Street], which is now the James," Flint said. "That's where I met Sammy Davis Jr., and he came over to the Baton. Kirk Douglas was in the Baton one night. I had to kick Chris Farley out, and it was so funny, because the night I kicked him out of the Baton the guy driving him said, 'Don't feel bad, this is the fourth bar he's been kicked out of tonight.' He'd sit on the floor and then he wouldn't get up, and he'd say, 'Tell everybody you danced with Chris Farley,' and I said, 'No, you tell everyone you danced with Jim Flint.'" (For a more complete list of famous Baton patrons, see Appendix.)

Other Female Impersonator Venues
Blue Dahlia

Flint explained the drag scene in Chicago in the early 1970s. "When I first opened, they had the Blue Dahlia on North Avenue [5640 West North Avenue]. They had the Nite Life on State and Walton [933 North State Street] and then the Isle of Capri on the South Side [14511 Western Avenue in south suburban Dixmoor, which was in business from 1968 to 1974]. Those were about the three going at the time."

The Blue Dahlia was owned by Emil "Moe" Monaco and was a popular jazz and drag club that featured such performers as Tony "The Jewel Box Revue" Midnite (1926–2009) and Maria Montez, "The Latin Dream." The Blue Dahlia was named for the Raymond Chandler novel and subsequent 1946 movie that featured Alan Ladd and Veronica Lake. The waitress and bartender was Margie Dahl. The bar was the one-time home of Chilli Pepper (pre-Baton) as well as popular entertainer Jill Christie. It had been around for years, and in 1955–56 the Blue Dahlia was considered the top female impersonation lounge in the country.

David's Place

By 1972, new female-impersonator bars on the scene included Sparrow's, House of Landers and then David's Place, near Sparrow's. "I remember when David's Place opened, they were kind of different," Flint said. "They weren't the usual bar owners that worked together. The rumor was they were going to put me out of business. And, of course, five or six of my employees and entertainers did go. Dina [Jacobs] and Audrey [Bryant] went to David's Place. That crushed me.

"I think when Tony Lewis left, that was the real crusher, because I always thought they were very loyal. I thought I was going to close, so I dropped the shows and spent two weekends here with 20-or-so good friends. Then I thought, 'What am I doing?' So I went out and hired a whole new cast and started over. It was Madalene Mitchell and Patricia D Roma and myself and a few of the stay-overs, and we started the show again. It wasn't the best, but we put it together. Three months later, David's Place folded, and the ones who left wanted back. A couple did come back, but a lot didn't."

Dina Jacobs was one of those who went to David's Place. "I don't quite recall why I left," she said. "I don't think it was money. I was never all that concerned about the money. I ended up going along with Audrey Bryant, China Nguyen, Tanya Terrell, Tony Lewis, Billy Denim and Taisha Wallace (who was also the dressmaker). The entertainers already at David's Place were Kiki St. John, Little Izzy (a "little person" drag queen), Ebony Carr. Ebony was the hottest thing in the show. Wayland Flowers even made a puppet of her! There was also Artesia Wells. She was so ahead of her time—hair, makeup, everything. She was so avant-garde, completely fresh and out of the box."

In Sukie de la Croix's "Gay Chicago Timeline" column of January 19, 2011, he noted: "A coffeehouse opens at David's Place, 5232 North Sheridan Road, as a home for the Loyola University campus gay group. David's Place was a drag bar that opened Nov. 10, 1972, and was co-managed by Earl Botrager (RIP 1994). An ad in Michael's Thing magazine reads: 'Cocktail lounge and restaurant extraordinaire. Chicago's most unique entertainment. Open 4:00 PM to 4:00 AM.'"

The Nite Life

Sukie de la Croix's August 13, 2003, "Chicago Whispers" column in Windy City Times included Bob M.'s memories of the Nite Life: "The Nite Life was a major drag bar located at 933 North State St. I don't know when it opened but it burned down early in 1973."

In de la Croix's September 13, 2000, "Chicago Whispers" column, Viki (aka Kiki) St. John recalled: "I was in the Nite Life with my friend Beverly one night. That was a straight bar with a drag show. We wanted to talk to the guys in the show when it was over. They had a cocktail waitress there who was a crossover. She was working there as a female waitress serving drinks. She worked downtown in an office during the day as a woman. She was saving her money to get the sex change. I don't know why, but the cops didn't know that was going on there. The show was just about over and we were waiting to talk to the guys, and Beverly said, 'I think we ought to get out of here right now.' So we got up and left. Five minutes later they raided the place. So we missed that one. They raided the place and they closed it down."

"There were so few nightclubs at that time, and at a lot of them, the entertainers weren't treated very well," explained Baton performer Shawn Luis. "I remember the Nite Life. Whitey was, I think, the owner's name. He treated his entertainers like prostitutes. Everything to him had a dollar sign on it."

Flint recalled: "The Nite Life was mostly hookers. The entertainers mostly stripped and then went out with the trade. If they went out with the trade, they had to give the owners a cut, and you kept the rest. That's how Whitey operated for years." Some of the popular Nite Life entertainers included Karen, Nicole, and Michelle as well as sometime Baton performer Sabrina Sabo.

La Cage

Then there was La Cage, which opened for a while at 50 East Oak Street. Thursday nights at La Cage featured La Soirée des Rêves Noirs ("the evening of dark dreams"). It was in business from 1980 to 1983 and was housed in the space that had been Barbara Eden's (I Dream of Jeannie) defunct restaurant Huckleberry's. After the purchase, the upstairs became a chic lounge and drag-show venue. It was also at La Cage that cult film star Divine started her nightclub act.

Sukie de la Croix's "Chicago Whispers" column in Windy City Times on June 21, 2000, included reminiscences from longtime Chicago female impersonator Lisa Eaton: "I worked at La Cage when Divine was there. La Cage was the most excellent female-impersonator lounge in the city of Chicago. It was located on Oak Street, right next to the Esquire Theater. Chilli Pepper told the guys who owned it, 'Oh, I've got this girl for you. She's great, you're gonna love her.' So I had my medication and I brought the house down and they hired me overnight.

"One day, La Cage called me up and said, 'We're letting all the girls off this week, because Divine is coming in and she needs all the time to herself.' They said, 'If you want to come in and see her tonight, come in.' I said, 'I'd love to meet her.' So she was downstairs in the restaurant with her wig off.

"When I met Divine she had a menu in front of her, and it was huge, and I said, 'Take the shark, girl, the last one I had swallowed a Puerto Rican. You'll love it.' She goes, 'OK, Judy, OK.' Then I was escorted back upstairs and she proceeded to go on, and she did 'Step by Step, Slowly I Turn' ['Native Love']. She had this big black wig on, like Ann Landers does.

"She was staying at the same hotel I lived at. I saw her crawling in at 4 in the morning once, shuffling her feet and heavy breathing. She said to me, 'Oh, hi, Judy.' Then she called me one night, and said, 'Hello, Angie.' And I said, 'No, there's no Angie here.' Then the phone rings again, 'Hello, Judy,' and I say, 'Hi' ... 'This is me, Divine. I need to know where I can buy size-13 pumps steel-reinforced. Just give me Chilli Pepper's number.' So I said, 'Oh, no, girl ...' She said, 'Oh, just give me her number.' I said, 'OK.' So she called, then Chilli calls me and says, 'Why were you so reluctant to give Divine my phone number?' I said, 'But you know how you are ... ' She said, 'But Divine's a star! She's a star!'"

(Harris Glenn Milstead, the actor and performer known as Divine [1945–1988], rose to prominence in such John Waters films as Pink Flamingos, Female Trouble, Polyester and Hairspray. Divine also toured extensively in such theatrical productions as Women Behind Bars and was enormously successful as a club entertainer. Divine died in his sleep of an enlarged heart on March 7, 1988.)

"The people at La Cage were going to do the same thing they tried to do with David's Place, namely to put me out of business, but it didn't last," Flint said. "By then I was already starting to build a name here because of the talk shows, and the straights were starting to come."

Sparrow's and Roby Landers

Dina Jacobs first met Roby Landers in Kansas City when she was part of the Jewel Box Lounge Revue. (The lounge was at 3219 Troost Avenue in Kansas City. The ads read: "Park in our big, lighted and patrolled lots in the rear and visit all 3 clubs in Mid-America's Greatest Fun Complex. The Yum Yum is next door south [3221] and the Cat Balleu is two doors south [3223]. More than 1,000 good seats!")

"I was still in Pearls of the Pacific, a touring group of Hawaiian queens," Jacobs said. "Because of the blue law [Sunday alcohol-sales restrictions] in Kansas City, the Jewel Box Lounge was closed on Sundays, and I remember Roby would always have everyone over to her place there. Later she came to Chicago to work at Sparrow's for Chuck Renslow and then had her own place with the House of Landers on Diversey. She asked me to come work for her. When I didn't, things were a little strained between us after that."

Chuck Renslow recalled bringing Landers back to Chicago. "When we brought her back from the Jewel Box in Kansas City to come to Sparrow's, she said she wouldn't come unless we found her an apartment," Renslow said. "She paid the rent, but we had to find it. The problem was that it had to be either first-floor or above a storefront, because when she made her own gowns she had a sequins machine that went thump-thump-thump. We finally found her a place on Broadway a couple blocks south of Montrose above a store, so at night she could sew and it wouldn't disturb anyone."

In Sukie de la Croix's "Chicago Whispers" column in Windy City Times on June 21, 2000, Lisa Eaton talked a bit about the House of Landers. "I met other people and they told me, 'Lisa, audition at House of Landers.' Well, I hardly had a wardrobe. I went in half-assed,

I wore sun hats and long skirts, boots and stuff, it was very '70s. I looked like a hippie imitating Liza Minnelli and Judy Garland. So then I started to go to thrift stores with a friend. The first audition, I didn't make it, and Roby said, 'You've got promise, though.' She liked my lip-sync.

"Roby Landers finally hired me when she saw that my wardrobe improved, and I learned some makeup tips. Roby paid us $100 a week, this was in '72, '73, and I roomed with Verushka, another queen that worked there. She was from South America. When they announced her name, they would say, 'The Latin Lovely Verushka, straight from Caracas, Venezuela.' We became good buddies. She was very jealous of me. Like if I'd leave her alone and want to go out, she'd get pissed off. We wound up fighting a lot. But we stayed together for a while."

Bar patron Richard Johnson remembered Roby Landers. "Oh, she was a lot of fun," he said. "Roby and her swizzle stick is what I remember most. She'd take it and slip it under her dress and then bring it out and wave it beneath her nose. She was always entertaining."

The House of Landers closed after only a couple of years, but in its heyday it featured such notable drag entertainers as Tillie the Dirty Old Lady, Jackie Knight, Ebony, Timi Saxton, Kiki St. John, Lisa Eaton, Jerri Anthony, Artesia Wells and Roby herself. After the eventual closing of the House of Landers, Chuck Renslow's ill-fated disco Zolar opened in the space. Uninsured, Zolar burned to the ground in a fire on March 21, 1976, a few months after it opened. Sources vary as to whether its cause was a spark from a passing train or faulty wiring.

Flint also worked with Landers for several years when Landers started his annual Halloween balls, and Flint was frequently an emcee. Later, Flint continued the Costumes on Review Halloween Ball tradition. Costumes on Review lasted at least until 1983, when it marked its 17th anniversary. (See Chapter 13.)

Togetherness

The attorney Ralla Klepak got involved with Flint in the Togetherness bar. "Jim came to me and we found an empty warehouse around 51 or 61 West Hubbard," she said. "We opened Togetherness as the first really elegant gay nightclub. It was for all people, men and women, female impersonators, all races. All people could come."

"It was not considered a drag bar," Renslow said. "It was a bar for lesbians and gay men and it had drag shows. The name Togetherness meant bringing all these groups all together."

"I went and managed Togetherness for Ralla Klepak," said Marge Summit. "I was working downtown in computers, and then after work I'd go home, and then around midnight I'd go into Togetherness and balance the money and place the liquor orders. I even worked there part-time as a bartender. When you walked into Togetherness, there was a low ceiling that ended after about 20 or 25 feet in, and then there were tables and chairs and stairs going up to a balcony that overlooked the stage. Roby Landers was there; Leslie Rejeanné, who did Diana Ross; Jan Howard; Audrey Bryant; and Tina King, who was the first drag queen I knew who actually had the operation and came back to show us. A lot of the girls worked there, before they went to the Baton after Togetherness closed."

In Sukie de la Croix's June 4, 2003, "Chicago Whispers" column in Windy City Times, he reprinted a column by That Girl called "Tuffy's Trivia," which weighed the merits of drag bars in Chicago. The column had appeared in the August 1972 first (and possibly only) edition of Tuffy This Month in Chicago: "Togetherness, 61 West Hubbard St., is definitely new to drag. The three cast members are individually talented, but very clumsy as a group. Tina King, a seasoned veteran to show business, recently retired and the show now lacks sparkle. Stacy Stevens [Flint recalled it as being in fact Nicki Carr] adds humor to Mama Cass and sheds new light on Barbra Streisand. LaVerne Sinclair is a double for Diana Ross and Jennifer Radclyff mimics some of the most well-known Black singers beautifully. Togetherness leaves much to be desired as a nightclub, poor lighting, close quarters and especially their less than generous drinks, and their only saving factor is the individual talents of their few entertainers."

Flint added, "I had a small interest in Togetherness with Ralla Klepak and then, soon after, it was too much for me, so I pulled out and kept the Baton, and Ralla kept it going after that."

Baton: The Turnabouts

The turnabouts were a popular event at the Baton. Flint had first "done" Felicia at a turnabout at The Chesterfield, which was an extremely important milestone in his life and career. Flint is someone who gravitates toward consistency in his life, so having turnabouts at the Baton seemed a wonderful idea. On those special evenings, the performers would tend bar and serve, and the bartenders and servers would perform.

The Baton "was like a drag version of Cheers—on hormones," said Warren Williamson. "I tended bar with Lotta Love and Billy Mann. I made a living working on Friday and Saturday night. I worked some weekday afternoons as well, but you didn't make anything in the afternoon shifts in tips. It was the only time I ever enjoyed my job. It gave me a whole different view of life. I was born to a right-wing fundamentalist family in Texas, so going to New York City and then Chicago and traveling really opened me up—but bartending in a drag bar showed me I had a lot more to learn.

"Jimmy was firing me every other day. Then he'd call me the next day and say, 'Where are you?' And I'd say, 'You fired me yesterday!' And he'd tell me to get to work. That used to happen all the time. I remember one time he didn't call me and it really shook me up, and I finally called him and he started laughing after a minute and said he didn't call just to scare me. Something else was, we also had those turnabouts at the Baton like he said they did at The Chesterfield. He threatened me into doing it, so I did. I'm more of a leather guy, so it didn't come naturally. Jimmy dressed and made me up personally. I did Jeanette MacDonald singing 'San Francisco.'"

"I think I wanted to see if he'd do it," laughed Flint. "We did it a few times here. Jesse and Bobby did it. Lennie did it, too. It was different. It worked then because the audience was more gay. With it being predominantly straight now, they really wouldn't get the issue."

Lennie Malina recalled the turnabouts. "Oh, yes, Jim making drinks and Chilli serving them," she said. "It was always a treat doing those because Jimmy was so happy, and when Jimmy was happy everyone was happy. There really is nothing like him with a smile on his face. Anyway, one turnabout, I remember Ikey [bartender Irene 'Ikey' Raczka] and I did 'Islands in the Stream,' and she was Kenny Rogers and I was Dolly Parton. Ikey would always get so nervous beforehand. A lot of times, for the turnabouts there, I would do Felicia on the roller skates with the baton. Or the other thing Jim would do, which was come out on roller skates and do a number in a wedding dress ['Go On With the Wedding' by Patti Page] and then at the end he'd lift up the dress and there'd be a big dildo. That was back when he liked being a little raunchy."

Sunday Night

"I remember, Sunday was also the day they had open stage, kind of an open microphone for guys who wanted to try their hand at drag," recalled Marge Summit. "We used to call it Creature Features because you never knew what you were going to see, and sometimes it was very scary. One time a guy who was cooking for me at the time did Miriam Makeba's 'Pata Pata' there. He was really good."

"Sundays were Guest Night," said Flint. "In the beginning we got a nice crowd, and people brought in other people to cheer them on. That brought in a mixed crowd and some interesting entertainers, but after a while we were only getting guys who wanted to throw a wig on and think they were pretty without putting any effort into it. We finally ended it, because it wasn't going where we wanted it to go. When it was going well, though, we had some great entertainment on Sundays—Bertha Butts, Virginia Slims, Kiki St. John."

The Sunday nights were also a sort of talent audition, though not as much as the Continental pageants have become. Shanté and Sheri Payne were Sunday regulars who eventually became full-time cast members.

Talk-Show Circuit

Flint described perhaps the most significant change in the popularity of the Baton: "We'd been on Irv Kupcinet's show a few times and knew Essee [Esther Solomon Kupcinet], his wife. I think Irv was in love with Chilli. [Irv Kupcinet was a columnist for the Sun-Times and well-known Chicago broadcast personality.] Our first show after that was Saturday Night with Jay Levine. I think Jay Levine was scared out of his tree just having us on there.

"About five years after we opened, Irv Kupcinet called me and said he was going to bring in a guest that night, and it was Phil Donahue and Marlo Thomas. After the show, Phil said he wanted us to go on his show. Not only did we go on his show, but we went on five or six times. That got people talking, and that's when I first met Oprah, in 1982 in Baltimore, and Sally Jessie Raphael, and then it was going from one talk show to another. I remember sharing the green room, the dressing room, at NBC Tower one time with Jerry Falwell. Phil said to me, 'I'm going to bring someone in, so don't be shocked.' I thought he [Falwell] was going to pass out.

"Phil Donahue was so great. He cared. He got more into your lifestyle and where you come from and what you do. Irv was a little like that as well. It was so different than when we went on something like Maury Povich. That was awful. With Maury it was not telling your story—all he wanted to do was ask, 'Are you a man?' That's all it was—'Are you a man?' And then, 'Are you a man?' And then, 'Are you a man?' Again I told the kids if they [talk-show hosts] don't want to talk to us about the entertainment factor and talk to us as people, we should stop going on there. Phil Donahue, though, was a great interviewer and so easy to talk with. He made a big difference in the success of the Baton."

"I was there when the Baton really took off," said Dana Douglas, a cast regular and eventual Miss Continental 1987. "Much of that happened when we went on the road. When we would go on these road trips from city to city, I was usually the driver, because I made a bad passenger. We went to Kentucky, Detroit, Baltimore, anywhere in that van. When we were home in Chicago, Jim was just our boss, but when we were on the road he treated us like superstars.

"We did The Jerry Springer Show before it became so trashy. We did a show in Baltimore, and that was when the hostess was Oprah Winfrey, before she came to Chicago. So, on her show Chilli did a number, which I think was Millie Jackson's 'Once You've Had It,' and I did one. Another time I did Cyndi Lauper's 'Time After Time' on a talk show. I remember because I wanted to do 'Total Eclipse of the Heart' but it was too long. Once we started getting on Jerry Springer, and then Oprah came to Chicago and we were on her new show A.M. Chicago, the Baton started becoming a tour-bus destination. That's when the Baton went from being a gay bar to being a mainstream show club."

The Rules

Flint clarified the restrictions for performing at the Baton, rules that have remained ironclad for more than four decades, even as ideas regarding drag and transgender identity have changed. "Enhancement is OK, but no complete surgeries," he said. "You can have top enhancement, bottom enhancement like hip implants, but not bottom removal. That's always been the case. We advertise female impersonation, so it has to go along with what we are. If anyone goes through with the surgery, they have to leave. Most leave on their own when they are getting the surgery."

There has been some talk that having an inflexible rule of this sort can be controlling and that having such a definition stands in the way of the natural course of greater fulfillment for some of the performers. Despite this, Flint maintains that it is and will remain the club policy. Flint said exceptions are made for special appearances, but none for regular cast members.

"Chanel [Dupree] had the operation, and she comes back and performs once in a while," he said. "I personally feel if you're going to go that far to be a woman, then you should not be performing in a drag show that says female impersonation. We advertise female impersonation, and once you become a woman, you're a woman. If one of the longtime cast members came to me and said they wanted to have it done, I still wouldn't make an exception. Maybe as a guest once in a while like Chanel and Lakesha Lucky—but to me that would be like deceiving the public. That's our policy, and that's what the show is about."

Some have said that the Baton policy is behind the times. One performer who wished to remain anonymous called it "ridiculous" and said that such rules are part of a larger attempt to "control performers' lives." The interviewee said several other venues have changed their performer policies to "male-born." Flint simply contends that "if they feel that way, then the Baton is just not the place for them."

Mercedes Tyler, who was Miss Continental Plus 2008, added: "I think one of the things that is interesting is just all the different levels of drag. The Baton caters to basically a straight audience, in that I think it's a lot of people going there wanting to see 'the freaks,' and the Baton has the skimpy costumes because the real questions are always, 'Oh, my God, is that really a guy?' and 'Where is it?'"

Bartender Tim Gideon hears it all the time and he knows what people come to see. "They all say, 'Oh, my God, I can't believe that's a guy, I can't believe that's a guy.' I hear that constantly. I get a lot of questions, which I always try to deflect, because a lot of what they ask is frankly none of their business. It can be very inappropriate. People will ask, 'Did they have this done? Did they have that done?' I try to be as tactful about things as possible, but that is really the performers' personal business. Mostly I'll just say the performers do their own makeup and hair."

"When you perform for a gay audience, it's very different," continued Mercedes. "Gay audiences for one thing have a different sense of humor. That's a big difference, plus they want to see the works. They want the big hair and the costumes and the jewelry. They want Vegas. I understand the Baton policy about only transsexuals because if you have the full operation, if you get a sex change, then you are in effect saying, 'I want to live my life as a woman,' so the irony of then making your living as a cross-dresser is kind of strange. Why would you want that, when having the procedure is to be a woman and no longer a man?"

The Basics

Performers at the Baton get a salary and tips. There are no benefits. Flint elaborated: "We did an insurance program for a while, but they didn't want to contribute into it, so they all got their own. Giving the girls days off is tough, because I don't want my show broken up on the weekend. We have so many out-of-towners, and they want to see the show, and all of our productions are built around all of them. Time off can be really hard on the weekends, Fridays and Saturdays especially."

Flint explained why the Baton is such a sought-after spot for performers. "The difference here is that here they have a five-day job," he said. "They don't have to fly here and get booked here and there. Sometimes they may get more money in a booking out of town, but by the time they pay their car and hotel and airfare and whatnot they don't make anything.

"The waiting list of people wanting to come here is unbelievable, because they like that steady job, and there are very few places that do that anymore. There's Parliament House in Orlando, where the performers work three or four nights, [performers at] Revolution in Orlando work three or four nights, and the other places are two or one night a week. Funky Monkey is also there, it is a restaurant that does more Kit Kat stuff. It's hard for kids to find a regular job. There is Vegas. They just started again at the Riviera. Everybody always tells me I should open a Baton there, but I have learned my lesson with out-of-town businesses. That was the worst business decision I ever made."

Men Seeking Impersonators

In an interview with Albert Williams in the GayLife issue of October 20, 1983, Flint discussed his clientele: "We have the kind that come in, the men who like only female impersonators ... they're straight men, but they have gay tendencies, but they don't want to admit they're gay, but they think of you as a woman. I mean, if I'm sitting here in drag as Felicia, they will talk to me. If I'm sitting here as Jim Flint, they won't have a thing to do with me. Their mind wants to be with her, not him. And sometimes it's very frustrating ... . They're all macho: air pilots, sports figures, just macho-type men."

"The number of men seeking transsexuals is greatly increasing," said Flint in a 2011 interview. "I wonder if a lot of it is, they're gay, but don't want to admit they're gay, so by having a woman that looks like she does, but has what they like—that way they are not gay. I had an entertainer for a while who had a boyfriend who was always saying he was straight, and I said, 'Listen, just a minute, you're not straight, your lover right there has the same thing below her waist that I have, so how does that make you straight?'"

Kelly Lauren, a one-time Baton performer who was Miss Continental 1988, explained. "It can be really difficult for t-girls to have relationships," she said. "A lot of t-girls escort. It can be a tough life. Something that is really tough about it is that there is no shortage of men who are looking for a girl with a little something extra, but it's rare to find a guy who doesn't care if other people know about it. That's the key. They don't usually want to take you out for dinner or go out in public.

"Most t-girls find that men want to keep them their little secret. There's no future there. Then sometimes with men it happens that when you meet them at a party or gathering or whatever, and they find out you are trans, they'll treat you like a prostitute. Seriously, not even knowing you, saying things like, 'Are you going to wear high heels and panties for me?' and things like that. I just tell them straight-out, 'Don't treat me like a hooker and I won't ask you for money.'"

Despite the odds, Flint explained that love is often found at the Baton. "There are a lot of romances, but long-term relationships, too," he said. "China met her mate there and has been in a relationship for 29 years. Dana Douglas met her partner here and they moved to Florida and he was a doctor, and she stayed with him until he passed away about a year ago. Cherine Alexander met Phil, and they were together at least 20 years. Men that want transsexuals or whatever need to find a place where they can find respectable ones."

The Bachelorettes

Many bars have seen the recent influx of bachelorettes as a detriment to business and to maintaining the gay bar atmosphere, to the extent that some North Halsted Street gay bars issued an edict against them. In some cases it was because of drunken behavior, and in others it was a political issue: The brides were celebrating a right the Illinois gay community did not have.

Flint said he never even considered banning bachelorette parties. "Why would I?" he asked. "They're a huge part of my business. More importantly, though, I'm against banning or discriminating against anybody. You control them and tell them, 'These are the rules, and you act accordingly when you're here or you leave.' You're a lady or a gentleman when you are here, but I don't believe in any sort of discrimination. We have fought too hard for our rights to turn around and start doing it against someone else.

"A few weeks ago we had all these white girls from the suburbs, and sometimes when they come in those bachelorette parties, they think they can do anything they want. We also had a lot of really lovely black ladies here at the same time. I said to my sister, 'I want to go get 10 of these black ladies that we have and put them onstage, so they can teach these young girls how to be ladies.' Some of the mothers are worse than the bridesmaids. We had one about a year ago who said the wrong thing, 'Fuck you,' and I kicked her out. The daughter said, 'What do you mean she's out?' I said, 'No one says that to me. I gave her three warnings, she's out.' I also told the bride that I pitied her. I said, 'If this is the way she acts here, how is she going to act at your wedding?'"

Parties of 10 or more prepay in advance, and a gratuity of 16 percent is added. "I have everything spelled out very clearly. Printed on our rules is also a statement saying that if you overindulge in liquor and get sick in the showroom, you are going to pay a $70 cleanup fee. It used to happen a lot. But now we've only had one in the past four months. I didn't think doing something like that was legal until I saw it on Judge Judy. It was a limousine service on the show, and right in the rules they had a cleanup fee. Also, when the slide show comes up, there is a slide that says, 'Be courteous to all of our guests.' You have to reinforce that. No standing in your seats, no pictures or video recording."

"For me it's easier playing for bachelorettes because they are always a new audience," explained performer Victoria LePaige. "The gay kids see so many different shows and girls, so they can be a little more critical. The smallest gesture can get the bachelorettes going crazy when the gay kids will want back flips. Bachelorettes want music they are familiar with. On Fridays and Saturdays I get so tired of doing Tina Turner, but they love her and I'm here to make money and please the audience."

"The bachelorette parties are easier. They're fascinated. It's new to them," said performer Maya Douglas. "As long as you do music they know—Top 40. If it's something they know and hear on the radio, they love it. I do Pink and Adele right now; Sasha does Katy Perry, Beyoncé. Mimi—we all try to keep it current. Ginger, Vicky and Sheri do more the characters Tina, Ross, Rhianna, and then Chilli does her act."

"Hallelujah for the bachelorette parties," said performer Sheri Payne. "They are so much easier to perform to. Gay people are more critical of their peers. They want you to jump through hoops and go that extra mile because they all think they can do what we can do, but they cannot. A lot of times, though, the women tend to go one way or the other—they're really into the show or they're standoffish. They either love the glamour or not. Sometimes they are intimidated by it.

"For the most part, the entertainers are treated very well," said Flint. "Sometimes the tips aren't what they would like, but they are not disrespected. The only real time the performers get treated shabbily is when one of the women will be jealous of the way they look. I remember one night my friend Joe Fraser brought in about 20 people. This one young guy and his girlfriend were with them. The more he drank, the more he forgot those were men up there, and he got so involved with tipping and everything, and when he came back to the table his girlfriend smacked him and ran out the door."

In a Chicago Tribune piece from April 7, 1989, titled "Gender Benders: The Showgirls Aren't Real, But the Glamour Is," reporter David McCracken wrote of this exact sort of conflict at the Baton: "'Sometimes a young couple will come in,' says Flint, 'and after a while the guy sort of forgets that's a man up there and gets very involved in the show. And the girlfriend gets very intimidated. We've had a couple of real scenes where people are storming out, shouting.'"

McCracken continued: "The ever-solicitous, ever-gabbing Chilli puts a different spin on the gender game: 'Women come here and are reminded of their own femininity,' she says in that throaty alto. 'It's like, before a woman gets married, she's concerned about looking good, she takes time with her hair and makeup—but after a few years, maybe she slacks off. Gets chubby. Then she comes here with her husband and sees him looking at the performers, really looking. And she thinks, 'What have they got that I don't?'"

In an interview with Albert Williams in the GayLife issue of October 20, 1983, Flint said: "A lot of women are very turned on to the makeup and the costumes. They say, 'I could look like that if I put a little work into it.' ... I think many, many times women take it for granted that they're women, and they don't take the extra pains or the efforts that we do because we're impersonating them."

"I loved watching all those people come in the Baton," said one-time manager Lennie Malina. "They expected to see some guy with 5 o'clock shadow in a dress and were always just blown away. I would be in the bathroom sometimes and I always overheard things like, 'Did you see the way George looked at that blonde?' or 'Did you see the way Henry was eyeing the legs on that Chilli Pepper?' Or I'd hear, 'Look at us. Those guys are amazing-looking. We need to do what those guys are doing.'"

Audience Memories

Candace Collins Jordan began her career as a Playboy Bunny at the St. Louis Playboy Club at age 19, transferred to Chicago at 20, became Playboy Bunny of the Year in 1976, and was the December 1979 Playmate. In the years following, she became a model, eventually signing with the Wilhelmina agency in New York. Jordan has been named one of the "25 Best-Dressed Chicagoans" by CS magazine, as well as receiving numerous other honors in and around Chicago. Jordan's blog, Candid Candace, was featured in Chicago magazine as Belle of the Blog. She is also a guest contributor on WLS-TV's Windy City Live.

Jordan, a woman-born woman, spoke of what first drew her to the Baton. "I was from a small town called Dupo, Illinois," she said. "I came to Chicago to work at the Playboy Club. I'd heard about the Baton and thought it might be fun and campy. I'm an only child, and what I really loved about it was that when I started going there, it felt like a second home. I recall Jimmy and Chilli from those days. In fact, Chilli introduced me to Oprah. The performers and Jim were all so sensitive and caring. I started to bring friends there. On our first date I brought my husband, Chuck, there. It was sort of a test. He passed with flying colors and we've been married since 1989."

Jordan continued: "I bring friends there. I've brought Jimmy Connors as well as Alex McCord and her husband [Simon] from The Real Housewives of New York [City]. Everyone always has a great time. The favorite people I ever brought there, though, were my mother, aunt and cousins. Being from a small town, they'd never seen anything like it. I just remember the joy and what a good time they all had and how nice everyone was. I think it really opened their eyes to a lot of different things.

"The greatest thing about the Baton, though, is the vibe. There is no negativity there. I was recently filming a Social Circles segment and interviewed Sheri Payne. I asked her what she liked about performing there, and her eyes started to fill with tears, and she said, 'I am just so thrilled that I can get paid to make people happy.' It was so moving.

"Then I asked Jim what he looks for in an entertainer and he said, 'I look for them to be on time.' It wasn't what I expected. I expected that he wanted them to be sexy or a great dancer, but no, it was punctuality. I think what he meant was, he looks for professionalism. It's a wonderful place, but it needs to be professional. It is a business and Jimmy is a good businessman.

"I rode on the Baton's Gay Pride Parade float and let me tell you, there is nothing like it—nothing. It was one of the biggest thrills of my life. Those performers are so revered it almost seems when you are riding with them on that float that all those hundreds of thousands of people are there cheering for the Baton. They're rock stars, people are going nuts, throwing things. It is always incredible."

Transgender singer Honey West explained her first experiences with the Baton. "I would come to the Baton after working at Gentry on Sundays," she said. "I'd come there a lot for the 8:30 or 10:30 show. I was completely star-struck by the whole thing. I was so green and so shy and so in awe, because the performers were these exquisite goddesses and I was always impressed by how kind and generous Jim was to me. These beautiful showgirls in their stunning couture gowns and how they would look in those outfits and put themselves together really amazed me. At the time, I was performing as a female impersonator, but I'd get ready in my basement, and what I wore to work would be what I came home in. I learned makeup through trial and error. I didn't have this sort of sisterhood that you saw at the Baton. I guess it always intimidated me a bit.

"One time after Gentry, I came to the Baton, and they used to have red neon around the mirrors in the room. Well, seeing all these amazing goddesses, I was so self-conscious and scared, thinking, 'What will I do if they come talk to me?' or whatever. I was feeling self-conscious, I suppose, so I started applying makeup. I kept doing it throughout the evening because I was sitting there watching these beautiful women with a mirror right next to me. Anyway, after the show, I went out to my car and looked in the rearview mirror and actually scared myself. It literally looked like Carol Channing had raped me in the bathroom. My lips were so red and so big. It was then I realized that sitting there, the red neon had erased the red of my lipstick, so I had been applying more and more and more throughout the evening. So, that was the night I also learned the valuable lesson that red neon can erase your lips."

"I'm a fan of the Baton from way back," said recording star Linda Clifford. "Then, years later, I was there for my daughter's bachelorette party. It's consistent, consistently entertaining. I love bringing friends there. It's always the same, and being there is being in an incredible fantasy world, like a dream. The entertainment, the makeup, the hair, the costumes, all of it impeccable. I have found myself in my own career trying to emulate some of the things the stars of Jim's show would do.

"I remember one of Jim's birthdays at the Park West and the place was packed. For this celebration, Jim had a gathering of friends come up and perform, and I came with a pianist and I got up onstage, and I think it was one of the first times people had heard me do something other than dance music and R&B. I did three standards. I remember doing 'Fever.' The other two I am not sure about. I think Jim was very pleased that I performed live rather than just using tracks. But the greatest thing was introducing my daughter Gina, who had just competed in the Miss Illinois pageant, and she performed 'And I Am Telling You I'm Not Going' from Dreamgirls. Well, here is this little thing in heels and a miniskirt, and when she opened her mouth, people didn't expect this big voice.

"Jim has done so much in opening the eyes of people to this wonderful world of entertainment. He doesn't get enough credit. He has done and continues to do so much for this city. I can tell you this much: This city is a better place because of him."

"I used to have a deli across the street, Au Marché [437 North Clark Street]," said Kim Turner. "I had that deli for seven years in the 1990s. The girls would come in to get food, but I had never been to the show. I remember I finally went on March 22, my birthday. Deborah [Decuire], my partner, was going there years before I met her. She was running with them since the 1980s. Well, they were all so welcoming there. When I first saw the show, I fell in love with the girls. The show was gorgeous, and the way they move and everything—it was thrilling. I got to know Jimmy, and every evening I would go back and forth. I didn't think of Jim as a business owner. I saw him as a friend and a family member, and he welcomed me there like a family member. He is a great person with a caring heart. We still go there faithfully."

Veteran club kid Zander Mander spoke of the lasting impact the Baton, Continental and especially Jim Flint have had on his life. "I basically have created a character, Zander Mander, that I could not get away with 30 years ago," he said. "Much of that was because of Jim Flint. Back then I'd go out in maybe a little eyeliner, a blue streak in my hair, some black leather or blue metallic pants, that was about it. What Jim has done through the Baton and through Continental has made it safer and more accepting for a professional club kid like myself. Now I can wear full makeup, eyes done up, corset, feathers, glitter, 6-inch heels, anything I want, because there has become a huge acceptance of drag in this town. Thirty years ago I would do this and people would reach for a baseball bat. Now I go out dressed the same way and people say, 'You're so fabulous, let me take my picture with you.' The queens and female impersonators were here first, but that acceptance has trickled down to the club kids as well. I learned so much from the girls. Not only fashion and makeup and hair things, but more the confidence to be who and what you are."

"I first went to the Baton shortly after I turned 21 years old," said Billy Fantastic (William Kucharenko). "My friend, David (Davita Jo), took me there, and we would watch the show weekly, usually on Sundays. From the moment I first went, I absolutely loved it. I quickly became friends with all the staff, both bar staff and entertainers. I grew to appreciate what female impersonation is, and most importantly, the people that do it. I met more and more people and finally Jim Flint. I was nervous at first because it was meeting the man behind it all and I didn't know what to expect. It was like meeting the Wizard from The Wizard of Oz."

Dorothy "Skip" Flint remembers the year they had a birthday party for her with a cake. "I don't really drink, but Jim got me drinking white zinfandel," she said. "I had too many that night and didn't want anyone to see me tipsy, so I went backstage to get my bearings so I didn't make an idiot of myself. I was sitting there seeing them all running around naked, and you realize they are so beautiful—but my God, they're men."

Scott Cooper aka Michelle Dupree, Miss Continental 1998, added: "When someone has a business like the Continental System, or the Baton or 3160, it doesn't happen by accident—not that much, for that long. That sort of success comes from the top down, not because people fear you but because they respect you and want to do a good job."

And the Winner Is ...

The unity and spirit of the gay community were also reflected in ways that extended beyond the corners of a specific neighborhood. A small indication of this "coming together" was seen in things like the annual Gay Academy Awards, presented directly following the Oscars telecast at the Baton. It began in 1973 and was done to help the Windy City honor its deserving entertainers, bartenders, waiters, gay organizations, publications and community leaders. Each year more than 1,500 ballots were collected at various sites around the city. As The Chicago Gay Crusader said at the time: "Gay Unity, Right On!"

Flint recalled the Gay Academy Awards. "We had people voting, with ballot boxes," he said. "It was a great thing for the community. It brought people together, it got them out. We'd have it here [at the Baton] and I'd have TVs around the room playing the Academy Awards, and everyone would get very dressed up and attend, and then afterwards we'd have our own version of the awards. We did that about six or seven years in the 1970s."

> **The 1974 Winners as reported by The Chicago Gay Crusader:**
> Entertainer of the Year: Chilli Pepper
> Amateur Entertainer of the Year: Lisa
> Best Bar: The Gold Coast and Up North (tie)
> Live Entertainer of the Year: Dina Jacobs
> Best Female Bartender: Nancy, formerly of Augie's
> Most Original Entertainer: Bertha Butts, Glass House
> Most Elegant Entertainer: China Nguyen, the Baton
> Waiter/Waitress: Joanne, at the Baton, and Caesar, at the Ritz (tie)
> Best Rising Newcomer: Chris Fontaine
> Bartender of the Year: Michael Karlin, Sunday's
> Musical Group of the Year: Andy Cahill & Jerry
> Best Girl Bar: Augie's
> Best Dance Performance: Peaches, the Baton
> Best Dramatic Entertainer: Audrey Bryant, the Baton
> Best Gown Design: Larry P. and Sal (tie)
> Best Publication: The Chicago Gay Crusader
> Best All-Around Female Impersonator: China Nguyen, the Baton
> In addition, a special Humanitarian Award was given to Chuck Renslow
> for his service to the gay community.

> **The winners in 1975 were reported by The Chicago Gay Crusader as:**
> Bartender of the Year: Ronnie, Up North
> Waiter or Waitress of the Year: Tony from the Baton and Corky from the Ritz (tie)
> Best Original Entertainer: China Nguyen, the Baton
> Best Rising Newcomer: Leslie Rejeanné, the Baton
> Best Personality of the Year: Bill, the Ritz
> Best Gown Designer: Larry and Stanley (tie)
> Best Dramatic Entertainer: Lotta Love, the Baton
> Most Elegant Entertainer: Chilli Pepper, the Ritz
> Best Female Impersonator: Jan Howard, the Baton

Best Dance Performer: Laura Merrill, the House of Landers
Entertainer of the Year: Peaches, the Baton
Group That Pushed for Better Rights in the Gay Community:
    The Chicago Gay Crusader.

The winners in 1976 as reported by The Chicago Gay Crusader from April of that year included:

Best Bar: Gold Coast
Best Women's Bar: His 'n Hers
Best Bartender: Ricky, Little Jim's
Best Female Bartender: Ikey, His 'n Hers
Best Waiter: Billy Mann, the Baton
Best Waitress: Elaine, the Oak Tree
Best Chef: Dennis, My Brother's Place
Best Disc Jockey: Michael, Sunday's
Best Original Entertainer: Dina Jacobs, the Baton
Best Dramatic Entertainer: Jan Howard, the Baton
Best Elegant Entertainer: Audrey Bryant, the Baton
Best Dance Performer: Orlando del Sol, the Baton
Best Gown Design: Larry Panice
What Group or Organization Has Pushed for Better Rights and Life
    in the Gay Community: GayLife
Best All-Around Female Impersonator: Jan Howard
Leather Club or Persons That Has [sic] Been Outstanding in
    Promoting and Expanding Leather Events: Second City Motorcycle Club
Entertainer of the Year: Jan Howard
Honorary Awards were also presented to Bertha Butts and Leslie Rejeanné.

Another honor went to "Person or Persons That Their Personality and Willingness To Help Others Have Made Them Outstanding in the Gay Community." Interestingly, in this category, which listed the nominees as Chuck Renslow, Felicia, Jack David, Wanda Lust and Mother Carol, no winner was listed.

Flint on skates at the Baton, 1970s and 1980s.

Flint does one of his popular baton-twirling-on-roller-skates routines at the Baton Show Lounge, 1970s.

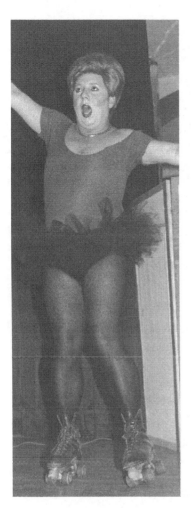  

The front of the Baton Show Lounge,
436 North Clark Street.

An early-1970s photo of Flint getting ready to go onstage at the Baton.

Charles Pierce performed as Bette Davis at the Baton, May 23, 1973. Here is a report on the performance in the July 1973 Mattachine Midwest Newsletter.
Photo courtesy of M. Kuda Archives

Above: Two ads for the Baton, in the July 1973 edition of The Chicago Gay Crusader.

Right: Notice for the Baton's hosting of a Miss Gay Chicago contest, in the November 1973 Chicago Gay Crusader.

Baton to hold Miss Gay Chicago contest

A giant step forward for gay unity has been announced by the Baton Lounge, 436 N. Clark St. The bar will be sponsoring a Miss Gay Chicago contest.

Contestants will be entered by any bar, business, or organization in the city and nearby suburbs. Proceeds from the pageant will go to Beckman House, a new community center planned in Chicago. The center will house the Gay Switchboard and provide a library. It will also house gay people for a couple of days and provide meals in emergencies.

The contest is scheduled for Feb. 14, 15, and 16. The winner will receive $300 and be sponsored in the Miss Gay America contest.

Several gay organizations have already expressed interest in participating in an effort to unite the bars with the groups while also aiding financially in community service projects. Organizations, bars, and businesses interested in entering the contest should contact the Baton, 436 N. Clark St., phone 644-5269.

Flint as "Felicia," 1970s.

THE Chicago Gay CRUSADER

25¢

MAY, 1974   THE TOTAL COMMUNITY NEWSPAPER ●   NUMBER TWELVE

CRUSADER WINS OSCAR

It was gay Chicago's Academy Awards night at the Baton, 436 N. Clark, on Apr. 2, right after the Los Angeles production was streaked by the *Advocate*'s Robert Opel.

With an audience filled with entertainers, bartenders, waiters, bar owners, gay organization leaders, and with over 2,000 votes cast, there was an air of excitement throughout the Baton's auditorium.

The first award presented was inscribed: "Group Pushed for Better Rights and Life in the Gay Community." *The Chicago Gay Crusader* was voted winner, and editor Michael Bergeron accepted the award. "Our slogan," he stated, "is 'the total community newspaper,' which means it is for the entire gay community, and I would like to thank the entire gay community for this award."

Felicia was the perfect host/hostess.
(Continued on page 8)

Editor Michael Bergeron accepts Oscar from Baton's Felicia

HAPPY BIRTHDAY TO US!

This is the 12th issue of The Chicago Gay Crusader, which marks our first year of publication.

The Chicago Gay Crusader was started in May 1973, and in those 12 months we have put out 11 issues (our 11th issue was a double-month issue because our staff was busy gutting Beckman House opened).

In our first year, we have discovered that the Gay Crusader has become an increasingly important asset to Chicago's gay community. We feel we have brought the gay community closer together through communication.

For the first time, we have a publication in which one can read things going on throughout the gay community without bias, without backbiting, without prejudice. We can f...

ANNUAL BATON AWARDS GIVEN

The *Gay Crusader* was the winner of one of the annual Academy Awards presented Apr. 8 by the Baton Show Lounge, 436 N. Clark St., before the customary packed house. The *Gay Crusader* won in the category of best publication.

In addition, a special Humanitarian Award was presented to well-known gay businessman Chuck Renslow for services to the gay community.

Awards were based on votes cast by patrons of cooperating Chicago gay bars. This was the third year the competition has been conducted by the Baton and the second consecutive year in which the *Gay Crusader* was a winner.

Other winners and nominees were as follows (a filled-in circle ● denotes a winner; there were ties in two categories):

ENTERTAINER OF THE YEAR
● Chili Pepper
○ China Nuyen
○ Leslie Rejeané
○ Peaches
○ Bertha Butz
○ Lady Baronness
BEST AMATEUR ENTERTAINER
● Lisa
○ Christine Knight
○ Erika
○ Raratunga
○ Maxine
BEST BAR
○ Sunday's
● Gold Coast
○ Bistro
● Up North
○ Carol's Coming Out Pub
○ Le Pub
○ Trip
○ King's Ransom
○ El Dorado
LIVE ENTERTAINER OF THE YEAR
● Dina Jacobs
○ Kiki St. John
○ Tony Lewis
○ Craig Russell
○ Michael Greer
BEST GIRL BARTENDER
○ Tina (formerly of the Baton)
○ Nancy (formerly of Augie's)
○ Judy (CK's)
○ Marge (His n' Hers)
○ Danielle (formerly of Augie's)
BEST GIRL BAR
○ CK's
● Augie's
○ His n' Hers

○ Lost & Found
○ Sue and Nan's
○ Closet
MOST ORIGINAL ENTERTAINER
● Wanda Lust (Man's Country)
● Bertha Butz (Glass House)
○ Felicia (Baton)
○ Ebony (formerly of David's)
○ China Nuyen (Baton)
MOST ELEGANT ENTERTAINER
● Audrey Brian (Baton)
● China Nuyen (Baton)
○ Shawn Luis (formerly of the Baton)
○ Terry Livingston (Glass House)
○ Kiki St. John (formerly of David's)
WAITER/WAITRESS
● Joann (Baton)
○ Skip (Baton)
○ Danny (Up North)
○ Gary (My Brother's Place)
● Cesar (Le Pub)
BEST MIXING NEWCOMER
● Chris Fontaine
○ Charonda
○ Dandé
○ Sandy of Milwaukee
○ Allison Brooks
BARTENDER OF THE YEAR
○ Dale (Up North)
○ Tony (Bistro)
○ Michael (Sunday's)
○ Les (Gold Coast)
○ Marge (Trip)
○ Louie (El Dorado)
○ Dwight (King's Ransom)
MUSIC GROUP OF THE YEAR
○ Sam & Trudy
○ Andy Cahill & Jerry
○ Gotham
○ Susie & Bob Moreen
BEST DANCE PERFORMANCE
● Peaches (Baton)
○ Audrey Brian (Baton)
○ Leslie Rejeané (Baton)
○ China Nuyen (Baton)
○ Ray Rast
○ Arteais Welles
BEST DRAMATIC ENTERTAINER
○ Audrey Brian (Baton)
○ Chili Pepper (Baton)
○ Jill Christie (Blue Dahlia)
○ Lisa Baton (formerly of the Baton)
○ Jodi Lee (formerly of the Baton)
○ Lotta Love (formerly of the Baton)
BEST GOWN DESIGNER
○ Taisha
● Larry P.
○ Sabrina
● Bill Haney

○ Stanley
○ Jay Lee
BEST LIGHTING
● Bill
○ Ralph
● Sal
○ Chuck
MOST PUBLICATION
● The Chicago Gay Crusader
○ David
○ In Touch
○ The Advocate
BEST ALL-ROUND FEMALE IMPERSONATOR
○ China Nuyen (Baton)
○ Jan Howard (Baton)
○ Taisha (formerly of the Baton)
○ Kiki St. John (formerly of David's)
○ Audrey Brian (Baton)
○ Shawn Luis (formerly of the Baton)
○ Michelle (Bite Life)
○ Sabrina (My Way Lounge)
○ Karen (Bite Life)
○ Liza Summers (Jamie's)
Categories were devised and affiliations of contestants supplied by the Baton.

GAY SWITCHBOARD
929-HELP

ACADEMY AWARDS PRESENTED BY BATON

Photographs by Bob Fundiller

DIGNITY / Chicago
Celebration

The Baton hosted an "Academy Awards" for Chicago's gay community in the 1970s. Here are clips about the event, and a ballot, from The Chicago Gay Crusader in 1974, 1975 and 1976.

14

FELICIA DOES IT 'MY WAY'

Baton boasts
'best in female impersonation'

BY FRED ALEXION

"Whew! Unbelievable! She's gorgeous!" gasped Jackie.

"You can't really tell, can you?" John leaned over to whisper. "What amazes me is the sincere honesty with which these people perform."

"That's why they're good," I answered back.

"Fantastic. I'm sitting here with my mouth open. I didn't come in jeans because my woman's intuition told me they would be hot," added Myra.

FELICIA

Conversations of this nature are common as I introduce friends, from time to time, to a unique but by no means new form of entertainment. It has even amused me to watch sometimes ignorant opinions change admirably during the course of a performance, as if I were the one being the teacher, when in truth it is the performers themselves who are making a statement through an art form that has been a part of theater and life itself from the very beginning—going through various stages of recognition, respect, and acceptance over the years.

There are many reasons for becoming a female impersonator, just as there are for wanting to do anything—money, identity, and recognition, or just simply to be true to yourself. No matter what you choose to do with your professional or personal life, the important thing is that you believe in it and are motivated by positive self-honesty.

CHILI PEPPER

When you are in the spotlight, it is hard not to be also the center of controversy, particularly if you're a gay male entertainer who's been given the title of "the madam of Clark Street." It's even more difficult when that title is surrounded by connotations which reflect your reputation for being a terror on wheels—someone not to cross if you can't take the sting of an acid rebuff.

However, with security and maturity come many surprising changes. It takes a big person to admit that much of one's difficulty in growth and acceptance was and is partly a result of one's own doing. No one can deny that owning, managing, or even working in a bar is one of the most difficult occupations, particularly if it is a gay bar that offers entertainment.

The numerous problems come from every direction, and it takes a strong, determined individual with guts to survive in a business where rumors (sometimes based on jealous rivalry from those insecure

JAN HOWARD

in their own identities) are aimed at putting you down, making you act understandably contrary to your nature.

No one knows this better than Chicago's own Felicia, who not only has added humorous glamour to the feat of twirling a baton while trying to balance on roller skates complete in tutu, but has also managed to give a Near North section of Clark Street the famous name of the Baton Lounge.

In its advertisements, it boasts the best in female impersonation—a boast which I can honestly say is true. The show presents the tops in its field of bar entertainment, but its success did not happen overnight for either the club or the entertainers who have made it what it is. Growth in any business is a struggle, but when the struggle is compounded by prejudice one's freedom of lifestyle and expression is limited.

PEACHES

Over the years, I have witnessed entertainers (the best and the worst) come and go and have seen the bars in which they were featured flourish or die for one reason or another—Sparrow's, David's Place, Togetherness, House of Landers. Only the best and occasionally the sturdiest (which are not necessarily the best) survive in this business—one which is continually striving for social acceptability and recognition as a legitimate art form in both the gay and straight worlds.

One has to admire a winner, especially if a person wins in spite of all the odds and has been called every name in the book, including a few that haven't been added yet.

Felicia (Jim Flint) credits his enduring success to the support of many of the city's well-known names, loyal employees, and audiences.

Starting out as a bartender at the Annex and later at the old Chesterfield, Jim was arrested seven times in a series of eight bar raids. In the big bar raid of 1965 he was jailed on a bum rap that took him through 23 courts at great personal financial loss before he enlisted the aid of Chicago lawyer Raila Klegak to clear him. During that period, Jackie Knight and Skip Arnold encouraged him to work as a female impersonator, doing guest spots and benefits. Working at Nan's Normandy as a bartender, Felicia's reputation grew as he frequently "carried on" behind the bar, entertaining the patrons.

"After five and a half years of working there, I decided to go on my own, and I have to thank Chuck Renslow because he helped me get my own place, the

first Baton on the corner of Clark and Hubbard. Chuck is responsible for many people making it on their own," Jim states.

"I'm indebted to the Lady Baronessa, Peaches, Jody Lee, and Jan Howard because these four entertainers stuck by me and put up with me during a period in my life when I really didn't know what I was doing. I almost went bankrupt two or three times, but we kept trying, and now five years later we are still here."

Jim considers Dwight (manager of the King's Ransom), Jack (owner of the Up North restaurant), David (manager of the Baton), Marilyn and Joann and numerous other employees personal friends he could not do without.

In the last five years, the Baton has expanded its quarters in a continual effort to bring one of the best shows in the country to Chicago, featuring from time to time more than 35 of this city's well-known entertainers and engaging special guest artists Michael Greer, Charles Pierce, Craig Russell, and Tiffany Jones as headliners for its own show.

CHINA NUYEN

The current cast at the Baton is certainly the most star-studded ever, presenting the Versatile Polynesian Lovely, Dina Jacobs (Miss Gay Chicago 1975); the Personality Plus of Miss Gay Illinois 1975, Peaches; the Blond Goddess Bombshell, Jan Howard; the Redheaded Vamp and Miss Gay Chicago 1974, Chili Pepper; the Fiery Fire Goddess, Countess of Hong Kong, China Nuyen; the Liza Minnelli Look-alike, Jody Lee; the Queen of Motown and Soft Soul, Leslie Rejeane; and the Lady of Sophisticated Elegance, Audrey Brian.

All these superlatives and a few more apply in each case, and while each of the entertainers is uniquely talented, all are distinctly original and appreciated for their differences by audiences who make them all stars.

Each gets his chance to stop the show with his own special obvious audience favorites: "This Is My Life," "The Best Thing You've Ever Done," "My Way," "Maybe," "Pillow Talk," "It Should Have Been Me," and on and on and on.

Jim, whose active life is the dual role of club owner and entertainer keeps him going 'til all hours, still finds time to attend classes at a local college and to be involved in local city politics, community fundraising and toy drives, promotion of an all-gay-girls' volleyball and softball team, the Baton's annual Academy Awards, and his annual creation of Costumes on Review every Halloween.

Costumes on Review has become one of the finest and biggest drag balls in the country. In the past few years, it has been presented at the Palmer House, Sheraton-Chicago, and Pick-Congress hotels with much success and enthusiastic recognition from both audiences and hotel managements, making it one of the biggest social events of the year.

The annual Academy Awards show was conceived three years ago by the Baton

SHAWN LUIS

to help the Windy City honor its deserving entertainers, bartenders, waiters, gay organizations, publications, and community leaders.

AUDREY BRIAN

Whether you're into female impersonation or not, it would be hard not to appreciate the people who own, manage, and operate the Baton Lounge. Even if you go just once for the experience, I am sure you, like others, will find something to appreciate and talk admiringly about.

Dina Jacobs beautifully sums up the philosophy of all who work there when she delivers a moving rendition of "My Way" in which she tells the audience that the most important thing for everyone to do is "to live, let live, and love, but to always do it your way."

[The author is staff writer and theater critic for David magazine. This is one of a series of features on Chicago-area gay bars and other businesses.]

MR. BISTRO
CONTEST

MICHAEL O'CALLAHAN and EDDIE DUGAN

MICHAEL CARDELLA ("Mr. Bistro") and MARK NARD (3d place)

RON JONES
Bartender at Bistro

Felicia and the Baton girls, featured in The Chicago Gay Crusader for April–May 1975.

Flint as Felicia, 1970s.

Dolinda Ko', Orlando del Sol, Flint and Joanna Caron, 1970s.

Flint with customers at the Baton.

Some raw layouts for promotional cards for the Baton.

Flier for the Baton shows, 2000s.

Flint as Felicia, 1980s.
Photo courtesy of Windy City Times.

Curt Mack and Delilah Kenney.

Flint with friend Mickey Day from Atlanta.

Flint's sisters Doris (left) and Dorothy "Skip" with Joe Fraser.

The Baton had a 42nd-anniversary celebration in 2011. Flint is pictured here with Dan Neniskis and Candace Collins Jordan.
Photo by Tracy Baim

Bob Waters, Ken Byrski, Dan Neniskis and Jim Flint at the Baton's 42nd anniversary, 2011.
Photo by Tracy Baim

Performers at the 42nd anniversary included, from left: Chilli, Sheri, Maya, Mimi and Victoria.
Photo by Tracy Baim

Flint on New Year's Eve, 2010.

A Baton logo.

Flint in front of the Baton.

Bea Holland performed at Smitty's, which later became the Baton Show Lounge.
Photo courtesy of Ralla Klepak

A 1970s signed photo from impersonator Charles Pierce to Flint. Pierce performed at the Baton.

A 1986 signed photo from Charles Pierce to Flint.

Impersonator Craig Russell also performed at the Baton. Shown is a signed photo to "Jim & Felicia" in 1973.

Joan Crawford signed this photo to Flint. She came to the Baton, and she and Flint also went to the Drake, among other places, with Richie Saunders.

Rosemary DeCamp, a radio, film and TV star, signed this photo to Flint. She visited the Baton.

Flint also met Sammy Davis Jr., who signed this photo to "Felicia," Jim's drag name, and visited the Baton for a show.

Jazz legend Sarah Vaughan came to the Baton and signed this photo to Flint after the two met.

Little Lil signed this photo to Flint in 1974. She was a Baton customer.

Singer Phyllis Hyman signed this photo to Flint. She attended shows at the Baton.

Flint with singer Linda Clifford, who attended Baton performances, including one for her daughter's bachelorette party. She also performed at Flint's birthday party at the Park West.

This photo is from Shirley MacLaine, who also came to the Baton.

Liza Minnelli, who came to the Baton and was also impersonated at the Baton by Jodie Lee.

Madonna with Jim Flint and the Baton performers, 1990s.

8

Baton: The Entertainers

At the foot of the carpeted stairs leading down from the rear of the Baton's stage is a small landing opening onto a larger room for guest artists. Low mirrors surround a long, flat wall table for getting ready. The walls are a vibrant spring green, and what is not painted is covered with glamour shots from various fashion magazines—the airbrushed faces of Madonna and Lady Gaga, Angelina, Halle, Raquel, Rhianna, Beyoncé and numerous others.

On the right side of this open area is the dressing room for the emcee and show manager. Currently it's Ginger Grant's dressing room. Previously it had been Leslie Rejeanné's and before that, Felicia's. To the left is a sinkless washroom, with just a toilet inside, and these walls are covered with beefcake shots—lots of Abercrombie & Fitch, cowboys, and sulking jeans models. No nudes. The Baton always draws the line at nudity.

Beyond this, a long hallway runs beneath the stage, passing eight dressing rooms, four on either side. Each girl decorates her own room to her taste. There are sequins, feathers, faux fur, wigs, scarves and shimmer for miles. Assorted makeup and brushes, tubes, powders and adornments cover every inch of dressing table in almost every room. The scent of sandalwood incense is in the air. On the wall hangs a clock; beneath it, a clipboard with the order for the night. It's changed for every show—three times every night. The show starts with a production number, followed by the individual numbers and culminating with the finale.

Sheri, Mimi, Maya, Victoria, Chilli, Sasha and, of course, Ginger are the current residents, but if those dressing-room walls could talk, oh, the tales they would tell of Monica, Shanté, Leslie, Cherine, Alana, Kelly, Tasha, Cezanne, Stacy, Ruby, China, Dana, Jodie, Terry and Flame, to name but a few.

In interviewing the entertainers for this book, it was said time and again that the stage show is great—but the real show is downstairs. There are revealed the lives, the drama, the antics, and there lies the heart of the Baton. It's time to slip behind the curtain and get a closer glimpse at some of the amazing talents and performers who have graced the stage at Jim "Felicia" Flint's Baton Show Lounge. More than 40 years of history are here—it's best to check your inhibitions at the door.

Jan Howard

Roger "RJ" Chaffin's "Impersonators Show Talent" article in the September 17, 1976, issue of GayLife featured a minibiography of the then-reigning blonde bombshell of female impersonation. "Yet another talented person at the Baton is Jan Howard," Chaffin wrote. "Born on the East Coast in Massachusetts, Jan left home at the age of 17 to join the Navy. After his three-year hitch, he left for California in search of fame and fortune. Nothing exciting happened, so he went to Denver, where he was soon to appear in his first drag show.

While in Denver, he felt he couldn't talk to people. They seemed very cold. Jan later found out that many people thought he was a lesbian. One day someone came right up and asked if he was a boy or a girl. He was then told that he should work in a show, looking so much like a girl. Jan said he really got turned on with the first show he did.

"From Denver he went to New Mexico, and then headed for Chicago. ... After auditioning for Felicia, Jan was hired, though he admits that his act wasn't very good at the time. People would come up to Felicia and ask why on earth he had hired Jan. But Felicia saw potential in him, which proved to be true; last year Jan was voted Entertainer of the Year at the 1976 Academy Awards [the Baton's version] ... ."

Bartender Warren Williamson recalled Jan Howard, "blind as a bat, and she couldn't wear her glasses onstage. She was so sexy, a Marilyn Monroe blonde. I remember when she did 'Blue Bayou' and she would be rolling onstage on these white fur pillows, and they somehow managed to do this ripple effect with the blue spotlights to make it seem like it was underwater. It was so beautiful."

Flint said Howard was in the service with him at Naval Amphibious Base, Little Creek, in Virginia. "I didn't know her as Howard. I saw her a couple times—but we didn't know each other then," Flint said. Later, he recalled, "she was working in drag at the New Jamie's [1110 North Clark Street] and said she wanted to come work at the Baton. I said, 'Jan, are you going to be able to see with your glasses off?' and she said, 'I'll manage.'

"Jan was one of those who got prettier as she became more polished. In every rehearsal I would tell people, 'You have to know your part, because if you don't, she'll fall right over you, and you'll both go tumbling and we'll have problems.' Because of Jan being so blind, I think everyone put more into rehearsal. They knew if it wasn't exact, Jan would run right into them."

In his "Baton at 40" piece in Ambush Magazine's issue of April 28–May 11, 2009, writer Gary Glitter said of Howard: "She was one of the first to take hormones and was called 'the Body Beautiful,' but she was so nearsighted that she had to count the steps to the front of the stage and several times miscounted and fell into the audience. They just picked her up and put her back and she continued on."

"When she would do a number, I used to carry a couple of those mesh table candles with me to the edge of the stage so she could see me to get the tip," laughed Marge Summit, who owned His 'n Hers bar. "I'd say, 'Come towards the light, Jan.'"

Dina Jacobs elaborated: "My favorite Jan memory was when we were all meeting to go out on the Belmont Rocks [then a popular gay sunning and cruising area on the Lake Michigan shore just south of where Belmont Avenue would meet the lake]. The cast was very close in those days and hung out offstage all the time. Jan said that on her way, this old woman stopped her and looked her up and down and said, 'How's the wig business?' Jan self-consciously said, 'Um, fine, I guess.' The woman looked at her a bit more closely and then scoffed, 'Yes, apparently,' and walked away in a huff."

"When we did productions, I was paired off a lot with Jan Howard," laughed Sabrina Sabo. "Everyone talks about her being so nearsighted, and that was true. But my favorite memory was when she did Sylvia's 'Pillow Talk.' For that, she would do it on this big pillow, and she ended up passing out onstage during the number. The full-cast production number was next, so we were all in the wings waiting, and I remember Audrey and Leslie eventually went out and dragged the pillow offstage with Jan still passed out on top of it. The audience loved it. They thought her passing out and being dragged offstage was all part of the act."

Years ago, the Baton dressing rooms were upstairs. Performer Shawn Luis recalled: "Jan and I had cubicles right next to one another, and then Chilli was on the other side. She used to get on our nerves. So Jan and I used to hang wreaths of garlic over the corner of our cubicle and hang little silver knives and used to say it was to protect us from the vampire, meaning Chilli, and then we would laugh."

"The first time we did a show down in Atlanta, they didn't know anything about queens having enlargements," said Flint. "Audrey [Bryant] and Jan both had them, and in Atlanta at the time you had to have a special permit in order to work. So we went down to the Atlanta Police Department to get the permit, and they saw the form and read it over and said, 'It says on here you're a boy,' and then gestured to their chests and said, 'If you're a boy, then what is this?' They just couldn't believe it. They made Audrey and Jan go get another ID, and so on the way down to go get the IDs, that elevator stopped on every floor because the policeman had called all his buddies and told them about us—so on each floor the elevator door opened and another group of cops were there to see us."

Chaffin's 1976 piece in GayLife went on to say that "Jan plans to undergo a sex-reassignment operation toward the end of the year. His parents were quite upset about this at first, but soon realized that Jan had to live his own life ... Jan told his parents about the change and the fact that he's gay all at the same time. Later he realized that it was quite a lot for them to take all at once. ... Howard continued, 'The most important thing for me to do now is to live like a woman all the time. When I go to the grocery store or to the movies, I have to be a woman. Operations scare me. I have never been too hip to operations, needles, or doctors, but if I have to do it to live the life I want to live, then I'll do it.' Planning to take a rest after the operation, Jan says she may go to work in a beauty parlor ... ."

"She was a beautiful blonde," said Ginger Grant. "Eventually she went to the Playboy Club [the original Playboy Club at 116 East Walton Street] and did a play called Pouff in about 1976. At the end of the show, they would say, 'It's not nice to fool Mother Nature,' and she would pull her dress up and show her genitals. She passed away from HIV years ago. After leaving [the Baton and Pouff], she stayed in Chicago but lived a very private life offstage."

Pouff cast member Mark Ward recalled: "It was a racy revue, with sort of a burlesque feel to it. Jan's lifting her dress was the culmination of the show. I remember, too, very specifically that it was 1976, because one day during rehearsal [December 20, 1976] Richard J. Daley died of a heart attack in his doctor's office right across the street on Michigan Avenue."

The nearsighted blonde bombshell who helped put the Baton on the map never had her sex-change operation.

Audrey Bryant

"From that era, I remember Audrey Bryant," recalled Marge Summit. "She worked at Vidal Sassoon as a receptionist, absolutely gorgeous. Then someone went to the Baton and saw her and reported her to her bosses, and she lost her job."

Shawn Luis recalled: "Audrey Bryant was so beautiful, breathtaking. She was so elegant and just had this air of grace about her. She would always breeze in 15 minutes before a performance and look absolutely perfect, and I would have to go there two hours ahead of time to get ready. I remember always thinking, How does she do that?"

"She was glamorous in this unique way for a drag bar," explained Kelly Lauren. "Audrey looked like a very glamorous doctor's wife. Very J. Crew and Dina Merrill."

Ginger Grant added: "Audrey Bryant looked great. She looked like Lauren Hutton. She modeled for the Sun-Times until someone found out she was a boy and they stopped using her."

"Audrey was very classy onstage and off, and that was something that was very rare in those days," said Sabrina Sabo with a laugh. "Even rarer was the fact that Audrey always minded her own business."

"Audrey Bryant was the fashion model of drag," Flint said. "The first time I saw her was at my Halloween ball at the Aragon. She was from Indianapolis, and she would come here and had this way of captivating everyone with that long swan neck. She was such a beauty. She went to David's Place [a rival impersonation bar] and never came back. After that, she went back to Indianapolis and then came back to Chicago after about five years. She said she gave up drinking and asked me if I would hire her back." Unfortunately, things never worked out for her to come back to perform at the Baton.

Joanne Caron

"Joanne Caron was another one from the early days," recalled Flint. "She was one of the wildest ones I ever knew. I had a great time with her. I think she was one of the only entertainers that did every fundraiser in town when there was something to do for the community. Very positive person. She was here in the mid-1970s. Then she moved to San Francisco and worked the clubs out there and eventually passed away."

Lynette Langston and Capuchine

"Lynette Langston killed herself, shot herself on the way to work one night," Flint said. "Her boyfriend was playing games with her that if she didn't do [what he wanted her to], he was going to get a real girl and all this." Cast member Sabrina Sabo also recalled Langston: "She was so striking, with the most beautiful eyes."

"Another entertainer, Capuchine, was probably one of the best strippers you ever saw," Flint added. "Small black girl and probably weighed about 100 pounds, and she would strip with one of those walking little barking dogs that would come right up to her crotch. So graceful and so much finesse. She could turn anyone on, she was so sexy. Did a great Diana Ross. She got involved with this guy who was selling drugs. I think she got killed because of all that, and this was sometime in the 1970s. Another tragic part of that was that her mother would not allow her to be buried as Capuchine. She was buried as a boy."

Wanda Lust

"The wildest one of us all was Wanda Lust," laughed Dina Jacobs. "Wanda was crazy. I remember her doing 'How to Use an Appalachian Dulcimer' at the Baton. Yes, it was an actual instruction recording that she did pantomime to. She'd do weird stuff, hilarious things. Way ahead of her time. She played all over Chicago."

Indeed, Wanda Lust was known to female-impersonator audiences from the Baton as well as Sparrow's and would later go on to DJ and work in the Man's Country bathhouse's Music Hall. She was a singer, dancer, comedian. Wanda Lust aka Stephen L. Jones also worked in the local gay community's VD van (in the mid-to-late 1970s), which traveled from bar to bar in the pre-AIDS era trying to get patrons to get tested for venereal diseases.

Karen Ross loved Wanda. "Oh, my God, she was hilarious—the whole concept," Ross said. "I'd be there tending bar at Sunday's and the VD van would pull up. You've got to picture this—a big VD van parked outside gay bars between 10 and midnight, trying to get people to get tested. And running around in the middle of all this, a really tall drag queen dressed as a nurse. Need I say more?"

Wanda Lust was even featured in posters around Chicago. They were an hommage to the Uncle Sam posters and read, "I Want YOU to Get Tested." It was an important time for the community because the groundwork for gay men's sexual health and awareness was being laid in the years prior to AIDS. Lust is thus remembered for her tireless work as an advocate for sexual well-being as well as for being an entertainer.

As for Lust's completely outrageous side, she is fondly remembered by many for riding on Man's Country's U.S. bicentennial Pride Parade float in 1976, dressed as Lady Liberty, draped in the flag but holding a dildo instead of a torch.

Lust moved to Kansas City in 1978, and on February 19, 1980, she was with her lover in a theater trying to watch a movie. Leather legend and Man's Country owner Chuck Renslow explained: "The guy behind her was making a bunch of noise, and she turned around and told him to be quiet. Then when they walked out of the theater, he stabbed and killed her. She died in her lover's arms waiting for an ambulance."

GayLife wrote about Lust's impact on Chicago, in a February 22, 1980, editorial: "Wanda gave many hours of his time towards good causes, such as Howard Brown Clinic's VD testing and treatment drives, Lincoln Park Lagooners' benefits, and the Frank M. Rodde III Memorial Building Fund. Wanda's last Chicago appearance was at Dragocious, a Rodde Fund benefit event. … Too often, drag is disparaged in our community, as an embarrassment, something to hide from the public, or a batch of frivolous, sexist froth. Not so, when so many performers, including Wanda, have given us all so much.

"Just as we have resisted the forces that would divide the S&M leather followers from the mainstream of gay community life, let us also resist separating female impersonators from the heart of our society. Because when Wanda Lust bled to death in his lover's arms last Tuesday, a little part of all of us died."

Peaches

Another entertainer from the early Baton days was Peaches, winner of such honors as Entertainer of the Year 1971 (tying with Dina Jacobs) at the Gay Academy Awards—the honor that was given out annually at the Baton for Chicago gay and lesbian entertainment and nightlife.

"One of the performers I really liked was Peaches," said Warren Williamson. "Oftentimes, after her performance, Peaches would come sit at the end of the bar. They all did after performing. That was a time for them to mingle with the clientele, but sometimes they'd just want to talk, so a lot of times I would talk to Peaches. She was such a sweet person with a lot of problems at home, and she would come to work way from the South Side. She and Leslie [Rejeanné] really took care of me. They would bring me boxes of ribs on the train sometimes from Leon's at 63rd and Cottage Grove."

"I saw her when I was moving into 55 West Chestnut," said Ginger Grant, who had known the entertainer from Atlanta. "I was in the hallway and heard someone say, 'Girl, leave my trade alone,' and it was Peaches, and she ended up living right across the hall from me."

"She was a dynamite entertainer, but she got involved with a person who did drugs," Flint said. "Some drugs came missing from these people, and they were actually going to shoot my light man Billy [Cooper] in the head because they thought he had taken them. They chased him in Lincoln Park underneath one of those stone bridges and, if some people wouldn't have come by, they would have killed him. It was horrible. Peaches quit right after that and joined the post office."

Taste of the Islands

Flint has always had a soft spot for Hawaii. Shawn Luis explained: "He has hired so many of us [Hawaiians] to work at the Baton—me, my cousin Dina Jacobs, China Nguyen (who has been a good friend of mine since we were sophomores in high school), Andrea Nicole, Roski Fernandez, Dolinda Ko', Lavina, Alana Kela, and those are the ones I know of."

Ginger Grant added: "Dina Jacobs, Shawn Luis, Cherine Alexander, Andrea Nicole, and China Nguyen all went to school together and held their books like girls. They were all mahu (which means transgender). They had classes together, and Cherine was in swimming, and China wanted to be in the roller derby, since that was a big thing in Hawaii at the time. They worked at The Glade. In that era they had a band and sang live. They all came [to the Baton] after that, and one queen would bring another queen, and they were all extremely talented. So, soon there were a lot of Hawaiians in the show."

Dina Jacobs

Dina Jacobs talked a bit about her journey to Chicago. "I left Hawaii and ended up being in a traveling drag show from The Glade called Pearls of the Pacific," she said. Pearls of the Pacific was not a welcome hit in Canada. According to Jenettha J. Baines' book The 100 Most Influential Gay Entertainers: "Her [Dina Jacobs'] run in Canada ended abruptly when the Royal Canadian Mounted Police of Edmonton, Alberta, came to the location where she and the other drag performers were living and told them they had to leave the area because one of the girls was caught prostituting, even though she was cited and released. The performers were escorted outside of Alberta and were told never to return again."

Subsequent travels took Jacobs to San Francisco and back to Hawaii and then to Kansas City. "We went all over. I came to Chicago in the end of 1970. A friend of mine, Roski Fernandez, was working at the Baton. On Sunday nights at the Baton they used to have this sort of open microphone for drag queens, and I performed. I remember I sang 'My Way' live, and Jim hired me the next day. Roski basically got me the job."

"Dina was amazing," Flint nodded. "Even as a big girl her face was gorgeous, and she could belt out a tune like nobody's business. She worked for me from 1971 to '75. And when Dina came, she brought China [Nguyen] and Shawn [Luis]."

Dina Jacobs gave some background on how she discovered the world of female impersonation. "Back in the '50s I saw Female Mimics magazine," Jacobs said. "It had a lot of pictures, and I remember one part showed Holly White, and it showed her in a blond wig in Germany with some other transgender people before the word was even around. Holly was posed with one leg on a table and the other leg down, long legs, black lace stockings, garter belt, bustier, and a blond wig. Then on the next page was the same girl without the wig. In a boy's haircut. Years later when I met Holly, I said, 'You know what, Mary, thanks to you I got into this.' She asked what I meant, and I said I saw Female Mimics magazine, and when I did she cracked up."

Jacobs also recalled the original setup of the Baton. "When you first walked in, there was a pool table. Backstage it was all so different," she said. "The stage curtain was so sheer you could actually see us through the curtain putting our music on. It had been called the Shack and looked like sort of a beach place, so I suppose it was kind of an omen all of us were coming there from Hawaii. You know, 'We've got this place decorated like a beach shack, so we better go hire some Hawaiians,'" Jacobs said, laughing. In the area where the showroom is today was a big round bar.

"Jim liked to shock me," Jacobs said. "I remember the day he took me to the Gold Coast [501 North Clark Street] and then downstairs into the Pit [the no-holds-barred lower-level sexual arena of that 1970s leather bar]. I was still a boy-boy then. I wouldn't wear makeup or clothes when I went out during the day. I had never seen things like that before. I was clinging on to Jim and he was laughing, and I couldn't believe it all. He got such a kick out of that.

"I'm sad we never took a cast picture of everyone in the show back then, but we never thought of it. We never thought of the next day back then. We were happy we were working. It was not as hectic as it is today. It was much freer. Everyone was more relaxed. We went to work, we got ready at work. I was still a boy-boy at the time. I never thought of electrolysis or hormones or anything like that, I just wanted to do drag. My cousin Shawn [Luis] and China had already started with hormones and everything. I did always hate shaving, though, and I always used to have to shave twice a day, once in the morning and then once before I would go onstage at the Baton."

Jacobs recalled something else the Baton did that was perhaps unique in those days. "We had switch shows with Sweet Gum Head in Atlanta, and all of us went down there, and the performers from there would come up here," she said. "That place was packed every night. Jim was the emcee. There was Peaches, Lady Baronessa, Audrey Bryant, Chilli Pepper, Jan Howard, Jodie Lee, Tony Lewis, Shawn Luis, China Nguyen and myself."

Flint said he showed Jacobs Atlanta and she fell in love with it. "And I said, 'Oh, she's going to take them all to Atlanta now. Wait and see.' So, sure enough, she tried," Flint said. "One time she got upset with me about something and said she was going to move to Springfield [in Illinois]. She said they promised her this whole show. So, three of them went, and they got there, and it was one night. She came back here. Dina got Orlando del Sol, the choreographer, to come over from Hawaii. She was always on the move. Dina went to David's Place for a while, then to Springfield, and then back at the Baton for a while. Then she ended up staying in Atlanta."

"I brought in a lot of talent," said Jacobs. "I brought people in like the seamstress and performer Taisha Wallace and Orlando del Sol, the choreographer, as well as talents like Andrea Nicole and Cherine Alexander. Shawn Luis came because of me."

In regard to her eventually leaving the Baton, Jacobs explained: "That was me. More than anything, I was restless. I was at the Baton, went to David's Place, came back to the Baton, and then Jim and I got into an argument and he fired me. That was when I went to Atlanta. I stayed there the next 24 years. Jim and I were very close for a while. If it wasn't for the Baton, I don't know where I'd be. He gave me the opportunity to become Dina Jacobs on the mainland. He made me see how special I was as an entertainer. I'm not pretty, I'm not thin, I don't have good hair—but Jim made me feel really special, and for that I'll always be grateful. It's made me stand taller. He gave me confidence about my talent. He made me feel like more than a drag queen, he made me feel like an entertainer."

Roski Fernandez

"Roski wanted to get hired here, and I just told her, 'I don't have an opening,'" explained Flint. "And she said, 'Well, can I do a guest spot?' I said, 'Sure, we have guest spots on Sundays.' That was when I was just making it and still lived in my dressing room upstairs. That Sunday night, I went to bed early, and all of a sudden I woke up to all this thunderous applause, and I called downstairs and said, 'What the hell is happening down there, Lotta?' [Lotta Love was a transgender bartender who worked at the Baton, not to be confused with Lotta Love Larry, who was a transgender entertainer at the Baton during the same period.]

"Lotta explained that I needed to come down and see this act. When I asked who it was, she said Roski Fernandez. So I came down and watched her next act. She was incredible. She would dance and do all sorts of things with a bottle of Drambuie on her head. She did the poi balls [where balls on a cord are swung around the body] and go down on her knees and roll over. She was incredible.

"Her [Roski Fernandez's] real name was Freddie Durano. She took over as choreographer at the Baton, but I had to calm her down because she started teaching the girls by taking a yardstick to them. She had a temper. I remember one time she and Wanda Lust really got into it in the dressing room, and she said, 'Don't mess with a Filipino or I'll stab you to death,' and tragically that was how Wanda Lust died a couple years later. She was the male lead dancer for the Bayanihan [Philippine National Folk Dance Company]. He was the lead dancer as Freddie Durano for years, and, of course, Mama—they called the choreographer [of the Bayanihan] Mama—she knew Roski during the transformation."

Fernandez was Dina Jacobs' show director in Hawaii. "When I started at the Baton in 1971, she was the choreographer. She was professional—a very tough teacher," Jacobs said. "Thank God, I didn't get the stick. I probably would have gotten it, but in Hawaii you either sang or you danced, we didn't have pantomime. So I sang and emceed. We worked together, but I wasn't really in the productions. She made everyone so professional. It wasn't just learning the steps. You had better be polished. We always had an ironing board and iron backstage at the Baton, even when I started. We could not go onstage with wrinkled clothes. We would be fined. Jim wanted that show so polished that there were fines for all those sorts of things, and Roski was the perfect person to help enforce them. More than all that, though, Roski loved performing. She would do the most amazing dances that people had ever seen. It was different and exotic.

"Roski started in the Philippines. She told me she went to this audition with her friend and ended up getting the part. Soon she worked her way up to the lead dancer. They traveled all over the world and then came to The Glade's show in Hawaii, and that was it. That's when she became Roski Fernandez. One of the girls in her troupe was named Roski, and that's how she got that name, and she just randomly picked Fernandez. Alfredo Durano was her real name.

"Roski had two apartments in Hawaii—one where she lived and one where she worked. The one she worked in was half a block away from The Glade. For the first six or eight months, no one even knew about her working room for tricks. That's what she called it, 'my workroom.' And the other thing with Roski—she had pictures of every guy she had been with. Every guy! Every man! Naked—neck to knees. She was crazy, but a complete perfectionist."

Flint recalled the raunchy side of Roski. "One time we were at a Continental, and I wondered where Roski was, and they said, 'Oh, she's already got a trick out by the White Castle.' Her whole thing was to put ice cubes in her mouth beforehand to add to the sensation of oral sex," Flint said. "She was a man-eater. In the old days she'd walk in the Baton audience; she would be looking to see who was there. I remember this one guy from Milwaukee, and his dick was so huge, and we all said, 'If anybody could handle it, it would be Roski Fernandez.' And afterwards we asked her, and Roski said, 'Oh, huh-uh, I couldn't do that. I grabbed it but that was all I could do.' She loved sex—and was so beautiful and talented. The year Shawn Luis won Miss [Gay] America, she should have probably won. They just couldn't get beyond how beautiful Shawn was, but Roski was by far the most talented."

Dana Douglas, a Baton performer and Miss Continental 1987, said that Fernandez was a taskmaster. "When Roski moved on, Orlando del Sol (who had been male lead) took over as choreographer," Douglas said. "Roski would smack you on the legs with a ruler if you weren't getting a step. She worked and got the productions together. Roski and Jim battled quite a bit because they were contemporaries, and she'd get drunk and tell 'Jim stories,' and I don't think he appreciated that too much. If I remember, that was right when Jim wanted to seek political office."

Jacobs added: "When we finally got to Atlanta, she had calmed down a bit, but I remember one day Amber Richards [Miss Continental 1991] came in and we were at The Cove, a 24-hour bar in Atlanta. Amber had to get home because she had rehearsal. She got there, and she was hanging and didn't get the step, and Roski hit her with her famous bamboo stick. Amber turned around and said, 'If you hit me one more fucking time with that bamboo, I'm going to make you eat it.' And Amber meant it. So, Roski didn't do that anymore.

"Roski had a horrible temper. In Atlanta, I was working with her at a bar called the Answer, and during her act this guy kept talking. She was glaring at him and eventually hauled off and hit him in the head with a board, so even though she was so talented they had to let her go, since there would have been lawsuits."

"Roski Fernandez was an excellent choreographer," added Heather Fontaine, a Baton regular and Miss Continental 1981. "I always like production numbers best, so I hired her to put a show together that we did weekends down here in St. Petersburg in 1995–96. We played different places down here like B.T.'s and Sharpe's and Tremors. She was much harder to like back when I was performing. I was not a dancer. It was funny. Roski oftentimes made me the lead, since the backup dancers used to have to do a lot more dancing. Some production numbers she wouldn't put me in at all for that reason. I knew her back in the late 1970s before Miss Continental. We knew each other from Atlanta and clubs like Hollywood Hots, the Locker Room and, in the earlier 1970s, Sweet Gum Head."

"I remember one time we were driving cross-country in that van," said Kelly Lauren, another Baton regular and Miss Continental 1988. "She never liked me, and that was putting it mildly. We were all sort of goofing around in the back, and as I remember we were flashing our tits to passing cars. She was in the front and said, 'What is going on back there?' I wouldn't tell her what was happening, I didn't want my girlfriends to get in trouble, too, so she turned around and threw a Big Gulp in my face."

Maya Douglas recalled the incident. "We were on the road, and either coming into or out of Providence, Rhode Island, Roski just threw a Big Gulp right in Kelly Lauren's face. I thought it was because Kelly wouldn't shut up. That was usually why she was on Roski's nerves. All I remember is she threw it right in Kelly's face and said, 'Are you cooled down now?'"

In Sukie de la Croix's May 14, 2003, "Chicago Whispers" column in Windy City Times, he wrote: "Roski Fernandez: Born in the Philippines, Fernandez was 1st runner up in the Miss Gay America 1974 contest. In January 1979, she performed at the Show of Shows at the Bistro, and earlier had been a regular onstage at the Baton. In March 1983, she appeared at Broadway Ltd. for their Spring Fair, which also starred Lenore Allen, Amanda Lustrelle, Tina Rae, Tanya Richards, Monica Mone't and 'Emperor I' Steve Allman." In 1988, she was at the anniversary party for the Normandy at 3400 North Clark Street.

Roski Fernandez, explosive and dynamic onstage as well as off, ended up in Las Vegas, where she performed in her final years before passing away in November 2010.

Orlando del Sol

Winner of the title Entertainer of the Year at the Gay Chicago Awards event in 1982, hosted by Gay Chicago magazine's publishers Ralph Paul Gernhardt and Dan DiLeo, Orlando del Sol was the male lead (with Ray West) at the Baton. Dina Jacobs had said she had a friend named Orlando from Hawaii. Flint told her to bring him to Chicago. "What Dina didn't tell me was that he was doing drag under the name of Coco," Flint said.

Dina Jacobs recalled: "I used to do his makeup. He used to be Coco. I brought him over. He was a male lead at The Glade, so he was Orlando before he became Coco and then went back to being Orlando again at the Baton. "

Flint saw del Sol as Coco one or two times and was not impressed. "I pulled him aside and said, 'Orlando, I'd love to keep you on as the male lead, but I don't think Coco will work.' Coco was just not my type. Orlando was so creative. He eventually became the choreographer as well," Flint said. "The numbers were up-tempo and creative. He was just fabulous. Things were flashy and fun and he got along with the girls a lot better than Roski. At the time, we had several Hawaiians here that were just magnificent. Shawn Luis, China Nguyen, Andrea Nicole, Dolinda Ko', Dina Jacobs, and Taisha Wallace. That brought a whole different flavor to the show. Orlando did some of our finest production numbers."

"I originally got into this because I was working with Roski Fernandez's wife [he married to stay in the country] in Hawaii," said Orlando del Sol. "His wife said, 'My husband has a dance company, and I think you would be perfect for it.'" The group was Kaisahan, and the group of 35 or 40 members toured the Hawaiian Islands and eventually went to Tahiti, where del Sol was basically Fernandez's male dance partner.

"I came to the Baton on December 4, 1975," said del Sol. "Dina Jacobs suggested that Jim hire me and I came, thinking I would be there for a month. When I arrived, the cast was Dina, Chilli (I remember the first thing Chilli did when I met her was show me her gold bracelets), Jodie Lee, Jan Howard, Audrey Bryant, and Leslie Rejeanné, and then Lynette Langston came on soon after. China had already left to go to Nite Life, and Shawn Luis had left as well.

"When I came, I was Coco, but actually I said I'd be more comfortable onstage as a man, so I was the male lead. The show at the time was so long. When Felicia was in it, it would literally be 2½ or three hours. Jodie would do medleys, and she was crazy—she would literally be pounding the floor with her hand during productions. Audrey was so lovely. Dina did her wonderful impersonations, like Peggy Lee. Leslie, of course, was Diana Ross. They were all terrific entertainers, but it needed to come together a bit.

"I offered to help choreograph production numbers, since that's what I was into, so that's what I started doing. I could see there was some room for improvement. Mostly they were very agreeable. Chilli was a bit hesitant but was very good at posing and crossing the stage with her arms extended. Audrey could be a little sour-faced about dancing, as well, but once the production was in place, she enjoyed it.

"Don Dauksha was doing the costumes, and things were really coming together—but Jim was still charging only a dollar to see the show. I talked him into raising the price. He was terrified that if he did he'd lose the crowd, so I think he ended up raising it to $2. Later, for a few months, we also brought in a male strip group called the U.S. Male Revue on Monday nights. When I was a leading man there, I danced and pantomimed. I didn't strip, though there were some leading men later who did.

"I also worked with Jim choreographing productions for his Toys for Tots benefits and Dragocious. Eventually, the shows at the Baton became so wonderful. I helped bring a lot of people over from The Glade in Hawaii. For a while we had several Hawaiians in the show. China and Shawn had left, but there was Cherine, Alana, Andrea and Dolinda."

His relationship with Flint wasn't always pleasant, del Sol recalled. "I remember one time we got into it, and I took all my costumes for the production numbers as well as my music tapes. Those were all my things. I picked it all up and stormed out, and at the time I was living with my partner, Ken, at 11 East Erie, and soon enough Jim and Billy Cooper were yelling up at me from three floors down. Eventually I came back a few days later."

Del Sol and his partner, Ken Nowakowski, have been together 35 years and met in 1976. "We met at the Baton," said Nowakowski. "I worked for UPS, and a friend of mine there was dating Dolinda Ko', though he was married at the time. He kept telling me he had this beautiful girlfriend and I had to come and meet her. I'd been to the bars before, and I knew of the Baton. Anyway, my UPS buddy brought me in there and introduced me around as his 'straight friend.' Then, from across the bar, I saw Chilli, and she said, 'Straight? I had him last weekend.' I corrected her that it was in fact the weekend before. She said, 'That's right, I'm sorry.'"

Del Sol added, "And then I came out of the dressing room and was introduced to Ken, and the first thing I did was went up and sat on his lap. And we've been together ever since."

Nowakowski continued, "So, after I'd get off of UPS during the day, I would come and help Orlando with the sets and costumes and things." Sometimes Nowakowski even helped with the technical aspects of the show. "One time [lights and sound man] Billy Cooper was gone, and so Jim had Lotta Love [the bartender] run the lights, and I did the sound. Well, Jim was performing that night and doing 'My Way.' When he would do that number, Orlando would be backstage to help Jim change, since in the piece he would go from drag into male clothing.

"Well, Lotta turned the lights up while Jim was changing. Jim was waving frantically, thinking that because the house lights were bright everyone could see him changing behind the fabric screen, which, of course, wasn't the case. No one could see a thing, because he wasn't backlit. So, Jim was gesturing wildly, Lotta couldn't tell what Jim wanted and couldn't get the lights any brighter, and then finally Jim yelled out across the audience, 'Lotta, my cunt!' thinking his genitals were being lit. Lotta turned to me and said, 'Did he just say what I think he said?' It was so funny."

Del Sol spoke of his eventual leaving. "I left the Baton in 1986. I felt like I had done my work there and they didn't really need me anymore. It was a good time." Upon leaving the Baton, del Sol was working at a Japanese restaurant and did a musical revue at a place called Nanny's, on Chicago Avenue near Damen Avenue. "I did that with Monica Mon'et, and the name of the show was Guys Will Be Dolls. I was so happy for my time at the Baton. If I hadn't come there, I would have never been where I am today, and I would have never met Ken."

Taisha Wallace

Like del Sol, Taisha Wallace was another performer who was onstage as well as working behind the scenes. Costumes for productions, sewing, and other wonderful creations for the shows were done at one time by Taisha as well as by Don Dauksha and Fred Legon. "Taisha Wallace was beautiful," recalled Flint. "She did a lot of the wardrobe. She was one of the Hawaiian girls who went down to Atlanta. She married a lesbian down there. She was working back in Hawaii at a gift shop for a few years but now she is back in Atlanta. Still so beautiful, though."

Sabrina Sabo

Sabrina Sabo was another Hawaiian entertainer who came to the Baton. "I was in Chicago from 1971 to 1982," Sabo said. "I lived on Chestnut with Andrea Nicole and Cherine Alexander. I was working the door at the Baton for a bit, left to go to the Nite Life [933 North State Street], came to the Baton as an entertainer, and then went back to the Nite Life. I liked the Nite Life because it was easier. It was all solo acts, no production numbers. It was more a strip-joint sort of place. I also did lights and sound there as well as perform. At the Baton I had a hard time trying to learn and remember all the production numbers. I did some Polynesian numbers and Hawaiian dances and some Natalie Cole. I loved hanging out at record stores, so I actually enjoyed finding things for other people to pantomime more. I often found things for Cherine.

"The toughest part for me about working at the Baton was having to go on either right before or right after Chilli. She always had the crowd right in her hand. Before, they were all hanging on to their money and waiting, and afterwards they'd just spent it all. When I worked there it was me, Leslie Rejeanné, Chilli Pepper, Audrey Bryant, Jan Howard, Lynette Langston, Jodie Lee and Cherine Alexander. Cherine was a wonderful entertainer. Actually, she gave Chilli a run for her money. The crowd came in to see Chilli and they would be screaming and just lining up for her—but Cherine won a lot of those people over. She had this way of going into the character of the song. She was really a wonderful, wonderful performer.

"Jim used to like playing tricks on me because he loved to get me mad. One time I was standing at the bar at the Bistro, and then I had this long, red hair. This guy came up to me and said, 'Are you Chilli Pepper, I love you.' And I said 'No, I'm not.' So then someone else came up and asked me if I was Chilli Pepper, and then another. Finally I turned around and screamed 'No, I am not Chilli Pepper,' and then I looked, and standing to the side in the bar was Jim, laughing. That's the sort of teasing he enjoyed."

Shawn Luis

Shawn Luis was another entertainer who came to the Baton in the great influx of island talent. "I met Jim in 1973 or '74," Luis said. "I am originally from Hawaii and came to California. After being there, I decided I was going to move to either New York or Chicago, so I came to Chicago first and went to the Baton Show Lounge. I was a licensed cosmetologist and didn't even think really about doing this professionally. I came right after my cousin Dina Jacobs had left for Atlanta with Lady Baronessa and Roski Fernandez. Jim said, 'Why don't you audition?' So I did. I did 'I Don't Know How to Love Him,' with a hula and a Tahitian dance. He hired me.

"James and I hit it off right from the start. He took care of me. He was kind of controlling, but he meant well. That's just how he showed he cared. With me, Jim wanted to make sure I was OK because I was naïve. He wanted to make sure guys didn't take advantage of me or that I wouldn't get hurt. That was such an important time for me. He really molded me as an entertainer.

"I remember when I told Jim I was going to take a vacation, and I went to California to visit my boyfriend. I was supposed to be there a week and I ended up being there for a month. When I came back, I walked in the door, and Jim said, 'You're fired.' I said, 'OK,' and went to get my things out of my cubicle, and he followed me into the dressing room and said, 'Where are you going?' I said, 'You just fired me.' He said, 'Well, just don't let it happen again.' And he put me back onstage that night.

"Another time right after China Nguyen started, I remember Jim was teasing me, saying that if I didn't enter Miss Gay America he was going to fire me. It was a four-day competition and they were so strict—curfew, no marijuana, and they kept you going all the time, out at the pool for photos, here for evening gowns, time for interviews. There were a lot of girls competing that year down in Atlanta, something like 58, and some really great performers like China Nguyen, Naomi Sims, Roski Fernandez, Rachel Wells and Chilli Pepper. Actually, that was one of the reasons for the friction between Chilli and myself. She would always say, 'I should have won Miss Gay America,' and I would say, 'Yeah, maybe you should have, but you didn't.'

"The truth was, I thought the real winner should have been Angie DeMarco, and she probably would have won it if she hadn't come in after curfew one of the nights. They were very strict about that sort of thing. After I won, I was back in Chicago going to some function, and I was wearing the Miss Gay America sash, and this old woman came up to me and said, 'You're so pretty.' And then she looked down and saw the sash and with the same smile said, 'Does that mean you're happy all the time?' I just smiled and said, 'Yes, yes, it does.'"

Shawn Luis also shyly added: "Not many people know this, but at one time after I won the Miss Gay America pageant, which was in 1975, Jimmy proposed to me. He put me in a beautiful long limousine and gave me two dozen red roses and said, 'Shawn Luis, I'd like to marry you.' It was so sweet, but I said, 'Jim, I can't.'"

"Jim was head over heels in love with one of my girlfriends, who was working for him on the show," said Sabrina Sabo. "Jim asked for my input on which ring should he buy for her. Someone was selling all these beautiful wedding and engagement rings. I picked out the one with the biggest diamond, since it was for my girlfriend/roommate, and Jim bought it for her."

Flint confirmed his proposal. "Shawn Luis was the only drag I ever fell in love with," he said. "She was gorgeous. One night we went to Milwaukee, and I always wanted her to enter the Miss [Gay] America pageant, and she said 'Oh, Jimmy, I can't do that.' I said, 'Yes, you can.' So we went there and were having dinner at M&M, the gay club. I said, 'You know, Shawn, you're really going to be pissed at me.' She asked me why, and I said, 'Because I entered you in the Miss [Gay] America pageant.'

"So, we all went that year. Shawn, China, Chilli—and Shawn was incredible. If it came down to talent, Roski Fernandez should have won, but Shawn's beauty was just so great there was no way anyone else could have won. I proposed to her later, but she was going to have the sex change, and that killed the deal. She was the only one I fell in love with that way. Now I won't even let them kiss me."

Luis continued: "I hadn't told Jim at the time, but I had decided a while earlier to have the transition surgery. I knew if I had that surgery I would have had to leave the Baton. It was something I had to do. I needed to be the butterfly and transform. So, once I decided that, I went to school during the day at Loyola and got a business management degree while working nights at the Baton. In late 1975, when I said I was having my surgery and leaving, he was angry for a long time. Jimmy can hold a grudge. We still talked on the phone and he would give me advice, but a lot of times one of us would hang up on the other. Now we have good rapport, though. Jim will always be a part of my life."

Luis recalled another incident involving the Miss Gay America title. "One time, I remember, I was at the Baton, and Jimmy came running in and said, 'Come on, Shawn. We have to go out to Midway Airport.' When we got there, it was because the Blue Angels, the jet pilots, were appearing there. There were all these other beauty queens there—Miss Chicago, Miss Illinois, and I just joined them. It was so funny. I was there posing for pictures, and no one was any the wiser."

"Shawn Luis is crazy, but in a good way," laughed Ginger Grant. "Jim sponsored her for Miss [Gay] America in 1975, and they are a strict contest. They don't want silicone or enhancements or anything. Shawn had silicone when she won the contest, and a couple months later she had her sex change and they didn't know it, so she was touring as Miss

America who supposedly had all these rules, and she broke them all. A beautiful woman, still, at 65 years old. She was another one who you would just stare at and not believe it was a boy."

As can be imagined with so many organic and synthetic hormones around, there was some tension and drama among the performers. "We'd have our ups and downs and fights, but we always tried to get through any conflict at the bar meetings," Luis said. "It was almost always professional and very rarely personal—usually it was the production number or who went where in the lineup. That sort of thing. That was such a formative period for me. The most important thing that Jim did for me and for so many at the Baton was that he makes the girls respect themselves, and what's more, he makes them realize that they deserve the respect of others. That was the greatest gift he gave me."

China Nguyen

"China is my best friend in the whole world," smiled Ginger Grant. "She's 65 years old and lives in Montgomery, Illinois, with her husband of 26 years. She has not had a sex change, but I say 'husband' because they have been a couple that long. She used to strip and do shows and then met this man from the Navy, and they got together and she became a beautician. They have a pool, and we have a luau at their place after Continental every year. She never has a bad thing to say about anyone.

"In her heyday, China would walk down the street and heads would turn, and she'd always think, Oh, they're clocking me, they know I'm a boy. I'd say, 'Honey, they're looking because you're a beautiful woman.'"

Andrea Nicole

A GayLife newspaper article about Andrea Nicole, "In Her Own Words" (February 9, 1984) by Albert Williams, begins: "Talking with Andrea one is struck by a street-wise, kinky sense of life's absurdities, an 'anything goes' craziness mixed with a pro's seriousness and dedication to craft. She's good and she knows it—and knows that she has to work for it, but that you can work and play too."

Nicole explained to GayLife a bit about what brought her to the Baton's stage: "'In Hawaii I was working as a hairdresser. My friends and I used to do drag on the weekends. We were weekend queens. Some friends of mine were working in a show but there was only one club on the island, so they got together in a traveling show and we worked all the islands. We were called 'The Fabulous Fakes'—can you believe that? I was probably 21. … I was always a chorus girl, I was never a lead. There was no miming in the shows. We were just a line. The solo acts were always the singers, the strippers.'"

Nicole also explained a bit about life at the Baton: "'People think it's funny when they look up on the stage,' she confides. 'But when you look out toward them it's a scream! We have a ball. We have this backstage motto: Get them before they get us.'" As to her plans for the future: "'I would have loved to be born a woman, to get married, to have that one person. But this is what I chose. I like women, but I feel there are enough women in the world now. Besides—life would never be as interesting as it is now.'"

In an interview for this book, Dina Jacobs spoke about Nicole. "We all went to high school together. I was a senior, Cherine [Alexander] was a junior, and Andrea was a sophomore," Jacobs smiled, recalling Nicole. "Many Andrea stories I could not tell you because I'd have to kill you later." She decided on a tamer anecdote instead: "I remember Andrea's sister would always come to school with drag-queen hair because Andrea was so into hairdos and French twists and clusters, and so she'd always practice on her sister, so Geri would always come to school with a different hairdo every day.

"She had a bad relationship in California, so I called and said, 'Mary, why don't you come to the Baton?' And she did. We all lived on Briar and Sheridan. It was Andrea, Orlando del Sol, Punipuni Pat ('punipuni' means 'liar' in Hawaiian) and myself."

Jacobs continued: "Andrea and I also went to work in Argentina together for a while. She was working at Queen Mary's in L.A. This agent came and saw her and said she wanted her to come to Argentina with three other girls. So Andrea, me, Brandi Lee, and China [Nguyen] went. Brandi and I sang and emceed, and Andrea and China were the variety act—they stripped, but clean stripping. China had a fire act. And Andrea just stripped down to a G-string and top and did it to Donna Summer."

"Andrea was a woman of substance," said former Baton manager Lennie Malina. It's clear she was one of Malina's favorites. "She was honest and forthright and just a genuinely good person without harsh words for anyone. We had a benefit for her after she got cancer, and Ikey and I flew to Hawaii and gave [the money that was raised] to her. Seeing this beautiful, statuesque woman sick and in that wheelchair was so hard."

Heather Fontaine recalled her time with Andrea Nicole. "When I won Miss Continental I was very young and basically had no idea whatsoever how to be a titleholder," Fontaine said. "Andrea was really nice to me when I came to the Baton, so sweet and nurturing. Some of the girls were kind of distant because I was a titleholder. That was tough because I was so far from home. Andrea was like a big sister."

Flint recalled her professionalism. "At rehearsal, Andrea was the first one here. She was always ready and able to separate our friendship from work," he said. "For that reason she was one of the performers who it was easy for me to go out with. We worked and we were friends, and she knew those were two different relationships. She sort of was a go-between for me as well.

"I remember one time we were at the Paradise, and the bartender, Mike, kept wanting to give me free drinks, and I went to the washroom and when I did, Andrea said to him, 'If you keep trying to give him free drinks, he's not going to sit with you, because he feels uncomfortable with that. It's not your booze to give away, and he comes out to spend money, not to get things for free.' Andrea would tell people things like that in my benefit."

"Her clothes were always impeccable," recalled Ginger Grant. "She could do anything. She'd go to a resale shop and buy a man's suit and bead the lapels, and it would be fantastic. She had that edge. Very sweet, nothing phony about her. She passed away in, I think, 1985. It was cancer. They discovered she was sick when she was a contestant in Miss Continental at the Park West. She was doing 'Memory' from Cats, and she had a harness on her, and they lifted her up to the ceiling, and when they did, the cancer or whatever was so bad in her lungs that she blacked out up there. By the time they had her down, she regained consciousness, but after that, she went to the doctor and found out everything. She went to Hawaii right away to be with her family, and her sister took care of her."

Sabrina Sabo recalled: "Andrea was beautiful, not the greatest at pantomime but absolutely gorgeous. She had a wonderful fashion sense. I remember when Cherine won Miss Continental in 1984. Andrea was so sick in Hawaii, and Cherine called her and asked what she should wear and do, and that was the year she won."

Ikey, the longtime Chicago bartender at His 'n Hers, Annex 2, Buddies', Annex 3 and 3160, recalled the time. "A bunch of the bartenders who were working for Jim, and a couple others, put on a show where we dressed as different characters to raise money for Andrea," Ikey said. "We ended up getting between five and six thousand dollars, and Lennie [Malina, manager of Annex 2 and the Baton at the time] flew to Hawaii [with Ikey] to give the money to her, and how grateful she was because she was really down and out at that point."

Ginger Grant agreed. "At the Halloween ball the next year, Jim had her as a judge, and by then she was pretty well gone," Ginger said. "She told us all, 'This will probably be my last year.' We have a luau every year, so that year we all sat around and ate and laughed and clowned and barefooted and acted crazy. It was a nice last memory."

"Jim flew us in from Hawaii and wanted her to be head judge at his Halloween ball at the Park West," explained Sabrina Sabo. "Andrea was in a wheelchair at the time, and the flight was so tough on her. I am forever grateful to Jim for paying our way and letting Andrea see everyone in the last days of her life. We stayed with Monica Mone't, who worked at the Nite Life. Andrea was so sick that she ended up not being able to be the head judge that night, but she got to see everyone. That was for Halloween, and we went back to Hawaii and she died on Thanksgiving Eve [November 27, 1985]."

Flint grew teary at the memory of when he heard the news that Nicole had died. "I was at the Limelight [the nightclub opened at 632 North Dearborn Street on July 31, 1985] the night they called and told Russ, the manager, to tell me Andrea had passed away," Flint said. "So I started drinking like crazy and got wiped out of my mind and passed out on the couch there. When they asked, 'What should we do?' Russ said, 'Let's just leave him here and let him sleep, and whoever comes tomorrow just let him out.'"

"Andrea Nicole has two nieces," Grant said. "One is named Andrea and one is named Nicole, and one looks like just like Andrea, and the other has the same mannerisms. It's very eerie."

Cherine Alexander

Cherine Alexander moved to Chicago in 1979 and remained in Chicago and at the Baton until 1984. Her trademark aggressive sexual energy onstage made her an extremely popular entertainer. Grace Jones, a leather-clad dominatrix and suggested kink were all specialties of hers.

In GayLife's Erotika feature (July 28, 1983), Cherine Alexander was profiled by Albert Williams: "'A good performer can grab the audience as soon as she comes out,' says Cherine Alexander, 'and carry them off to wherever they're going and bring them back.'" In the Williams piece, Alexander went on to say: "'[I] started cross-dressing in high school. I couldn't wait for weekends, to go out and play. ... They had this bar, called The Glade, which was a show bar ... . To me it [cross-dressing] wasn't something sexual. It was just something that I felt within. I felt more attractive as a woman. I didn't, you know, hate my organ. I didn't feel like a typical pre-op transsexual. There have been some people that I've met that find it a sexual fantasy, but to me it's a way of life … . And my feelings are feminine, my intuitions are female ... it's something that I don't even think about at all.'"

Alexander continued: "'At the Baton everybody's got their own style, which is good, because everybody flows together and they work together. Sometimes there are similarities, but everybody seems to project their own imagery … . I'm the kinkiest one in the show, really.'"

As to the tour buses full of Baton customers: "'When they do come in, they expect to see men that look like men that are dressed in women's clothes. And when they first see the girls coming out one at a time, they kind of sit back, they're shocked. And then they try and find fault. And if they can go beyond that and just look at the talent itself, then they appreciate it. If they start looking for fault, then they miss the whole illusion. They get intimidated. You have to bring them out of that and make them feel comfortable—and then you can play with them,' she says slyly. How does she do that? 'I guess a lot of eye contact. And—you play with them by um, being suggestive. If you can pull that off without making them feel intimidated, and let them know that you're still a guy, then they feel comfortable. Otherwise they get intense. They do ... you have to hit them slowly.'"

"Cherine was a great entertainer. She had tons of charisma and would do Tina Turner and Grace Jones a lot," added Kelly Lauren.

"Cherine and I kept in touch after she came to California, up until her death," said Heather Fontaine. "She was so amazing. She had this confidence onstage that was wonderful. She and Chilli both have that quality."

Stilettos and Sneaks Blog
Alexandra Billings writes about Cherine Alexander: Passing It On
Posted October 31, 2010

[This post is reprinted with permission and has been slightly edited.]

I had no idea what they were talking about. I stood there looking at them both like they were nuts. A beauty pageant for transsexuals? What? What is it exactly they do? Walk around in picture hats trying to whisper like Marilyn Monroe?

I didn't want any part of this.

I was four years out of high school and working at a club on the North Side of Chicago called La Cage. It was the early '80s and everyone and their mother were either having sex with total strangers, or shoveling heaps of cocaine up their noses. I was doing both. Our club was a hot spot at the time, but it was nothing compared to the Baton down on Clark Street. This was where the stars performed. The divas. The entertainers who resembled living Barbie dolls. The Tribune, Phil Donahue, Irv Kupcinet, they all frequented the Baton. Although Ginger, Candy, Patti and Lisa and I pretended it didn't matter, it did. We were still small-time. Second-rate. The place to go when you couldn't get a seat in the main theater. You had to make reservations to see a show at the Baton; to get a seat at La Cage, you needed to give good head.

And so, at the corner of the bar, after closing one Friday night, my friend Cesar and my boyfriend at the time tried to lure me into my first big competition.

"Well, let's at least go see what we're up against," I said grudgingly.

The next week, the three of us bought tickets and arrived at the Park West, which is a [900]-seat house in a fancy part of Chicago. As we took our seats, the music filled the space, and as if someone had let the door open on a transsexual convention, 26 of the most insanely beautiful women popped out of the wings on either side of the stage, draped in white, and paraded in front of us smiling, waving and throwing their delicious trains from side to side. Screams, whistles, cheers and hollers rang

"Cherine told it like it was, no holds barred," said Lennie Malina "She was open and honest and we loved each other. She was a great performer and a wonderful person."

Former Miss Continental Dana Douglas agreed. "I moved in with her when I came to Chicago. I did her costume the year she won Miss Continental. She had so much style and class. She was the one who taught me onstage confidence," Douglas said.

Flint said that on the night Alexander won Miss Continental at Park West, for her talent number "they threw her in a cage with a leopard and flipped it around, and they turned it around and she was gone and the leopard was in there, and they turned it around again and she was in there but the leopard was gone."

Judy Walker was a well-known madam. "I ran a house of prostitution, large call-girl operation, in the city of Chicago for many years," Walker said. "Started before my marriage. I had, as clients, men from all over the U.S., from in and out of Chicago. Movie stars and politicians. I had some of the girls at the Baton working for me."

"Cherine was one of her girls. There was some bigwig with the county that she always would tie up. A few Baton girls worked for Judy," said Flint.

"She used to be a stripper because she had the moves and everything," said Ginger Grant. "She was off the wall. She would do Grace Jones or wear a beautiful gown and then strip and start crawling around on the floor like a snake. She had this great aura, way ahead of her time. She battled AIDS for years and was blind for many years. Her boyfriend died, and then about six months later she died [in October 2010]. They cremated her and spread her ashes in the ocean."

through the rafters. Every single one of them was astonishing to look at. I actually had to rub my eyes a couple of times to make sure I was seeing what I was seeing. After all, I was just a little kid from Schaumburg, for Christ's sake.

"Are you kidding me?" I said to my boyfriend under my breath.

He smiled, and took my hand.

And did another line.

I wasn't that. I was a lot of things, but a raving beauty I wasn't. I wasn't tall and luxurious, and to be perfectly honest, I didn't know that I wanted to be. It looked like a heavy burden. I don't think that I cared that much. I had just befriended Michael Sanders (a friend still to this day) and he was constantly trying to pull me out of my pink-and-red stage. I couldn't match a color with a Garanimals set. I had no taste. None.

(And to be truly honest, not much has changed. Getting dressed for any kind of gig or function is still a nightmare for me. This is why I have my gays.)

But I wanted to act, I didn't want to waltz up and down a runway in a G-string. My lip-syncing consisted of monologues I stole from the TV and put on cassette tapes. I did Sondheim and Weill. I fancied myself Vanessa Redgrave, not Raquel Welch.

Let's face it: I was full of my own crap at the time.

I was also terrified.

I had only been transitioning for three or four years and I was completely unsure of myself as a female or as an actor. Even though I had been in the theater with my father as a child, taking my art seriously wasn't at the top of my list. I pretended I knew what I was doing, and to everyone around me I was self-assured and confident. Inside I was a bundle of confusion, rage, fear and paranoia. And deep down, I wanted desperately, more than anything, to be a "beauty." To be worshipped. To be adored. To be flipping my train and pulsating down a runway to the homey sound of catcalls and perverse whistles. To be exactly what I had been criticizing at the time as "trash" and "nonsense." I hated it so much because I wanted it so much.

I was also so loaded with drugs you could have squeezed the heroin out of my own anus. And involved with a man who whispered sweet nothings in my ear, and then threw me down the stairs and punched me in the face in the middle of a grocery store.

I was in the center of a tornado with no signs of it stopping.

And as we sat with our drinks in our hands, the three of us ogling the bathing suits, the evening gowns (which were unreal), finally came the talent portion. And somewhere, in the middle of the 26 contestants, popped this dark, tan, glorious woman with piercing brown eyes, moving her mouth to Laura Branigan. I was mesmerized. It wasn't really about her beauty for me, there was something else happening. Something unexplainable. Something truly compelling. There was something that seemed to dig deep in me, hold onto me, and propel me forward toward her. And I wasn't the only one. The audience lost their collective minds. She slithered and posed, gestured and pulsated, reached out toward us in a way that few performers have an ability to do. She was giving us something that night. She was handing something over to us, and for me, that night, sitting at that table, in the midst of those [900] screaming Mimis, I felt as if she was handing it over specifically to me. It wasn't just a performance, it was an experience.

"Who IS that?" I asked Cesar in a half-whisper.

"Oh, girl. That's Cherine Alexander. She's It," Cesar said breathlessly.

And she was. She was It.

The next year I entered the pageant, and lost.

I entered Miss Continental the following year—and lost. However, that year, my blond-haired, blue-eyed pal Kelly Lauren and I were asked by the owner of the contest to come and work for him. His name was Jim Flint, and he owned the Baton.

I'd finally made it to the main stage.

The week Kelly and I arrived at the club, I think I owned four dresses, all with detachable ruffles, and a couple of old wigs that looked like the cat had been chewing on them for about a week. Kelly was much more prepared than I was. There was little room in the downstairs dressing rooms, and some of the girls were leaving but hadn't quite taken everything out just yet. It was a changing of the guard, so to speak. The old generation was going, and a new one was on its way. At the time I had no idea what that really meant, especially to the women nearest the exit, but as I look back on it now, I can finally feel the weight of that night. I remember their faces. The look of horror and strange relief. The fear that nothing might lie ahead for them. What to do when you're transgendered in 1989 and you don't do a boffo

Liza Minnelli impersonation? Where do you go? Who'll take you in? Contrary to popular belief, we can't all work at McDonald's.

And no one really looks fabulous in that paper hat.

Strangely, Kelly and I were to share Cherine's old dressing room. Cherine Alexander, the first huge performer, the first real Drag Star I was witness to when I was barely into my 20s, was packing her bags as Kelly and I glued our lashes on in front of her mirror.

The night her bags sat outside our room was the night of my first show at the Baton. I was terrified. There were always huge production numbers with hats and dancing boys, and the last thing I wanted to do was parade around half-naked pretending to be glamorous. I was still at war with that part of myself, and the mere mention of push-up bras sent me into a tizzy. I just wanted to do my 'All About Eve' speech and get the heck out of Dodge. But ... there was a sense of joy for me. There was Cherine. This was her space and I was in it. I wasn't too high not to notice that and know that it meant something.

I had watched Cherine for the last week in the wings when she was performing her Grace Jones, or her Eartha Kitt. I studied her. I marveled at the dollar bills being thrown at her feet by lines of both men and women. Her eyes flashing and those gorgeous, long fingers caressing her face as she jutted her chin toward the sky. And I practiced as I watched. If I was anything back then, I was a good mimic. And a good thief.

So ... I stole.

Blindly.

And as her suitcases sat outside our dressing room, and the girls were saying goodbye, I walked up to Cherine. She was wearing a long, black trench coat to protect her from the sharp Chicago winter whipping up outside the club. It was close to the overture for that night, and I hadn't really spoken to her at all. So I gathered my courage, and finally said something:

"Cherine. I just want you to know. I'm stealing blindly from you."

Cherine looked at me and smiled. Her eyes squinted and she touched my chin with those beautiful fingers, lifting my face up to the light in that badly lit hallway.

"Oh, Tita—it's not stealing if you do it from the heart. That's called: passing it on."

And she disappeared into the dressing

room down the hall.

(Just so you don't think it's a misprint: "Tita"—pronounced "Tit-ah"—is a Hawaiian word meaning "sister." We had many girls from the Islands at the Baton, and this was a term of endearment from all of them. Cherine used it wisely and with great emphasis.)

The next time I saw her was about three years later. I was a bit more secure in my job, and my cocaine addiction was now in full bloom. When she came to do a special concert, we were all fluttering around downstairs preparing for her return. Although I never really knew her that well, I was thrilled she was coming back. I had such huge respect for her, and she really changed me in a way that was a bit unexplainable.

This time, I walked down to the end of the hall the night of the show where she and Leslie were dressing and gabbing. Leslie Rejeanné, who did a knockout Diana Ross (although not ever to be compared with my own Drag Mother Diana McKay), was the emcee and our fearless leader. She held the highest spot at the Baton beside the great, legendary Chilli Pepper. Leslie was given free rein to make the schedule for the evening, deciding who gets which spot, deciding on the production numbers for that night, and generally keeping up morale, which at that time, as loaded as we all were, and as full of our own ego as we all were, was herculean to say the least.

Leslie and I ended up being great friends, and to be invited into the dressing room at the tip of the hallway without a password was true status at the club. Leslie's laugh and her ability to cherish friends was something that stayed with me through many dark days. And to this day, it's hard for me to listen to Bette Midler's version of "Superstar" without hearing the sound of my own heart breaking a bit.

I knocked, and Leslie opened the door. There was Cherine, sitting at Leslie's makeup table, half-dressed and pointing to her own half-bald forehead. Most of her hair had fallen out, and she had some lesions on her neck the two of them were attempting to cover up with pan stick No. 5.

My mouth hung open.

I knew what this was. I knew what this meant. We had all begun to lose people. I knew what the signs were. The disease at that time was still called GRID, but the word AIDS had recently been splashed all over the front page of Time magazine not too long ago. This wasn't just gay men dying now. This disease had no prejudice. But I had nothing to say. Nothing formed in my mouth. I stood there. Frozen.

"It's OK, Tita, it's only me," she said, smiling. "Got a Zsa Zsa Gabor wig handy?"

That was the last thing she ever said to me, and that was the last time I saw her alive.

Cherine passed away last Friday morning [in 2010].

My heart is in a strange place because as I said, she wasn't someone I spoke to often. In fact, even when I moved to California and was only minutes away from her, I never visited her. Not once. She was an enigma to me. She was otherworldly. I met her at a time when I was transforming into something I had always felt was true, and she was the first person I saw who was happy, gorgeous and a brilliant entertainer. She was my first role model, of sorts.

I only knew her through her work. I only touched her through the architecture she and I shared. I only kept her with me by adopting her shapes, her gestures, her internal tempos. I said maybe three or four pieces of text in total to her, but she remains a massive part of my history. I am forever changed by her and forever different. She is ingrained in my soul. And that has nothing to do with time.

I can't forget her. So I posted what I could find of her.

Strangely, as it was with every encounter I had with Cherine, this number was the exact number I saw at the Park West that very first night I went to Miss Continental. I can't believe I found this. I'm still in a bit of a state of shock. I remember that night like it happened last week. I can smell it, hear the crowd screaming, feel my pulse racing, knowing that if SHE could do that, if there was someone that looked that gorgeous, that was that enigmatic, that knew how to give that gift freely and without hesitation, then there was hope for all of us. It wasn't merely about moving your mouth to other people's music, it was about going forward into it.

And now that I've found this clip, now that I can share it and the story of Cherine and what she meant, I feel her voice very close.

"OK, Tita. I'm passing it on."

(To view the video/clip discussed, go to YouTube.com and search for Finalist #24, Cherine Alexander's Talent, for Miss Continental 1984–85.)

Dolinda Ko'

"Dolinda Ko' had the best body," said Flint. "It was the only time we ever got busted here. She was talking to this cop, and Andrea said, 'I think that's a cop.' So Andrea went over and cautioned Dolinda not to talk to him. Then Dolinda went backstage and then a little later was back out again talking to him, and I guess gave him her number. And she was 'soliciting,' but we got it dismissed. Now she's a bus driver in Hawaii and is a true Hawaiian mama and weighs about 350 pounds."

Dana Douglas recalled: "Dolinda had an amazing body. She wasn't real talented but she was a sweet and friendly sexpot. She wasn't a pageant sort, she just liked being a girl."

"Dolinda was a local in Hawaii, so she spoke with a broken Hawaiian-English accent, so she could be hard to understand sometimes, but very sweet," added Heather Fontaine.

Ginger Grant agreed. "Dolinda had a Raquel Welch body. Lovely," she said. "Those Hawaiian girls were ahead of their time. They had implants and hips and hair to their waist. We saw Dolinda about 10 years ago in Hawaii, and Jim said, 'Ginger, close your mouth.' I couldn't believe it. She was bigger than me. She drove a bus for handicapped children, and her hair was gray."

More of the Many Baton Stars
Bertha Butts

"I worked with so many great entertainers and just great people. Jan Howard, Stacy Stevens, Peaches, Chilli Pepper, Audrey Bryant, Lotta Love, and big Bertha Butts," said Shawn Luis, becoming suddenly enthusiastic about Butts, the House of Landers veteran, Baton regular, and popular 1970s–'80s entertainer. "Bertha was phenomenal. I was always amazed at how incredibly she could move for a big person. What a performer!

"Bertha Butts was gigantic," said Flint. "She moved to Atlanta. She was a huge man and made the prettiest woman, and could she entertain! She could move every bit of fat on her body. And in the daytime she was a macho man. Her eyes—she painted these huge arching eyebrows, painted wild like Divine, and this was before Divine."

Tony DeSario, a former Mr. Continental (2005–06), worked with Butts at Illusions in Atlanta. "She was terrific and so much fun," he said. "So many of my best friends from that time are not with us anymore."

Lotta Love

Shawn Luis also recalled Lotta Love, a 1970s performer.

"Lotta was big and tall with a beautiful smile," Luis said. "He was very troubled. He still came in to work as a guy. He had a boyfriend, and the boyfriend was in love with the male side of him but not the female side. I think he ended up committing suicide."

Flint clarified some confusion regarding the Baton staff in the early days. "There were two Lotta Loves. There was Lotta Love the bartender, and Lotta Love Larry. Lotta Love Larry was black and an entertainer."

In a Chicago Gay Crusader piece in 1973, Michael Bergeron profiled the captivating

Lotta Love. The piece began: "Felicia announced her to the stage. 'And here she is, from K-Y Flats at the Lawson YMCA, the tall, tan, and terrific Lotta Love.'" The piece continued, describing how Haitian-born Lotta Love/Larry was 6 feet 4 in heels: "She started at the Baton with her best friend Peaches doing both dramatic as well as comic pantomiming of songs. The former gang member, ballet instructor, and go-go boy was working his way through college (majoring in physics) by performing at the Baton at the time of the article and even played on his college football team." Lotta/Larry closed the interview by saying, "'I'll always be grateful to Peaches for giving me the courage and the stamina and determination to get onstage in front of people in female attire and perform, and I'll always be grateful to Felicia for allowing me to have the stage to do the performing.'"

Flint described the other Lotta Love: "She was a transsexual bartender. She was so big, nobody would dare to start anything. She was about 6 feet 3. I remember one time this guy came in who wanted to get tied up and abused, and he was in love with me. So we went up to my dressing room, and I tied him up, and I got a phone call, and I had to run up north really fast, so I took off and forgot about this guy tied up in my dressing room. Lotta Love called me up at about 3 a.m. and said, 'Jim, we're getting ready to close, what should I do with that guy?' I said, 'What guy?' Lotta replied, 'The guy that is tied up upstairs.' I had completely forgot about him, so I said, 'You know, Lotta, you always wanted him. Just untie him and take him home with you.' And so she did."

Heather Fontaine

Heather Fontaine explained how she came to work at the Baton in February 1982.

"I moved to Chicago during my reign as Miss Continental and then left when I gave up my crown the following Labor Day," she said. "When I moved to Chicago, I was having problems, and one of my implants ruptured and I was in the hospital. Felicia came and visited me and even paid me while I was in the hospital. I eventually had them removed and replaced with silicone. When I came here I didn't have a lot of costumes, so Felicia lent me the money to have some costumes made.

"She was really good to me. She was very good to all the girls. When I was there it was Leslie, Sherì Payne, Andrea Nicole, Cherine Alexander, Orlando del Sol, Dolinda Ko', and Chilli Pepper. I used to do different things—a lot of theater, Evita. Some 1960s girl-group things. I didn't really do the top hits of the day or anything. I'm a clown and I love to make people laugh, because I think it makes everyone comfortable. I remember the dressing rooms used to be upstairs and I shared a big one with Sherì, Cherine, Andrea.

"After I gave up my title, I moved to San Antonio, Texas, and worked at a place called Sunset Boulevard before moving out to California. There weren't a lot of queens in the early 1980s, with breasts, doing shows down in Texas, and so they paid well. I had one show a night, which would consist of two numbers, and that would bring in $250. So, basically, you only had to work a couple nights a week to have a good income. That's changed, though. I don't do shows much anymore. When I get the itch, there's a bar here, but trust me, I have done enough shows to last me a lifetime."

Leslie Rejeanné

Roger Chaffin's "Impersonators Show Talent" piece in the September 17, 1976, issue of GayLife featured the following minibiography of Leslie Rejeanné. (Leslie's surname was spelled a variety of ways in programs, news articles, and publicity of the day—Reggina, Reginet, Regine, Regina. Sometimes her printed name carried an accent, and sometimes not. It was pronounced "ray-jen-NAY.")

"Born in 1954 and raised in Chicago, Mahogany [aka Rejeanné] came from a very large family of nine boys and one girl. Leslie has always dreamed about being an entertainer from the time he saw Diana Ross and the Supremes on television ... . At that time the girls were on the Hollywood Palace, and Leslie turned to his mother after the show and said, 'Mommy, I want to be just like them.' His mother chuckled, not dreaming that later she would see her son onstage performing as Diana Ross.

"At the age of 17, Leslie started working the bars with Bertha Butts, later doing a spot for Roby Landers. Next came a spot at Felicia's. Leslie was scared to death, but Felicia asked him to come back on a Saturday night and play the big crowds. He went over big, but the following week he did not return. At the time he was just learning to sew and he wanted something nice to wear. That something nice didn't turn out so nice, so he didn't go back. Feeling bad and embarrassed, he stayed away for a while.

"He finally landed another spot at Roby's House of Landers, and it happened that Peaches (a performer at the Baton) and Bertha were in the audience. They saw Leslie after the show and told him how much Felicia was interested in him and that he should go back and talk to Felicia again. The outcome of the ensuing conversation was that he started working several days later, and three years later is still making the audiences stand up and shout for more.

"Leslie thinks that a lot of people have the wrong ideas about what female impersonators are really like. 'Lots of people think that we are snotty, deceitful and nasty, most of all stuck up on ourselves and what we have. But we're not. I'm always just me. I really don't think you can change a person inside. If you are going to be nice, be nice no matter what you have or what you are.'

"From 'Love Hangover' to 'Ain't No Mountain High Enough,' Leslie controls your emotions, your inner thoughts. She makes you focus your attention on her and on the song she uses to get her message across. Ross may be boss, but Mahogany is solid entertainment."

Eventually, Rejeanné went from being a dynamic entertainer to taking over as emcee of the show after Felicia retired. In his Chicago Tribune piece of April 7, 1989, titled "Gender Benders: The Showgirls Aren't Real, But the Glamour Is," reporter David McCracken wrote: "Few emcees male or female or in-between can work a crowd as well as the superlative Leslie [Rejeanné], originally from the Robert Taylor Homes on the South Side. Flint says: 'A lot of her emceeing she got from me, watching me carrying on with people. But she's put her intelligence and her wit to work, and she's probably one of the most charming when it comes to talking with people. She can make you feel good or she can snap back—if someone wises off, she's got the lip to come back at 'em. Any good emcee enjoys that happening, because it gives you something to react to.'

"Leslie was doing some serious, good-natured reacting during her intro to the 12:30 show, playfully chiding one couple too interested in each other—'Y'all cut that out, this is a family show'—and taking on one of the more outspoken women in the back, who had apparently been very much reminded of her own femininity. Unfazed, Leslie turned her rather vulgar comment into one of the funnier bits of bitchery that night. But in general, the aura of tolerance and good feeling at the Baton is practically palpable. And when Leslie sings, or appears to sing, 'I Love You Just Because You're You,' and the audience members line up for a hug or a kiss on the cheek, the Baton attains a kind of weird grandeur that is singularly American."

There were many great entertainers in those days. One-time Flint partner and bartender Warren Williamson recalled some of the talent. "Leslie Rejeanné was magnificent," he said. "She was Diana Ross, she out–Diana Ross'ed Diana Ross. She did all her numbers. She looked and did it better, with a presence onstage that was just superb. They used to stand in line to tip her $20 bills."

"When I was at the Baton, I was always so impressed with Leslie Rejeanné," added actress and singer Alexandra Billings/Shanté. "At the time, she was really sort of the director and stage manager of the show. She put the show together. Did the lineup and made sure the shows had a beginning, a middle and an end.

"My wife, Chrisanne, always used to come and see me at the Baton. She was always so impressed with Leslie. Leslie had a gentle and kind, an open persona that was very rare in drag in those days. Then it was more about aggression and attacking the audience. That wasn't Leslie.

"Chrisanne used to love when Leslie would do Bette Midler's 'Superstar.' When she did it, she would come in at the back of the bar, with a cigarette, in a pin light—it was wonderful. So, every time Chrisanne would come in, she would send a note down requesting that Leslie do that number. Now, mind you, this was usually the last of three shows at the very end of the night when there could be a very small audience, and no matter how tired she was or what was going on in her personal life, Leslie would do that for Chrisanne because that's the sort of person she was.

"Another time, there was a birthday. Now, understand that, over 20 years ago, coming out as gay was a big deal, but coming out as trans was huge. If being gay was considered second-class, we were considered third-class, so many of the girls had families who disowned them. So, one of the girls working there at the time was Chanel Dupree, and I remember it was her birthday and Leslie gathered us all together and said, 'This is what we're going to do. You [pointing at one of us] are going to do streamers, you are going to do signs, you are going to get the cake ready,' and on and on.

"So, when her birthday came around and Chanel was onstage for 4½ minutes doing her number, each of us was downstairs frantically doing our one thing, and when she came down I will never forget the look on Chanel's face. She was just so surprised. Not just that—she was shocked that anyone would go to these lengths for her. And we as her family, under the guidance of Leslie, had taken the time and energy to plan and execute it."

Kelly Lauren added: "We were very close, and she was an amazing person. We would go to one another's dressing room and talk and have an ear to listen or a shoulder to cry on. I was always afraid I would be fired and have to go back to Houston. She told me, 'Miss Kelly, if you are good enough to work at the Baton, you are good enough to work anywhere. If there is one thing Jim knows, it's how to spot talent.' When Leslie and I would get together, we would also do pounds and pounds of cocaine. After work a lot of times we'd also go back to her place and smoke pot until the sun came up. I think the drugs eventually began to affect her performances somewhat, or at least her reliability."

"I met Leslie the first year I was in Continental. She was my best friend when I was in Chicago," said Dana Douglas. "She was a child of the projects, street-smart, and had no fear. Leslie looked nothing like Diana Ross, but I did her hair and makeup, and she had this amazing skill or confidence to somehow convince people she was Diana Ross. Her personal life was a mess. She was so ghetto offstage and never managed to shake the projects. She dated lots of guys and was never faithful and partied way too hard. That was her eventual downfall, was all that partying."

Flint agreed. "I only fired one performer, and that was because of drugs. It was Leslie. It was horrible. I loved her and she had a tragic story, but the drugs just got so bad that I had to let her go," he said.

"My favorite Leslie memory, or at least the one that comes to mind, was sitting in the back seat of a car talking with her," explained Lennie Malina. "I was talking and saying, 'You're on the top of your game and just enjoy it, savor it.' She had a tendency to always go back or think in the future and I just wanted to tell her to enjoy this, that she was really it, at the peak. That's where we all were back then, though. We were all avoiding where we were and not paying attention to the good things that were happening. We were all going so fast and never really stopped and looked around and thought, 'Oh, this is really great.'"

"Leslie was run down by a car on the South Side," said Marge Summit. "I never knew if it was an accident or not."

"She seemed like she was in the process of getting her life back together. She was doing her laundry, and she was hit by a car and flew into the path of another car. I heard she died instantly," said Kelly Lauren.

Flint grew wistful when recalling Rejeanné. "Leslie and I are both from the same kind of families," he said. "Very large families with the mother as the dominant worker and kept us going. Brothers in jail. We grew up in public housing. We related to each other quite a bit. She was a true friend. She always had a gift of gab to her and did the best Diana Ross. She gave 110 percent every time, and that was whether she came in and things were horrible, when she got onstage she was incredible. There was no one like her and there never will be."

Chilli Pepper

Chilli Pepper stories are plentiful, and her persona is legendary. No one who knows or who has met her is indifferent.

There are tales of how Chilli hooked up Oprah Winfrey with her fashion consultant and how they became pals back when Winfrey "used to have a life." Chilli's biography for the Chicago Gay and Lesbian Hall of Fame reads: "Chilli was one of the first local media personalities to take up the issue of AIDS awareness, helping to bring HIV/AIDS into the homes of Middle America at a time when the president of the United States [Reagan] was not publicly acknowledging the epidemic. Mentions in the Chicago Sun-Times (Irv Kupcinet's 'Kup's column'), the Chicago Tribune (the 'Tower Ticker' and 'Inc.' columns), Chicago's neighborhood Skyline newspaper, and People magazine, plus television appearances on Phil Donahue's, Oprah Winfrey's, and Jerry Springer's shows as well as Chicago's WGN-TV (Channel 9)—all at a time before Rock Hudson's death and its revelations rocked the non-LGBT world—brought Chilli into the forefront of the fight to confront AIDS.

"When Donna Karan wanted to make a statement at the opening of Barneys New York's

Chicago store, she called on Chilli to model as a mannequin in the main display window at the store's launch party, which also benefited the Design Industries Foundation Fighting AIDS (DIFFA). In 1979, when Michael Butler premiered the movie Hair in Chicago, Chilli was the 'Premiere Entertainment' and introduced drag to an audience who may have thought 'drag' applied only to car racing or having a bad day."

In "Pumpgirls and Cheeseburgers," a Mimi O'Shea (pen name of Jeff McCourt) piece in GayLife on June 27, 1985, the writer took Chilli to her favorite place, the Pump Room. She is well-known there. A 5-by-5-inch color photo was hung in the bar, depicting Chilli, Nan Mason, and Pudgy, the article said. Amid familiar greetings, Chilli was escorted to Booth No. 2 (Booth No. 1 being always reserved for Irv Kupcinet) and ordered a cheeseburger. In the piece, Chilli was reported as saying, "Thanks to Felicia [Baton owner Jim Flint], I am allowed to create my own personality onstage. All of us at the Baton do this. Felicia has always been wonderful at allowing each of us that creative freedom—and it works."

The article said the performer's name, Chilli Pepper, comes from an experience Chilli had on a beach in South America with a friend. "I was sunning and became very, very red. My companion told me I looked as red as a chili pepper. I blushed and took the name," Chilli said. She said she created a character somewhat similar to Joan Collins' Alexis Carrington on TV's Dynasty: "It took me a long time to create this cartoon. It's a cartoon that works for me. ... I like clear vocals in my numbers. I like strong individual performances: Mary Wells, Phoebe Snow, Linda Clifford are big favorites of mine. Gradually I developed this thing for Millie Jackson. Show tunes are not my forte. Production numbers [with the entire cast] still frighten me. When I first arrived at the Baton, Felicia had an established show with fabulous group numbers. I became less afraid with lots of practice, but I still love to go it alone."

O'Shea's piece continued: "Chilli flashes her rings designed by Steve Feinstein. She then orders a piece of apple pie to go. It arrives wrapped in the shape of a ring, along with a courtesy box of chocolates from the management." When asked to give advice to new performers, Chilli replied: "Get a job in a factory. Get out of town. Go home, the market here is saturated."

Chilli calls Oprah Winfrey a friend and, even more impressive, Winfrey calls her a friend as well. Chilli has been on the TV legend's show an astounding seven times. She's been in People and in Playboy. She's been on Joan Rivers', Phil Donahue's and numerous other talk shows. She's known in the finest restaurants. The best way to describe bridging the gap between female impersonator and mainstream matron seems to be a good amount of talent and a great amount of chutzpah.

"When I first went and saw Chilli, it was at the Blue Dahlia," said Flint. "I brought her here, and Jan Howard did not like her, so I told Chilli I didn't think it would work out. Then I went to the Blue Dahlia a few more times and watched her and went to Jan and said, 'Jan, I don't care if you like her or not, she's coming to work here.'"

Chilli initially came to Chicago to become Miss Gay Chicago. After winning the title (in 1974), she stuck around. She was only at the Blue Dahlia a short while before coming to the Baton. She still enjoys it.

"The crowd is the best part of this job," she said. "A woman came in a few months ago and said, 'Do you remember me?' and I said I didn't, but she said she had come in with her mother about a month ago. Of course, my next question was, 'How is she doing?' She said her mother had passed away a couple weeks ago. The woman added, 'But I had to come back and say thank you, because you posed for pictures with her and that made her so happy.' Those things are the biggest compliments. See, so sometimes they give me money and sometimes they leave me with something else. Those are the best tips."

As Chilli spoke, it became clearer that what she does is indeed pantomime, but far more interpretive, like a hybrid of improv and performance art. "I make faces and interact to get a reaction," she said. "If I try to be glamorous, or flirt or be mean, I am looking for a reaction. Not everyone understands this, not everyone has the same sense of humor. I like to be an artist. The people who understand me enjoy it because they see what I am doing. It would be nice if we just have to look good, but there is more to it. There is art. And it is an art where we have to jump up and down in high heels. It is what it is."

Chicago performer Honey West said: "One of the most amazing things I saw was the night Chilli Pepper made me really understand and appreciate the art of lip-sync. She was doing the Bonnie Raitt song 'Something to Talk About,' and what was so cool is that when you have a set song with set vocals and set places where the vocalist breathes and such, you don't really think of being able to change it. But as I sat there that evening, I watched Chilli interpret that song three or four different ways depending on who she was singing to.

"She'd perform it one way to sort of chastise some people who were talking in one part of the bar, and then she saw a cute guy elsewhere and she sang it like, 'Hey, let's give them something to talk about,' in this flirtatious way. But she did all this with a static recording. It was amazing. She stuck to the song and yet was not limited by it, and I found that completely fascinating in a theatrical way.

"I mean, as a cabaret singer I perform songs and change the way I word things or the volume, and I can break in between and talk and draw people in in different ways. Chilli was having that level of interaction but with this prerecorded material. I've heard it a hundred times in my career, people say, 'You're really talented because you really sing,' and I said, 'No, that's a real talent, there's a real art to lip-sync. You just don't realize it. Try it, go home and pick a song you know like the back of your hand, and perform it to the record in a mirror. It's not so easy.'"

Bonnie Raitt is indeed one of Chilli's favorites. "I am fond of Millie Jackson, she is probably my very favorite. Interesting stuff, things that tell a story. I love Linda Clifford, and Loleatta Holloway," Chilli said, adding: "The biggest compliment I ever received was from Millie Jackson. She had me open a concert for her once, and afterwards she said, 'When I was watching you, I forgot that it was my voice.'"

Chilli, also the very first Miss Continental (in 1980), admits that the crowd has changed in the years she has been at the Baton. The formerly gay show lounge became more and more of a tourist destination and then finally a place for bachelorette parties as well. "The crowds have changed with the [AIDS] plague. How could it not have changed? It was so sad. It was a party, and everyone just wanted to have a good time. Then everyone was dying, but they were dying out of love. Now we have a different sort. They come and hopefully enjoy and maybe learn a little something about themselves, how to walk in heels, how to put on makeup. And maybe if they have children that are gay, they will learn to be a little more tolerant."

Former Baton bartender Warren Williamson said Chilli was always the big attraction. "I remember watching Chilli, and she would not even be able to hold her tips," he said. "There were \$20 and \$50 bills one after another, and every once in a while a guy would go to give her a single, and she would throw the dollar bill back at him. She'd have these wads of bills and go and drop it in a box behind the curtain and come back out to collect more. She was something else, and still is. She's still kicking those legs up. Those late-night shows had well-known professionals [in the audience]—architects, doctors, entertainers, the real upper crust of society."

Shawn Luis remembered: "We all wanted to be entertainers, but Chilli wanted to be a star. When she would start going on like that, Peaches and I would just look at each other and roll our eyes."

Dina Jacobs volunteered her take: "I never quite understood Chilli. There was always a sort of shield or cover around her, like she was never quite comfortable with us.

"I do remember one time, though. We were with Lady Shawn [who would eventually become Miss Gay America 1981] at the Fontainebleau Hotel in Miami Beach, and we were watching Miss Gay Florida. There were two camps that night—there was Bobbi Lake and her friends, and Cuban Michelle and her friends. The two groups were getting out of control with their cheering.

"Well, then from behind us come tomatoes thrown at the stage, and the people who really threw them ran, and when everyone turned in shock and anger, there were the three of us. We took off running, and one thing I'll say is that Chilli was the fastest   she was out the door with her coat and purse and across the street before Lady Shawn and I had even gotten out of the building."

"I love Chilli Pepper," Kelly Lauren laughed. "She invented the word 'regifting' and brought schmoozing and networking to an entirely new level. To put it simply, Chilli is a genius at knowing how to work it.

"My favorite Chilli memory was, there used to be this boy queen named Lisa Eaton who supposedly was a great Judy Garland impersonator back in the day, but when we knew her she was a drunk. Anyway, Chilli liked bringing her downstairs and playing pranks on her. She would get Lisa singing 'Rose's Turn' from Gypsy, and when Lisa would open her mouth to hit that note of 'Here she is, BOYS,' Chilli would stick a feather from a boa in her mouth so Lisa would sputter. She played that prank a couple of times."

"Chilli is an individual all on her own," Flint said. "She has a long reputation. She is accepted out in public at the best restaurants. She promotes herself well. She's not bashful—she's out front doing it."

"Chilli was always a loner, a loner and an icon who doesn't care what people think but at the same time does," said former Baton manager Lennie Malina. "She'd come there to work, and that was about it. It was not to socialize."

"Chilli is truly brilliant and one of the great comedians and stage performers in the genre," said Alexandra Billings. "And Chilli also changed the course of my life. One night, we were doing the show at the Baton, and there was a theatrical producer in the audience. He gave Chilli a script and said, 'Here you go—this show is really big in New York, and we want you to star in the Chicago premiere when we open it here.' So by this time I had my own dressing room, which was right across from Chilli's, and I saw her in there with a script and I said, 'What are you reading?' And she replied that it was a new script a producer had given her, which seemed very good.

"So I didn't think anything more of it, and then three or four days later the script was suddenly on my dressing room table, and I said, 'Chilli, someone put your script in my dressing room.' She told me she did. I said, 'But they gave it to you, they want you.' She replied, 'They want me, but they need you.' She did one of her great gestures with the nails and the rings and said, 'You need to do it, you need to move on,' and that script was for Vampire Lesbians of Sodom.

"I auditioned for the part and got it, and it ran at the Royal George for three years and really resurrected my acting career. Everything snowballed from there—from that extremely generous gesture from Chilli. So, in many ways, she changed the course of my life."

Speaking of giving the script to Alexandra Billings (then Shanté), Chilli said: "I thought that she should take that journey. She was fantastic. She was a great actress. I told them to see her. They wanted me, but I said, 'No, you have to see her.' I insisted. And they did, and that is that."

"Chilli is a trip," laughed Dana Douglas. "Her middle name is 'take me, give me, buy me.' I learned from Chilli to always ask for something if you want it. If you don't ask, you won't know—so she'll be somewhere and say, 'I like this, can I have it?' 'I like that, will you buy it for me?'

"Oh, and she is deathly afraid of planes and elevators. She'll use an elevator but needs an elevator buddy, and she will cling to you the entire time she is riding in it. When I would go with her she would dig in and, let me tell you, you felt it. When I knew her, her fingernails were 14-karat gold. Literally, they were made of gold, and those golden claws held on tight. In fact, the reason I first met Jimmy was because Chilli will always get people to drive her places rather than fly, and when Jim saw me in Miss Florida in 1981 it was because he'd driven Chilli down there.

"Chilli performing in her heyday could go out onstage and just say 'bring me' and make a gesture with those fingers and rings, and they would come with hundreds of dollars and diamonds and bracelets. Her birthday parties were legendary and always at some estate. There would be a throne set up, and she would literally be showered with gifts, mostly jewelry. So, different mansion, different estate, same throne. The one who gave Chilli the best gift would then be her companion for the party, so it would become these great competitions between a lot of very powerful and influential people.

"I think, the year I remember most, I bet she was given seventy or eighty thousand dollars' worth of jewelry. Her lover for a long time was the jeweler Steven Feinstein [who died several years ago], and he gave her that huge ring she wears with the diamond C with Pepper running down it in emeralds and rubies. When I left town, I gave her a $3,000 Oriental rug for her place.

"She is living her fantasy, and she has to have millions. She's collected jewelry always, and now it's gems—but before, it was gold. Before Mr. T gained notoriety and became bouncer of the year, which brought him into the public eye, he was here in Chicago. We knew him and he didn't wear the gold then, but Chilli did. I think he may well have gotten that gold-chains thing from Miss Chilli Pepper."

"Chilli's birthday parties are a trip," added Cezanne. "I remember the one where a bus actually came and brought us to an estate. It was a complete five-star meal and very elegant, and, of course, the gifts. I could not believe what I was seeing."

Flint laughed when he told one story about a Chilli birthday. "I went to a birthday party for one of my entertainers back in the 1970s," he said. "I was playing a joke and rang the doorbell and said, 'Is Mr. Feinstein in, please?' They said, 'He's here.' And I said, 'Tell him the Chicago police are here. We've had some complaints, we're on our way up in the elevators.' And they said, 'Sir, we'll get him.' And I said, 'We'll talk with him when we get there.' By the time I got to the door, I heard toilets flushing and this and that, and everybody was throwing their marijuana and everything else down the toilet, and when I walked in I said, 'Chicago police.' They never invited me to another birthday party."

"Jewelry is a passion of mine," admitted Chilli. "It always has been. It's not an investment, it's always a gift. To make something like this," she said, pointing to a huge diamond-pearl-and-gold ring (one of the many she was wearing), "that will move like this," she said, moving the head and the tail of the turtle ring, "I think jewelry is eternal, or at least more eternal than we are. If we go tomorrow, this will remain for another hundred, 200, 300 years or more. Look at King Tut's jewelry. That's still around. This is something that will stay. I like things to be long-lasting and consistent like this, I like friendships to be like that. And love to be like that."

Former Baton regular Tasha Long recalled first coming to Chicago to work at the Baton: "Chilli's dressing room was right across from mine. I didn't know anybody in the city, and Chilli said, 'What are you doing for Christmas?' I said, 'I don't know.' She said, 'I do. You're coming with me.' And she took me with her to a friend of hers for dinner. It was so nice. She had a present for me, and they had a present for me, and really made me feel good and so not alone at the holidays. I was so grateful for that."

"My cartoon," as Chilli called her persona, "can be a little rough around the edges. Not everyone can be Julie Andrews, but deep down I am a good and a kind person. People don't want everything nice. I have fun. Not everyone understands, not everyone sees beyond the cartoon. "How much of Chilli is me and how much is creation depends on who is watching and what they bring out in me. If you are interested in knowing me, you get me. If you only want the cartoon you see onstage, that is what you get. Any description of Chilli must come from the audience, from you. Chilli is a response. Chilli is a mirror. This is my art, this is what I use to perform."

She continued: "I'm not naked. That's not what I'm selling. This," gesturing to her face, "this is what I use. I make an expression and I see how they react. When I see people respond, then I know where to go. That's how you perform. The key is seeing yourself through their eyes. If you judge me because you think I care about this or that, or judge me because of who I hang out with, I don't care. It's taken me years to get acceptance. That is going to be handed down to other people. That is another and maybe a larger way of being kind."

Maya Douglas

"I had won Miss Continental in 1985 and came to the Baton in 1987 through Shanté," said Maya Douglas. "Dana Douglas and, I believe, someone else had just left. Shanté was pushing for me to work there, and finally Jim let me give it a try in October 1987. It was the first time I'd ever lived away from home, and I really missed my friends and family. It was such a tremendous learning experience, but let me tell you, you had to get on your game quick or you didn't last. When I started, it was Chilli Pepper, Shanté, Leslie Rejeanné, Sheri Payne, Kelly Lauren, Alana Kela, Ginger Grant. And Ray West was the male lead.

"I have great memories of all those years. One was a production number. We wore halter tops. It was Leslie, Chilli, Shanté, Kelly and myself. We were posed up the stairs, and I hit the step and my heel broke off, it just broke right off, so there I was with one shoe. I just started laughing, and Leslie turned to see what was going on and when she saw, she took her shoe off. Then everyone took a shoe off, and eventually we did the number with all of this kind of hobbling, because we were all only wearing one shoe. The audience loved it."

Her favorite celebrity memory was of the night Madonna was in the house. "Mimi Marks was doing her in the show at the time," Douglas said. "They were in town filming A League of Their Own, and they took basically the whole back half of the bar, and they came in after the show started. Mimi had gone on, and the crowd had realized Madonna was there. I was on next, I think. I remember I was doing Grace Jones' 'Love on Top of Love,' and the curtains parted, and I was standing there, and everyone was turned around looking at Madonna. I couldn't be mad, because I would've done the same thing. After the show, she came downstairs to the dressing rooms, and we were all standing around like schoolgirls, and then she said, 'You girls are fierce,' and once she said that, it was like she was one of us.

"So many celebrities. I remember when Robert Wagner and Stephanie Powers came in and got a photo—Robert Wagner got a little handsy. His hand was on my butt."

Cabaret performer Beckie Menzie recalled Douglas. "One of the things I used to do was sort of put my men through a test," Menzie said. "I had my husband (then boyfriend) come and hear me sing at Gentry, and then if he was OK with that and things started to become more serious, I took him to the Baton. It was a litmus test, because I work with a lot of different sorts, mostly gay but some transgender, so he needed to be accepting. I could never be serious with someone who wasn't comfortable. So, that's where I brought my second husband. Well, Jim put us right front and center that night, and Maya Douglas was performing, and let me tell you, she worked Earl for, I bet, a hundred dollars in tips that night."

When Douglas left the Baton eight years later in 1995, she was Miss Gay USA. "They [Miss Gay USA and Miss Continental] were sort of competing competitions," explained Douglas. "Anyway, one night after that, Jim and I had a huge blowout. It was the anniversary weekend of the Baton. My boyfriend at the time and his family were going to be there, and my sister was in town, and we were sold out, and I asked Bobby the manager if she could sit with them or, if not, could she sit at the bar. He said, 'We'll see.' Well, Jim overheard and said, 'Absolutely not.' And I turned around and said, 'That figures.' I was about to take a month leave of absence for Miss Gay USA touring, and he said, 'When your leave is over, don't bother coming back.'

"He chased me downstairs, and we had a huge blowout in my dressing room. I said, 'What have I ever done? When have I asked for anything? I am always on time, I work hard.' I had been offered a job in Dallas the week before, so right then I decided to take it. I went back up crying and called from the pay phone in the lobby about the job. Then I talked to my boyfriend, who told me to just do the show. So I went back down and after all this, Chilli had heard and came in my dressing room and said, 'Are you OK?' I said I was fine and that I had another job.

"Then Jim came down a few minutes later and apologized and said he was sorry, he was under a lot of pressure with the anniversary and all. I said, 'No problem,' but I turned back to the mirror and finished doing my makeup. That was my last night there until I came back in 2007. I found out after I left that some other girls wanted my dressing room, and Mimi told me Jim said, 'She'll be back,' and left it empty for six or seven months before he'd let anyone move in there."

Douglas spoke of her eventual return. "I was making good money in Dallas, and then the management changed and they started cutting my nights. By then, Jim and I had completely made up," she said. "I'd been back for all the Miss Continentals and performed a few weekends at the Baton, and was there for his 60th birthday. Anyway, when all these changes were happening at the club in Dallas, I was talking to the head judge Skip [Mackall] at Miss Continental, and he said, 'Call Jimmy, I'm sure he'd take you back.' So I did. He said, 'How soon can you take care of things down there?' And it so happened that I came back for the anniversary in 2007, so it was almost 12 years to the day that I left.

"It was nice. He needed some performers around that time, too. Kelly Lauren and Chanel and Shanté had left, and he needed a headliner and, because of the titles, I was a name. In those 12 years I'd been gone, I had been Entertainer of the Year [1997], Miss Universal Show Queen [1999], and Miss Continental Elite [2006]. The Continental Elite title really sort of brought my career full circle."

Douglas said it was a big change between the time she left the Baton in 1995 and when she returned in 2007. "Oh, definitely a drastic change in the audience and the neighborhood," she said. "It always used to be packed with a gay audience, and it was a smoke-filled room. Lots of couples. Now it's smoke-free, bachelorette parties and things, but Jim has evolved with the times and kept it successful that way.

"As to the cast, it hadn't changed too much. When I left, it was Mimi, Chilli, Monica, Ginger, Sheri. And Victoria had just started. So when I came back, it was pretty much the same girls. The only new one was Sasha.

"Jim will also check how someone is going to work out from guest spots and he'll ask us what we think. When someone new joins, it's like a new family member. He considers this family and he wants it to be comfortable."

"Maya is probably the only one I know at her age that still has the face she had when she was first here," said Flint. "That face is magnificent, you can do anything with it. She stays beautiful, beautiful, beautiful. Maya went on to Dallas and won every crown she could in every other pageant and then came back and won Continental Elite. She started with Continental and when she won it she was the weakest Continental I ever had, but she ended up getting better and better as a performer and winning Continental Elite. When she won she said, 'This is my finish.'

"Maya is the most consistent person. She's always got a new wardrobe. She makes everything she wears. She's just different and always glamorous. A lot of different hair changes, she's not afraid to change and do new things. That can be rare for longtime performers."

Ginger Grant added: "Maya Douglas and I met in 1984 when I first entered Miss Continental. I knew just a few people, and Maya didn't know anyone, and we both sat in the back during registration and we bonded. She takes care of herself and sews. That girl has money in her bank account."

"All the production wardrobe I take care of, and a lot of the girls have their own people who make their individual stuff, but Maya makes all our production outfits," said Flint. "She does a great job because she knows what the girls like and the way to fit them. She can go home and make them and come in and maybe spend a half-hour redoing something, and then it's all done and that's how good she is with it. So it's great to have Maya around and it gives her a lot of extra money, too."

"I have made everything in the productions for the past three years," Douglas said. "I made the curtains on the stage, I even made Jimmy's shirt he wore on the Pride Parade float [in 2011]. I always loved to sew. My mother was a seamstress and it was something I needed to do when I started going to bars. That's when I started making clothes. I've done a lot of evening gowns, things for the Kit Kat Lounge [3700 North Halsted Street].

"I am sort of lazy about sewing. I live in a duplex, and the entire downstairs is my sewing room. The thing is, after something like New Year's or the anniversary at the Baton where I have to do 20 costumes, I get tired of it.

"I've had a couple signature gowns. There's the red chain gown, which was basically two pieces of red fabric, one up the front and one down the back and held together on the sides by chains. Then I also did a copy of the J. Lo gown with the plunging neckline that went to her waist. I did that in a nice tropical green. I think those were my favorites.

"In the 1980s when I was here I didn't do as much. I've been doing a lot more since I came back, and my sewing capabilities have improved so much."

Miss Continental head judge Skip Mackall explained how it was Maya Douglas who made him understand female impersonation.

"Maya Douglas showed me the humanity of this. Coming into all this, it can just seem so out there, and I really didn't understand," he said. "Then one time Maya said to me, 'You know, I didn't change. I'm the same self I was as a child, only when a little boy was looking in the mirror, he was seeing a little girl. This didn't change who I was, or my values, or even what foods I like to eat. All it did was make the outsides match the insides. It all felt completely natural. I was becoming who I was, not becoming someone else.'" Mackall added that it was sort of his "aha" moment about the entire phenomenon.

Douglas sighed when she summed up the Baton experience. "I would have to say that if it wasn't for Jimmy I wouldn't have a career," she said. "I was from upstate New York. It was 1985 and he took a chance on me. I won Miss Continental and started working at the Baton and left, but now I'm back and he's become like a second father to me.

"He didn't have to stick with me, or any of us. People have been fighting for years to come work at the Baton. Trust me, there is a long, long line. Everybody wanted and still wants to be at the Baton, but he stuck with us. People always ask me how to audition for a job here and I say, 'Well, you really don't, Jimmy just sort of adopts you.'"

Ginger Grant

Ginger Grant is Jim Flint's right-hand person, and no one is more cognizant of that fact than Flint. "Anything that I can't do, Ginger can do," Flint said. "Ginger is good at fashion, Ginger is good at decorating, Ginger is good at this and that. At emceeing she is better than I ever was. She knows enough Spanish now that she can go with the Spanish.

"Being a full-blooded Greek, when the Greeks come in she can start speaking Greek, and when she does they go crazy. Even when the Japanese come in or the Koreans or Filipinos—she always has a few words or a saying someone can connect with."

Warren Williamson remembers when Grant first started coming into the Baton in the mid-1970s. "I was carding her because she didn't even look 18," he said. "She used to hang around at the end of the bar and watch, just fascinated. I said, 'Someday you might be up there,' but Ginger would always say, 'Oh, no, I couldn't, not me.' And now she's the emcee."

"I started coming here in either 1974 or 1975 on New Year's Eve. I was amazed. It was a whole new world," said Grant. "Nobody cared how you were or your size or color. I was so entertained, and it wasn't just because they were men. It had nothing to do with that. It just looked like so much fun. I liked the entertainment and the theater of it. I'd been class clown and entertained in my own way my whole life. At the time, I worked at the Millionaires Club, which is the same owner who has Carson's Ribs.

"When I used to come in the Baton, there was an entertainer named China Nguyen from Hawaii, and with her came a new choreographer from Hawaii named Orlando. We were sitting around the bar one night, and he said, 'Oh, you are so pretty, pretty face. You should try it,' and that was it. I didn't need more coaxing at that point. They put makeup on me and it was a hobby for years. That was my first time dressing up. I did a Dionne Warwick song. As to the name, we were sitting around and I always liked Ginger Grant from Gilligan's Island. She was so glamorous.

"When I first started, I did guest spots every Sunday until it finally became something. As I said, I was at Millionaires Club, and I opened all the Carson's Ribs places at the time. I got tired of working 80 or 90 hours a week. I put in for a vacation around Mother's Day, and the day before I was to go on vacation my boss said, 'You can't go. If you go, you're fired.' I said, 'I'm sorry, I'm gone.' Then when I came back he said, 'No, I was only kidding,' but I had made up my mind. I said, 'No, it's time.'"

Dana Douglas recalled Grant with a smile. "She was a comedy act and she became a regular my last year there," Douglas said. "She was also an amazing chef and did all the cooking for Carson's Ribs—in those old Carson's TV commercials, the hands you see brushing on the sauce are actually Ginger's hands. She was always a real sweetheart."

"I worked for a show bar out in Wheeling for about nine months," said Grant. "This was probably in 1985 or '86. It was a place called the Final Approach in the [Palwaukee Motor Inn], and it was dinner and a show. We were filling it up, too, but there were other problems. The people who ran it owned a lot of strip clubs out there also, and there was talk that they were having card games and this and that. I worked out there with seven other kids, and then on a Tuesday morning I got a phone call to go get my things, because the FBI was closing it down. At that time Jim was short and asked if I could work on Fridays and Saturdays for a couple of months. Then Dana Douglas quit and I went full-time.

"I really started on North Halsted Street. I used to tend bar at Christopher Street [3458 North Halsted] with Tommy O'Connell and did a show later. We had so much fun and made a fortune. When I worked there, I was in drag, and that was when it was one room with a bar and a little stage on top. I worked there Monday nights. They wanted to get all the industry people in. I finally left when they wanted to become a 4 o'clock bar and I didn't want to tend bar until that late. It was fun for about a year. I also did shows here and there at Club La' Ray [3150 North Halsted] and, before that, I worked at Trianon [3150 North Halsted] and Vortex [3631 North Halsted].

"I used to have a problem with drugs. I fell in love with somebody, and I never did anything until I met this person. I'm not blaming him, I did it, but for three years I rocked and rolled and had a good time. Jim had a lot of reasons to fire me. I showed up to work, but I was not doing my job properly. Before that, we were good friends, but we really grew closer after that when I got sober. I've been clean and sober over 20 years now. That's when we started traveling together and watching out for each other.

"I started working as emcee in the early 1990s because Jim let the previous emcee go (Leslie Rejeanné). It was the first time I believe he ever fired a performer. So then he came to me and it was a Friday night, and he said, 'You get up there and you be funny.' One on one, it's easy to make people laugh, but onstage was different. Entertaining was no problem, because you didn't talk, but once I hit the stage as an emcee and I saw all these people sitting there saying, 'Hey, impress me,' it was tough.

"The first month or so, it was probably a two-second monologue, fast, fast, fast and then the next girl. That's what I told them all at the time, was, 'Be ready.' Now I enjoy it. Even if I am in a bad mood, it's like therapy. I had a problem with a stutter years ago and I think this helps. At one time I was very fearful of it, but I think facing it and overcoming it makes you love it more. Also, because of my size, my weight—society sometimes looks at size and likes to stereotype right away."

Grant said that, as emcee, she lines the show up. "We all work together down there, but I am show director," she said. "I decide what we're going to do productionwise and make sure the show starts and finishes on time. The girls pick their own numbers, but the productions I pick out. I determine the order of the performers as well.

"When I emcee now, I say, 'This is like fairyland here. We don't care about the color of your skin or your race or gender or anything. If you have a problem with that, when you come in, you leave it all outside—just come inside and have a good time. It's magical in here.' There sometimes are people who come who aren't sure what we're doing, so I feel they should be educated the proper way. So, to do that, you just talk to people.

"I know emcees across the country who like to swear, and this and that, and comment about vaginal areas and all that. People don't want that. They are here to be entertained. There was a guy who came in the other night who said, 'Oh, you drag queens are fabulous.' I said, 'We're not drag queens.' I consider myself a female impersonator or an actor. I think we're beyond that, really. I think anyone who puts time and effort into trying to be good and perform or it's a lifestyle, we're not drag queens, we're impersonators."

Once Grant landed at the Baton, she said she "found a home. This is also one of the only clubs in the country where we can get a paycheck and it's not going to bounce. We're here to work, and you learn that real quick. In January, when we have four people in the audience on a Wednesday night, we still get a paycheck on Saturday. Jimmy takes the loss; we don't.

"He's my best friend and an incredible boss 98 percent of the time, and then that other 2 percent Felicia comes out, and you want to slap the bitch. When he's Felicia he'll blow over anything. Even when he's right 95 percent of the time when he blows, it's how he blows that is the problem. I'm not a fighter, Jim likes people to fight. He loves to argue with people. I don't argue, I pout. That has caused some problems sometimes, but they always blew over.

"Jim and I think alike. I think part of the reason we're close is we're both businesspeople, and I don't let business and friendship cross the line. I'm here when you need me. You need me to mop a floor, I'll mop a floor. That's the way I was at Carson's. That's my work ethic. With these shows and contests, a lot of times we're [Flint and Grant] the last ones out the door at night and the first ones here the next morning, and we may be fat and old but we still do it. We're not afraid to work and we're both doers. What I don't know, I will learn.

"We work together and also go on trips together. Usually we go to Florida a couple times a year. We used to always go to Hawaii, but that nine-hour flight has become too much for me. When we go to Florida, we'll go down on a Friday in September, and Jim will come back on Wednesday, but I will stay another five or six days. That's my rest time. I rarely leave the hotel. We do it right after Miss Continental, so when we go down there we're still 'on,' but by the time I leave I am done. We travel in a pack. We watch each other. We have beautiful dinners. We have a nice time doing nothing."

Grant reflects on the impact Flint and the Baton have had on her. "Jimmy and this place changed my life," Grant said. "The Baton gives you an avenue, and then you do what you want to do with that. It's a platform. That's what Jim gives you, is the sort of outline. Jim isn't going to make you change your breasts or take hormones or do electrolysis or anything. All he does is give you the basics, the opportunity. As to promoting yourself as a product and what is 'Ginger Grant' or 'Mimi Marks' and 'Sheri Payne' or whoever—that's up to the person."

Sheri Payne

Sheri Payne has decided to pronounce her first name "Cherie," with a stress on the second syllable, since her 50th birthday. "An ex-lover used to call me Cherie instead of Sheri, and I kind of liked it," Payne said. When interviewed for this book, she had time for just a quick chat as she did her blocking—her "paint by numbers [makeup]. I've got a 1-to-10 process."

"I credit my coming here to my foster brother Donald Henderson. He brought me here," Payne said. "Actually, I'd been exposed to it before then, though. I grew up on the South Side, and one night we went to the Jacques [Cristion] ball at 63rd and Cottage Grove at the Grand Ballroom. There you could see female impersonation in the black community. That was the first time I can remember seeing drag, and then my mother used to also take me to the Jewel Box Revue at the Regal Theater when they would sometimes come to town from Kansas City.

"I didn't know what drag was at the time, I was too young. After my brother brought me here to see the show, I was in awe. We went home and started playing around, and he put red lipstick on me. I think that's when Sheri Payne was created. At first it was Cherry, but there was another entertainer on the scene at the time named Cherry who was kind of gross, so I decided to become Sheri.

"I was hired in 1980 and probably started coming down here in 1977. I saw the show, and that was it for me. I always felt like a girl but I never dealt with dabbling into whether I was a boy or girl. I was always just me.

"You can never have a [single] favorite memory being here. You meet so many people, I think it all blends together. I'll be down here and have a catty moment with somebody, and then joking, and then I'll be down here with Janet Jackson and it's all happening right here in downtown Chicago. It's fabulous. On the other hand, there's getting ready in four minutes for the next number and girls falling down the stairs or forgetting they're in the next number. It's crazy, always something crazy. You stick around long enough and you'll have a Baton dressing-room moment.

"One time I was standing here getting ready and I was talking to Monica Munro when her dressing room was right across the hall, and I had my big Whitney hair on, and Monica said, 'Sheri, honey,' and I said 'What, girl?' and she said, 'Girl, your hair is on fire.' And I looked in the mirror and screamed. I had just sprayed my wig and was leaning close, to do the makeup, and talking to her out the door and not paying attention. I must have put my wig against the hot mirror lights, and poof. The whole wig was buzz-cut black. I couldn't feel a thing because there's a cap and then a big wig and all."

Payne has a favorite Jim Flint memory. "She's such a stickler that the curtain has to be just right, behind me," Payne said. "When I come out I sometimes sort of throw the curtains back behind me, especially when I'm doing something dramatic like Whitney. Well, the curtain got bunched on one of the stairs, so the illusion of the curtain behind me was off. Well, he went to adjust it backstage, and there's a couple steps, and then the curtain lands, and then there's the stage. All of a sudden the crowd is going up. I'm thinking the audience is going up for one of my Whitney routines. Not so. What happened was, he fell down those stairs and rolled out onto the stage behind me while I was performing. Literally he rolled onstage like a barrel, and it took her a while to get up because she kept slipping and that only made it funnier. I thought they were going up for me. I turned around and saw him, and let me tell you, we were all peeing on ourselves, it was so funny.

"I have to say Whitney Houston is my favorite to do. Before her, it was Diana Ross. My favorite Whitney Houston number is 'I Have Nothing' from The Bodyguard, where she is sitting in the chair in the black suit looking magnificent with those pretty white teeth. She looks just like me. She looks like me because I'm older, you know.

"One thing I will say, Jim Flint has an eye for a queen. His choice is never off. Sometimes he'll bring them in for a couple guest shots and ask us our opinion. Mostly he wants to make sure everyone gets along, because this is family. With the talent, he sees something we don't see. Some have an eye for art or an eye for something else. He has an eye for a queen. He can sit and watch the national pageants and tell you who is going to win, the moment they walk out onstage."

Payne also talked about the crowds. "The most usual question they ask is definitely 'Where is it?' 'Are those yours?' 'How did you do it?' 'How do you make yourself up?' It's OK, though, because I was asking the same questions when I was coming here. People want to know. How I answer depends, sometimes I tell the truth and sometimes I just make stuff up, but they can tell when I'm making it up."

Gesturing toward her small and cluttered dressing room, Payne said: "This has been my home for a long time. That's something you don't forget, is getting your own dressing room at the Baton. When I first started working here, they had Sunday-night guest night in the late 1970s. I would come every week and I must have done that a couple of years. I was not going to give up. The girl who had this dressing room before me was Leslie Rejeanné, and she called me Eve Harrington, so now I call Victoria [LePaige] that, even though she has done triple what I have done in regards to the pageants and all that. Anyway, when I started, I was working at Walgreens at the time as a cashier. [Eventually] Jim asked if I wanted a job and brought me here and said, 'If you want a job, this can be your dressing room.'

"At the bottom of the stairs to the dressing rooms is a large general room with mirrors, and that is the guest dressing area. That's where I used to get ready. A guest is usually one number, and they're not part of the production, so all you need is a place to get dressed and put on the makeup. Regulars each have their own rooms.

"It's a fast-paced show and you have to perfect your craft. Mainly, though, you have to be an entertainer inside. Most of us were in dance. Mimi was a gymnast, Victoria was a dancer, everybody was in the performing arts. You can be beautiful and have great clothes and everything else, but if you don't have that innate entertainer thing about you, you're just not going to make it. I was always a dancer. After I first did the splits, I would watch TV, do my homework, and all day hold the split so I wouldn't lose it. My mother thought I was crazy."

Payne also spoke about her working relationship with Flint/Felicia. "I did not like when Felicia did the show. She was a tyrant," Payne said. "You talk about fast-paced. She changed between every number, thinking she was Loretta Young or something. Twirling on those roller skates and squealing like a little old pig." Payne let out a high-pitched "wooooooooo, ahhhhhh."

"When she did the show, we'd have five or six different production numbers," Payne said. "Chilli and Leslie always said to me, 'You may hate doing this at this pace, but it's going to make you a rounded entertainer.' I think the show even ran two hours then. It was a bigger cast, and then we had leading men as well."

Payne said: "My mom is religious, and from her aspect she just doesn't want us to burn in hell, but other than that, I am her child no matter what I do. She taught us to love and not to talk about anybody, because you are never better than anybody else. That's how we were brought up. It's strange, too, I didn't even know what black and white was until Martin Luther King got killed. Race was never discussed in our house. So then, when that happened and it came up in school, I finally thought, 'Is that what this is all about?' We always just thought people were people, and we thought right.

"We may be going at it down here, but when we hit that stage we hold hands. That says a lot. Everybody fights. My mom always told me the tongue is the most foul thing in our bodies. That the worst things will come out of our mouth without even thinking about it sometimes."

Payne paused from applying her "paint by numbers" and laughed, trying to sum up her relationship with Flint: "He gives me the hardest time, but I think that's because he loves me the hardest. That's what I always tell him."

Flint spoke kindly about Payne and her troubles.

"When Sheri Payne hits the stage, she probably gives 110 percent every time. There are times when I can get after her because she's late a lot and this and that. But when she hits the stage, she entertains everyone and is full of energy," said Flint. "For years I didn't talk to Sheri, because she was running with the drug crowd. So I told her, I said, 'Sheri, I don't like your crowd, I don't like you, and I don't like that—but you're good for the show, so as long as you do your show and don't bring that in my show, you are always welcome to be here.'

"Sheri got caught up with this guy who then fell in love with this woman, and the boyfriend and the other woman set a bomb to try and kill the woman's husband. Sheri got involved because the woman and him were writing checks on the husband's account. There was so much bad publicity for a while that I didn't know if I ever wanted her back, but they kept her [Sheri] locked up in federal jail for about three or four months."

Lucio Guerrero reported on the case in a February 21, 2003, Chicago Sun-Times article: "A female impersonator said he went on a crime spree with a male lover because of love and didn't think about the consequences. Frances Joseph Burkhart, who for more than 20 years has been known as Sheri Payne on stage at the Baton Show Lounge, said Thursday he knew Sienky Lallemand was involved in credit scams but helped him anyway during their four-year romance. 'I did mostly anything that he asked me to do,' Burkhart said. 'I was in love with him.' Burkhart testified Thursday in the trial of Lisa Toney, another one of Lallemand's lovers, who is accused of conspiring to kill her husband, Marcus Toney, with Lallemand's help."

Payne's involvement with Lallemand was peripheral to the murder case. Lallemand allegedly conspired with Lisa Toney to kill her husband, Marcus. Payne had been involved with Lallemand previously in a credit card scam but had steered pretty clear of the law since her brush with the Indianapolis police. Joy Bergmann wrote, in a Chicago Reader article of May 9, 2002, under the headline "Seduced," that Payne, after Indianapolis, had "a few arrests for minor offenses like shoplifting and disturbing the peace, but no convictions. She kept working her flawless Whitney Houston impersonation at the Baton. Though their romance had ended years earlier, she still kept the door open for Sienky Lallemand.

"So when he called the afternoon of January 13, 2000, and asked if she wanted to make a little money, she accompanied him to the Harris Bank on Monroe. According to court testimony, Sienky now had his hands on a fraudulent credit card. The account was in the name of Marcus Toney, but the name on the card—the 'authorized user'—was that of a former girlfriend of his, a Chicago police officer.

"Sheri presented a fake ID bearing the name of the ex-girlfriend and obtained a $4,000 cash advance. Two hours later Sienky entered the same bank, went to the same teller, received a $2,500 advance on another credit card for which Marcus Toney was liable, and was recorded on the same surveillance tape. The following night Sienky checked into the Fairmont Hotel, charging the $1,400 suite to one of Marcus's cards."

The subsequent trial for the murder of Marcus Toney by his wife and Lellemand caused headlines a decade ago. Payne has chosen to put this regrettable incident behind her and continues to exude a friendly spirit, professionalism and the highest of entertainment standards as a regular at the Baton. Payne is grateful to have what she has and to still be able to do what she does. "It was difficult," she said. "I appreciate Jim standing by me through that, but you make mistakes and you live and you learn. I'm grateful to Jim for keeping my job open through all that. I was used. I was vulnerable.

"That can all change out there in the world, but the only thing that changes here is the music. You have to be a special girl to work at the Baton. We have been in business over 40 years. It's all about touching the people. I remember September 11, 2001, and not knowing what to expect when I came to work, and the place was jam-packed, all three shows. All that week. I think that right there says something about this show and what this place gives to people."

Alana Kela

Ginger Grant, who was very close to Alana Kela, spoke about the former Baton performer. "I met her the first time in Hawaii," Grant said. "Her hula was magnificent and she probably had 48DDs. Her femininity and costuming were amazing."

"She was this gorgeous brown goddess," recalled Alexandra Billings. "She was from Hawaii and this wonderfully complicated person who did these great authentic, traditional Hawaiian songs and dances. Well, at the Baton we were always sort of nudged to do new material, freshen things and all that, so one time I said to Alana, 'How come you don't have to do new songs? Why do you just get to keep doing your Hawaiian songs and dances?' She turned to me and said, 'Because I'm brown and special.' She was so funny. We became great friends. Oh, God, she had a temper on her, though. Do not piss off Alana. I have seen her throw brooms across the room in anger."

"Alana was so graceful," Kelly Lauren said. "She floated across the stage, simply glided. Her head never moved when she walked. When I worked there, we used to call her The Informant because she would tell Jim everything we did. Jim usually likes to have someone in that role. She moved to New York and eventually came to a terrible end."

"Alana Kela was a gigantic personality," added Flint. "Her folks owned all the boat service in Kauai. She came here to be an entertainer and then moved to New York to become a madam, and I think she was treading on other people's territory, and they killed her. About a week before that, we went to New York and we had dinner with her at Frankie and Johnnie's on 45th and 8th [Avenue], a great little steakhouse. Richard Dreyfuss was at the next table. We had a great night, and then the next week she was killed."

"It was Thursday night, and John Bradley (who was a designer and friend of hers) and I were going to New York on Friday to visit her," explained Ginger Grant. "I talked to her that day. Alana was a prostitute, a high-priced call girl, and the phones were ringing and she said, 'Oh, the police told me to shut down today, and I'm not shutting down.' They told her to shut down or there would be problems. She said, 'I can't, I have to work, I've got to make money.' When the guys would call, she'd keep them on the phone and see if she thought they were legit, and if they were she'd have them come to the corner of 70th and Columbus and call from the pay phone, and she'd look out at the phone booth, and if they still looked OK she'd have them come across the street and press her buzzer.

"Anyway, the night before we were going there, at about 1 a.m., another Hawaiian girl who lived there called me and said Alana was shot. It could have been the madam. Alana was working with a madam who got in trouble and Alana bailed her out financially, so when Alana worked, all the money would come to her." Grant dismissed the widespread rumors that Kela was shot for attempting to steal the black book of the madam. "I've heard that, too, but it's just not true."

Grant continued: "I also think it somehow involved the police. About a year after the murder, another Hawaiian girl was having coffee, and this man came up and started talking to her, basically hitting on her. They started talking about Hawaii, and he said there used to be a girl from Hawaii living in his building. The Hawaiian girl played along and said, 'Oh, really?' And then the guy said, 'Yes, but this girl wasn't a girl.'

"He said that he came home from work at 10:15 on the night Alana was murdered and got there the same time police arrived. He said she was lying in the stairwell and the police lifted up her dress so they could see her penis and then went in her apartment and ransacked it. So they knew she was a guy and knew her line of work. It was weird, too, because I went to identify and claim the body. In New York you see a photograph, you don't actually see the body. Well, at first they wanted to know about her and the case, but then it suddenly became not even about her. They wanted to know how the phones worked, because she'd get 300 calls a day. [There was an ad in an adult magazine.] They wanted to know what she was doing and how the ads worked.

"I do think that whoever killed her knew her, or at least was invited into her place. She had a long, narrow apartment, and at the end was the kitchen and then moving forward was the bathroom, and then what we called 'the workroom,' and then her bedroom and then a living room on the other end. Whoever shot her, shot her from the living room. She was shot once in the front and two times in the back and she ran out the building and down two flights of stairs, and that's where they found her. I had to call her family, and they were Mormons. They said they knew it was going to happen because of her lifestyle.

"There is so much speculation about her death. Also, about two months before she was killed, Alana was on a talk show, and it was about high-class call girls, and they had some straight call girls as well as some queens. Alana was sitting there very quietly because she was always acting like a lady. Then someone said something about how they're trash and who they date, and Alana said, 'I date very influential people—judges, lawyers, politicians, actors, Mafia, everything.' I sometimes wonder if someone was worried that she might eventually talk."

Dana Douglas recalled a softer side of Alana. "I loved Alana," Douglas said. "She was the nicest, with a heart of gold. One of the things I did for a while after I moved down to Key West was, I bred exotic birds, and Alana's husband—well, her longtime boyfriend—came to work for me, so she would visit quite a bit." Douglas added with a laugh, "Alana was a true Hawaiian girl, and by that I mean all are welcome."

Dana Douglas

Dana Douglas started at the Baton in 1984. "[Jim] wanted me to come to Chicago, but that was a long way from home, so I went to Atlanta instead and started working at Baton South there," Douglas said. "That closed after only a few months. When I came to Chicago, I didn't know what to expect. Jim was a fan of mine and he played it up. He put up posters saying I was coming and told the other girls, 'Dana Douglas is coming, she'll show you what glamour is.' So, he was sort of keeping them in line by promoting me.

"I was on the bottom of the totem pole, though, so when I came in I started doing some different things. They had Chilli, and then the rest of the cast when I got there was mainly black and Hawaiian, so I was the blonde. I started doing things like 'Teach Me Tonight' and old disco. The crowd started to catch on to what I was doing very quickly, so I started working my way up the ladder. I worked at promoting myself, too. Nights off from working there, I'd go to the then-hot nightspot the Limelight and worked there as living art in the entrance.

"I had come to Chicago after breaking up with my boyfriend of seven years in Atlanta, and so I moved up here to be a superstar and to find a rich boyfriend. And that's sort of what I did. I met Dr. James Slaff my first month at the Baton. We dated for two years and then moved to Key West. We were together 26 years until he died in 2008. He was a wonderful man, a scientist who worked for the government and worked for the NIH [National Institutes of Health] and published all this research without government approval about AIDS, in a book called The AIDS Epidemic [1985]. He thought it was important for the public to know, and didn't really consider the consequences, and as a result the government fired him.

"He wrote the first book about the epidemic back when it was still called the gay plague. He said it is not a gay disease but a disease spread sexually through whatever means. He was right, too. He had a photographic memory and was a brilliant scientist, but he had no common sense. He was such a genius that he lacked some socialization skills.

"When he first came in the Baton, he was looking for Andrea Nicole. He had dated her for a year, so when he came in that night looking for her, he found me. Andrea, by the way, did an outstanding Cher. Anyway, he was goofy and sort of nerdy and he was so aggressive, too, but he turned out to be the love of my life. You just never know sometimes. He went into private practice in Key West and then had some substance-abuse problems and went into rehab up in Gainesville and started a private practice again up there as a leading gastroenterologist and then died of a stroke in 2008."

"I got to know Dana Douglas well because, soon after she came to work at the Baton, I entered the Miss Gay Chicago contest, and Dana did my makeup and hair and I won," said Ginger Grant. "Dana was and is a good businesswoman. Very statuesque, very theatrical, great clothes. She could dance a little bit but she was more a beauty. She was beautiful enough where she could just stand there."

Flint said Douglas would do Evita. "She was a 6-foot-2 blonde bombshell," he said. "I remember one time they had an idea for Valentine's Day, and a friend of mine, Nancy Reiff, got a call that they wanted someone to be a Cupid and hand out balloons at the State of Illinois Building. [Reiff then ran the company Balloons to You.] So Nancy suggested Dana, who was a huge hit and wore this little white outfit and wings and was walking around handing out these balloons, and all the men were on her. Two weeks later, the lady who set this up found out Dana was a transsexual and called up Nancy and said, 'I didn't know that was a transsexual. You are never getting another booking from me again.'"

When asked what she would advise a novice performer, Douglas, who was also Miss Continental 1987, said: "Perform by looking into the light as if it is someone you know. That way it looks like you're looking at everyone. Don't go looking for people for tips, because you probably won't see them anyway. When their hand comes into the light, that's when you realize they're standing there."

"I owe so much to Jim Flint," added Douglas. "He was such a contributing factor to my life and did so many wonderful things for me. I don't know where I would be if it weren't for him. I'm not one who forgets. If he needed me, I'd be there at the drop of a hat."

Kelly Lauren

On the official Baton Show Lounge/Continental site, 1988 Miss Continental Kelly Lauren said: "So many things have changed in female impersonation in the last 20 years.

In Houston, my hometown, female impersonation was virtually nonexistent. The crowds had become extremely cliquish and never really understood me as an entertainer. I moved to Chicago in 1985 and joined the cast of the Baton. In Chicago, one can do a song the crowds have never heard of and it will be well-received. I was so thrilled because I could finally support myself as an entertainer—doing what made me happy. ... In Houston, I only worked in shows occasionally for little or no pay. Houston never took me seriously. Tiffany Arieagus [Miss Continental 1982] told me, 'Miss Kelly, you have to go away from home to be appreciated,' and she was right!"

"I worked at the Baton from 1985 to 1989," Lauren explained in a 2011 interview. "I came here at the same time as Shanté. We were hired the same day. I remember when I first started it was a kind of blonde rivalry between myself and Dana Douglas. I wasn't a classically trained dancer, but I was cute and energetic and graceful. I remember one time I was thinking about doing an exact creation of the Madonna 'Open Your Heart' video with the chair and the dance and the exact costumes, everything. I said I was doing that, and Dana was saying, 'Oh, I think that's a bad idea.' Basically she was trying to sort of plant seeds of self-doubt in me.

"There was some rivalry there. It wasn't just her. There were some jealousies about boyfriends and who was the star and all that. There could be a lot of mind games. I was so excited, though. I was a showgirl, but we worked hard. It was three shows a night. There was an opening number and a closing production and then another one in between and usually two individual numbers for each entertainer. It was a lot, but it was so exciting."

Dana Douglas said of Lauren: "Kelly was very sweet, really strange. She was a lost child. Very talented but she had no family structure, so she always seemed to me like a little girl. She moved in with me for a while. Kelly came in to replace me when I was getting ready to move to Key West in 1986."

"I probably started a couple months after Kelly Lauren and Shanté. Those two! They were different then. They were so much wilder than I was," said Ginger Grant.

Flint agreed. "Kelly Lauren was wild and still is wild. We have our ups and downs. I say, 'Call me in the office,' and she'll call me at 6 at night when I'm taking a nap. We get along much better now, though," Flint said.

"I worked there 4½ years and I was in the doghouse more often than I was in Jim's good graces," said Lauren. "He would say nice things about me to other people, but never to me. To other people he would say things like, 'You watch her, one day she will outdo all of them,' but he'd never say something like that to me.

"My favorite memory of the Baton were the dressing rooms downstairs. How could it not be? There is that long corridor with doors along each side. The dressing rooms were different shapes, but they are basically like big walk-in closets. We could each decorate our dressing room however we liked. I was like a kid in a candy store every time I went down there. It was just so amazing. It was funny, too. A lot of times you could smell the pot smoke and then someone would say a catty comment and it was so funny—right away you would see all these hand mirrors stick out of the doors so each girl could see who was saying the catty remark or what the reaction would be.

"One of Jim's favorite things to do was to hide in my clothes rack in the dressing room behind the gowns when we were all onstage for the closing production number, and then he'd jump out and scare me when I came back."

Lauren agrees that she was a wild child at the Baton. "Oh, yes, I was wild. There's no denying that," she said, citing as an example one of the more memorable evenings out with the girls. "We socialized quite a bit. I did anyway with Dana and Shanté. I remember one time Dana, Shanté, Alana Kela, Sheri Payne, Leslie Rejeanné and myself all thought it sounded like a good time to do mushrooms and go see Poltergeist II. It was not a good idea. We acted like such fools. The only thing that didn't happen that night was that we didn't get kicked out of the theater."

Shanté / Alexandra Billings

Alexandra Billings is one of the great Baton success stories. She is well-known as the first trans woman to have played a transgender character on television. Her credits include roles in Grey's Anatomy, ER, Nurses, Eli Stone and Karen Sisco, as well as the made-for-TV movie Romy and Michele: In the Beginning.

In addition to teaching at the illustrious Steppenwolf School West in Los Angeles, Billings has also starred in numerous stage productions (Gypsy, Who's Afraid of Virginia Woolf?, Gertrude Stein and a Companion, and others), including her one-woman autobiographical show. She is also an accomplished cabaret singer and has recorded CDs that include The Story Goes On and Being Alive. In 2002 she was given the New York MAC Hanson Award as a cabaret artist of the year. She is also the proud recipient of a Jeff Award (for Chicago theatrical excellence) and five After Dark Awards, as well as being the subject of the Emmy-nominated documentary Schoolboy to Showgirl.

Shanté aka Alexandra Billings recalled coming to work at the Baton. "I had been working at Club Victoria [3153 North Broadway, which opened in March 1983 and was the former gay club Crystal's Blinkers] and performing since 1981, and at that time the Baton had sort of an open-stage deal on Sundays," she said. "It was where young drag queens could come and basically audition, or at least perform. Jim was usually there, and I remember being so intimidated by him when he stood in the back. He stood there with his arms crossed like Edward G. Robinson.

"I was doing crazy stuff, not really drag. I would tape-record scenes from movies and then act them out onstage and set them to Sondheim music. Strange stuff. Anyway, so I went there every Sunday night for almost a year and finally got up the nerve to approach Jim and ask what he thought or if he had any notes.

"He said three things: get better costumes, learn how to do your hair, and do something from this century—so I took his advice. I had someone make me some costumes, had a friend show me some things with my hair, and then I started doing Eartha Kitt. That was really what got me noticed or at least made him see some potential in me."

"Shanté was a great Eartha Kitt. Shanté as an entertainer was just wonderful, so different and fantastic," agreed Flint.

"Kelly Lauren and I started the same day," said Billings. "Kelly was a shoo-in. I sort of coasted in because of circumstances and because he needed a few new girls to replace three who were leaving, which were Dolinda Ko', Cherine Alexander and Andrea Nicole. He said he was taking us on a trial basis and made that very clear. We were here but if we didn't work out we were gone.

"I remember the first night, Kelly and I moved into Cherine's dressing room because she was leaving, and all of a sudden we heard Jim coming downstairs to the dressing room. I was so nervous and when I get nervous my solution is to start cleaning something. So Jim comes down and Kelly is lovely and very outgoing and was sort of this 'hello, darling, hello' combination of Marilyn Monroe and Tallulah Bankhead in the hallway. And Jim said, 'You need to calm down,' which sort of set the tone and was the theme for most of their relationship. I on the other hand was basically wedged in the dressing room closet/clothes rack.

"Jim came in and said, 'What are you doing?' and I was so nervous that all I remember saying was, 'I, umm, am alphabetizing my gowns.' I was completely crazy with nervousness, but that made him sort of chuckle, and that made me zero in on that and think, Hmm, now that was a way I could survive here. If I could make him laugh.

"Jim was always very good at seeing a niche in the performers and sort of rounding out his cast. There was a slight overlap, but not really, with Dana and Kelly. Dana was this showgirl, this tall, willowy living Barbie, this Amazon who would step onstage, and it was like with Mimi Marks, there would just be gasps—she had this amazing, statuesque beauty. She was huge and gorgeous, but the best thing about Dana was this beauty and then juxtaposed to this sort of Elaine Stritch trucker voice, so she looked one way and then would open her mouth with a voice that said, 'Now get me a cigarette before I bust you in the face.'

"Dana was so interesting, too, because she had this sort of Southern gentility and manner about her, but at the same time the heart of a stripper. She and Leslie Rejeanné were best friends. Kelly, on the other hand, was obsessed with Madonna—that was her thing. But yes, the beautiful-blonde thing still caused a bit of a rivalry. There was definite tension there."

"Shanté and I were close friends," added Dana Douglas. "And at the same time she was extremely jealous. She was so much more talented than I ever was. She had more talent in her little finger than I do altogether, but I was a showgirl, a 6-foot-tall-in-my-stocking-feet showgirl, and she wasn't. She was a great actress and entertainer, and it really hurt her that someone less talented than her could win Miss Continental. She was always trying to outdo and she did … .

"In those years, I remember the porn star Rick Donovan. [Rick "Humongous" Donovan was the XXX star of such features as Dynastud and The Bigger the Better.] He was at the height of his fame, and he was bisexual, and he came in the Baton, and there were hardly any people in the audience, but we all wanted him. He was cute and was hung like a horse. We all tried to get him, but he only had eyes for Shanté—and Shanté got him. She flaunted it and rubbed it in our face, and I can't say I blame her. I'd have done the same thing."

"Jim was someone who actually helped turn my life around," said Billings. "At the time, I was dating a drug dealer and we were holed up in this hotel on a three-day binge. I don't know if you've ever experienced this, but when you wake up out of a coke binge you have no concept of time. So I went to the lobby and they said I had a message from Jim Flint. So I called him and said, 'What's going on?' and he said, 'Shanté, you're fired.' I asked him why, and he said, 'Because it's Sunday, you disappeared for three days! It was like you fell off the planet!' I begged him not to fire me, 'Please, Jim, I can't afford it.'

"He was so mad. He said, 'This has never happened before, let me think about it.' So I called on Tuesday and he said, 'I will take you back if you clean up your act. I'll let you back through those doors, but I have no tolerance for that drug, so you can either keep doing that drug or you can walk through these doors to your future—but not both. It's your decision.' So, actually, that was a key moment in my life, and I have to say if it wasn't for that ultimatum I'd most likely be dead. He definitely changed the course of my self-destructive behavior."

Chanel Dupree

Chanel Dupree was another Baton favorite, as well as Miss Continental 1990. "She won my first Halloween ball when she was 16," said Flint. "Later she became a regular at the Baton. She was the sex symbol. Chanel is in her own little world when she's onstage. She wants to be perfect, impeccable, and better than everyone else. Her sister Betty ended up having the sex change, too. I don't think the third, Maria, ever did, but all three sons went into drag. It was like another performer I had working for me at one time, Ruby Red. It was her, and then all three of her brothers went into drag."

Candace Collins Jordan joked: "I've said that if anyone could steal my husband away it would be Chanel Dupree. Her hair, her makeup, wow—she was it on a stick. I remember when she did 'Vogue' with a different and unique choreography. It was amazing. The audience went wild. Then, when you meet her and discover she's a great person as well, that just seals the deal."

Maya Douglas recalled her favorite Chanel moment, prefacing it by saying that many times her favorite memories of the Baton are the "outtakes." "We were doing 'One Night Only' with Leslie as the lead, and Chanel and I were the backup, and we used to come across the stage on the sides and come down," Douglas said. "We had these really pretty black-and-glitter gowns, and the bottom, it was all netting and tulle. Chanel was in front of me, and she got caught in the tulle and fell into a roll and could not get up, because she was completely caught in this netting. It's a challenge to look glamorous when something like that is happening."

Flint explained that after winning the Miss Continental title, Dupree eventually left the Baton because she went through with the sex-change operation the following year and fell in love with a man in Florida. "She's very happy with her life down there now," he said.

Monica Munro

In the parade of international queens during the opening number of Miss Continental 2011, the former winners all "represented" different countries—France, Italy, Spain, China, Mexico, Zimbabwe and so on. Miss Continental 1993, Monica Munro, represented Lebanon. As she paraded down the runway to applause and turned to join the lineup of former Miss Continentals, Munro extended each of her arms and, with her back turned, flipped off the audience. "Classic Monica," laughed veteran club kid Zander Mander.

Victoria LePaige recalled: "I used to sometimes come to the Baton before I worked there. Monica Munro was my favorite. She would always do the unexpected onstage. She commanded your attention. The white girls always want talent like Monica or beauty like Mimi."

Miss Continental 1999, Tommie Ross, agreed: "Monica Munro was creative, innovative and just so commanding onstage. You were always mesmerized by what she would do."

"Monica is my auntie," added Baton server and bartender Cai Holyon. "She's one of the people who really does listen to me. When you are her friend, you truly know that she'll look out for you and have your back. She's very nurturing and a great entertainer, but although she has that nurturing side, she also has this other side. As an entertainer she's very edgy. She can also be edgy as a person and does have a sharp tongue. She will tell you what she thinks, and Monica will tell you the truth. She'll say, 'I don't care if the truth hurts, I'm telling you the truth.'"

Ginger Grant recalled Munro when Munro was a boy-boy: "She entered a contest in New York and, at the time, she was in foam rubber from her neck to her ankles and said she would never have silicone, and two years later … ."

Choreographer Harrison McEldowney said that one of his favorite things to do is go downstairs at the Baton. "In the first dressing room on the right beyond Ginger's—it used to be Monica Munro's and now it's Mimi Marks'—I like to go in their dressing room and just sit there and listen to the performers and feel the atmosphere," McEldowney said. "It is so soothing for me. I was a show-business kid and I've done it my whole life, so for me it's like being backstage in a Busby Berkeley musical, with showgirls running around half-dressed and laughing, and the sometimes bitchy comments—the glamour and the excitement of it all."

Tasha Long said: "Monica was outrageous and flamboyant. My favorite memory of her was down in the dressing rooms—it was so much fun, because we would be getting ready, and we would be asking her questions like we were interviewers, and she would answer as Cher. She does a great Cher voice. It was hilarious."

"Monica Munro is one amazing talent," said Zander Mander. "If you go on YouTube and type in Monica Munro HellRaiser, a great video of her comes up. When club kids or young queens want to learn how to be fabulous, I say watch this and learn. She was a huge mentor to me. She also was the one who taught me to say 'fuck you' very properly. We sat down one evening for cocktails after a Christmas party, and she has a very dangerous sense of humor. She said something, and I said, 'Fuck you,' and she said, 'No, not like that, like this.' Then she turned from me and very slowly gave me the finger and said 'fuck you' with her eyes and just the trace of a quirky smile. No words were needed, and truthfully, when Monica gives you that look, even the finger isn't necessary."

Mimi Marks

The celebrated beauty and performer Mimi Marks has won an array of titles, including Miss Continental, Miss International Queen, Miss Cosmopolitan and The World's Most Beautiful Transsexual. She is featured in the Janet Jackson video "Rock With U" and is reportedly the first openly transsexual runway model, working for Ford Models. She performed and has appeared on numerous talk shows—even co-hosting with Jerry Springer. Mimi Marks has made the tabloids for dating Dennis Rodman.

Flint beamed when he spoke about Mimi. "Mimi Marks has come so far. I had to go to Milwaukee to get her," he said. "I took Ginger up there three times and said, 'Ginger, there's this blonde up here who I think could be a big entertainer someday,' but she was so awful-looking and so homely and had no wardrobe. And Ginger saw her and said, 'Are you sure?' I said, 'Look at her dance, she's really got talent.' She doesn't dance as much now, because she doesn't have to, she's so beautiful. On the fourth time, Ginger said, 'OK, let's call her.'

"So I called her and said, 'Mimi, this is Jim Flint from the Baton. Would you like to come down and work with us?' She didn't know what to say. I said, 'We'll get you a couple gowns.' She came down, and two weeks after she was here, she just started going and going and working with the other girls that were here at the time, because she wanted to be as pretty as them. When you come here, you have all the teachers helping you, and Chanel was around helping at the time.

"Mimi is probably one of the prettiest impersonators I've ever seen. Her gowns, her bodywork, her makeup, her hair, everything about her. It was a great transformation. You wouldn't believe it was a little boy from Iowa."

"I'm from Waterloo, Iowa," said Marks. "I graduated high school in 1985 and, in 1986, started going to the bar there, which is about as big as this dressing room. They had shows, and so they kept asking me to be in them, because I was in gymnastics growing up and a dancer, so I was into arts and did community theater. All the queens were wanting me to be in the show, and I was thinking, 'I'll never do that.' Even though I knew on the inside that I felt like a girl. I think I was afraid that if I ever did that, I'd never stop. In Waterloo, Iowa, I didn't know how that would go over.

"Soon enough, they had me onstage doing a show, and from then on I never stopped. I moved to Cedar Rapids. All these people were queens but lived as boys. I didn't know anything about hormones or anything like that, but there was one queen there who years before had lived in California as a woman and taken hormones but then had to come back to Cedar Rapids for family. So I only knew a bit from her.

"Then we went to Milwaukee to see a show, and I fell in love with it. It was a place that actually had a show every week. They had two bars—one was Club 219 and the other was La Cage. We went to both shows and then I went back to Cedar Rapids, and all I just wanted was to go back to Milwaukee. They had talent nights there [in Milwaukee] on Wednesdays and you could win money, so I wanted to do that. I went back a month later. One week, I entered the talent at La Cage and won, so then I decided to stay and do the talent competition at Club 219. Then the next week, I won there, and they asked me right then if I wanted to be a member of their show. I just ended up moving there.

"Within a year Jim, Chilli, Dana Douglas, Tandi Andrews, Maya and Cherine all came to Club 219 to do the Continentals on Review show. I was probably the youngest person working there at the time. We were all in the dressing room because they were all getting ready and we were in the corners watching, because we just wanted to see, and we were saying, 'Oh, my gosh, I can't believe they're here.' I was just in the corner not saying anything, and Jimmy said, 'I want to see her perform.' He'd met all the other girls before, but I had never met him. He asked the show director, Ginger Spice, and she said, 'Perfect, Mimi would love to perform.'

"I was so intimidated to perform with these girls in the same show. The girls I was working with helped me put myself together and loaned me their best costumes. They just said, 'Go out there and dance as much as you can.' I used to do back flips and everything back then. Everyone was so nice to me, and gradually I started coming here [the Baton].

"I came with some girls from the show on a weeknight. There was hardly anyone in the audience, it was a third show, and so now for those same shows, sometimes when it's hard to get yourself up to performing for that last show of the night, I like to remember that was me. I was someone in a third-show audience, and what I saw really changed me."

"Mimi Marks is lovely," said Ginger Grant. "I've known her since she was a boy. We have a good friend who lives in Milwaukee, Ginger Spice, and that's where we first saw Mimi. She came and stayed with me when I was living in Boystown [in Chicago's Lakeview neighborhood] during my drug days, and I would not give her any drugs, and she was mad, and I said, 'No, if I did, your drag mother would kill me.'"

"Jim had me come and fill in when girls were on vacation," Marks said. "I worked a couple of weekends here. In 1990 I entered a pageant here, Miss Cosmopolitan, and I won, and he asked me onstage that night in front of everyone if I would be interested in moving to Chicago. Within two weeks I packed up my two boxes of stuff and moved."

"When she first came to the Baton, they were calling her the new Kelly Lauren," said the real Kelly Lauren. "Sometimes we were mistaken for one another, which I always took as a huge compliment. She is so lovely."

"You feel like a member of the cast immediately because you're in the show a lot," explained Marks. "When I started working here, the newest girls went on first, they were in the productions. As the new girl, you were the one to do stuff. In the start, my schedule was to be in the opening production, come offstage, change, then I was first girl onstage.

"From Day One I learned to be quick, fast. That's the way it runs. A lot of the girls were tough on you because this is a dog-eat-dog world, and you have to be able to roll with the punches. I learned so much. I'm so thankful for that. Now I can go do shows anywhere in the world, and some of these girls need five songs or 45 minutes to get ready, and I'm like, 'Are you serious? We change our clothes, our hair, everything in four minutes sometimes.'

"When I first came, Maya and Chanel helped me out a lot. My roommate Kim Cleveland really helped me. Alana Kela and I had a sponsor here named John Bradley, who helped me out a lot. He helped me get a place to live. When I started going on hormones and all, Jimmy found a girl for me who did all of our stuff for us. Her name was Michelle. I found out later Jimmy told her to always take care of me, take me under her wing, and not let me get too crazy. Of course, because I wanted to do all that stuff, the lip injections, everything. Everybody else was doing it, but Jimmy told her to not let me do that. Now I'm grateful that he did.

"Every year for the past 21 years I've seen that Irish temper of Jimmy's. I swear I have been fired and/or quit every year in the past 21. He and I go at it.

"Last year at Continental time, I was emceeing. I will tell the people when I am emceeing that you can't tip the contestants, but if you feel like tipping them you just come to me, and I'll put it in the ATM machine right here." Marks gestured to her generous cleavage. "Then they can withdraw it later. So it became this thing where I'd say, 'ATM-ing, the ATM machine is open.' I was doing that last year. He wanted the show to start and the show wasn't starting. I was emceeing, and he saw me doing that and thought I was begging people for money.

"We got into a knock-down, drag-out fight, screaming 'fuck you' at the top of our lungs. It was the Sunday night after the preliminary, and we came back here [to the Baton], and I was emceeing here as well, because Ginger didn't work. It happened backstage here. I was so mad. I said, 'I'm fucking leaving. I hate this place,' and he said, 'If you leave here, you're never coming back,' and I said, 'Thank you for your permission to never come back.' Oh, we went at it!

"I came down here and had all my makeup off in three minutes, and then they called me and said, 'Jimmy wants you to come to the office next door.' It all got resolved immediately. I was there for Continental and rehearsal.

"We just go at it, though. I am a strong-headed person, so I speak up, I don't sit there and take it like he wishes I would do sometimes. Now, he will call me prior to a meeting and say, 'Mimi, the meeting has nothing to do with you. Don't freak out.' If it has something to do with the show, like girls are late getting on the stage or there's too many slow numbers, it doesn't have to do with me, but it still has to do with the show. I'll be the voice. Sometimes it's gone a week or two where it can be chilly between us, but it never means anything."

Marks said her Madonna moment was her favorite time at the Baton. "I was doing Madonna for Madonna," she said. "They had made such a big deal about her coming here, but no one was supposed to know, the public or media, but we knew. It was all hush-hush. We knew she would be here in the second show, so I wasn't in the opening. I just got ready, and then the second song, Jimmy called and said, 'Put Mimi on next!' I had to go on ahead of time. I was doing 'Vogue.'

"I remember thinking when I came out, I just hope the people respond when they realize I am doing Madonna and the crowd doesn't do something horrible like do, 'Oh, her!' and she's sitting here—that would be awkward and terrible. They cheered, though, and I was doing the number, and all of a sudden I could see one person walking down the middle aisle, and all of a sudden I realized it was her, and everything seemed to be in sort of slow motion, and I remember thinking, Should I keep performing? What do I do? Should I stop and say 'nice to meet you,' or what?

"Then she started tipping me and handing me bill after bill. No one knew who she was, but people pay attention when the person keeps tipping. All of a sudden people started to realize that was who it was, and when she turned around to go walk back, the whole place stood up and were screaming. It was crazy! That was a highlight.

"I once got $1,100 from one person. It was this guy who would always come and take the money and put it all over you. And that day I was not in the mood for him to stand there the whole time and put dollar bills all over my costume. So he came up with a wad of dollar bills, and I just thought, Ugh, and sort of stepped back. Then he put that stack of ones away and pulled out a banded pack of hundreds and handed them to me like that. And the whole time he was putting those $100 bills on me, I was thinking, 'Oh, my God, oh, my God,' but you have to play it very 'oh, whatever.' So he gave me that pack of hundreds and then one more, so it was $1,100.

"Another time I remember, on my birthday I'd gotten all these great tips, because it was my birthday. I had just gotten offstage from doing my number and made hundreds of dollars. I had a candle in my room, and I went to do something and turned around, and then I turned back around, and my whole dressing-room table was on fire. I started putting it out and didn't even realize it when it was happening, but what had burned was my stack of money! I was so devastated and sad. The girls all chipped in, and at the end of the night they gave me an envelope that was all money." Then Marks added, yelling in the downstairs dressing room for effect, "And that was the one nice thing these girls have ever done."

Mimi Marks and the Baton performers did a lot of talk shows in the 1980s and 1990s, "when they were still normal," she said. "Jerry Springer was cool, I had some great times with him and even co-hosted the show with him in Daytona. I was on his show seven or eight times. One of my best friends originally worked for Jenny Jones, and Chilli, Sheri, Monica and myself went on that show. Then my girlfriend went on to become the senior producer at

Jerry Springer. I was on there a few more times than I probably would have been if she wasn't my friend. She was asking me and calling in favors to appear. It was fun at first, and then the talk shows changed and became nothing but 'that's a man!'

"In reality, I've heard every question. I've been asked them all, and I don't mind answering if they're sincere. But if you're an asshole, ugh. I hate when people ask, 'What bathroom do you use?' What do you think? What's the better situation here, me in the men's room or me in the women's room? Or I will be in something like this," gesturing to her low-cut black spaghetti-strap dress, and then her breasts, "'Are those yours?' Really? How do you think I would possibly take these off?"

Cai Holyon explained that Marks is also her drag mother. "Yes, although I am a woman, Mimi is my drag mother. I was her only drag child for years. She's my drag mom, my mom, and my big sister. It's a prestigious thing to be somebody's daughter. They advise and look out for you. In this community it's usually a younger drag that you're trying to help groom or make look like you, but in my case it was different. I was the daughter that wasn't the drag. I was the daughter that was the girl.

"So, since I don't want to look like her or be an entertainer, I'm very low-maintenance. Mimi now has four drag children, and three aren't even drags. It's low-maintenance for her, and then on Mother's Day it's 'what are my children going to bring me?' Trust me, on Mother's Day she is well taken care of—she gets flowers and cards and the whole nine yards.

"Family is very important to her. I've taken her home to Iowa. She's very connected with her family and very family-oriented. She loves her mother to death, her sisters, her nieces, her brothers. They all accept her, they all love her, very, very tight family. I remember watching an interview on America Tonight with Mimi and her mom, and this was in the early 1990s, and her mother called her 'he' at the time, which was so interesting because she would never think to do that now. That was 18 years ago, though, and in that time things have evolved in her family. All the nieces and nephews are all 'Auntie Mimi' and 'Auntie Mimi' from the time they are little."

Flint said Marks went back to her 20-year high-school reunion a couple of years ago. "She didn't want to go, and the girls kept calling her up because everyone in Waterloo has been in here [the Baton], and finally she decided to go," Flint said. "So she went and they wanted her to come out to the bars, and she said, 'No, I think I am going to stay in a more controlled atmosphere.' She told me, 'Jim, it was such a treat to go and see everyone looking so old, especially the guys.' She said she couldn't have had a better time that whole weekend and they all treated her like she was a goddess. It was very important for her."

Cindy Barbalock, promoter of the South East Continental contest franchise, summed up her adoration of Mimi Marks succinctly: "She exemplifies everything that the art of female impersonation is about. Her beauty inside and out is perfection."

"There are so many, many [Flint memories], I can't tell," said Marks, pulling her legs up beneath her on the chair. "I guess it was that first day, his saying, 'I want to see that girl right there perform.' It changed my life. I never imagined that I would be able to do this for a living. I always thought it would be fun to do, but I never imagined that 25 years later I would still be doing this and have had a nice career doing it. He gave me that opportunity."

Victoria LePaige

Sixteen-year Baton veteran Victoria LePaige said that when she was in high school she was into Tina Turner. "This was during her 'Private Dancer' days, and that's who I usually do at the Baton," she said. "Tina, Phyllis Hyman and Diana Ross on occasion. I love that this can be my life. I so admire Jim because he's taken something that I love, female impersonation, and made it respected. He took what was once something that many people did not respect, and made it something to be proud of. He's made it the epitome of what a great show should be, with the gowns and the production and frowning on profanity onstage. The Baton is still there, and that says something. It has withstood the test of time."

LePaige, who was Miss Continental Plus 1996 and Miss Continental a decade later, explained how she first started doing female impersonation. "I had some girlfriends that I used to dance with in a company called the New Breed dancers," she said. "One of my girlfriends, whose stage name was Friday Foster, started doing this. I was one of those who was saying, 'I will never do this. I will never do drag.' Then one of our girlfriends painted one side of my face and I've been doing it ever since—that was over 20 years ago.

"Dressing up was another avenue for me to express who I was and what I enjoy doing. I studied dance, did plays, and this was another way to creatively express, to perform. The best part about working here for me is dressing up. I love dressing up. With the wigs and sparkly clothes and feathers and all that—I live for that."

LePaige recalled her early days at the Baton. "It was here that I really learned to appreciate female impersonation. At the Baton it was a job, and a job that was taken very seriously. I am not from the area, and I remember I was hired in May, and probably that December we had the first really severe snowstorm in Chicago, and I called Ginger and said, 'Do I still have to come in to work? It's snowing.' She paused and then said, 'Yes, baby, I know it's snowing, but this is your job. Rain, sleet, snow—the show must go on!' It's true, too.

"Working there grooms you—five nights a week, three shows a night, and that show is structured and polished, and everything is so tightly run. The overture begins promptly at 8:30, and seven minutes later we had better be out of our dressing room and upstairs for the opening production. Jim is a stickler for being on time.

"It has been very interesting, working for him all of these years. I know I have not been one of his favorites, but we have a mutual respect for one another. I have a large amount of admiration for him because he has allowed us to take pride in what we do and elevated female impersonation over the years into something that can be respected. ... He does not hire girls who are not respectful for what they do, and the whole Continental System is about being respectful and about being a lady."

LePaige continued with a cast memory from the 1990s. "One time, Jim took us down to Peoria to show us off," she said. "It was sort of like, local boy makes good. It was myself, Monica Munro, Mimi Marks, Ginger Grant, Sheri Payne, Chilli Pepper and Ruby Red. Well, there was a huge snowstorm, so, the night we were going to perform, the audience was really small. That never mattered to Jim. He always said, 'You don't know who is in that audience, so always put on your best show,' and we did. Those people lucky enough to be there that night were floored! They saw some real talent that night. Jim always demanded the highest of standards, and it is always a thrill to be a part of that."

"Oh, that Christmas party in Peoria," laughed Flint. "We went to my favorite restaurant, Big Jim's. We went down and had a great dinner, and then a couple of them went to the casino, and then we ended up at The Fox [pub], and there were maybe 10 or 15 people in there, and all of a sudden they realized who we were and put a number on, and the performers were jumping onstage. Those people got quite a show!"

"Truthfully, the dressing room is the show," LePaige said. "The things that go on behind the scenes in the dressing room are so much more entertaining than what happens onstage. These are all intelligent and witty people you are working with, and some of the things that come out of their mouths on a regular basis are unbelievable. Ginger is even funnier offstage than on. We pitched it as a reality show to Logo, VH1 and Bravo, and nobody picked us up. I couldn't believe it. I thought it would be perfect. It's really a family. We fight, we love and we have a common thread of putting on a good show, and no matter what is going on, we are up there on time, smiling and laughing and giving people their money's worth.

"Jim and I have had a couple of falling-outs. When I was Continental Plus, he fired me at one point, and even before that first month was up. We made up. When I first started working here, we were in rehearsals and he got into it with Mimi, and she walked out of rehearsals screaming and cursing. Then, the next week, the same thing happened with Monica, and then it happened with Ruby Red—and I was like, 'Whoa, am I sure I want to work here?' But he's much more relaxed these days than he was 15 years ago.

"When I first started this, before I ran for any pageant or started working at the Baton or anything, I said to one of my friends, 'I am going to have a beaded gown in orange, yellow, red and green. I'm going to have every color.' I deserved that and, because of this place, I have those. I love that. I always wanted to play dress-up, and now I can get paid for it. So, thanks to Jim for my playhouse."

Cezanne

"Jim and I went to Calumet City to check out Cezanne, and we hired her," said Ginger Grant. "She was here for a while and then left and came back. [She's] a very good entertainer. She did Janet Jackson for Janet Jackson, 'I Get So Lonely.' She did J. Lo. Great energy, and an incredible dancer."

"Yes, I did 'I Get So Lonely' for Janet Jackson, and it was awesome," said Cezanne. "Some of her dancers had seen me in 1999, and they told Janet about me, and then she came in a few weeks later. Unfortunately, my mother had a stroke that week, and I was home in Kentucky at the time. I got a call from Jim, who said, 'Your twin sister is here,' and I didn't understand what he meant because I'm an only child. Then it clicked. Well, I came back in a few days, and that Thursday she came back again with maybe one dancer and a bodyguard. She was so kind and generous."

Ginger Grant added, "Yes, when Janet Jackson was here we all sat on the floor and ate fried green tomatoes with her."

"One of my favorite moments was the night Cezanne won Miss Continental," said Flint, speaking of her 1994 victory. "The question she had was, 'What are the three most important things in your life?' And she said, 'My health, my family and my dignity.' She answered without the slightest pause and said it without the slightest thought or hesitation, and that was really wonderful. I was so proud of her that night, because she had been in Continental once before and came in second-to-last or something. So, it really showed how much she had grown. She was always quiet, always professional, one of those entertainers that was great to work with because she never gave you any trouble."

"When Jim was looking for a dancer, he and Ginger came and saw me in a club I was working at in Calumet City called the Bank Lounge [200 State Street]," said Cezanne. "I remember they liked me but didn't like that I danced in granny boots, but it was 1991 and I was doing Paula Abdul. That was just the style. When I finally auditioned for Jim, it was with Amy DeMilo. I started in November of 1992, the day President Clinton was elected, and I left in 2002. I moved to Orlando and, after six or seven years, moved again, and I am now working at The Connection in Louisville. I am the sort of person who tends to want to try new things. It was a wonderful experience, but after 10 years and five days a week, three shows a day, I was ready for something different. I was also a little over the Chicago winters.

"I had a wonderful time at the Baton. I came there when I was around 26 or 27, and it was also when I began transitioning [to female]. I am so very grateful that I had a job, that I could afford to transition into the person I wanted to be in my various stages of growth, in an environment that understood and accepted. It was a place where you didn't have to explain everything like I would have had to do if I was working a 9-to-5 in an office or something.

"I must say that in my career—I've worked at almost all the places with running shows—the Baton is something very special. Most places don't have a regular show or cast. It's one or two nights a week and it's not as professional. Jim gives you that professional environment, those tools, and he allows you to do things and experiment with it. You get so much experience. Think about it—five days a week, three shows a night for 10 years. I got a lot of experience at the Baton. It prepares you for anything and everything. I am always impressed, too, that the motto is that if there are five people in the audience or 200 people, they're here to see the show and you still give your all. Those people are still paying for the illusion and for the entertainment, and it is your responsibility to give them your best. That's a very important thing, a crucial thing to instill in performers.

"Jim is very good at filling a style to fit in the mold of what is missing in the show. When I came, he needed an energetic dancer. I did a lot of Paula when I started, some Janet. What happens is, you begin to see the other entertainers and their style, and then you realize how you can broaden your repertoire to grow and enhance yourself as a performer without overlapping. When I started, Sheri Payne had left for a while and then she came back; we may have overlapped a bit, but Jim kept us both in the show."

As to her favorite thing about working there, Cezanne said she "loved the camaraderie I felt with the other girls at the Baton, especially Mimi. The year I met her, we were both in Miss Continental, which usually makes people competitors right away. It can mean tension when you meet, but we hit it off right away. By the time I moved up there, we were friends. We had a lot in common, a lot of growing-up experiences, and being a theater kid, we just clicked as friends and have been great friends ever since.

"That's what these relationships are, too. It's not just co-workers, it's friends and it's family. I remember when I was in Miss Florida one year, I was performing, and I looked out in the audience, and so many of my friends at the Baton had come down to see me—Jim, Ginger Grant, Mimi Marks, Monica Munro, Victoria LePaige. That meant so much to me, that they came down for that."

Tasha Long

"I was at the Baton in 1996 and '97," recalled Tasha Long. "I remember it was a lot of work. I was the new girl, so I had to open the show after Ginger's introduction and the production number. It was changing and getting ready fast. So, doing that for a year was an amazing course in being on time, being ready and being professional. Everyone there taught me by example. You really had to be on your game as a performer. It really prepped me for when I won Miss Continental in 1997.

"I loved working the anniversary shows. It was doing those productions that you really realized how the other girls worked and how they learned. It also gave the group a real sense of unity, with helping each other with costumes and picking out music. It gave you a sense of family—not only among the performers that were there at that time, but with all the other girls who had graced the stage. So, there was all this history of entertainers that had come before you. It came with a real sense of pride to be part of this line.

"The time at the Baton was also huge for me personally. When I moved to Chicago I was pretty androgynous, and working there was sort of what took away the last parts of maleness about me. Monica helped me a lot. She gave me a lot of her older clothes.

"I was really in training as a transgendered individual, which can be really tough if you aren't around girls who have or are going through the same thing. Working there just made it a part of life, and you were working with people who were doing the same thing. It was normal, and that made it so much easier. With me, that became part of my daily routine. I was learning how to live my life. So, those girls and that Baton environment taught me the ropes both as a person and as an entertainer."

In a Chicago Tribune Arts & Entertainment piece on June 7, 1998, Sid Smith profiled Tasha Long. "Is mine a comfortable life? I love it. … It's hard. Not the money part. I make enough to pay my bills. But the pressure. We do three shows a night, five nights a week," Long told the paper. "And living your life as a woman offstage is hard, too, trying to interact with society and getting everyone to accept your lifestyle. Even in Chicago. A lot of people I meet assume I'm a woman, but not everyone. I don't exactly have the softest voice around." Onstage she transforms into Eartha Kitt, Whitney Houston or Dionne Warwick. "Offstage, she's more like the girl, or lady, next door," the Tribune article stated.

"I grew up in Birmingham and went to school there," she told the Tribune. "I wanted to be a cosmetologist. While I was in beauty school, a friend of mine suggested I enter a contest. I'd never done drag. But I always dressed more unisex. I went, lost, entered again, lost again and finally won my third time out. A couple of weeks later, I was offered a job." The Tribune said that was 1983, and contests, tours to other cities and night performing soon wrecked Long's school credits. "You could say I've used what I learned about hair and makeup in another field. Getting started in Alabama wasn't as hard as some might think—there's a strong tradition of drag throughout the South."

Long entered Miss Continental seven times, the first time in 1983. "I didn't know what I was doing that first year," she told the Tribune. "In other contests, there are rules insisting no surgery or alterations or hormone treatments. The Miss Gay America Pageant is still like that. But when I came here, I saw beautiful girls with lovely bodies and gorgeous hair. They looked just like magazine cover women. I gagged. I didn't even make the Top 10."

The Tribune continued in its 1998 article: "A year and a half ago, Long moved to Chicago and began living her life as a woman full-time. She finally won the Miss Continental title in September. Now 34, she, too, has undergone hormones and surgical augmentations, though not surgery. She may never do that."

Regine Phillips

"In 2002, I was in Miss Florida Continental, and Jim and Ginger were there," recalled former Baton regular Regine Phillips. "After the contest, Ginger said, 'We are having Windy City Continental next weekend. You should think about coming up and competing.' So I did, and it was at the Baton, and I competed and won every category. Then I went back home [to Pensacola, Florida], and about a week later Tim Gideon from the Continental office called me and said Mimi had to have surgery and asked if I could work as a replacement on Friday and Saturday night.

"I was so thrilled! It was a dream of mine. So I went and performed. Then I was leaving to go back home on Monday, and before I left I went to the office to thank everyone, and Jim said to me, 'You know, there's an opening here.'

"I couldn't believe it. I was so excited, but I needed to think it over. I know I was grinning ear to ear. I was working as the show director at The Connection in Nashville and had worked hard for four years to get that position, but it didn't take me long to decide to come to the Baton.

"I was there from February 2002 to 2006. I did J. Lo and Janet, Top 40, high-energy dance music. My favorite memories were when I would hear the overture and it was almost showtime. There was so much excitement. Ginger would rev up the audience. The rush of performing there was so great. The regulars were nice, too, some that would say things like, 'I am always glad when I come in here because you can put a smile on my face.' Things that made you feel good. It was wonderful working there. When I eventually left, it was to be closer to my mother and family in Nashville."

Sasha Colby

Flint talked about the "newest" regular Baton cast member, Sasha Colby, who has been with the show almost five years.

"Sasha called me up from Hawaii and said she wanted to be hired here," Flint said. "She came here and, after seeing her dance, there was no way of keeping her out of the show. She's so energetic and a fresh face. She does Beyoncé and Katy Perry.

"The one thing about the show is that I like everyone to be different, and when Sasha Colby first wanted to come, Regine Phillips was here. They would have been too similar. When Regine left and Sasha showed up, it worked really well. Sasha sent her résumé to come here, and we saw her at Continental. Sasha took Regine Phillips' place after she quit. Regine was an incredible dancer who went back to Nashville."

"I was born and raised in Hawaii," Colby said. "I actually grew up in a dance studio there. All my friends wanted to get off the rock of Hawaii and get to the mainland and make it big as dancers. I realized while I was dancing that I was supposed to be a girl. I was getting those kinds of overwhelming feelings, so I started transitioning while dancing. That was when I was about 18 or 19.

"Then my friends started going to L.A. and dancing backup, and I thought, 'What can I possibly do to be the best I can be and make this dancing work for me?' So, I loved watching pageants and loved Continental. At about 17 or 18, I saw my first pageant on video, and my drag mother in Hawaii sat me down and we watched them all. She told me all about this place," gesturing to her dressing room in the lower level of the Baton.

"The Baton is the place to be. If you are anyone in our business, you go there, so that was my goal. I was doing shows in Hawaii underage. I did the show and then they would escort me out the door because I wasn't old enough to be there. I met Dina Jacobs in Hawaii, and she told me more about the Baton.

"As soon as I turned 21 and was able to run in Continental, I did. Actually even before—I was so eager. I won the prelim at 20, and so I could compete in Continental when I was 21. I did, and ended up in the Top Five. I loved it. I got bitten by the Continental bug. I've been in it three times, and the last time I was first runner-up. So hopefully I'll keep moving up, which would be really nice—and not fall back.

"I remember the day I got hired. I was living in Tokyo, Japan, with a friend of mine, and I had already done Continental, so my name was out there. Then I got an email from Yoshiko Oshiro [Miss Continental 2002], saying, 'Talk to Ginger and Jim, because Regine Phillips just left the Baton. They're looking for a dancer girl and they thought of you but didn't think you would ever move to Chicago.' I immediately jumped on the computer and emailed and wrote this crazy 'What do I have to do to get hired there? I will do anything' email. I got on a plane, went back to Hawaii, got my stuff, got on a plane, and came here. It was that fast, less than a week's time. He [Flint] said he liked my energy and needed a dancer, and I love to dance, so it was a perfect fit.

"Being from Hawaii, I had never really experienced winters. I came here in February and walked off the airplane literally in jeans and flip-flops. Everyone here was so sweet. When they realized that, they all brought clothes and coats, Sheri, Victoria and Chilli, and everyone else, even the bar people, and they gave me all these things. It felt like home and like something a family member would do for another family member right from the start."

Sasha rolled her enormous eyes and smiled. "Seeing all these heroes in the flesh, like Mimi Marks and Sheri Payne and Chilli Pepper and everyone, I was and continue to be overwhelmed," she said. "I had heard stories about them, but now I am with them. I remember, early on, Jimmy telling me to 'keep quiet and pay attention to the girls downstairs and you'll go really far. Hang around with the good girls who aren't caught up in all different things and you'll do great.'"

Colby also explained how coming on as the new girl felt and works in regard to music. "There's an unspoken thing," she said. "We all know our lane of why we're in the cast. We're all different. I won't do Whitney Houston or Tina Turner and they won't do some crazy song no one's ever heard of. I like some wilder things, but I love Beyoncé, Katy Perry. I like different house singers, electronic things. He'll give us a lot of slack musicwise as long as another girl isn't doing that performer.

"He'd rather we shy away from profanity. He wants us to be classy, but nowadays you have to evolve with the audience. I guess he used to be a little more raunchy than he is now—but not with a lot of the profanity. That's what so much of the music is today. People want to see music videos or something they would see in a concert.

"I try not to butt heads with Jim too often, but every once in a while we do. One time, there was this boy that was in the bar that I didn't get along with, who was on me and harassing me a little bit, and I was at the end of my rope with it. We had already had a couple confrontations outside of here, where he had come to other jobs and things. So, I did not want to see him. He was here on a third show on a Saturday, and I walked up to Jimmy at the bar and said, 'He needs to go.' And I didn't realize how I said it, my tone—just that 'you need to get rid of him.'

"Jim flipped on me. He said, 'This is my fucking bar, and don't you fucking yell at me and tell me kick out a paying customer because you don't like him—no.' Then I went off back and said, 'So that man's $5 is worth more to you than your employee!' Back and forth, and it got emotional really fast. Then five minutes later he said, 'Well, I didn't mean all that, but if you have a problem just let me know and come to me.'

"With my friends who are dancing backup with different artists, like for Janet Jackson, we'll be talking and I'll say, 'God, I wish I had that job, you travel and you're doing this and that.' They tell me, 'But you are onstage with a freedom to dance whatever you want to dance and look however you want to look. We're contracted to do the same thing every day in the same way.' I guess I really love the freedom to be in charge of whatever I want to be for that time onstage. He gives us the platform."

Colby's most memorable moments are when she meets celebrities. "Yes, and they come down here and want their pictures taken with us—like Jennifer Hudson, Janet Jackson, Queen Latifah and so many others," she said. "I am completely star-struck when that happens.

"I'm here five nights a week, and I book out [get booked for out-of-town engagements] every now and then. I work at Roscoe's and then bartend at Cocktail, so it can be a lot—but I love it. The Baton has really offered me a lot of opportunities to go other places in different cities, and people will want to book me simply because being a Baton performer is on my résumé. This career is what you make of it, so if you're a go-getter, you'll reap the rewards from it."

Flame Monroe

"I used to do glamour drag and now I do standup comedy," explained one-time Baton performer Flame Monroe. "I worked there in 1992. It was rocky at times, but I learned so much there—how to be on time and how to be a professional. Working there taught me to have great confidence in myself as a performer. I have enormous respect for Jim and all he has done for the art form of female impersonation. He has really raised it to a new level. Our relationship was tumultuous, to say the least. We are both control freaks, and that is not always the best for a work relationship. One thing I will say is, Jim has an eye, a vision for what a performer can be. He can see the potential. It's an amazing skill."

"Flame Monroe was so great," said Flint. "I think she hurts herself sometimes. I've heard she's a great father for her children. We were both strong personalities and would butt heads—oh, would we butt heads. She was an incredible dancer and just fantastic onstage."

Jodie Santana

"I met Jim in 1995," said Jodie Santana. "I was working at a club in Rock Island, Illinois, called J.R.'s Nightclub, and he was there at the gambling boat because he likes to gamble, you know. He said, 'You should come visit us at Continental.' So then in 1996, I came and competed the first time.

"Oh, Jim has a good taste in food, too. I remember one time during the holidays I came up and was doing some sewing for the Baton, and he ordered us a pizza with white sauce and Italian sausage. I still think about that pizza. I love food, too. When I was working there as a performer, Mimi would always talk me into bringing in food. I love to cook and I am known for my chicken and dumplings. Mimi liked it so much that when I'd bring it in, she'd set it on her hot rollers to keep it warm. Jim used to get on me for that, too, since we're not supposed to have food in the dressing rooms. He'd say, 'Jodie, you're going to bring in the rats!'

"The biggest thing I remember about the months I was working there was, he always wanted us to be ladies. At least that's what he'd focus on with me. He'd say, 'We're not a strip bar so don't come out and take your clothes off. That's not what this place is about.' He would say he wanted people to come into the Baton to say, 'Can you believe that is a man up there and that he can be that beautiful and with a body like that?' Jim would always say, 'You don't need to take your clothes off to do that. You are too beautiful and talented for that.' He does not like a dirty show.

"I remember one time, I finished my number and he came flying down into the dressing room and said, 'You will never wear that on the Baton stage again! This isn't a whore bar. These people aren't looking for that.' He was right, too. It was this black patent-leather nasty outfit, and it was trashy. I would get mad at him plenty of times, but once I took the time and stepped back, I could see he was right. He just wanted me to be better, and make me the best I could be.

"I remember my second day at the Baton. I came in, and there was about a 25-minute rehearsal for a production number to 'Giving Him Something He Can Feel.' Afterwards I said, 'Oh, when are we going to be doing this?' And they said, 'Mary, we're doing it tonight.' That night, during the number, it was so sweet—Victoria LePaige and Sheri Payne kept their hands on my back and moved me to let me know where I was supposed to be, so I didn't get in trouble. That's the way it is there, though. You learn fast, you be on time, and you be a lady.

"Jim paid me the biggest compliment this year after Continental Elite. When I came off the stage he said, 'You looked just like Zsa Zsa Gabor up there. And she was such a beautiful woman in her prime.' Another time I was competing, and for my talent I did Dorothy Dandridge doing 'You Do Something to Me.' After the number, I was down in the dressing room getting changed for the next part of the contest with another contestant, and Jim came down and he was singing the song. When he left, the girl I was changing with said, 'Well, I guess we know whose talent he liked.'

"I have been in the Top 12 of Miss Continental six or seven times and been in the Top Five of Elite twice. I keep coming back because it really does feel like family. I like these people and truthfully, and this sounds hokey to say, but I don't care if I ever win either of those titles, because Jim hiring me to work at the Baton was the biggest compliment I could have ever been given. It really has been the highlight of my career. After I was there about seven months, my stepfather died, and I had to come back home to Southern Illinois for a while. Jim understood, and in fact he said that appreciation of my family is one of his favorite things about me."

Tajma Hall

"I first heard about the Baton from Victoria Parker," said Tajma Hall, who was Miss Continental Plus 2007. "She was going to compete for Miss Continental Plus 1996 and asked if I would be in her talent portion. She told me that it was being held at the infamous Baton Show Lounge. I had never heard of the place and had no idea what made it famous. She then told me it was a show bar for female impersonators and it had been visited by some of the world's most famous people. I was so excited to come and see such an amazing place!"

Hall first met Flint when she moved to Chicago about 10 years ago, in 2001. "I was very intimidated by him but knew I had to meet him," she said. "I found my way to the Baton Show Lounge on a Saturday night and the place was packed. I stopped and introduced myself as I was leaving. He said, 'Nice to meet you,' and kept moving the crowd along.

"Jim has allowed me to come work there and emcee there many times. I am a part of the family. I would say I am the alternate cast member. I work for many of the girls when they are out of town and fill in for Ginger when she is away. The Baton, Jim and the cast have all had a huge influence on me. I have grown so much in this art form since moving to Chicago and working at the Baton. I love Jim, I love the Baton and I love the cast—they are all dear to me."

Felicia

One-time Jim Flint boyfriend Warren Williamson spoke about Flint's alter ego, "Felicia." "He was just so great, ridiculous but at the same time great," Williamson said. "He had on a poofy skirt, pigtails, and they put freckles on him. He'd do a double baton onstage. Then, at the end of his act, they would light the batons on fire. After a while people would come from miles away to see his act."

"He didn't do it very often but I remember, when the anniversary was coming up, Jim announced he was going to perform that night as Felicia," said Alexandra Billings. "It was fun. He got ready down in the dressing room. Chilli did his hair, and Leslie Rejeanné did his makeup, and everyone was helping. Felicia was wonderful, very old-school glamour—sort of Arlene Dahl meets Ethel Merman, so it was old-school glamour but with an underlying 'but watch it or I'll box your ears' edge to it.

"Anyway, as it got closer and closer to Jim's time to go on, he was so nervous. I mean really nervous—he was down there and just talking a mile a minute and saying, 'I don't think this is going to work. I think this will be awful. I'm not sure about this and I'm worried about that.' He was just going on and on. Finally, I caught his eye in the mirror and said, 'This is going to be much better than what you think.' And still talking to me in the mirror with perfect timing, he said, 'Yes, but I think it's going to be awful.' And we just laughed. He ended up being terrific."

Tommie Ross had the chance to see Felicia at the Baton anniversary during her reign as Miss Continental in 1999. "I saw Felicia that night with the skates and the flaming batons, and let me tell you, I was very impressed!"

"Technically, I retired Felicia in 1985," said Flint. "That was my last time, because I was going to run for County Board and didn't think I should be doing drag. I did the roller-skating with the batons a couple times after that for fundraisers or anniversaries, but it was really when I retired Felicia. Truthfully, I don't miss it, either."

Server and bartender Cai Holyon added: "I've seen him do his number in his roller skates once as Felicia after he retired. I think it was the Softball Follies. He can skate and twirl a baton better than I ever thought he could, and he was so cute in his bathing suit with a tutu over it."

"When I was with him, Jim would always do the closing number of the show, and so in those years I would always do his makeup and hair and cover up his tattoos, like those two spiders over his nipples. I used to always joke with him—one for hot and one for cold, that's what I always told him," laughed Dana Douglas.

Choreographer Harrison McEldowney recalled: "I'd heard about Felicia but I had never really seen her until there was a benefit fundraiser for the gay [softball] league, called the Softball Follies, and Jim performed as Felicia in that, with the batons and the roller skates, and I was amazed. He was really good."

"I remember when Jim would do a number. He would come out on his roller skates with the baton, it was usually to 'I'd Rather Be Blue' from Funny Girl," said Kelly Lauren. "He also would do 'I Am What I Am' from La Cage sometimes. He'd wear street clothes and then a sequined coat with a rounded collar when he'd do that number. Those are the two things I remember him doing the most."

"I actually think Jim was happiest as Felicia," said former Baton and Annex 2 manager Lennie Malina. "You could see it. That Felicia character was such a kick for him, his passion. When he sang 'I Am What I Am' in character, that was his essence."

Male Leads

"Tony Lewis was probably the most beautiful male lead we had," gushed Flint. "He was a golden blond with the blue eyes. People couldn't take their eyes off him. He left to go to David's Place. Then after that, he got rather ill, and we didn't see much of him after that."

Dina Jacobs added: "I used to sing with Tony. We were doing an album together that Chuck Renslow, the owner of the Gold Coast and Man's Country, was producing. I remember it was when the song 'Then Came You' was popular, because that was on the radio and he wanted to do it. We rehearsed at the Dewes Mansion [503 West Wrightwood Avenue] on the top floor in that ballroom, and I just remember us being in that huge ballroom, and we were tucked away in a corner of it with the piano—that place was amazing."

Jacobs grew teary-eyed at recalling her favorite story about Lewis. "When we first moved to Chicago, we didn't know anybody," she said. "It was Andrea Nicole, China Nguyen, Cherine Alexander and myself. Tony and his boyfriend Russell lived upstairs from us when we lived on Foster and Sheridan.

"It was Christmas Eve and we heard a knock on the back door, but we didn't know the neighborhood, so we didn't answer it. And then Tony called up and said, 'Ho-ho-ho, this is Santa Claus, you have something on your back porch,' and we opened the door, and there was a Christmas tree and some presents. They had decorated the tree and everything. It was so sweet that he and Russell would go and spend money on us. I will never forget that sweet act of kindness."

"They used to say 'Ray West with the hair chest.' He was one of the most popular male leads at the Baton. Oh, God, he was amazing," exclaimed Dana Douglas. "He was the male lead, an early Marlboro Man who looked like Tom Selleck. He got himself a rich husband."

"Ray did George Michael, 'Careless Whisper,'" recalled Maya Douglas, "And he'd strip, and when he did he would have the women lined up. He was very, very handsome."

"He was a little diva. I loved her, sexy to death. Sort of Burt Reynolds–looking," said Sheri Payne. "He had sort of a Vegas shady edge to him, so we had to watch her and keep her in her place because we are family here."

"Ray West came from Detroit," Flint said. "He was so well-known when he was here that socialites and everyone would come to see him. His lover was one of the brothers from the Como Inn [a large, popular Italian restaurant in Chicago that closed in 2001 after 77 years], and they bought a huge estate in the Florida Keys. Whenever Ray got onstage, he was so incredible the customers would stare. They tipped him so well because he was not only great onstage, but he also had the personality to go along with it. He would do some regular numbers, some semi-strip numbers, and was also the male lead in the show when there was a man involved with the girls. The nice thing about Ray was that he made the girls look like girls because he was such a man himself."

Flint also recalled another early male lead, Marty Helton. "He was the greatest male dancer, bodywise he was perfection," Flint said. "I used to take him to Florida with me a lot, because I was dating Jack Campo's lover at the time and I figured if I had this guy with me no one would suspect. But he'd go out, and then I would go out and do my thing. We got to be great friends, and then he went to Detroit. I went to a bar there one night, and there was Marty Helton in drag. His drag name was Aura Lee. I almost fainted. I couldn't believe it. For a while he was going to come back and work at Dominick's in the floral department, but he never did. He's passed away now."

Paul Lopez, a former male lead at the Baton, first met Flint at the Baton for a pageant in 1990. "After winning my national title of Mr. Gay All-American, I toured the country performing in 2001 and 2002," Lopez said. "Shortly after that, Mr. Flint had me come do a few guest spots at the Baton to see if the crowd would take to me, and they did. I made so much money in tips I couldn't believe it. The ladies that came to watch the show made me feel like a star, as did all the girls in the show.

"I was male lead in the show for about a year. I always did a lip-sync number like Ricky Martin, Enrique Iglesias or Michael Bublé. My moneymaker was a Ricky Martin mix, where in the middle of the act the song 'Shake Your Bon-Bon' would come on, and I would strip down to a leather outfit with leather chaps and leather G-string.

"Working for Jim taught me to be on time, to be more professional, and it made me want to be even better at whatever I do. I work with high-school students now, and I used a lot of what I learned from Jimmy in my teachings.

"The New Year's Eve shows there always especially made me feel like part of a family. New Year's Eve was so awesome because we all worked so hard to do all kinds of new productions, and even if some of us did not get along at the time, that night everyone got along, and we all gave each other hugs and kisses, just like a family. I actually caught Jimmy backstage that night with the mic, doing the countdown. I made sure I was the first to wish him a happy New Year that night. He actually can be a little shy, so it takes him a few minutes to come out and wish everyone a happy New Year in person.

"Jimmy has made such an impact on the gay world. Here I am in Colombia, and drag queens here know about the Baton and Continental pageants. I think every female impersonator in America dreams about working at the Baton or becoming Miss Continental. It makes them dream but it also makes them work hard, due to the fact that he sets the standard high for all of them. But by doing this, I feel he created something beautiful for the GLBTQ community, where people can be entertained or where a young person can dream of being a great entertainer and can achieve that goal at the Baton or at Continental, because that's how it was for me."

Choreographer Keith Elliott

Keith Elliott, choreographer and founder of Dance for Life, a 20-year-old annual AIDS fundraising event, explained how he came to assume duties as Baton choreographer.

"I was hired as a backup dancer for Ginger Grant in Miss Continental in the mid-1980s," Elliott said. "It was when she was doing 'No Bad News,' from The Wiz. So I started working with Ginger and doing some more things, like choreographing her 'If My Friends Could See Me Now' number the following year. I started meeting and interacting with Jim more and the other cast members, like Chilli. Then, when Orlando was leaving, I was offered a job at the Baton. So I choreographed at the Baton a total of nine years and at Miss Continental a total of 13 times, I believe. I loved working on the big opening production numbers for Miss Continental and Continental Plus. Eventually I moved on to focus on Dance for Life, and then Harrison McEldowney took over as choreographer.

"The performers at the Baton are all so wonderful, because they are at the top in their chosen profession. People look at the Baton and Jim Flint, and what he created is really what the art form is all about. Jim taught me that if you are going to make this your profession and want to make the illusion, you need to respect it. You need to be professional, be on time, present yourself well, and respect yourself, as well as others and the art form. If you want it to be a vocation, that is what it takes and nothing less. You had better believe rehearsal was Thursdays from 2 to 4, and Jim would pitch a fit if anyone was late.

"My favorite time at the Baton is when everyone is just calm. The hormone shots can work everyone up a bit and make them in a work or networking mode, and constantly on. That can be a little draining. So, I loved those quiet moments when things were low-key and when I felt we really connected.

"I think I bonded most with Ginger and Mimi. Ginger, because she sort of was my entree into this world, and Mimi, because we are very like spirits. Also Monica and Maya, just because they have that amazing performer ability and this attitude that just goes for it. Sheri Payne has always been so consistently sweet, and that smile of hers is amazing. It's been fun knowing Chilli as well. I run into her all the time on the street—it's sort of fun to see and chat with her outside of a professional mode.

"One of my favorite numbers I choreographed at the Baton was a production with Ginger in the lead, and it was done to the song 'Who Stole the Jam?' It was very retro and wonderful. Another great number was put together by Tony Savino and myself, and we did it for Maya Douglas' talent in Entertainer of the Year. It was a 1940s swing production number with 12 sailors that strip down, and we took this to Ohio and the crowd went crazy. It was great. Later we did a scaled-down version here [at the Baton]."

Maya recalled, "Yes, Keith is a great choreographer. He was a young, fresh choreographer and worked with Continental and then came to the Baton. He's very sweet. He was great to work with and so talented. When he was doing my talent for that show, I would work Saturday nights and he would want me at his house at 10 on Sunday morning. He'd have a pot of coffee ready and he'd say, 'OK, let's go."

(The Entertainer of the Year is not to be confused with the similarly named Gay Academy Award category of the 1970s. EOY began as a contest system in 1990, with promoters and preliminaries similar to the Continental System.)

Elliott laughed about one of his favorite Flint memories. "I remember one time Jim, Chilli, Ginger and I were sitting at the Baton, and Jim turned to me and said, 'Girl, you don't have a drag name,' and I said, 'Well, I don't do drag,'" Elliott said. "He completely ignored me and said, 'You are a one-name girl—Chrissy!' And then I think Ginger said, 'Yes, Chrissy, but with no H—Crissy.' And they were all laughing.

"Well, I didn't think anything of it. So I am walking down the street on Clark and I go by El Jardín and I hear this loud voice yell, 'Crissy! Crissy! Hey, girl!' and it was Jim, and when he yelled it, people turned to stare at me from what seemed like every possible direction. I was so embarrassed, I just thought, 'Oh, God!'"

Eventually, Elliott gave up his duties at the Baton as well as Miss Continental to devote more of his time and energy to Dance for Life. Dance for Life is a multiple-dance-company event that Elliott started in 1991 to raise awareness as well as funds for HIV/AIDS prevention and care, all while promoting the art of dance in Chicago.

Choreographer Harrison McEldowney

Harrison McEldowney met Jim the first time while working as backup dancer for Lady Catiria in 1995. This was the year she gave up the Miss Continental crown at the Blackstone Hotel. At the time, the Baton choreographer was Keith Elliott, who was also doing his Dance for Life. Elliott and Todd Keich used to also do a fundraiser for Dance for Life called Dance Divas, which was held at the Baton. In this event, men from several dance companies performed as their favorite divas. McEldowney did Ann-Margret, and Cassie from A Chorus Line, and choreographed the show.

"What impressed Jim about my work was that, for the production, the members of various dance companies learned this show and did it in basically two days to be performed the following Thursday. It was fast," McEldowney said. "He also liked that I worked and got along well with the Baton girls.

"What happened was, Keith told Jim he was leaving to focus more on Dance for Life and recommended me. Jim called me and asked me if I would be interested in the job. I said that I would, and he said, 'Great, see you Thursday.' It was very classic—few-words Jim.

"That was in 1997, and the girls working at the Baton at the time were Tasha Long, Ginger Grant, Chilli Pepper, Monica Munro, Victoria LePaige, Sherì Payne, Cezanne and Mimi Marks. They liked me because they considered me a 'fishy' choreographer, meaning that I choreographed for women, and since these performers lived most of their lives as women, they wanted choreography that reflected that and not choreography that was for men who dressed as women.

"We rehearse once a week for the weekend show, and if we are learning something we can get the basics down in about two hours and then spend the next few rehearsals perfecting it."

"They come in every Thursday and work from about 1 to 4, and then if we need extra rehearsal they'll schedule them," said Flint. "After certain events, we let it go a bit, because we have enough productions. We had our anniversary and New Year's, and we start with some new things for Continental in September—out-of-towners come and they want to see new things."

"Harrison and I work next to each other at the Continental contest for hours while we do the cattle call. He never gets stressed," said Ginger Grant. "I am a person to scream. Harrison is there getting the acts on, he's there to sweep up with a broom, he's there to tell the emcee the next contestant is ready. He's doing this and that. He is there."

Flint laughed: "Something that shocked me about Harrison was, about three years ago I went on a Royal Caribbean cruise, and I'd gone out the night before, and as I was waking up I heard this voice, and I thought, 'What the hell is Harrison doing in my room?' What I didn't realize was that when you're on that cruise line and you wake up, it was him saying 'Hi, I'm Harrison McEldowney, and these are the shows we're doing.' He's also the choreographer for the cruise line."

"Another vivid memory of Jim is New Year's Eve at the Baton," McEldowney said. "Every year he does a backstage countdown, 10-9-8-7, and it never matches anyone's clock, but I always go backstage because he is always back there with the microphone, and I always give him a hug and wish him 'Happy New Year.' He is usually tearful and retrospective, and I know he is thinking about all the people he has lost, and that always gets me—just that small moment of intimacy, that hug, and then I go back out to the party on the main floor.

"I think the first time I realized how much Jim really meant to me was one of the first years I was working there. Jim was at the front door, and there was some sort of problem with the seating, and he went over to the table to see what was wrong, and the woman at the table got up and took a swing at him.

"Well, I was sitting at the end of the bar near the door, and I hopped up, and Jimmy and I took her outside. I remember when I jumped to his assistance, my main reaction was, 'How could she do that?' Meaning, how could she do that to someone who has helped our cause and community so much?"

'The Girls at the Baton'

"The two favorite productions I have done for the show have been the two original numbers we recorded," said McEldowney. "The first one was, Becky Menzie did a wonderful song she would sing at Gentry [712 North Rush Street] called 'The Girls at the Baton,' and she talked about Chilli and Mimi and the rest of the girls in it. We went into the studio with Becky and recorded the song and built a production around it. The other one would be the original song we wrote and recorded for the 40th anniversary, and it was simply called '40-Year Anniversary Song.'"

"Cheri Coons and I wrote a song called 'The Girls at the Baton.' I was so thrilled when they decided to do it as a production number for their anniversary," added cabaret legend

Becky Menzie. "There are three female voices in the recording we did of the song, and then when we came to see the production and I saw Mimi Marks matched up with my voice, I was over the moon. Let me tell you, the Baton is so iconic and well-known that I can take that song anywhere in the country, not just the Douglas Dunes, but anywhere, and it still gets a laugh. Because everyone knows about the Baton."

'The Girls at the Baton'
by Beckie Menzie and Cheri Coons

A girlfriend of mine took me out for the
   night
Because I was lonely and blue.
The good seats were gone for the
   Chippendales' show,
So we went to a nightclub she knew.

No, I'm not a girl who dreams of the stage,
I've always been shy and retiring.
My friend said she thought the show was
   a drag,
But I found it very inspiring.

'Cause now, I want to be just as pretty
As the girls at the Baton
Who put satin dresses on
And smoke from diamond cigarette
   holders.

I want to be just as curvy
Where their plunging necklines drop
With enough right stuff to stop
The dress from falling off of their shoulders.

Six foot three
And every inch a goddess,
I want to cop their style.
Men would kneel,
Tuck twenties in my bodice,
And ask me in return for just a kiss and a
   smile.

I want to be as coquettish
With the grin that opens doors
And the skin in which the pores cannot be
   seen.
I want to sing Judy Garland songs
Dressed up like Liza—is that so wrong?
I want to be just as pretty
As the girls at the Baton.

I sneaked past the guy at the dressing-
   room door
And looked for the girls at the show.
I thought they would teach me the tricks of
   the trade,
The things every woman should know.

The girls were all gone, excepting for one,
A fact I found very surprising.
And what caught my eye as she zipped up
   her fly
Was something there was no disguising.

She said, "You too can be just as pretty
As the girls at the Baton
Who put everybody on
And keep them busy guessing their
   genders.

"You too can be just as slinky
In your sequined gown from Saks
With enough bikini wax
To keep you rolling,
Bumpers to fenders."

Ginger knows,
And so does Chilli Pepper,
That men still love Old Spice.

They're the pros,
So watch their every step, girl.
At that age, you'll be lucky to look half as
   nice.

You, too, can be as bodacious
With a little nip and tuck
If you pad and paint and pluck strategically.
You, too, can strut with your falsies on,
Dressed like the harlot of Babylon.
You, too, can be just as pretty
As the girls at the Baton.

Creating a Family

As evidenced by many of the stories from performers and staff at the Baton, as well as the recurring staff members' names in many of Flint's numerous other business ventures, his employees become family. "I left my family at 14, and then at 17 I left for the Navy, so I missed out on a lot of family stuff. I guess I've always tried to create a family," said Flint.

"Part of the appeal," added Maya Douglas, "was also that you become a family and Jim does become a sort of father. My family accepted me, so I was lucky, but I still miss them, being so far from home. This was my new family, and it has always meant a lot to me."

"You really do become a family," explained Alexandra Billings. "You spend more time with these people than with anyone else. We were working so many days, three shows a night. It was a lot. In that work, you are your own writer, producer, dresser, director, makeup artist, etc., and as a result you begin to depend on the opinion of all these others and the presence of them to better yourself as a performer."

"It was a totally dysfunctional family, but somehow when you put all those dysfunctions together, it all worked," said former manager Lennie Malina. "I'm talking mainly about the upstairs, the staff rather than the performers. The downstairs was part of the family, too, but in a different way.

"Some of those dysfunctions—well, there are no boundaries at the Baton. I remember one time I had a new girlfriend and came in sort of smiling, and Jim said, 'Lennie got some last night!' Then he said louder, 'Hey, everybody, a round of applause—Lennie got laid last night.' It was crazy and wonderful and it sometimes sounds bad when you talk about it, but it was family and I wouldn't change my time there for anything."

"All of us spent every single day together for years and years and years," said Cai Holyon. "We are like a big dysfunctional family where we want to kill each other every day or we love each other every day, and you deal with people's quirks and problems.

"To have this relationship with someone and then see how the audiences react to some of the girls—I forget sometimes what the audience sees. The audience is thinking, 'That's a man,' and to me I'm saying, 'That's just my friend Mimi, my sister, or whoever.' I am always working here either as a server or as a bartender. I've sat in the audience, I think, twice since I've been here. It's a completely different thing from working, because you block everything out and watch the illusion they are giving."

Ginger expounded a bit on the subject. "We're with these people five days a week, seven hours a day," she said. "Oftentimes we're with these people much more than with our own families. We have our mood swings, our good days and our bad days, but we're basically family, and Jimmy is like the mother. I might not get along with every one of them all of the time, but we've got each other's back."

The Guy at the End of the Bar

"A few years ago I wanted to do a show with my great friend Honey West," said Alexandra Billings. "So I went to one of Jim's clubs [3160] and wanted to speak to the manager. Well, when I came through the door, who was at the end of the bar but Jim. Immediately, of course, I wanted to start cleaning something, but I walked over, and he hopped off his bar stool and gave me a huge hug and said, 'It's so great to see you. We watched you on ER and I'm so proud of you. Your career is going in so many great directions.'

"We sat there at the end of the bar and talked, really talked for a long time. It was just an amazing experience to have this peer conversation with this man who had been so important in making me who I am. He saw something in me that no one else really saw and at a time when no one else saw it.

"He really gave me the confidence to find my own authentic voice. He gave all of us professional lights, professional sound, a professional environment and allowed each of us to become our own entity, our own commodity. He was one of my mentors. We learned how to make it work—how to create very quickly and do it under pressure and to do it without complaining."

Billings continued: "As I sat there talking and listening with Jim, I thought, This guy is a true legend. He's a savvy businessman, and just think of the bravery—to open that kind of bar, at that time, and turn it into this amazing source of revenue.

"Really, I see him as a simple man who had a huge dream. I admire his tenacity, but at the end of the day he's the guy sitting at the end of the bar—and who also happens to own the place."

Doing It His Way

When Flint entertains as Felicia, he often performs the song "My Way." His friend Ken Nowakowski redid the lyrics of the song for Flint. Below are Nowakowski's lyrics and his explanation for them.

Wait now, Billy! / Don't dim the lights. / I won't leave them / in confusion.
My friends, / forgive me now / if I choose to part / with this illusion.
You laughed, / you had your fun, / but before you sprout / your wings and fly away
Take some time / to hear me out— / please— / see things my way.

What about you? / Your childhood stories? / Can they all / be happily written?
With me, / I recall the image / of a small-town boy / who never fit in.
In Peoria / it didn't play well, / so I hopped a bus / and hit the highway!
Now I'm Chicago's hostess / with the very mostest /—well, / this is my way!

Yes—I saw sad nights / when audiences were few
And cloudy days / when bills were overdue,
But I stayed — / I staked my claim, / and each problem / I overcame.
I fought off strife / to win this life, / and this life goes my way!

In these gay years / history was made, / and I played my part / to make things better.
Some say, / "Life is a drag"— / well, I know it is. / I'm a trendsetter!
After Stonewall, / we picked up clout, / and when AIDS struck, / we learned to shout.
"We may be down / but we are out!!" / And we'll never— / never die away!!

Wipe away the makeup, / off with the curls,
Strip away this jewelry, / my diamonds and pearls,
Next comes the fabulous / designer gown, / and the façade / comes tumbling down.
Felicia's gone / but Jim Flint goes on— / And I did it my way!!

"These lyrics were written for Jim because he had seen so many performers onstage using this song to make it an effective and sometimes very powerful statement for their need to use female impersonation as a means of expression," Nowakowski said. "Dina Jacobs considered 'My Way' her anthem. When Jim mentioned possibly performing this number using personalized lyrics, I told him that I would see what I could come up with. In composing the lyrics, I had discussions with him so that I could understand a few things about his childhood and his early years in business.

"These lyrics were written in the early 1980s when all the Chicago gay bars were losing employees and patrons to the AIDS epidemic. Jim and I agreed that mentioning this in the song would add strength to what would essentially be a very biographical performance. We had all by that time lost very close friends to the disease.

"This performance was designed to take place before the last production number of the show. Felicia would be dressed in a full gown with all accouterments attached. She'd first pantomime one of her regular songs—but instead of exiting the stage when that number ended, the lights would shift to just a spotlight directed at her, and the intro to the instrumental recording of 'My Way' would begin playing through the sound system. She would look up to the light booth, address Billy Cooper, and then begin speaking to the audience.

"While she performed the dialogue of the first stanza, a simple dressing screen with black borders and opaque white fabric, similar to those seen backstage in movies and television shows, was moved through the curtains at stage left. Orlando crouched behind the screen, ready to help Felicia make a quick transition from woman to man.

"With the start of the second stanza, Felicia moved behind the screen and, while reciting the song, began her metamorphosis. The last stanza was most effective as Felicia wiped away her makeup, stripped off her wig and pulled a bracelet from her arm while reciting the appropriate lyrics.

"By the last line, she stepped out from behind the screen as Jim Flint, dressed in a shirt and pants as if ready to go out to have dinner at a neighborhood restaurant. I stood in the audience during the premiere performance to feel the response—it was an instant hit that seemed to have appealed to everyone there."

Baton male dancers in the 1970s: Little Jimmy, Tony Lewis and Ricky Love.

Baton cast, 1970s. Back row, from left: Leslie Rejeanné, Jodie Lee, Lynette Langston and Chilli Pepper. Front: Jan Howard, Orlando del Sol, Felicia, Audrey Bryant.

These five photos: Various Baton casts, 1970s.

Dina Jacobs, 1970s (above) and 1979 (below).

Cherine Alexander, 1970s.

Jodie Lee, 1970s.

Jan Howard, Jodie Lee, Chilli Pepper and Audrey Bryant, 1970s.

Leslie Rejeanné, 1970s.

Jodie Lee, Peaches and Lynette Langston, 1970s.

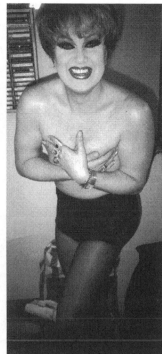

Chilli Pepper images from 1970s through 2000s (with Orlando del Sol in first photo).

Lady Baronessa Maria Andréa

To Timmy: My love to you always
Lady Baronessa

Clockwise from top left:

Lady Baronessa, 1970s.

Lisa Kirk, 1970s.

Entertainer Lotta Love in the August 1973 Chicago Gay Crusader.

Lynette Langston, Chilli Pepper, Jan Howard, Leslie Rejeanné and Jodie Lee.

Peaches, Dolinda Ko' and Andrea Nicole, 1970s.

Shawn Luis, Jim Flint as Felicia and Roski Fernandez, 1970s.

Shawn Luis, 1970s.   **Orlando del Sol, 1970s.**   **Peaches and Jan Howard, 1970s.**

Jan Howard, a Baton performer in the 1970s, performed in a show called Pouff at the Playboy Club in 1976–77. Larry Townsend of the Chicago Tribune described it in his January 28, 1977, review as a "wild, zany, anything-goes show filled with a frenzy of topless performers of all three sexes."
Photo courtesy of Mark Ward.

Alana Kela, 1980s.

Andrea Nicole, with Jim Flint, a month before her death in late 1985.

Andrea Nicole, 1980s.

Andrea Nicole, 1980s.

Baton cast, 1980s. Back row, from left: Leslie Rejeanné, Kelly Lauren, Ginger Grant (back), Maya Douglas, Roski Fernandez, Chilli Pepper. Front, seated, Shanté and Chanel Dupree.

Baton casts, 1980s.

Baton cast, 1980s. Back row, from left: Roski Fernandez, Chilli Pepper, Leslie Rejeanné and Kelly Lauren. Front: Maya Douglas, Shanté and Chanel Dupree.

Baton cast, 1980s, with designer Bob Mackie. Back row, from left: Dana Douglas, Chilli Pepper, Bob Mackie, Leslie Rejeanné, Orlando del Sol. Middle: Ray West, Sheri Payne and Alana Kela. Front: Shanté and Kelly Lauren.

Dana Douglas and Ginger Grant, at the State of Illinois Building in Chicago, pictured in the February 20, 1986, Windy City Times. Douglas played Cupid in a Valentine's Day promotion coordinated by Nancy Reiff's Balloons to You company.

Baton Show Lounge regular Dana Douglas played Cupid in a Valentine promotion at the State of Illinois Building. 'Balloons to You' co-ordinated the event with 'Ginger Grant' assisting.

Ginger Grant, 1980s.

Kelly Lauren, 1980s.

Left and above: Maya Douglas, 1980s.

Shanté and adult film star Rick Donovan, 1980s.

Above and below: Roski Fernandez, 1980s.

Shanté, 1980s.

Sheri Payne, 1980s.

Victoria LePaige, Monica Munro, Cezanne, Ginger Grant, Mimi Marks, Sherì Payne and Chilli Pepper.

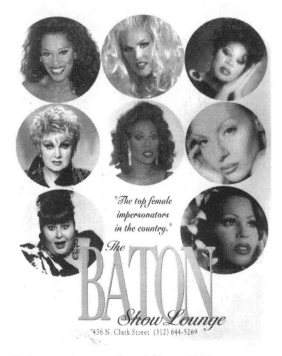

Baton cast promotional fliers, 1990s.

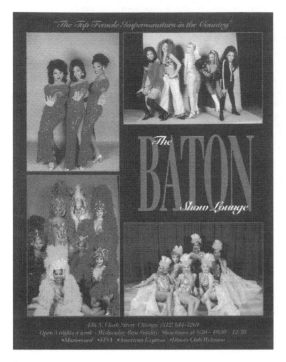

Baton cast promotional fliers, 1990s.

Above and above right: Cezanne, 1990s.

Chanel Dupree, 1990s.

Above and below: Ginger Grant, 1990s.

Left and above: Maya Douglas, 1990s.

Mimi Marks and Ginger Grant, downstairs at the Baton, 1990s.

Mimi Marks, 1990s.

Left, right and below: Monica Munro, 1990s.

Above and right: Sheri Payne, 1990s.

Regine Phillips, 1990s.

Flint and the cast, 1990s.

Choreographer Keith Elliott, at the Baton, 1990s.

A cast photo session, 1990s.

Tasha Long, 1990s.

A cast photo session, 1990s.

Mimi Marks at the Baton, 2000s.

Monica Munro, Sasha Colby, Mimi Marks and
Maya Douglas at the Baton, 2000s.

Baton performer Jodie Santana.

Ginger Grant at the Baton, 2000s.

9

Baton Personalities Outside the Spotlight

As with most of Jim Flint's business establishments, the Baton has a relatively small staff turnover. As server and bartender Cai Holyon observed, "Someone usually has to die or move out of the city for someone to change their position or even their section at the Baton." People stay for years—and not two or three, but more like 10, 17, 20 or more.

There is a strong sense of family among the co-workers, and with that comes a strong sense of commitment to the functioning of the place and to putting on the show. A lot of people rely upon the production and, for it to function smoothly, people have to do their jobs. It is very rare for someone to call in sick.

There is little to no backup in any position. Someone works the ticket booth and the phones; someone works the door; one and sometimes two work as bartenders; one and sometimes two, as servers; and someone is on lights and sound. With such minimal coverage, missing work for an unscheduled reason is much frowned upon. People will show up and work through almost any ailment out of dedication, though some may say out of guilt or dread of the repercussions. Everyone on staff is very familiar with Flint's self-described "Irish temper," and staff members tend to go to great lengths to avoid it.

Former manager Lennie Malina called the upstairs crew a "completely dysfunctional family, yet somehow, when all those dysfunctions come together—it works." Whatever the recipe, Flint must know the proper ingredients.

Getting to know and learning about the cast of characters upstairs—the folks pouring and serving the drinks, selling the tickets, and doing the lights and sound—proved no less colorful than meeting the cast in the dressing rooms downstairs. Here is a small sampling of that "supporting" cast.

Richie Saunders

"Oh, yes, the doorman," laughed Warren Williamson. "'Grandma Richie' was always what we called him. He was a little, bent-over man who would sit there and knit and take the money as people came in, and half the time Jimmy was going out to apologize to people for his not letting people in or offending them."

"We used to have him at the door, but his mouth was so wild and he was so crazy and offensive that I finally made that ticket booth so he'd stop offending people. That didn't work," confessed Flint. "Lesbians would come in and he'd say, 'Oh, here come the cunt-lappers.' He'd say things like, 'Go in, sit your black ass down, and don't forget to tip the waiter.'

"One night we had a group of eight people in, and he was waiting tables that night. They left, and he ran out after them and said, 'Did you leave anything at the table?' They said, 'Oh,

I'm not sure,' and came back in and were looking all over. Finally they said, 'Why? Did you find something?' And Richie said, 'No, I asked because I'm still looking for the fucking tip.' That was just how he was. He would say anything to anybody. And to this day people come in and talk about the abuse they took from him."

"Richie would say the most obnoxious things, and he expected people to realize or get his sense of humor," said former manager Lennie Malina. "That's what it was, too. He meant to be funny. Well, not everyone understood that. Most just thought of him as this old gay man being weird or they took offense, and it was easy to take offense." Some took his comments as racist and others as sexist.

"Richie Saunders was a trip. He could be so mean, but he also had the greatest stories," laughed Cezanne. "He liked me and I think it might be because I tend to be very calming and diplomatic. I think he also liked me because he said I looked like Raquel Welch."

Flint had known Saunders since The Chesterfield. He'd brought him to Sam's as well. Flint shakes his head: "Richie was Richie. I went with Joan Crawford and Richie to the Drake a few times when Joan would come to town in the late 1960s or early 1970s," said Flint. "They got along very well. He knew her from years back in Hollywood. Every holiday she would send Richie a card and an autographed photo. Afterwards, when the book [Mommie Dearest] came out, I asked Richie about it and he said 95 percent of it was true, because the studios would cover everything up."

Dana Douglas recalled her own Saunders memories. "Richie was the bitterest old thing on this earth. 'What the fuck do you want?' 'Fuck you!' 'Get the fuck out of my way!' That was Richie," she said. "The thing is he was really sweet and didn't mean any of it. He cried when I left the Baton, and I was so moved by that."

"He used to like to pop out his teeth at people," said Maya Douglas. "He liked me, though, since I gave him a ride home a lot of times."

Saunders died about 12 years ago. "He had all kinds of ailments," said Cai Holyon. "You would have to walk him to the bathroom because he claimed he couldn't walk there on his own. Then he'd be in there for 20 minutes and then would sit at the end of the bar and have someone, sometimes even customers, take him back to the booth."

Rumor had it that if no one would come by to walk Saunders to the restroom, he would pee in the garbage can in the ticket booth.

Holyon continued, "The ticket booth! The charge machine we used was at one time behind him in that booth, so you would have to reach over and swipe the charge. When you did, he'd grab your crotch or your boobs. He'd call people horrible names and say horrible things you would never say to anyone in a million years. 'Does your cooze get cold in that skirt?' 'Does the wind blow up your cooze in that dress?' Awful things—and he'd call complete strangers terrible names. He did it all the time.

"Ginger would say, 'You are a wrinkled old man,' and Richie would fling open the door of the ticket booth and yell from the booth to the stage, 'You'd be wrinkled, too, if you weren't so fat.' He'd literally scream it across the bar."

Ginger Grant recalled: "About a year after Richie died, the Riverdance people came in and they said, 'We tried to get reservations a few months ago, and we called and asked for the Baton [pronounced by them with an Irish accent as in Baton Rouge] Lounge, and the person said, "If you can't fucking pronounce it, then don't come," and hung up on us.' That was Richie."

"We'd have meetings and Jim would say 'Now, Richie, you just sit there and you don't say anything,' and Richie would say, 'Fuck you,' and then just start giving his opinion on whatever the subject happened to be. Richie had something to say about everything," said Cai Holyon.

Heather Fontaine laughed. "Richie was a trip," she said. "The things he used to say to people on the phone. When they asked who was in the show that night, he'd always say I was a Tab Hunter impersonator. He was quite a character."

Flint added: "Oh, God, Richie was bad but when he got paired with his sidekick Sandy, who was a bartender at the Nite Life—things were completely out of control. One time he got drunk and hopped in the back of a car and said to take him to 5050 North Sheridan, and the cop turned around and said, 'You've got five seconds to get out of this fucking squad car.'

"He and Sandy would get even crazier at the Nite Life. They'd order pizzas and put pubic hair on them and serve them to customers there. Another time, Sandy was cooking and turned on the oven and got to talking, and by the time he lit the match for the stove it blew up and went through to the apartment next door.

"Another time, [Sandy] bought this new Magnavox TV and got it home and kept trying it, and it wouldn't work and wouldn't work. He had it about a week before he called Goldblatt's and said, 'You sold me this thing and it doesn't work. Now, if you can't fix this thing, I want my money back and this out of here.' They apologized and said they would send a serviceman right away, and so they did, and when the repairman came out he said, 'Sir, you have to plug this television in first!'"

"Jim and Richie were together a long time," said Holyon. "Jim took him about everywhere he went. They were together for 40 years! Think about it—that's a long time, that's a relationship. With Richie it really was about loyalty. Jim would never turn him out. Jim and Richie. There are a couple people that haunt this place. Richie is one, and Billy Cooper is the other."

Billy Cooper

"When I first started, one of the things they told me about Billy Cooper was, 'Don't give him any money, don't give him any cigarettes, and don't give him any liquor,'" said Holyon. "He was one of the few people I know of who was fired from this place. He was fired right in front of me in the lobby at the Park West for trying to order Dom Perignon and having it put on Jimmy's tab."

Flint maintains that, like many fired Baton employees, Cooper was rehired and that he had just gotten "very drunk that night."

It was also said that Cooper was sometimes prone to steal. "Now we can leave our tips on our tables in our dressing room, but when Billy was here we couldn't do that, he'd steal our tips," explained Ginger Grant.

"Billy Cooper was very nice," Flint said. "He was a genius at working that booth. No one could do it like he did. He always liked to help the girls and eventually got a little too mixed-up with drugs. All the problems came from that. One time the drug dealers thought he stole the drugs, and they were going to kill him. Billy was always here and always ready to work. Even on all the holidays, he was with his Baton family. He would want to cook and bring in greens and all of that."

Community activist and Baton patron Lori Cannon recalled Cooper: "He was the premier sound-board and lighting master, a genius at featuring his girls in his own way and making sure each was special. What worked for Cherine Alexander might not work for Alana Kela and he knew it, and they knew that he knew it."

Holyon added that working the light booth is the hardest job in the place. "Billy had the hardest job here. If you work the light booth, you have to put in the tape for the music and get the next tape ready so there is no lull in the show. So, when one tape stops, the next one begins. You have to turn the backstage lights up for the girl getting offstage and get the lights ready for the girl coming onstage.

"It's a lot of work and it all has to be timed just right. Then you have a girl telling you at the last minute that she wants to change her number, and they run up and give you a different tape, so it's change the number in the order of the acts. We still use tapes, because CDs can skip. Also, with CDs you have the carousel, and it has to revolve, and that causes a lull in the show, and Jim does not like lulls in his show."

Lennie Malina said: "Billy was like me. He had no other life but the Baton, and partying. That's what life was, for a lot of us. The Baton was his house. It was where he lived, and in that sense we were roommates."

Billy Cooper, the sound and light man who contributed so much to the wonderful Baton productions, passed away from AIDS complications in the early 2000s.

Bobby and Jesse

Bartenders Jesse Dugan and Bobby Glaze are also key figures in the story of the Baton. "Bobby was a bartender I met in Atlanta at a bar called the Answer," Flint explained. "Then I opened the Baton South down there for a short time in the front part of the Redoubt Atlanta. It was probably only a few months. When I decided to close it all, because I was losing money, Bobby said he wanted to come to Chicago. So he came here and, later on, he met Jesse.

"They were probably the two wildest people who ever worked for me, and that's saying something. Bobby was the calm one and Jesse was the wild one. If they were sober they were wonderful, but if they were drinking it was a calamity. They worked here for years. Then Jesse got very sick and passed away, and Bobby still lives in Chicago. Bobby was one of the people I could depend on for years until he just was drinking so much. Now he's given up drinking altogether.

"When those two were together, you never knew if they were going to start fighting or smash this or that, and they'd have parties and fight. They probably had more coffee tables in one year than anybody I know, and frying pans. Jesse always wanted to give everything to anybody. He'd never say no.

"I think he was barred from most places on North Halsted because, once he got drunk, anything could happen. Once, he was trying to get into Christopher Street and they wouldn't let him in the door, and he was screaming, and he took off his leather jacket, and his shirt, dropped his pants, bent over and mooned them and then took off running. You never knew what he was going to do."

Holyon agreed that those boys were wild. "Bobby and Jesse were the most volatile things in this place for years!" Holyon said. "Bobby Glaze was from Charlotte, North Carolina, and worked for Jimmy in Atlanta and then was here about 20 or 21 years, and his lover Jesse worked here for about 17 or 18 years. They drank together and fought together. People would purposely sit at the bar to watch them fight.

"Cezanne lived with them, and she said, when she would come out of her bedroom, there would be things smashed all over the place. Every coffee table was smashed into pieces. I've seen them pick up bar stools and run after one another. I've seen one pee on the other one. I've seen them drink more alcohol in one sitting than I've ever seen anyone drink in my life. Crazy things. Jesse got caught sucking dick in the alley behind Johnny Z's on videotape. When they drank, anything could happen.

"Bobby and Jesse would pick up hustlers on the corner, and Jesse would give them a $5 deposit to meet them back at closing and take them home. Then Jesse wouldn't have money and would want Bobby to pay for his hooker, and then they would be fighting.

"One time I woke up at around 11 a.m. from passing out at their house, and there was a naked hustler passed out in the living room. My purse was way up on this cupboard because they didn't want the hooker to get it, and then Jesse and Bobby were beating the fuck out of each other, and that was a daily thing with them. That was how they lived their lives."

Dan Neniskis added: "They were a couple. Good bartenders, but they would go out and get shitfaced and get to fighting. About every other week, one of them would show up with a black eye."

"Bobby got fired," said Holyon. "I got suspended for a month and Bobby got fired. We were at a party, and I was a no-show, no-call, and Jimmy told me I was suspended for a month, so I went to Wisconsin, and Bobby got fired. Jesse always blamed me after that for Bobby getting fired, but it wasn't me. It was a lot more than that one incident. Bobby had been fucking up for years."

Maya Douglas shook her head remembering them. "Bobby and Jesse, partners forever," she said. "Bobby was manager and they were both bartenders. They always fought. Jesse was always drunk.

"They would always have Thanksgiving dinner for us. They would work the night before and go home and cook this amazing feast, and there would always be at least 20 or 30 people there. They would even have to-go plates for people who had to work, and they'd bring more food into work for us the next day.

"They were absolutely wonderful, troubled but so wonderful. You could always count on running into them on the street, drunk."

"They loved having holiday dinners," added Cezanne. "I remember Roski [Fernandez] used to always make the Filipino dish pancit when we had holidays. That happened a lot at Bobby and Jesse's, and a lot of time it would be work people, since most [of us] lived quite a ways from our homes and we often only had a day or two off."

"And whenever they would have a party or get-together, the rule was, 'Don't be smoking any of that stuff until after Jim leaves,'" laughed Flint, "because I am so anti-drug."

"I lived with Jesse and Bobby for about a year when I first moved here," said Cezanne. "Yes, they could be volatile, but my parents had a volatile relationship as well, and the bottom line was that they loved each other. In a way, they became sort of parents for me. They could say anything they wanted to one another, but you better believe nobody else better be saying something. They were very loyal to one another."

Joanne De Corey

Any recounting of the Baton staff would not be complete without remembering Joanne De Corey. The popular Baton waitress was also named "Trash of the Year" at the Gay Chicago Awards contest in 1982, hosted by Ralph Paul Gernhardt and Dan DiLeo.

Lennie Malina recalled one side of Joanne. "Yes, she could party. Believe me, I remember Joanne passed out with her pantyhose around her ankles," Malina said. "She was that sort of partier. However, she was an amazing individual. She took her job at the Baton very seriously. She was a genius. She had a memory for a face and names. People might come in once a year; she'd remember their name and most impressively what they drank, and whether they wanted it with a splash or a lime wedge or whatever. Just one time and she would remember. It was an incredible skill.

"Another vivid memory I have of Joanne was when someone left her a 15-cent tip, and she chased them out the front door of the Baton and threw it at them and said, 'You must need this more than I do.' She had a heart of gold, and her word was gold. You could always count on her. No question. When Joanne said she would do something, you could consider it done."

"She worked here as a waitress and then came back and worked the door for a while. She also was a bartender [and manager] at the Loading Dock [3702 North Halsted Street]," said Grant.

"Joanne De Corey was one of our waitresses here," Flint said, smiling. "You might have a packed house and she could still handle that whole floor all by herself, an amazing waitress. Later she went on to work at Loading Dock. Marvelous and intelligent. Her family disowned her when she was 16 or something for being gay and transsexual. These guys caught her one time by Bughouse Square and put lighter fluid on her and set her on fire, so she had some scars. Those guys went to jail. She was a longtime volunteer at Open Hand GroceryLand; she died a few years ago from AIDS complications."

Vital Bridges/Open Hand volunteer coordinator Lori Cannon recalled Joanne fondly. "Joanne ended her days as one of the finest examples of community service, dedicated to helping other men, women and children with AIDS," Cannon said. "She worked at the Open Hand GroceryLand food depository and took her responsibility to show up and do an exemplary job very seriously. She began as a bagger, brought on more volunteers, and became the premier receptionist. Whatever needed to be done, Joanne would do it. No question, no hesitation, she saw the bigger picture and would do whatever it took to make the clients' lives more comfortable."

Joanne De Corey was also profiled in the 2001 book Living With AIDS under the name, Joanne McAllister. The profile says the Forest Park, Illinois, native was honored as a devoted volunteer at both Open Hand and Test Positive Aware Network (she was named Volunteer of the Year by both organizations).

In a one-page interview, De Corey was asked about AIDS and the effect it had had on her life. When asked how HIV challenged her, she answered: "I don't see it as a real big challenge, it's just what you have to do. HIV has helped me with being comfortable with everything. I don't know why, but I realized what was important and what wasn't important. Being at the bars, being out, is not important."

De Corey went on to say that she was fine with having another year or possibly two left to live. When asked how she got to that point of acceptance, she answered: "You make lemonade. Ya know, you just make lemonade—and it's always been that way. This is the hand you're dealt, you deal with it. I've learned to be happy with what I have."

De Corey continued to contribute to the community to the best of her ability and lived another seven years with AIDS before passing away peacefully July 3, 2008.

Billy Mann

"Another bartender at the Baton was Billy Mann," Flint recalled. "Billy Mann worked at Sam's and then here. He was from Marseilles, Illinois. He was a great friend and a lonely person. He loved to drink straight vodka with a Coke chaser. He worked at the Redoubt for a while, too.

"I remember one night when I was still at The Chesterfield, he came in and was so excited and said, 'Oh, this guy asked me out for dinner.' I asked him where he was going, and he said he didn't know. So he got all dressed up and said he thought they were going to a place called the Crystal Palace. I said, 'Oh, I never heard of it.' So he came back the next day and said the guy came and picked him up and they went out for dinner, but instead of the Crystal Palace, the name of the place was White Castle.

"Poor Billy. He drank so much. When he was working at the Redoubt, I remember we closed for Christmas and he went home to his family. The next day he called and said, 'Jim, I can't come back right away, because they are going to do some tests and I have to be in the hospital.' I said, 'Fine, Billy, just let me know.' About three days later, he died of cirrhosis of the liver, and when they went in his house up on Fremont [Street] there were 1.75-liter [approximately 59.2-fluid-ounce] bottles underneath the bed and stacked high in the closets, where he drank that much vodka all the time."

Lennie Malina

"When I started working for Jim, I had left His 'n Hers and was debating between the Baton and the Bushes [3320 North Halsted Street]," Malina said. "I went through the pluses and minuses, and the deciding factor was that the Baton was established. I started as a bartender but, less than a year after that, I became manager of the Baton as well as the Annex 2. I gave that job 100 percent—beyond that, even. It was my life. It was nine years without a day off, or when I did have a day off it was to do some Continental preliminary in Florida, so it wasn't much of a day off at all."

Flint recalled Lennie with a smile. "Lennie went with us on a Florida trip," he said. "She was the only real woman with us. The girls were all out on the beach at Fort Lauderdale, and they were all out there sunning their breasts and showing them off—Chanel Dupree, Maya Douglas, Shanté and Ginger of course. The lifeguard was loving it, so he didn't say anything. Then all of a sudden these two little kids saw them and thought they were all Playboy bunnies. When the girls saw that, they screamed and covered themselves. Those kids followed us around for hours."

"I trained the staff as well," said Malina. "It sounds like a lot because it was. At the time, it was my family and my life. I had no other life, but there was such a feeling of family that it was OK. It was more than my job or my career. I was very close to the performers there—Andrea, Cherine, Leslie and Sheri. Ikey [bartender then at Annex 2] was my partner, and we saw each other at work."

"Lennie Malina, who was my lover at the time, was the manager of both Annex 2 and the Baton," said Irene "Ikey" Raczka. "Jim always says anymore that he can't take vacations, because he doesn't have someone like Lennie to run the places for him. Let me tell you, when it comes to dedication you could never ask for anything more. She would run it like it was her own business and work so hard for him."

"Part of this period, too, was when Jim was running for political office [mid-1980s], so he was around even less, so I was really in charge of things," said Malina. "I remember one time, boy, we got into it. The police all of a sudden decided they were going to come into clubs and everyone had to have an ID, whether it was a 25- or a 90-year-old. Everyone had to have one or they would close the place down. That was the new rule, and there was a lot of talk that it was going to be enforced. So, when I was taking reservations for the Baton, I told every person that it didn't matter what age you were, that you had to bring a driver's license or ID because of this new city rule.

"Well, Jim got wind of that, and I got the wrath of God. He had connections, so that probably wouldn't have happened to him anyway, but he told me, 'I can't believe you are saying that to our customers and turning them off from coming here.' And I told him, 'Look, you left me in charge and I did what I thought was the right thing to do.' We got into it, but it was like all our fights. We never stayed mad at one another for very long.

"I recall another time there was a gas leak between shows, and this was when people were still smoking up a storm at bars. So the Fire Department had to come, and they checked everything out and cleared up the leak. I remember standing on top of the fire truck with a megaphone, telling the 10 o'clock crowd that it was OK, the show would be starting but we would be seating about 10 minutes late. I told them because we just had a gas leak that there would be no smoking or lighting of anything during the show. And for the most part, people just sort of shrugged and came in anyway. I was so surprised that no one wanted their money back or wanted to reschedule.

"The job just got to be way too much after a while. If I gave less, it might have been OK, but I couldn't. I had to give it my all. There were so many times I tried to quit and Jim wouldn't let me. I would literally throw my keys at him and he would ignore it. Neither of us was acting very adult at the time.

"Strange dynamic there. Jim liked to stir things up. Sometimes I think he would create drama just because he liked the excitement. That was definitely a part of the mix.

"I worked there from 1979 to 1987, and then my mother passed. I kept telling Jim I was going to leave and to let me train someone. I finally just had to give him the keys and walk out, because he would never listen.

"Then he put his sister on the door, and he took over. I traveled around for a few months, mainly up the East Coast with just a pup tent, a stuffed animal and some clothes. I came back a while later and was working at Buddies' [3301 North Clark Street] and then part-time at the door at the Baton before moving to Germany."

Caissa Holyon

"Everyone calls me Cai. I came here from Milwaukee," said Cai Holyon. "I started here in May of 1992 and I had only been 21 for a couple of months. Jim needed a waitress. A mutual friend, Suzi Arnold, played on Jimmy's softball team, and I got the job, and that's how I met everyone here.

"When I first started, I was just so into the show. I was so enamored with the girls and so young. I was actually raised by a couple of drag queens.

"It's tough sometimes being the only girl, because although they may be impersonators, you have to remember that they're all men. As the only woman, I have experienced sexism, and I don't think a lot of it was intentional, but I think there is a sort of male entitlement, and I didn't know how to deal with that.

"I'm a crier. I'm one of those people that if you hurt my feelings I'm going to cry, and since they're all guys, they don't get it. There's an emotional aspect that sets me apart. Plus, as a biological woman, you go through different things in life that men just don't understand."

As to the sometimes-volatile nature of the Baton, Holyon laughed. "Sometimes I'm the peacekeeper in this dysfunctional family and sometimes I like to stir it up," she said. "Sometimes I'm the defiant one. I have a big mouth and I tend to have the most volatile fights with Jimmy because of this. I open my mouth and don't know when to shut up. That's caused us to have huge blowouts, but then five minutes later we're saying, 'I'm sorry, I love you, I'm sorry,' and we're fine. I've been fired six or seven times easily. 'You're suspended!' 'You're fired!'

"About two weeks ago we got in an argument, and he told me I was off for a week, and I said fine. One time we got in a huge fight outside, screaming. We were both wasted and I have no idea what it was about, but we were screaming at one another and crying and screaming and crying and shouting, 'How dare you!' Then he said, 'If you go in there and tell anyone we were fighting, you're fired,' and I said, 'Fine. I'll be fired.'

"I went in and said one thing, and it was 'goddamn, you said something,' and I said, 'I didn't say anything,' so then the shouting started all over again. That time was bad. It can be bad, but it means nothing. It's always over stupid stuff. The second one of us raises our voice, the other one gets so defensive that it erupts."

As to growing up at the Baton, Holyon said: "It was really rough in my 20s and it also entailed a lot of drinking. We all grew up together. Mimi, Monica, Cezanne and myself were a core group that hung out together, did things together, worked together. We used to go to Frankie Z's [435 North Clark Street] almost every night after work.

"I remember one time, though, we went to the Closet [3325 North Broadway] because we didn't want to go to Berlin [954 West Belmont Avenue] or Manhole [3458 North Halsted Street] and we needed a 4 o'clock bar. We bombarded the Closet, and we were with a couple other bartenders and servers from here. Wherever we'd go we would just be crazy. At the Closet that night, I bet the bartender made $300 in tips from us. We were literally putting wads and piles of cash on the bar."

As for the Baton, Holyon said: "I like bartending best, but I think I make more money working the floor. Gratuity is an automatic 16 percent, but you are welcome to leave more, and I am a good server, so I do have a lot of times where I get more. I serve anywhere from 45 to 50 people. I bartend on slower nights, Thursdays and Sundays. Chad and I are the fastest. They're tugging on you, pulling on you: 'Where is the bathroom?' 'Why can't I take pictures?' Taking pictures, that's a big one. Most of the performers try and have some control over their image."

"People love to take unflattering pictures, or maybe they just do [take bad photos]," said Ginger Grant. "A lot of times if you're on the stage above them and doing something, it's easy to get a bad shot. It is disruptive to the entertainers, and we like to be in charge of our image. We have to have some control over how we are presented to the public."

"They'll try to take pictures anyway," added Holyon. "They will wait until your back is turned but they'll try again. Chad [another waiter] just puts his hand in front of the camera. The clients will oftentimes openly defy you. We have to ask that they sit down in their chairs and be courteous so other people can see the show.

"The bachelorettes are more likely to get drunk and unruly. I had someone throw up last week. It happens all the time. It was right after we got new carpet, and she puked right in the front in the middle, during the opening production number on a slow night where there were only about 15 people here. Two days later, same thing. A woman was slumped in her chair and there was puke on the floor. It was really getting out of hand, so finally Jim just added a cleanup fee of $75 if that happens.

"It can get pretty wild in here. The craziest thing that ever happened was, 20 black girls and 20 white girls got up on their chairs and were ready to fight, because of the chair between the two groups and who was going to get that chair and who was going to move down. Lennie Malina was working the door and she went in. I don't know how she did it, but she somehow defused the situation.

"We make all the drinks one by one by hand, so it can be pretty hectic for a bit—especially with the bachelorette parties. You'll get an order and it will be one dry martini, one virgin strawberry daiquiri, one margarita, one strawberry margarita, one regular strawberry daiquiri, and one virgin strawberry margarita, all in one order. Hypnotic drinks are huge right now. They are the ones with the glow sticks. Those are $12.

"I think I am a little better with doing this because I do both. I respect the amount of work the bartender has, and I also know what the server is going through on the floor, so I am pretty good at knowing what it's like. I have perspective both ways. I am the only person that does both.

"We're always busy on Saturdays 365 days a year. In the spring and summer it tends to be more bachelorette-y and white girls, and the fall and winter tend to be more black girls. Lots of women, very rarely groups of men. I had a lot of men this past Saturday, and that was about 15 men all night in three sittings of a section of 50, and 15 was a lot, so that says something.

"We work with such a small staff. You schedule your days off and you can't call in sick. You have shifts; that's your shift and you show up. We've worked with every ailment you can imagine. There is nobody to replace you if you're sick. Nobody changes positions. Somebody literally has to die or move, for you to get a different station. Richie Saunders died, and Chris Garcia now works in the booth, and I got Chris' station. People stay here a long time."

In describing the difference between the two door positions, Holyon explained: "Working the door is where you stand at the podium and take IDs and mark off their seats on the seating chart. The booth is where you're in the box and sell tickets through the window. Chris Garcia has been in the box for 12 years, from 6:30 to 2, selling tickets and answering the phone.

"I don't know what else to say about the place other than, it has become such a huge part of my life—work and personal, and all that gets completely mixed up here. On one level it's a job, but the thing about working here is that there are so many other levels."

Kim Cleveland

"When Billy Cooper got fired, Kim Cleveland worked the light and sound booth, but mostly she worked the door," said Grant.

Flint added: "Kim Cleveland is probably one of the most talented people I've ever met for makeup and hair. She used to paint me when I'd get in drag. Nobody can do it like she does. She's Mimi's roommate and, when she comes to the Baton, you can always tell because all the girls' hair and makeup is even better than usual. Years ago she did lights and sound and did the door. For years and years nobody even realized Kim was a boy."

Tim Gideon

Tim Gideon came to Chicago from Tennessee for a visit and ended up going to work for a company in Evanston before getting involved in the bar scene, when he went to Carol's Speakeasy [1355 North Wells Street]. "I was David Boyer's assistant and worked in the office during the day and did all the liquor and all of that," Gideon said. "In the evenings, I worked at the bar at night and managed sometimes. I worked at a bar in Tennessee at 18, so I did have some experience in the environment.

"Carol's was fun, probably 95 percent gay, and Friday was dollar-drink night, which was always packed. I remember one time, for one International Mr. Leather party, we must have had 1,600 people in there—busy, busy place. Then when the stuff happened with Jeffrey Dahmer, that's what closed it. [After his capture, it was found that the popular club had been a "hangout" of serial killer Jeffrey Dahmer.]

"Oh, they were big there [at Carol's] for Halloween. We decorated for that for months. One time we did Indiana Jones and changed the place to fit with that theme, with cardboard on the walls and painted caves and boulders everywhere. Another year we did Batman. Another year we did Star Trek.

"I've worked here for Jim Flint since the 1990s. I started mainly with River North Travel agency and then went to the Baton about 1999. River North Travel started slowing down, and then when the airlines put all the caps on the commissions to something like $10 a ticket or whatever happened, we stopped. That was about 2005. Prior to that I did all the travel tickets and things for the Continental girls and all that. We don't have our [River North Travel] license anymore to sell tickets. Anymore, with everything online, it is so much cheaper for people to do it on their own anyway.

"At the Baton, I started as bar back and moved to bartender. I worked in the office Monday through Friday and then at the Baton on Friday and Saturday nights. Right now, the most popular drinks at the Baton are the hypnotic drinks, because they have glow sticks in them. If you take one tray out with the blue glowing drink, then all of a sudden they all want them. Those drinks feature all different kinds of vodka—bubblegum, cherry, pineapple, coconut—and they're very sweet.

"The shows are 8:30, 10:30 and 12:30 and, since the show is 90 minutes long, once the people leave we are cleaning and turning everything over for the next show, and everything is very precisely timed. Ten minutes to set the room and 20 minutes to seat the whole show. The latter two shows are tougher; the 8:30 is easier because they trickle in. I don't think we ever started a show late since I've been here—or very rarely, like once a decade."

"Slap on your lashes, put your dick up. We got a show to do," laughed Ginger.

"If the first number is not on 20 seconds after that overture, there goes Jimmy to see what the problem is," Gideon said. "And he will not be happy. There was only once that the show started late, when an amplifier went out and they had to change it. And one night my biggest nightmare came true, and they had me do lights because Jermaine had family problems."

Gideon also spoke of some changes to the bar itself. "The stage was moved back a little so there is more room for seating, and the bar has been extended—8 feet were added to the length of the bar, and the stage was shortened by about 5 feet. That was done after the incident at the E2." (On February 17, 2003, 21 people were killed and dozens injured as a result of a panic following a fight at the E2 nightclub at 2347 South Michigan Avenue.) Gideon continued, "More room was added for the existing client tables and not for any additional tables."

Gideon said that things "don't change much here. That's part of the charm, I think. The productions change, but not the spirit. I love when they have new productions. When they previewed the 'Single Ladies' production, the audience went crazy. Same for 'Cinema Italiano' from Nine—with all the red, and Mimi is totally nude in a red bodysuit with lace and the long sequined sleeves, and all the girls have matching dresses. The audience really goes up for that. To be here and see how people react—it feels pretty great to be a part of that magic."

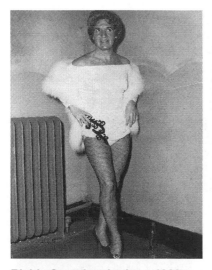

Richie Saunders in drag, 1960s.

Richie Saunders, 1990s.

Jim Flint and Richie Saunders.

Richie Saunders working the ticket booth at the Baton, 1990s.

Ginger Grant and Roy, a bartender at the Baton.

Lennie Malina.

Ken Nowakowski, Orlando del Sol and Ginger Grant.

Jesse Dugan.

Designer John Bradley and Mimi Marks.

Bobby Glaze.

Jim Flint's sister Serena works the door at the Baton.

Chris Garcia.

Cai Holyon.

Tim Gideon.

The Baton staff have fun on Halloween.

Flint with Billy Fantastic (William Kucharenko).

10

The River North Area

Jim Flint was a pioneer in the 1960s and 1970s development of Chicago's Near North Side business district. The area the Baton is located in is now unofficially called "River North," but when the bar started in 1969, it was a dangerous and risky place to open a business.

"The Seventies were a good era for the Near North neighborhood, but going back ten years and a few blocks up the street, things were not so rosy," wrote RJ Chaffin in his article, "A Slice of History: The Near North," in the GayLife issue of February 22, 1980. "Clark Street north of Grand but south of Chicago Avenue once wore the dubious honor of being the city's 'worst half mile.' A reporter for Chicago American informed readers that in July of 1961, 380 autos and trucks were stolen in that area; 13 persons were robbed at gunpoint; 108 residences and businesses were burglarized; 81 purses were snatched; and three women were raped (two more fought off their attackers). The hustling in this area was extreme."

It was in fact the gay bar business that began to turn that worst half-mile into the real-estate gold of River North today. Two of the pioneers in the district were the Baton at 430 North Clark Street and the Gold Coast at 501 North Clark. The first live DJ disco in the gay community came in 1972 with P.Q.'s, at 661 North Clark.

Another huge change in the neighborhood came the following year. Eddie Dugan's Bistro ("Nice people doing nice things for nice people," said the advertisement) opened its doors at 420 North Dearborn Street on May 31, 1973. The Bistro was the Studio 54 of Chicago, attracting celebrities and a different sort of gay crowd—those who wanted to dance. The Bistro was the focal point of the Chicago boogie-oriented nightlife until its closing on May 31, 1982.

The Bistro featured Lou Di Vito, the self-taught disc jockey who went on to win the top-DJ award from Billboard magazine. The website discomusic.com displays a clipping from an unidentified publication of the era, which mentions the award and praises Di Vito. It reads: "He [Di Vito] uses 1100 Technique turn tables that he would not trade for anything and has a pre-amp for each with a very elegant monitor system. His booth is encased in a plexi-glass, all of the speakers are J.B.L.'s including the 32 super tweeters in the ceiling. The Bistro definitely has one of the best sound systems in the nation."

Bistro DJ Jeff Berry shared his memories of that time. "When I moved to Chicago to work at Dugan's Bistro as alternate DJ for Lou Di Vito, I would often be at the Bistro even on my nights off, to listen to the music or watch the shows, if I wasn't working coat check," Berry said. "Dugan's Bistro was known as the 'Studio 54 of the Midwest.'" In the book Out and Proud in Chicago: An Overview of the City's Gay Community, Berry wrote: "On any given night you might bump into members of the Rolling Stones, Joseph P. Kennedy II, Bette Midler, Sylvester, Barry Manilow, Elton John, or Rudolf Nureyev, among others. All could be seen rubbing elbows on the dance floor or in the VIP lounge with newly liberated members of Chicago's gay community, as well as straight folks from the suburbs. At the same time you would be entertained by beefy dancers and the Bearded Lady, and mesmerized by the lighting wizardry of T.L. Noble under snow machines and NERF cannons."

In the Chicago Tribune's Variety section of March 23, 1980, Barbara Molotsky wrote of the Bistro: "One of the city's liveliest discos, Bistro is responsible for Chicago's birth of boogie. It continues to maintain great music offerings at the hand of deejay Lou DiVito and a most interesting crowd. Opened in 1973 by Edward Davison [Dugan], it was the first big disco in the city then catering to gays. Now it is a melange of every preference. The Bistro rocks 7 nights, providing some of the most unusual sight and sound entertainment around. There's a cover charge of $3 on weekends, $1 on Thursdays and Sundays, and no cover Monday–Wednesday."

On the disco.com website, patron Bruce D. explained that the second-to-last song played at the Bistro before it closed was "Don't Take Away the Music" by Tavares, and everyone in the DJ booth, including Noble and Di Vito, broke down crying. Then Di Vito laid the needle on the very last song played at Bistro, "Last Dance" by Donna Summer. After it ended, Di Vito sealed the disc in tape and wrote on it that the record would never be played at Paradise (2848 North Broadway), the new Dugan–Di Vito venue. The Bistro was their baby.

"I remember Bruce well and can attest to what he says," said Jeff Berry. "The only thing I'm not sure about is the Tavares song. I was down in the basement talking to Eddie Dugan at the time, but that sounds about right. I know that Diana Ross' 'Ain't No Mountain High Enough' was one of the last three songs, probably before Tavares."

In the September 1973 issue of The Chicago Gay Crusader, columnist Margaret Wilson, a member of Chicago Lesbian Liberation, wrote about a new lesbian bar in the area—Ms., at 661 North Clark Street, which took over from P.Q.'s. Marge Summit and Chee Chee were owners. Summit later opened His 'n Hers, which over the course of its history had three locations: 2316 North Lincoln Avenue, 944 West Addison Street, and 5820 North Broadway. The Ms. float in the 1974 Gay Pride Parade was controversial. The lesbian newspaper Lavender Woman condemned the float with a label of "most insulting to women" and "most messed-up lesbians of 1974."

"That was so stupid," scoffed Summit. "It was because Ms. [the bar] had won this award as best lesbian bar, so there was this lovely dancer from California, and I painted her gold and put her on the float like an Oscar or an award. She was wearing pasties and a G-string but the rest was all gold, and whenever the float would hit a bump her boobs would bounce, and people would say, 'Oh, my God, she's real!' I thought it was cool and fun, and the thought of them taking offense really pissed me off."

When asked how she came to own the Ms. bar, Summit said: "I was at P.Q.'s and talking with Paul—who wasn't the owner, he was just the guy on the license. I said, 'You got a good business here,' and it was, the place was packed all the time. But I said, 'When Eddie Dugan opens the Bistro a couple blocks away, you are going to be able to run through this place with a pool cue sideways and not hit a soul.' And that's exactly what happened. So, after Togetherness closed, I came back to P.Q.'s, and the real owner said, 'Let's talk about it.' I said, 'OK, the deal is, I will run it for you, but I run it my way. If I run it, you stay out of it and only come for your pay when it's closed.'

"When I moved in, it was such a toilet, such a pigsty. I had a good business for a year or year and a half. I had celebrities come in, like comic Rusty Warren and cabaret singer Frances

Faye. Then another bar [C.K.'s, at 1425 West Diversey Parkway] opened and took all my best clients. I was left with a bunch of rough kids. Finally, I was tired of having to frisk everyone at the door for weapons, so I decided to close and open His 'n Hers on Lincoln. As far as I knew, we were mostly all fronts [for other owners]. The first bar I ever really owned was His 'n Hers at the second location underneath the Addison el stop by Wrigley Field."

Another staple of the area was the leather dance bar Ozone, at 112 West Hubbard Street. "It was a great dance club," recalled Paul Yinger. "You entered through the alley, and it was amazing to be there, because upstairs there was a railing that went all the way around and you could look down at the dance floor, and there was another nice bar upstairs there."

During the heyday of disco, members could see Sylvester in concert at Ozone for $5 ($8 for nonmembers). Bart Lombard, a former bartender at the Ozone and then general manager of three of Dr. Steve Rempas' bar businesses, shared some of his great memories of tending bar at Ozone, in Sukie de la Croix's September 3, 2003, "Street Walkin' With Sukie" column in Windy City Times: "In addition to Sylvester, there were concerts by the late disco diva Vicki Sue Robinson and the attractive gay singer Paul Parker, among them.

"I started working in the bars in Chicago in 1977, Alfie's and Le Pub, as well as the old haunts of the Brownstone, Cheeks, Glory Hole, Loading Zone, Ozone and finally as general manager of Dr. Steve's Loading Dock, Men's Room and Halsted's," said Lombard. "I left Chicago in 1988 but the memories of those days are still vivid, where the bar employees were 'celebrities' of sorts and the bars merely served as their home base. ... The first gay bar I went to was actually by mistake; it was Alfie's [at 900 North Rush Street] in 1976. ... What followed was an 11-year odyssey of the Chicago nightlife and my personal journey as a gay man living in a time of outrageous hilarity and antics, yet monumental change ... .

"I met Dr. Steve Rempas after I was hired to bartend at Ozone. ... We became very good friends and I can tell you that Ozone was the wildest bar I had ever worked. The M.A.F.I.A. club [Mid-America Fists in Action, for men interested in the art of handball] would gather at our bar every Friday night, and for a brief time Ozone was THE bar in Chicago.

"I'll never forget the night I really got to know Dr. Steve ... a couple of other bartenders from Ozone were off and having a drink at my bar. In the corner of my eye, I could see the upstairs of the bar being swarmed by the Chicago Police Department. Not wanting to be arrested, I asked the one off-employee, Les, to 'watch my bar for a sec' and then ran to the basement and hid in the basement ceiling while Les and everyone else working there were arrested. It was scary then, but so funny now, because I was hiding in the ceiling of the office basement, and the police were there below me allowing Larry to count the bar's receipts for the night and put them in the safe, and I can remember the police saying they were missing one bartender but couldn't find him.

"So I whispered down to Larry, 'Larry, it's me, Bart. I'm in the ceiling,' and he said 'Stay there.' So I did, for what seemed like an hour. The police had left, the bar was locked and I was locked inside, so I called the owner, Dr. Steve, and told him my plight, and he drove down and unlocked the bar and got me home. Les, however, didn't think my switcharoo was too funny, as he ended up spending the night in jail."

A Starbucks now stands at the corner of Hubbard and Clark streets, the old location of Sunday's, 430 North Clark, where DJ Artie Feldman spun. Even earlier, the old Baton had been there, in the days when it was called Smitty's Show Lounge, and it became the Ramrod after the Baton moved. Sunday's was easily recognizable by the upside-down Old Style beer sign hanging above the door. "I think I put that up originally when that was the Baton," said Flint. "The only reason I did it that way was to bring attention to it."

Karen Ross recalled: "I worked at Sunday's, first as a cocktail waitress and later as a bartender. It was actually called Sunday's Child because of that old poem that starts, 'Monday's child is full of grace' and ends with 'And the child born on the Sabbath day is fair and wise and good and gay.' We had so much fun, a great crew—David Peckham, Michael Karlin, Robin Ward, Jack Williamson and Chuck Rodocker. In fact, when Chuck [Rodocker] left to go to Redoubt and later open Touché on Lincoln, I got promoted from cocktail waitress to bartender. Sam Olin was the manager."

Beside Sunday's, the lesbian bar Marilyn opened at 432 North Clark Street in 1981. It was a 4 a.m. bar, touted as "a disco room for hot women only!" The same year, Druids moved in around the corner at 112 West Hubbard Street. It featured live music as well as 25-cent beers on Sunday nights. It had formerly been The Ranch, 112–114 West Hubbard.

Across the street was My Brother's Place, 111 West Hubbard, described at the time as "a quiet little restaurant with exceptional food—not cheap, but good."

Bill Kelley remembered: "It was on the second floor, very well decorated, and it was a gay restaurant and I liked that. It wasn't a coffee shop but an actual gay restaurant. I remember in the entranceway there was an urn of huge peacock feathers as a decoration."

My Brother's Place had great bartenders, Jerry Lee and Gary; a very popular chef in Dennis; plus waiters Jim and Bill.

"I can tell you about My Brother's Place," Marge Summit said. "Good restaurant there on the second floor. In fact, that's where I saw Cardinal [John] Cody. [Cody was the Roman Catholic archbishop of Chicago from 1965 until his death in 1982.] He used to bring his hustlers in there for dinner. He was there in a full-length black mink coat. People don't want to hear that. He tricked with Jerry, the bartender there, and I said, 'Jerry, you're a good-looking guy. What are you doing seeing the likes of him?' and he showed me this gold necklace he was wearing and said, 'That's why.'"

The bar directly below was Oasis, 111 West Hubbard. Also in the area were places such as a venerable gay bar called The Haig, 800 North Dearborn Street, with a "cocktail lounge" neon sign that once elicited tongue-in-cheek comment from a Chicago Daily News gossip columnist in the early 1970s when some of its important letters burned out. The building at 61 West Hubbard was the site of Togetherness, and later Stars, and then The Roadhouse, described as "a friendly neighborhood bar atmosphere in the heart of Chicago's gay night life."

The Trip, at 27 East Ohio Street, was the focus of a court case taken to the Illinois Supreme Court (see Chapter 3). The New Jamie's, 1110 North Clark Street, featured some cross-dressing as well as some hustlers. However, the hot bar for picking up rent boys was the New Flight, 420 North Clark. It was a notorious hustler bar advertised as "a friendly place to meet people—where you always get treated fairly." Eddie Dugan, owner of the Bistro glitter palace, was heard to have aptly described the New Flight as "a bar without gimmicks. Just hustlers!" The New Flight's logo featured Pegasus, the winged horse that sprang from the neck of the mythological Medusa when she was beheaded by Perseus. It was a mainstay of the River North gay area starting in 1975.

Richard Cooke recalled: "The New Flight on Hubbard was the place to pick up hustlers. You'd go there and get a beer and then go to the back by the pool tables. That's where all the best-looking hustlers hung out."

In the same area was Alfie's, 900 North Rush Street, "Chicago's Hottest Cocktail Bar," where the disco DJs were Peter Lewicki, Michael Graber and Sam McGill, and where Pepe Peña (future co-owner of Sidetrack bar) used to tend bar. Alfie's featured dancing and live entertainment as well as Monday Madness, at which all drinks were 75 cents. According to Sukie de la Croix's April 9, 2003, column in Windy City Times, "On October 22nd 1980 Alfie's was closed down by the IRS for nonpayment of taxes. A public auction of the equipment seized by Federal authorities was held Nov. 6 on the premises of the bar."

A popular 1970s gay black disco, the Ritz, was at 933 North State Street and featured Quad-Sound. The staff included Bill, Dave, Gail, Gary, Corky, Popcorn and Jay Jay. It was described as a friendly neighborhood bar during the day, and at night the large rectangular island bar and medium-sized dance floor took on a disco mood. On September 2, 1981, the Ritz was destroyed as a result of arson. A GayLife article from September 18, 1981, reads: "Detectives of the Chicago Police Department's Bomb and Arson Unit determined the origin of the September 2 fire by observing burn patterns in the dance floor area. When floorboards were pulled up, they said gasoline had seeped through. ... Earlier lab reports had confirmed that the June 2 fire had been deliberately set, according to investigators."

There were many other gay bars close by, including the strip-drag nitery Nite Life (933 North State Street) which became Walton Street Waterworks in 1984. Among the rest were Harlow's (which eventually replaced The Trip at 27 East Ohio Street), Icon (710 North Clark Street), Sir Bentley's Pub (640 North State Street), The Gate (650 North Dearborn Street), Big Daddy's (848 North Clark Street), Foster's (868 North State Street), Welcome (22 East Chestnut Street), the Loading Zone and later the pretty step-down bar TJ's on Oak (46 East Oak Street), Poofy's (508 North Clark Street) and Ifs, Ands and Burt's (5 West Superior Street).

In Sukie de la Croix's May 14, 2003, "Chicago Whispers" column in Windy City Times, he wrote: "Stage 618 at 618 N. Clark St. had its Grand Opening on Jan. 2, 1976. The bar featured go-go-boys Bobby, Jimmy, Joey and Greg, was advertised as being 'completely gay-staffed' and was rumored to be 'syndicate owned.'" Nevertheless, for a while the well-known gay activist Ira Jones took an active management role there.

The Inner Circle opened on Valentine's Day of 1975 at 233 East Erie Street with Andy Warhol superstar Holly Woodlawn appearing there for the first two weeks. (Earlier, the bar had been in two other locations: on Armitage Avenue near Clark Street and then at 1842 North Wells Street.) As reported by Sukie de la Croix in his February 26, 2003, column, other acts at the Inner Circle included comedian and actress Marilyn Sokol, female impressionist Arthur Blake, Betty Rhodes (the cabaret singer who died of cancer in January 1988), and Gotham, an openly-gay-male musical and comedy trio. The bar included a small dance floor and served lunch and supper. It was gutted by fire (arson suspected) that May.

For a while, at the King's Ransom (20 East Chicago Avenue), every Sunday was Hot Pants Night. The bar had popular Chicago bartenders Dwight Smith and Stan Walker. Danny Pierson, another personable bartender there, was supportive of Mattachine Midwest in the 1960s and '70s. The King's Ransom also was the second gay bar in the city (after the Normandy) to allow same-sex dancing.

In Sukie de la Croix's "Chicago Whispers" column in the Windy City Times of September 19, 2001, "Wally" described the King's Ransom in a bit more detail: "It was very calm there, and was what they called, at that time, a wrinkle room [a bar frequented by older patrons]. I hit it off there too because there were people you could actually talk to, have a decent conversation with.

"The bar itself was a kind of horseshoe, but at an angle. It was on the garden level, and you had to go down a couple of steps to get into the bar. You walked in and there was a living room set up with a couch and then you went down a couple of steps to the bar. There was a fireplace in the corner.

"It was very pleasant and to me they were old men, but now they'd be young men to me, because most of the clients were in their mid-to-late 30s, or early 40s. I enjoyed it there, because I fit in, but I fit in most any place. I used to go to all the bars. The Near North Side was my kingdom, whether it be the Gold Coast, the Haig, the King's Ransom, whatever ... ."

On the seamier side of things were Leslie's Adult Books (731 North Clark Street), the Adam Adult Movie Arcade (49 West Chicago Avenue), the Adonis Bookstore (6 East Walton Street), the Ohio and State Health Club (9 East Ohio Street), and the Wacker Health Club (674½ North Clark Street), which in its 1974 GayLife newspaper ad boasted "over 40 years at the same location."

C.H.A.P.S. at 116 West Hubbard Street claimed to be "more than a bathhouse ... more than a bookstore ... ". C.H.A.P.S. was a private club with an alley entrance and a $5 membership. Originally, prices varied. From 8 a.m. to 6 p.m., rooms were $6 and lockers $3, a slight saving from the $9 and $5 regular prices. Wednesday and Thursday specials offered rooms for $7 and lockers for $2. Eventually, a much simpler flat fee of $4 for lockers was implemented, though room prices continued to vary.

The Newberry Theatre was located at 854 North Clark Street—"all the best in all male films." The Newberry opened in 1914, had seating for approximately 700 and was named for its proximity to the renowned Newberry Library. It became a porn theater in the early 1970s (briefly straight, then gay) and closed around 1977. The building was subsequently demolished.

The nearby Image Theater (originally the Standard Theater, built in 1913), at 750 North Clark Street, also boasted the finest in all-male erotic entertainment; it was open noon to midnight with special midnight showings on weekends. Admission was $6. In Clark Street's earlier skid-row days, when the theater would still attract a mixture of gay and derelict customers, it sometimes had almost as many gay men in its basement restroom as it had men who were awake in the auditorium. In July and August 1981, police raided the Image on "prostitution" charges. At that time, because sodomy was no longer illegal and solicitation to have unpaid sex wasn't a crime either, a common harassment technique was to up the ante by alleging that men illegally offered or agreed to have sex for money, which was illegal. This type of police entrapment took place over several decades.

Chuck Renslow's businesses in the area included partnership in the nearby Club Chicago baths, 609 North LaSalle Street, which advertised, "When you're ready for the real thing ... " and "Club Baths is a good place to come!" Renslow also opened the Barracks Hotel, "a hotel for men," at 506 North Clark Street—basically a hookup spot, right across from his Gold Coast bar. He also was an owner of the token-taking XXX peep-show arcade called the Machine Shop, 504 North Clark, so named because of all the machinery needed to run the many projectors, as well as a smaller sister establishment, the Tool Box, 404 North Clark, which featured plastic glass partitions between booths and glory holes aplenty. (It was the Tool Box that ushered manager Roger "RJ" Chaffin into the video business. He eventually opened RJ's Video, which then moved from the Near North Side on Clark Street to 3452 North Halsted Street.)

Renslow also ventured into the restaurant business with the Grubsteak, 508 North Clark Street. A description said that "delicious ground beef sandwiches stand out here, with other items on the menu too. Reasonable prices, Western decor. Not fancy. Open after bars close for late-late night eating." Also closely associated with Renslow was the Bob Maddox and Frank Goley leather store, Male Hide Leathers, which began as the Leather Cell in The Pit of the Gold Coast before outgrowing the space and taking a storefront at 66 West Illinois Street, though it was still connected to The Pit via an underground passage.

Steve Toushin of the Bijou Theatre recalled the neighborhood. "It was great. There was nothing like it," he said. "It was all warehouses, so it would be quiet after everyone left work, then about 9 it would come to life and stay hopping until 5 in the morning. I had two businesses down there, both massage parlors and whorehouses: Big Bertha's at 109 West Hubbard and the Crazy Horse Saloon at 114 West Hubbard, right next door to the New Flight. … And when the Crazy Horse closed, I eventually opened a bathhouse called The White Elephant [Bath Lounge] in that location for a while."

In the counterculture progression of the area, it's important to mention the opening of O'Banion's in June 1978 at 661 North Clark Street. According to the Chibarproject.com: "Following the demise of Chicago's first punk club, Le Mer Vipere [La Mère Vipère,] when it burned down in 1977, a new bar by the name of O'Banion's opened up at the northeast corner of Clark & Erie in River North and quickly became a Chicago legend. O'Banion's was not exactly 'aesthetically pleasing' or even 'clean,' but it did play host to a litany of local talent and national acts like the Dead Kennedys, Hüsker Dü and The Replacements. This was a far cry from its previous incarnations as a gay bar [P.Q.'s and Ms.], the largest strip club in Chicago and at one point a 'Bugs' Moran hangout. As punk rock yielded to new wave, so did the neighborhood to gentrification and O'Banion's was sold and turned into an upscale restaurant. Though it only existed for four years [closing in February 1982], its influence on Chicago music can be felt today in such venues as Metro, Empty Bottle, Neo and Exit."

The gay community was at the very center of this new direction in music. O'Banion's predecessor, La Mère Vipère, was the world's first punk dance club. It began as a gay bar, a satellite of another gay bar owned by Noë Boudreau named the Snake Pit (2132 North Halsted Street). La Mère held its first "Anarchy Night" on Mother's Day 1977, at the suggestion of Mike "Sparkle" Rivers, a La Mère bartender who also worked at Sounds Good Records, one of the few Chicago record stores to carry the latest punk releases from England.

The noted New York drag artist and playwright Charles Busch (Psycho Beach Party, The Tale of the Allergist's Wife, Vampire Lesbians of Sodom, etc.) was a Northwestern University graduate and, while still living in Chicago at the beginning of his career in 1976 and 1977, performed on La Mère's stage. One production was Old Coozies, his short one-act, two-actor takeoff on the Bette Davis and Miriam Hopkins film Old Acquaintance. Another was his short play Myrtle Pope: The Story of a Woman Possessed, in which he and fellow actors parodied Hollywood women's movies.

Jumbo Jarry's Hot Dog Stand had opened back in June 1962 when the area was still "Chicago's worst half-mile." It offered hot dogs and meatball sandwiches, Italian beef, chicken, chili, fries and by several accounts even a drug dealer on the premises. Seeing the transformation of the neighborhood, Jumbo Jarry's changed along with it, becoming a huge gay hangout and eatery pre- and post-barhopping. Jumbo Jarry's tolerance was even expressed in its slogan, "Your sex life is none of our business, but our hot dogs are." The stand was across the street from the Gold Coast bar, and its front windows were prime real estate for watching the street action.

"Jumbo Jarry's was nasty," Richard Cooke said. "I think Jumbo Jarry's was just painted on the door. They had those long fluorescent lights, and there were a lot of those No-Pest Strips hanging from the ceiling filled with flies. You ordered at the window and then they had a standing window ledge, so you stood there and watched all the leathermen outside connecting. The other thing about Jumbo Jarry's was, you must never, ever order the chili."

Lori Cannon added, "And their fries—best grease in the Midwest … of course, we were all so liquored up that any selection would be scrumptious!"

Warren Williamson agreed. "You know, I still remember those burgers, they were so bad they were good," he said. "Almost 40 years later, and I can remember the taste of it. I'd die for one of them. And their chili dogs."

The late RJ Chaffin shared his memories of that time: "After a big night, everyone who closed the Gold Coast, Redoubt, or even the Bistro would all go get something to eat either at Jumbo Jarry's, or they'd go hang out at the Oak Tree on Oak and Rush [streets]."

Baton emcee Ginger Grant recalled meals with the Baton doorman Richie Saunders at the Oak Tree. "That was always a big social place for people who worked and partied in the area. Many times, a few of us from work would go there and people would eavesdrop because Richie was so crazy, and he'd turn around and scream, 'Pull up a chair so you can fucking eavesdrop properly.'"

"We would close at 5 a.m. on Saturdays [Saturday nights]," said Patrick Finnegan Renslow, speaking of the Gold Coast in a 1995 interview with Jack Rinella. "The sun would be up [by the time we got out of there] in the summer, and we would go to a place called [the] Little Corporal on Wacker Drive [1 East Wacker] for eggs Benedict and then go to bed about 10 and wake up at 5 or 6 p.m."

Another iconic establishment in the Baton neighborhood was right across the street. Anyone at the Baton will attest to the importance of Frankie Z's (435 North Clark Street) in the story of the Baton. The popular Near North bar-restaurant with a neighborhood feel was there for decades before closing in early 2011. As a result, it became a popular post-work destination for many of the Baton staff.

"Oh, yes, Frankie Z. When he first opened, I would go over and talk with him, and I knew his brother because they owned Z's on Dearborn [Street]," said Flint. "They were there for years and years. I had this crush on this straight guy. He was just like his dad, a real jewel. I'd walk in at 11 or noon and he'd say, 'Let's have a cocktail, Jim.' And I'd say, 'No, Mr. Zimmerman, I can't drink this early.' Frankie was very much like his dad."

Cai Holyon added: "My biggest memory of all of us is just going out night after night after night. We'd all hang out at Frankie Z's almost every night after work—Cezanne, Mimi, Monica, Jesse and Bobby. We hung out at Frankie Z's because it was right across the street. It closed only a few months ago after 35 years. For 10 solid years it seemed like we would go there every night after work. It was a straight bar but he was an excellent neighbor and he loved Jimmy."

Community activist Joey McDonald remembered another feature of the neighborhood back in the day. "There was a drug store called Cosmo's [Cosmopolitan Drugs] on the corner of Clark and Chicago, and I remember the name because in their window they had a T-shirt with hippie stick-figure people on it, and where the eyes were supposed to be were flowers, and the logo on the T-shirt was 'I Get My Drugs at Cosmo's.' I bought that T-shirt and wore it. The great thing was—everyone got it and thought it was funny," he said.

This cluster of gay and lesbian businesses and other establishments was more than just a shopping or partying district. The ramifications and underlying effect were much more profound. This conglomeration of taverns and other venues brought people together as never before and helped accelerate and solidify a sense of gay unity in Chicago in the pre- and post-Stonewall era. We saw our numbers. We felt the sense of community. We were growing and boldly making ourselves known by in fact claiming a territory. It was from these bars and businesses that a political consciousness grew and was strengthened.

Gay organizations came to the Near North area as well. For a while, Mattachine Midwest met in the area at the Red Cross headquarters at 43 East Ohio Street. Mattachine Midwest was one of the first enduring gay organizations in the city and was in existence from 1965 to the mid-1980s. It was formed chiefly by a civil-rights activist and star encyclopedia salesman named Robert Basker (under the pseudonym Robert Sloane), aided by such others as Ira Jones and Pearl Hart.

Mattachine Midwest began as an organization dealing with gay political matters and social-service needs. The goal was "to improve the 'legal, social and economic status of the homosexual.'" Besides offering referrals to sources of legal, religious, psychological and other professional services and holding monthly socials, it focused on the escalating police harassment at the time and produced a politically conscious newsletter. Eventually the group moved more from the political arena and into the education and social-service sectors. Mattachine Midwest was key to laying the foundations for future GLBT organizations.

One of those subsequent groups, which also operated in the area, was the Chicago Gay Alliance. Co-founded by activists who included Gary Chichester, Jerrold E. Cohen, and Nick Kelly, CGA created Chicago's first gay and lesbian community center, which existed from 1971 to 1973. According to Cohen's Chicago Gay and Lesbian Hall of Fame biography, "While walking his dog, he happened on a house for rent at 171 West Elm Street. That house became the city's first Gay Community Center." The two-story brick cottage was used as a meeting place that hosted rap groups, consciousness-raising sessions, social events and the convening of various organizations. CGA had pride events as well as movie nights and even a gay art fair, and it tried to model its social-change efforts on those of New York's Gay Activists Alliance.

Flint's Baton Show Lounge also provided a meeting space for numerous groups and organizations (sporting, political, social and other types) during this time. It increasingly became a hub for community activity and involvement. It was an especially popular venue for community fundraisers of every sort. This active presence as a meeting place only increased as AIDS came to the fore during the 1980s.

"The area was incredible," Karen Ross said. "Everyone got along. All that mattered was that at the end of the weekend you knew you would be back again the next weekend. There was no place better. Kids today don't know what they missed."

Marge Summit added: "You could go in anywhere, any bar, and you always knew people. You had friends everywhere because everyone was friendly. We were a tight community. If someone was in a jam, you would help them even if you didn't know them. That's just what you did as a community."

Left: Jim Flint in front of the Baton and River North Travel, 1990s.

Below: A photo strip with images of the outside and inside of the River North Travel and Baton locations on Clark Street.

11

Miss Continental

The annual Miss Continental contest, started by Jim Flint in 1980, began as a direct result of the Miss Gay America pageant.

The Miss Gay America pageant was first held at the Watch Your Hat & Coat Saloon in Nashville in 1972. Norma Kristie, representing Arkansas, won the title that year, and in 1975 Kristie purchased the pageant from the previous owner.

As the pageantry system continued to grow, it evolved along the lines of the mainstream Miss America contest, with regional contests sending state representatives to the national competition. Contestants were judged in categories of interview, evening gown and talent, with a sportswear/contemporary-fashion category added later.

Because of the regulations of the Miss Gay America contest, many professional female impersonators were barred from competing, because they had surgical enhancements or used female hormones. The title guaranteed the winner bookings at every state preliminary held during the titleholder's year. For the winner, the MGA crown turned what was often local and sporadic work into a full-time job.

Since many transgender performers who have had enhancements or hormone treatments rely upon such bookings as a primary source of income, it seemed only natural that a system would evolve to meet their needs. But the birth of the Miss Continental system wasn't quite as clean and natural as one might hope. It involved Jim Flint and his temper—and his efforts resulted in a new national pageant system.

Birthing Pains

"I entered [Miss Gay America] because in the late 1970s I wanted to see what it was like," said Flint. "The rule was, you had to be there at 8 a.m., so we got there at 8 a.m., so there were something like 16 people not there. So then we were going to wait until 1 o'clock at the Sweet Gum Head in Atlanta." (The Sweet Gum Head opened in 1971 at 2284 Cheshire Bridge Road and was Atlanta's premier drag club–disco.)

"So, I went along with that. It got to be 1 o'clock and they still weren't there, so then they said we are going to give these people until 7 that night," Flint said. "So, I raised my hand, and the person at the pageant said, 'What's the problem?'

"I said the problem I had was that the rule was 8 this morning. 'We flew all night, we worked until 3:30 in the morning. We caught the first flight, and this little queen over here took three or four buses to get here. We're all here. That was the rule and I think the pageant should be closed now. If they're not here, they're not here.' She took a vote on it and we won, so they closed the pageant [to latecomers].

"I also felt there was some discrimination going on. There were people right there that they wouldn't let in because they'd had body enlargements. One had silicone. Another was taking hormones. I said, 'You are discriminating against them, but you are discriminating against us also by having the pageant open [to those who are late].'

"As the pageant went on that week, I remember sportswear was the category. To me, that was swimsuit or wet suit, but this little girl from Indianapolis had a red blouse on and jeans and boots and a lasso. They thought of sportswear as suits with fur and whatnot—like something you would wear to a sporting event or the races. This judge was standing in the hallway, and she was just criticizing this girl, and so I said, 'Do you think it is right for a judge to be out here criticizing a contestant like that?' She said, 'What do you mean?' I said, 'You're really putting that little girl down, and I think of it as sportswear, too.'

"She told me I should be quiet or she'd disqualify me. I said, 'No, you don't have to do that because I am getting out right now.' I said, 'You shouldn't even be judging the pageant and talking like that. Two weeks ago you were so drunk at a pageant you set your fur on fire.'

"About that time the owner of the pageant came up and was about to open her mouth, and I said, 'Don't say one word, because I've been waiting to slap you upside the head for three days.' So we walked out. Leslie [Rejeanné] and I both walked out. We went and were getting our things, and then the owner said, 'You can't take your stuff out until the pageant ends,' and I said, 'You and who else are going to stop us?' So we left."

"When he started Miss Continental at Miss Gay America, I was there," said a future Mr. Continental, Tony DeSario. "Trust me, there is an entire lobby full of people to corroborate this story. There was no way not to notice. He shouted at Norma Kristie in that lobby, 'I'll start my own contest, and it'll be fair and better than anything you've ever done.' And he did, too. Continental has a reputation for being classy, and it is the cream of the crop when it comes to pageants."

A Glittering Debut

By this time, Flint was a successful businessman as the owner of several gay bars, and he also had event experience, having run his Costumes on Review balls in Chicago since the late 1960s.

"After my problems with Miss Gay America, my friends said I should start my own pageant," Flint said. "The two to really encourage me were Ernesto Perez and Woody Brooks in Atlanta. Ernesto was a Cuban designer who did window design at a lot of the bigger stores. He got me going in the beginning. They both encouraged me and said they'd help me start a pageant. Then Raphael Velasco from San Antonio, Dan Fraser from Orlando, Skip Mackall, and Allan Gelman, who owned Twit magazine [a Texas gay and lesbian entertainment news magazine]. It was hard on those guys, since they were all involved in Miss Gay USA. They were helping me but still wanted to keep their loyalty."

(In 1985, Miss Gay America promoter Jerry Bird purchased the bankrupt Miss Gay USA pageant. In the mid-1990s, the Miss/Mr. pageant became Miss Gay USofA after a cease-and-desist demand was made by Miss USA owner Donald Trump.)

"Skip, Dan, Raphael and Allan all really got behind me and showed me how to explore and get others around the country to start a franchise or get involved in the Continental contest," said Flint. "I couldn't have made it without those guys and their advice, support and expertise."

In 1980, Flint created the Miss Continental USA contest. He vowed to make it inclusive of all levels of female impersonation, with enhancements and hormones allowed, but no surgical genital removal. Contestants were scored in interview, swimwear, talent and evening gown categories, plus an onstage question for the finalists. The first Miss Continental was Chilli Pepper, who won the title from the pool of 14 contestants gathered for the pageant at Chicago's Park West music venue. Chilli has never had implants, and several who have subsequently won the title have not. However, in the years since its inception, the Continental Pageantry System has become renowned for its "titty girls," or pre-op transsexual contestants.

Flint named the pageant Miss Continental in homage to one of his favorite bars, which was a home away from home when he was in the Navy. "I'd leave base every night and we'd all meet at the Continental on Boush Street in Norfolk, Virginia. I was an impressionable age, late teens, early 20s—and it sure made an impression. I loved that place. For a contest name, Continental had a good ring to it because it sounded so inclusive.

"I talked to them over at the Park West [322 West Armitage Avenue], and we got the room. We only had 13 contestants and a winner, but it was a big success. Chilli Pepper was our first Miss Continental, in 1980. Every year it just seemed to keep getting bigger and better."

When Chilli Pepper won the title, her court was second runner-up Dina Jacobs and first runner-up Andrea Nicole.

The Park West was and continues to be a popular venue for many of the Continental pageants. Former Park West special events coordinator Barbara Supeter recalled the early years. "The Park West opened in, I believe, 1977 or '78 and quickly closed because the reviews were something like, 'They have a million-dollar joint with a nickel sound system.' So I came on after they closed and were ready to reopen in March 1979," Supeter said. "I began as a receptionist and eventually became special events coordinator.

"I started working with Jim almost immediately. I recall the first Miss Continental, the Halloween balls, some sort of drag fashion show, as well as several fundraisers for Jim. He always had the crowd. What a force of nature. It amazed me how he would run around and seemed to be wildly throwing all these things together and yet somehow, by the fact of his doing it so many times or maybe by his sheer will, it would come together into a wonderful show.

"As events coordinator at the Park West, I would have a lot of meetings with Jim, and I'll never forget him always coming in with his pants and polo shirt, and then the first time I saw him as Felicia, Chilli Pepper pointed and said, 'There she is, that's Felicia,' and I couldn't believe it. I didn't recognize him at all.

"Jim had a temper and he could explode. I remember the first time it happened to me. Oh, the size of it just crushed me. I was so hurt, and Chilli pulled me aside and said, 'Oh, no, honey, he don't mean it.' And he doesn't. He blows up and then is over it, and it's on to the next thing."

A Tight Ship

"Something else we wanted to do different with Continental is, so many of the other pageants went on for four or five days—talent would be one day and swimsuit might be another. It would just go on and on," explained Flint. "The other contests go from Monday to Saturday. Ours is Sunday and Monday. All of the Continentals are two days. We go two days, have more contestants, and finish it in three to four hours.

"All the preliminary competition happens the first day—we do interviews, talent, swimwear, formalwear. And then the next day we have the competition—we have the parade of candidates, pick the Top 12. Then the slates are wiped clean and they do swimwear, talent, formal-wear—we pick the Top Five, and then there is the final interview, and then we name the runners-up and we have the new Miss Continental.

"It's simple, it's fast, it's exciting. I think it also gives the performers a good taste of what the fast-paced nature of this business can be like, if they don't already know. Contestants are marked down for being late. On several occasions, that has determined the finalists."

"At Continental, we always compete with ourselves from the year before, so really the next year's contest begins a week after the contest is over and the tape or DVD for that competition is put together," Flint pointed out. "We're always looking to expand and improve."

Currently, Continental has four separate contests or pageants. "We have Miss Continental, of course," said Flint. "Miss Continental Elite is for female impersonators over age 40, and that one is great because it's really the seasoned veterans. They know all the tricks. There is also Mr. Continental for gay men. Miss Continental Plus is for performers 225 pounds or over. We have had to check that a couple times. We have a scale right there.

"On other occasions, for the general Miss Continental, a couple queens have told me a couple contestants have had the operation. So we took them in the back with two other people and checked them to make sure they hadn't had the operation. We've had a few transition after their year as Continental, like Chanel Dupree, Lakesha Lucky and Chena Black. Sometimes, people who aren't secure about themselves when they enter will often find reasons to challenge someone else."

The Continental System is based on a 150-point method. The interview is worth a maximum possible 25 points, with the judges looking for intelligence as well as personal charm during the session. "On the personal interview, we have them go in five at a time, so it's a competition," said Flint. "It's a balance that you're looking for.

"You can't just sit there and not join in, but at the same time you don't want someone who is overbearing. As a representative of Continental you want someone who can communicate well with people. During their year they are going to be attending all the preliminaries and entertaining, but they are also going there as a spokesperson, so the ability to connect and communicate is very important."

The swimsuit category is also worth a potential 25 points. The scoring areas are selection of bathing suit; poise, personality and presentation; and hair and makeup. Evening gown carries a potential 40 points, with the key scoring areas being originality and elegance of gown; poise and presentation of contestant; and presentation as formalwear and not theatrical costume.

The final category is talent, which is worth the largest number of points, a potential 60. Contestant talent is judged by scoring every aspect of talent performance, including artistic achievement in song, dance, pantomime, comedy, etc.; costume, makeup and hair; and special effects. When it comes to talent, Flint was also quick to point out: "You have to judge the person and not the overall talent, meaning not all the dancers but the person, because when they go on the road they aren't going to have all those backup dancers. The production should showcase the talent and not overshadow it."

For the Top Five finalists, the final interview question is worth an additional 40 points and is based on the intelligence and completeness of the answer as well as the contestant's poise and charm while answering. The questions can be about anything, are usually serious in tone, and tend to be geared toward getting a clear sense of the contestant's personality, while testing the contestant's grace under pressure. For example, in 2011 the final questions at Mr. and Miss were "How forgiving are you of friends who disappoint you?" and "When was the last time you cried and why?"

Miss Continental is held every Labor Day weekend along with Mr. Continental, which became an annual contest in 2004. Easter weekend is the time for Miss Continental Plus, which began in 1991, and Miss Continental Elite, which began in 2004. In 2011, the contests were at the Park West and at the Vic Theatre, 3145 North Sheffield Avenue. Over the four-day weekend, the first two-day contest is held on Friday and Saturday; the second, on Sunday and Monday. They require separate admission payments and are usually at different venues. All four contests have remained and will continue to remain in Chicago.

"I always wanted to keep it here because people love to come to Chicago," Flint said. "We have much more than most cities have to offer. It's central. I think the contests that change locations every year—I think it hurts them. We put our tickets [for the Labor Day competitions] on sale the Thursday after July 4, and we're out of our 800 reserved tickets in an hour and a half. We also don't have a lot to put on sale that day, because we have a lot of people that come back year after year. They want their tables. It's like Wrigley Field, you let me know and you get your table back."

In the four different Continental pageants, contestants can win more than one crown and title—but not within the span of a year. For example, a former Plus can go on to be a regular Miss Continental, as happened with Lady Catiria, Miss Continental Plus 1993 and Miss Continental 1995, as well as Victoria LePaige, Miss Continental Plus 1996 and Miss Continental 2006. A former Miss Continental can also go on to become a Miss Continental Elite, as has been the case with Maya Douglas, Miss Continental 1985 and Miss Continental Elite 2006, and Danielle Hunter, Miss Continental 2000 and Miss Continental Elite 2007. Contestants also often compete numerous times before winning the title. In fact, it is extremely rare for someone to win the title on the first try.

A qualification is that you cannot have won that particular contest before, but you can enter numerous times and enter different contests. Mokha Montrese, Miss Continental 2010, competed 14 times before she won. Tasha Long, Miss Continental 1997, took about eight times. Armani, Miss Continental 2009, competed eight times before winning. Alexis Gabrielle "Gabby" Sherrington, Miss Continental 2011, was an eight-time contestant as well.

After being named, winners are scheduled to appear and perform at all the other preliminary contests. They are flown in by the promoters, are put up, and usually do two or three songs. The reigning titleholders are paid, wined and dined, and travel to many places—Hawaii, Puerto Rico, Texas, Canada, New York and more. They see and meet people whom in the future they can call for bookings. It is a great networking opportunity, as is the contest itself.

"Anymore, the actual people I book for the Baton as guests or for regular spots are from the Continental System, because it is guaranteed they are going to be the best," Flint said.

The Parade of Continentals

Although to some it may be just a title, to many involved in the Continental System it's much more. Like many of Flint's undertakings, Continental is often referred to as a family. So, here are some of the diverse members of this eclectic family—some of the titleholders, competitors, judges, promoters, technicians, choreographers and even members of the audience. It is a contest but, more than a competition, it is a celebration, an extended family reunion that takes place twice a year, and one that continues to grow with each passing year.

"Of course, it was the start of everything, and there was no thought of what to expect," offered Miss Continental 1980, Chilli Pepper. "When I won, for my talent I did Linda Clifford's 'Red Light' from Fame, and everyone said I shouldn't because it was too new, the movie was just out. But I felt it, so I went with my heart. That is how I choose. Choreographer Randy Duncan was a backup dancer and Joseph Holmes was my choreographer." Holmes was the founder and artistic director of the modern dance company bearing his name. He died of AIDS in April 1986 at age 38 and was succeeded as artistic director by Duncan.

"I remember Chilli's production number at the Park West," said Baton choreographer and performer Orlando del Sol. "It was to 'Red Light,' and my partner Ken [Nowakowski] did the props, which were a big clock and the doorway to a hotel."

R&B recording star Linda Clifford said she was terribly flattered when she learned Chilli had won with pantomiming one of her songs: "It's a huge compliment," she said.

Chilli also mused about the pageant over the past several years. "It has changed," she said. "It is nice to have been at the start, the first. Now it is about the production more than the personality. Now you spend $30,000 of yours or a promoter's money so they can say they have the winning queen. It's different. I don't know if I'd be willing to do something so grand."

"I won Miss Continental in September of 1981," said Heather Fontaine. "I was the second, and I think the first one to go through the preliminaries and everything. I did Marilyn Monroe for my talent, 'Diamonds Are a Girl's Best Friend,' and had the pink dress from Gentlemen Prefer Blondes made and everything. I had no idea what I was getting into. I was Miss California and then they just sort of sent me to Miss Continental. But I had no idea. I was very young at the time—22 or 23."

"She was the best Marilyn Monroe imitator I have ever seen in my life. When Heather performed, you just couldn't believe it was not the actual Marilyn," recalled Flint. "Except Heather was maybe even better-looking."

Fontaine, who came out of virtual retirement to perform for a very appreciative audience at the Miss Continental 2011 pageant, said: "Jim always joked that when I toured and went to preliminaries that I always forgot how to find my way back home. I'd stay over if they asked me to perform that coming weekend. Sometimes I'd stay two or three weeks. When they asked me in my interview part of Miss Continental, I said I would promote unity among queens, and that's what I was trying to do.

"I remember staying in Norfolk a couple weeks, and the bar owner there had Mamie Eisenhower's burgundy limousine, and they used to drive me around in that. It had those sort of doors where both front and back doors open from the center, in the middle. They'd take me wherever I wanted to go in that thing and treated me like royalty. Felicia did freak out a bit, but she understood. I was building a bridge. I was doing these shows and staying over and really cementing a relationship with Continental and all these preliminary pageants and places. I was a goodwill ambassador."

Miss Continental 1985, Maya Douglas, explained how she came to win the pageant. "I met Jim when I first competed in Miss Continental in 1984, coming in sixth behind winner Cherine Alexander. I was so intimidated," she said. "I was just this 22-year-old kid from upstate New York (Rochester). I remember I did A Taste of Honey's 'Sukiyaki' and an All That Jazz number. I was so naïve. I didn't know clothes. My gowns were a black velvet fitted evening gown with these glittery hot-pink wings on the front that sort of extended from the waist up. It was the sort of thing where when you saw it you would just say 'hello!'" Douglas laughed. "Those pink wings must have extended a foot on either side. My other gown was a black-and-gold brocade with a Latin flair and lots of ruffles along the bottom.

"The next year I came out and just wanted to get in the Top Five. Then when the Top Five finalists were announced, I was so excited because I kept thinking, 'Oh, I got a prize!' Then they called the fourth runner-up, and then the third, and it was myself, Alana [Kela] and Candi [Stratton] on the stage. When I won, I was so flabbergasted. I spent that year traveling around to other pageants. It really showed me the world. I was 23 and hadn't really ventured much from Rochester.

"Then when my year of travel was over, I went back to Rochester, and it seemed really small. I loved my family and friends there, but it was just—not so glamorous. I was working doing drag at two places there. One was a place called Joe's Disco, and the other place was called Backstreet. Well, Shanté was making an appearance at Backstreet, and she kept telling me, 'Move to Chicago.' Finally I agreed and moved here without a job, but Jim soon hired me."

Douglas went on to win almost every major title in the field. She was Miss Gay USofA, National Entertainer of the Year and Miss Universal Show Queen. "When I won Miss Continental Elite in 2006 [21 years after being Miss Continental], it felt as though my career had really come full circle, and that was the phrase I used in my acceptance speech. I really wanted to win it in 2005, figuring it had been 20 years since Miss Continental and 10 since I was Miss Gay USofA. I thought the math would be good. But Jim wasn't allowing former Miss Continentals to compete in Elite in 2005. That didn't happen until the following year, so as soon as he changed that rule I won it in 2006. I think my favorite of them all was still Miss Continental, because it was really the one that launched my career."

Douglas explained a bit about her transformation over the years. "I started going to bars when I was 17 or so, and it was 1980 and kind of the start of punk. Punk rock was exploding," she said. "I was skinny as a rail and very androgynous-looking. I was going to hair school, so I had crazy hair that was purple in the front. There was a grand opening of a new club in Rochester, and some friends and I decided to dress up, so I did, and that night the management asked me if I wanted to do a show the next month.

"At the time, drag in Rochester was still very 1970s. I was doing Grace Jones and Blondie, and the other performers were all with the big hair doing Petula Clark. The crowds loved me, but not so much the other Rochester queens.

"Then came Miss Continental a couple years down the line. I didn't have any hormones until 1987, and then I had some silicone injections in my hips and in 1989 my first set of implants. That really changed my whole performing persona, the whole show dynamic. I became more comfortable in less fabric and wanted to show cleavage and curves. I really opened up as a performer about then and became much more confident. I am just so amazed by all of it. I never expected my life to take this path, but I'm glad it did."

"Tandi Andrews was probably one of my favorite entertainers of all time," said Flint. "She is one of the ones who really put Continental on the map. I'll never forget the year she came into town. She won the preliminary in Atlanta and came into the Baton in this little off-the-shoulder sort of sundress. She introduced herself and said, 'Hello, I'm Tandi Andrews. I'm competing in the contest tomorrow.' I said 'Oh, great,' and didn't think much of it. Then the next day she got onstage and did 'The Music and the Mirror' [from A Chorus Line], and she danced and she danced and she danced. She was Miss Continental 1986. [Andrews also went on to become Miss GayUSofA in 1992.]

"One time I was with a couple straight friends, and we were walking down the corridor at O'Hare, and all of a sudden Joe elbowed Fred to look at this woman. I knew who they were eyeing, but I didn't say a thing. She got about 10 feet in front of us and then she said, 'Jim,' and threw up her arms. Joe said, 'No!' and I said, 'Yes.' They had no idea. Tandi was like that, though. She actually won a Miss Virginia Beach contest against 17 girls, and even they didn't know at the time she was a boy.

"After she won the [Miss Continental] pageant, she took over emceeing and did such a great job. After she passed away [from AIDS in 1999], we did some clips of her emceeing Continental. We did it at the start of the contest that night, because we didn't want to bring everyone down, but yet we wanted to pay her tribute. The place, everyone, just stood and started applauding. That's how great she was." Flint grew tearful and added, "You just knew she was in the room that night."

More Continentals

Dana Douglas met Jim Flint at the Miss Florida F.I. pageant in 1981. It was there that Flint first became a fan of the tall, blond female impersonator. The following year, he became one of her sponsors for the Miss Florida F.I. pageant, and that year she won.

"I went to Chicago the following year, and that was my first time in Miss Continental, and I placed in every position in the thing before I won," said Dana Douglas. "I have a complete set of those trophies. Fourth runner-up, third, second, first, and I finally won in 1987. It's so funny: I came back out of retirement a few years ago and I was at a Mr. Continental, and one of the contestants came up to me and said he was such a fan and all, and then he said, 'I was born the year you won the contest.' I just held my smile and said, 'Thanks.'

"Kelly [Lauren] came in to replace me at the Baton when I was moving to Key West in 1986. I gave my notice in September, and my last day was going to be New Year's Eve. Part of the reason for my leaving was James. [Douglas' husband and partner was the HIV pioneer and noted gastroenterologist Dr. James Slaff. In 1985 he worked for the National Institutes of Health and helped educate the first generation of AIDS activists with his 1985 book The AIDS Epidemic.]

"James wanted me to come to Key West, and my giving notice was partly, too, from losing Miss Continental that year [1986] to Tandi Andrews. I should have won that year, and Jim [Flint] put $22,000 into my winning it, but he knew if I won I'd leave the Baton. So, after that, I was so mad [that I lost] I thought, I am going to leave anyway, and so I gave notice.

Then the next year, I came back from Florida and won it by a landslide." Douglas' talent segment is still talked about today: a musical production to 42nd Street.

Joey McDonald recalled helping Dana Douglas in 1987's contest. "I remember going over to Joanne De Corey's house several nights after the Loading Dock closed and helping her sew the sequins on the netting, as well as the flowers that covered the breasts and crotch of Dana's outfit and also on the netting for her scarf," he said. "Dana and Joanne were friends from the Baton. I remember, too, that Tracey Ross [from Star Search] was one of the judges that year, and she was in awe and kept saying, 'That is not a man! No way! That's a woman.'"

"As Miss Continental, I did my job," said Douglas. "I went to every preliminary, sometimes two or three states a day! I was a professional and I worked my butt off at it. I remember when I was Miss Continental, I stayed with Jimmy [at his home]. We don't hold grudges.

"I was in his guest bedroom, and I must say with being with James [my husband] in Key West I was living like a glamorous rich lady. I had jewels and clothes. That morning I heard something, and I opened my eyes, and Jim and Dan were sneaking into my room, and I heard Dan say, 'Look at what she's sleeping in,' and I was in a custom-made satin negligee nightgown with a train and a matching coat—I had three of them made, one in red, one in black and one in yellow. When Dan said, 'Look at what she's sleeping in,' I heard Jim whisper, 'That's because she's a lady.' I knew what I was doing. I'd dressed like a queen and rolled my hair and all before I went to bed the night before, because I wanted to look like a goddess when they came in to wake me, and I did.

"I went back to Miss Continental for my 10-year anniversary in 1997. I also returned in 2006 when Tulsi asked me to. It was like coming home again, because I had been out of it for so many years. I stood around that night and collected money for eight or nine minutes after the song had ended."

Douglas' beloved husband, James, died in 2008 at age 54. Currently, Douglas works in the antiques business and is hunting around to land a reality show. "Can't you see it?" she said. "A reality show about an antique auctioneer by day and a drag queen by night."

Kelly Lauren comes to Miss Continental every year. "It's exciting because every year a new girl is added to our select group of performers for the big production number. I won in 1988 in my fourth attempt at the crown," she said.

"My big blowout with Jim happened when I was Miss Continental in 1988," Lauren said. "I had this boyfriend at the time who was trouble, but I wouldn't listen. I loved this guy, but Jim was just relentless, telling me he was no good and that I was a disgrace to the title and everything, so finally I told him, 'Fuck you, fuck the Baton, and fuck Miss Continental.' I was screaming and crying, and Jim said to me, 'Oh, my God, isn't it a little early for the Oscars?' One thing I will say, he is funny.

"I was so mad that I didn't go back to give my crown to the next Miss Continental. I stayed at a barbecue in Milwaukee instead. I just didn't think what I did with my personal life and who I dated was any of his business. I love Jim, but we were always fighting about something, and that was the last straw. I just couldn't take any more of what I perceived as his interfering."

In a January 17, 1990, article in the Chicago Tribune's Style section, "Glamazons: Here She Comes, With a Few Hundred Pounds and a Massive Will to Win," Richard Knight Jr. wrote: "[Flint] will brook no resistance to his authority: Kelly Lauren, 1988's Miss Continental, is nowhere in evidence at this year's festivities. Rumors buzz that she has been fired for not showing up at appearances, for 'bad conduct.' Flint says that 'she has a boyfriend and she's very insecure. No one even missed her,' he sniffs.

"Perhaps not, but just to make sure, Flint announces that all the contestants have signed what amounts to a morality and scheduling clause: 'We have very high standards and we want them safeguarded. Miss Continental will have to travel a lot.' In other words, no show means no crown."

"We had one Miss Continental whose lover decided to do drag, and I'd go to a preliminary and the lover would walk in, and then Miss Continental would come in, shlepping the bags," said Flint, referring to Lauren. "I didn't think it was right. She'd get him on the judging panel, and he wasn't qualified. I never fired Kelly, she just didn't show for the contest. I never wanted to do that after they won. Then, another time, she came back, she got onstage and stripped naked, and I almost banned her that time. But I gave her another chance and she's really straightened up."

On the Baton Show Lounge website, Lauren stated: "When I was Miss Continental, I failed miserably and let my insecurities, weaknesses, naivety and drug/alcohol abuse ruin the experience, and I let everyone down, most sadly myself. If I had it to do all over ... Maybe one day I can redeem myself of my greatest achievement: being crowned Miss Continental. In the last 13 years I have been clean and sober and am grateful to have survived as so many have not. I give Alcoholics Anonymous all the credit for teaching me how to live a life free from drugs & alcohol—which is so prevalent in this lifestyle. I do not think I am better than people who still party, it just no longer worked for me, and I did not want to be miserable anymore."

Try and Try Again

Flint spoke about another Baton favorite of the era. "I really wanted Shanté to be Miss Continental so badly that year [1988] and if John Bradley had not designed that evening gown she would have won it all," he said. "That gown just looked like a knocked-up poinsettia or something. It wasn't flattering."

"I loved that gown, though—it was a blood-red, floor-length gown with giant sort of leaves coming out around the shoulders," said Shanté, who now goes by the name Alexandra Billings. "I think the reason so many people voted against it was because it was too much of a costume, but I loved it. I remember in the preliminaries Kelly Lauren won the swimsuit and evening gown, and I won the talent, so we knew it was pretty much between the two of us.

"When I was first runner-up to Kelly, it was a mighty blow. That was the third time I'd been a runner-up. So I went to Jim and said, 'That's it, I'm done. No more pageants.' I was newly sober and it just wasn't worth all the hassle. I will never forget the look of disappointment on his face.

"Then he said, 'One more time and I'll take care of everything.' So we went and entered Miss Florida F.I. [Female Impersonator], which is a huge deal. It's a big, big pageant, and up until then no one from outside of Florida had ever won. Well, Jim paid my airfare, paid for new costumes, flew my dancers down, put me up at an amazing hotel, makeup artist, everything."

Flint said Shanté "was magnificent, and she won" the Miss Florida title.

"So after I won, I went back to this amazing hotel room with this gigantic tiara and a nice big check, and I was alone," Billings said. "Not one person from the pageant was there to congratulate me—none of the other contestants or anyone. It was so depressing. Then Kim Cleveland, who was doing my makeup, came in and said, 'Oh, congratulations,' and everything, and saw I was depressed and asked me what was the matter. I said, 'Look around.' And she said, 'Oh, yeah, that's weird.'

"So we sat there for a while, and all of a sudden there was a knock on the door and there were three dozen red roses from Jim along with a note that said, 'I always knew it. Jim Flint.' That completely turned it all around, and even now I sort of get choked up remembering how that made me feel and for it to come at that time when I really needed something."

(On the Miss Florida F.I. website, the year 1989, in which Shanté won, is missing entirely. The listing runs consecutively from 1973 down to the present year and simply lists Lakesha Lucky 1988 and then Chena Kelly 1990. Apparently the contest was held under a different name the year Shanté/Billings won, but she is still omitted from official listings by the pageant owner and executive director, Victor Zepka, who no longer recognizes Shanté/Billings because she apparently did not come back to give up the title.)

Billings also shared her experience of being a Continental judge. When asked to grace the judges panel, she reportedly quipped, "They want me to judge? How can I pick a winner? I only know how to be first runner-up." Billings, who never won a Continental title but who has had a long career onstage, in TV and in film, explained in a more serious tone: "It is a big deal. All the judges met, and we discussed just how seriously we took the point system. The hardest thing I had a time judging was the talent. Sitting as a judge was odd, too, since I know what it's like to be up there—how difficult it is up there and also how tough it is to lose."

By 1990 it was clear the pageant was getting bigger and the bar had definitely been raised on what it took to compete and, more importantly, on what it took to win. In "Glamazons: Here She Comes, With a Few Hundred Pounds of Sequins and a Massive Will to Win," Knight wrote in the Tribune: "The pageant is in its 10th year, has grown from 14 contestants to 44. Owner and creator Jim Flint says that the best thing about all this hoopla over a bunch of boys dressed up as girls 'is pride. We've become open about our gay lifestyles … . You naturally want positive role models on all fronts.'"

Talent, it seems, had especially come of age. Knight's piece continued: "Flint recalls that once the contestants were content 'just doing a number'—lip-synching to a tape and acting out the song. Now however, 'talent' has come to mean lavish production numbers.

"And lavish means lavish: Ginger [Valdez] recreates 'Madame Butterfly' complete with rickshaw, 4-foot fans, giant paper umbrellas and a Chinese dragon. Aggie Doon ('Miss Manhattan') struts and shimmies through a 1920s speakeasy, ends up shooting her lover and frying in the electric chair to the tune of 'What I Did for Love.' ...

"But simplicity still has its place. Lauren Michaels does a ballet number sans set and back-up boys and actually gets up en pointe and stays there while singing 'Some Enchanted Evening.'"

Knight's piece also mentions that sitting on the judges panel that year was Robyn Douglass, the Breaking Away (1979) actress, who probably got her Continental judge seat on account of her performance as a male impersonator in the 1984 TV movie Her Life as a Man.

Bigger and Better

"The first time I met Amber Richards was when she was in Gay Miss America, competing from Indianapolis," said Flint. "Amber was always a fan favorite. She gave people what they wanted. She didn't give people slow songs. She did big things, wild things, flamboyant costumes. She never gave a bad performance and became the darling of Atlanta after she moved there.

"The year she won Miss Continental, when it came to the time for the Q-and-A and Amber was in the Top Five, I said to someone, 'Well, I know she's going to get this, because that queen can talk and she won't stop talking.' And I was right. She won the pageant that year with her answer."

Amber Richards, who was Miss Florida F.I. 1985 and Miss Continental 1991, worked at Flint's Baton South in Atlanta, among other places. Richards died of smoke inhalation from a house fire on May 13, 1996.

Chicago choreographer Keith Elliott recalled a talent number performed by Mimi Marks, Miss Continental 1992. "I loved doing the number from The Will Rogers Follies with Mimi Marks the year she won Miss Continental," he said. "We fought like cats and dogs, with me constantly wanting her to do more and she always wanting to do less. I remember I wanted her to do a front walkover, and she eventually did it. We laugh about it today when we see each other."

"My favorite memory of Miss Continental was my very first year. I had never seen talent of that caliber," said Miss Continental 2005, Domanique Shappelle. "It was 1992, the year Mimi Marks won, and she was incredible. She did a number from The Will Rogers Follies, and it was the production to end all productions. There were at least 15 backup dancers, the women were all in white and wearing sort of Daisy Dukes–style shorts, and the men were in white with the shirt open low—it was all white and blue, and Mimi had white cowboy boots on—it was so great. It reminded me of the Dallas Cowboys Cheerleaders."

Marks talked about the obligation behind her eventually winning the crown. "It was exciting," she said. "The traveling was great, and at the same time it was tough. I'd never really flown much. I'd never flown at all before moving here [to Chicago] and I got a booking in Florida. For me, it was also at the very start of my career. I came here [to the Baton] in 1990, and I won the title in 1992, and I was still new and fresh, so it was a great way to start off—winning, and traveling, and meeting everyone.

"The hardest part of the title was also the traveling and meeting so many people as well. I had a boyfriend at the time who was crazy because he was so jealous. He'd be pissed because I was gone, but then when I came back with the lovely money it was suddenly fabulous. That didn't work out.

"And that was also the year I learned Jim [Flint] is horrible to fly with. He's great because he knows so many interesting things about the different places. However, he needs basically no sleep, and so we'd be on a plane and I'd start to doze off, and he'd always nudge me and say, 'Mimi, are you asleep? Mimi.' It drove me crazy."

"One of my favorite moments was in 1993 when Mimi Marks was giving up her Continental crown," said regular pageant attendee Ed Cavaliere. "They had a final number and she came out in a strapless red gown, and the stage was all bathed in red lights, and the Continental crown was on her head. Then the Continental crown was lifted into the rafters by wires and in its place was an identical crown in red. The place went up for grabs. It is that sort of classy thing that people can count on at the Miss Continental pageant."

"In 1986 I started performing and soon realized that being a titleholder was a smart career move," said Cezanne. "It increases your notoriety, your visibility, your marketability and, as a result, your income. Becoming Miss Continental was also good for me because I was sort of struggling with the transition of who I was and who I wanted to be, and that was the direction I wanted to go. The first time I entered, I didn't know what I was doing. The second time I was still green. By the third time, when I won [1994], I had already been Miss Gay USofA, so I was ready.

"I remember when I won Miss Continental, [Miss Continental 1984] Cherine Alexander had come into town for the event, and everyone was so excited to see her. When it came time for Jim to announce the winner, he stepped up to the microphone and announced the new Miss Continental is—'Cherine Alexander,' and of course he meant 'Cezanne.' It's dubbed over in the video and all, but at the time it shook me a little.

"I loved my year as Miss Continental. Monica Munro crowned me. I love to travel and see things, and you go everywhere for it. Some of my favorites were D.C., Hawaii, Puerto Rico. Jim is an amazing tour guide and he loves doing it. He exposed me to so many different things. The two biggest things were the Vietnam Memorial in D.C. and then when Jim took me to the Pearl Harbor exhibit. Jim got a real kick out of showing me attention because of the couples who were always around, and no one thought a thing—the husbands were checking me out but not knowing. Jim loved that.

"When I lost my mother in 2008, I was so depressed. I had lost my dad before, and that was when my mother started getting sick, and I was an only child. When Mom got sick the Friday before Labor Day, I phoned Jim and told him I couldn't make Miss Continental that year. Jim adored my mother, and at the contest he had a moment of silence for her and said a prayer for her, and then later some of the performers did a show to raise some money for her funeral and burial, and Jim added some money to it as well. That was so moving to me, that they would help me in this time of need when I was so down. He called and checked on me. It was an act of kindness I will never forget."

The Show Must Go On

"My first time in a gay club, I was still a senior in high school," said Continental contestant Amy DeMilo. "I saw my first drag queens and show that night." Once the show ended, DeMilo asked about performing and was told about a talent contest the following week. "I was there looking like a train wreck and feeling like a million dollars ... . I was asked what my name was and told them my boy name. They laughed and said, 'Your stage name.' I said I didn't have one, so I was given the name Amy, and I've been her for three decades. I knew the first time I entertained that this would be my path in life."

DeMilo, who was Miss Florida F.I. 2000 and Miss Gay Florida USofA 2010, has competed in Miss Continental four times. DeMilo's favorite Continental memory is from 1992. "The year Mimi won, I tied with Tasha Long for fourth runner-up. When they called the lineup, they forgot to call me as tied, so, after the first runner-up was called, there stood Mimi and myself staring at each other. It's a precious moment caught on film."

DeMilo said her favorite Flint memory was of when he took her and Cezanne to dinner and then to a club with Bob Mackie to see Tandi Andrews perform. DeMilo praised Flint: "Jim is such a great man and has done so much for the female impersonation industry, making it better, bigger, and more accepted as an art form."

"Lady Catiria ruled New York! She was a hot and spicy Puerto Rican performer," said Ginger Grant.

Flint recalled the unforgettable entertainer Lady Catiria Reyes, who died in 1999 at age 40. "She was one of those people everyone fell in love with," Flint said. "She was Miss Continental Plus first [in 1993], and then she started losing weight. When she lost weight, she decided to run and won Miss Continental [in 1995]. At that point in time, she got very ill, and she kept telling me she had bulimia. I remember we went from Washington, D.C., down to Norfolk and she was so sick, so I went out and got all this food so there was plenty on her dressing table and in the hotel.

"I didn't know it was HIV. She did not tell me she had HIV until a week before she gave up her crown, because she said, 'You have so much to worry about that you don't have to worry about me, too.' Then in her farewell speech at Miss Continental, she kind of read [told off] a few people who spoke badly about her illness. She was one of those people no one said a bad thing about."

Head Continental judge Skip Mackall recalled his friendship with Lady Catiria. "Everyone was coming back for the contest and she was going to be there," Mackall said. "People were worrying about how they should act when she was clearly so sick. We were all out for breakfast and the whole 'how should we treat her' issue came up, and I remember Jimmy said, 'Everybody is going to be that person one day. And when that happens, what they'll want is to be treated like they would normally be treated—not any differently. With all that going on in their lives, what they are going to want is just a usual day.' And he was absolutely right."

Lady Catiria's victory was also one of pageant regular Ed Cavaliere's favorite Miss Continental memories. "In 1995, when she came back after winning Miss Continental Plus and after losing the weight and competed and won Miss Continental, it put a lump in my throat. She looked absolutely beautiful and was as kind and as friendly as could be. I remember, when she was called as one of the finalists, the air of confidence she exuded. She was so poised and held herself so regally. That look of confidence on her face was just dynamic."

Catiria lost a reported 82 pounds to compete in the Miss Continental pageant. As recounted on the Internet Movie Database website: "During her farewell performance at the 1996 Miss Continental pageant, [Catiria] wearing a black rhinestone gown bordered with a large red rhinestone band symbolizing the AIDS Ribbon, aroused the crowd with a classic song rendition while a recorded message from herself played softly, divulging [to] the over 2,000 crowd that she had been diagnosed with AIDS." According to queermagnet.com, Catiria performed regularly at Escuelita in New York City and was also featured playing herself in the 1995 film To Wong Foo, Thanks for Everything! Julie Newmar.

The IMDB site also contains a personal quote from the icon herself, "The key to life in general is education, ignorance is weakness and we should make no room for that in our lives."

Regine Phillips, who was a Baton regular from 2002 to 2006 but was never crowned Miss Continental, spoke about competing in the contest for the first time. "I first met Jim when he was a judge in the Miss South Alabama contest," Phillips said. "He introduced himself after the contest. I remember in that show that Chanel Dupree was the special Miss Continental guest. I was so amazed by her. She was so gorgeous, with a great body and an incredible costume. The way she carried herself and her personality, she was just it.

"The first time I entered Miss Continental was in 1996. It was such an experience being there. I wasn't expecting anything. I only had two weeks to get ready for the pageant. I lost my jewelry, my evening gown was ripped, I had an old bathing suit. I drove from Pensacola, Florida, to Chicago to compete. I did a Pocahontas theme for my talent and did 'Colors of the Wind.' I did my best and gave it my all, but I saw how talented everyone was and did not expect anything. So, when I was named as one of the Top 12, I was so surprised. Having that happen pushed me to work harder, because I got a taste of what it was like and that the judges saw that potential, that talent in me. I just wanted to get better and better. I ended up coming back and competing in Miss Continental seven times and got as high as second runner-up in, I think, 2006."

Tasha Long, a Baton cast member who was Miss Continental 1997 and Entertainer of the Year 2004, recalled first meeting Flint, in 1988. "I was so nervous, because this was my first pageant and it was a Miss Continental preliminary in Montgomery, Alabama," she said. "I had heard all about this man, and when we were introduced he was so nice and said to me, 'You have a winning smile.' I always was grateful to him for that, because it made me feel so good at a time when I was so nervous."

Are You a Queen?

On the Continental website, Michelle Dupree aka Scott Cooper (Miss Continental 1998) commented on his beliefs about changes at Continental. "I think the biggest difference between a reign as Miss Continental today versus 10 years ago is that I wonder how my win would have been viewed in light of the gender issues I faced," Cooper said. "I think we all recognize the fact I was met with a great deal of resistance when I won because I live my life as a man.

"In recognizing the resistance I experienced, I believe I am even more sensitive to the plight of our transgender brothers and sisters who face discrimination every day in the workplace, social settings and in relationships. I wonder if it would have been as much of a big deal now as it was then. I still believe I have to work harder in some ways, but my Continental sisters, all of them, never make me feel like I don't belong. That's a family. That's a sisterhood."

Dupree's year as Miss Continental was a very busy one—the entertainer was also cast with Robert De Niro and Philip Seymour Hoffman in the comedy crime drama Flawless (1999). As Scott Allen Cooper, he was billed eighth, as the character Ivana. On the Internet Movie Database website, the description of this Joel Schumacher film reads: "An ultraconservative police officer (DeNiro) suffers a debilitating stroke and is assigned to a rehabilitative program that includes singing lessons—with the drag queen next door."

Cooper was interviewed for this book, and he spoke about how his journey began. "I met Jim at Miss Continental Plus the year Erica Christian won in 1994," Cooper said. "A friend of mine, Angel Sheridan, was competing, and I went with her on the interview. We got to talking and I said to Jim, 'I have to leave town Tuesday morning because I have a show on Tuesday night.' And Jim turned to me and said, 'Oh, are you a queen?' And I feel as if I have spent the 18 years that followed trying to answer that question. At the time, I was in La Cage off-Broadway, and at the time I didn't even have a drag name, because in the La Cage circuit you just use your regular name.

"So, in 1996 when I went to Miss Continental and competed and made the Top 12, I knew my destiny. Then I took 1997 off, and the next year I came back in 1998 and won.

"It was a sort of scandal because I did not live as a transgendered person. I had no enhancements, took no hormones, didn't have implants. Miss Continental had been sort of a safe haven for those transgender people who were in that category [who were taking hormones, who'd had enhancements and who were living their lives as women]. So here I was, this boy from New Jersey who won on talent and interview. They had a hard time with me because I had broken through this sort of sacred ground, and there was a lot of opposition. Security was tight that night, and they got me out of the theater quickly, and I got into a cab with [head judge] Skip Mackall and, on the way to the victory party at the Baton, I had only one thing to ask Skip, 'Was Jim happy?' When I asked him, Skip said 'Yes, he is.' So I knew Jim had my back.

"Personally, I couldn't believe I won. Everyone, including my friends, didn't think it was possible. They said, 'You'll never win, but you'll get a lot of work because of it,' so I went in looking to get bookings.

"After I won, what would happen was, word would get out, and I would see the audience and they would be sort of there with their arms crossed. I did not have the same reception as many. I was not a long-standing contestant. I didn't have a long history with the pageant system like so many of the others. No one considered me a real threat until the final night. Once I won, I think I had more to prove. I never missed a plane or a taxi or an engagement. I never wanted the door to be opened for there to be any question that I didn't deserve the title. I took the title and responsibilities of Miss Continental very seriously. I was on a mission.

"When I first performed at the Baton, I remember sitting on the bar stool, and Bobby Glaze came over to me and said, 'These people don't understand you, they have a lot to learn about talent.' And I told him, 'Bobby, I will win them over, and I will do it person by person and preliminary by preliminary, but I will do it.'

"A year later, I was back at the Baton at the last preliminary, and the crowd went crazy. I sat at the bar and said, 'See, Bobby, I may be sitting on the same bar stool as last year, but this time I got them.' Jim was behind me the whole time. He always complimented me in front of people and was sure to say what a great job I was doing. I never once felt Jimmy didn't have my back.

"When I gave up my crown, before I performed my final number I said, 'I didn't come to change things, I came to be a part of things.'

"There is great camaraderie between winners because we are all part of this family that share a common experience. Only the others can really understand it. Mokha Montrese and I were just talking about this. We said, 'You want to win so bad, because you think at the time about what it can do for you and how it's going to change you,' but it changes you in ways you don't expect. It's nothing like you expect. It's like trying to explain the way something tastes, you can't really. What's difficult about it and what's wonderful about it are not necessarily what you expect.

"I remember when Tommie Ross came to me after she had won, the year after I did, and asked if I had any advice, and I thought, 'Are you kidding me? I am not worthy!' She asked what she should do that night, and I said, 'Just be Tommie Ross. Just go out and be you.' That's important.

"There is a lot of disguise and costumes in this business, so the semblance of realness that a Miss Continental brings to the stage is the most important thing. And if you look, no one who has won this contest has ever been a carbon copy of anyone else. We are allowed to be ourselves and we are never expected to be anything else.

"As to the man, I cannot say enough. Jim is not only generous financially but also emotionally. So many people have careers based on his good fortune. Being Miss Continental taught me that all things are possible, and that's a lesson I took to heart. It is what actually led to my being able to be a father of two today."

Winning Numbers

Tommie Ross is one of the most popular contest winners, as Miss Continental 1999. Ross also has become a respected judge of the pageant, with a presence that exudes integrity and class. Ross explained a bit how she first met the man who would be so important in her life.

"When I began, I was just Ross and did Diana Ross," she said. "After about four or five years, I became Tommie Ross. When I first met Jim, I was Miss Gay USofA in 1988 and I think I was at the Miss Florida [F.I.] pageant. I was sitting behind Jim and a couple of girls. Anyway, the girls kept getting up and moving around during the show, and Jim was getting annoyed until he finally said, 'I wish you two would just sit down and behave like this lady here,' and he gestured to me. Then he asked who I was, and I introduced myself. That compliment was my first meeting of Jim Flint."

Ten years later Ross was crowned Miss Continental. "I must say that, with the Miss Continental pageant, the way Jim treated me surpassed the treatment I had at every other national pageant," she said. "I was treated with respect and like an absolute professional.

"Part of my duties as Miss Continental was to go and entertain and appear at smaller competitions across the country that are sort of feeder pageants to Miss Continental. I was crowned in September, and that following July I was involved in a car wreck and was unable to finish my reign. When I finally gave up my crown at the ceremony, Jim got very emotional when he spoke about wanting to take me to Puerto Rico and Hawaii and how my accident prevented that."

The show was at the Vic Theatre the night Ross gave up the crown. "We set up a little dressing room on the side of the stage, and she came on and did her number," Flint said. "I told her, 'We're going to have you here if we have to bring you in an ambulance.' If you didn't know she was hurt, you could never tell. When she did the opening number, the girls glided around her.

"That year Scott [Palmer] and I took her and Chevelle Brooks, who was reigning Continental Plus, to Hawaii and on the Navy boat, and not one person clocked them [knew they were not female-born women]. Because of the way they look and the class they have, no one would ever pick up that they were boys."

"He eventually did take me to Puerto Rico on his own sometime later and paid for everything," said Ross. "We went sightseeing and really enjoyed our time there. I will tell you this—he has more energy than anyone I know. He can go to bed at 5:30 and be up at 8. His following through on that promise [to take me to Puerto Rico] really showed me the kind of man he was."

Ross explained her perspective on the other side of things, as a Continental judge. "I am pretty strict as a judge because I really feel if the girls are competing on a national level they should be performing at a very high level," she said. "There are certain expectations. The details all must be perfect. I tend to weed out the ones who are just not ready."

"The first year I entered the Miss Continental pageant was the year Amber Richards won [1991]," said Danielle Hunter. "Every year at contestant registration, Jim talks about how important it is to be on time and basically gives a little lecture. Well, every year he talks about using only hand-held props and then tells the story of this queen who came in with props that were bigger than the whole stage and took 45 minutes to set up and who then was the worst talent he ever saw. That was me. I was a baby.

"I didn't understand what was going on, and it wasn't until 2000 that I won Miss Continental. About the fifth or sixth time I entered, I could tell I was starting to get a following, that people were following my progress and watching me improve. I learned and practiced and kept my eyes open. I was determined. I won on my seventh try.

"The biggest advice I have for the girls entering is, 'Get ready for the speed of it.' Jim runs a fast, efficient contest, and he has it down to an art form. Very few girls are able to keep up their first time out, and if you're not ready when he calls your number, they move on.

"During the year of Miss Continental, my favorite part was the travel and also becoming close to some of the girls at the Baton. I meshed well there and fit in. It was very comfortable for me, and I didn't have to work to become a part of things. I became particularly close to Monica Munro. We hit it off. I would see her all the time when I came to the Baton, and then I was also flying up and staying with her for preliminaries, things like that. We became family.

"When it came time to enter Elite in 2007, I was looking for a pageant to do. I wanted to travel again, and as a personal note I had a job in Florida but I needed a break, a change. So, I looked around at the other contests and figured that I wanted to be around people I liked and I wanted to be treated in a way I like to be treated. Continental Elite was the logical choice, so I entered and won Miss Continental Elite in 2007.

"I don't think Jim understands the effect he's had on people's lives. I come from a town of 300 people and was raised Pentecostal. I had been tortured and ridiculed my entire life. When I moved away, pageants and drag were one of the first things I discovered, and it became family. For the first time, I was accepted and not taunted and tormented. With Continental, it brings all that together. Jim gives outsiders a place they can call home."

Moving On Up

Miss Continental 2001 proved to be a great success story for the Continental System.

Candis Cayne was born Brendan McDaniel in Maui in 1971. She left Hawaii for Los Angeles after graduating from high school. In L.A. she trained as a dancer before subsequently moving to New York to make a name for herself as a choreographer and female impersonator. She appeared in the documentary Wigstock in 1995 and as Diva in the comedy-drama Stonewall (1995), as well as in the film To Wong Foo, Thanks for Everything! Julie Newmar (in which she was billed as Brendan McDanniel) that same year. She began transitioning to female in 1996 and appeared in the documentary Dragtime in 1997 along with playing the title role in the indie production Mob Queen. The film Charlie! followed.

"I was living in New York City and really hadn't heard much about Continental, because the transgender people I knew in Manhattan weren't really pageant people," Cayne said. "Then actually Lady Catiria told me I should enter, she sort of planted the seed. Anyway, there was a time where I wasn't really doing anything, and I met promoter José Abraham and he said he wanted to take me to Continental. So, I competed in a preliminary and I won it and came to Chicago to the pageant.

"Seeing all the magical, gorgeous girls when I got to Continental was what made me really want to be a part of this family. That first year I came, I was first runner-up, I believe, and then the following year I won. I was and am a dancer and actress and had worked hard enough at my craft so the talent part of the pageant didn't really frighten me. The hardest part for me was the thought of spending $4,000 on a gown or learning what to do with my hair and all of that. The hard part was getting down what the Continental look should be.

"Once I won, it felt amazing to be a part of the Continental community and family and be a part of this little but very important piece of history called Continental. The only downside of the title—and this really isn't a downside but more just part of the job description—is that you do travel every weekend.

"I have known Jim 12 years, and as long as I have known him he has always been deeply supportive and very understanding of my quirks, like getting so involved with the moment that I forget to follow through with a promoter or return a phone call. But Jim understands that, as part of me."

After winning Miss Continental in 2001, which featured as her talent performance a wonderful rendition of the Ann-Margret number "Appreciation," Cayne worked the Continental preliminary circuit and continued to perfect her craft. "The best part of it all, though, was that Jim genuinely seemed as excited to have me in the Continental family as I was excited to be a part of it. That meant a lot," she said.

Cayne went on to star in the 2007 RuPaul film Starrbooty as well as an episode of CSI: NY the same year. In 2007 and 2008, Cayne really came into the spotlight as Carmelita Rainer, a trans woman having an affair with New York Attorney General Patrick Darling (William Baldwin), on 11 episodes of the ABC prime-time drama Dirty Sexy Money, which made her the first transgender actor to play a recurring transgender character in a prime-time series.

The same year, she also had a guest role on the series Sordid Lives. She also had a recurring role as transgender character Alexis Stone in Season 6 of Nip/Tuck in 2009 and has since had roles in the series Drop Dead Diva. She continues to make independent films as well as perform in clubs worldwide as a result of her fame and Continental title.

In regard to increasing trans visibility, Cayne has appeared on shows as diverse as The View, Entertainment Tonight, Access Hollywood, Good Morning America, Inside Edition, RuPaul's Drag U and Chelsea Lately, among others.

"I don't really like the term 'female impersonator,' primarily because I don't think I am impersonating anyone," said Cayne. "This is who I am. I was fortunate as a transgender person to have a very loving and accepting family. It was around the mid-1990s that I realized I was not really happy unless I was all glammed up. I remember I was in my apartment and had candles lit and I was looking at myself in the mirror, and I decided I did not want to grow old as a man, I wanted to grow old as a woman. I had a girlfriend who was transitioning at the time, and I called her up and said I wanted to do it.

"I started hormones shortly after that. It was scary because I was an actor and dancer, and by doing this I could very likely be throwing my career out the window. That wasn't an issue, though. I decided it was what I had to do and that whatever happened, I would face it. I'd be strong, professional, and work at my craft, and things would work out.

"It has limited me to a certain degree. Even after Dirty Sexy Money, finding acting work can be very hard. There is certainly a tendency to pigeonhole performers. Auditions are difficult. I wouldn't presume that I have opened doors for transgender performers in the future, but I'd like to think that maybe I've opened some minds and eyes."

No Business Like Show Business

Yoshiko Oshiro had been a part of the Paper Doll Revue in Hawaii. The beautiful entertainer won an impressive number of pageants, including Miss Universal Show Queen (1986), Miss Galaxy International (1992), first runner-up to Queen of the Universe (1992), Miss Tuberose Galaxy (1992), Miss Hawaii Continental (1994), Queen of Queens (1996), Miss Hawaii Continental (1998), Miss Illinois Continental (2001), and Miss Metropolitan Continental (2002), which was the preliminary that led to her being crowned Miss Continental in 2002.

"I always say I started my transformation at 17 when I started taking hormone shots and by 20 I'd already had breast augmentation," said Oshiro. "I really knew I wanted to be a woman since before elementary school, since I wanted to be a cheerleader instead of a football player, and since instead of playing with caterpillars I wanted to use chalk and crayons because I loved the pretty colors.

"In high school, I would wear straight-leg jeans and then a shirt tied in a knot in the front. When my sister would go out, I would put on her dresses and heels. I used to love watching her put on her makeup and paint her nails. It wasn't really a decision. It was something that happened naturally. A decision would have to be to change from that direction. In 1985, at 20, I entered my first pageant because a girlfriend of mine wanted me to enter the Universal Show Queen contest.

"I first learned about Continental when I went over to my girlfriend June's house and watched a Continental video. I was amazed. I wanted to be a part of it. I entered for the first time in 1994 and was a big mess. I was overly confident and thought I knew everything and got there and realized the level of competition. It humbled me and made me want to work to be better and earn the title.

"The reason I wanted to be Miss Continental changed over the course of competing. At first it was because it seemed so grand, but then it became a challenge, a goal, and something I needed to accomplish as an individual. It was a competition within myself. I won in 2002, the sixth time I competed."

For her talent that night, Oshiro danced to excerpts from The Fifth Element, followed by a club mix from Red Alert and then a breakdown by Jennifer Lopez. However, Oshiro received especially high marks for her Q-and-A, handling a volatile situation with poise and intelligence.

In 2002, as the crowd chanted "Flame! Flame!" for contestant Flame Monroe who failed to make the Top Five, Oshiro was the first of the Top Five to come onstage for the final question. "The crowd was shouting," she said. "I stood there, completely in the middle of this controversy and just focused on grounding myself and maintaining my poise. The question was about voting and why we should do it. I said something like voting was important because it was a way to express our rights and opinions as citizens of this country. I said the freedom of speech and to express ourselves should not be taken for granted. I said that is why people have the right to voice their opinion, like being unhappy their candidate was not in the Top Five."

Judge David Hudspeth recalled: "I remember the year Flame Monroe was not in the Top Five, and the audience was packed with her fans and supporters. They began hooting and yelling and stomping, and I really thought there was going to be a riot. I remember I was sitting at a table between a bodybuilder and a personal trainer and thinking, 'I am so glad to be sitting where I am now.' Jim handled it well. He went out there and said, 'We are not continuing until you shut up. It is so disrespectful for you to be behaving this way, especially for the contestants who worked so hard to get here.'"

"When this was going on, Jim was backstage, and he was so shaken," said judge Skip Mackall. "It really hurt his feelings that the crowd would protest like that when he had started this whole contest as a way to give these girls this great avenue to raise their self-esteem and put themselves together as a package and give them this platform to promote themselves. For him to go through all that and the audience to revolt really shook him."

"The year I didn't make the Top Five, I thought they were going to tear the place apart," recalled Flame Monroe. "Truthfully, I loved it. At the time it felt to me like I had won the contest, because fans had never acted that way for any queen that didn't make the cut. It certainly threw Jim."

"When I was named Miss Continental 2002, it felt like the end of this 10-year process, so it was actually a feeling of relief," said Oshiro. "I was still a country girl. In the area of Hawaii where I was raised, we had to take a bus to go to the closest mall 30 minutes away and, when we did that, we used to get all dressed up because it was so exciting. So, being Miss Continental was a challenge with all that travel, but the Continental family helped to guide me, and Jim would meet me at different places. It always gave me such a feeling of being protected to know he would be there.

"He came to many of the preliminaries I had that year. We ate a lot—we'd go to Cracker Barrel and Steak 'n Shake and White Castle. We always had a blast. He'd get mad sometimes, especially when he drove, because I traveled with these two huge trunks and he'd always say, 'Yoshiko, you are so tiny, why do you have such large trunks?' and he'd grump about it a bit, but then he would calm down two minutes later.

"The nicest thing about Miss Continental is that it has allowed me to become a teacher and an inspiration to younger girls in the contest. They ask advice and they listen to what I say as a titleholder, so I have become a sort of mentor. Seeing those girls with all their potential and energy, I want to be there for them. When I look at them I can remember the way I felt, and know how important words of advice can be."

Miss Continental 2004, Erica Andrews, remembered first meeting Flint "through a dear friend of mine, Raphael Velasco, who ran a club [The Saint] and was a pageant sponsor in San Antonio. They were very good friends. Jim was also very good friends with my drag mother,

Tandi Andrews [Miss Continental 1986], who used to emcee Miss Continental before she passed away. Jim used to come down, and we would all go to the Tip Top Diner and sit and have a wonderful meal and share stories.

"I remember first working at the Baton in 1996 to cover while a Baton girl came to Texas. I was young and very nervous, and in Texas we do our two numbers and call it a night. At the Baton it was two numbers plus production numbers, and there were three shows a night. So it was a good learning experience for me. It was also playing to a different audience, a broader one. There were bachelorette parties and bridal showers. It was very new.

"I first competed in Miss Continental in 1999, and then again in 2001, and finally I won in 2004. By that time both my mentors, Raphael and Tandi, had passed away. I was sort of their offspring, their drag daughter. Tandi taught me so much about doing things the right way—about changing your look, about never being seen before a performance, since it detracts from the effect.

"When I finally won in 2004, I won by myself with no dancers. I couldn't afford them. Raphael had been my biggest sponsor and paid for so much of everything. He passed away in 2003, so I was on a budget. I tried to save what money I could, but I was also a provider for my mother in Mexico. The night I won, I told Jim, 'Tandi and Raphael are watching from above,' and gave him a big hug."

Longtime pageant judge Denis Sabol recalled Andrews. "One of my favorite Continental memories was when Erica Andrews came out in her swimwear. She had a Native American/ Cher sort of feel to it, yet it was very revealing and very classic. When she did her turn and walked, I just went 'wow!'" Sabol said.

"I remember that bathing suit," said Andrews. "I was paying so much of my own money. I wanted to save and have a fabulous everything because it was going to be just me. So I had a designer suit made, and that cost between $700 and $800. Anyway, I decided to save that for the final night, and I'd wear one I made myself the night of the preliminaries. It was sort of edgy and I thought it would work.

"It was an orange-and-black tiger-print one-piece, but the only part connecting the top and the bottom was a strip down the front, the sides were open. The fabric was from what was left of a gown, and I think the top part was just that fabric sewn on top of a bra. I had chains around my waist and had a sort of synthetic foxtail hanging from one of the chains, and so when I came out I was sort of twirling that foxtail on the side like a cool cat. My choker was a vintage belt that I had rigged in the back. My shoes were fashioned with rhinestones and chains I added.

"The entire suit cost me maybe $30. When I was named winner of the swimsuit in the preliminary, I knew I had to wear that same suit again for the finals, so the designer suit stayed in the box the entire pageant. That's the story of the cutting-edge swimsuit. It was all illusion, and it was all me just putting things together on a budget."

Judge David Hudspeth recalled his favorite Erica Andrews moment. "A few years before she'd won, Erica Andrews was in the finals and, in the Q-and-A portion, Jim asked her a question about a current issue in Little League baseball, and she was completely stumped," he said. "She ended up answering the question as though it was 'Why should you be Miss Continental?' Well, a couple years later she was back, and Jim asked her the final question, and this time it was a question about Continental, and she looked at him and said, 'I've been watching CNN for two years, and this is what you ask me?'"

Andrews is now also a promoter with the franchise Miss Texas Continental (with Javier

Castillo). She has been on The Tyra Banks Show as well as The Maury Povich Show several times. She also periodically does makeup for the Povich show, a position she got when on her second appearance she refused to be made up by his people. "It must have made an impression," said Andrews. "Since then, he'll fly me in specially to do the girls' makeup."

She was featured in the 2006 Showtime documentary Trantasia and had a juicy role as Emma Grashun in the 2010 revenge-horror-exploitation opus Ticked-Off Trannies With Knives. She is lovingly referred to as "the most beautiful drag queen in captivity." Renowned for her unique routines, Andrews' well-known performances include her Mommie Dearest boardroom–Shirley Bassey mix to "I (Who Have Nothing)" for the 2006 National Entertainer of the Year pageant. Her many titles include Universal Show Queen (2004), Miss Gay USofA (1999) and, of course, Miss Continental 2004.

Andrews mentioned Flint's love of practical jokes. "He had so much fun prank-calling me during my reign as Miss Continental," she said. "He'd change his voice, and he would say he needed to speak to me and then say things like there was a problem with my reign as Miss Continental and that I wouldn't be able to keep the title anymore and that I'd have to surrender my crown. Eventually, I caught on to him.

"I so admire Jim. For so many years he has given all us entertainers the chance to make a business out of what we do. He brings to it his reputation and this wonderful history. He makes it credible and consistent. He has made it a known product."

The Process of Becoming: Coming Into Their Own

"The year I won, it was a big deal because I was such the underdog," said Miss Continental 2005, Domanique Shappelle. "I had competed three times before that and never made the Top 12. So, when I won, it was very unexpected. It was a total shocker, and I almost fainted. The two runners-up, Sasha Valentino and Alexis Gabrielle Sherrington, had both been first and second runners-up in the two previous years. The thing I did differently the year that I won was my talent. I did 'Everybody's Girl' from the Broadway musical Steel Pier. It was a striptease and I won the talent. It was pretty risqué. I had six dancers with me, and it was all in red and black and feathers and had a sort of flamenco, Spanish tang to it.

"I have gone back to the pageant every year since, and currently I own two preliminary pageants—Continental Kentucky, which has a Plus and Miss category, as well as the Pacific Coast Continental, which has Mr., Miss, Elite and Plus categories.

"Jim is good and fair and knows this business inside and out. The best thing about him is that he has never lost touch with the performing aspect of it. He respects the girls to such a high degree, and in return he demands professionalism.

"Jim also is a great insurance for the Continental System, which means that if the promoters don't come through with the money for the winner, Jim will see they are paid, though chances are that promoter will have their license to own a Continental prelim revoked. The preliminary will remain, but under a different promoter.

"If a promoter chooses to, they can change the name of the preliminary. For example, when I won Miss Continental in 2005, I represented Miss Virginia Icon. Prior to that, the contest in the area had been Miss Hampton Roads, but the promoter had never won a title with that name for the previous 14 years, so he decided to change it.

"The Miss Continental pageant also has a reputation for its amazing opening productions. With most pageants, you might have people coming in later. At Continental, people are there

20 or 30 minutes ahead of time. There is no lollygagging. It's a whole different attitude. They are in their seats and ready, because they know the opening production will be something."

Victoria LePaige explained her dual reigns as Miss Continental Plus and Miss Continental. "I won Miss Continental Plus in 1996," she said. "I was 26 years old at the time. The whole experience was so rewarding, but I was green. I was learning on the job and sort of faking my way through it. I was still in the process of becoming.

"Jim saw the promise in me during that time. I think he saw my eagerness to learn. He hired me at the Baton, and the girls you work with there are the best so, to be considered among the best, you need to perfect your craft and find your niche among those wonderful entertainers. The talent there pushes you to be better.

"What happened was, after 10 years of working at the Baton, I became much more polished. I worked alongside many Miss Continentals like Mimi Marks, Monica Munro, Chilli Pepper, Tasha Long and Cezanne. I saw how hard they worked, and I soaked it all up like a sponge. Then in 2006 I became Miss Continental, and by the time I won that title I knew I deserved it. I was ready.

"Presenting yourself as a former and getting the respect and admiration of your peers is wonderful. That comes with the Continental title. After I won Continental Plus, I never thought I would be a regular Miss Continental. I never thought it would happen for me. I was actually running for the pageant on a rebound because I didn't win another pageant. Me being me, I put all of my preparation and money into it. I don't put limits on myself. I'm not saying I'm a plus girl or a regular girl. I am a competitor regardless of size. I don't get caught up in that. You may look at me as a full-figured entertainer, but I don't see myself that way. I see myself as an entertainer—period."

Aurora Sexton, National Entertainer of the Year 2011, said she moved to Chicago because of the reputation of Miss Continental as well as the Baton. "I am so grateful to Jim for this wonderful exposure and the chance to really show this as an art form as well as a business," she said. "I worked at the Baton in the summer of 2010 for six months. It's a lot of work, good work, and I learned a lot from the performers. Jim runs a tight ship and he can be demanding, but it is only so the show will be flawless.

"I had a lot of out-of-town commitments, so I couldn't accept the full-time position that was offered me. As it was, that six months I was working nonstop—Kit Kat on Mondays and Tuesdays, Hydrate on Wednesdays, Spin on Thursdays, and the Baton the rest of the week. I was also juggling the out-of-town gigs.

"I have competed in Continental three times and have made the Top Five once. This year I am not eligible, since I am the reigning National Entertainer of the Year. Let me tell you, Continental is the school of hard knocks, and it makes you a better performer, and it also really challenges you. It helped me build a name and a reputation and allowed me to live a very nice lifestyle. It's an expensive endeavor, but if you are really serious about this as a career then it is an investment."

"I have been aware of Continental ever since I first started entertaining," said three-time contestant Shantell DMarco. "I remember, when I first moved to Orlando, I heard it called the Super Bowl of drag. I wanted to be a seasoned entertainer before I even showed up there. With that caliber of performer, I didn't want to just show up randomly."

"The first time I competed was in 2006. I made the Top 12, and then the following year I competed I made the Top Five, and then the next year I made the Top 12 again. Then I took three years off, but I am going to come back and compete again in 2012.

"I love the professionalism of the contest. I love that it is on schedule. I can't believe I'm saying that, because normally I am not the kind of person that likes structure. I am Cuban, and usually we are late for everything. Entering Continental made me manage my time better.

"I was first interested in drag at about 17. I was interested in the glamour and the glitz and wanted to be a part of that, but I never thought the female impersonation stuff would happen. When I started having those feelings, my biggest fear was relationships. I had a boyfriend at 18 and we broke up because of it, because I started wanting to look like a girl. A lot of gay men don't like that. It broke my heart.

"I started hormone shots at 19. Then there was 'how is this going to affect my relationship with my family?' It was very scary. I didn't know. No one wants to lose their family. It turned out they respect me more now because I am doing what I have to do to be happy."

Through the Looking Glass

"I first became aware of Continental when I saw a poster for a Toronto preliminary in July of 1997," said Tulsi, Miss Continental 2008. "I was already dressing up as a girl and had just started taking hormone shots, but I was not doing shows. I remember I went to that preliminary with a drag-queen friend of mine, and she was talking to Paris Frantz, who was Miss Continental and entertaining that night. I thought, What is this girl doing talking to my drag-queen friend? I didn't think she was a female impersonator.

"Two years after that, I entered my first prelim, which was in Toronto, and I got fourth runner-up, but there were only five girls. I did everything myself, but I did meet Michelle Dupree and Monica Munro, who were there. Then, two weeks later, I went to Detroit and competed in Michigan Continental, and that was when I met Jim for the first time. He was so complimentary and gagging over me that I thought he was a chaser, a pervert. Then I heard he wasn't into the girls, but he used to be one of the girls. He wasn't a chaser, he was a sista!

"In 2001 I competed in Continental for the first time, and I was terrified. I was not prepared for that audience. When they were reading the Top 12, I was saying, 'Don't say my name, don't say my name'—and they didn't. Then I came back in 2003 and took it a bit more seriously. I won best interview, but I still didn't make the Top 12. I kept coming back, and won best interview several times but didn't make the Top 12.

"Something that used to happen every year at Continental was, we'd have rehearsal and it was early in the morning, and Jim would be taking roll to make sure everyone was there, and everyone would say 'here' one after another. Every year when Jimmy got to my name, I would shout out 'hello, Jimmy!' and it always used to make him laugh.

"When I came to Continental in 2008, I was a lot more relaxed. I got a sponsor, so a lot of the financial burden of competing was off of me. It just seemed like everything came together for me. I was ready. There is no key to winning Continental. You have to do it in your own way and follow your own path and instincts. I had to take my time and grow as a performer. I seemed to focus on each category one at a time."

Judge David Hudspeth reminisced: "One of my favorite Continental memories was the year Tulsi won. She came out in the evening-gown portion in this yellow, ruffled ball gown, and as she moved to the end of the runway she very gracefully just sank down into the dress.

It was so stunning you could hear the gasps. I was sitting next to Monica Munro and had a bruise on my arm from where she grabbed me so tightly."

"I loved that gown. It was huge. You could have run a marathon in it," said Tulsi. "It just floated. I had only tried the gown on once since the fitting. That move was completely unpremeditated.

"Becoming Miss Continental was interesting because up until then it was like seeing only one side of the mirror. Winning was like stepping through the looking glass. It opened my eyes to everything Continental. It's prestigious, but it is also a job, a gig. Everybody is looking at you, and there are a lot of expectations. I felt all that weight, definitely.

"The key for me was to stay above it and keep a positive attitude. The traveling and socializing alone can become a nightmare if you let it, but it is definitely a goal worth achieving. I'd like to think I brought a lot of personality and character to the title. I was good at connecting with people, and at the end of the day that's what it's all about."

"When I was in fourth grade, I remember, all my friends were girls, and I would ask them to bring me a dress to wear. So, when I think about it, I have been transgender most of my life," said Miss Continental 2009, Armani.

"When I was 18, I was living with four other queens in a two-bedroom apartment," she said. "They were all entertainers, and I was working at a karaoke bar as a waitress. Well, the place was bought out, and the new owner of this straight bar fired all the transgender employees. The old owner had kind of a thing about transgender waitresses, so there were a few of us.

"Around this time, three of my roommates were getting ready to perform at a Continental Airlines Christmas party. One of my roommates got sick, and they needed a third girl. Basically, it came down to 'you don't have your rent money, do this show and we'll call it even.' So I stepped in and did the show, and I got the best response of all my roommates. I made a quick $300. So my career as an entertainer really started out being about money.

"The first system I competed in was actually Gay USofA. As I got in the field and started meeting more and more people, they all started saying, 'You are so Continental.' I was so flattered, because those girls were so wonderful.

"The first year I competed in Continental was the year Michelle Dupree won [1998] and I made the Top Five. Being in the Continental System taught me right away to be prompt. I used to be one of those people who was 20 minutes late for everything. Not in that system. All the systems have their pluses and minuses. Continental taught professionalism and, to be one of the best, that means being on time.

"I competed a total of eight times. I was all over the place in how I did. I was first runner-up in 2007. Then I took a year off to focus. I wanted a house and a car and a stable life. The amount of money I was spending on Continental was huge. I could have had a five-bedroom house and a pool and a maid for the amount I'd spent. My lover was sick of spending all his money on my pageantry, too. I made a vow that this was it. I was entering one last time, and if I didn't win, so be it. That was the year I won.

"For my talent, I did Michael Jackson. It was a 'Billie Jean' mix. I was going to do him anyway, but then just two months before the pageant that year, he died. My talent went over really well, but I don't know if things would have turned out differently if he hadn't died. The minute they called my name, time stopped. I see pictures of people hugging me and things, but I don't remember. I was blank, in shock. I knew I delivered the best that I could, but it is a pageant, so nothing is guaranteed.

"A funny story about my gown. In 2002, Yoshiko Oshiro, the reigning Miss Continental, came to Raleigh, North Carolina, for a preliminary and performance, and Jim was there, too. Well, Jim took us all to Macy's. He said, 'I can't believe you girls go out and spend three to five thousand dollars on a gown when a lot of times you can find wonderful things right on the clearance rack.' Then he found this gorgeous purple-and-fuchsia gown for $89.

"I ended up competing in it that year at Continental, but I didn't win. Seven years later, we were in the middle of a recession. I took that gown and had it revamped into a modern gown. When I won, I went up to Jimmy and asked him if it looked familiar. He said, 'Vaguely,' and then I told him it was that gown updated. He couldn't believe it.

"My favorite part of my reign was the preliminary in Hawaii. It was very different than the contests here on the mainland, where everyone seemed more out for themselves. There, it was such a place of love. The queens were helping each other with makeup and doing each other's hair. It was a real sense of family. Once a week, all those queens went to the beach together and had a cookout. It was just so much positive energy, just a really beautiful society of queens.

"I remember my last preliminary during my reign was in Chicago, and I was getting ready to fly out of O'Hare, and they canceled my flight. They were setting up cots and telling us we could spend the night there and then fly out in the morning. Well, Jim heard about this and called me. He told me to get in a cab and come to the Baton. He said we'd have a nice evening and he'd get me a place to stay. He said, 'Miss Continental is not sleeping on a cot in the airport.' That says something right there."

Persistence Pays Off

Mokha Montrese won the Miss Continental crown in 2010 on her 14th attempt. "I found myself searching for something," she said. "I always got something out of competing. Every time, I learned something—what wasn't working, or I received some helpful advice. It was always a positive experience. I met friends, I met new people who inspired me. I'd been in the Top 12 maybe eight times and then the Top Five probably five times.

"When I finally won, I remember I was very hot, literally burning up when I made the Top Five. Then it all sort of became fuzzy. I heard 'wah wah wah' where you can't really hear voices. It was not until the DVD came out that I heard my name being called as Miss Continental. I remember the Park West felt like it exploded, though. The crowd went crazy.

"Transitioning [to female] was extremely difficult for me. I am from New Orleans and was living in Birmingham, Alabama. Prior to transitioning I had been a professional ballet dancer and then a dance teacher. I lost my job. I lost most of my friends. My family distanced themselves. I still have not seen my mother. We have talked on the phone in the past year, but that is it. I just saw my sister for the first time in 17 years this past year.

"When I transitioned, I didn't know what to expect. I never really wanted to do drag shows, but I had to, because it seemed the choices were either showgirl or prostitute. I was a dancer, I knew how to entertain. Being a showgirl and having the crowds like and tip me is what led to the pageants. I looked at it from a dancer's point of view, as a way to network, get bookings, and hopefully increase my income. Somewhere along the line, it became a spiritual journey as well.

"That's what made me so emotional when it came time for my year as Miss Continental to end. By the time I won, I was not the same person that I had been when I first competed in 1993. In fact, it was a complete 180. It was so clear to me that it had been this journey. It showed me where I had come from, where I had started, and all the accomplishments and validation that went along with that. It was overwhelming."

Hello, Gabby

The evening Alexis Gabrielle "Gabby" Sherrington was crowned Miss Continental 2011, the program could well have been called Hello, Gabby! given the crowd response. For her talent, Sherrington pantomimed a Broadway-quality production number of "Hello, Dolly!" re-recorded and rephrased as "Hello, Gabby!" with references to Jimmy Flint and Ginger Grant and a special guest appearance by Mr. Continental 2007, Simba Hall.

With the final refrain of "Gabby will never go away again," it was quite apparent that Sherrington was indeed here to stay. The veteran Continental competitor (it was her eighth time in the contest) and frequent runner-up finally won the crown—and the crowd—that night. By the time her name was announced as the winner, she had the audience at the Vic Theatre on their feet and chanting her name.

"When I was 16, I saw a video of the Miss Continental pageant from the year Chanel Dupree won," said Sherrington. "Once I saw it, I knew I had to be a part of that. I had never even seen drag performance before. That was definitely a defining moment. From that moment on, I was inspired, and becoming Miss Continental was the dream I began working towards."

In an interview with CarrieFairfield.com, Sherrington, the former Miss USofA 2004, Miss Black Universe, and Miss Black America Plus and the future Miss Continental, spoke about how she first discovered "Gabby."

"It all really started at a talent show that my high school, Paxon High [in Jacksonville, Florida], was hosting," she was quoted as saying. "The theme of the talent show was Putting on the Hits. I performed the song 'How Can I Ease the Pain' by Lisa Fischer. Initially I was a bit nervous but, me being the person I was, I wanted to perform something different and edgy (which is what I am known for) and, needless to say, everybody fell into my character and illusion! I honestly do think that is the point that Alexis Gabrielle Sherrington began to take shape."

After winning in 2011, Sherrington spoke about her experience in Continentals past. "I first competed at Continental in 1997," she said. "Competing in this system was great. It groomed me as an entertainer and as a professional. The main thing I learned from that experience, up until the night I became Miss Continental, was to believe in myself. We're often our own worst critics, and that can make you bitter. You have to have a tough skin and refuse to give up on your dream. A lot of times, if you want something, you are going to have to work for it. That time and competing those years made me see how much I wanted it."

Sherrington's favorite memory of Flint is from the contest in 2004, the year Erica Andrews was crowned. "Jim has this tendency to botch names," she said. "For the longest time, because my name is so long, he always just called me Alexis Sherrington. That year when I made the Top Five he said my entire name. When he announced me as Alexis Gabrielle Sherrington, I knew I had arrived.

"Something else Jim does which is so great is, he comes down to the dressing rooms during the competition, and he'll talk to the girls as though they've been friends forever. That makes me respect and love him even more—just that he takes the time to go to the dressing rooms and acknowledge the girls and let them know that he appreciates their efforts and the fact that they are here in his contest competing. That says something about the man."

When asked on the CarrieFairfield site why she continued to compete in the Continental System rather than trying for another title such as Entertainer of the Year or Universal Show Queen, Sherrington replied: "Continental is my long-term goal. It is something that I have a burning desire to represent and, not to sound arrogant, but I feel that I have earned the right to be part of such a prestigious group of entertainers that are the former Miss Continentals."

Prior to her victory, Sherrington took off three years because of some personal issues. "I knew that I could not reign successfully without my home base taken care of," she said. "I had to be ready both personally and physically. When I finally heard my name called as Miss Continental, I felt relief. I had been close several times before, so I didn't want to presume. I was in shock as well, and then to feel the crowd and all that love and support and hear the applause, it was really amazing to have something you work so hard and long for to suddenly come true. I'm looking forward to a phenomenal reign."

One of the Top 12 performers the night of Alexis Gabrielle Sherrington's crowning was Tatiana Braxton. Amid the many musical and dance numbers performed by the finalists, Braxton did something unique, a dramatic reading from For Colored Girls Who Have Considered Suicide When the Rainbow Is Enuf, by Ntozake Shange. It was Braxton's fifth time in the pageant and fourth time in the Top 12. She has yet to crack the Top Five. "I usually land right around the same area, sixth to eighth place," she said.

She first competed in 1998. "I was a dresser and entered a preliminary on a dare. I won," said Braxton. "What happened was, my career was going so fast, and I just ended up at Continental without the experience. I didn't know what to expect. I got there and looked around backstage and all of a sudden it hit me, 'Oh, this is the big time, this is really professional.' That time I did not make the Top 12.

"I didn't compete again in Continental until 2006. In those eight years, I polished myself as an entertainer. It's important to remember that Continental is a business. It is professionally run, and I think sometimes there are larger issues at hand than merely what's happening onstage, like what sort of image the pageant wants to project, or who or what kind of girl they may be looking for.

"The fact remains that if you are in this business, this is something that will be good for you. It reaches so many people and such a diverse crowd, especially now with the DVDs and everything. People write me all the time saying they have seen me at Continental or they watched a tape of the program. Being in Continental gives a performer a great amount of visibility and exposure. It's good publicity and a great marketing tool. It gets your name out there. It keeps you relevant, it gets you bookings and it looks good on your résumé. It is a smart career move."

Also competing that night was Tiffany T. Hunter, who did an energetic musical number from Legally Blonde. It was Hunter's third time in Miss Continental. The first two times, she made the Top 12, and this time she was second runner-up.

Hunter said of her beginnings: "I loved watching shows and started to acquire costumes from the professional queens, but I didn't know how to get my start. In May 2003, a friend of mine asked me to perform in his benefit show. I agreed, of course! I got someone to paint my face and spent days planning my debut. Looking back on it, my preparations make me laugh. However, I loved the feeling of being onstage, and Tiffany T. Hunter was born!

"I'm originally from St. Louis, Missouri, and pageants are very popular there. One of the first pageants I was exposed to was the Miss Missouri Continental preliminary. I was immediately interested in it and started watching pageant tapes of other prelims, and the national pageant as well. I wanted to compete because of the prestige Continental holds in our community.

"One of my favorite memories of Jim was at Miss Missouri Continental 2009. This was my first year competing and, as if I wasn't nervous enough, he came to watch the preliminary. When I was done with my talent, I could see where he was sitting, and he was standing up from his chair applauding. To have someone as highly respected as Jim Flint applauding something I did was an incredible feeling and let me know I was on a good path."

As to the benefits of competing in Continental, Hunter replied: "Competing for Miss Continental has had a significant impact on me not only as a performer, but in my personal life as well. It has fine-tuned my craft, whether it's a certain look I am going for or a dance move I should no longer do. Also, it has perfected my organizational, time-management and money-management skills, to name a few."

Hunter is preparing for her fourth return to Miss Continental in 2012.

Miss Continental Plus

Started by Jim Flint in 1991, Miss Continental Plus is a title reserved for those performers weighing 225 pounds or above. Since many female impersonators in the field were larger, and size as well as born-gender can often be a part of the illusion, Flint thought it would be another way to celebrate the art and expand the Continental family. It is held over Easter weekend. The criteria for judging are the same as for the Miss Continental pageant.

"I was surprised when I won Miss Continental Plus," said 1991 winner Ginger Grant. "Everyone thought I would win, but I still wasn't too sure. I wondered if it would matter that I worked here [at the Baton]. At that time there weren't many bookings for Continental Plus. Now there are almost as many as Continental." Grant said her memories of the year were mainly of meeting people and having them "wine and dine you and treat you so grandly. That Continental title really does come with a pedestal."

Miss Continental Plus 1997, Dena Cass, said she met Flint about 20 years ago when she came to the first Miss Continental Plus, the year Ginger Grant won. "I am a plus-sized entertainer and was really impressed with how everyone was treated and the way the contest was run," she said. "So, I came back the following year and got second runner-up.

"Then in 1997 I won the title of Miss Continental Plus. It was such an amazing experience. I traveled all over the States and Puerto Rico, and it really opened so many doors. Jim showed me how entertainers should be treated. Before that, I was OK getting ready in an alley or a flooded basement, and that can still happen at some places, sometimes it's unavoidable, but Jim set the standard of how it's supposed to be.

"It was amazing to be a part of this family, because that's what Jim has done, too. He's given so many of us families. He gives us a home and makes us feel loved. It's the same thing with working at the Baton. You become family. I don't have family, so it means that much more to me, I suppose. I have breasts and I've altered myself. When I told my family I was going to do this, they said, 'If you do this, you can't come home again.' So, I thought, 'I can either make you happy or make me happy.' I had to choose me. I had to be myself.

"In 1998 and '99, I worked at the Baton, and I was born just a little farm boy from Iowa, so to meet all these entertainers, like Teri Hatcher and Janet Jackson, when they came to the club, was overwhelming.

"Since being Miss Continental Plus, I have gone on to win other titles as well. I was Miss USofA At Large in 1998, Miss International Plus in 2003, and in March 2011 I was crowned Miss All American Goddess At Large. Jim was the one who started it all. I just love him. He's down to earth and just so funny and entertaining, even when he's not trying to be."

Tumara Mahorning, Miss Continental Plus 2000 and Showgirl of the Midwest, performs at the Grey Fox in St. Louis. "I met Jim when I was helping out contestants at the 1995 Miss Continental pageant," she said. "I walked right into him, and later someone said, 'Do you know who that is?' and then they told me. I thought, 'Oh, lovely.'

"Five years later, I entered my first time and won Miss Continental Plus 2000. I said that if I entered I was going to do things the way I wanted to do them, and that's what I did. For the first night of talent, I did The Cranberries' 'Zombie,' and I was wearing burlap and had a straw wig, and my dancers were in body bags. I got a standing ovation but I didn't know what to think, because when I came offstage, Jim said, 'Well, that was interesting.' Then the next night, for talent I did Eartha Kitt's 'Le Danseur de Charleston' and did a Charleston and was very glamorous. I wanted to do two very different things.

"I have so many great Jim memories. Ten years of his mispronouncing my name!" It's pronounced like Tomorrow (but a slang-tinged Tomorra) Morning. "My favorite memory, though, was, I was backstage at the Park West, and Carmella Marcella Garcia [Miss Continental Plus 1995] was announcing me, and I went to walk out onstage and someone was standing on my train. It was Jim, and he was in the middle of a conversation with Ginger. I was whispering to him to move but he couldn't hear me, and he didn't move. Then all of a sudden I heard Carmella yell from the stage, 'Get off of her train!' And Jim turned so red and said, 'I am so sorry.'

"I remember another time Jim and I passed each other at O'Hare Airport. We were both there to go to a preliminary in, I believe, Ohio, and we were wearing the same fur coat! One of the funny things about traveling as Miss Continental Plus was going through security, because I had this huge crown and jewelry and makeup and I was a man. I live as a man but perform as a woman. So anyway, it got to be such an issue that I just started traveling with pictures because that sort of explained things. As a result, I signed more pictures at airport security than anywhere else. Also, travel is very expensive now with the extra baggage, especially if you live as a man and have to ship that much more, with the padding and everything.

"I think my favorite Jim memory, though, was when I went to my first preliminary as Miss Continental Plus 2000 and Jim presented me with money as well as flowers. He introduced me and said I was the most articulate Miss Continental he'd ever had. I felt part of a family and extremely welcomed.

"The Continental family is what we rightfully call ourselves and there are emails and birthday cards and Christmas cards. If there is any drama, Jim says, 'Leave it at the door.' People always say to me that I should enter another contest, and I always answer that with a simple 'why?' Once you are part of this family, nothing else really compares."

On the Road Again

"This coming year will mark my 25th year as an entertainer," said Miss Continental Plus 2003, Victoria Parker. "Even as a kid I was always a ham. I was a child performer and effeminate, and the first show I went to I thought, 'I can do that.' So, I talked to the people doing it, and they put me in the show, and that was my debut in 1987, at Lynn's Lounge in Fayetteville, North Carolina. I loved it right away but also realized it was a lot harder than I thought. There was a lot more to it than just dressing up. It was dressing up and then performing. It's all about entertaining people. That's still my favorite part of doing this, just looking out at people and knowing that you're entertaining them.

"I first met Jim at Virginia's Continental Plus preliminary in 1996. I won, and he came backstage afterwards and talked with me and said I reminded him of himself when he first started doing drag. I was just so flattered.

"Then I came to Continental Plus that year and, after the first round of things at the contest, Jim was on the stage and announced that from then on he would be giving an interview award at the Continental contests and it was all because of one contestant, who had so impressed him and the judges in the interview—and it was me. I couldn't believe it. So I was the first one that ever got that award, and now they give it out every time at all four Continentals.

"That year I ended up getting first runner-up in the contest. Then I came back the next year and got fourth runner-up, and the year after that I didn't even make the Top Five. Then I decided to take some time off and figure out what I was doing wrong, or not doing right, anyway, because I was moving backwards. So, I didn't compete for four years and got more experience. Those four years I helped other contestants in the contest, so I still came, but I didn't compete. Then the next time I came, in 2003, I won. When I won, Jim gave me a big hug and said, 'I was waiting for you to come back.' I think all that time I was really just getting ready, getting the experience that the Continental System expects of you as a winner.

"Winning really made me step up my game, because suddenly there was so much to live up to. It challenged me. I wanted to be an excellent representative of the system and uphold all my duties as well as live up to the expectations of the audience.

"Jim is hard to work for, in that he demands excellence of his titleholders. He keeps a firm hand on us and runs a tight ship. My very first prelim, I slept right through my alarm and missed my flight, so I had to call the office and get them to rebook me, and, of course, Jim answered the phone. He was a little terse, but when I saw him later, he was fine. He lets you know right away that it's a business and that you need to be on your toes and be the person they want you to be as Miss Continental Plus, meaning a professional.

"It was a wonderful experience. I think there were 15 preliminaries in my year, and so I traveled all over and got a lot of experience. My being Miss Continental Plus opened a lot of doors. It led to my being in the movie Trantasia [Showtime, 2006], which led to my being in the documentary Pageant [2008], which led to my being cast in RuPaul's Drag Race. That was a very humbling experience, being the first one cut during the first season—but it was also wonderful to be a part of the first reality show to feature drag queens.

"Jim deserves a lot of thanks for establishing, promoting and providing a great system for furthering the art of female impersonation. So much of the progress we have made goes right back to him. I salute him."

Desiree DeMornay shared her experiences. "For my talent when I won Miss Continental Plus in 2006, I did Barbra Streisand's 'The Main Event,' and I'll never forget the standing ovation I got when I finished," she said. "Then, when Jim read my name as the new Miss Continental Plus, I remember thinking, 'I have been waiting to hear that!' I had competed before and ended up winning on my seventh try.

"My favorite part of being Miss Continental Plus was the traveling and the meeting people and entertaining at so many new places. I loved, loved, loved my reign. I loved having people at the airport meet me with signs saying Miss Continental Plus and then taking limos. It was really wonderful for me personally and also to represent such a polished and classy pageant. My only complaint is that the year went by too quickly.

"I love Jim Flint's wit. It took me a while to understand that sometimes when he's being serious he's really being funny. Once I understood that and started to catch on, he was hilarious to me."

Making Dreams Come True

"I was introduced to drag by Tiffany Arieagus, Miss Continental 1982," said Miss Continental Plus 2007, Tajma Hall. "I watched her perform at the Offshore Drilling Company in Myrtle Beach, South Carolina. I approached her, and we began talking about many different things. She was extremely nice and personable. Out of the blue, she asked me if I had a girlfriend. I told her no, and she asked why a pretty girl like me did not have a girlfriend.

"I told her I was really a boy, and then she asked what my drag name was. I told her I did not do drag, and you should have seen the look on her face! She told me that a pretty boy like me should definitely be doing drag. She spun me around and said, 'Dear, your drag name will be Tajma Hall—first name Tajma, last name Hall.' I was mortified and told her I had no interest in doing drag. She told me it would happen, and I left the club in fear of what just happened. Well, some years later, I started the art form, and my name was indeed Tajma Hall.

"In 2003, after being around the Baton and all the girls, I decided I was ready to enter Miss Continental Plus. It was an amazing experience. I made the Top 12 my first year and felt I really made a name for myself in the system. I went back the following year, allowing so many people to influence me and what I presented. I made the Top 12 again, but was very disappointed in myself. The following year my mother became very ill, and I had to sit out. My heart was not with pageantry, it was with my mother.

"In October 2006, I decided it was time to become an official part of the Continental family. I entered Miss Dreamgirl Continental Plus [a Continental preliminary], won four of the five categories, and was crowned the winner. I was very excited but knew I had my work cut out for me. I had an amazing team behind me, and Jim Flint gave me words of encouragement the entire year. He was very supportive and made me realize I could do it.

"In April 2007, my dream came true. Again, I won four of the five categories and was crowned Miss Continental Plus. My favorite memory is hearing Jim Flint say, 'And your new Miss Continental Plus 2007, Tajma Hall!' I can still hear him saying it, and it still brings tears to my eyes. I had an amazing reign and it changed my life forever."

Hall, who said she is "living her life like it's golden," also won the title Miss Gay USofA At Large 2009. About her affiliation with Continental, she said, "Now, Jim allows me to emcee Miss Continental, Miss Continental Plus, Miss Continental Elite and Mr. Continental. I also emcee prelims to the national pageants. I am very involved in the Continental System and I would not have it any other way."

"I competed in Miss Continental Plus for the first time in 2007 and made the Top 12, and then the following year I came back and won. I am one of those people who, if you show me directions once, I can find my way, and that's really what I did the first time," said Miss Continental Plus 2008, Mercedes (who later added Tyler as her last name). "I learned what was going on and how things were done. The next year, I was fortunate enough to have people who believed in me. I got a costume designer and choreographer and for my talent did a Bette Midler medley of 'Friends,' 'In the Mood' and 'Sing, Sing, Sing.'

"One of the most touching moments at a Continental pageant was the year when Jim gave a speech about us all being a family. That year, both Cezanne's parents had died and, after Jim's speech, all the former Miss Continentals and Miss Continental Pluses went through the audience collecting money to pay for the funeral. It was very moving and so true. Continental is a family, and that's not to say that it is perfect and there aren't conflicts. It has plenty of that, too, just like most families.

"The year I won Miss Continental Plus, I had kind of a rough time, because at the time I was living my life as a man and I had literally come from left field, so I didn't really have a name. I was not always—shall we say, graciously received. However, Jim always had my back and always went to bat for me. I really had to work to prove myself that year, but I did.

"Sometimes it was so grueling. I remember once, over a four-day period, I flew on a Friday from Chicago to North Carolina to West Virginia to perform at West Virginia Continental Plus, and that ended about 3 or 4 a.m. Then the next morning I flew from West Virginia back to North Carolina and on to perform in Toronto, and then was there the next night for Canadian Continental Plus, and then flew to Miami for the Miss Florida Continental Plus.

"I saw Jimmy there and said, 'You know what? I am going to stay here for a week. I don't have any bookings right now, I have worked my butt off, so I am going to just get a hotel here and lie on the beach for a week.' He ended up paying for my hotel room and giving me some spending money and said, 'Have a good time.' It was so sweet."

"I started doing female impersonation because I was a makeup artist, and I started playing with makeup on myself. I was in theater in high school and all that, so that was my niche. What happened was, Halloween became talent shows, and those became pageants," said Roxxy Andrews, Miss Continental Plus 2010.

"I didn't actually compete in a Continental preliminary until 2008, when I represented Metropolitan Continental Plus in Florida. I went to the pageant Easter weekend in Chicago, and I ended up getting third runner-up but, more importantly, I got my name out there. Becoming part of the Continental System did that for me right away. People who saw me in the pageant started calling and booking me, 'Oh, we saw you at Continental Plus, and we'd like you to come to our club,' that sort of thing. So, that year, I traveled, since I hadn't been much out of Florida before then. With so many pageant winners coming from this state, we joke that it must be something in the Florida water.

"Anyway, the next year, I went back to Continental Plus, and that year I got third runner-up as well. Again, my bookings and experience increased, and what I was doing, which I didn't realize at the time, was making myself ready for when I did win. I won on my third try and became Miss Continental Plus in 2010. Those years leading up to it gave me the self-confidence I needed and increased my professionalism to the degree that I felt ready. That isn't something you buy or something you do, it comes from within. That's what you learn from experience, and I don't think it can really be taught.

"When it came time to step down as Miss Continental Plus, I literally had a breakdown onstage. It was so moving to know that I had done my job and now I was a member of this elite sisterhood. I didn't want it to end, but at the same time it was clear that it was someone else's turn.

"I am going to come back in 2012 and compete in Miss Continental. I want to show that just because I am a Plus doesn't mean that I am lesser than or can't compete next to a smaller competitor. There's this mistaken idea that being a Plus girl means it's easier to win. I want to show that nothing changes because of size. I want to break down those walls.

"Continental is the best system out there. It is literally what every entertainer wants to walk into. Things run smoothly, it is professional, there is help ready, things start on time, it's not five days long, there isn't too much talent onstage. It's all balanced really well. I'm the type that when I get ready to perform, I want it to happen. I don't want to have to stand around for hours in a gown and wait. There's other pageants, too, where it is a big party or the judges are drinking during the contest. You don't see that sort of thing at Continental.

"I love the illusion of all this—the clothes, the hair, the shoes. I love making people smile. I learned a lot from my drag mother, Erica Andrews.

"There are so many amazing things about Jimmy. The fact that he created all this is a big part of it, but then there are so many other things, like, he is the only person I know who can go to all these different cities, rent a car without a navigation system, and know exactly how to get and where to turn to be where he needs to be. I've traveled with him, so I know. The other thing that impressed me traveling with him was that he may not always remember a name, but he never forgets a face. Once he's seen you, he's seen you."

"I first heard about Continental in 1986," said Miss Continental Plus 2011, Chelsea Pearl. "I was in Indianapolis, where I was for 18 years, and I was in the cast at a place called the 21 Club. Chilli Pepper actually was a guest, and the first thing she said to me was, 'Oh, you're so Continental,' meaning the pageant. I was so flattered. Since then, it became a sort of dream.

"I first met Jim Flint in 1991 or '92 when I was competing in a contest called Miss Chubby World [a prelim for Miss Continental Plus at the time]. I ended up coming in first runner-up [behind Gina Nate]. What was so impressive was that after the contest, Jim came up and said he enjoyed my work. Then he went and picked up my suitcases himself and put them in the trunk of his car and took me back to my hotel. It is still my favorite memory of him, because it really shows the kind of classy and hands-on sort of guy he is. That was when I first met him. What a first impression!

"It's, like, when you go to the contest, at Continental every time, there is Jim walking around, greeting people, thanking them for coming. If you are there early, you'll see him moving the tables or doing this or that. It's the same with how he treats the girls. Jim knows he needs girls to have a pageant, and he is very encouraging and caring and makes sure that they are recognized. He thanks them for being there, and that's huge. It's amazing he hasn't become jaded after doing it for so long, but he hasn't.

"I first competed in Miss Continental Plus in 1998. I was second runner-up, then first runner-up, then second runner-up, and then the next time I didn't make the Top Five. Afterwards I had a lot of people telling me negative things. They said, 'Don't go back,' and, 'See, they don't want you'—that sort of thing. It wears on you and sometimes you start to feel you are not worthy when you hear that enough. Thankfully, I didn't listen, because the next time I went I ended up winning. It just shows you that dreams come true. That would be my message, I suppose.

"Being Miss Continental Plus has been so overwhelming. People talk to you differently. There's a whole new level of respect, and the admiration so many of the girls have to those who carry this title is so flattering. As to the plans for my year, Continental sort of takes care of itself. My goal is not to disappoint. Jim has never disappointed me, so I don't want to disappoint him. I want to be the best representative I can be. I also want to keep encouraging other girls and let them know that it can happen for them, too. I think of those negative voices talking to me, and I just want to let them know that a quitter never wins. It's that simple."

Continental Elite

Continental Elite is a two-day contest Flint established to take place over the four-day Easter holiday weekend, to balance the two-day Miss Continental Plus. Elite is a contest for the seasoned performance veterans. It is for female impersonators age 40 or older, to celebrate those contestants whose experience and knowledge of the art form is titleworthy.

"I had heard about the Continental System in New York back in the 1980s. I was still living in Puerto Rico, but I would come into town periodically for guest spots at Escuelita, a Latin club in Manhattan [at 301 West 39th Street]," said Miss Continental Elite 2005, Barbra Herr.

"In 1990 I moved to New York, and at the time I never thought of entering a contest, because I didn't like the thought of being judged or competing," Herr said. "Well, I entered a few anyway and never won any of the early ones. Then in the late 1990s, I met José Abraham, who is a wonderful promoter. He changed my view of the pageants. I had also met Jim and Ginger before, when they'd traveled to New York.

"The first time I went to Continental was the year Tommie Ross won in 1999. I was in the prelims seven years in a row, and it was so nice and wonderful. I got pageant fever. I always placed in the Top 12 and was in the Top Five twice. Then Jim convinced me to enter Continental Elite in 2004. So I entered, and that was my sixth time. I didn't really want to do it until I won Miss Continental and, at the time, Continental Elite was still very new, but Jim didn't have that many contestants, and so he convinced me, and then I came in first runner-up, alternate to Nikki Adams. When I came back to Elite the following year, I won.

"When I won Miss Continental Elite in 2005, truthfully it didn't feel like Miss Continental. There weren't a lot of prelims. It was great to be a part of the court and all, but I didn't travel much. But from competing in Continental so many times and having a name and a good reputation from that, people flew me in anyway, and as a result, when I left Elite there were 12 Continental Elite preliminaries, so I guess I did my job well.

"Whenever Jim comes to New York, we love to go shopping and to lunches and great dinners. Let me tell you, Jim knows how to take a girl out. Then we usually have several drinks afterwards. My favorite Jim memories, though, are just those conversations. We are both very straightforward and unyielding. We're both left liberal Democrats, so we can discuss politics for hours, and we are both huge baseball fans, although I am a Yankees fan and he's a Cubs fan. He's definitely a Cubs fan."

"I got my name Electra from one of the strippers in Gypsy," said Miss Continental Elite 2010, Electra. "At the time, I was opening for Eartha Kitt, the real Eartha Kitt, and I was doing all these impressions and look-alikes, and a regular name just didn't seem to fit for me, so my manager at the time said we needed something with a bit more pizazz—especially if you're opening for Eartha Kitt. We decided on something one-name. Well, I said, 'How about Electra?' and that's how it started.

"I first met Jim at the Miss Florida pageant in 1993. It was the first pageant I ever entered, and Jim came up to me afterwards and told me I should have won. I would go to different pageants and events and see him, and he would always say hello and was a perfect gentleman. In 1994 I won National Entertainer of the Year, and I was in Chicago for the Miss Continental contest after I won, and Jim asked me if I'd walk the stage and wave and wear my crown [as National Entertainer of the Year]. So, after that, he said, 'When are you going to be in one of my pageants?'

"Well, I didn't really see myself as a Continental type. I didn't have breast implants and hips. I was a comedienne when I would emcee, and mostly I performed as look-alikes. I do about 25 different ones—currently I'm doing Bette Midler in Atlantic City. But I also do Judy Garland, Marilyn Monroe, Liza Minnelli, Lucille Ball, Joan Crawford, Bette Davis, Carol Channing. The point is, I wasn't Continental, in that I couldn't just stand there and look gorgeous and sell a song. I love watching it, but it just didn't feel like me, but I told Jim that if I ever decide to enter a Continental he'd be the first to know.

"Well, my mother had been very ill for quite some time, and I took care of her. While that was going on, I sort of pulled back from performing at anything, except on a local level just to bring some money into the house. Before she died, she encouraged me and told me that I had to go back out, that I had a life to live. She died on April 4, 2009, and a year later, over Easter Sunday weekend, I was crowned Miss Continental Elite 2010. Easter Sunday 2010 was also on April 4.

"I was 51 at the time I became part of the Continental family. When I entered, I said to Jim, 'See, I always keep my promises.' I was so moved. The night I won, when he saw me all done up, he said to a friend of mine, 'Oh, she looks beautiful.' That did it for me. It's even sweeter when you've never been seen that way.

"Now, what I really want is for Jim to get back on his skates so we can do a skating number together. Jim with his skates and baton again, that would be terrific."

"I was a girl long before I hit the stage, but Victoria Lace and Armani are the girls that got me to do drag seriously," said Miss Continental Elite 2011, Daesha Richards. "I wanted to be a dancing diva like them, but I ended up becoming a walk-real-fast diva. Some girls dance and some girls walk—I walk, but I do it fast. I first started performing as a favor for a friend, as a backup dancer. From that day on, I was hooked.

"This was my third time competing for Elite. This year was different because I was moving to Atlanta and wanted to start my life over with a new home and a new place in drag history. Continental is the top of the ladder no matter what title you hold—Miss, Mr., Plus or Elite. I wanted to leave New York on top of the world, so I did the contest again, and God blessed me and I won.

"The week before, I got a really bad infection and was so sick I could not get out of bed, and on top of that I had to pack because I was moving the week after the pageant. So, going to Chicago, I felt like I was dying. If it were not for my friends that were there with me, I would have just stayed in the bed in the hotel. Criss Mapp, Princess Janae and Jasmine International got me through the weekend. Without them I would not have made it. Thank God for real friends.

"My duty as Continental Elite is first and most importantly to inspire other girls that are 40 and over to compete next year. This might sound like an easy job, but it is not. A lot of girls my age feel they have to compete with the younger girls to stay on top. In some cases that is true, but in this case it is not. There is a place for Elite girls; we just have to claim it and make it our own."

Mr. Continental

In the mid-1980s, Flint produced a Mr. Continental contest. "Christian Winkel, the leatherman I had such a crush on, won, and Jeff Stryker the porn star was first runner-up," Flint said. "It never really took off after that."

More than a decade later, things had changed. The Continental System of pageantry was well-established. Other pageant systems featured a Mr. contest. People had suggested a Mr. competition to Flint on several occasions. Finally, in 2004, he decided the time was right. The Mr. Continental contest resumed. "We decided to make it Labor Day weekend, along with Miss Continental."

The Mr. Continental event requires that the contestants be gay and over 21. The gay stipulation has occasionally caused some questions about a contestant's qualifications, similar to the issues of gender equipment that sometimes arose in the Miss Continental. "A couple years ago we had a Russian opera singer from New York. There were questions, but then we watched who he went with every night and realized he wasn't straight," said Flint.

Like the other Continental pageants, contestants from various Mr. preliminaries compete for the title. For the actual scoring of the contest, the same judging categories and percentages are used, except instead of evening gown, the men compete in formalwear.

"Now in Mr. Gay USofA they have a Mr. Gay USofA At Large, and people are calling me to ask when Continental is going to have a Mr. At Large," added Flint. "I am a large man, but I don't find anything compelling about seeing another large man do a number as a big man or coming out in a bathing suit. I have the large for ladies because there's an illusion to it. Since the men have no illusion, I don't understand what difference size would make."

The start of Mr. Continental was a bit rocky. Carl Harris was Mr. Continental in 2004 but was unable to continue his reign, so Ray Mathews, as the alternate, took over the duties.

According to CarrieFairfield.com, Carl Harris was dismissed and stripped of his title. The site reported that Flint sent a letter with $1,000 of Harris' remaining prize money and said that, because he was the new pageant director for Mr. & Miss Black USofA, he was no longer needed.

When asked about the circumstances in an interview for this book, Flint responded: "I couldn't have my Mr. going around the country promoting another pageant. He could not fulfill the contract, and so Ray Mathews was appointed."

Antonio Edwards, who also held the titles Mr. Gay All American in 1998 and Mr. Gay

USofA in 2001, was well aware that Flint had started a Mr. Continental. "Then, in the summer of 2004, Carl Harris, who at the time was Mr. Continental, told me I should enter," said Edwards. "That next year, I competed and won on my first try. For the talent portion, I sang a song called 'Per Te,' which in Italian means 'For You,' and that was kind of risky because at the time I sang it in Italian. One of my favorite memories is standing with Jim on the stage at the Park West for the pictures."

"It was a wonderful year," said Edwards (Mr. Continental 2005). "I traveled across the country representing the system at states with preliminaries and met with promoters. I was living in Roanoke, Virginia, at the time, and another thing I did was drive everywhere. When I would have a prelim, the promoter would fly me to Dallas or Chicago or wherever, but between those contests I went to the contests for other systems, like Miss Gay USofA and Miss Black America, and wore my sash and my medallion and made other systems aware of the presence of Continental, since I was only the second Mr.

"By doing that, the nice thing was visibility, but also it was showing those other systems that they were being supported as well. I think that was important." Edwards' actions may indeed have carried extra weight and importance, cementing any breaks in the pageant community in the wake of Carl Harris' dismissal.

Edwards added: "I have come back to Chicago every year since I won, for not only Mr. and Miss over Labor Day weekend, but also Elite and Plus during Easter weekend. Whenever I come to Chicago, before I even go to my hotel or anything, the plane lands, I take the train in, and the first thing I do is go right with my bags to the Baton, go back to the office, and sit on the floor by Tim [Gideon] and Scott's [Palmer] desks and catch up with Jim and everyone. Just that catching up and carrying on is so nice.

"The 30th anniversary of Continental was an amazing event. To be there during that weekend, you really felt the history and the feel of family. It started when I was 15 and still in high school, and yet it's still going on today. That's something. That's an accomplishment."

"I remember Jim walking through the door of Illusions in Atlanta, where I worked," said Mr. Continental 2006, Tony DeSario. This would have been sometime during the early 1980s. "It was the biggest show club in the country, down on Peachtree Street—Diana Ross, Chaka Khan and Gladys Knight came there. It was about five times the size of the Baton, and the stage was about as big as the one at the Park West. Our regular cast was 15 girls and six guys, and we had an on-staff seamstress and choreographer. We had enormous productions, salary with insurance.

"It was like the Hollywood of drag down there at the time, with people like Hot Chocolate, Tiffany Arieagus, Tandi Andrews, Bertha Butts, Rachel Wells, Dana Douglas, Amber Richards, Chena Black and so many others. Into this walks Jim, with Chilli on one arm and, I think, Andrea Nicole on the other, and they were just over the top, the girls in their gowns and furs and diamonds, and even in that environment Jimmy's entrance made you say 'wow!'

"Around that time, I started competing in pageants. I was young and talented but thought it was mostly a bunch of musclemen in Speedos. Well, I had talent, so I competed if it was a night I didn't have a show. It was usually a minute and a half in a suit, then a minute and a half in a swimsuit and then sing a song.

"A lot of times, those contests paid $500 for first, $250 for second, and $150 for third. So, I looked at it as getting good pay for basically five minutes of work. So, from 1981 to '84, I did that as supplemental income. When you enter a contest, you have to have a sponsor, and since I worked at the place where a lot of the contests were being held, they couldn't sponsor me—so I asked Jim. Many times I won, and when I did, I'd give him the plaque to hang in his club. Soon Jim wanted to sponsor me all the time.

"I wanted Jim to have a Mr. Continental [contest]. I left Atlanta in 1985 and moved to Las Vegas and went between there and L.A. for the next three years. While I was there, I heard about a Mr. Continental [the year Flint's leather paramour Christian Winkel won], and then I didn't hear anything more.

"About 1990, I moved back to Atlanta and was working as show director at LaVita's and was there about three years. The shows down there were drying up. In my opinion, it was because the queens started being in charge of the shows, and not businesspeople. The queens were lazy, and the productions went away and it was just one individual number after another. It was ugly to watch, because sometimes they would just walk around from table to table and basically stand there and be snapping fingers for money. The only thing that wasn't that way was the Stars of the Century show. And this was down from probably five or six places that had big impersonator shows at one time.

"After that, I was the singer in a corporate band [one that plays for corporate parties] for a while. Then a Nashville producer heard me and wanted me to do a country album. I had a No. 33 song with 'Drive' in 1995. I recorded under the name Tony Hoops, because they didn't want me as Tony DeSario traced back to the impersonator shows and gay contests.

"I toured for a year and got really soured on the business. I opened for big names and went to some big parties, but things would happen, like, they would send a car, and in the back seat would be a woman who was my supposed 'date' for the evening. When I went anywhere, they told me how to walk and talk and where to be seen and what to wear. Eventually I'd had enough.

"In 2001, I returned to Atlanta and was the general manager of a place called the Jungle. Once I was there, I started booking events, and one of the shows I booked was a Continental preliminary. The [2005] Mr. Continental was Antonio Edwards, and he was talking to me and said I should think about [entering the competition]. I said, 'Are you crazy?' I said I was 42. He said, 'This is different, Tony. It's not about body or youth. They want an intelligent man with talent to hold this title.' That night Jim came in for the prelim as well, and he asked me why I wasn't entering."

Flint said he had been trying to get Tony DeSario in the contest. "He told me, 'Jim, I am just too old. I could never compete with those young kids.' I told him that maybe he couldn't compete in the swimsuit, but he could in the interview, the talent, and the formalwear," Flint said. "I said, 'When it comes to the Q-and-A at the end, you know you can talk.' I said, 'All you have to do is stay halfway in the swimsuit. You've got everything else going for you.'"

"I said, 'Well, I've asked you to do things for me, so I'll do this for you, but only the one time,'" explained DeSario. "So I entered a preliminary and won.

"When I got to Chicago, none of the guys entered in the contest had heard of me. I had basically been off of the stage for 10 or 15 years. They thought I was someone's sponsor or something. They laughed and made fun of me. I expected that. During the first night, I sang 'Superstar' by Luther Vandross at the Baton and got a standing ovation, and they had to wait for people to calm down."

The next night on the bus on the way to the finals at the Park West, Flint asked if anyone was going to change his talent from what he'd done in the preliminaries. DeSario raised his hand. At the first opportunity Flint pulled DeSario aside and asked him if he was sure he wanted to change his song. Flint knew DeSario had won the talent and had a good idea that his version of the Vandross song was wonderful enough to win him the contest overall. DeSario remained firm in his decision to change his song.

"I said I was sure. I knew what I was doing," DeSario said. "That night I sang 'Bridge Over Troubled Water,' and I always have to play with the sound people because my voice is very loud, and I knew that when I hit that powerful note it would blow the sound out, so I told them to turn the sound on the down side. Well, when I got to that part, I had the microphone down at my side, and they could still hear me in the balcony. The house went nuts. And I won.

"The thing is, after the Continental contest, when you appear somewhere—whether it's Arizona or New Mexico or Texas or North Carolina—they play the video of the contest in the club before you get there, to sort of get people excited. So, they would all want to hear me sing what I sang on the tape, so by the time my year was over I was so tired of singing 'Bridge Over Troubled Water' that just the intro could make my blood curdle.

"After I won, I ended up getting fired [from my regular job] for missing time from work. I'd just got a new home and a new car down in Atlanta, and I was scared. I called up Jimmy and he said, 'Pack a bag and come up here, and I'll book you for a month.' So he did. I think I played the Baton the whole month of October. Then Jimmy booked me at show clubs around the country. I was always on the road. He had me sing at the Gay World Series and at Soldier Field when the Gay Games were in Chicago. He gave me the chance to sing for some major crowds. By going that extra step of booking me that year, he saved me."

"I competed in Mr. Continental in 2004 and got second runner-up," said Simba Hall. "It was my very first pageant. I was attracted to it because at that time in Mr. Continental the talent had to be live. There was no lip-syncing. That rule changed in 2007."

In 2005, Hall didn't compete at Continental. Instead, he became Mr. Renaissance. He wanted to build up his name and reputation before returning. However, he did attend the contest and watched Antonio Edwards sing "Per Te." Seeing Edwards named the winner excited Hall.

"I realized I could win Mr. Continental doing a talent that was closer to my classical roots," he said. "The next year I entered and sang 'Ave Maria' and got first runner-up to Tony DeSario. I was so disappointed and considered not coming back. The following Easter, I went to the Miss Continental Plus pageant. I ran into Jim there, and he said he'd heard I might not be entering the contest that year. He told me he thought that would be a shame. That was so nice of him that I ended up entering. That was the year I won and became Mr. Continental 2007."

As the drag son of Tommie Ross, Hall said the most important thing the former Miss Continental taught him was, "You have to show people how you want to be viewed." Hall explained: "For example, I want to be seen as a distinguished, talented, dedicated and classy man. If that's the image I want to convey, I need to do it through the way I dress and speak and carry myself onstage. Marketing yourself means presenting yourself as a clear package, a clear image."

Hall shared his favorite memory of Flint as well. "We both love to gamble," Hall said. "One time, we were leaving Chicago to head to one of the casinos down near Indianapolis. On the way, we stopped at a Steak 'n Shake. I had never been to one before, so once we sat down Jim gave me the whole story about his working there on roller skates. I was laughing so hard I couldn't breathe. Then he told me I had to try a strawberry shake. Well, I didn't really like shakes that much, but this one was made with fresh fruit. I loved it. Now, not a week or two goes by that I don't have to go to Steak 'n Shake for a strawberry shake."

Hall is retired from competing but holds seven national titles, including Mr. Gay USofA 2010. "Each system is special to me," he said, "but Continental is by far the classiest. It is a pageant I could invite my mother to, and trust me, my mother is a Holy Roller. It is the closest thing this world has to a crossover pageant."

"When I competed, Jim embarrassed me after the preliminary because he was telling people I did Michael Jackson better than Michael Jackson and should be in Las Vegas," said Rasean Montrese. "When I won Mr. Continental in 2008, I did 'Beat It' into 'Billie Jean' into 'Thriller.' Actually, when he said that to me about Las Vegas, that was what started the wheels turning about my going to Vegas, which I eventually did. I even had a 45-second bit part in Disaster Movie [2008] as Michael Jackson, which came about because Jim allowed me to use the clip of myself performing at Mr. Continental as my audition tape for the role."

Judge Shawn Batton vividly recalled Montrese's talent. "The year Rasean Montrese was competing in Mr. Continental, he did his talent preliminary night at the Baton," Batton said. "Rasean did Michael Jackson for talent, and the crowd went nuts. After his talent, the judges, simultaneously, looked at each other in awe of what had just happened. It was the only time I can remember that ever happening."

Montrese, who was also National Entertainer of the Year 2005, said that something else that changed for him "was just being Mr. Continental. After I won Entertainer of the Year, it was sort of 'great, see you next year.' With Jim, he was much more involved. One thing that set him apart, too, was that he was looking not only for an entertainer, but also for a gentleman. He didn't want just sexy and nasty, he wanted someone who would represent the administrative side as well as the entertainment aspects of the title. That really impressed me.

"Jim has changed the internal and external perception of the pageantry system. He took something which was known as being just sort of campy and brought this class, grace, beauty and sophistication to it. He made that the standard."

Stepping Stones

"I had been a part of the Continental competitions for a while as a background dancer and choreographer," said Nick Gray, Mr. Continental 2011. (Miss Continental is awarded the same year as the title, while Mr. Continental wins in one year for the next year's title; thus Gray won in 2010 for Mr. 2011.) "I worked with Armani and did her 'Happy Feet' number at Continental 2009. I worked with Alexis Gabrielle Sherrington and Shantell DMarco as well. Jim noticed me and asked if I had ever thought about competing in the Mr. Continental pageant. A good friend of mine is David 'Freklz' Hunter, who was Mr. Continental in 2009, and I thought, 'I can do that. I am a dancer and choreographer by profession, and I can be a good business representative because of my business degree.'

"At the competition in the formalwear, I remember walking across the stage and looking regal and trying to prove to the audience and the judges and to Mr. Flint that I was the one. It's in your carriage and the way you conduct yourself and speak. For my talent, I did this chair dance to 'Dear Goodbye' by JC Chasez. It became this dance about the relationship I had with my ex. I still have people who talk to me about that today.

"I met so many amazing people during my reign. It was very different from being a background dancer to being in the forefront. It made me go from being a dancer to being an entertainer. As a dancer, you are working for someone else, and as an entertainer you are in charge. As an entertainer, you have a freer range, and approval comes not from the choreographer but by the audience watching you.

"I remember, my first preliminary, people expected certain things from me, and as an entertainer I am very eclectic. Because I am black and come from Jamaica, people expected one thing, and I danced to 'Black Hole Sun' by Soundgarden. But that song moved me. I find a beat that turns on my body, not sexually but as a dancer, and once I do, that's it. That makes me move.

"I also wanted to go through the year keeping my clothes on. Everybody wanted me to be naked all year, but I stayed in my clothes. It has been a great job opportunity for choreographing and dancing, and it has also been a great steppingstone. By asking me if I ever thought about competing in Continental, Jim gave me a nudge. He saw my talent and capability, and that really helped me have the confidence to see that I was a good fit for the title and had a lot to offer.

"In my year, I wanted to show that the guys are a symbol of excellence as well. The guys don't dress up, we aren't illusionists. But I wanted people to realize we bust our butts and work just as hard as they [the female impressionists] do."

Philip Alexander, Mr. Continental 2012, said he was in the Navy and stationed at the Pentagon when he came into the gay community through the pageant system. "I was first there as a backup dancer the year Antonio Edwards won," Alexander said. "I thought, 'I can do this. I'm going to try.' So, I competed and didn't make the Top 12, and it sort of filled me with negativity. I came to sing and wow the judges with my voice. It doesn't work that way.

"I competed again and made the Top 12 but not the Top Five. Again I was brought down, and what I didn't realize was, what you have to do is get a feel for the system. The system is actually grooming you to re-evaluate your stuff, not through actual comments by the judges' score sheets, you don't get anything like that. It's more by learning through the feedback of people, learning what people to listen to, and what is constructive and what is critical. There's a difference.

"After my second time, [judge] Jim DeMundo came up to me and asked if I was going to compete again and said, 'You've grown so much as a performer, I really think you should give it another shot.' Then I talked to Nick Gray, and he inspired me again, and I said, 'I will do it with a great promoter behind me,' and so I became Mr. Big D Continental Alternate for John 'Messy' Stevens."

For his talent, the tall and elegant Alexander sang a stirring rendition of "The Prayer" (originally done by Celine Dion and Andrea Bocelli), which received a standing ovation. His performance made him a crowd favorite, but what made him the clear winner was his answer to the final interview question about forgiveness. In his clear and heartfelt response, Alexander spoke of reaching out and forgiving the mother who gave him up for adoption, and how that act of forgiveness had subsequently lifted a weight from him and brought wonderful things into his life. The conclusion was that forgiveness can be difficult, but it is essential in order to grow as a person. At the close of his answer, the crowd went wild.

The morning after his victory on Labor Day weekend 2011, the new Mr. Continental said: "I have been so grateful to win, but grateful that I did it with a clear sense of deservedness.

That's huge. The competition was a bloodbath. I was scared to death because the talent, the looks—there were so many great contestants. So, to win from that caliber of men really makes it that much better. It also makes the job of Mr. Continental that much easier. When people are happy that you have won, they are much more responsive and receptive.

"I foresee this coming year as the biggest year for Mr. Continental yet. I'd like to inspire quality contestants to enter. I think that is done any number of ways. When I was Mr. State of Florida Continental, I got emails all the time with questions about competing. Sometimes making a difference for someone in competing is as simple as being available, as answering their questions, and inspiring them to be their best—not their best as they think they should be, but the best as themselves, as an individual."

Also competing that night in 2011 for the title of Mr. Continental was Noah Lee Richards. Richards first became aware of the Continental contest when his gay mother (an adopted mother, similar to a drag mother), Daesha Richards, began competing in Continental Elite during Easter weekend of 2009. "The more I learned about Continental, the more excited I became," said Richards, who had previously competed in Mr. Latino Universe in 2009.

He decided to enter Mr. Continental the next Labor Day weekend. "I made the Top 12 in Mr. Continental 2009. I was thrilled, because that first time I was mainly looking to get experience and to grow as an entertainer. The next year I was second runner-up, and then in 2011 I was first runner-up," said Richards, who did a rousing dance number for his talent performance.

"The thing I like about Continental is that each winner is unique," Richards said. "What I learned in competing several times was that I needed to be more confident, not confident as a sort of persona, but confident in myself and of who I was. They were not looking for me to be anyone else. I liked the fact that I could stay who I was and still win this contest.

"I may not be as strong or as muscular or as masculine or have as deep a voice, but I am just as much a man. I represent something that goes deeper than just the look of a body and a face. I represent those who maybe are doubting themselves because they are not all those things we think a man should be.

"Jim and Ginger have been nothing but supportive and encouraging. I was talking to Ginger on the phone before the contest this year. She said, 'Jim is right here, do you want to say hello?' So Jim got on the phone and he asked how I was doing, and I said, 'Great,' and he said, 'And remember, Noah, keep it butch.' And we laughed. And then he said, 'I love you, Noah, you're great.' Just to hear something like that is wonderful. He's not looking for anyone to be anything other that what they are. He is looking for someone to be the best they can be."

The Judges

Time and again, Jim Flint is referenced as knowing how to pick a queen. Although he is not involved as a Continental judge, he often does have an eye for the contestants who display that certain Continental something—a spark or flair or level of sophistication that has come to be associated with the pageant.

"I guess, when I look at somebody, I don't see their looks," Flint said. "The first thing I see is their talent, and that's not necessarily what they are doing. What I notice is the way they carry themselves and the way they project themselves onstage. Some people carry themselves in a very positive way and others in a very shy sort of way. I look for that outward sort of thing, for a contestant who carries themselves like a Continental."

Regarding the judges themselves, Flint explained how he chooses them. "First of all, I look for judges with integrity. They need to not talk about contestants outside the competition. If I think your scores look like they are fixed for one individual, I remove [that judge]. I look for knowledge. Have they been around drag awhile? We've had Tracey Ross from Star Search; and Bob Mackie, the designer; the actress and singer Alexandra Billings, who competed as Shanté. Ericka Dunlap was our head judge one year [Miss America 2004]."

In all of the Continental pageants there are five preliminary judges, and the final night of competition there are seven individuals who have the honor, as well as the challenge, of sitting on the judges panel.

Singer Linda Clifford has also been a judge. "When Jim first asked me to be a judge at the Miss Continental pageant, I said, 'I don't know how qualified I am. I mean, I love being there, but I don't know how qualified I am to judge.' He said, 'You are a performer and you know what's good.' So I went and judged a few times," Clifford recalled.

"The hardest thing about it was seeing the girls who didn't make the Top 12. Then you get down to the Top Five, and you just start thinking about how much went into this for each contestant. This isn't your everyday performing—the hair, the costumes, the talent— everything is glamour and excellence, way over the top. Then to think you have to narrow it down to one person. It's tough but, I think, every year I was a judge we got it right."

Sometimes, getting it right means speaking up despite the awkwardness of the situation. "One time, the scores were entered incorrectly," said Flint. "When I was handed the Top 12 and started reading off the names, the judges started saying, 'Something is wrong.' So Raphael Velasco and Skip Mackall, who was my head judge at the time, thought the scores might have been added incorrectly, and they were right. Linda Clifford was on the panel that year, too.

"So, when we found out there was a problem, I decided I had to go out there and be honest. I figured there would be a few that would scream and holler, but the others that know it's always fair will come back, and we'll end up selling out faster because of that. That's exactly what happened."

Veteran judge Skip Mackall recalled the evening. "We were going to go high-tech and bring computers in to help tabulate the scores," he said. "The pageant was huge that year, a solid 40 contestants. We'd done all the preliminary judging, and when they were naming the 12 finalists on the stage and at about the fourth or fifth name I said, 'Something is not right.' This is in front of the huge crowd there for the event. I went up and said to Jim off microphone, 'I think something happened, I don't think these are the right names.'

"Jim stopped the whole thing right there. It turned out, the person who did the data entry had done it incorrectly. Jim made this announcement that this was an honest contest and there had been a mistake. The votes were recounted, and Jim said, 'I know these contestants want to be finalists because it was fair, not because of a computer error.'

"It was just a wonderful speech and I remember sitting there thinking, 'This guy is great.' I mean, it would have been just as easy to go ahead with those 12 and choose from there, but he wanted to do it fairly and the right way, even if it meant this public admission that things had gotten screwed up. That's integrity. When we talked about it later, he said it showed the same thing about me and my coming up to him and saying that I thought there was an error in the computer tabulations. He said that I could have just as easily sat there and not said a word."

Mackall currently serves as head judge and has been involved with the Continental System for 20 years. "I met Jim in 1992 when a friend of mine, Denise Russell, was coming to compete in the Continental Plus pageant," Mackall said. "She lived right above me, and he sang so wonderfully—live, as a man—I said, 'Can you take it up an octave?' It ended up I sort of went along and helped manage Denise that weekend.

"I met Jim and found out we had a lot in common. We both liked sports, we were both involved in and had judged beauty pageants. I came from a musical-theater and ice-skating background, and this entire Continental world of pageants just amazed me. After I left, he had someone give me a call to come back and judge the Miss Continental pageant. That was huge. You never forget your first Miss Continental pageant.

"When I came into this, I did not realize how professional it was going to be. Jim knows all aspects of the business. He knows all the people who have regionals. The event itself is run like clockwork. It starts on time, there are no lags. Something interesting is, whether he realizes it or not, Jim has created a pageant that emphasizes something he likes in people, and that is the ability to communicate. That's why there is the interview in the preliminary and the final questions during the pageant."

Mackall expanded on his point about professionalism: "One year, I remember we had chosen the 12 for the semifinals and we had rehearsal before the show at the Park West. One of the Top 12 finalists showed up late, so that meant points were deducted from her score, and the one who was originally the 13th in ranking made the Top 12. Well, the person who made it in was not really someone you would want representing your pageant, but that night she was outstanding and ended up winning. Everyone knew how tough it was going to be, and there were problems that year. So, Jim was running around, and I ran into him backstage, and he let out a sigh and said, 'What the fuck did you do to me?' I told him I did what he told me to do. 'I voted for the person who did the best in the contest tonight.' He looked at me and said, 'That was exactly the right answer.'

"Once they have made the preliminaries and the finalists are chosen, it becomes a level playing field. I try and judge each element and category separately, and the scoring is really set up to work well that way. So, I don't vote for the contestant, I vote for the talent, the interview, the swimsuit presentation, etc. I take it very seriously because I try to keep in mind that these people are doing what I wouldn't do. They deserve my time and respect."

Offering his assessment both of the Continental System and of Flint himself, Mackall added that "the Continental System is a way to give a lot of people a job and allow them to make a living and be accepted as they are. Jim has built a huge forum for that and for people to be more comfortable in their own skin and live their lives with dignity. He's changed so many lives that way and provided a way for so many to become who they want to be.

"Jim shows how life can be when you live without boundaries. You give him a hurdle and he'll jump over it. I call him the maestro sometimes, because he is like a conductor who takes all these different instruments and puts them together and somehow makes this wonderful music. None of the elements match, there are people from every sort of background and interest and ethnicity, and yet it becomes this family.

"Armistead Maupin has this great line about our logical and biological families. That's what Jim has done. He has given a logical family to a lot of people who many times have been abandoned by their biological families just for being who they are. Jim is a perfect example of the impact one person can have on the lives around him. I met him at 27 and thought I knew it all. He was that one person you meet who changes everything."

"I first met Jim in 2002 when one of my friends, who competed in pageants as Erica Cartier, took me to the Baton," said judge Steve Moore. "It was very much a quick meeting. Then through the years I have become good friends with many of the contestants and people involved in the pageants, so I started judging preliminaries here and there. Then Maya Douglas and Louis [Lee] Boroff started suggesting to Jim that I would be a good judge for Miss Continental. The first year, I was in line as an alternate judge for finals, and I got a call at 4 that afternoon that I was slated to judge that night. I was so excited. It was something to cross off my bucket list because I really had wanted to judge a national contest.

"It was tough. When you judge preliminaries, it seems that at every competition there are one or two that really stand out as national material. Well, Miss Continental is all those contestants, and for the final nights you are looking at the Top 12 of that group. The level is just so high. Finals night, I am looking at the same thing as the audience. The score sheets sort of guide you, but there is no lesson on how to do it. No matter what the category, I look for poise and charm and I guess I'm thinking, 'Is this person a female, or an overbearing male in a dress'?'

"When I first started judging contests, Tajma Hall was one of the judges at a pageant we did in Indianapolis, and when she introduced me as a judge she introduced me as a former Falcon model. I had never done porn; it was just Taj having fun. But, she said, all through the night people were coming up to her and saying, 'Oh, yeah, I have several of his videos.'

"Anyway, somehow Jim heard about this, and when he introduced me in 2010 as a Miss Continental judge he said, 'And with us to judge this evening is Steven Moore, airline pilot and former Falcon model.' I'm not a shy person, but I was so embarrassed. I thought it was hilarious that Jim had that playful of an attitude, that he had heard this, and sort of kept the joke going. Now I've even had people on Facebook say they own some of my videos."

"I met Jim for the first time at the preliminary at Cleveland in 1996. It was the year Victoria LePaige won Miss Continental Plus," said Denis Sabol. "I had worked judging pageants on a city, state and regional level, but didn't enter the national level until 2003. I remember I was driving and Skip Mackall called and said they wanted to get my information because I was going to be on the panel that year. I had previous experience being pageant coordinator for Skip's Starmite Productions. That's really how I got to know Jim. It was funny. After they asked me, I wondered if I'd have to have training or something—no, it was full force. I think I did all four that year.

"I was most apprehensive about the interview portion in the preliminaries. I had judged contests on different levels, but not of this caliber. At a city or state level, I'd ask things like 'Why are you here?' and 'What inspires you?' That sort of thing. My first national contest, I just listened to that portion so I'd get an idea of what the other judges were asking. Now I ask things like, 'What three things do you need to complete your job at work?'

"I think my favorite to judge is the Elite, since it's for contestants 40 and over, just seeing the amount of energy they put into it and that they've been around and have managed to keep it fresh. That's wonderful to see.

"I remember that first year I judged nationally. We all went to the Baton, and then afterwards we went to a piano bar that was nearby. Some of the entertainers from the contest went along with us. Someone from one of the papers was there, and they wanted to get a picture, and I sort of stood off to the side, and Jim said, 'Denis, you come here. You're part of this family now.' I'll never forget how that made me feel, and it's true. It is a big family, and these pageants are big family reunions—even if it is a lot of work to judge."

Judge David Hudspeth met Flint through Skip Mackall. "Continental was at the Riviera [Theatre] that year," Hudspeth said. "I remember that, in the midst of everything, Jim stopped when he was walking up the aisle and wanted to know if I was having a good time and enjoying the weekend. He asked how had the city been treating me. It just struck me as so nice. Wherever Jim is, he always seems to be at the hub of activity, but despite that, he always wants to make sure you're having a good time, and he wants you to know that he recognizes and appreciates that you're there.

"I like being a judge, because I don't ever want a winner where people think, 'What the hell were they thinking?' With the knowledge that they will be representing the pageant and the system, I look for consistency. I am from Akron, Ohio, and when we get a national pageant titleholder here, it's a big deal. I don't want someone to come up to me after the titleholder visits and say, 'Really? That's who you chose?' I don't want to pick someone who will disappoint Jim, the system, or the people who will see that winner during their reign.

"I spend two or three weeks coming up with my interview question. I want to know who you are and what you believe, not that I necessarily need to agree with you, but so I can get a feel for you and that you express yourself articulately. Last year in Plus and Elite, my question was, 'In the business you're in, many performers are working under the table and not paying into Social Security and Medicare. Given that, if that person then gets ill, what do you think is society's responsibility to them?'

"I constantly marvel at Jim's stamina. One night, we closed the Baton and he told me he was going to go home and lie down for a bit, and then said he was going to go to services the next day and asked me if I wanted to join him. I asked when the Mass was, and he said, 'I think the first one is at 5'—less than three hours from then!

"Every once in a while you meet someone who is in perfect sync with what they are doing, and that's Jim. He just loves putting people at ease and entertaining them."

"I started coming because I was involved in fashion and productions," said 2011 first-time judge Harvey Washington. "I have been coming to the pageant for 20 years, since Mimi Marks was crowned [1992]. Finally, the year Tasha Long won [1997], I said I had to meet the person behind this amazing contest, and I met Jim.

"My favorite moment was in 2007 when Jim brought me up onstage before the winner was announced. I had a $1,200 Louis Vuitton bag that I was giving the winner. I joked that the receipt was still inside if they wanted to return it. That got a big laugh. Necole Luv Dupree was the winner that year.

"The hardest part about judging was knowing so many of the girls, but I just had to block all that out. I had to take it away from the personal level and make it about business. A lot of money is spent on people coming to the contest and everything, and I really wanted to be sure that it was fair and that it was done right. As a first-time judge, it really did make me see how fair everything is and what a solid system it is.

"Because of his passion and his commitment, Jim has given the gay community a voice. He has given people the chance to be who they want to be and be proud of who they are. He's made people see the gay as well as the transgender community in a new light. He broke down barriers. What happened was, doors opened and, just as importantly, when they opened, people were able to walk through the front door rather than through the back door."

"I was in Little Rock, Arkansas, at a pageant. I was a background dancer for a friend of mine who was competing, Kirby Kolby," said one-time promoter and current judge Robbie Ham. "Kirby introduced me to Mr. Flint, and I said, 'Pleased to meet you, Mr. Flint,' and shook his hand, then went about my business. I think he was used to people fawning all over him because of who he was, but I was just respectful but busy doing my business. That impressed him. Through friends, he invited me up to Chicago that year to the Miss Continental pageant, and it was really the start of a great friendship. I was still in North Carolina but started coming up there for pageants and to visit.

"If you've ever visited with him, Jim has this gift of making Chicago seem like the greatest place in the world. He really makes it interesting, takes you to all the best places and really shows it off. He makes you love Chicago. He would take me to the piano bar at The Drake, and Gentry, and all sorts of wonderful places. So, I started thinking about moving up here, and he was saying to me, 'Come up here, things will be better, brighter.' He gave me the courage to move based on just this great friendship. I've been here since 2007. I am a hair stylist. Jim was my first customer. He used to send people to me when I was still at Salon 1800. Though I no longer work at a salon, I still go to his office and cut his hair.

"Jim showed me you could support and sponsor female impersonation without doing it yourself. Jim loves it. He loves the entertainment aspect of it. So, for about three years, from 2002 to 2004, I owned a regional Miss Continental preliminary in North Carolina called Miss Emerald Coast Continental. I would work it out of Legends nightclub in Raleigh, where I tended bar, and Jim would always come and support the event. Now that I am up here, I have been a preliminary and finals judge at Miss Continental the past three years.

"The best thing about being a judge is being so close to the contestants, and the worst is that it is a very small world and people all know and mentor each other. It's tough to vote someone poorly because they simply weren't doing well that night, even when you know they are capable of more. Jim is very adamant about everyone coming in on a level playing field. I do believe the way he has it set up makes it the fairest contest. There are five preliminary judges and then seven final judges, and those final judges are all seven different people from seven different cities, seeing seven different things in seven different ways—and on top of it all, the highest and lowest scores are dropped.

"After being around pageants for so many years, I must say I can usually pick out the top three with no problem. What makes a winner is consistency and the fact that they have managed to level themselves into a consistent performer and have branded who they are and what they do, like Mimi Marks or Tommie Ross."

Keven Callahan has an extremely impressive résumé, which includes being NBC Universal's director of merchandising. He has also served as creative director at Crabtree & Evelyn and manager of visual merchandising at Bath & Body Works and at Giorgio Beverly Hills. Callahan currently manages visual merchandising for Gucci's seven Florida stores. He also heads up StudiOut, the largest LGBT employee group under the worldwide NBC Universal umbrella.

This year he added judge for Miss Continental to his résumé. Callahan had been a judge in previous years at various pageants and preliminaries in Florida. "I'd been brought in by Dan Fraser [Continental promoter] to judge some contests at Southern Nights, which is now Revolution Nightclub in Orlando," he said. "I had actually been the preliminary judge for many of the contestants who went on to greater success at Continental."

It was at a regional contest this year in Florida that Flint asked Callahan to be a national judge. "We had just named the winner at the preliminary, and I desperately had to go to the bathroom, so I was out of my seat and headed to the washroom and Jim got onstage," Callahan said. "Someone pulled me out of the bathroom at the last minute, because Jim was asking me from the stage if I would be a judge that coming Labor Day weekend at Continental in Chicago. I yelled yes from the back of the club and quickly ran back in the bathroom."

When it came to being a judge on the national level at Miss Continental, what Callahan didn't expect was just the amount of concentration needed to take in all the performers and give each the full focus they deserved. "That was harder than I thought. These people spend a lot of time and money to be there, and I owe it to them to give each my full attention.

"The other judges were very welcoming to me. I think the only two I knew before this were Tommie Ross and Skip Mackall. I judged both days, and it was so exciting. The night of the finals, I was all dressed and ready to go two hours ahead of time, and I am one of those people who is never ready two hours early. I was like a little kid."

Although he knew many of the contestants, some quite well, Callahan said it wasn't hard to put that aside. "It was easy for me to extract the friendship from their performance. This contest system overall is by far the fairest I've been involved in. It is professional, organized, on time and, because of all that, it is that much more legitimate. It commands respect."

Honoring Velasco

Another important part of the Continental pageant history was the presentation of the Raphael Velasco Award in honor of the late judge and promoter from San Antonio. It was given to commemorate an individual's contribution, promotion and recognition in the art of female impersonation.

"We stopped giving the Raphael Velasco Award now," said Flint. "It was done on personality as well as accomplishment. Raphael owned The Saint in San Antonio. He really helped me understand a lot about this business. Every Monday night we'd talk on the phone, and when we talked we would talk drag. He was a wonderful man and a great friend, just a terrific individual.

"I remember we were at a preliminary in California, and Michelle Dupree (Scott Cooper) was with us, and I said, 'Something is wrong with Raphael, because every time I turn around he wants to go to church.' One day he must have gone to four Masses. He wasn't feeling good, so I said, 'Well, Michelle is a nurse.' Michelle wanted him to go to the emergency room, and he did not want to go at all. He died the following week. I miss him so much, I couldn't go back to San Antonio for several years.

"I stopped giving the Raphael Velasco Award because too many were deserving of it and I didn't want to hurt anyone's feelings."

Erica Andrews, Miss Continental 2004, was mentored by Velasco as well as by the late Tandi Andrews. On the site ClubLuxor.com, Erica Andrews was quoted as saying this of

Velasco: "Raphael Ruiz de Velasco. The first time that Raphael ever saw me do drag, I was at a talent night at the Paper Moon around 1989–90. He walked me down the stairs, tipped me a twenty-dollar bill, and kissed me on the right cheek. I had no idea who this man was, but I was intimidated and afraid of him. ...

"As a friend, he was the best friend that any queen could ask for. As a mentor, the best support and the best adviser for me. As a businessman, I studied his techniques, his ways, and the ability to negotiate. I learned never to settle for less [than] I am worth. He always said to me, 'Erica, there is a difference between friendship and business. Know how to separate the two.'"

Promoters

"I always try to do a little more with my promoters to keep them involved. I probably try to go to 75 percent of the preliminary pageants around the country," Flint said. "You know how Continental to me is like a family. The same is true with a lot of the promoters. They have their own families of people who then come to Continental and share friendship and laugh. [Promoter] Alyson [Thomas], for example, puts so much into it and brings you two or three terrific contestants in every contest. She loves the art."

"They call me the Jackie O of drag because I look like the mayor. I am very conservative and understated in the way I look and dress," said Alyson Thomas. "In 1991, I was friends with Amber Richards and I went to watch the pageant and support her, and I fell in love with the system and the girls. From 1991 to '99, I went to every pageant and really enjoyed them. Then there was an ad in the local newspaper looking for promoters in North Carolina. A friend said, 'Alyson, you should buy this.'

"So, in 1998 or '99, I called up Jim and we hit it off, so I decided to become a promoter. And that following year, I ended up bringing Danielle Hunter to Chicago and she won Miss Continental. I got the formula, the knowledge, the experience, and as a result of sponsoring a winner my preliminaries grew. I started having prelims for other titles in the Continental System as well. My winners were consistently placing. Then, two years later, I ended up buying the South Carolina prelim as well. Partly that was selfish, because I didn't want to compete with anyone else in the Carolinas.

"What happens when you purchase a franchise is, you then create a name, which Jim either approves or disapproves of. They used to be simply the state names, but lately they have become creative with other names. [For example: Lucho's Continental, Big D Continental, Dreamgirl Continental, North Shore Continental, etc.] Then you create a pageant with the same rules, regulations and requirements as the rest of the Continental System. Your pageant would have the same categories of judging—interview, talent, swimwear and evening gown. You also agree to bring the titleholder to the national pageant. You have a prize package which will include entry fee, airfare and hotel at the Continental contest.

"That's the minimum, but when I have a candidate I go well beyond that. Also, during your preliminary, you may not have any talent onstage that is not part of the Continental System, so there could not be a performer or an emcee who was just a friend or someone local unless they are a part of the Continental System or family [meaning they have competed in one of the Continental pageants on a national level].

"What happens is that if you do it right, it grows and grows. I know what it takes. For

Alexis Gabrielle 'Gabby' Sherrington, that was a $20,000 investment in her and in myself and in the Continental System. I support all my winners. I give them guidance, I review their music, I coach them, and I pay for everything. My reputation for supporting my winners is impeccable, and as a result I get a lot of entries in my preliminaries.

"I support them every step of the way. I am with them [in person] or, if I'm not with them for some reason, I'll want them to call me. 'How did your interview go?' 'Who do you feel is your biggest competition?' 'What is your contestant number?' 'Are you on time?' 'Do you need me to give you a wake-up call?' 'Take a picture on your phone and show me how you look before going into the interview.' I want to know all of this. This is the sort of thing I expect from them, because it is my name and Jim's name and the Continental System's name that is out there.

"I take this very seriously. Since this is an investment for me as well, they are basically applying for a job. I have a Miss, Mr., an Elite and a Plus franchise. If I send two candidates, one will be from North and the other from South Carolina. They will be basically the winner and the first runner-up. But if I don't feel the first runner-up is worth the investment and is not ready for a national competition, I won't send them, and I'll be very frank about it. This is expensive, and if I am going to back them I have to be able to believe in them to do it 100 percent, and sometimes that doesn't happen with the alternate.

"When you come to my preliminary you need to present a business plan for your Continental package. For me to sponsor you and for you to be a part of this system, you need to show me what you are going to do for the system and for Jim as well as for me. You need to make me believe.

"I will not sponsor anyone who I feel would be lowering the standards of the system. If contestants are not up to the standards, the system cannot flourish. What you do after the pageant is your own business, but while you are there you are working. You are not there to party. I know how the system works and am ready to help people who are willing to work. I take care of everything I can so my contestants can be relaxed and do the absolute best they can in the contest."

Thomas reflected on her favorite moment as a part of the Continental System. "It was when Jim presented me with the Raphael Velasco Award in 2006," she said. "I had been calling myself the Susan Lucci of Continental because I had pageant winners, but I had never won any of the preliminary awards for myself. When Jim called my name that night, it really didn't register at first. I went up there, and he was just beaming when he gave it to me.

"He said how much I reminded him of Raphael, and I was fortunate enough to have known Mr. Velasco when he was alive. Jim said I had the same intelligence, class, dedication, sophistication and respect for the art form. When he gave me the award, he gave me a kiss, and there is a wonderful picture of him kissing me onstage at Continental, and that is my favorite Jim Flint memory because, after so long, I finally felt he understood me as a person."

"I first came to Continental 20 years ago when I did hair for Christina Piaget, who was in the contest from New York City. It was a magical thing and I fell in love. It was so glamorous and elegant and rich in beauty," said promoter José Abraham.

"I always liked hair and makeup and helping the girls, and Janette Valentino told me she was going back to Panama and asked me if I wanted to be a promoter. That was 16 years ago and I've been doing it ever since. I now have five different contests—City Lights Continental, New York New York Continental, Latina New York Continental, Puerto Rico

Continental, and Caribbean Continental. I send candidates to Miss and I have had two Elite winners, Danielle Hunter and Barbra Herr.

"My favorite moment as a promoter was when Candis Cayne won the crown. She was my queen. My other favorite moment would also have to be when I won the Raphael Velasco Award the first year it was given out. It meant so much to me because I so love the art of female impersonation.

"My favorite Jim memory is similar. He came to my house in Washington, D.C., and I cooked for him and we had dinner. He told me that as a promoter he admired me because I love what he loves, that I work for the contest with my heart and not for the money.

"I usually bring four or five girls to the contest. I spend so much of my own money so I can put 100 percent behind each contestant. I treat them like a queen and give them everything they need. They always respect me, and in all the years I have been doing this, I have never had a fight with any of my queens. Promoters are there to help the girls and out of love for Continental. There is no money in this. I was so pleased this year. Four of the contestants I brought made the Top 12, one made the Top Five, and one won talent.

"At my house I have a lot of my sons and daughters. I have 29 queens and 14 young men in San Cartier House [in Washington, D.C.]. They call me Father. We watch the pageant videos and prepare for pageants. I told them that 'one by one I will bring each of you to the pageants,' and one by one I am. We're happy together. We have performers, dancers, some sew and do costumes, some do hair and makeup. I teach them what I know, and the deal is that we all are there to support the other. I also tell them that if they are in my house, they have to go to school. I will not help you if you aren't in college or school. No drugs, either, and that you always are happy for the success of another member of the San Cartier family. No jealousy.

"The first daughter I had in my house, Lorena San Cartier, is the mother of the house. Many of the sons and daughters were thrown out by their families because they were not accepted. They did not have people who loved and respected them, but they get that with me.

"I think of Ricardo, who wanted to come into my house, my family, when he was 21. I said, 'I will let you come in if you stop doing drugs, and you go to school and you become a nicer person.' Now he is in a university and off of drugs.

"I know how that can be. I was 15 when I was thrown out of my house because I was gay, and I never did anything bad. I vowed to prove to my family and the world that I can do it myself, and I did it. I am now helping others to do it as well. We are family and we are also all part of the Continental family."

Promoter and sometime judge Jim DeMundo also shared his Continental memories. "The first year I went to the contest was the year Mimi Marks won," he said. "The professionalism and the sense of family really appealed to me. And the performers were beyond compare. There were winners like Monica Munro and Cezanne. They made me want to get involved. I liked the way Jim ran it. He was very personable and charismatic.

"This will be my 17th year as a promoter. Jim and I had met through the WCAA softball league, and I helped him with his team. We talked a bit about Continental and about Pittsburgh and about how they didn't have a contest in 1995. So I ended up starting one.

"This preliminary has been all over. The Metropolitan Continental contest began at a bar in Pittsburgh called the Metropol. I worked that out of there for three years and then moved the contest to Dayton, Ohio, to a bar called Jessie's Celebrity. That was a real powerhouse place. We used to get so much support and so many contestants, it really thrived there. The owners thought they were going to make it really big, so they opened another place in Las Vegas, and it ended up going under and they lost the bar in Dayton as well. Then for four years I was in Chicago, and the contest was out of there, and since leaving there I've been down in Orlando.

"When it comes to winners, I know about 90 percent of the time. Sometimes I'm surprised. However, it's interesting. You may not agree at the time with who should have won, but when the tape or the DVD comes out and you watch it, it's always clear that the best that evening, the person who was supposed to win, has won.

"I was so moved when Jim awarded me the Outstanding Dedication to The Continental Pageant Award. When it was renamed the Raphael Velasco Award, I won it again. So I have been given that twice, which has so touched me. I think I have won it for running the fairest and most professional preliminary in the Continental System. I am also currently the longest-running preliminary with the same owner.

"The thing I always tell my Metropolitan contestants who then go on to Continental is, 'There can only be one winner, so if you go there and whether you come in first or dead last, as long as you feel you did your personal best, I will be proud of you.' And it's true. All I ask is that people take it seriously, professionally and do the best they can. That's all you can ask of anyone."

Promoter and judge Shawn Batton first met Flint when he came to the Continental Plus pageant in 1991 to be with and support his friend Chelsea Pearl.

Batton recalled "the year Erica Andrews won Miss Continental in 2004. My friend Mercedes [later Miss Continental Plus 2008] asked me if I wanted to see the Miss Continental pageant. She bought general-admission seats, and I believe it was at the Vic. We were waiting in this long, long line while the VIPs, promoters and Jim's associates went on ahead. The seats we had were way, way in the back of the balcony, and I was getting very frustrated.

"At intermission we went down to the lobby, and I said to Mercedes that we were just going to stay here and see the rest of the show. We did, and it was great and, when we left, I said to her, 'I am going to be sure I never have to have seats like that at this thing again. I am going to buy a preliminary and become a promoter.'"

Batton started Shining Star Continental in July 2005. "I knew what I was getting into, because I had been a promoter for other systems in years prior, but I didn't expect the sort of involvement you get with Continental. There is so much guidance and interaction, not only in a professional capacity, but it fosters this friendship and closeness between all the parts of the system. The Continental group is really a family. There is a wonderful sense of camaraderie."

As to the man himself, Batton continued: "Jim Flint can talk to anyone about anything— he can go right from evening gowns to sports and back to food. He loves his jokes, though. Once, he called me at work from a private number and left a voice message. He disguised his voice and claimed to be from the IRS and that I was to give him a call and left a number at River North Travel that I didn't recognize. He got me good that time. I called him back but was shaking in my boots.

"My favorite Jim memory is from the Baton anniversary party about four years ago. Jim made a very moving speech from the stage and mentioned all these people who were near and dear to his heart, and he mentioned me among them. I was so touched that he felt that way. I am honored to know him."

"I first became aware of the Continental in 1995, and then I was incarcerated," said promoter Louis (Lee) Boroff. "When I was in prison [for theft, forgery and then armed robbery], I wrote to the Baton office and explained that I would like to be kept abreast of what was going on in the Continental pageant, since I knew a lot of the girls. They were so nice. They would send me the Continental program every year.

"I started going again when I got out in 2006. That's when my real relationship with Jim Flint began. I started taking pictures at the contest and learned what an amazing man he is. I really look up to him as sort of a father figure. In 2008, I moved to Chicago. Jim calls me Candi Baker, since that was my drag name and because I bake cookies and cupcakes all the time. I learned that in prison. Educated myself from Martha Stewart.

"When it came to being a promoter, it took a long time to convince Jim that I was ready and was in the right place in my life for this, but Jim believes in giving people a chance, and I passed the test eventually. Jim gave me an opportunity. He even signed the paperwork that allowed me to get an apartment in the city. He believed in me, and that belief ignited the spark I had in myself.

"I had been photographing Continental and various events for 2½ years when I began Mr. and Miss North Shore Continental in 2011. I am sending the titleholder as well as an alternate to both pageants. This coming year I am adding an Elite and a Plus as well."

Promoter Dan Fraser said he had heard about Jim Flint, the Baton Show Lounge and the Continental Pageant System for many years. "My first experience was sponsoring Lakesha Lucky the year she won," he said. "Two of my best friends were her backup dancers, Von Gretchen and the late, great Tasha Diane. We were so proud of Lakesha.

"One weekend, Tiffany Arieagus was the special guest at Southern Nights [in Orlando, Florida], a club where I was the general manager. My friend Greg Moore, who was a former resident of Chicago and now an Orlando transplant, led me to my first introduction to Jim. It was Friday night, and Greg, who worked part-time for the club, approached me and informed me that we were going to have a special guest in the audience that night. I quickly put together a VIP table and set it up with a bottle of Dom Pérignon.

"Our guest for the evening was none other than Jim Flint. I was nervous meeting the famous icon from Chicago. I watched the show with him, and luckily we became friends. We had so many things in common: female impersonation, the nightclub business, and the love of a good meal with friends.

"Over the years, I quickly became a regular at the Baton, meeting new friends. The employees and entertainers at the Baton are like my Chicago family. In addition to being a promoter, Jim has honored me with the opportunity to judge his contests on more than one occasion as well as to be the contestant coordinator. With Jim, it is always a sure bet that the conversation will be enlightening and ultra-entertaining."

Seven years ago, promoters Eric Gorczyca and Keith Combs bought the Stonewall Nightclub in Huntington, West Virginia. The former owner was eager to sell. The couple purchased the bar without knowing much about the pageantry system, but wanted to bring a contest to West Virginia.

Gorczyca explained: "I researched all the systems—USofA, Miss Gay America, and National Entertainer of the Year—and Continental seemed the most straightforward. We had our first preliminary in 2005 and have a Miss Continental as well as a Miss Continental Plus. Last year we had our first titleholder, Chelsea Pearl, who was Miss Continental Plus. We have also had a couple first runners-up. Sasha Colby represented our West Virginia preliminary, as well as Roxxy Andrews the year before she won.

"When it comes to having someone represent West Virginia in my preliminary, I would rather send someone who would not do as well but who is willing to give it their all than someone who might do better but isn't willing to put forth the effort. The amount I involve myself depends entirely on the contestant. With someone like Chelsea, I could never hope to know as much about female impersonation as she does. She's been doing it for years. I gave her some tips; some she used and some she didn't. She's the expert. Other contestants want a little more input and guidance. Each girl has to figure out her own recipe for success.

"Now we book entertainment at the bar every weekend, and they are not always from the Continental System, but the vast majority of the entertainers are. It can be pricey, but exposing the area to that level of entertainment has had a positive effect on business."

Since purchasing the Stonewall Nightclub, the couple (who have been together for 10 years) have also purchased the Atmosphere Ultra Lounge in Charleston, West Virginia. "The thing I did not expect going in this Continental System were the friendships that would develop. I expected it to bring business, I didn't expect it to bring friends.

"It is at once very professional and at the same time has the feeling of family. That comes from the top. That's what you get from Jim. The promoters are a welcoming group and I usually talk to Jim a couple times every day. He's taught me a lot about the business.

"Jim is easily one of the greatest men I've ever met. He is kind, considerate and forgiving. He taught me to be positive and keep moving forward. I know that even if I stopped being a promoter tomorrow that I would still come and visit Chicago because of him and will always have the pleasure of calling him a friend."

Robert Waters and Ken Byrski have been friends of Flint's for years, and later became promoters. Waters first heard about Flint and the Baton from the media. "There was this show talking about men who actually looked like women. Well, a little later my sister moved to Detroit, and I moved here with her," Waters said. "There was a place in Detroit at the time called Todd's Sway Lounge, on the east side of town. Jim came into town for the pageant, and that was when I met him."

"Since there was no one representing Detroit and since this city has a large contingent, we decided to start a preliminary. We started a nightclub called Zippers in 1997," said Byrski. "We had a contest one Sunday afternoon and decided to ask Jim about starting a preliminary. He has set rules for the preliminary—how much money you pay the winner, what you're responsible for. There are guidelines. If you want to go over and above that, it's fine, but he does have minimums.

"We're currently in the process of selling Zippers. Things are economically pretty tough in the Detroit area, but if someone needs a sponsor, we will sponsor them for the contest. We actually had four contests. Robert did Miss Michigan Continental and Miss Michigan Continental Plus, and I did Miss Great Lakes Continental and Miss Great Lakes Continental Plus. Each has their own crown, their own title, their own money and their own schedule responsibilities."

Though they are connected to Continental as promoters, the vivid memories Waters and Byrski have of Flint have been the vacations. "We've had wild times in Toronto and Niagara Falls," said Byrski.

Flint affirmed that the trips with Waters and Byrski are indeed wild: "The situations we all get into are always just way out of control."

"The best times, though, are just when we are sitting around a pool talking. We don't even need to go to a fancy restaurant," said Byrski.

Waters agreed: "That's right. We can all have just as much fun at White Castle or McDonald's."

"Jim calls a lot," added Byrski. "He's a friend who's always there. He flew in for my mother's funeral and called all the time when Bobby's brother died. I'm two weeks older than Jim, so every year at 12:01 on my birthday he calls and says, 'So, how's it feel to be two weeks older than me?' We talk on the phone every day, a lot of times two or three times a day. His big thing is, when we call and ask what he's doing, he'll say, 'I'm at work—after all, I'm a trained professional.'"

Memories

Following are more memories from people associated with the Continental System.

"With Miss Continental, it turned out to be bigger as it went on, because since the production was being filmed and then produced, the departing Miss Continental became more ambitious. She wanted a bigger and bigger opening production number and to do much more than simply walk onstage," said choreographer Harrison McEldowney. "Sometimes I have butted heads with people. For example, Chanel Dupree and I are very much alike, very fiery and volatile."

Choreographer Keith Elliott recalled doing Monica Munro's production number for Continental, "and it was this futuristic thing, and she was coming out of a shell. This was years before Gaga, by the way, and it was to a Janet Jackson number. We were wearing unitards and Jason masks from Friday the 13th, and we had those dryer tubings on our costumes as well, to look even more futuristic. Anyway, one of the dancers, right before we were ready to go on, said she had to go to the bathroom. I said, 'We don't have time, we're on now.' And so we went on, and she ended up piddling herself during the number onstage at Miss Continental. That was pretty memorable.

"I applaud Jim Flint because I understand what it takes to be the founder of something and to keep it going, and to keep it going with your initial vision intact. People might come in and want to change it, and things can come along here and there to improve on it—but it is still that initial vision, that idea. I know how tough that can be from Dance for Life. It takes tenacity to keep something going. He has taken this and turned what he loved into an art form, not only at the Baton but with Continental as well. That's heroic."

Devoted Continental fan Ed Cavaliere has attended every Continental pageant except the first two. "I have seen the show tighten over the years, and it always has a level of professionalism, standards and talent that just keeps improving," he said. "I always look forward to the evening-gown portion. Just the creativity and elegance you see on that stage is amazing.

"I remember Tulsi coming out in her yellow gown—very few use lemon yellow, and this gown was gorgeous, an ideal choice for her. I also was completely blown away by Yoshiko Oshiro, who wore the most gorgeous pink gown. It was so classy and understated, and as I sat there looking at her, [I was] thinking, 'That is a woman.' I could have taken her anywhere, to any event.

"I'm always so impressed by Jim at the contests as well. A lot of times when people have achieved a certain level of success and have arrived, they have an attitude about them. Not Jim. He's out mingling with the audience, taking the time to talk to everyone. Asking, 'How are you doing? Are you enjoying the show? Did you have any problem getting here?' That personal touch means so much. He shows everyone they are valued as a person and seems genuinely grateful for their being there."

"Things can sometimes get a little tense behind the scenes around Continental time," said pageant ticket head and Baton employee Cai Holyon. "I was in the office about three years ago during Continental season, and everyone was working so hard, and without thinking I said, 'God, Jimmy, I need a haircut,' and he said, 'I'll cut it.' Then he got a pair of scissors and came up behind me and cut my ponytail off! He just reached over, grabbed it, and chopped it off with the scissors. The next day I had to have it cut professionally. He is not allowed to touch my hair ever again."

Theresa Altgilbers from Jam Productions and the Park West said she first met Flint through the Miss Continental pageant at the Park West. "He scared me at first, because he can be pretty bossy and has a strong presence," she said. "As I got to know him, I found his bark is worse than his bite. I don't know if I want him to know that. I feel like it's easier to work with him when he thinks I'm a little afraid of him. In the past several years, he has given me, Jam and the Park West a shout-out at the anniversary party, saying that he hates me, but with a smile. I suspect he secretly enjoys working with me, although I would never make him admit it."

Flint has nothing but praise for Altgilbers. "She is one of the hardest-working women I've met in my life," he said. "She'll pick up a table and clean or whatever. She will do anything for you. We deal with her. She is above and beyond when it comes to your event, and if it's not done right, she'll do it. Another year something happened with the toilets, and she was in cleaning the bathrooms."

Altgilbers, director of sales for the Park West, where Flint has held so many contests over the years, recalled a wonderful moment from a Continental Plus pageant. "Usually I am busy watching the crowd or the door or the technical aspects of the show and don't pay a lot of attention to the talent, but one year I caught the end of the opening number, which was some sort of nautical theme," she said. "When Jim came out onstage, his back was to the crowd in a full yellow fisherman rain gear, and then he turned around and he was the Gorton's Fisherman [the seafood pop-culture icon]. He's often at the podium or onstage in a host capacity, but I'd never seen him be part of the actual show.

"Also, we try not to have a new sound engineer do the Continentals, because there are so many different CDs or tapes for approximately 30 talent numbers and then the swimwear and gown music. It's a very tricky job. Jim will call out and sometimes insult the tech staff from the stage on the mic if there's a glitch."

Park West owner Jerry Mickelson said his company deals with Flint in the context of entertainment. "We have worked with him here at the Park West so many times for so many different events and occasions," he said. "He wants everything to come off perfectly, not only the way it looks, but that it comes off perfectly for the performers as well as for the audience—and rightfully so. That is why he's a leader in the field. He is demanding. He wants it perfect. If there is a problem with something, we have to be sure to rectify the situation for the following year. If we didn't meet his level of expectation, he wouldn't be working with us. Yet he doesn't demand anything more from anyone than he demands for himself.

"How do you describe Jim Flint? He's indescribable. He's gregarious, he's outgoing, he's loyal, he's honest. He's all these great qualities you don't see a lot of anymore, especially in a lot of businessmen."

Backstage contestant handler and helper Billy Fantastic (William Kucharenko) explained: "Each Labor Day and Easter weekend, I look forward to Continental. I was first asked to help out in 2004 shortly after coming to the Baton. I help out backstage, working with Ginger to make sure the contestants are lined up and ready so the pageant goes as smoothly as possible. I absolutely love being behind the scenes, with the contestants—the current, the reigning, and the formers. All the hard work that is put into competing for such a prestigious title as Continental is really something quite amazing.

"A memorable time for me was at one of the Continental brunches. Pictures were being taken of the Continental family and promoters, and Jimmy passed by me and said, 'Come on, be in this picture, you are a part of this family.'"

"One of my favorite parts of being in the contest is Billy Fantastic," said Miss Continental Plus 2011, Chelsea Pearl. "He is the backstage coordinator and quite a personality. We connected immediately. He makes sure everyone is where they're supposed to be and that the girls know they are on in two songs or whatever. He is on top of it. Billy is nothing but good energy for the girls, and backstage that is always appreciated."

Paul Lopez, a former male lead at the Baton, shared his favorite memory from a Continental pageant several years ago. "I have hosted the Miss Continental pageant a couple times," he said. "One time, I was hosting it at the Vic, and there was a contestant doing a Donna Summer medley. As I looked across the stage, there was Jimmy in the other wing, dancing away and looking happy as can be. It made me giggle, and when he saw me he gave me this wonderful smile that made me laugh."

"It is a family. It's so great seeing these people every year, and sometimes twice a year," said Flint. "The pageant goes on Friday through Monday, and that is just such a rush seeing and catching up with everyone. After everything ends on Monday, on that Tuesday we all do something, and then on Wednesday we all go with the Hawaiians that are in town to the suburbs and have a cookout.

"By Thursday, when they are all gone, I am so depressed. It is a real letdown. I love being with the people, so it can be tough when it's over. It was that way with the leather runs when everyone left town, and it was that way with the softball tournaments. And it's really that way with Continental. It's depressing because everyone goes back home, and those are people you love and look forward to seeing so much. That's another good reason to have it two times a year. Continental has become so much more than a contest. I never could have planned or imagined this."

The first Miss Continental contest, in 1980. Winner was Chilli Pepper (center), with 1st runner-up Andrea Nicole (left) and 2nd runner-up Dina Jacobs.

Miss Continental 1980, Chilli Pepper.

1981's Miss Continental finalists. Heather Fontaine (fourth from left) won the contest.

Miss Continental 1983, Chena Black.

GayLife / Thursday, September 8, 1983   **5**

Street Talk

The 4th Miss Gay Continental USA pageant presented topnotch entertainment by some of the nation's top female impersonators. Previous years' winners appeared to award prizes and perform for the crowd at Park West, including Chili Pepper, Heather Fontaine, and Tiffany Ariagas. Chena Black was named this year's winner, Cherine Alexander won first runner-up, Dana Douglas second runner-up, Andrea Nicole third runner-up, and Dolinda Ko fourth runner-up. The gala event was produced by a team of first-rate talent, headed by Felicia. (Photos: Melvin Simmons, Bob Bearden)

Above: Miss Continental 1985, Maya Douglas.

Right: Coverage of the 1983 contest in GayLife, September 8 edition.

Alan Gelman (from left), Raphael Velasco, Jim Flint and Dan Fraser.

Judge and promoter Raphael Velasco and Tandi Andrews, Miss Continental 1986.

Left and right: Miss Continental 1987, Dana Douglas.

Flint with Miss Continental 1997, Tasha Long.

1985 at Miss Continental. Judge Ana María Polo, promoter Danny Winthrop and Maria (last name unknown).

Flint with Miss Continental 2002, Yoshiko Oshiro.

Flint with Erica Andrews and judge Skip Mackall.

Baton performer Flame Monroe, whose avid fans chanted 'Flame! Flame!' at Miss Continental in 2002 when Monroe failed to be named one of the Top Five finalists.

Tommie Ross, Jim Flint and Erica Andrews.

Miss Continental Plus 2010, Roxxy Andrews, with Flint.

David Sandling of Houston's Miss Southwest with Flint.

Mimi Marks, Jim Flint and Candis Cayne at Continental 2011.
Photo by Hal Baim

The cover of the 2011 Miss Continental program book featured 2010 winner Mokha Montrese.

Mr. Continental 2012, Philip Alexander. The men are selected in the year ahead of the title year, while Miss Continental is from the same year.
Photo by Kat Fitzgerald

At the 2011 Labor Day weekend Continental events, many of the past Continental winners gathered together.
Photo by Hal Baim

At the 2011 Labor Day weekend Continental events, most of the Continental promoters from across the country gathered together.
Photo by Hal Baim

Finalists at the 2011 Miss Continental contest, held at the Vic Theatre.
Photo by Kat Fitzgerald

Heather Fontaine, Miss Continental 1981, performed at the 2011 contest.
Photo by Kat Fitzgerald

Miss Continental 2010, Mokha Montrese, performing at the 2011 contest.
Photo by Kat Fitzgerald

Contestant Alexis Gabrielle "Gabby" Sherrington at the 2011 Miss Continental contest.
Photo by Kat Fitzgerald

Alexis Gabrielle "Gabby" Sherrington wins the 2011 Miss Continental title, after multiple attempts. She's pictured with Jim Flint.
Photo by Kat Fitzgerald

Mokha Montrese at the 2011 contest with (from left) Monica Munro, Michelle Dupree and Tommie Ross.
Photo by Kat Fitzgerald

Maya Douglas at the 2011 Miss Continental contest.
Photo by Kat Fitzgerald

Miss Continental 2001, Candis Cayne, performs at the 2011 Miss Continental contest.
Photo by Kat Fitzgerald

1980
Chilli Pepper

1981
Heather Fontaine

Tiffany Ariegus
1982

Name also spelled Arieagus.

1983
Chena Black

Cherine Alexander
1984

1985
Maya Douglas

Miss Continental

Former Winners

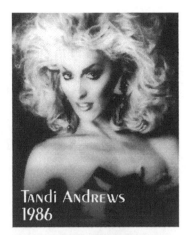

Tandi Andrews
1986

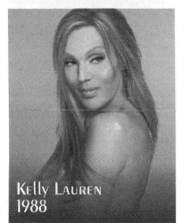

Kelly Lauren
1988

Dana Douglas
1987

Miss Continentals

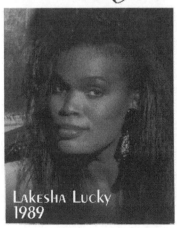

Lakesha Lucky
1989

Chanel Dupree
1990

Amber Richards
1991

Mimi Marks
1992

Monica Munro
1993

Cezanne
1994

Lady Cateria
1995

Paris Frantz
1996

Tasha Long
1997

Name also spelled Catiria.

Michelle Dupree
1998

Tommie Ross
1999

Danielle Hunter
2000

Candis Cayne
2001

Yoshiko Oshiro
2002

Erika Norell
2003

FORMER Miss Continentals

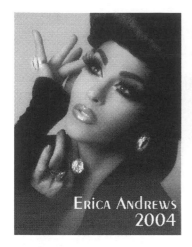

Erica Andrews
2004

Domanique Shappelle
2005

Victoria LePaige
2006

Necole Luv Dupree
2007

Armani
2009

Mokha Montrese
2010

Tulsi
2008

GINGER GRANT
1991

Celebrating 20 Years!

DENISE RUSSELL
1992

Lady CATERIA
1993

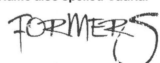

Name also spelled Catiria.

PLUS FORMERS

ERICA RENEE CHRISTIAN
1994

CARMELLA MARCELLA GARCIA
1995

VICTORIA LePAIGE
1996

Dena Cass
1997

Terrie Williams
1999

Santana T. Summers
1998

PLUSFORMERS

Tumara Mahorning
2000

Angel Sheridan
2001

Chevelle Brooks
2002

Victoria Parker
2003

Angelica Sanchez
2004

Amaya
2005

Desiree DeMornay
2006

Tajma Hall
2007

Mercedes
2008

PLUSFORMERS

Coco Van Cartier
2009

Roxxy Andrews
2010

Chelsea Pearl
2011

Nikki Adams
2004

Barbra Herr
2005

Maya Douglas
2006

ELITE FORMER WINNERS

Danielle Hunter
2007

Michelle Fighter
2009

Angel Sheridan
2008

Electra
2010

Daesha Richards
2011

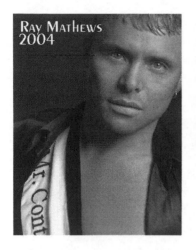

Ray Mathews
2004

Antonio Edwards
2005

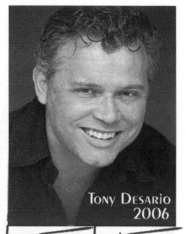

Tony Desario
2006

FORMER MR. CONTINENTALS

Simba Hall
2007

Rasean Montrese
2008

David "FreKlez" Hunter
2009

Name also spelled Freklz.

Christopher Iman
2010

Nick Gray
2011

12

Other Businesses, Partnerships and Family

Jim Flint opened a leather bar, the Redoubt, in 1976. "Redoubt" is derived from the French "redoute," meaning a military fortification, The bar was much smaller than the Gold Coast, Chicago's first gay men's leather bar.

"We could probably fit 30 upstairs and maybe 40 or 50 people downstairs in the Bunker," Flint said. "It was on the corner. Mike's Rainbow Restaurant was in the front, and the bar was in the back. So we had a side entrance at 65 West Illinois [Street]. It had been a bar before I moved in there, and I think I opened it for $4,000. You couldn't turn it down for $4,000.

"I chose [the name] Redoubt because it was a bunker surrounded by the enemy, and at that time the Gold Coast was really big in one direction and then the Bistro was real big in another. Not that I thought of them as enemies, but it seemed like a cute little place in the midst of all that was going on."

Flint said he told Chuck Renslow, owner of the Gold Coast, about the new bar, "and Chuck was fine with it." Renslow confirmed this, adding that at that time, the Gold Coast was so popular and crowded that they had to turn people away. As it turned out, the Redoubt was a great venue for overflow and for people to go back and forth between the two. The same was true for Male Hide Leathers and later the nearby leather dance club Ozone.

Another motive for Flint to open the Redoubt was simply his immersion in the leather lifestyle. "I fell in love with a leatherman," he said. "There were a couple of them, as a matter of fact. The real big one was eventually first runner-up to International Mr. Leather the year Luke Daniel won [1982]. His name was Christian Winkel [representing the San Francisco Eagle]. I thought he was the most magnificent man I'd ever met in my life.

"Christian was living in San Francisco and tending bar at a club, the Pendulum [4146 18th Street], in the Castro. Eventually, in 1984, he was the first Mr. Continental, and [porn legend] Jeff Stryker was the first runner-up. After that, I couldn't get Mr. Continental off the ground, because everyone thought to enter you had to be of that stature, so we quit it for a few years. I used to visit Christian out in San Francisco. He was gorgeous, with a heavy German accent. He'd say, 'Jim, we go here tonight, yes.' And then we used to get on the back of his bike and ride all over San Francisco."

Flint was into the whole leather club scene. "I wouldn't have opened the Redoubt if that didn't interest me," he said. Indeed almost a decade later, in 1985, Flint emceed the International Mr. Leather contest as Felicia. When he recalled the event in the book Leatherman: The Legend of Chuck Renslow, Flint said, "I only hosted it the one time and thought it was incredible." The entertainment that year at IML was Judy Tenuta; an all-male clogging dance troupe from Atlanta, called the Buffalo Chips; and juggler Robert Gruenberg.

The Redoubt's notable features included the down-and-dirty, "anything goes" downstairs, the Bunker. It had midnight drawings on Wednesdays, wooden nickels, T-shirts, and even a piranha tank behind the downstairs bar. "People used to love to watch feeding time, when we would give the piranhas some goldfish to eat," Flint said. An advertisement of the era boasted that the Redoubt featured "surprise guests by the basketful."

Something else people tend to remember about the Redoubt was the door. "Dan Lauing designed the outside door at the Redoubt," explained Flint. "The thick wooden door was weighted and attached by pulleys with cables, which ran along the ceiling, then down behind the bar. When the door opened, the cables would tighten and the counterweight would rise behind the bar. It was very dramatic. There was no getting in the door without being noticed. Mainly it was a conversation piece. People talked about it and were coming there just to see the damn door." Lauing was also the man who designed the grottoesque whirlpool for Man's Country in 1977.

A one-time bartender at the establishment, Dan Neniskis, clarified another bit of Redoubt décor lore. "There was no giant butt plug in the Bunker! On the way downstairs, there was a rail, which was actually about a 15- or 20-foot limb of a cherry tree, and at the end of this sizable piece of lumber there was carved the shaft and head of a dick," he said. "Like the Gold Coast, the Redoubt's Bunker went underneath the vaulted sidewalks in the area and it would leak when it rained, so eventually we had to close one of the rooms."

At the Redoubt, there was also a little room downstairs by the heater with a narrow entrance. "You could go in there and do whatever you wanted to," said Flint. "It was a playroom. We could've easily gotten busted but we didn't. If anyone was coming in who was suspicious or looked like a cop, the bartender would buzz down as a warning, but we didn't have any problems. I allowed women in the bar, but they were not allowed to go downstairs, though a couple of them still did."

As with most bars, a big factor in the success of the Redoubt was some very popular bartenders—Jackson Fleener, Roger Messer, Harley McMillen, Chuck Probert, Dan Neniskis, Harry, Bobby Lee Smith, John Harr, Chuck Rodocker and Flint's former lover Warren Williamson.

Flint recalled: "Jackson Fleener and Roger Messer were my roommates for a while. I had this big apartment at 1030 North State, so we all lived together for a while. Jackson was all about complete freedom, everything went with him. Full of energy, a good person to have fun with, but he got on drugs. Jackson had so many boyfriends that would come and stay all night."

"I was one of his boyfriends. I met him at the Redoubt," said community activist and patron Joey McDonald. "I was so mesmerized by him. He flirted with everybody who came in the bar, but I thought it was just me. He used to give me free drinks all the time. I was crushing on him big-time. I was intimidated, though, because the gay stuff and especially the leather stuff was all very new to me, and he looked like a big, dominant leather top, and that sort of frightened me. It wasn't until later I realized he was more a switch-hitter. Jackson at the Redoubt and Jim Dohr at the Gold Coast were my two big bartender crushes at the time."

"Eventually I had to let Jackson go because of the drugs," said Flint. "Annex 3 was where I finally had to let him go. They caught him out back selling drugs. Later I was going down to Florida to a Miss Florida pageant. They called and told me Jackson was put in the hospital. I got on the phone and called him and said I'd be back on Thursday. I said, 'As soon as I get back we'll straighten this out,' but he passed away that week. It was too much cocaine. This kid was so charismatic, but it just ruined his health. He had a horrible upbringing, at least that's what he told me.

"Roger [Messer] was my manager at Redoubt. He was a former Mr. Windy City [in 1978]—so handsome. Then he worked for me at Annex 2 as well. He got sick with HIV and eventually left and went to California, and he couldn't handle it anymore and killed himself. He threw himself over a wall. It was so sad."

Chuck Rodocker spoke about this period in his life in a 1995 interview with Jack Rinella. "I worked at the Redoubt just after it opened for about six months," he said. "And that was the same time that Wally Thomas had taken over or reopened Touché. Touché was over on Lincoln Avenue [2825 North Lincoln]. The King's Ransom people originally made it gay. They ran it for about six months. And it wasn't successful, because you have to realize that the neighborhood at that time was very blue-collar, to a point of being redneck." (Under Rodocker's direction the revamped Touché flourished in the location until fire destroyed it on March 3, 1990. The blaze began in the early morning hours after closing, in a heating-and-electrical storage area before spreading to the alcohol inventory. When the alcohol exploded, the roof of the bar caught fire. After the conflagration, Touché relocated to its 6412 North Clark Street location.)

Dan Neniskis started at the Redoubt in an unplanned way. "I was here one night, and Roger Messer, one of the bartenders, came up to me and said someone was sick and could I tend bar? So then I started working downstairs. That was probably around 1979 or 1980," he said.

Warren Williamson used to tend bar there a lot during the day and then tend the Baton's bar at nights. "Redoubt was a shot-and-beer sort of place. Anybody could do that, and I liked it there, but at the Baton you needed a bartender who had some experience, so I worked there nights," Williamson said. "At the Baton, all the girls were always ordering things like International Gold Cadillacs and things like that."

"I think I got a part-time job at the Redoubt because I was not working at the time and Jim knew I could use the extra money," said Harley McMillen. "I worked as a bartender on the weekends in the bar downstairs. I was right in front of the piranha tank. The Redoubt was also the only place that I was able to fulfill a fantasy and, after the bar closed one night, I screwed one of the young guys on the pool table. Nice for me. I never told Jim."

A Redoubt patron, Curtis Kath, recalled bartender Bobby Lee Smith as a man of small stature and big heart. "He always looked as if something was on his mind, almost sad, and yet anytime I was in his presence, whether at the bar or at El Jardín restaurant, he would break into a smile from ear to ear," Kath said.

"Bobby Lee worked for me at the Redoubt," said Flint. "A great guy. I knew him as a waiter at El Jardín. He worked for a while at the Bistro, too. Then, Ben Allen wanted him to open [a bar] with him at Clark and Deming [2546 North Clark Street]. Bobby got sick and would never admit it. Even when Ikey and I would visit him in the hospital, and this was up until two days before he died, he would never admit it was HIV."

"John Harr was also a bartender for Jim Flint at the Redoubt, as well as Chuck Probert," said Kath. "Harr was a classmate of mine [at mortuary school] and introduced me to my first-ever gay bar, Sam's." Kath remembered that Harr was from a pig farm in Southern Illinois and was known as Ma Harr in mortuary school.

Paul Yinger, aka adult film star and personality Steve "Titpig" Hurley, first met Jim Flint soon after coming down from the Upper Peninsula of Michigan in May 1980 for a University of Chicago fellowship in respiratory care. "One night I decided to go out with some of my new friends, and as fate would have it, that night was also the night of the 1980 Mr. Redoubt contest.

"When I went in the Redoubt, I'd never seen anything like it. It was the first time I'd ever experienced anything leather. I remember the downstairs was dark and exciting. I couldn't believe people were actually having sex, though it was hard to tell because it was so dark. The only light downstairs seemed to come from the piranha tank behind the bar.

"I entered the contest that night and won, but it wasn't held at the Redoubt— it was held at the Baton, because they had a stage. The first prize was a pair of leather chaps from Male Hide Leathers, which I still own today. I remember it was on a Monday because they didn't have a drag show and that it was in mid-May. International Mr. Leather was that coming weekend, but the old Mr. Redoubt was entered in that contest. The month after that, I won the Mr. Windy City contest, and that came with a prize of $700, and with that money I moved permanently from the U.P. and got a job at Northwestern, and my life just took off."

"The Redoubt reminded me of about as old-school a leather bar as you could have in Chicago," said Joey McDonald. "You saw a lot of guys with flogs and handcuffs in their pockets. The Gold Coast was more playful and had a more big, open, airy feel. There was art on the walls. It seemed more welcoming, so I felt more comfortable there, because I wasn't sure I belonged at the Redoubt.

"The Redoubt was more ominous and dark and had more of a dungeon feel. The guys there seemed to be really more into a certain dominant-submissive headspace. The piranha tank sort of sums up the feel. It was very 'the hunter and the hunted' at the Redoubt, it had that chase-and-be-chased tension."

Yinger continued: "It was dark downstairs at the Redoubt, and the bar was at the end of the stairs with a railing around the perimeter. There was a cell room on one side, adjacent to the bar. Once, I was about 23 at the time and cute, and these guys just grabbed me and dragged me back there and held me down and played with me and sucked me off, and once they got me off, they just went back to drinking or whatever. It was much wilder than anything I had experienced before. There was nothing like that in the U.P.

"My duties as Mr. Redoubt were to make a few appearances. I remember some Colt models would come into town and I would do things with them. I really remember Colt film star and model Clint Lochner and the couple wonderful nights we had together. Jim took us out to eat at the Pump Room, and then afterwards we went back to the Redoubt for some sort of show or appearance."

Flint adds: "Oh, my goodness, when Clint Lochner, the Highway Patrolman from Colt, was here, I hired him one time to come do my contest. He was here and he came in my bedroom. He looked at me and said, 'Aren't we going to ...' And I said, 'No, no—I hired you to do the contest, not to do this.' I wanted to, though—I should have."

There were no arrests or incidents at the Redoubt. "We could have gotten arrested there. We had a sex room downstairs, but the cops just didn't bother us," Flint said. "There were payoffs, and the neighborhood had changed by 1976. There was a [police-connected] bagman in the area that came to all the bars and would take it. We actually didn't deal with the police directly. As soon as we opened, the payoffs started." (See Chapters 3 and 4.)

In a 1996 Jack Rinella interview, Male Hide Leathers co-owner Bob Maddox discussed the increasing business for his leather specialty clothing store. "The time was right, and there was no one else around, and we happened to be in the right place at the right time," Maddox said. "Of course, being in the Gold Coast, that was the place to be in those days until, you know, eventually, the Redoubt came across the street on Illinois. That, of course, brought more people in, and people had a second place to go, and if things weren't happening at the Gold Coast they'd walk over to the Redoubt for a while, and then they'd come back over there and vice versa, so they played on each other well."

"It was a very hot bar on Saturday and Sunday afternoons—being near the Gold Coast, Male Hide Leathers and Ozone," recalled Warren Williamson. "The Redoubt would get all this leather traffic going back and forth.

"We used to get all sorts in there. I remember one old guy. He seemed almost a derelict. I mean, sometimes he'd even come in with no shoes, but Jimmy was a soft touch. He'd always let him in and then, when he'd get too drunk, Jimmy would be the one to tell him to leave. I'll never forget this guy. You wouldn't think anything to look at him. Downstairs above the trough urinal we had a chalkboard, where people wrote things or what they were looking for or whatever, and he wrote:

> "When the frost is on the punkin',
> That's the time for dickie dunkin'.
> But when the weather is hot and sticky,
> That's the time for dunkin' dickie."

"I still remember that, how many years later? I remember thinking it was very clever and that it really impressed me," said Williamson. "I think it sticks in my mind, too, because it was really when it sank in that people may look one way, but there may still be a lot going on upstairs."

"The same year I entered the Mr. Redoubt contest, I met a boyfriend named Scott Daniels who was also in the contest," said Yinger. "He lived in the Lawson YMCA, which was such a wild place. Rent there was $50 a week or something. Scott was a waiter-hustler-hairstylist and just another part of my education about the city. We were together for about six months, and then after him I met Bob Rosloniec, my lover of 13 years who passed away in 1993. The hard thing about this is that it was such a good time, but it also became a very bad time as well. I started to lose a lot of friends. Jim lost a lot of friends, and he was always very good about helping with memorials and things."

In addition to Yinger, other Mr. Redoubts included Michael Meacham Hage in 1981 and David Morgan in 1982. "Another of the Mr. Redoubts was the lover of Larry Eyler. That was Gary Lewandowski," said Flint. "I knew Richard Speck, John Wayne Gacy and Larry Eyler. Gary was saying how Eyler took him out in the country in Indiana and said he was going to kill him, and he cried and said he had children, and he ended up not doing it. He came back, and I said, 'How in the hell did you ever stay with him after something like that?'" Few believed Eyler was actually capable of the monstrosities he spoke about. Eyler was eventually convicted for the torture, murder and dismemberment of 16-year-old Danny Bridges in August 1984.

Redoubt Moves to Halsted

"I eventually moved the Redoubt over to 440 North Halsted, near Grand," said Flint. "Eddie Dugan also said he was going to move the Bistro over there because this area [River North] was changing, but he never did. I was over there for a good year or two, but I just decided to get out of that location and close the Redoubt."

"I was still dating Jackson [Fleener] at the time he was bartending over there," said Joey McDonald. "When the Redoubt moved, the feel changed. It went from being a dungeon to being more of a neighborhood bar with a leather theme. They had a stage at that Halsted location as well. I remember because I came in one time and Jackson actually got up on the stage and serenaded me and did a little dance for me. The song he sang was something early-new-wave."

"I helped design the new location," said Neniskis. "It was a very large bar, and I worked with the prison-bar motif. We had a lower level there and, of course, brought the carved cherry handrail leading downstairs. There was also a restaurant at this location. It was a bar and grill, so the Redoubt served food as well.

"There was no separate entrance for the restaurant—it was a part of the bar, and there was fairly high-end dining there, and you could either eat at a table or the bar. The chef was Robert Koral. We had a brunch and an evening menu. Sadly, we moved to this big location just as AIDS started becoming known and everyone was too scared to go out."

Harley McMillen also remembered: "Yes, I moved to the Redoubt's new location as well. We had the restaurant and it was all very nice, but the old Redoubt had a lot of cross traffic between places. There was nothing there [at the new location]. The Bistro was supposed to move there but never did. It was not in the best area, either. The timing was just wrong."

"My mom cooked at the Redoubt in the new location," Flint said, smiling. "I loved for my mother to do the soups and sometimes hamburgers, but mainly we loved to have her doing the soups. She went in during the day and felt like she was in charge when she was doing that, and trust me, she was having a field day. She'd cooked for a large family and did that at the hotel back in Peoria, so she loved it."

Redoubt Goes South: Atlanta

Flint also opened a Redoubt in Atlanta in 1982. "I did that mainly because I always wanted to go to Atlanta," Flint said. "Everybody wanted me to have a bar there. I was close to one of the guys with the Atlanta Motorcycle Club. They didn't have a good bar to go to, so I decided to do it. Dan Adelezzi wanted to manage it down there and, as good as it was, the money never seemed to be coming back here. It always seemed to be in debt.

"Finally, I just decided I couldn't absorb the debt anymore, so I just wrote off the losses and closed it. It was very successful for the short time it was open, a little less than a year. I had to fight a lot of the owners there who were telling people that I was part of the Mob and that the Syndicate was backing me. It was just bad out-of-town management. I couldn't watch things."

Flint's boyfriend Scott Palmer recalled the place. "In Atlanta, Jim basically got robbed blind because he wasn't there to oversee it," Palmer said. "It was a great bar and was packed all the time. Also, I think the bar owners were sort of afraid of him. They seemed to think he was some sort of Mob type down from Chicago to take over things in Atlanta."

"I'd see him at softball events and then, when he opened the Redoubt in Atlanta, he asked me if I would work [there] part-time 4 to 10 p.m.," said Mike Denny. "So I became a bartender there. A while after that, he tried to open the Baton South, so I would work Redoubt and then weekends on Fridays and Saturdays I worked the Baton South. I remember him as coming in about once a month to make the rounds."

The entire Baton South–Redoubt Atlanta complex was "an old drive-in [theater]. The parking lot was huge, and the concession was where the bar was," recalled Dan Neniskis.

"Parking was a huge necessity in Atlanta, because everyone drove," added Flint.

"It was such a strange setup," said Lennie Malina. "It was an old drive-in, and you entered through ground level into the Baton and then went down to the lower level, and that was the Redoubt. So it was truly a bunker or fortress in Atlanta. I remember the way it was set up in the office there. I would be sitting in the chair and could hear voices behind me. Because it was underground, the ventilation system and the grates were something like a block away, you'd hear these weird, muffled conversations people would be having over there. Very strange."

"Originally he had it as Redoubt Atlanta, and then Baton South," added Neniskis. "Dan Adelezzi was this handsome, tall and slender guy who was in Chicago Knights and who was running things down there for Mr. Flint. But they didn't much like the way Mr. Flint came in. He was a Yankee and he just sort of came in town and was going to do all this. It was not appreciated."

Since the front part of the complex was the Baton South and the other part Redoubt Atlanta, Neniskis said, "I think he was doing a sort of leather-and-lace thing at the time. The Baton South failed miserably, and the Redoubt eventually failed as well."

Dana Douglas said Flint hired her for the first time in 1984. "He wanted me to come to Chicago to the Baton, but that was a long way from home, so I went to Atlanta instead and started working at Baton South there," she said. "We were in the front part of Redoubt, and the leathermen from the Redoubt were allowed to come to the front and see the show, but the queens weren't allowed back in the leather part."

"Amber Richards and I changed that," laughed Dina Jacobs. "We went and told all the leather boys that rule. They were all friends of ours, and all we wanted was a drink. We were starting to do all these benefits for HIV, or whatever it was called then, so we were well-known in the leather community. We didn't want to go cruise anybody as much as just duck back there and get a drink. So what happened was that eventually they started boycotting the place, and then the Eagle opened, too, in Atlanta."

Jacobs recalled that the cast of the Baton South was Joanna Caron, Dana Douglas, and Chena Black (Miss Continental 1983), with Ron Sanford as the leading man. The final member of the Baton South cast, Amber Richards, later went on to become Miss Continental in 1991.

"It closed after only a few months," said Dana Douglas. "In my opinion, part of what happened was that Jim came in and said, 'I'm Jim Flint and I'm from Chicago and I'm going to open this place,' and expected people in Atlanta to care. People took offense. This was the South, and the way of doing things was different than they are in Chicago. People stayed away from the show, despite the fact that it was a good cast. Bobby Glaze helped run the Redoubt and Baton in Atlanta. We came up here together."

"Bobby Glaze came out of all that," laughed Flint. "Bobby was a bartender I met in Atlanta at a place called the Answer. Then I opened the Baton down there for a short time in the front part of the Redoubt Atlanta. That was probably only there for about four months. It was the room in the front of the bar. Then I decided to close it all because I was losing money and I couldn't keep track of it. Bobby said he wanted to come to Chicago, so he came here, and later on he met Jesse, and they were with me here at the Baton for a long time."

"Jim sent me to Atlanta to save the Baton-Redoubt complex down there," said Chicago Baton and Annex 2 manager Lennie Malina. "I went there and was going to save the place, and so I called all the crews together and gave a pep talk and said we were going to turn the place around. Literally, the old manager had left, I drove down there, and walked cold into a place I didn't know to try and save it. I was on the phone with Jim (when I could get him) to try and get advice.

"Eventually he told me he wanted to close, so only a few weeks after my pep talk I also had to fire both staffs, close the bars, and get rid of everything or bring it back to Chicago. I remember, in each of the two spaces, all I left was a light bulb."

Annex 2

Annex 2, which opened in August 1981, was on that Hubbard and Clark street corner where Starbucks is today, at 430 North Clark. "I opened it there because the Baton was next door," Flint said. The space had been occupied by the original Baton. Following the move from 430 by the original Baton, the space had become the Ramrod. When it closed, former Flint co-worker Sam Olin then had opened Sunday's, which Annex 2 replaced.

Once Annex 2 opened, Flint had a leather bar, an impersonator bar, and a dance bar all within a block of one another.

"Jim Flint made everybody realize that a show bar and a leather bar and dance/party bar were all the same thing," said Joey McDonald. "There was no doubt what kind of bar you were in when you were in it, but he blended those different facets. The twink drag and muscle boys at Annex 2 and female impersonation at the Baton and the leather gear at the Redoubt—it all blended. We all put on something, and we're all still part of the group. He celebrated each one, but didn't let that limit who a person could be. Same with a baseball jersey—another outfit."

Despite thinking he was once offered as a "sacrificial lamb" by members of the Dallesandro family and despite the ensuing legal hassles at their Annex bar, Flint had fond memories of the original Annex. It was the bar that "broke him in" as an official Chicago bartender, so he decided to pay it homage with the name Annex 2.

"I wanted to name it that because that's where I got my start, so I went to Nick and asked him if I could use the name," Flint said. "He gave me permission. I like having things connect that way, like with Miss Continental being named after the bar in Norfolk [that Flint frequented when in the Navy]. I like to sort of have that tie to the past."

Taking ownership of Annex 2, Flint expanded, which involved breaking down the wall between what was once Sunday's and the defunct Marilyn's and making it all into the Annex 2. The Marilyn's space at 432 was turned into the dance floor. GayLife of August 28, 1981, described the Annex 2's interior when it opened on Wednesday, August 19: "The bar's hot new decor features a basketball court—hoops, lockers, and all."

The grand opening included plenty of complimentary cocktails and great hors d'oeuvres. The bar featured a little of everything. There was Monday-night football with a 9 p.m. buffet. On Tuesdays, all team members who wore their team shirts got 75-cent drinks. Wednesday offered all well drinks for 75 cents. Behind the bar were some of the most popular bartenders of the time, including Irene Raczka (Ikey), Pepe Peña, Kenny (Diana Hutton), Roger Winans, George Medeiros, J.P., Rusty and popular Redoubt bartender Jackson Fleener.

Ikey talked a bit about first coming to work for Flint and about Annex 2. "I first met Jim in 1978 when I was working at His 'n Hers," she said. "When he met me he said, 'When can you start come working for me?' I said, 'I have a job.' He said, when I left that one, to come talk to him. So later, when I left His 'n Hers after an altercation with [owner] Marge [Summit], I eventually started working for Jim at the Annex 2 on Clark and Hubbard."

"I had gone to His 'n Hers on Lincoln Avenue [2316 North Lincoln] when it was by Children's Memorial [Hospital]. Both Ikey and Lennie worked there," said Flint. "I'd have a hamburger and got to know them. Ikey was the favorite of all the guys. She's just got that way about her. It's something a good bartender just has. She's still working, and she'll be 70, and she probably has the first penny she ever made, too." Ikey works for Flint at his 3160 bar now.

"I worked as a bartender at Annex 2 for six years," said Ikey. "It was a great bar. That was when bars were bars. Now, people want to be entertained. In those days, people came in and they met people and hung out and made their own fun. Now it's work to keep them coming back, but not in those days.

"You came in at the corner into the bar. That's where I worked, and there were a couple video games in there. Pac-Man, I remember, was there. Then there were sliding glass doors [on the north wall], and that led to the dance bar, and that was where Frankie Knuckles [among others] DJ'd. Then there was another pair of sliding glass doors, and that led into the Baton.

"I remember bartending with Roger Messer. What a sweetheart. He was tall, 6-feet-3, and gorgeous and built. He had a bushy mustache but was a big teddy bear. Really, just a gentle giant."

The disc jockeys at Annex 2 were local personality Joseph LoPresti, Steve Adams, Frank Lipomi, Brian Barber and Frankie Knuckles. "I love Frankie, and he got his start there," Flint said.

According to his official website biography, Knuckles is a DJ, producer and remix artist. Knuckles was instrumental in developing house music (electronic disco-influenced dance music) as a Chicago DJ in the 1980s and helped popularize it in the 1990s with his work both as a producer and as a remixer. In 1996 he was inducted into the Chicago Gay and Lesbian Hall of Fame. In 2005 he was inducted into the Dance Music Hall of Fame.

Bill Sheehan worked the door at Annex 2, along with Dan Neniskis. "Working the door at Annex 2 wasn't as easy as it sounds," explained Neniskis. "In those days Hubbard [Street] was where all the hustlers hung out, especially at the New Flight down the street. Those boys were known to pick pockets and steal money off the bar, that sort of thing. So, part of being the doorman there was to keep the hustlers out.

"There were double sliding glass patio doors on the brick wall between the bar and the dance floor, and then eventually another set of sliding glass patio doors were installed, and there was access through more sliding glass doors from the dance floor of Annex 2 into the Baton. It's the sort of thing that would never pass [buildings] code today."

"The Sunday tea dances were so popular at Annex 2," said Ikey. "That was when it was busiest. They'd start at 4 and then wind down about 10, when everyone was bombed and calling it a night because they had to work in the morning."

Lennie Malina was manager of both the Baton and Annex 2. "My favorite thing to do at Annex 2 were the tea dances," she said. "I designed a lot of them. I remember for a while we had a truck-stop theme, and we suspended the front part of a semi above the dance floor along with various parts of the truck itself, like the steering wheel and side mirror and stuff. Then, in the first room where you came in, we decorated it like a truck stop with booths and checkered tablecloths, and ketchup and mustard and napkin dispensers in each booth.

"I also cooked for those tea dances, and I don't cook—but there I was, suddenly cooking spaghetti for a couple hundred people."

"We used to do acid at the tea dances," said Joey McDonald. "I remember one time specifically. I think this was 1982. All my friends were wearing black spandex shirts and I was wearing a red one. Roger [Messer] gave us all shots, which were called Christmas Trees, and right when we did the shots was when the acid kicked in. There was too much going on in the bar, so I remember we all ran outside and, right when we did, a firetruck was going by and we couldn't believe that the firetruck had a disco light on top of it.

"We ended up walking up and down Clark Street until it started to get light outside that night—and then we went to Man's Country."

Neniskis recalled some happenings at the bar. "There was certainly a colorful clientele," he said. "One time this huge white queen named Sugar was in there rip-roaring drunk and high on drugs, too, maybe, but he picked up the Pac-Man machine and was going to throw or tip it on top of someone, so we got him, and then the cop cars came and they took Sugar away.

"I used to work as a funeral director and embalmer, and so one Halloween we did the Annex 2 up just like a funeral home, and there were seven caskets arranged around the bar. There was one set up with a spray of flowers and the two torchiers on either side and the lighting, everything was prepared like the viewing of a body. People could actually get in the casket and have their picture taken as a souvenir."

Flint said his mother, Pearl, thought it would be fun for her to lie in one casket and Baton doorman Richie Saunders to lie in the other. Flint called Saunders on the phone to see if he'd be willing. "Pearl was on the extension," Flint recalled. "I said, 'You know, Richie, Mom wants to have a photo of you in one coffin and her in the other,' and he said, 'You know, there's two things I don't do—I don't lay in coffins and I don't eat pussy.' And on the extension my mother said, 'Thank God for that, Richie.'"

In an effort to mix things up and keep people coming that December, Annex 2 had a Victor/Victoria Holiday Ball featuring black, white, and gray attire and a musical program by Brian Barber. There were leather weekend specials as well, with discounts to those in leather or uniforms. Despite the ideas and promotions and whatnot, there was no denying that the neighborhood was changing. The cross traffic from one nightspot and gay haunt to the other just wasn't there anymore. The Baton was surviving because of the tourism—it was a destination spot. The gay clientele was moving north to the Lakeview area.

After closing the Annex 2, the dance-floor area at 432 North Clark Street once more was separated from the corner space (430) by a wall, and the 432 space became Flint's River North Travel.

Jack Delaney and Dan the Man

After he dated Warren Williamson in the 1960s, Flint dated a few other men.

"I ended up meeting a guy named Jack Delaney [in the late 1970s], and I stayed with Jack for a while," Flint said. "Then we went to El Jardín one night. We were there with my best friend at the time, Pat. Well, Pat got up to go to the bathroom, and he said, 'Why don't you tell Jim before I get back?' Well, he came back in a minute and then said, 'Did you tell him?'

"Finally, I said, 'What's this all about, tell me what?' Pat said, 'You know that guy that I said I met last week and that I've been dating?' I nodded. He said, 'Well, his real name isn't Dave. His real name is Jack.' And I looked at Jack, and he looked down and said, 'Jim, it just happened,' and I said, 'Yeah?'

"He asked me if I was upset. I said, 'I'm not upset at all. I'm going to drink my margarita, pay the check, drive you two motherfuckers to your car, and I don't want to talk to you again.' Later we did talk, but I said, 'Just don't ever lie to me again. If it's the truth, tell me the truth.'" (Pat Griffin, Delaney's partner, died in 1997.)

"During the 1980s, Jim and his partner Dan spent many a Thanksgiving at Pat and my apartment, condo and then house," Delaney said.

"When I started dating Dan Neniskis," Flint said. "I thought he was the weirdest person in the world, because I left the Redoubt one night with Roger Messer and we went up to the Bushes on [3320] North Halsted. We were just having a cocktail, and this guy walked over and said, 'Can I buy you a drink?' I said, 'What do you want to buy me a cocktail for? You're in my bar every night and you won't even say hello.' He told me that here [at the Bushes] we were on equal turf, so he could talk to me. Later I did take a drink, and as I was drinking it, I turned to Roger and said, 'Who in the hell is this strange one?'"

"I knew of him, the persona," said Neniskis. "It was Memorial Day weekend and we were at the Bushes, and I just went up to him and grabbed and shook his hand and introduced myself. I knew of him, and by that I mean I knew Jim Flint as the owner of the Redoubt.

"At the time I had no idea about the Baton or Felicia. When I did find out, it sort of intrigued me more. In those days, it seemed there were disco dollies, leather guys and impersonators, so when I started going to the Baton after we began dating, it opened up this entire world. I was fascinated."

"I am the type that's never really had a type. What attracted me to Dan was his big ears. I am a big ear freak," laughed Flint. "Ronald Reagan was an ear freak. At Ronald Reagan's funeral, his son said, 'Didn't you know my dad was into earlobes? Can't you see him sealing some deal by grabbing a guy's ear?' After he said that on TV, I got about 10 calls of people saying, 'Jim, you're not the only ear freak.'"

Neniskis recalled their days of dating. "We used to go for car rides a lot, and we also used to go to Navy Pier back when it was just a dump, and right where the Ferris wheel is was a little fried-shrimp place that gave out their food in those greasy little bags," he said. "We did that a lot.

"I remember we would get together, and he started telling me to watch out—that people would try and break us up and say things about me. It happened, too. People would say things and gossip, spread rumors that would take me down and not make me or Mr. Flint as desirable. They told me, 'You're one of Jim's many boy toys,' that kind of thing. The worst thing that happened, though, by far, was a five-page letter I got about 18 years ago, which I still have, from someone who told me to step aside, that he knew Jim would be better without me."

Scott Comes to Town

Flint has had, to put it mildly, a very complicated love life.

Flint spoke about what was going on personally for him back during the height of the AIDS epidemic. "It was such a horrible time. Everyone was getting sick," he said. "Dan got very sick, and I thought he was going to die. I'd been through so many deaths, and in a weak moment I met Scott. I knew him from before, because I hated his guts. He played softball against us, and he and I almost got in a fight when he ran into my first baseman, I thought, deliberately."

Scott Palmer said he's known Flint since 1985 or '86. The two officially met in the heat of an argument. Palmer slid into Flint's first baseman when playing for an Atlanta softball team. "He came flying out and we had words," Palmer said. "That's how we first met, screaming and yelling at each other, and 26 years later we still scream and yell at each other, but we get along.

"I had a lover in Atlanta who passed away in 1988, and I moved up here in 1989 to take a job with a law firm. I ended up going with a different company that developed intellectual-property software.

"During that time frame, I was ready to start playing softball again, and Jim was really the only one I knew here from softball or that had a team. I saw him at the old Gentry on Rush. I was in there with my adopted godfather, and I said to him, 'I'd like to play, but I don't know if I want to play with him or not, because we've had words back and forth,' and my adopted godfather said, 'He's a pretty nice guy.' So, I had my adopted godfather give him my number and say that when softball starts to give me a call.

"Delilah, who worked at the Annex 3 at the time, called me when the season came around, and I went out and started playing ball with the Annex 3 Blues, and we developed our relationship. We are totally opposites. I'm very introverted and reserved and more corporate-oriented. Jim is out and in your face."

Flint explained his relationship with Palmer. "We went to a tournament in Birmingham, Alabama, and I put certain people in rooms together, and Scott switched rooms with who I was supposed to room with, and so when I got there, surprise. I had a new roommate. We ended up being friends, and one thing turned into another," Flint said.

"We were booked to go play some games and we got booked in the same room, and that's when the relationship sort of began," added Palmer. "I switched rooms with someone but did not realize that was what I was switching to. I did not mind it, but I did not switch specifically to be with Jim."

There are 23 years' difference in age between Flint and the younger Palmer. "He's the youngest man I've ever dated," said Palmer. " He was only 49 when we first started a serious relationship. Prior to that, I'd never dated anyone under 55 or so. My lover in Atlanta was 57 when we met and 62 when he died."

Flint said things have been going on with both Dan Neniskis and Scott Palmer ever since. "Scott has a separate place in Sandburg Village," Flint said. "He works as my assistant here [at the Continental-Baton office], and he does his thing and Danny does his thing, and it all works somehow. I don't know how it works, but it works somehow."

Neniskis strongly disagreed with that scenario. "I was never sick, and time has not smoothed things over. There is animosity. I was bumped out of the way and we were all battling, and finally I said to Scott, 'Fine, you want him, you take him and see how easy it is.'

"We lived at 1835 West Erie in a three-flat upstairs from Jim's mother. After she passed, we got a place in Orleans Court over on Grand and Orleans, and now we are in Buena Park and have been in the Montrose and Dayton area for 22 years. Scott was on East Ohio in a high-rise there and then got a unit in Sandburg Village."

Flint said he and Neniskis "have been together for 35 years. I don't know if you want to say it is a lover relationship or a partner relationship. I say it is more of a companion relationship. He has his bedroom and I have my bedroom. He has his washroom and I have my washroom. But it is a compatible relationship."

"Guess I am going to win in the end. We [Jim and I] have a shared mausoleum crypt, just the two of us," added Neniskis.

"I'm going to be buried in Queen of Heaven, where Al Capone is buried, in Hillside," explained Flint. Commenting about the two men, he said: "They hate each other because Dan fell in love with Scott, and Scott was drinking, and Dan bought him a sweater for Christmas, and Scott lost it, and they've hated each other ever since. I've lived with Dan for 35 years but we haven't had sex in 34 years. That's why I don't understand all the jealousy."

"The first few years were very nice but, after that, we had a lot of pressures from outside," said Palmer. "One, because my job was taking me all around the United States as well as a lot of time in Europe. Our company was growing, and there were only five people developing the software. As the company grew, I automatically fell into the role of going out and doing installations, and setting up the networks and training the attorneys and paralegals how to use the software so that it was functional. We spent as much time together as we could, and typically that was softball. I would try and schedule my work around softball tournaments. Jim would often fly and meet me in different cities.

"The small U.S. firm I was with had a senior partner that was retiring, and by that time we had major clients around the U.S., Europe and Asia, and our software sold for $300,000 a package, but they were ready to get out of the business, so we were sold to a separate entity, a law firm from Brussels and Barcelona. I went over and met with them. They wanted to give me a raise, but the catch was to live permanently in Germany or Brussels.

"I'd had too much. I'd been in Europe for a month and had already planned on going home for Christmas, and during this time Jimmy and I had been talking all through this, and Jimmy's answer to being unhappy was, 'Just quit!' Well, you can't really do that in the corporate world.

"At any rate, I returned home, saw him briefly, and had planned on flying to my parents' house in Alabama. When I stopped by the office briefly for a few things, they said they wanted me to go to Seattle on Christmas Eve. I'd have never gotten home. I'd had enough and walked out and basically did nothing for three or four months.

"Jim at the time had the travel agency [River North Travel, 432 North Clark Street], and that system needed to be upgraded, so I did that and upgraded it to a whole different platform for him. I rewired and restructured the office as he wanted it at that time. Back then, there were four desks in the front where the agency was primarily located. Then Jim had his office in the back.

"Re-networking and restructuring the office took a few months, and then it was going into Continental time. I looked at what they had at the time and, then, Continental basically ran off a copied sheet of paper with tables laid out on a basic rough design, and when a table was sold it was marked off. It was run well, but the front-end part really needed to be tweaked. So Jim asked me what I could do for that.

"So I went out and got him the software he needed and set him up and got him a complete mailing list and got that going. One thing led to another needing to be done, and now it's so many years later, and I'm still here."

River North Travel ended around 2003 or 2004. "We stopped when the Web really got up to speed for people booking online," Palmer said. "They could get better deals than what you could get by dealing directly with the airline. We booked Continental tours, hotels and flights—but River North Travel also did a lot of other corporations in the area. I brought my entire company's business to River North because of Jim."

At the time, River North Travel was also popular with gay and lesbian travelers, booking RSVP cruises and customizing LGBT travel and vacation packages for the individual. It was also a great venue for community generosity.

"Back in 1993 we were organizing the Chicago contingent for the national march on Washington for GLBT rights," said Chicago activist Victor Salvo. "Among other things, we were working to raise enough money to send 50 PWAs [people with AIDS] to Washington so they could participate in something that would ordinarily be too costly for most of them. We went to see Jim at River North Travel to discuss our goals.

"He immediately took the lead in making those arrangements and put up the money to secure airfare and hotel accommodations for the 50 slots while we worked to raise the money. And when we fell a little short of the goal, instead of cutting the number of seats, he paid the difference out of his own pocket. [Salvo recalled the difference as being roughly the cost of air and lodging for 13 PWAs.] As long as I live I will never forget his generosity—especially because he never wanted to be acknowledged for it."

Palmer said that, now that the travel agency is no more, his main duty is to be the one who gets yelled at. "Jim has an extreme temper, and a lot of times the public doesn't see it," Palmer said. "Through the years, you develop a tough skin if you are around him or in a relationship with him. He may scream at you for three to five minutes without even breathing, but then, if you give him two or three minutes, he'll apologize. It'll come out, and when it comes out it will often be directed at me or people close to him.

"He can get mad about anything. A lot of times, things will build and reach a point and he'll just explode. It could be hassles with getting things done and ordering something and not have it be here on time.

"I used to think I wanted to live with Jim, but after all these years I don't know. Jim is a very clean person. He'll shower several times a day, and his clothes and everything are very clean. But he likes to do things like leave wet towels on the floor or bed. Those are things that get to me. For cooking, he can turn on a microwave and maybe fry an egg. Laundry, you can forget about. If you can't take it to the cleaners, he probably couldn't tell you what to do with it.

"Things with Dan [Neniskis] can be rather complicated. I just deal with it. I laugh at him, mostly because I don't know what the guy is so concerned about. He has nothing to lose. Jim and his businesses fully support him.

"He's always hated me and for no reason. He and Jim weren't even together when Jim and I started seeing each other. They were roommates and they still are. They had a little two-year relationship and that was that. The easiest way to think of it is, Dan moved in with Jim and didn't move out, and Jim would not put anyone out. I had no idea that they were anything but roommates, because that's what they are.

"Three or four years into it, things were getting crazy. I used to live on Chestnut, and my doorman would tell me things like, 'That same guy is back.' Dan would literally just walk around my building and wait for Jim to come out. You could see it weighing on Jim, to the point when I just said, 'Whatever, if it makes Dan happy and it makes your home life happy, then just let it be.' It's been 21 years of that."

Palmer said a medical condition makes travel difficult for him. "Typically we go to Naples, Florida, for a few days and Cape Cod for a week and Boston for Christmas," Palmer said. "Jim and I have the majority of our arguments when we are in the car, because his driving scares the shit out of me. I never know where his brain is, because he has so many things going on. Is he concentrating on the phone call or the road or looking over there? Typically, it comes in the car, and it comes when I hit the imaginary brakes on my side of the car and yell or whatever.

"He'll get out of the car and leave it in gear. He's done that and I've still been in the car, and it starts moving and he's just standing there talking. That's even happened when he's been talking to the police after getting pulled over.

"I think we were in Phoenix another time—I know it was a ball tournament—and we had a little bit of time to kill before our flight, and Jim wanted to stop at the casino for a few minutes. By the time we got out of the casino, we hit traffic, and there was some construction as well. We're trying to get to the airport, and Jim missed the exit. That was, of course, my fault because I should have told him.

"Anyway, he made his own little turnaround by the median, and we got on the rental-car road, but we got on it going the wrong direction. It was a Hertz, and, thank God, Hertz was the first one on the rental-car road, but since we were going the wrong way, Jim barreled in there the wrong way and went over the one-way spikes, and all four of the tires blew. He got out like nothing was wrong, gave them the keys and said 'I'll pay for it later, I'm late,' and we left.

"Another time, we were driving from Philadelphia to Manhattan, and it was a rental car, and in the car with us was a friend, Bill Clayson. Anyway, it started raining and Jim got flustered and couldn't find the wipers, and he ended up getting so nervous he just took his hands completely off the wheel and said, 'Scotty, what do I do? What do I do?' I reached over and grabbed the wheel, and Bill in the back seat said, 'Now, Jim, the first thing you do is put your hands back on the wheel.' That's what driving with him is like sometimes.

"One of my favorite Jim stories is, we were visiting our friend Chuck Dema in Manhattan, and the name of his place is the Dugout, right down in the Village. Chuck was actually one of the founders of national gay softball when his New York team challenged a San Francisco team.

"Anyway, there was a dance floor upstairs at this bar, and Jim and I aren't big dancers. So Jim propped himself on this ledge and sat right on top of the red-ink pad that they would use when they stamp someone's hand. Well, he was wearing light-colored khaki shorts at the time. So we told him about it and he didn't believe us. We ended up going to a few more bars, and I remember at the Spike and the Eagle they looked at Jim and the red stain on the rear of his shorts, and then they looked at me like I'd done something to him. I just shrugged. Finally, at the end of the night, he realized I'd been telling him the truth.

"Up until a few years ago, we normally do Cubs spring training every year. Sara [Davis] will go with us, and she's like my adopted grandmother. In her eyes, I can do no wrong. She likes to watch Jim and I interact, especially in the car.

"I actually have a matching Cubs tattoo to Jim's on my calf. And in 1991 I got a heart tattoo on my back with JWF [Flint's initials], where Mom would be on a heart tattoo.'

"Jim is such a generous spirit. He's paid tuitions for school for people. And when people ask him why, he will say, 'Well, they seem like a good kid and that's the only way they'll get to do it.' Through the years, he has done so many generous things. We used to do a lot of Cubs games. That's how we spent a lot of our summer afternoons. If we couldn't go, Jim would sometimes find some kids who would never have the opportunity to go. His seats are top-of-the-line, right over the first-base dugout. He'd find three kids and go up to them and ask them if they would behave if they went to a Cubs game. If they said yes, he would give them tickets to the game that day."

Pearl Dies

On December 19, 1987, Jim's beloved mother, Pearl, died. She lived at 1835 West Erie Street, in the unit directly beneath Flint and Neniskis.

"I didn't know my mother was sick," Flint said. "I remember going over, and the Christmas tree wasn't up, and Mom wasn't feeling good that week. I took her to see Dr. [Robert] Murphy right away. He wanted her to go to the hospital. She was supposed to go in the hospital two days later. Dan and I went to my mother's. We went in, and she walked out to the kitchen table and started saying, 'You know, Jim, I wouldn't want a son any different in my life. You've been wonderful to me, and I'm so proud of you.'

"Then the phone rang. It was her sister, and she asked my mom what she was doing, and she said, 'Oh, I'm just sitting here telling Jim and Dan how good Jim has been to me all my life,' and then she took a deep breath and fell right into my arms. Dan called 911. The paramedics worked on her for 45 minutes, but there was just no bringing her back. Dan and I went to the funeral home and made all the arrangements.

"Dan had been an undertaker and studied it and everything, so he knew just what to do and what needed to be done. Eugene Sawyer was mayor at the time, and he ran a bus from City Hall to the funeral home because my sister worked there and because I knew so many people at City Hall. That night, Dan asked if I wanted to ride in the hearse to take my mother down to Mason City. I said, 'Danny, I love my mother but I can't ride in a hearse.' I just couldn't. She's buried in Mason City right next to my dad."

Annex 3

Flint tried his hand at another version of the Annex brand.

"I was closing the Redoubt at 440 North Halsted," said Flint. "And Teddy's [a closed gay bar] had been at 3160 [North Clark Street], and it was for sale. The landlord asked me if I wanted to take it over. This was in September 1985. I thought at first I'd do a sports bar. I did do a sports bar there for a long time."

Neniskis clarified: "Then in 1986, when the Annex 2 closed, we moved all the coolers and tables and even liquor north to the former Teddy's at 3160 North Clark, and that became Annex 3. My name went on the license. When we moved up here, there was a bar called Thumbs Up on the corner, and then Club La' Ray [3150 North Halsted Street, "Music, Videos, Dancing & More"], and earlier in that [La' Ray] location was Trianon, where DSW [shoe store] is now. Irene's Diamonds [3169 North Halsted Street] was where the Lucky Horseshoe is.

"When we first came into the former Teddy's space, it was like a Twilight Zone episode. Everything was thick with dust, but there were glasses on the tables, cigarettes in the ashtrays, straws in the glasses—it was literally as though someone had just come in one day and told everyone to go. We changed it all. It was made sort of chic, at least by the décor-of-the-day standards. Everything was pink and blue, chrome, neon, angled. Our slogan became, 'A neighborhood bar on a busy street.'"

Paul Yinger also recalled Annex 3. "Oh, sure, I remember it pretty well. It was convenient, since my lover and I moved up to Barry and Broadway. I remember it being much more modern than most of Jim's other places. There was glass and mirrors, and even the downstairs dance floor was nice and bright. It was a fun place."

"At the Annex 3, we eventually found our niche with the dart league and as a sports bar," said Neniskis.

Palmer laughed. "We were dart champs probably five years running, and Jim was on the team, but during a big game or tournament he would get so nervous that he used to drive around the block to calm himself down," he said. "This was before cell phones, so one time when we were in the playoffs against Charlie's [3726 North Broadway], every time he came around the block, someone would have to run out to the car and tell him what was going on, because he'd get too nervous standing there."

"I started phasing out the sporting thing, it sort of lost interest among those people," said Flint, hinting perhaps at his greater disillusionment with the gay sports leagues in general. "At one time I turned it into a piano bar for Tony Zito, but Tony was dying of AIDS at the time and was very harsh to people sometimes. I'm sure it was the medicine more than anything."

Zito was well-known in Chicago's musical and cabaret circles. He had been a draw at Flint's former place, the pre-Baton venue Smitty's Show Lounge. The December 20, 1992, Chicago Tribune obituary for the 48-year-old composer and cabaret performer states that Zito was a member of the original Chicago cast of Hair in 1969. In 1975 he won a Jeff Award for best original music for his score for a production of the play Under Milk Wood. The article said Zito taught vocal ensemble and piano theory at Columbia College and worked as a performer at Yvette restaurant, 1206 North State Parkway.

Annex 3 did what it could to last. "We tried different things after that. Did a lot of amateur drag. We were experimenting and trying to find something that worked," said Neniskis.

Bill Kelley recalled that Annex 3 had one evening a week for the organization Asians & Friends–Chicago, "an organization that my partner Chen [Ooi] and I have been members of since the beginning. I believe the nights we met there were Fridays." Begun in 1984, Asians & Friends–Chicago "assists in developing friendships through social, cultural and educational activities."

Despite the varied attempts and the changes, nothing seemed to be working for Annex 3. "Eventually, after Tony Zito, I changed it back into a sports bar," Flint said. "Then the final thing was when I let Danny start taking it over, and then he got to where he couldn't handle it and it started going down. Then I had one of the bartenders rip me off for about $6,000 by not counting booze. I just wanted to wipe the slate clean and make it something else altogether."

Another Redoubt

In 1993, a few years after the opening of Annex 3 at 3160 North Clark Street, Flint decided to open yet another Chicago incarnation of the Redoubt, his former leather-Levi's-uniform bar. He chose to open the tavern at 1315 West North Avenue.

"It was probably only open 18 months or so. That's about how long Jim will give a bar to turn a profit," said Neniskis. "It was just so out there at the time, between Elston [Avenue] and the river and right by the Kennedy [Expressway]. It was the current site of the bar Exit and across from where a Home Depot is now. At the time, that spot where the Home Depot is was a toxic dumpsite.

"That area had so many prostitutes. I became good friends with a lot of them and their pimps. I used to let them come into the bar, but they could only use the two stools closest to the door. They couldn't use the bathroom, and no matter what they ordered it would be $7.

"There was one of those huge 24-hour adult bookstore-arcades across the street, so we'd get some traffic from there. Basically, though, it was a typical leather bar stuck out in the middle of nowhere. The bartenders were Frank Kellas, Tom Recca, Jerry Gitney and myself."

Joey McDonald recalled: "Yeah, I went to that location of the Redoubt a couple of times. It was a pretty rough-and-tumble neighborhood. It was unsafe and I would never go unless someone drove. I wouldn't even take a taxi over there."

"The biggest night we ever had at the 1315 Redoubt was when we had a John Wayne Gacy execution party," said Neniskis. "We had it the night of his actual execution. We had a painting John Wayne Gacy had done on display. I got a life-size skeleton and dressed it as a clown and put it on a gurney with an IV stuck in its arm. [Bartender] Frank Kellas provided the IV bottle."

The skeleton was the centerpiece of a buffet of strawberries and fried chicken, which was what Gacy had requested as his final meal. "That was our moment of glory at the 1315 Redoubt. Channel 7 news even came out for that," added Neniskis.

Gacy was executed May 10, 1994.

3160: The New Bar

When the Annex 3 model failed, Flint kept the bar but picked a new name, 3160.

"Jim wanted to change the general format," said Neniskis, "so these past five years we've been 3160. That's one of the ways we've always been different. I will tend to say 'measure twice and cut once,' and Jim will cut sometimes without even measuring. It's been a piano cabaret bar ever since. He really loves cabaret performance, so it's perfect for him."

"There's a history behind that," said Palmer. "As I said, I always have dated older men. So I opened Jim's eyes to clubs all around that were aimed at the older and mature men/younger men crowd. Like the piano bar This Is It in Milwaukee, or places in Manhattan like the Townhouse and the Regalese. This 'older men and the younger men who like them' world was all new for Jim. When we were looking to change the Annex 3 and find a new niche, Ginger, Jim and I were sitting around thinking about it, and that was the seed of it, going after the mature crowd. 3160 isn't really that at all, but that was sort of the initial inspiration.

"It's called 3160 because we had a concept for a piano and cabaret bar but we never did come up with a name. I was downtown getting the license and on the phone with Jim, and we were brainstorming to think of a name, so finally I just said, 'It's at 3160 North Clark, why don't you just call it 3160 Piano and Cabaret Bar?' So that's what we ended up naming it."

Flint is very excited about 3160. The venue takes live entertainment in a new direction for him. He traces his fondness for vocalists and cabaret entertainment back to his youth. "It was Your Hit Parade with Dorothy Collins and Gisele MacKenzie and all of them. In the 1950s that was all we had," he said.

(As a television show, Your Hit Parade ran from 1950 to 1959, primarily on NBC but also briefly on CBS. It began in 1935 as a radio program. According to Chicago's Museum of Broadcast Communications, "The TV version featured the top seven tunes of the week and several Lucky Strike extras. These extras were older, more established popular songs that were very familiar to audiences. The top seven tunes were presented in reverse order, not unlike the various popular music count-downs currently heard on radio.")

"We didn't have a TV when I was growing up, but our neighbors did," said Flint. "It was one of those ones with a tiny, tiny screen, and it always had Your Hit Parade on Saturday nights. I just loved all those songs. I said I want to be one of those one day, but I didn't have the voice. I tried it a few times. I still sing in the bathroom."

"This is the third place I've worked for Jim! There was Annex 2, Annex 3, and now 3160. Can you believe it?" laughed Ikey. "We're like some old married couple, God forbid. Jim and I have always had a love-hate relationship. Six months of the year, we love each other, and the other six months we can't stand the sight of the other. He loves to bicker. He will come in and start yelling that we don't have this or that and tells the customers he has to come in to keep me in line. People love it. It's like we have an act going."

"I tease Ikey almost every night she works," Flint said. "I go in and say, 'I'll have a grasshopper' or 'I'll have a brandy Alexander.' She'll say, 'Fuck you.' I always tell her I'll get Hanna at the Drake to come train her how to make these drinks."

"Oh, my God, and does he love pranks," said Ikey. "I can always tell when he's got a good prank going, because he will be sitting there at the end of the bar and I'll see his belly start to shake and jiggle, and I know. Then comes that big smile. He's just a real treat. All that side stuff is just the way we show how much we care for the other.

"Sometimes, though, we have bigger fights. One time about three years ago, I was sick and it was snowing out, and I called in and said I wasn't feeling well, and Jim said, 'OK, then stay home.' So then the next day I didn't feel well and I called in, and Jim said, 'Goddamn it, I knew you were going to call in.'

"I said, 'Listen, Jim, you know me. I want my money. I'd come in with my left arm cut off.' So he complained some more and I said, 'You know what, Jim, you can take your job and shove it.' He said, 'You know what, Irene,' (he always calls me Irene when he's mad), 'I'd think twice before saying that.' And then I said, 'Well, I mean it, I quit. And merry Christmas to you!'

"So a week and a half later I called and said, 'Hey, Jim, how were your holidays?' And he said, 'Horrible, on account of you,' and I said, 'Good to hear that, because mine were horrible because of you, too.' Eventually it all got settled.

"He likes the drama and all that, but at the same time he is so loyal. When he loves you, he loves you, and I know today if I quit I could go back to him in five years and he'd find something for me. I've been working for him for so long. I worked at Annex 2 downtown for six years, then I went to Annex 3 for four, then I was at Buddies' [a non–Flint-owned gay bar at 3301 North Clark Street] for 12 years, and then now I've been back to Annex 3–3160 for another 10, so I must like something about the guy."

Nowadays, 3160 is providing a hot venue for some of Chicago's top cabaret and piano entertainers. Currently, 3160 features live music five nights a week. It offers a relaxing lounge atmosphere with the added perk of no cover charge.

Legendary vocalist and recording artist Audrey Morris was performing in the mid-1950s at a club on Rush Street called The Sands and sometimes, for the same owners, at a place they had on Division Street called The Dunes. Mr. Kelly's was across the street from The Sands at 1028 North Rush. Mr. Kelly's was not doing very well, so the owner approached Morris and asked if she wanted to come over. She did, appearing there periodically and amid tours until Mr. Kelly's closed in 1975. When asked what makes a good cabaret performer, Morris explained, "It's understanding the lyric and then making the lyric personal, so then the audience can listen and make the lyric personal to them."

Morris first went to 3160 to hear Paul Marinaro. "I started going there to see Paul. He is in a time warp," she said. "He loves all the music of the 1940s and 1950s. I agree with him. Who can compete with the music of Hart, Gershwin and Cole Porter? So, he called me up to the microphone, and I performed."

 Paul Marinaro came to Chicago from Buffalo, New York, in 2000. "I saw him a few years ago at the Gentry on State Street," Flint said. "He was so beautiful, that voice. I think Paul just needs one song made to make it, huge. I think he will make it to the big time. He has it all—the charisma, the looks and the voice."

"I first met Jim in early 2006," said Marinaro. "At the time, I had heard about 3160 opening, but wasn't aware of who Jim was. He immediately offered me a job, and I started working for him at 3160 in April that year. It's been my musical home ever since." Marinaro said Billie Holiday, Ella Fitzgerald, Frank Sinatra and Anita O'Day are among his musical idols. Of the legendary vocalist O'Day (1919–2006), Marinaro said: "Seeing her perform for the first time was, without a doubt, one of the biggest thrills of my life.

"While most live music venues or cabarets have either closed or replaced the piano with a DJ or jukebox, Jim has continued to give us a home. Being a straight-ahead, jazz-influenced singer, I realize that the audience for such music is unfortunately dwindling or scattered. Jim has never asked me or any of my musicians to change it up, nor has he ever interfered with anything we've wanted to do or try as musicians.

"He's given us complete freedom and support. When I wanted to add a bass player to our weekly gig, it was done. When I want to bring in special guests, done. Add a drummer for the night, done. I've heard enough stories and have enough of my own experiences in dealing with clubs and club owners to know how rare that is."

"It's a wonderful place to perform, because the crowd really listens," added Morris. "I know Jim because Jim is not an absent owner. He would be right there at the end of the bar and he listened. He always really listens. His singers who work there just think the world of him, and in this business, good bosses can sometimes be scarce."

"Judy Roberts and I started performing a song for Jim called 'Here's to Life.' I think it's a perfect song for him," said Marinaro. "We've since recorded it for him as well. It's 'his song' and he never fails to request it. I love singing it for him, because I can tell how much meaning that song has for him." The vocalist-pianist Roberts relocated to Phoenix in 2008.

Marinaro said that his favorite memories with Flint involve what happened after hours, "when we would sit and visit and Jim would regale us with many of the wonderfully entertaining stories of his life—whether it be with just me, my musicians, or legendary performers like Judy Roberts and Audrey Morris. On many occasions I would often sit back and listen to Jim and Audrey reminisce about the good clubs and the good old days. They always remember the same places, people, and events."

Marinaro added: "One might assume that because of who Jim is and because of all he's meant to and for the gay community, he would relegate himself to all things gay. It isn't true of him at all. Whether it be at the Baton, pulled up to the bar at the Drake Hotel, at Wrigley Field, or at a sports bar someplace, he has friends from every conceivable walk of life.

"With every group of them he remains the same, conducting himself with dignity and self-respect and an expectation of the same from those around him. More than once he's expressed to me his dislike of vulgarity or distasteful behavior. In many ways it's a surprising dichotomy. Despite everything, the boy from Peoria is an old-fashioned kind of guy, and a very classy one."

"When Jim asked me to come sing at his 70th-birthday party [in 2011]," Morris said, "I was so excited, and mainly I was worried about making a mistake. Deeper than that, I just kept thinking, 'I hope he knows how fond we all are of him.' Jim's taste tends to be along the lines of the Great American Songbook, so that night I ended up doing two ballads, 'I Can't Get Started' and 'Reaching for the Moon.'"

Flint said the first time he heard Morris was probably at the London House, a jazz club and restaurant on the southwest corner of Wacker Drive and Michigan Avenue, and he later saw her many times at Mr. Kelly's. "I went there a lot and even saw Barbra Streisand there before she was famous," Flint said. "I was even there for the closing act of Mr. Kelly's. It was Damita Jo and impressionist Arthur Blake. So, every night, I would go and sit with Damita until the show was over, because she always wanted to have people to support Blake."

(Born Arthur Blakely Clark, Blake was a noted female impersonator onstage, onscreen and in nightclubs, who was known to do more than 150 impressions, including many parodies of female stars from the golden age of Hollywood. According to the website at http://members.cox.net/foxy1/blake.htm, Blake appeared in such films as Port of New York with Yul Brynner, Harem Girl with Joan Davis, and Diplomatic Courier with Tyrone Power. Blake also appeared with Jayne Mansfield in her Las Vegas act, and his former piano accompanist later found fame as Liberace.

(When asked how he got into the business, Blake replied, "My grandfather had a fire escape that overlooked a burlesque theater." Blake said that from age 4 he sneaked into the theater. He was caught by his family, but he learned that he was allowed to continue to peek if he regaled his family with impressions of what he saw, and he would re-enact the entire burlesque revue. As an adult, Blake played in major clubs and theaters on three continents. He died in 1985 at the age of 71.)

After a show at Mr. Kelly's, Damita Jo would come over to the Baton. "I fell in love with her because of songs like 'Yellow Days,' '[Nobody Knows You When You're] Down and Out,'" Flint said. "I enjoyed her music so much, and then her child came down with sickle cell and she got off the circuit for several years. I think it was in the late 1970s when she tried to make a comeback at the Playboy Club here, and she was one of the last acts they had before they closed it. She and Shirley Bassey were my favorite entertainers."

(Damita Jo [DeBlanc] was born in 1930 and died on Christmas Day in 1998. The R&B diva was active from the early 1950s and released several albums in the 1960s. According to StarPulse.com, she remains best-known for the million-selling 1960 hit "I'll Save the Last Dance for You," her response to the Drifters' "Save the Last Dance for Me," as well as 1961's "I'll Be There," the answer song to Ben E. King's "Stand by Me." She also had a hit with the 1966 English-language version of the Jacques Brel song "If You Go Away.")

Honey West performed at 3160 with Alexandra Billings (Shanté) "and we had a wonderful show there. It really is one of the coziest places to perform. I love it. Performing there with Alex was a dream. We're best friends and have known each other for years, since probably the early 1990s.

"I remember when we were playing at 3160, it was two weeks after I got a face-lift, and my plastic surgeon was in the audience. We were talking to people during the show between numbers, and I introduced my sister. And then I introduced my plastic surgeon, and [Billings] said, 'I can't believe you just introduced your plastic surgeon, nobody does that.' I said, 'Why not? He's my doctor. My gynecologist is here, too.' She said, 'Your gynecologist?' and I said, 'Yeah, he's a specialist.' It's amazing the lines you can come up with on Vicodin and vodka."

"I first met Jim when he was opening 3160," said performer Amy Cole. "Paul Marinaro was performing at Gentry, and Jim was going to be there with the intent of listening to performers for his club. I was at 3160 on Thursday nights and some Fridays for about the first two years it was in business. I did mostly progressive pop with piano and vocal. I also did a lot of improvisational things with cards in the audience, and I would have them write things about their lives or about their friends, and I would make up little songs on the spot. It was a huge opportunity for me to perform regularly, doing what I want.

"Jim was always so generous and supportive and encouraging. He has provided this wonderful space for people to come and listen to performers. When you see it from the outside, it is a little surprising that there is going to be this intimate room where people actually listen, where you are not going to be competing with a TV or dance music.

"Jim would drop in and hear us. He was always very approachable. He cared about the individual performers and it was a nice, personal connection. Sometimes the owners are more peripheral, or they book you but there is not a feeling of being a part of a family. Jim gives you that. I am still part of his birthdays and special events and am grateful for that."

"As a singer I've had many ups and downs, both personally and professionally," added Marinaro. "Since I've known him, Jim has been a constant support. Just knowing that my musicians and myself have a musical home each Wednesday night continues to mean so much to me. I'm not fully sure Jim knows how much it means to us."

Jimmy Russell in front of the Annex 2 bar, 430 North Clark Street, 1980s.

Flint with the winners of Mr. Annex 2 in 1982.

Flint with staff and the winners of Mr. Annex 2 in 1983.

Above: A business card for Annex 3.

Right: Mr. Redoubt 1980, Paul Yinger.

Flint (left) with Mr. Redoubt 1982 winner David Morgan (center).

Harley McMillen tending bar at the Redoubt in Chicago, 1980s, with the piranha tank behind the bar.
Photo courtesy of Harley McMillen

Flint with Mr. Redoubt 1983 and runners-up.

Flint with Mr. Redoubt winners, 1984.

Christian Winkel, 1970s, Flint's inspiration to open the Redoubt leather bar.

Flint employees Irene "Ikey" Raczka and Lennie Malina, 1980s.

Flint with Roger Messer, who was Mr. Baton and a longtime Flint bartender, in the late 1970s.
Photo by Tom Coughlin, Gay Chicago Archives

A business card for River North Travel.

Flint with a group of friends, 1980s. Back row, from left: John Shanahan, Jackson Fleener, Flint, Dan Neniskis and Harley McMillen. Front: Stan Fronchaz and Woody Lorenz.

Flint and Jack Delaney, circa 1980.

Above: Annex 3 patrons, including Mike Meismer (right).

Right: Flint as Felicia, with Dan Neniskis.

Paul Marinaro, Flint
and Judy Roberts at
3160, which replaced
Annex 3 at 3160 North
Clark Street. Marinaro
and Roberts have
performed at 3160.

Flint with Dan Neniskis.

Flint with Dan Neniskis at a slave auction for charity, at the Gold Coast bar.

Flint with Scott Palmer.

Flint with Scott Palmer at a softball tournament, 1991.

481

Scott Palmer.

Flint with his mom, Pearl, and Dan Neniskis.

Flint and Dan Neniskis
with Flint's sisters Dorothy
"Skip" and Doris.

Pearl Flint, Jim's mom.

13

Community Involvement

In addition to Jim Flint's entrepreneurship as a bar owner and Continental creator, and besides his involvement in sports groups, political organizations and electoral campaigns, Flint also was a founder, member or leader of gay and AIDS community organizations starting in the 1970s. These included the Chicago Knight gay motorcycle club, Tavern Guild of Chicago, the Dignity/Chicago Catholic gay group, Chicago House and Costumes on Review (which actually began in the late 1960s).

Flint's bars served as de facto community centers, with dozens of groups using the Baton for both meetings and benefits for their own causes. In addition, Flint opened his doors to benefits for individual people coping with AIDS, cancer or other issues. In the days before multimillion-dollar institutions serving the Chicago LGBT community, the Baton and other bars really were "home" for much of the community—a place to be accepted, a place to get help and sometimes a place of last resort for those ostracized and disowned by their families of origin.

In response to a January 30, 1986, GayLife newspaper question about the future of the gay community, Flint responded: "Bars and bar staff will play a major role in the gay and lesbian community because of the great volume of people they come in contact with, and the money that generates in bars for fundraising efforts."

While the community has grown beyond the once almost impermeable boundaries of bar culture, the bars today still provide an important space for building and growing a sense of community.

Costumes on Review: Halloween

Before there was the Baton, before there was Miss Continental, there was Jim "Felicia" Flint's Costumes on Review, a Halloween contest covered not just in the gay press, but sometimes in the mainstream media. The events grew to some 2,000 attendees at their peak.

There were other famous balls and female-impersonation events in Chicago held during this era, including an annual Halloween ball by Jacques Cristion on the South Side. In the 1950s, female impersonator and costume designer Tony Midnite not only defied police by performing in drag, but also brought the famed Jewel Box Revue to town for a sold-out run. By 1975, Finnie's Club, creator of Chicago's longest-running Halloween ball, marked its 40th anniversary, an event covered in the November 1975 issue of The Chicago Gay Crusader. As late as the 1970s, the Finnie events drew thousands each year to the cavernous Coliseum, which stood at East 15th Street and South Wabash Avenue until its 1982 demolition.

In the 1970s, female impersonator Roby Landers held Roby's Ball, including in 1975 a ball at Chicago's Playboy Club. Flint emceed at some of Landers' events, and Landers was involved in the early Costumes on Review shows. In September 1972, King Enterprises presented a "Miss Gae Universe Pageant" at the Aragon Ballroom, with guest emcee Roby Landers. Those listed as organizers were Bill Holmes, Don Dunfee and Doris Furbush.

Flint started his contests in 1967. The earliest competitions Flint held were in partnership with the Fleischmanns, property owners with whom Flint had dealt over the years. They worked with Flint on the show when it was at the Aragon Ballroom, 1106 West Lawrence Avenue.

"Jim wanted to do a big drag ball at the Aragon Ballroom," said Sam's bartender Stan Walker. "It was while he was working as a bartender at Sam's, and he convinced Wally and Al [Fleischmann] to get involved and sell tickets over the bar. [They] had all the seating and tables laid out and everything [at the Aragon]. So, the day of the event we had to set up and break down this massive event, because paying for an extra night rental was so much. But it was a huge success. I don't even know how much money they raised. There's a picture of me onstage from that night in a sailor outfit and Jim in a black dress, and even Al Fleischmann was a part of the show."

Marge Summit recalled the event. "I just remember it and thinking that nobody had ever done something like that on that scale in my memory, not in a straight venue," she said.

"The Halloween drag ball started at the Aragon in the mid-to-later 1960s," Flint said. "I used to have it, and everyone came out to the ball. Great costumes. After the Aragon, I moved to the hotels on Michigan Avenue, and it was like a Hollywood premiere, because people would stand and stare and applaud. I used to have over 100 contestants just walk the runway, and they were judged on evening gown only or costume only—two divisions.

"The great thing about those was, since it was Halloween you could have a big drag party and get away with it, since it was technically dressing up for the holiday. I had the seating chart and sold tickets at Sam's. The Fleischmanns backed it. It was their show until I moved to the hotels; then I started doing the backing. We set everything up and broke everything down in one day.

"One year we did it at McCormick Place, and all the tables were just the opposite of what I requested on the phone, so about four of us just started turning all the tables. The union people came out and said, 'You can't do that,' and I said, 'Go fuck yourself, this is my event and we're doing it.' We revised that whole room in under two hours because if we had waited for them it never would have gotten done. And then eventually I went to the Park West."

Because these events were not held at bars until they moved to the Park West, there were no age restrictions, so there were times when even a teenager won, such as future Baton performer Chanel Dupree.

The Chicago Gay Crusader covered Felicia's seventh, eighth and ninth Costumes on Review from 1973 to 1975. Pictured in 1974 were Felicia, "Queen of the Ball," and Ralla Klepak, the 1973 queen. The special guest at the 1975 event was Air Force Technical Sergeant Leonard Matlovich, who was fighting for his right to serve as an openly gay man in the U.S. military. The 1975 event was at the Pick-Congress Hotel, and it raised $1,100 for Matlovich's defense fund.

Flint was among several local supporters of Matlovich during his visit to Chicago in 1975, and he hosted a benefit for him at the Baton. Other benefits during the November 14–16 weekend were at Chuck Renslow's Dewes Mansion and at Mattachine Midwest President

Guy Warner's apartment. Jack David of the Up North bar and restaurant catered the parties. A check for $3,500 from the November 14–16 weekend events was given to Matlovich, and Mattachine thanked David, Flint and Renslow, "who once again gave of their best on behalf of Chicago's gay community."

Just a few weeks before his Chicago visit, Matlovich had been on the cover of Time magazine on September 8, 1975, which was an inspiration to the still-young modern gay-rights movement. This was the first time an openly gay person was on the cover of a mainstream U.S. newsmagazine. In 1980, Matlovich actually won his battle after many years of legal maneuvers, but he decided to take a buyout from the military rather than risk their drumming him out for other causes. He died of AIDS complications on June 22, 1988, just short of his 45th birthday.

His gravestone's epitaph is a frequently quoted inspiration to those who worked for decades to lift the military's gay and lesbian ban: "When I was in the military they gave me a medal for killing two men and a discharge for loving one." The ban on gay and lesbian service members, which had been modified during President Bill Clinton's administration to an unworkable Don't Ask, Don't Tell compromise in 1993, was finally and fully removed in 2011 under President Barack Obama (although the new policy does not protect transgender service members).

GayLife covered the 10th annual Costumes on Review in its edition of November 12, 1976. The event was held October 30 at McCormick Place, with "hundreds of gay and straight people … every segment of the city's gay community seemed to be present somewhere in the throng, including members of some of the motorcycle clubs. Many female impersonators were on hand, such as the Bearded Lady; Tillie, the dirty old lady; Mother Carol; and the entire cast of the Baton. A number of Milwaukee entertainers were also present along with that city's 'Mr. Groovy Guy.' Emceeing the show was Felicia herself (Jim Flint) in a succession of gorgeous dresses, even a leather number complete with chains." Also attending were Eddie Dugan, Jack David, Chuck Renslow, "Little Jim" Gates, Bill Kelley, Robbie Crystal and Ralla Klepak.

"Entertainment for the evening was provided by the cast of the Baton and was choreographed by Orlando del Sol," GayLife reported. "The first event of the evening was the costume contest with many beautiful and interesting entries. Several costumes with peacock themes won the runner-up prizes but the first prize went to an entry entitled 'Winter, Spring, and Summer' which portrayed, with imaginative use of feathers and layers of costume, a cocoon and a butterfly. In the streetwear competition (covering everything except long gowns) the winner was Margo.

"Highlighting the evening was the queen competition with many lovely entries. The judges had a difficult time deciding the winner and did not choose the entrant who got the most audience response. The audience seemed to favor a red-gowned beauty who was chosen runner-up and who rudely stepped on his bouquet and walked out of the room followed by some of his disappointed and unruly followers. The winner, who graciously ignored the commotion created by this unprofessional conduct, was attired in a stunning white creation decorated with fur."

McCormick Place was also the location of the 1977 Costumes on Review. The Chicago Tribune reported on the upcoming event in its October 14 edition, saying the contest is "the largest ball of its kind in the country and attracts people from at least 18 states, including Hawaii." The Tribune said more than 2,000 people attend the gala event, which features a masquerade and female impersonation categories.

Cheryl Lavin wrote in the Tribune piece, "Costumed Treats You Can Trek To," that the previous year "a butterfly that metamorphosed onstage into representations of the four seasons won the masquerade competition. A sequined peacock with a 10-foot feather spread won second prize.

"Past winners in drag competition have been decked out in form-fitting dresses, jewels, wigs, and makeup. Many of the city's hairdressers and designers turn out to see the imagination that goes into the outfits. Flint will be doing all the commentary wearing four specially made gowns.

"The first, second, and third prizes for female impersonators are $1,000, $500, and $100. For masquerade they're $400, $200, and $100. Trophies are awarded for best gown and hairdo.

"Reserved table seats are $10; general admission is $9. Tickets are available at Baton, 436 N. Clark, 644-5269, or at the door. The doors open at 7 p.m. and the show begins at 8."

The 1978 event included special guests Pudgy and Sam Hill and was at the Radisson Hotel, 540 North Michigan Avenue. It benefited the Tavern Guild's Frank M. Rodde III Memorial Building Fund. The 1979 event was also at the Radisson.

From 1980 to 1985, Costumes on Review was at the Park West music venue, 322 West Armitage Avenue.

GayLife featured an interview with Flint by Albert Williams in its October 20, 1983, edition.

"Felicia is a brassy, bawdy yet motherly entertainer in the Totie Fields tradition," GayLife said. "Flint … is a quiet, laid-back man with an amused look and an elaborate Cliff Raven tattoo. To many, Flint epitomizes two 'extremes' of the gay experience—leather and drag— and he doesn't hide it, either. In fact, a highlight of the Baton's shows is Felicia's occasional performance of 'My Way,' in which he changes onstage from his gown into a basic leather-Levi's outfit."

Flint told GayLife he developed his Costumes on Review after seeing some of the drag shows when he first visited Chicago, including one at the Coliseum in 1957. "Flint joined forces with noted impersonator Roby Landers to produce a show at the Aragon, and then Flint went on his own, always seeking to make the show more professional, more elegant," GayLife said.

Flint identified himself as a gay male in the GayLife piece, but in one interesting quote, he also discussed female impersonation as "a business, a profession. … But sometimes I say when I get to be 50 I might become a woman, see how the other half lives." When he transforms, however, Felicia ends as soon as the makeup comes off, "and I become him again, who wants to go out and seek the adventures and excitement and my sexual desires," he said.

Flint's connection to Roby Landers continued in 1979, when Flint received the Roby Landers Award during the Tavern Guild of Chicago's annual Dragocious benefit in September.

By the mid- to late-1980s, Costumes on Review gave way to the growing Miss Continental franchise (Continental had started in 1980).

Flint's bars participated in other pageants and contests, including the Redoubt's entering contestants for International Mr. Leather. In 1973, the Baton sponsored a Miss Gay Chicago contest, with the winner representing the city in the Miss Gay America contest. The Baton's Shawn Luis won Miss Gay Chicago in 1974, and that year she also won Miss Gay America. (The timing overlapped a bit, and the Miss Gay America designation did not exactly coincide with the part of the year in which Miss Gay Chicago was selected, so the local and national title years did not always match.) The next 1974 Miss Gay Chicago was Baton performer Chilli Pepper, and in 1975 Dina Jacobs won (representing The Chicago Gay Crusader).

The Baton even hosted a "Ms. Butch & Ms. Fem Contest" for lesbians in 1974.

Chicago Knight M.C.

In 1971, the Chicago Knight Motorcycle Club was formed by a break-off group of Second City Motorcycle Club (which had been founded in 1963). The Knights lasted until 1990. During the 1970s there were several other Chicago gay motorcycle clubs, including Circle, Cossacks, Hellfire, Tradewinds, Rodeo Riders and Chicago Pride. The Gold Coast was the home bar of the Knight club, which was primarily social and for men into the leather scene. But the group also had altruistic goals, including fundraising for the annual Toys for Tots campaign in the 1970s and 1980s.

Flint hosted many Knight events at his bars, and he was elected president of the Knight club in 1976.

The Knight bylaws said the club was "to conduct projects of a public service or charitable nature to benefit legitimate charities and to promote the good image of the Club."

The Knights sponsored a Toys for Tots benefit for the first time in 1971 in the basement bar (The Pit) of the Gold Coast. The events ran for 15 years, and Flint was instrumental in their success. Toys for Tots is a large-scale mainstream campaign for children's charities. While many groups use the name, the best-known is the Marine Toys for Tots Foundation, started in 1947 by Marine Corps members and veterans.

On November 28, 1976, the Knight club was joined by six other motorcycle groups for a Toys for Tots benefit at the Baton—the club members once again dressed in drag for the show. As Tom Peters reported for GayLife on December 10, "On stage, wigs and gowns found themselves competing with tattoos and moustaches, but who noticed? When the cause is correct, no one stands on ceremony." Flint's Felicia "stole the spotlight" with a great performance, according to Peters.

In 1977, Jim Flint's Baton bar hosted what was billed as the Knight's fifth annual Toys for Tots benefit on November 22.

The 1981 event was also a success, with dozens of performers and Flint, "whose graciousness and witty banter pervaded the entire show" as he emceed the 2½-hour event, according to a report in the December 18, 1981, issue of GayLife.

In 1982, the benefit raised $22,000 for various toys charities, including the Salvation Army. The Knights received media coverage that year after the Salvation Army refused its $1,400 donation because of the nature of the gay club. The Army claimed the decision was in "harmony with our philosophy," and the anti-gay nature of the Salvation Army has been under scrutiny ever since. Jim Piehl was president of the Knights during this time.

Gay activist Harley McMillen spoke about the Knight club to Sukie de la Croix for his

"Chicago Whispers" column in the Windy City Times issue of September 27, 2000. "Jim Flint was involved with the Chicago Knights," McMillen said. "He was very instrumental in the Toys for Tots program. We would raise money in the holiday season and we chose different organizations and hand delivered the money to those organizations.

"One year we wanted to give money to Cabrini-Green [public housing projects on the Near North Side], for toys, and so we went to Jesse White and he had us deliver directly to the families, and that was the one and only time I walked through Cabrini-Green. But it was that kind of an organization, where we were directly involved in what we were raising and where the money went.

"We did try to give money to the Salvation Army and they refused it because of who we were. We got quite a bit of publicity over that. Even Mike Royko wrote about it in one of his [Chicago Sun-Times] columns, in terms of 'why wouldn't they take the money, and what about the people that need help?' The general public opinion was very much in our favor. Since then I have never given the Salvation Army a dollar, but that's just my personal thing."

In making the donation, the Knight club did inquire about the financial situation of the Salvation Army's youth program, and GayLife, in a September 3, 1982, editorial, wondered if that request for information was what was really behind the refusal of funds. Did the Army have something to hide?

Sukie de la Croix also reported that the Salvation Army's Lieutenant Colonel Earl A. Polsley, the day after he returned the check, backed down and told Piehl he had made a mistake and wanted to correct it. "Piehl demanded an apology to the gay community. None was given and so the Chicago Knight club issued a press release on Aug. 27. Mike Royko's column appeared in the Sun-Times Sept. 1, 1982," de la Croix wrote.

The Salvation Army and Cabrini-Green were just two of many charitable recipients the Knights donated Toys for Tots money to (or tried to, in the case of the Salvation Army). Other beneficiaries over the years were the Northwestern University Settlement House for children, the American Indian Center, the Jesse White Youth Center, the Uptown Community Center, Misericordia Home, Little City, Little Brothers of the Poor and individual families.

Flint recalled his role in starting the Chicago Knights annual Toys for Tots events. "Part of my passion came from remembering when I was a kid and how we were so thankful to get things from the South Side Mission in Peoria," Flint said. "We just got bigger and bigger. It was so beautiful to do this, and we always chose some families ourselves, and we would buy all their gifts and their food, bringing those baskets in Cabrini-Green with Jesse White right there.

"I knew Jesse as the state representative in that district and, of course, I helped him during his election. He also had the Jesse White Tumbling Team at the time. We went with Jesse, and those families were so appreciative. We even went to the Robert Taylor Homes [a public housing project on Chicago's South Side], and I was petrified because of what you hear, but we were fine. Helping those families was so great. It was really what Christmas is all about."

Jesse White, who is now Illinois' secretary of state, still remembers Flint from those 1970s and early-1980s Toys for Tots fundraisers, and he also is still upset that the Salvation Army turned back those dollars. "We'd go to the Baton and see the show, and during the show they would call the recipients [of donations] to the stage, and we'd thank the community," White remembers. "I won't ever, ever forget the caring and giving spirit of the gay community when it came to helping kids in need. I know kids who would not have [had] toys at Christmas. They made it possible for them to have something."

Long-time Chicago gay activist Gene Janowski was a fellow member of the Chicago Knight club with Flint. Janowski was the founder of the Stonewall Memorial Bookshop, housed at the Knight Out bar, 2936 North Clark Street, in the 1970s. Later, the bookstore was renamed the Source when he turned it over to Harold Meyer, the bar's proprietor. Janowski performed in several of the Toys for Tots events.

"Jim was always there for his community," Janowski said. "Politically, he was one of the earliest members to stick his neck out on our behalf, at times when it was dangerous to do so. The money he made always made its way back into the community through other businesses and charities. On a personal level, Jim was always willing to help out a community member in need and will always be a treasure to the gay community. And as Felicia, Jim still looks drop-dead gorgeous in a gown."

The Prairie Fire Review was another event held by members of the Knight, Second City and Pride clubs. Once again, motorcycle-riding, tattoo-emblazoned, hairy club members dressed in drag for a good cause. The 1977 theme was "Chicago's Gangster Era, 1920s and 1930s."

Jim Flint did not ride a motorcycle, but he was attracted to the men who did—and at the time, he owned the Redoubt leather bar in Chicago. He went on a lot of the club runs (as a passenger) to nearby cities and towns, and even longer runs to Texas, North Carolina and Georgia. Certainly, sex was part of the attraction for the men involved in these clubs, but there was a social component. Baton performer Ginger Grant attended one of the Knights outings in Gurnee, Illinois. This was a perfect combination for Flint—leather and lace, two of his many interests. He considered leather just another form of drag.

Ginger Grant related one story about Flint's performing for the Knights.

"Jim performed that night along with some of the leather guys in drag," Grant said. "Orlando choreographed for them, and they put on a show for one another on a flatbed truck beneath the stars. I remember Jim fell off and knocked out his teeth and spat them out and finished the show." With Flint, the show always must go on, and he did not go to the hospital. Grant was intimidated by the testosterone-fueled atmosphere: "It was all this leather-and-Levi's stuff. I was so scared. I went in my car and locked the windows and put towels up."

The Scroll, the Chicago Knights newsletter, listed members of the group in 1976, including Lord Knight Harley McMillen, Square/Sheriff Chuck Probert, Scribe/Tax Collector Jim Piehl, Charter Member Harry Mickelson, and members such as Jim Flint.

It was never down-and-dirty fighting between motorcycle groups, but they did compete. Flint's companion Dan Neniskis explained how the various motorcycle and BDSM (bondage/domination, sadism/masochism) groups worked.

"The main rivalry was one of what each would do for the community, so although it was this sex/leather group, in most cases it was charity-based," he said. "To that end, we'd do shows and food drives, events and various things to help raise money to donate, and then we as the Knights would meet and decide what three or four organizations we wanted to give the money to. And it would usually be about eight or ten thousand dollars, which was a lot in those days."

The Chicago Knight club disbanded in 1990. Many of the motorcycle clubs—made up of men more willing to be on the "cutting edge" of sexual experimentation, according to Harley McMillen—were ravaged once AIDS started to be diagnosed in the 1980s.

Flint's involvement in other groups always included a continuation of his charity work. For example, the Windy City Athletic Association, which Flint led intermittently for many years, promoted the co-benefits for Toys for Tots and Chicago House in 1987 at the Baton. The Knight club had stopped doing Toys for Tots, so Flint picked it up as part of WCAA.

Tavern Guild

The Tavern Guild of Chicago was a very important part of the city's late-1970s to late-1980s gay community. While it served as a social and networking organization mainly for employees of gay bars along with some owners, it also raised critical money for community charities.

Its most significant accomplishment came in 1977 when the Tavern Guild established the Frank M. Rodde III Memorial Building Fund, with the goal of opening a gay community center. Frank Rodde was a popular bartender at the gay bar Carol's in Exile, at the intersection of Addison Street and Broadway, who had been brutally stabbed to death in his apartment on April 2, 1977.

After two years and numerous fundraisers, the Guild turned over operations of the Rodde Fund (which had amassed around $80,000 at that point, Flint said) to Gay Horizons, which meant that future donations would be tax-deductible because of that organization's recognized Internal Revenue Service status.

The turnover also broadened the fundraising base beyond the Guild, but it kept some ties to the Guild through shared membership. The Tavern Guild and many bars continued to raise money for the Rodde Fund for a number of years.

Eventually, the Rodde Center did open, in May 1985, with Gay Horizons as a tenant, in a building complex at 3223–29 North Sheffield Avenue. Its purchase price was $422,500. But that building was sold (in late 1989 for $540,000) under questionable financial circumstances (some estimates put the value of the property at that time at more than $700,000).

The proceeds (estimated at $169,000, giving the Rodde Center $287,332 in assets by 1990) were exhausted during failed attempts to operate or purchase a new center. It took until 2007 for another community center to open—this one created by Center on Halsted, which is in fact the newest name for the Gay Horizons corporation, but with a leadership transformation.

The Rodde Fund itself existed as an Illinois corporation from 1979 to 1995, when it was involuntarily dissolved by the secretary of state, apparently for failure to file annual reports. Beginning in 1990, its registered agent was the late Al Wardell, a longtime co-chairperson of the Illinois Gay and Lesbian Task Force and a posthumous inductee into the Chicago Gay and Lesbian Hall of Fame.

He served as the fund's executive director in 1990–91 while it ran a scaled-down version of the Rodde Center in rented space in Suite 1200 at 4753 North Broadway. Wardell died of AIDS complications in 1995. Michael Harrington was the final board president of Rodde. He stepped down in early 1994, with the agency's funds depleted and no community center on the horizon. The Broadway rented space was closed.

The Tavern Guild of Chicago conducted many enjoyable ongoing and special events. One annual event was Dragocious, held for a few years at the Baton and featuring popular bartenders doing drag. In 1979, the Gay Pride Band opened the show with "Over the Rainbow." Chipp Matthews, Jim Flint performing "His Way," Tony Lewis, Rene Van Hulle (who co-founded the Tavern Guild) and Ben Allen were among those onstage. In 1980, highlights included Cesar (who used the surname Vera, but whose real last name was Ubalde) singing "Grand Avenue," Chicago Molly and Michael K., according to GayLife's October 5 report.

In 1980, GayLife reported May 2 on the first Metamorphosis benefit event at the Aragon, sponsored by the Tavern Guild. The benefit featured entertainment in a carnival-like atmosphere, but it also included volleyball, with teams sponsored by Good Shepherd Parish Metropolitan Community Church, Dignity/Chicago, the Baton and Lincoln Park Lagooners. Chicago's first "royal court" was crowned, with Emperor, Empress and Ms. titles going to, respectively, Steve Allman (sponsored by Cheeks and Zazoo's), Joanna Caron (the Baton and the Oak Tree Restaurant) and Nancy Reiff (the Baton), according to GayLife's May 9 issue. The Gay Pride Band and the Windy City Gay Chorus were among the entertainment. Five percent of the money went to the Tavern Guild, 25 percent to the Rodde Fund, and 70 percent to other lesbian and gay organizations.

The guild raised money not just for the Rodde Fund but for many charities. For example, in 1980 it distributed more than $21,000 from the Metamorphosis event. Those receiving funding included the Rodde Fund ($5,500), Gay Horizons ($3,000), the Illinois Gay Rights Task Force ($2,000), Howard Brown Memorial Clinic ($2,000), Toddlin' Town Performing Arts–Chicago Gay Pride Band and Windy City Gay Chorus ($1,500), Dignity/Chicago ($1,000), Good Shepherd Parish Metropolitan Community Church ($1,000), the Lesbian Community Center ($1,000), Mattachine Midwest ($1,000), the Rogers Park/Edgewater Gay Alliance ($500), the Windy City Rainbow Society of the Deaf ($500), the Pride Week Planning Committee ($500), the Gay and Lesbian Coalition of Metropolitan Chicago ($500), Evangelicals Concerned ($500), Affirmation/Chicago ($500) and the Northwestern University Gay and Lesbian Alliance ($100).

The money was distributed July 14 at a cocktail party held at the Baton.

The Tavern Guild received the Group award at Gay Chicago magazine's 1978 awards event.

Howard Brown and AIDS Fundraising

Even before the community had heard about AIDS, gay men were facing other health challenges. The community and its bars came together starting in the mid-1970s to sponsor a traveling van to encourage testing for VD (venereal diseases). Jim Flint's Baton was among the bars that hosted the van on its rounds.

Flint also supported blood drives in the community just prior to the identification of AIDS. The gay and lesbian communities often helped mainstream causes, and donating blood was just seen as being a good citizen in those days. No one knew that some of that blood was carrying a potentially deadly virus. The Baton was among the businesses that sponsored plaques awarded to the groups getting the highest number of donors to the blood drives, held in 1981 and 1982.

As soon as AIDS (at first called GRID, for gay-related immune deficiency) was diagnosed in Chicago, the city's bar owners and community leaders began to step up. At the time, Harley McMillen was executive director of Howard Brown Memorial Clinic, which was ground zero for tactics and support needed in the early years of AIDS. First mentioned by the U.S.

Centers for Disease Control in June 1981, the disease that became known as AIDS struck fast in Chicago's gay male community, especially among its leather and bar sectors. Jim Flint was a frontline witness as the disease cleaved a gruesome path through the gay male population.

"When AIDS started in Chicago, he was at the forefront of doing fundraisers for us, either at the Baton or running the slave auction at the Gold Coast that I participated in," McMillen said.

On May 2, 1982, the Baton raised $1,600 for the Howard Brown facility with "An Evening of Cesar—Flying High." More than a dozen performers donated their time. Cesar Vera was producer, and Orlando del Sol did the choreography. Flint and his bars had helped Howard Brown throughout the 1970s, so this was not unusual, but it was just the start of a larger-scale effort with AIDS on the horizon.

Strike Against AIDS was a big annual event held in the 1980s. It was focused on a communitywide bowling-pledge competition at Marigold Bowl, but it included activities at area bars, such as Jim Flint's Redoubt bar. It started as a benefit for Howard Brown's AIDS Action Project but eventually helped other AIDS agencies as well.

The first Strike Against AIDS, held March 10, 1984, was started by Marigold's owner, Bob Fagenholtz. He approached Dan DiLeo of Gay Chicago magazine and Erin Criss of GayLife newspaper with the idea. The first event featured Mayor Harold Washington's gay liaison, Kit Duffy, as scorekeeper, with dozens of well-known politicians and entertainers bowling for the cause.

Individuals were bowling as representatives of their host bar or business. So, for example, Alderman Bernie Hansen bowled for Christopher Street; Dick Uyvari, for Gay Chicago; Bud Kaz, for GayLife; Michael Franz, for Feinstein Jewelers; Olga Flannigan, for Augie/CK's; Marge Summit, for His 'n Hers; RJ Chaffin, for the Tool Box; Eddie Dugan, for Paradise; Gary Boots, for Man's Country; Bill Sheehan, for the Windy City Athletic Association; Frank Bostic, for Touché; Judy Petrovski, for The Closet; Rudy Johnson, for the North End; Chicago Molly, for Carol's Speakeasy; Alderman David Orr, for Opal Station; John Cieplak, for Sidetrack; Victoria Cazel, for the Illinois Gay and Lesbian Task Force; and Jim Flint, for the Baton. Chicago Beverage Co., distributor of Miller beers, donated $1,000 for the event, and Anheuser-Busch, which brews Budweiser, donated $1,500.

This was a mix of gay, lesbian and straight persons, from nonprofits, bars and other businesses. In 1984, this was a unifying effort of a sort that had been only infrequently seen in the previous decade (mainly for the Pride Parades and the 1977 anti–Anita Bryant demonstration).

The Strike events were held for several years. In 1986, the Redoubt hosted the kickoff events, and Budweiser donated $27,000 that year.

On Memorial Day in 1985, Jim "Rusty" Russell, a close friend of Flint's, organized Chicago's participation as part of an international Mobilization Against AIDS. About 600 people attended Chicago's candlelight vigil May 27. Flint said Russell was himself very sick with AIDS complications at the time, but somehow he gathered enough energy to coordinate the event. Russell spoke at the event about his "lonely journey" of accepting his diagnosis. Flint was also among the speakers.

At the event, Flint attacked those bars that refused to help community charities. "They take your money every night and never come out," he said. By pressuring involvement from these holdouts, "we'll get rid of this and we won't have any more of this tragedy in our community."

Flint also took it upon himself to produce AIDS brochures to put out at his and other bars around town in the mid-1980s. "Jerry Williams and I would go to San Francisco and go to groups and ask if we could reproduce their pamphlets. We'd bring back a copy and make 25,000 or 30,000 more," Flint said. "We did this for over a year, putting out pamphlets. …

"These young kids today think it's over, and it really isn't over, because we don't talk as much about it. When you've seen 500 or more of your friends pass away, and you are getting older and you think these were the people you were supposed to be getting old with—it really gets to you.

"I think the one that hit me hardest was Jimmy Russell. He was in Chicago Knights and played on my softball team, and he started the first candlelight march. I remember the first time in Washington I went to see the NAMES Project Quilt. I saw five-or-so people I knew, and I couldn't take it anymore. I walked away. It got to the point where I would go to a softball game or tournament, and I didn't even ask where so-and-so was, because I didn't want to hear. You thought, but you didn't know."

In July 1985, Chicago Sings Against AIDS was held at the Park West. Jim Flint and some of his performers were among those donating their services for the event, a benefit for Howard Brown Memorial Clinic's AIDS Action Project.

Chicago House

His being part of the group that founded Chicago House, a home for people with AIDS, was one of Flint's crowning achievements.

One evening, Flint was with a few friends on the patio of Adrene Perom's Big Red's bar, discussing some of the service gaps facing people with AIDS, many of whom were ostracized by their families and had no safety net to keep them off the street in their final days. The group of friends decided housing was needed, so they called for a meeting at the Baton Show Lounge to discuss forming an agency for housing those who were affected by AIDS. Chicago House and Social Service Agency came from these early meetings.

"We were on the back patio at Big Red's when it was on Halsted Street [3729 North Halsted]," Flint said. "We were saying there should be a residence for people who are gay with AIDS. That was when the crisis was really becoming known, and there weren't a lot of places for these guys." Those gathered included Flint, Chuck Probert, Chuck Kaiser and a few others.

"I said, 'This is a little too big for us, our involvement should be to get other people involved, so why don't we move the next meeting to the Baton?' I called Arlene Halko, who worked at Cook County Hospital, and I called John Chester, Jack Delaney, Pat Griffin and a few of those people, to see if we couldn't get a lot more people who had a lot more power than we did and see if we could do it."

Meanwhile, Thom Dombkowski's connection to AIDS was very personal. He had been exposed to HIV, the virus that causes it, by at least two lovers—Phil Spence and Patrick Rossi. Rossi died, after being in terrible pain, on June 9, 1985, just a few months before Dombkowski began his involvement with Chicago House. (Dombkowski lived 20 more years and died of AIDS complications at age 55, on April 20, 2006.) In the obituary for Rossi, Dombkowski said the community needs to have a discussion on how to help people with AIDS deal with the myriad issues facing them, from insurance to health care and housing.

"As a result of that obituary, which was in Gay Chicago, there was a community forum that was called," Dombkowski told Jack Rinella in a 1996 interview. "Harley [McMillen] and Jim Flint and I and Big Red met at Big Red's patio and put the agenda for it together. And [Steve] Wakefield was involved in it as well.

"And it was done from the stage at the Baton, over three meetings, over the course of a month. Out of that, there was one group—we found a group of seven people who were basically social workers and religious types who didn't have an ounce of business sense between them, who were already working towards something. There were several of us from the leather community who were interested in this sort of thing. So we started to hook together and took it from there. Chicago House was incorporated September 9 of 1985. By the day after Thanksgiving, we had raised $75,000 and we were on our way."

Three of Flint's close friends through his previous activism were part of those early Chicago House meetings: Jack Delaney, John Chester and Arlene Halko. Chester and Halko were actually Flint's "godfather and godmother" through his involvement in Dignity, Chicago's gay Catholic group. Delaney eventually became board chairman of Chicago House.

"When [AIDS] began to appear in Chicago, it was so frightening that often lovers, families and friends shunned the afflicted person," said Halko, owner of Piggen's Pub (674 West Diversey Parkway) and a longtime lesbian activist. Halko died in 2007, but her memories were recorded for a Chicago House brochure.

"In many cases those in whom the virus took up residence were destitute," she continued. "We [the members of the gay community] felt that we had to do something to help these, 'our people.' A call went out to meet at the Baton. The place was packed.

"That night was an incredible experience. We set up groups to take up specific tasks. … About 10 of us agreed to undertake the permanent housing problem. That was the night Chicago House was born." Other people at the meeting focused on related AIDS issues, such as food, medical assistance, counseling, legal help and more.

"Chicago House was started at a community meeting at the Baton," Chester said. "Jim was very important to the founding of Chicago House. He let us have the meetings there free, and there were no scheduling issues. We set up meetings all the time, and advertised in gossip columns and with fliers, and could count on the space. Jim was at some of the meetings. He would bring it down to 'who is going to do this, how will it be paid for,' the practical things. People would dream big, the very best, but we couldn't afford it."

While Flint did not stick with Chicago House as an organizer, what he did was to provide the needed early boost—free meeting space, and then a huge gala kickoff fundraiser held December 1, 1985, at Limelight nightclub, 632 North Dearborn Street. This event was the last of a weeklong series of fundraising events at area businesses, including tag days at bars, and a total of $27,000 was raised through all the efforts. Chicago House Fundraising Chair Thom Dombkowski, who later became executive director of the agency, said the money raised was enough to open a facility in 1986.

The Limelight fundraiser, "It's Up to Us," was conceived and chaired by Flint, according to the December 5, 1985, GayLife report on the event. "Flint … along with Bob Strada, Judy

Walker and the boards of Prairie State Democratic Club and Windy City Athletic Association brought several hundred people out in the first snow storm of the year to donate their $25 to the cause. … Flint and Strada … introduced an unending flow of entertainment." Performers from the Baton donated their time, as did singers Caron and Nan Mason, Cats cast member Calvin Remsberg and disco stars Pamala Stanley and Paul Parker.

Given Flint's political connections (that week he also filed papers to run for a seat on the Cook County Board of Commissioners), several elected and appointed officials also attended, including Aldermen Bernie Hansen, Martin Oberman and Jerry Orbach; state Representative Ellis Levin; state Senator William Marovitz; county commissioner candidates Charles Bernardini and Sid Ordower; and Tom Coffey from Mayor Harold Washington's office.

The cancer-related death of female impersonator Andrea Nicole was announced at the event. Flint and Dombkowski each donated $500 to a Nicole fund at Chicago House.

Dignity/Chicago

A crush on a man brought Jim Flint to the Roman Catholic Church.

"My father and mother were Methodists, my grandmother was Pentecostal, Assemblies of God," Flint said. "But I was fascinated with the Catholic Church probably when I was 7 or 8 years old. I always dreamed of being a Catholic brother someday, going to do a mission."

In the 1970s, Flint met Jack Delaney, a member of Dignity/Chicago, a gay Catholic group. "I fell in love with Jack, that's why I got involved with Dignity," Flint said. "We dated for a short time. A lot of my greater friends came out of that. Arlene Halko, Pat Griffin, John Chester, who was my mentor in a lot of things I did."

Flint was a board member for Dignity, and he was baptized in the 1980s by the Reverend Michael Jacobson, at St. Sebastian Church [Dignity's meeting space at 824 West Wellington]. The church was eventually demolished after a devastating fire in 1989. Arlene Halko and John Chester became his godparents through the conversion process.

"I was with John Chester. We went out drinking to the Baton," Delaney remembers. "John was very interested in politics, so Jim let him in free. Jim came over, he was giving us drinks. John said, 'My politics got us in free and your blue eyes got us free drinks.' That was 1978 or '79. We became friends, we dated a few times. He started going to Dignity because I was very active with Dignity at the time, as was John. Jim converted to Catholicism."

Chester explained the godparent situation. "It was very, very strange, the two of us [Chester and Halko] walking behind Jim on his way to be baptized," Chester said. "One of the nice things is, when you are baptized, it wipes away all the things you've done before. His eyes kind of glazed over, it looked like he was remembering, and he goes, 'Ohhhh. That's quite a slate to wipe clean.'"

Flint was very committed to the Catholic Church. "When I went to Mass, I wanted to be in the first or second row, I wanted to hear every word," he said. Flint first joined the local Dignity board in July 1980, the same year Delaney served as president of the chapter. Flint hosted a fundraiser for Delaney at Annex 2 in August 1981, the year Delaney was running for the national Dignity board.

Flint's influence was also felt in the overlap of Dignity with politics—some politicians attended Dignity events and forums. Representatives Elroy C. Sandquist Jr. and Woods Bowman attended the fundraiser for Delaney at the Annex 2.

"The Catholic Church can do ritual pretty well," Chester said. "Jack was Jim's inspiration to join the church, but Jim was active in Dignity for a few years, and I had the impression he really liked going there and having this hour of preaching and ritual, which was very different from the world he lived in or moved in—but it was still very much like drag. The priest in robes is another kind of drag, and certainly the ceremony, staging and music is comparable."

Jim Bussen, an important leader in both the local and national Dignity organizations, said that when Flint decides to get involved in something, "he kind of twirls in. He did a lot to help organize committees, and social events, stuff like that. He was not a lead—he didn't want to be overshadowing others' work, but he worked with these people." Bussen said Flint did take a lead role on the committee working on the big communitywide Orange Ball fundraisers during the 1970s.

Flint had left Dignity by 1986, when Cardinal Joseph Bernardin stepped his foot into the gay-rights ordinance battle in the city, lobbying against the measure and causing the bill to lose in the City Council that year. (See Chapter 5.) Bernardin also eventually forced Dignity out of the church literally and figuratively—members had to join a new group, Archdiocesan Gay and Lesbian Outreach (AGLO), if they wanted to be part of a group sanctioned by the Catholic Church, or to meet in a Catholic facility.

The division continues today, with separate gay Catholic groups—one supported by the church, the other on its own. Flint was gone from the group by the time Bernardin divided it. Delaney was on the national board when the Dignity-AGLO split happened.

Birthday Celebrations

Jim Flint's annual birthday celebrations, held on or around July 27, are legendary. They have ranged from bar crawls among his establishments to large-scale galas at the Park West. Almost every year they have served as a benefit for some cause or politician.

Flint's 1975 birthday celebration was held at the Baton and was covered in The Chicago Gay Crusader. The paper said more than 20 entertainers came to mark the occasion, including Jodie Lee, Shawn Luis, Roski Fernandez and Vera of the Snake Pit. Flint was in his Felicia drag for the occasion.

Comic legend Pudgy and pianist Sam Hill appeared at Flint's 1978 birthday party at the Baton.

His 1982 birthday featured parties at his bars Annex 2, Baton and Redoubt, as a benefit for the Gay World Series softball tournament that was coming to town the following year. The same bars marked the birthday in 1983, and that year's beneficiaries were the Windy City Athletic Association and the Greater Chicago Gay and Lesbian Democrats. Flint was a part of both groups.

Flint's 1984 birthday observance moved to a larger location, the Park West, 322 West Armitage Avenue. The event was a benefit for the Andrea Nicole cancer fund.

The 1985 event, also at the Park West, was a benefit for Chicago House and Flint's Redoubt softball team. The Joseph Holmes Dance Theatre performed.

Cabaret professional Becky Menzie said her favorite memories of Flint were of when he used to come to the old Gentry on Rush, at 712 North Rush Street, or later when Gentry was at 440 North State Street. "A lot of times it would be late on Monday, and some Mondays we were the only ones there," she said. "He would start telling me stories about his life here in Chicago and would literally have me transfixed.

"I sang for his 60th birthday party at the Park West, so he had a couple of the girls go on and do their numbers, and then came me, so I went out and started singing 'The Girls at the Baton,' and I couldn't believe it when people started coming forward to tip.

"I wasn't dancing or anything, but they came forward to tip me, and let me tell you I made a lot of money. I was just shoving it down my cleavage, and then I got backstage and I pulled it out and was about to hand it to Jim to give to him for his birthday, and he said, 'No, all the girls get to keep their tips.' I thought, 'Man, I am in the wrong profession. Nobody tips like that at Gentry.'"

Dozens of groups benefited from these annual birthday celebrations, which also were a chance for Flint's friends to come from all over the country to enjoy Chicago in the summer. Since Flint traveled so much for his softball and Continental pageants, his network of connections around the country grew each year.

At Flint's 70th-birthday celebration in 2011, he asked people to donate to the campaigns of Chicago's two openly gay aldermen, Tom Tunney and James Cappleman. Several hundred people were in the audience, there to enjoy a birthday filled with cabaret professionals, female impersonators and other entertainers.

Getting Roasted

In an article in the January 21, 1977, edition of GayLife, Managing Editor Ron Anderson wrote of a roast of Jim Flint held at Little Jim's bar, 3501 North Halsted Street. It gives a nice taste of the decade and of the role Flint played in it:

"Little Jim Gates, who is always coming up with new, fun events at his bar, has started a series of celebrity 'roasts' honoring various Chicago personalities. The first one he chose was Jim Flint, also known as 'Felicia,' proprietor of the Baton Show Lounge. Many of Jim's closest friends gathered at Little Jim's to pay tribute to him as one of the most important gay businessmen in Chicago.

"Among those who helped to 'roast' Jim Flint were Lena from Pepper's, Orlando del Sol (choreographer at the Baton), Marge Summit from His 'n Hers, Ricky from Little Jim's, Frank Thomas from Second City, Paula Carol [actually Karol], Craig Kelso from The Pride, Joann from the Baton, Gloria James, and the voice of Bristol Lee.

"Many of the most cutting remarks lose their effectiveness when transferred to the written page where you miss the inflections of the 'roasters'' voices and the looks on Jim's face, but some are worth repeating. Referring to Jim's sponsorship of a girls baseball team, Marge said that he is 'the only man who makes money being a woman and then sponsors a bunch of girls dressed up as boys.'

"In the first of the many references to Jim's roller-skating, Marge also mentioned that you can always tell when Jim is at the Gold Coast because 'his roller skates are double parked outside.' Paula [Karol] reminisced about the good old days at Togetherness and the Baton and about Jim's casting auditions. Craig Kelso told the crowd that Jim doesn't have wrinkles around his eyes anymore because he wears his wigs so tight that they erase the laugh lines. He also mentioned that there was a little yeast in the silicone that Jim [received], so 'under the hot lights he looks like a brioche in heat.'

"Craig also delighted the audience by saying that Jim has 'documentary beauty.' 'With his roller skates and flaming baton, he looks like the Hindenburg coming in for a landing.' Gloria James warned the 'roasters' that they better be careful because Roby Landers was once white until Felicia roasted her. Several references were also made to Jim's position as Lord Knight of the Chicago Knight club.

"After responding to his 'roasters' remarks with some zingers of his own, Jim made a pitch for unity in the gay community and for participation in the mayoral election which will come up in April. He said that this is a chance for the city's gay people to make their presence known. He also put in a plug for support of the city's gay-owned and gay-operated businesses.

"The evening reached the perfect balance between sarcastic humor and genuine affection. With a person as well known as Jim Flint it is relatively easy to make biting humorous remarks. In Jim's case it is also just as easy to pay genuine tribute to all the things he has done for Chicago's gay community."

Other Support

Since his move to Chicago in the 1960s, Flint has also supported and been part of many other projects.

Flint said he was in Chicago's first gay pride march on June 27, 1970, organized as a commemoration of the 1969 Stonewall Riots the previous year in New York City. The march was from Washington Square Park (also known as Bughouse Square) to the Civic Center Plaza (now named Daley Center Plaza).

The first gay pride parade in Chicago was on the sidewalk. An actual street parade was not until the following year. In 1970 the dozens of spirited and chanting marchers made a point to walk past the Lawson YMCA and a theater on Chicago Avenue showing the camp trans film Myra Breckenridge starring Mae West and Raquel Welch and based on the Gore Vidal novel.

Once the parade moved into the streets there were the usual marchers and banners and convertibles, but Chuck Renslow decided to do something a little different. He put a friend's backyard gazebo on the back of a flatbed truck and had several of his female impersonators from his bar Sparrow's pose alongside it, and Chicago had its first gay pride parade float.

When that march later became an annual parade in Lakeview, Flint and his Baton showgirls were among the first contingents with a full float, in the mid-to-late 1970s, and they have been a popular entry every year since. Flint also gave funds to the Gay Pride Week Planning Committee during its formative years, and he was among those thanked in ads from the committee.

Flint said that at first, some people in the community tried to ostracize those they did not think represented it well to the mainstream. "They didn't want the drags or leather in the first few parades—then who is going to be involved?" Flint said. "And where do you put me, I'm involved in both? We finally got over that issue."

The Lincoln Park Lagooners, Chicago's oldest gay recreational sports association, held some large-scale community benefits in the 1970s. Winter Carnival in 1976 and its Cruisin' the Nile in 1977 are still remembered for bringing the community together. The events benefited local charities, especially Howard Brown Memorial Clinic. Flint's bars were regular supporters of these efforts—his Baton is listed in the top category of partners for the Carnival and Nile benefits.

Flint helped out gay media during their fledgling days, hosting benefits and parties for GayLife and The Chicago Gay Crusader, in addition to taking out advertisements. The December 15, 1975, turnabout at the Baton, where entertainers became servers and waiters, and the waiters and servers became entertainers, was a benefit for the Crusader. When the winningly cantankerous employee Richie Saunders came out to sing "God Bless America," he received tips from almost everyone in the crowd. In 1982, Flint's Annex 2 bar hosted the holiday party for GayLife, with political leaders and entertainers among the guests.

In 1974, The Chicago Gay Crusader had a list of "top 10" thank-yous to community members who supported its efforts to publish a gay and lesbian newspaper. Flint was fourth behind Jack David (of the Up North), Woody Moser (of the 21 Club) and Chuck Renslow. Activist Gary Chichester was fifth. The paper's comments about Flint read:

"Felicia has always tried to bring entertainment to Chicagoans. At the same time, he has often raised money for gay causes.

"When the Gay Crusader decided to open Beckman House [a community center located at 3519½ North Halsted Street] in Chicago, Felicia believed in the need also. He threw a benefit for us, which raised enough money for the security deposit and rent, thus becoming one of the businesses that got solidly behind a gay community center for Chicago.

"Felicia has always been generous to the Gay Crusader and its projects through publicity, advice, and cooperation. We thank you, Felicia."

Flint opened his Baton Show Lounge to other entertainment in the 1970s and 1980s—theatrical productions from various local theater companies. The Baton did not have its own shows Mondays and Tuesdays, so theater productions were usually on those nights, mainly by the Speak Its Name company. In 1980, Speak Its Name presented these shows: Lanford Wilson's The Madness of Lady Bright, John Bowen's Trevor, and Robert Patrick's Fred and Harold. For five weeks in March and April 1981, a staging of the Richard Hall play Love Match was presented at the Baton. Also that year at the Baton, the group performed Noël Coward's Mad About the Boy, and in 1982 there was a Speak Its Name production of Cabaret, the musical by John Kander and Fred Ebb that was based on a John Van Druten play and derived from Christopher Isherwood's The Berlin Stories.

The second anniversary of the Chicago Gay/Lesbian Community Band was celebrated with a concert at the Baton on February 16, 1981. In addition to the band, other performances were given by the Windy City Gay Chorus and the Artemis Singers.

Flint was also among the people at the first meeting of Chicago's Mattachine Midwest, in 1965. He was not an active organizer of the group, but he was a member and distributed the Mattachine Midwest Newsletter at his businesses. Before he was an owner, he also encouraged the straight owners of the bars where he worked to at least carry the publication, even if it was kept hidden behind the bar and available only to those who asked for a copy.

Mattachine Midwest, which borrowed its name from the national Mattachine Society, an early gay-rights group, hosted Flint as special guest speaker in January 1986. According to the March 5 issue of GayLife, Flint spoke about his life as a bartender and owner.

ONE of Chicago was the local chapter of the national ONE Inc., which was organized in 1952 in Los Angeles. In 1958, the national group won an important U.S. Supreme Court case against the Los Angeles postmaster that established the right of gay publications to use the mails. The Chicago chapter was largely subsidized by Paul R. Goldman, a non-gay lawyer with a large gay clientele, and it conducted monthly social meetings that often included guest speakers. Flint also supported the chapter's efforts, including its 1974 banquet. Others at that event included out-of-town gay movement leaders Eldon Murray of Milwaukee, Frank Kameny of Washington, D.C., Tom Smith of the National Gay Task Force, and Morris Kight of Los Angeles, as well as Chicago-based author Valerie Taylor and many other Chicago leaders.

The ONE chapter continued to operate until at least the 1980s, and in 1979, Flint attended its September 7 meeting to discuss the recent appearance by Flint and some of his Baton cast members (Jodie Lee, Leslie Rejeanné, Lavinda and Chilli Pepper) on the Irv Kupcinet television show.

From the late 1970s for at least a dozen years, Chicago also had a Mr. Windy City Contest. During the evening, Gay Chicago magazine presented its annual Gay Chicago Awards. Flint was often an emcee for these awards. Mr. Baton, Roger Messer, won the 1978 Mr. Windy City contest, held at the Radisson Hotel. The contest was originally sponsored by Eddie Dugan of Dugan's Bistro and Mother Carol. Later events were co-sponsored by Dugan and Flint along with Gay Chicago's Ralph Paul Gernhardt and Dan DiLeo

Flint won a Gay Chicago award in 1982 as Owner of the Year. In 1981 he had won as Organizer of the Year. He was inducted into the awards' Hall of Fame in 1986.

Speaking of halls of fame, Flint was also among the first year's inductees into the city of Chicago's Gay and Lesbian Hall of Fame, the only such municipally sponsored event in the country. The inaugural induction took place in 1991 under Mayor Richard M. Daley's administration.

The Metropolitan Business Association was Chicago's first non-bar gay business organization. It started in 1978, and its first board officers and directors were Chairman Chuck Renslow, Vice-Chairman James Gates, Secretary George Harvey, Treasurer Walter Almquist, and board members Jim Flint, Robert Maddox, Adrene Perom and Bert Spitz.

The MBA endorsed Chicago participation in the first gay and lesbian March on Washington, in 1979. That March on Washington effort was discussed at a public meeting July 24, 1979, at the Baton. Flint said he has supported Chicago's efforts in each of the LGBT marches on Washington since, which occurred in 1987, 1993, 2000 and 2009.

On June 5, 1979, Flint was co-leader of a protest against the Chicago Police Department's harassment of gay bars (see Chapter 3). As part of the efforts, which were coordinated by the ad hoc group Gays and Lesbians for Action, an advertisement ran in GayLife on June 22, 1979, thanking those who contributed to the protest event. More than three dozen businesses and groups were listed, including the Baton and the Redoubt. Gays and Lesbians for Action (also known as Gays and Lesbians in Action) continued for at least a couple of years more— Flint and his colleagues Doris Shane and Delilah Kenney are listed in a thank-you ad by the Illinois Gay Rights Task Force for their efforts helping support state gay-rights-bill lobbying work. The ad appeared in the June 26, 1981, issue of GayLife. (The ad also announced the change of the task force's name to Illinois Gay and Lesbian Task Force.)

Chicago's Good Shepherd Parish Metropolitan Community Church, part of the MCC gay church network founded by the Reverend Troy Perry in Los Angeles, held several 1970s fashion show benefits at the Baton. The fashions ranged from leather to gowns, and outfits came from a range of "name" companies including Bigsby & Kruthers, The Gap and Male Hide Leathers.

Adrene "Big Red" Perom was the original pie-toss queen of Chicago. She started hosting pie-toss benefits at her Big Red's bar in the 1970s, and Jim Flint was a regular victim for a good cause, including the Rodde Fund.

The executive committee of the Gay and Lesbian Coalition of Metropolitan Chicago published a letter in the November 9, 1979, issue of GayLife thanking Flint "for opening up the Baton to us to hold our meetings the last several months. This has been a generous and supportive gesture, and we want Jim and the community to know that we appreciate it and do not take it for granted."

In 1977, Flint was among those supporting and attending a huge anti–Anita Bryant protest at Medinah Temple, where the orange-juice spokeswoman was featured as the star attraction at a Shriners event. The Gay and Lesbian Coalition of Metropolitan Chicago and GayLife newspaper helped coordinate the protest, which with several thousand demonstrators was the biggest the Chicago gay community had seen up to that point.

Bryant, the 1958 Miss Oklahoma beauty-pageant winner, went on a crusade against gay rights in the 1970s. She worked to successfully repeal the Dade County, Florida, gay-rights law in 1977, resulting in nationwide protests against her. She was also a spokesperson for the Florida Citrus Commission, and as a result many protesters used oranges in their creative attacks on Bryant, such as "Anita Bryant Sucks Oranges" buttons and shirts. A nationwide boycott of oranges was organized by gay activists. Two large Orange Ball events were held in Chicago that raised money to fight her efforts and received cooperation from Flint. Because of the controversy she had stirred, Bryant's contract as orange-juice spokeswoman was not renewed when its term ended in 1979.

When the city's gay-rights bill was reported favorably by a City Council committee in 1979, GayLife wrote an editorial thanking various activists for their efforts. Among those thanked were "Jim Flint, Delilah Kenney and Bill Kelley, for devoting countless hours," along with John Chester, John Donovan, John McCaffrey, Charlie Mehler and more.

Aftershock was a series of events held to benefit gay groups in Chicago the weekend of October 7–9, 1983. Several bars joined forces for the events, including Flint's Annex 2 as well as his Redoubt, which was in its new 440 North Halsted Street location. Paradise Chicago, Sidetrack, Buck's, Christopher Street, Loading Dock, Manhandler, Dandy's, and Bushes all had events, and there was also a Lake Michigan cruise on the Star of Chicago, leaving from Navy Pier.

On January 13, 1986, Flint was among those honored by the Northside Concerned Citizens group. Another honor Flint received came in October 1985, when the Chicago Gay Men's Chorus made him an honorary member of the group.

Flint stepped up to raise a reward for the capture of three men who shot and critically wounded gay bar customer Ron Cayot after he left a bar on Halsted Street in 1992. Additional money was raised to help cover his medical expenses. Cayot survived for several years, but he was permanently injured. "We will not tolerate thugs coming into our neighborhood and preying on our customers," Flint, as organizer of the fund, told the Tribune on April 6, 1992. As the Tribune reported February 11, 1993: "Cayot holds a finger to his throat to cover the surgical hole through which he usually breathes. It is the only way he can force air through his surgically reconstructed larynx. 'I wish I could show them exactly what they did to my life,' he croaks. 'They destroyed me.'"

"I probably helped 40 or 50 nonprofits over the years with benefits at the Baton," Flint said. "I also have helped when individuals have needed it. When Cezanne's mother and father passed away, we did an event to help cover the burial expenses. We did this when a woman lost her home in a fire on the South Side."

The Baton showgirls, with support from Flint, also attended many benefits around the city and suburbs. Ginger Grant, Chilli Pepper, Mimi Marks, Maya Douglas and almost all the Baton regulars over the years donated additional time to hundreds of community events, large and small.

All these efforts were a critical part of community-building. When Flint started, there were very few people willing to be out in the media (especially with their real names), and few people stepped forward to raise significant money for the community. Most of the wealthy potential donors were closeted, and foundations and corporations would rarely fund gay or AIDS causes, so it was the gay bar and business sector that stepped in to fill major gaps in the community's needs.

"Coming from a large family, who had nothing, I just felt I had to help," Flint said. He couldn't always say yes, but "you do the best you can. You had a good week at the business, you helped."

Flint said now the community is a lot bigger and stronger, with several openly gay and lesbian elected officials and many more openly LGBT-owned businesses. But still, he said, "we've got to be more accepting. The Halsted thing upsets me a lot. [In 2011, the community experienced many divisions along racial lines, with some Halsted-area residents blaming a perceived increase in crime on the African-American youth hanging out in the area.] They want to make it as a racial thing, I don't think it's a racial thing.

"I guess for me, I didn't even know what racial was until I moved to Chicago. In Peoria, where I went to school and grew up, we just didn't have that sort of thing. At the Baton we certainly don't have it, because our audience here—the first show could be all-white, second all-black, and third fifty-fifty.

"We've come a long way in our community in acceptance, and we have a little more to go. Although sometimes in the 1970s I think we had stronger friendships come out of it, it was a smaller community, and we all had to stick together more. Where today it's sort of cutthroat, and some people are using their social networks to attack people."

One Life, Well Lived

Summing up a person's life, whether in a short article or a lengthy book, is not an easy task, but it is all the more difficult when that person has touched so many other lives. Flint, who left home at 15 and left for the Navy at 17, seems to have worked like a weaver, constantly crafting new networks of family, both chosen and biological, throughout his 70 years. During our interviews for this book, Flint's chosen friends, as well as those on opposite sides of rancorous community battles, provided their own views about the contributions of this intriguing figure in the Chicago community.

Longtime Flint friend and political colleague John Chester said he believes Flint "opened doors for the community that broadened it out somewhat away from the lakefront, because his business was recognized as a successful business downtown. He is a strong, forceful person. ... Also, in terms of the tourist and entertainment industry, the Baton put Chicago on the map."

Sidetrack bar owner Art Johnston, despite all his differences with Flint, especially around sports leagues, said that he was "thrilled to be part of the same community that Jim has been a part of. Jim was brave, and outspoken, and fearless at a time when most people in our community were not. I think back about a comment said a couple years ago, 'I remember back in the 1970s, if I got home at the end of the day and I had not been fired or beaten up, that was a good day.' In that era, Jim Flint was not about to be shut up by anybody. I admire him for that.

"Even though I disagree with him on issue after issue, I admire that he was never going to be told to shut up, or told that female impersonators are not part of the community, etc. By his own example I think he encouraged many people in our community—especially those not in the mainstream, more on the edges, like female impersonators—he encouraged them to know that this was their city, too. We all owe him a great deal of gratitude."

Transgender activist Helena Bushong is torn about the role the Baton has played for her community. Flint has provided jobs for many performers over the years, but he also requires that if they go through the "bottom" surgery, they have to leave the show because there is no more illusion, no more "impersonating" women—they are fully women. Many clubs now allow their performers to transition to female and still perform, but the Baton is one of the last to keep that line in the sand.

"There are transgenders who have no intention of getting surgery—they're comfortable with it [the Baton policy]," Bushong said. "But I know a lot of ladies who are not very comfortable with that. But the Baton pays good and we have trouble getting jobs, and the Baton leads to other possibilities for the girls."

Bob Kuzas, a straight man involved in mainstream Democratic politics, first became familiar with Flint in the 1980s. He contrasted Flint, who campaigned and lost as an openly gay man, to the late Cook County Treasurer Edward Rosewell, who was a closeted gay man but very successful at politics. Kuzas ran Rosewell's 46th Ward committeeman's office, and then from 1992 to 1996 Kuzas was 46th Ward committeeman.

"I would have to tell you he was pretty active in all communities," Kuzas said of Flint. "Many issues ran parallel, and in stride with the gay community, and Jim was in the forefront of all of that. He took many chances with his own life and career, trying to make sure there was equality. Not just for the gay and lesbian community. For Rosewell, it was not until the end of his life that he was openly out, but he came from a different generation of politicians. ... He was the No. 1 precinct captain in the city, and [Mayor Richard J.] Daley gave him rewards for that, and asked him to be treasurer of Cook County. So he felt an obligation to the original Daley to keep his sexuality to himself. ...

"Jim Flint brought it right up and put it in your face. He was a pioneer in the gay movement. Flint's impact was courage. In one word, he had courage. He showed guts, balls—you gotta remember, he had a lot at stake, with liquor licenses, business licenses, etc., he put his whole livelihood at stake for a cause he believed in."

Errol (Stoney) Summons calls Flint "Uncle Jim" as a term of endearment and respect. "Actually my friend Vince Sanchez introduced me to him as Uncle Jim at a gay softball tournament in Houston," Summons said. "We hit it off right from the start and over the past 10 years or so I have been honored to call him friend.

"My favorite Jim Flint story?" asked Summons, who is African American. "Well, I travel quite a bit for work and, wherever I would go, Jim would tell me to try this restaurant or go to that sports bar. He loves recommending places. Anyway, one time Vince [Sanchez] and I were in Raleigh, North Carolina, and we went to a restaurant and we told the management there that our Uncle Jim Flint had recommended it.

"So, later they called Jim and said, 'There were a couple guys in here who said you were their uncle. Now, I can see how maybe the one guy could be your nephew, but I see no way on God's green earth that other fellow could be related to you.' Jim still laughs when he tells that story.

"The best thing about Jim is his persona. He is so giving. My favorite part of knowing him is just watching him interact with other people—with promoters or the girls or even with anyone. I am an outsider to all that—but I am an outsider who has had the good fortune to have crossed paths with him in this life."

Like many of Flint's closest friends, Janet Maguire from Boston met him through sports, in her case at a Boston College vs. Notre Dame football game in the late 1990s. She visits with Flint on his frequent trips to the East Coast.

"I have never met a finer gentleman who would help anybody," Maguire said. "He has helped people financially, giving people jobs. He's probably the least, most unassuming person I've met. He has no boundaries on race, religion, etc. I know he's helped his sisters and brothers, family, and nieces and nephews. He has supported different people politically. He has a gamut of friends—like his friends in Boston, some are rich, some are paupers."

This is not to say all is rosy in the life of those who orbit around the enigmatic Jim Flint. But regardless of the arguments and internal struggles, no one can deny that Flint has added immeasurably to the lesbian, gay, bisexual and transgender communities of Chicago and nationally. He's not done yet, either, but his contributions up until now are enduring.

Flint, interviewed almost 30 years ago in the October 20, 1983, issue of GayLife newspaper, reflected on his way of dealing with the world:

"Being a businessperson, you're constantly making the decisions, that sort of thing. So you look for somebody that once in a while can tell you what to do and take the upper hand. ... And I'm a strong Leo, so it takes a very, very strong person to conquer [me]—and on top of it, I've always been a bitch! You know that. You either like me or you don't like me, it's nowhere in between."

Coverage of Felicia's (Jim Flint's) 7th annual Costumes on Review Halloween ball, in the November 1973 Chicago Gay Crusader.

Chanel Dupree won the Costumes on Review at age 16, mid-1970s, pictured with Jim Flint as Felicia (left) and Chilli Pepper (right).

Jim Flint as Felicia, Richie Saunders and Chilli Pepper at a Costumes on Review.

1974 Costumes on Review coverage in November's Chicago Gay Crusader.

FIRST PHOTO: Baton's Felicia, The Queen of the Ball, last year's queen and Chicago attorney, Ralla Klepak.   SECOND PHOTO: Third runner-up and first runner-up.   THIRD PHOTO: Best Costume award (couple in foreground), first runner-up (background) and Ms. Klepak.

Roby Landers, Jennifer Radcliffe and Jim Flint, at a 1970s Costumes on Review.

An advertisement in GayLife newspaper, September 7, 1979, for Felicia's Costumes on Review.

FELICIA'S COSTUMES ON REVIEW

Photos by MARK ZIMMERMAN

OVER 100 GOWNS

1975 Costumes on Review coverage in November's Chicago Gay Crusader. Air Force Technical Sergeant Leonard Matlovich is pictured with Flint in the top row (third photo).

A 1980 flier for Felicia's Costumes on Review.

Felicia at a Costumes on Review at the Pick-Congress Hotel, 1970s.

Costumes on Review, circa 1980. From left: Jack Delaney, Jackson Fleener, Flint, Chuck Probert and Roger Messer.

Flint dressed as a clown for a Toys for Tots benefit at the Baton.

June 1976 edition of the Chicago Knight Motorcycle Club's newsletter, The Scroll.

At a Chicago Knight Toys for Tots benefit, held at the Baton.

Members of the Chicago Knight Motorcycle Club, 1970s. Flint is in the front row, middle.

Chicago Knight Motorcycle Club's Toys for Tots benefit in December 1975, pictured in the January 1976 issue of The Chicago Gay Crusader.

The Tavern Guild of Chicago's board, pictured in this Midwest Times 1981 photo by Erin Criss. Back row, from left: Chuck Probert, Chuck "Kitty" Kiser, Chuck Rodocker, Tyrone Sinclair and Chipp Matthews. Second row: Teddy Hall, Delilah Kenney, Flint and Cesar Vera. Front: Bill Maggio.

Tavern Guild's Dragocious fundraiser, advertisement in the September 25, 1979, issue of GayLife.

Flint as Felicia (as the Statue of Liberty) at a Chicago Knight Motorcycle Club Toys for Tots benefit.

16   ONCE AGAIN,

Chicago walks away with Miss Gay America Pageant

"Miss Gay America — 1974"
Shawn Luis
of
"The Baton"

Shawn Luis was congratulated on winning the Miss Gay America pageant, in the June 1974 issue of The Chicago Gay Crusader.

The 1975 Miss Gay Chicago Pageant. From left: Flint, Diana (Miss Mattachine Midwest), Jim Gates, Lisa Somers (Miss Snake Pit), Eddie Dugan, winner Chilli Pepper and Michael Bergeron of The Chicago Gay Crusader.

These two images: Chilli Pepper (spelled "Chili" here) wins Miss Gay Chicago and is given a sendoff for the Miss Gay America pageant, in the March–April 1974 edition of The Chicago Gay Crusader.

Mitzi Monet, Roski Fernandez, Wanda Lust, Jim Flint, Dina Jacobs and Peaches at a 1970s Miss Gay Chicago Pageant.

The Baton held a benefit for The Chicago Gay Crusader newspaper in December 1975, covered in the January 1976 Crusader.

Flint was among community leaders thanked by The Chicago Gay Crusader in 1974.

Flint (top row, second from left) was among many local and national figures at this 1974 benefit for the gay group ONE of Chicago, pictured in the May 1974 issue of The Chicago Gay Crusader.

MATLOVICH BENEFITS

AT DEWES MANSION

Ex-Air Force T.Sgt. Leonard Matlovich was in Chicago during November to raise funds in the name of gay civil rights. He is fighting to overturn the discharge which the Air Force gave him because of his gayness.

AT THE BATON

Fundraising events were hosted in Chicago by Chuck Renslow and other residents of the old Dewes mansion, 503 W. Wrightwood Ave., by owner Jim "Felicia" Flint at the Baton, 801 N. Clark St., and by Mattachine Midwest president Guy Warner at his apartment. Jack David of the Up North catered the parties. Mattachine Midwest coordinated the benefit series.

AT MATTACHINE PARTY

Air Force Technical Sergeant Leonard Matlovich attended several benefits in Chicago in late 1975, including one at the Baton, as covered in the January 1976 Chicago Gay Crusader.

"Nurse" Wanda Lust and her VD testing and education van went to several gay bars in the 1970s, including the Baton. This ad is from the September 17, 1985, GayLife.

Love Match was one of many plays that were performed on off nights at the Baton. Flint donated the space for the productions. This ad is from GayLife, March 20, 1981.

Jim Gates, owner of Little Jim's bar, 3501 North Halsted Street, hosted a series of roasts for well-known gay Chicagoans. Jim Flint was roasted in 1977. Gates is pictured with Flint at the roast.

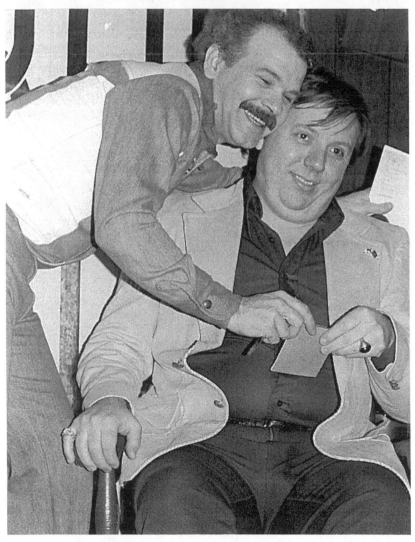

These two pages: Flint and his Baton entertainers in Chicago's Pride Parade, 1970s to 2000s.

Photo by Greg Elin

Photo by Kirk Williamson

Jim Flint, Jim Piehl and Harley McMillen at an early-1980s AIDS fundraiser.
Photo courtesy of Harley McMillen

An ad for an AIDS benefit slave auction at the Gold Coast, mid-1980s. Flint often was the emcee for these auctions.

Strike Against AIDS flier from March 8, 1984. Jim Flint, representing his three bars, was among those bowling for the cause.

Flint (center, with Harley McMillen on his left) at the 1985 AIDS Memorial March and Rally.
Photo by Jack Sitar, Gay Chicago archives.

Early 1980s: Judy Walker and Jimmy Russell, who organized Chicago's first AIDS Memorial March and Rally, in 1985.

This December 5, 1985, edition of GayLife had four stories on the cover, and Flint was connected to all four. He was coordinator of the Chicago House launch benefit, he was in the meeting with Senator Paul Simon, he was kicking off his County Board race, and his former Baton entertainer Andrea Nicole had died of cancer.

Flint, pictured in the December 5, 1985, Windy City Times, as coordinator of the Chicago House benefit at the Limelight, with Jackie Sapien and Thom Dombkowski of Chicago House.
Photo by Lee A. Newell II

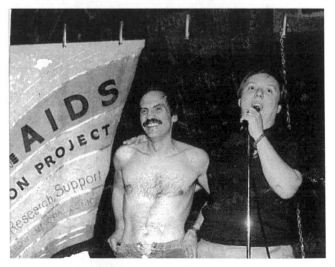

Gay Chicago's Dan DiLeo with Jim Flint at an AIDS benefit, early 1980s.

The 1986 Mr. Windy City
Awards, which also featured
the Gay Chicago Magazine
Awards. In front row are Ralph
Paul Gernhardt (from left), Jim
Flint, Eddie Dugan and Dan
DiLeo. The Mr. Windy City top
three are standing.
Photo courtesy of Gay Chicago
archives.

The 1987 Mr. Windy City
winner was activist Paul
Adams (second from left),
and in back row (right) is
performer Rudy de la Mor.
DiLeo, Flint and Gernhardt
are in the front.

THEY CAME FROM ACROSS THE CITY AND ACROSS THE COUNTRY TO SAY:
HAPPY BIRTHDAY, FELICIA

Photos by Robert Vandiver

OVER 20 ENTERTAINERS CAME TO SAY
HAPPY BIRTHDAY TO CHICAGO'S
"FABULOUS FELICIA"

JODY LEE WAS ONE OF THE FIRST
ENTERTAINERS TO WORK FOR FELICIA

VERA OF THE SNAKE PIT COMMANDED
A STANDING OVATION

ENTERTAINERS CROWD AROUND FELICIA
BACKSTAGE AT THE BATON

TWO WINNERS CONGRATULATE A WINNER:
SHAWN LUIS, "Miss Gay America, 1974",
FELICIA, AND ROSKI FERNANDEZ, first
runner-up, "Miss Gay America, 1973"

Jim Flint has been celebrating his July birthday in very public ways for decades. The celebration is always a benefit for some group, politician or cause. Shown is coverage from the September 1975 edition of The Chicago Gay Crusader.

Flint's birthday was promoted in an ad in GayLife, July 23, 1985.

Mimi Marks at Flint's 70th-birthday party.
Photo by Hal Baim

Sasha Colby at Flint's 70th-birthday party.
Photo by Hal Baim

Above: Attorney Ed Mogul (left) at Flint's 70th-birthday party.
Photo by Hal Baim

Left: Tommie Ross at Flint's 70th-birthday party.
Photo by Hal Baim

Flint celebrated his 70th birthday at the Park West in 2011.
Photo by Hal Baim

The sign outside the Park West in 2011.
Photo by Hal Baim

Flint with his sisters Doris and Dorothy "Skip" at his 2011 birthday party.
Photo by Hal Baim

Maya Douglas at Flint's 70th-birthday party.
Photo by Hal Baim

Appendix

Locations where Flint worked in 1960s:
21 Club, 3042 West Irving Park Road
Annex, 2865 North Clark Street
The Chesterfield, 2831 North Clark Street
Drake Hotel's Club International, 140 East Walton Street
Gold Coast, 1110 North Clark Street
Hollywood Bowl, 1130 North Clark Street
Millionaires Club, 600 North Michigan Avenue
Normandy, 744 North Rush Street
Sam's, 1205 North Clark Street

Businesses Flint owned or co-owned:
3160, 3160 North Clark Street
Annex 2, 430 North Clark Street
Annex 3, 3160 North Clark Street
Baton Show Lounge, 430 and 436 North Clark Street
Baton South, on Ponce de Leon Avenue in Atlanta
Continental Pageant System: Miss Continental, Mr. Continental,
    Continental Elite and Continental Plus
Costumes on Review
Redoubt, 65 West Illinois Street, 440 North Halsted Street, 1315 West North Avenue
Redoubt Atlanta, on Ponce de Leon Avenue
River North Travel, 432 North Clark Street
Smitty's Show Lounge, 430 North Clark Street
Togetherness, 61 West Hubbard Street

Organizations Flint led at one time:
Chicago Knight Motorcycle Club
Prairie State Democratic Club
Tavern Guild of Chicago
Windy City Athletic Association

Organizations Flint helped found or on whose board he served:
Chicago House
Dignity/Chicago
Metropolitan Business Association

Celebrity Visitors to the Baton

Following is a list of some of the well-known individuals who have been spotted attending performances at the Baton Show Lounge over its 42 years.

Al Lewis (Grandpa Munster)
Alex McCord and Simon van Kempen
Ana María Polo
Bob Mackie
Candace Collins Jordan
Carol Channing
Carol Marin
Cassandra Peterson (Elvira)
Charles Pierce
Chita Rivera
Chris Farley
Craig Russell
Da Brat
Damita Jo
Dennis Rodman
Dinah Shore
Dolph Lundgren
Ericka Dunlap
Esera Tuaolo
Frances Faye
Gale Sayers
Goldie Hawn
Grace Jones
Harold Washington
Irv Kupcinet
Jack Brickhouse
Janet Jackson
Jennifer Holliday
Jennifer Hudson
Jill St. John
Jimmy Connors
Joan Crawford
Joan Rivers
John Cusack
John Karlan
John Larroquette
Jose Cardenal
Josh Brolin
Judy Tenuta
Kate Shindle
Katt Williams
Kendall Gill
Kirk Douglas
Lauren Bacall
Linda Clifford
Liza Minnelli
Loleatta Holloway

Loretta Swit
Lorna Luft
Luc Longley
Luther Vandross
Madonna
Mariah Carey
Mark Saxenmeyer
Marlo Thomas
Martha Wash
Merri Dee
Michael Greer
Minnie Driver
Mo'Nique
Muriel Clair
Oprah Winfrey
Paul Lynde
Phil Donahue
Phyllis Diller
Phyllis Hyman
Pudgy
Queen Latifah
Rick Donovan
Robert Cazimero
Robert Wagner
Rock Hudson
Rod McKuen
Roger Moore
Rosanna Arquette
Rosemary Clooney
Rosemary DeCamp
Rosie O'Donnell
RuPaul
Rusty Warren
Sammy Davis Jr.
Sarah Vaughan
Shirley MacLaine
Stephanie Powers
Steve Kerr
Tamron Hall
Ted Kennedy
Teri Hatcher
Tim Curry
Tippi Hedren
Tommy Tune
Tracey Ross
Wolfgang Puck

Entertainers at the Baton

The following are the entertainers who have been part of the cast at Chicago's Baton Show Lounge since it opened in 1969.

Amanda Winters
Andrea Nicole
Audrey Bryant
Aurora Sexton
Basha
Big Jimmy
Brenda Steele
Candi Stratton
Cezanne
Chanel Dupree
Charles Pierce
Cherine Alexander
Chilli Pepper
China Nguyen
Craig Russell
Dana Douglas
Dena Cass
Dina Jacobs
Dolinda Ko'
Flame Monroe
Ginger Grant
Heather Fontaine
Jan Howard
Jimmy
Joanna Caron
Jodie Lee
Jodie Santana
Lady Baronessa
Lynette Langston
Lavinda
Leslie Lasalle
Leslie Rejeanné
Lotta Love
Madalene Mitchell

Marty Helton
Maya Douglas
Michael Greer
Mimi Marks
Monica Munro
Nikki Stevens
Orlando del Sol
Patricia D Roma
Paul Lopez
Paula Sinclaire
Peaches
Pudgy
Ray West
Regine Phillips
Ricky Love
Ronnie Russell
Roski Fernandez
Ruby Red
Sabrina
Sam Hill
Samantha George
Sasha Colby
Sasha Valentino
Shanté (Alexandra Billings)
Shawn Lewis
Sherì Payne
Stacy Stevens
Tasha Wallace
Tony Lewis
Tony Zito
Victoria LePaige
Virginia Slim
Wanda Lust

People Interviewed for this Book

More than 150 interviews were conducted for Jim Flint: The Boy From Peoria, all during 2011. Following is a list of those who were interviewed, and most of them are quoted in this book.

A.J. Epstein
Alexandra Billings (Shanté)
Alexis Gabrielle Sherrington
Alyson Thomas
Amy Cole
Amy DeMilo
Antonio Edwards
Antonio King
Armani
Art Johnston
Audrey Morris
Aurora Sexton
Barbara Supeter
Barbra Herr
Becky Menzie
Bill Svetz
Billy Fantastic (William
  Kucharenko)
Bob Guilford
Bob Kuzas
Bob Nickelson
Bob Strada
Bobby Glaze
Burton Natarus
Cai Holyon
Candace Collins Jordan
Candis Cayne
Carol Haddon
Cezanne
Chanel Dupree
Chelsea Pearl
Chilli Pepper
Chris DePaepe
Chuck Renslow
Cindy Barbalock
Curtis Kath
Daesha Richards
Dan Fraser
Dan Neniskis
Dana Douglas
Danielle Hunter
David Hudspeth
Deborah Decuire
Dena Cass
Denis Sabol
Desiree DeMornay

Dick Decker
Dina Jacobs
Domanique Shappelle
Doris Flint
Dorothy "Skip" Flint
Ed Cavaliere
Ed Mogul
Electra
Eric Gorczyca
Erica Andrews
Erin Criss
Errol (Stoney) Summons
Flame Monroe
Frank Snyder
Frank Zimmerman
Gene Janowski
Ginger Grant
Greg Moore
Harrison McEldowney
Harvey Washington
Heather Fontaine
Helen Shiller
Helena Bushong
Honey West
Ikey (Irene Raczka)
Jack Delaney
Jan Berger
Janet McGuire
Jerry Leppek
Jerry Mickelson
Jerry Williams
Jesse White
Jim Bussen
Jim DeMundo
Jim Flint
Jim Henritze
Jim O'Connor
Jodie Santana
Joe Fraser
Joey McDonald
John Chester
John Keys
José Abraham
JT McWilliams
Judy Roberts
Judy Walker

Keith Elliott
Kelly Lauren
Ken Byrski
Ken Nowakowski
Keven Callahan
Kim Turner
Kit Duffy
Larry Scantland
Lennie Malina
Lilia Delgado
Linda Clifford
Lori Cannon
Louis Lee Boroff
Marcia Hill
Mark Ward
Marge Summit
Maya Douglas
Mercedes Tyler
Mike Denny
Mike McHale
Mike McRaith
Mike Meismer
Mimi Marks
Mokha Montrese
Nancy Pribich
Nick Gray
Noah Lee Richards
Orlando del Sol
Paul Lopez
Paul Marinaro
Paul Yinger
Philip Alexander
Ralla Klepak
Raquel Rodriguez
Rasean Montrese
Regine Phillips
Richard Cooke
Richard Johnson
Rick Garcia
Rick Welch
Robbie Ham
Robert Waters
Roxxy Andrews
Sabrina Sabo (aka Lizares)
Sam Coady
Sara Davis

Sasha Colby
Scott Cooper aka Michelle
  Dupree
Scott Palmer
Shantell DMarco
Shawn Batton
Shawn Luis
Sheri Payne
Simba Hall
Skip Mackall
Stan Walker

Steven Moore
Suzi Arnold
Tajma Hall
Tasha Long
Tatiana Braxton
Theresa Altgilbers
Tiffany T. Hunter
Tim Gideon
Tom Chiola
Tommie Ross
Tony DeSario

Tulsi
Tumara Mahorning
Victor Salvo
Victoria LePaige
Victoria Parker
Warren Williamson
William B. Kelley
Yoshiko Oshiro
Zander Mander

In addition, there are a few people quoted from interviews conducted in the 1990s by Chicago historian Jack Rinella, excerpts from 1990s and 2000s interviews by Sukie de la Croix for his Windy City Times column, and text quoted from individuals interviewed for Leatherman: The Legend of Chuck Renslow.